CODE OF ALABAMA

1975

With Provision for Subsequent Pocket Parts

Prepared Under the Supervision of

The Code Revision Subcommittee of
The Legislative Council

Robert H. Harris, Chairman

by

The Editorial Staff of the Publishers

Under the Direction of

A. D. Kowalsky, S. C. Willard, W. L. Jackson,
K. S. Mawyer and T. R. Troxell

VOLUME 17A

1989 REPLACEMENT VOLUME

*Including Acts through the 1989 Regular Session and
annotations taken through Southern Reporter,
Second Series, Volume 539, Page 143*

THE MICHIE COMPANY
Law Publishers
Charlottesville, Virginia
1989

Table of Titles

In Addition, This Publication Contains

Table of Contents

VOLUME 17A

Title 32.

Motor Vehicles and Traffic.

TITLE 32.

MOTOR VEHICLES AND TRAFFIC.

CHAPTER 1.

GENERAL PROVISIONS.

1

§ 32-1-1. Repealed by Acts 1980, No. 80-434, p. 604, effective May 19, 1980.

§ 32-1-1.1. Definitions.

The following words and phrases when used in this title shall, for the purpose of this title, have meanings respectively ascribed to them in this section, except when the context otherwise requires:

(1) ALLEY. A street or highway intended to provide access to the rear or side of lots or buildings in urban districts and not intended for the purpose of through vehicular traffic.

(2) ARTERIAL STREET. Any United States or state numbered route, controlled-access highway, or other major radial or circumferential street or highway designated by local authorities within their respective jurisdictions as part of a major arterial system of streets or highways.

(3) AUTHORIZED EMERGENCY VEHICLE. Such fire department vehicles, police vehicles and ambulances as are publicly owned, and such other publicly or privately owned vehicles as are designated by the director of public safety or the chief of police of an incorporated city.

(4) BICYCLE. Every device propelled by human power upon which any person may ride, having two tandem wheels either of which is more than 14 inches in diameter.

(5) BUS. Every motor vehicle designed for carrying more than 10 passengers and used for the transportation of persons; and every motor vehicle other than a taxicab, designed and used for the transportation of persons for compensation.

(6) BUSINESS DISTRICT. The territory contiguous to and including a highway when within any 600 feet along such highway there are buildings in use for business or industrial purposes, including but not limited to hotels, banks or office buildings, railroad stations and public buildings which occupy at least 300 feet of frontage on one side or 300 feet collectively on both sides of the highway.

(7) CANCELLATION OF DRIVER'S LICENSE. The annulment or termination by formal action of the director of public safety of a person's driver's license because of some error or defect in the license or because the licensee is no longer entitled to such license, but the cancellation of a license is without prejudice and application for a new license may be made at any time after such cancellation.

(8) CONTROLLED-ACCESS HIGHWAY. Every highway, street or roadway in respect to which owners or occupants of abutting lands and other persons have no legal right of access to or from the same except at such points only

and in such manner as may be determined by the public authority having jurisdiction over such highway, street or roadway.

(9) CROSSWALK.

a. That part of a roadway at an intersection included within the connections of the lateral lines of the sidewalks on opposite sides of the highway measured from the curbs or, in the absence of curbs, from the edges of the traversable roadway;

b. Any portion of a roadway at an intersection or elsewhere distinctly indicated for pedestrian crossing by lines or other markings on the surface.

(10) DEALER. Every person engaged in the business of buying, selling or exchanging vehicles who has an established place of business for such purpose in this state and to whom current dealer registration plates have been issued by the department of revenue.

(11) DEPARTMENT. The department of public safety of this state acting directly or through its duly authorized officers and agents.

(12) DIRECTOR. The director of public safety of Alabama.

(13) DRIVEAWAY-TOWAWAY OPERATION. Any operation in which any motor vehicle, trailer or semitrailer, singly or in combination, new or used, constitutes the commodity being transported, when one set or more of wheels of any such vehicle are on the roadway during the course of transportation, whether or not any such vehicle furnishes the motive power.

(14) DRIVER. Every person who drives or is in actual physical control of a vehicle.

(15) DRIVER'S LICENSE. Any license to operate a motor vehicle issued under the laws of this state.

(16) ESSENTIAL PARTS. All integral and body parts of a vehicle of a type required to be registered hereunder, the removal, alteration or substitution of which would tend to conceal the identity of the vehicle or substantially alter its appearance, model, type or mode of operation.

(17) ESTABLISHED PLACE OF BUSINESS. The place actually occupied either continuously or at regular periods by a dealer or manufacturer where his books and records are kept and a large share of his business is transacted.

(18) EXPLOSIVES. Any chemical compound or mechanical mixture that is commonly used or intended for the purpose of producing an explosion and which contains any oxidizing and combustive units or other ingredients in such proportions, quantities or packing that an ignition by fire, by friction, by concussion, by percussion or by detonator of any part of the compound or mixture may cause such a sudden generation of highly heated gases that the resultant gaseous pressures are capable of producing destructive effects on contiguous objects or of destroying life or limb.

(19) FARM TRACTOR. Every motor vehicle designed and used primarily as a farm implement, for drawing plows, mowing machines and other implements of husbandry.

(20) FLAMMABLE LIQUID. Any liquid which has a flash point of 70° F., or less as determined by a fagliabue or equivalent closed-cup test device.

(21) FOREIGN VEHICLE. Every vehicle of a type required to be registered hereunder brought into this state from another state, territory or country other than in the ordinary course of business by or through a manufacturer or dealer and not registered in this state.

(22) GROSS WEIGHT. The weight of a vehicle without load plus the weight of any load thereon.

(23) HIGHWAY. The entire width between the boundary lines of every way publicly maintained when any part thereof is open to the use of the public for purposes of vehicular travel.

(24) HOUSE TRAILER.

     a. A trailer or semitrailer which is designed, constructed and equipped as a dwelling place, living abode or sleeping place (either permanently or temporarily) and is equipped for use as a conveyance on streets and highways; or

     b. A trailer or semitrailer whose chassis and exterior shell is designed and constructed for use as a house trailer, as defined in paragraph a., but which is used instead permanently or temporarily for the advertising, sales, display or promotion of merchandise or services, or for any other commercial purpose except the transportation of property for hire or the transportation of property for distribution by a private carrier.

(25) IMPLEMENT OF HUSBANDRY. Every vehicle designed and adapted exclusively for agricultural, horticultural or livestock raising operations or for lifting or carrying an implement of husbandry and in either case not subject to registration if used upon the highways.

(26) INTERSECTION.

     a. The area embraced within the prolongation or connection of the lateral curb lines, or, if none, then the lateral boundary lines of the roadways of two highways which join one another at, or approximately at, right angles, or the area within which vehicles traveling upon different highways joining at any other angle may come in conflict.

     b. Where a highway includes two roadways 30 feet or more apart, then every crossing of each roadway of such divided highway by an intersecting highway shall be regarded as a separate intersection. In the event such intersecting highway also includes two roadways 30 feet or more apart, then every crossing of two roadways of such highways shall be regarded as a separate intersection.

     c. The junction of an alley with a street or highway shall not constitute an intersection.

(27) LANED ROADWAY. A roadway which is divided into two or more clearly marked lanes for vehicular traffic.

(28) LICENSE or LICENSE TO OPERATE A MOTOR VEHICLE. Any driver's license or any other license or permit to operate a motor vehicle issued by the director under the laws of this state, including any nonresident's operating privilege as defined herein.

(29) LOCAL AUTHORITIES.

     a. Every county commission; and

b. Every municipal and other local board or body having authority to enact laws relating to traffic under the constitution and laws of this state.

(30) MAIL. To deposit in the United States mail properly addressed and with postage prepaid.

(31) METAL TIRE. Every tire the surface of which in contact with the highway is wholly or partly of metal or other hard, nonresilient material.

(32) MOTOR VEHICLE. Every vehicle which is self-propelled and every vehicle which is propelled by electric power obtained from overhead trolley wires, but not operated upon rails.

(33) MOTORCYCLE. Every motor vehicle having a seat or saddle for the use of the rider and designed to travel on not more than three wheels in contact with the ground, but excluding a tractor.

(34) MOTOR-DRIVEN CYCLE. Every motorcycle, including every motor scooter, with a motor which produces not to exceed five brake horsepower nor to exceed 150 cubic centimeter engine displacement, and weighs less than 200 pounds fully equipped, and every bicycle with motor attached.

(35) NONRESIDENT. Every person who is not a resident of this state.

(36) NONRESIDENT'S OPERATING PRIVILEGE. The privilege conferred upon a nonresident by the laws of this state pertaining to the operation by such person of a motor vehicle, or the use of a vehicle owned by such person, in this state.

(37) OFFICIAL TRAFFIC-CONTROL DEVICES. All signs, signals, markings and devices not inconsistent with this title placed or erected by authority of a public body or official having jurisdiction, for the purpose of regulating, warning or guiding traffic.

(38) OWNER. A person, other than a lienholder, having the property in or title to a vehicle. The term includes a person entitled to the use and possession of a vehicle subject to a security interest in another person, but excludes a lessee under a lease not intended as security.

(39) PARK or PARKING. The standing of a vehicle, whether occupied or not, otherwise than temporarily for the purpose of and while actually engaged in loading or unloading merchandise or passengers.

(40) PASSENGER CAR. Every motor vehicle, except motorcycles and motor-driven cycles, designed for carrying 10 passengers or less and used for the transportation of persons.

(41) PEDESTRIAN. Any person afoot.

(42) PERSON. Every natural person, firm, copartnership, association or corporation.

(43) PNEUMATIC TIRE. Every tire in which compressed air is designed to support the load.

(44) POLE TRAILER. Every vehicle without motive power designed to be drawn by another vehicle and attached to the towing vehicle by means of a reach or pole, or by being boomed or otherwise secured to the towing vehicle, and ordinarily used for transporting long or irregularly shaped loads such as poles, pipes or structural members capable, generally, of sustaining themselves as beams between the supporting connections.

(45) POLICE OFFICER. Every officer authorized to direct or regulate traffic or to make arrests for violations of traffic regulations.

(46) PRIVATE ROAD or DRIVEWAY. Every way or place in private ownership and used for vehicular travel by the owner and those having express or implied permission from the owner, but not by other persons.

(47) RAILROAD. A carrier of persons or property upon cars other than street cars, operated upon stationary rails.

(48) RAILROAD SIGN or SIGNAL. Any sign, signal or device erected by authority of a public body or official or by a railroad and intended to give notice of the presence of railroad tracks or the approach of a railroad train.

(49) RAILROAD TRAIN. A steam engine, electric or other motor, with or without cars coupled thereto, operated upon rails.

(50) RECONSTRUCTED VEHICLE. Every vehicle of a type required to be registered hereunder materially altered from its original construction by the removal, addition or substitution of essential parts, new or used.

(51) REGISTRATION. The registration certificate or certificates and registration plates issued under the laws of this state pertaining to the registration of vehicles.

(52) RESIDENCE DISTRICT. The territory contiguous to and including a highway not comprising a business district when the property on such highway for a distance of 300 feet or more is in the main improved with residences or residences and buildings in use for business.

(53) REVOCATION OF DRIVER'S LICENSE. The termination by formal action of the director of a person's license or privilege to operate a motor vehicle on the public highways, which termination shall not be subject to renewal or restoration except that an application for a new license may be presented and acted upon by the director after the expiration of the applicable period of time prescribed in this title.

(54) RIGHT-OF-WAY. The right of one vehicle or pedestrian to proceed in a lawful manner in preference to another vehicle or pedestrian approaching under such circumstances of direction, speed and proximity as to give rise to danger of collision unless one grants precedence to the other.

(55) ROAD TRACTOR. Every motor vehicle designed and used for drawing other vehicles and not so constructed as to carry any load thereon either independently or any part of the weight of a vehicle or load so drawn.

(56) ROADWAY. That portion of a highway improved, designed or ordinarily used for vehicular travel, exclusive of the berm or shoulder. In the event a highway includes two or more separate roadways the term "roadway" as used herein shall refer to any such roadway separately but not to all such roadways collectively.

(57) SAFETY ZONE. The area or space officially set apart within a roadway for the exclusive use of pedestrians and which is protected or is so marked or indicated by adequate signs as to be plainly visible at all times while set apart as a safety zone.

(58) SCHOOL BUS. Every motor vehicle that complies with the color and identification requirements set forth by statute or regulation and is used to

transport children to or from school or in connection with school activities, but not including buses operated by common carriers in urban transportation of school children.

(59) SECURITY AGREEMENT. A written agreement which reserves or creates a security interest.

(60) SECURITY INTEREST. An interest in a vehicle reserved or created by agreement and which secures payment or performance of an obligation. The term includes the interest of a lessor under a lease intended as security. A security interest is perfected when it is valid against third parties generally, subject only to specific statutory exceptions.

(61) SEMITRAILER. Every vehicle with or without motive power, other than a pole trailer, designed for carrying persons or property and for being drawn by a motor vehicle and so constructed that some part of its weight and that of its load rests upon or is carried by another vehicle.

(62) SIDEWALK. That portion of a street between the curb lines, or the lateral lines of a roadway, and the adjacent property lines, intended for use by pedestrians.

(63) SOLID TIRE. Every tire of rubber or other resilient material which does not depend upon compressed air for the support of the load.

(64) SPECIAL MOBILE EQUIPMENT. Every vehicle not designed or used primarily for the transportation of persons or property and only incidentally operated or moved over a highway, including but not limited to: ditch digging apparatus, well boring apparatus and road construction and maintenance machinery such as asphalt spreaders, bituminous mixers, bucket loaders, tractors other than truck tractors, ditchers, levelling graders, finishing machines, motor graders, road rollers, scarifiers, earth moving carry-alls and scrapers, power shovels and drag lines, and self-propelled cranes and earth moving equipment. The term does not include house trailers, dump trucks, truck mounted transit mixers, cranes or shovels, or other vehicles designed for the transportation of persons or property to which machinery has been attached.

(65) SPECIALLY CONSTRUCTED VEHICLE. Every vehicle of a type required to be registered hereunder not originally constructed under a distinctive name, make, model or type by a generally recognized manufacturer of vehicles and not materially altered from its original construction.

(66) STAND or STANDING. The halting of a vehicle, whether occupied or not, otherwise than temporarily for the purpose of and while actually engaged in receiving or discharging passengers.

(67) STATE. A state, territory or possession of the United States, the District of Columbia, the Commonwealth of Puerto Rico or a province of Canada.

(68) STOP. When required, means complete cessation from movement.

(69) STOP or STOPPING. When prohibited means any halting even momentarily of a vehicle, whether occupied or not, except when necessary to avoid conflict with other traffic or in compliance with the directions of a police officer or traffic-control sign or signal.

(70) STREET. The entire width between boundary lines of every way publicly maintained when any part thereof is open to the use of the public for purposes of vehicular travel.

(71) SUSPENSION OF DRIVER'S LICENSE. The temporary withdrawal by formal action of the director of public safety of a person's license or privilege to operate a motor vehicle on the public highways, which temporary withdrawal shall be for a period specifically designated by the director.

(72) THROUGH HIGHWAY. Every highway or portion thereof on which vehicular traffic is given preferential right-of-way, and at the entrances to which vehicular traffic from intersecting highways is required by law to yield the right-of-way to vehicles on such through highway in obedience to a stop sign, yield sign, or other official traffic-control device, when such signs or devices are erected as provided in this title.

(73) TRACKLESS TROLLEY COACH. Every motor vehicle which is propelled by electric power obtained from overhead trolley wires but not operated upon rails.

(74) TRAFFIC. Pedestrians, ridden or herded animals, vehicles, streetcars and other conveyances either singly or together while using any highway for purposes of travel.

(75) TRAFFIC-CONTROL SIGNAL. Any device, whether manually, electrically or mechanically operated, by which traffic is alternately directed to stop and permitted to proceed.

(76) TRAILER. Every vehicle with or without motive power, other than a pole trailer, designed for carrying persons or property and for being drawn by a motor vehicle and so constructed that no part of its weight rests upon the towing vehicle.

(77) TRANSPORTER. Every person engaged in the business of delivering vehicles of a type required to be registered hereunder from a manufacturing, assembling or distributing plant to dealers or sales agents of a manufacturer.

(78) TRUCK. Every motor vehicle designed, used or maintained primarily for the transportation of property.

(79) TRUCK TRACTOR. Every motor vehicle designed and used primarily for drawing other vehicles and not so constructed as to carry a load other than a part of the weight of the vehicle and load so drawn.

(80) URBAN DISTRICT. The territory contiguous to and including any street which is built up with structures devoted to business, industry or dwelling houses situated at intervals of less than 100 feet for a distance of a quarter of a mile or more.

(81) VEHICLE. Every device in, upon or by which any person or property is or may be transported or drawn upon a highway, excepting devices moved by human power or used exclusively upon stationary rails or tracks; provided, that for the purposes of this title, a bicycle or a ridden animal shall be deemed a vehicle, except those provisions of this title, which by their very nature can have no application. (Acts 1980, No. 80-434, p. 604,

§ 1-100; Acts 1981, No. 81-803, p. 1412, § 1; Acts 1985, 2nd Ex. Sess., No. 85-998, p. 366, § 1.)

Commentary

Except where otherwise noted, the text of these definitions was taken from the most recent version of the Uniform Vehicle Code (UVC), promulgated by the national committee on uniform traffic laws and ordinances and the national highway traffic safety administration. The UVC has been employed nationally as the standard to improve and update traffic and motor vehicle laws.

Subdivisions (1) and (2). "Alley" and "arterial street" are not defined by the previous Alabama statutes.

Subdivision (3). This definition is very similar to former section 32-1-1(1).

Subdivision (4). This definition differs from that in former section 32-5-290(d) with respect to wheel diameter (20 inches under prior law, while 14 inches by chapter 5A.)

Subdivision (5). Identical to former section 32-1-1(2).

Subdivision (6). This term was defined in former section 32-1-1(3). The definition provided in subdivision (6) changes the old requirement from 50 percent of frontage for 300 feet to a total of 600 feet frontage collectively on both sides of the highway and at least 300 feet on one side of the highway.

Subdivision (7). There was no corresponding law in Alabama at the time of enactment.

Subdivision (8). This was previously called a "limited-access highway", identically defined by former section 32-1-1(15).

Subdivision (9). The term was identically defined in former section 32-1-1(4).

Subdivision (10). Nearly identical to section 40-12-240(1).

Subdivision (11). No change was made from the prior statute, section 32-1-1(5).

Subdivision (12). The UVC section 1-109 uses the term "commissioner", whereas Alabama uses the term "director", identically defined in former section 32-1-1(6).

Subdivision (13). There was no prior Alabama counterpart to this definition.

Subdivision (14). Identical to former section 32-1-1(7).

Subdivision (15). Not previously defined by Alabama statutes.

Subdivision (16). Not previously defined by Alabama statutes.

Subdivision (17). Very slight variations from section 40-12-240(2).

Subdivision (18). Nearly identical with former section 32-1-1(8), except that this definition adds the phrase "by percussion."

Subdivision (19). Identical to definition in former section 32-1-1(9).

Subdivision (20). Identical to definition in former section 32-1-1(10).

Subdivision (21). Not formerly defined by Alabama statutes.

Subdivision (22). Identical to former section 32-1-1(11).

Subdivision (23). This definition replaces two separate definitions, sections 32-1-1(12) and 40-12-240(14); both varied substantially from this section. "Highway" and "street" [see subdivision 70] are identically defined, and thus synonymous.

Subdivision (24). This term was defined in section 40-12-240(5), but has been revised to conform to the UVC.

Subdivision (25). This term was not previously defined in the Alabama statutes.

Subdivision (26). Former Alabama law, section 32-1-1(13) was identical except that it did not contain paragraph (c).

Subdivision (27). Identical to former section 32-1-1(14).

Subdivision (28). Alabama section 32-7-2(3), the preexisting section, did not enumerate that license was issued by the director.

Subdivision (29). Former section 32-1-1(16) was similar.

Subdivision (30). This term was not previously defined by the Alabama statutes.

Subdivision (31). Similar to former section 32-1-1(47).

Subdivision (32). This definition replaces the various and varying definitions found scattered throughout the preexisting Alabama statutes. Sections 32-1-1(20), 32-14-2(1), 32-18-1(3), and 40-12-240(7).

Subdivision (33). Similar to former section 32-1-1(18).

Subdivision (34). Similar to former section 32-1-1(19). This subdivision differs from the prior law in the addition of the word "brake," which is designed to indicate horsepower developed by the engine, as measured at the drive shaft, and the addition of the phrase "nor to exceed 150 cubic centimeter engine displacement" as well as the prior weight limitation of 200 pounds which is designed to correspond with section 32-12-20.

Subdivision (35). Identical to section 32-7-2(5).

Subdivision (36). Identical to section 32-7-2(6), except for minor difference in word usage.

Subdivision (37). Virtually identical to former section 32-1-1(21).

Subdivision (38). The former definition, section 32-1-1(22), varied considerably and included a mortgagor entitled to possession. Revision has been made to conform with adoption of the Alabama Uniform Commercial Code, section 7-1-101 et seq.

Subdivision (39). Similar to former section 32-1-1(23).

Subdivision (40). This subdivision simplifies and clarifies the definition in section 40-12-240(12) ("private passenger automobile").

Subdivision (41). Identical to former section 32-1-1(24).

Subdivision (42). No substantial change has been made but this definition replaces sections 32-1-1(25), 32-7-2(9), 32-14-2(3), and 40-12-240(13).

Subdivision (43). Replaces former section 32-1-1(26).

Subdivision (44). Similar to former section 32-1-1(27).

Subdivision (45). Same as former section 32-1-1(28).

Subdivision (46). This definition limits use of road to those with authorized authority and differs from former section 32-1-1(29) which defined road as not open to the public.

Subdivisions (47), (48) and (49). These three terms are virtually identical to former sections 32-1-1(30) through 32-1-1(32).

Subdivision (50). Not previously defined by Alabama statutes.

Subdivision (51). Identical to section 32-7-2(11).

Subdivision (52). Similar to former section 32-1-1(33), but removes requirement for dwellings to within 200 feet apart.

Subdivision (53). Not previously defined by Alabama statutes.

Subdivision (54). This is a much more detailed definition than former section 32-1-1(34) and is based on UVC § 1-156.

Subdivision (55). This subdivision is identical to the definition in former section 32-1-1(35).

Subdivision (56). This subdivision is identical to the definition in former section 32-1-1(36).

Subdivision (57). Similar to former section 32-1-1(37), except that in the former statute a safety zone was not necessarily set apart of a roadway.

Subdivision (58). This definition is more specific than former section 32-1-1(38), but varies from the UVC section 1-160 which makes reference to the regulations established by the national commission on safety education of the National Education Association, Washington, D.C. 20036. This subdivision permits the department of public safety to promulgate such regulations.

Subdivision (59). No definition of this term under former law, but see section 7-1-201(37).

Subdivision (60). No definitions of this term formerly appeared in Alabama's motor vehicle laws. But see section 7-9-105(h).

Subdivision (61). Alabama previously had two conflicting definitions of this term. The definition contained in section 40-12-240(15) differed from and has been replaced by this subdivision which is identical to former section 32-1-1(39).

Subdivision (62). Identical to former section 32-1-1(40).

Subdivisions (63), (64), and (65). No definitions of these three terms appeared in the prior Alabama statutes.

Subdivision (66). This subdivision separately defines "stand or standing" and "stop or stopping", whereas these terms were defined together by former section 32-1-1(42).

Subdivision (67). Section 32-7-2(12) omitted reference to Puerto Rico.

Subdivision (68). Identical to former section 32-1-1(41).

Subdivision (69). See comment to subdivision (66) above.

Subdivision (70). Not previously defined by Alabama statutes. Note that this is the same definition as that for "highway" [see subdivision (23) above]; thus, the two terms are, for the purposes of this title, synonymous.

Subdivision (71). Not previously defined by Alabama statutes.

Subdivision (72). The former definition was substantially different from this subdivision. Section 32-1-1(44) was unnecessarily restrictive and has been changed to conform to the UVC.

Subdivision (73). Not previously defined by Alabama statutes.

Subdivisions (74), (75), and (76). Identical definitions of these three terms were found in former sections 32-1-1(45) through 32-1-1(47). Another definition of "trailer" with a minor variation appears in section 40-12-240(18) and for use in the motor vehicle license section.

Subdivision (77). Not previously defined by Alabama statutes.

Subdivision (78). Alabama formerly defined "motor truck" in former section 32-1-1(48), and excluded vehicles weighing less than 1000 lbs. This subdivision provides a much simpler version.

Subdivision (79). Identical to former section 32-1-1(49).

Subdivision (80). Not previously defined by Alabama statutes.

Subdivision (81). Alabama had two varying definitions of this term; former section 32-1-1(50) and section 40-12-240(22). They were very similar to this definition.

General comment. Because streetcars are no longer in use in this state, the term "streetcar" is not defined here, and its former definition in section 32-1-1(43) has been repealed.

Code commissioner's note. — Acts 1980, No. 80-434, p. 604 repealed § 32-1-1 of the 1975 Code and enacted a new provision containing definitions which has been codified above for purposes of consistency with the treatment originally accorded the repealed section as enacted by Acts 1927, No. 347, p. 348 and amended by Acts 1932, Ex. Sess., No. 58, p. 68 and Acts 1949, No. 517, p. 754, § 1.

Editor's note. — Most of the cases cited below were decided under former § 32-1-1.

There is no legal distinction between "highway" and "public highway," but "highway" is generic term for all kinds of public ways and phrase "public highway" is tautological expression, since all highways are necessarily public. Sexton v. State, 239 Ala. 662, 196 So. 746 (1940).

Roadways of military installations are highways within state and subject to its traffic laws. Hilyer v. Dixon, 373 So. 2d 1123 (Ala. Civ. App.), cert. denied, 373 So. 2d 1125 (Ala. 1979).

Public road includes road dedicated to public by prescriptive use. — A public road would include a road dedicated to the public by its prescriptive use for a period of 20 years. Clark v. State, 25 Ala. App. 30, 140 So. 178 (1932).

It is character rather than quantum of use that controls in determining whether way is public or private. Liberty Nat'l Life Ins. Co. v. Kendrick, 282 Ala. 227, 210 So. 2d 701 (1968).

Placing of stock gaps or gates to control livestock would not keep a road from becoming a public road where it was evident that by placing the stock gaps beside the gates there was no interruption of the use by foot or automotive vehicles. Liberty Nat'l Life Ins. Co.

v. Kendrick, 282 Ala. 227, 210 So. 2d 701 (1968).

Unabandoned dirt road formerly part of public highway. — Where record is devoid of any evidence tending to show that the dirt road, formerly constituting a part of a public highway, and in fact still usable by the public, was ever abandoned, it must be concluded that the dirt road out of which the plaintiff emerged was a public road. Traylor v. Butler, 291 Ala. 560, 284 So. 2d 263 (1973).

Notwithstanding the fact that a public roadway had been altered by construction of a new road and the old road had been put in partial cultivation and was no longer kept in repair by the county authorities, the old road did not thereby lose its character as a public way. Traylor v. Butler, 291 Ala. 560, 284 So. 2d 263 (1973).

Company road as private road or driveway. — Company road constructed to allow company equipment access for logging operations, which was privately maintained and was used for vehicular traffic by the owner and those having express or implied permission from the owner, was not governed by the provisions and specifications of the Alabama Manual of Uniform Traffic Control Devices, as it was a private road or driveway, and not a highway. Thompson v. Champion Int'l Corp., 500 So. 2d 1048 (Ala. 1986).

Insufficient allegation of public highway. — A complaint alleging that plaintiff when injured "was driving along a road which was generally used by the public," "and the defendant was driving along said road in an automobile," does not allege that the road was a public highway nor that plaintiff was not a trespasser. Stewart v. Smith, 16 Ala. App. 461, 78 So. 724 (1918).

Police officer authorized to move illegally parked vehicle impeding traffic. — Where defendant's vehicle was parked illegally on the shoulder of a public highway during "rush hour" with the driver's door opened partially out in the roadway, obstructing traffic, and the vehicle was impeding traffic and posing a danger to other traffic, as well as to defendant and his passenger, who were asleep, any police officer, as defined by subdivision (45), was authorized to move such vehicle, or require the driver or other person in charge of the vehicle to move it to a position off the paved or main-traveled part of such highway. Martin v. State, 529 So. 2d 1032 (Ala. Crim. App. 1988).

Motor scooters included in category of motorcycles. — See Standifer v. Inter-Ocean Ins. Co., 37 Ala. App. 393, 69 So. 2d 300 (1953).

Area deemed neither residence nor business district. — See Klein v. Harris, 268 Ala. 540, 108 So. 2d 425 (1958).

Definitions not useful as to Sales Tax Act. — Definitions of "semitrailer" and "trailer" cannot be considered useful in determining the legislative intent in case of the Sales Tax Act levying a tax upon truck trailers and semitrailers. Haden v. Lee's Mobile Homes, Inc., 41 Ala. App. 376, 136 So. 2d 912 (1961), cert. denied, 273 Ala. 708, 136 So. 2d 920 (1962).

Cited in Kennemer v. McFann, 470 So. 2d 1113 (Ala. 1985).

Collateral references. — Products liability: sufficiency of evidence to support product misuse defense in actions concerning commercial or industrial equipment and machinery. 64 ALR4th 10.

§ 32-1-2. Liability for injury or death of guest.

The owner, operator or person responsible for the operation of a motor vehicle shall not be liable for loss or damage arising from injuries to or death of a guest while being transported without payment therefor in or upon said motor vehicle, resulting from the operation thereof, unless such injuries or death are caused by the willful or wanton misconduct of such operator, owner or person responsible for the operation of said motor vehicle. (Acts 1935, No. 442, p. 918; Code 1940, T. 36, § 95.)

I. General Consideration.
II. Owner, Operator or Person Responsible.
III. Guest.
IV. Willful or Wanton Misconduct.

I. GENERAL CONSIDERATION.

Section not violative of equal protection. — Prohibiting recovery from owner or operator of motor vehicle for injuries to guest, unless caused by wanton misconduct, is not violative of equal protection provisions of state and federal Constitutions on ground that guest is deprived of right of damages from subsequent negligence which still exists as an action of trespass, since there is sufficient difference between a "guest" and a "trespasser" to make them separate classes in prescribing police regulation. Pickett v. Matthews, 238 Ala. 542, 192 So. 261 (1939).

Police power is sometimes superior to personal and property rights, which not infrequently yield to the general welfare. Pickett v. Matthews, 238 Ala. 542, 192 So. 261 (1939).

Thus state may change rule of common-law duty. — The state has the right, by exercise of police power, in interest of general welfare, to change rule of common-law duty even though such change deprives one of a claim for personal or property damage. Pickett v. Matthews, 238 Ala. 542, 192 So. 261 (1939).

Legal duties not preserved by due process provision. — Constitution 1901, § 13, which provides "that every person, for an injury done him, in his lands, goods, person, or reputation, shall have a remedy by due process of law," preserves the right to a remedy for an injury. Thus when a duty has been breached producing a legal claim for damages, such claimant cannot be denied the benefit of his claim for the absence of a remedy. But this provision does not undertake to preserve existing duties against legislative change made before the breach occurs. There can be no legal claim for damages to the person or property of anyone except as it follows from the breach of a legal duty. Pickett v. Matthews, 238 Ala. 542, 192 So. 261 (1939).

And there is no right to have existing statute continue in effect without repeal or modification, except as to a cause which has accrued and vested. Pickett v. Matthews, 238 Ala. 542, 192 So. 261 (1939).

Except as to vested rights. — Undoubtedly the right to the remedy must remain and cannot be curtailed after the injury has occurred and right of action vested, regardless of the source of the duty which was breached, provided it remained in existence when the breach occurred. Pickett v. Matthews, 238 Ala. 542, 192 So. 261 (1939).

Province of legislature to repeal guest statute. — Under the distribution of powers section of the Alabama Constitution, it is within the province of the legislature to ascer-

tain and determine when the welfare of the people might require that the guest statute should be repealed. Beasley v. Bozeman, 294 Ala. 288, 315 So. 2d 570 (1975).

Supreme court would notice change of conditions. — Supreme court would take judicial notice of fact that in 1915, when supreme court opinion was written holding that statute imputing negligence of operator of motor vehicle to occupant who was not a passenger paying fare on vehicle regularly used for public hire was an unwarranted and unjust discrimination against persons riding in motor vehicles, the highways were not infested with "hitchhikers" obtaining free rides from operators of motor vehicles. Pickett v. Matthews, 238 Ala. 542, 192 So. 261 (1939).

Purpose of section. — The purpose of this section is to prevent generous drivers, who offer rides to guests, from being sued in what often are close cases of negligence. Roe v. Lewis, 416 So. 2d 750 (Ala. 1982).

Construction of section with intent and purpose in view. — As the use of automobiles became almost universal, many cases arose where generous drivers, having offered rides to guests, later found themselves defendants in cases that often turned upon close questions of negligence. Undoubtedly the legislature in adopting this section reflected a certain natural feeling as to the injustice of such a situation. The terms of the section should be construed with their intent and purpose in view, and the purpose and object that the legislature had in mind sometimes throws light upon the meaning of the language used. Blair v. Greene, 247 Ala. 104, 22 So. 2d 834 (1945); Sullivan v. Davis, 263 Ala. 685, 83 So. 2d 434 (1955); Boggs v. Turner, 277 Ala. 157, 168 So. 2d 1 (1964); Roe v. Lewis, 416 So. 2d 750 (Ala. 1982).

Strict construction required. — The guest statute is in derogation of the common law and as such should be strictly construed. Roe v. Lewis, 416 So. 2d 750 (Ala. 1982).

Section does not create defense of contributory negligence. — When the statute requires willfulness or wantonness, it does not change the principles which apply to such an action, and does not create the defense of contributory negligence, which is not applicable to a count of that nature under other circumstances. Shirley v. Shirley, 261 Ala. 100, 73 So. 2d 77 (1954).

When section must be pleaded. — Where complaint did not allege that plaintiff was riding as a guest in the car without the payment of compensation therefor, if this section applied, the duty would be on defendants to plead it unless the complaint on its face showed its application. Penton v. Favors, 262 Ala. 262, 78 So. 2d 278 (1955).

Complaint held sufficient. — Complaint that plaintiff was an invited guest riding in defendant's car, which was driven by him, and that "defendant wantonly injured plaintiff by causing his automobile to overturn, thereby injuring plaintiff" (described in detail, and that) "she suffered all of said injuries and damage aforesaid, as a proximate result of the wanton act herein complained of" sufficiently showed that the act was itself wantonly done. Dean v. Adams, 249 Ala. 319, 30 So. 2d 903 (1947).

The allegation that plaintiff was a "passenger on a share expense basis" is of such certainty as to apprise the defendant that the plaintiff was thereby asserting that he was not riding as a guest of the defendant. Wagnon v. Patterson, 260 Ala. 297, 70 So. 2d 244 (1954).

Where a count alleged that injury was wantonly inflicted by heedlessly or recklessly operating the car, it would have been a harsh construction to hold that a second phrase, "heedlessly or recklessly," emasculated the charge of willfulness and wantonness clearly expressed in it. Brooks v. Liebert, 250 Ala. 142, 33 So. 2d 321 (1947).

Damages. — Proof of willful and wanton negligence in an action under this section does not exclude the awarding of compensatory damages where there is proof of such compensatory damages. Shields v. Castleberry, 41 Ala. App. 390, 133 So. 2d 516 (1961).

As to punitive damages for wantonness along with compensatory damages, see Clinton Mining Co. v. Bradford, 200 Ala. 308, 76 So. 74 (1917); McDonald v. Amason, 39 Ala. App. 492, 104 So. 2d 716, cert. denied, 267 Ala. 654, 104 So. 2d 719 (1958).

Cited in Chapman v. Nelson, 241 Ala. 21, 200 So. 763 (1941); Bell v. Brooks, 270 Ala. 691, 121 So. 2d 911 (1960); Alabama Farm Bureau Mut. Cas. Ins. Co. v. Mills, 271 Ala. 192, 123 So. 2d 138 (1960); Bagley v. Grime, 283 Ala. 688, 220 So. 2d 876 (1969); Western Ry. v. Still, 352 So. 2d 1092 (Ala. 1977); Phillips v. Unijax, Inc., 462 F. Supp. 942 (S.D. Ala. 1978); Grantham v. Denke, 359 So. 2d 785 (Ala. 1978); Maffett v. Roberts, 388 So. 2d 972 (Ala. 1980).

Collateral references. — 60A C.J.S., Motor Vehicles, §§ 399.1-399.14. 61 C.J.S., Motor Vehicles, §§ 486(1), 493.8.

8 Am. Jur. 2d, Automobiles & Highway Traffic, §§ 465-559.

Emergency rule as applied to automobile drivers. 6 ALR 680, 27 ALR 1197, 79 ALR 1277, 111 ALR 1019.

Owner or operator of automobile and passenger as joint adventurers, 48 ALR 1055, 63 ALR 909, 80 ALR 312, 95 ALR 857, 138 ALR 968.

Who is a guest within contemplation of statute regarding liability of owner or operator of motor vehicle for injury to guest. 82 ALR 1365, 95 ALR 1180.

What amounts to gross negligence, recklessness, or the like, within statute limiting liability of owner or operator of automobile for injury to guest. 86 ALR 1145, 96 ALR 1479.

Who is entitled to benefit of "guest" statute. 109 ALR 667.

Distraction of attention of driver of automobile as affecting question of negligence, wantonness, etc. 120 ALR 1513.

Position of car on wrong side of road or encroachment across center line as gross negligence, recklessness, or the like, within guest statute or rule. 136 ALR 1256, 6 ALR3d 832.

Gross negligence, recklessness, or the like, within "guest" statute or rule, predicated upon manner of operating car on curve or hill. 136 ALR 1270.

Liability for injury to child by automobile left unattended in street or highway where child was in relationship of guest of driver prior to injury. 140 ALR 549.

Intoxication of defendant as defense to action under automobile guest statutes. 141 ALR 58.

Conduct of operator of automobile at railroad crossing as gross negligence, recklessness, etc., within guest statute. 143 ALR 1144.

Host and guest relationship between parties to "share-a-ride" arrangement within statute or rule regarding liability of driver or operator of motor vehicle for injury to guest. 146 ALR 640, 161 ALR 917, 10 ALR3d 1087.

Commencement or termination of host and guest relationship within statute or rule as to liability for injury to automobile guest. 146 ALR 682.

Defective brakes as gross negligence, wilful or wanton conduct within meaning of guest statute. 170 ALR 628.

Custom or practice of drivers of motor vehicles as affecting liability to guests or passengers. 172 ALR 1141, 77 ALR2d 1327.

Member of family riding in car driven by another member as within guest statute. 2 ALR2d 932.

Liability under guest statute to automobile guest injured by falling from or through door of moving automobile, where claim of gross negligence, wilfulness or wantonness is made. 9 ALR2d 1343.

Payments or contributions by or on behalf of automobile rider as affecting his status as guest. 10 ALR2d 1351.

Guest's knowledge that automobile driver has been drinking as precluding recovery, under guest statutes or equivalent common-law rule. 15 ALR2d 1165.

Driving motor vehicle without lights or with improper lights as gross negligence or the like warranting recovery by guest under a guest statute or similar common-law rule. 21 ALR2d 209.

Protest by guest against driver's manner of operation of motor vehicle as terminating host-guest relationship. 25 ALR2d 1448.

Physical defect, illness, drowsiness, or falling asleep of motor vehicle operator as affecting liability for injury under guest statute. 28 ALR2d 33.

Domestic servant as guest of employer under automobile guest statute. 49 ALR2d 341.

Continuation of relation of passenger or guest after alighting from automobile. 50 ALR2d 981.

Liability of motor vehicle owner or operator for personal injury or death of passenger or guest occasioned by inhalation of gases or fumes from exhaust. 56 ALR2d 1099.

Mutual business or commercial objects or benefits as affecting status of rider under automobile guest statute. 59 ALR2d 336.

Applicability of guest statute where motor vehicle accident occurs on private way or property. 64 ALR2d 694.

Vehicle owner or his agent having general right of possession and control as guest of driver within automobile guest statute or similar rule. 65 ALR2d 312.

Intoxication, unconsciousness, or mental incompetency of person as affecting his status as guest within automobile guest statute or similar common-law rule. 66 ALR2d 1319.

Applicability of guest statute and its requirement of gross negligence, wanton or wilful misconduct, or the like, to owner's liability for injuries to guest in vehicle negligently entrusted to incompetent driver. 91 ALR2d 323.

Choice of law in application of automobile guest statutes. 95 ALR2d 12.

Last clear chance in actions by motor vehicle passenger against host-driver. 95 ALR2d 617.

Standard for judging conduct of minor motorist charged with gross negligence, recklessness, willful or wanton misconduct, or the like, under guest statute or similar common-law rule. 97 ALR2d 861.

What is "motor vehicle" within automobile guest statute. 98 ALR2d 543.

Liability, under guest statutes, of driver as owner of motor vehicle for running over or hitting person attempting to enter vehicle. 1 ALR3d 1083.

Speed alone or in connection with other circumstances, as gross negligence, wanton-ness, recklessness, or the like, under automobile guest statute. 6 ALR3d 769.

Burden of pleading and proving guest status, or absence thereof, under automobile guest statute. 24 ALR3d 1400.

Right of third person to recover contribution from host-driver for injuries or death of guest, where host is not liable to guest under guest statute. 26 ALR3d 1283.

Nonmonetary benefits or contributions by rider as affecting his status under automobile guest statute. 39 ALR3d 1083.

Status of rider as affected by payment, amount of which is not determined by expenses incurred. 39 ALR3d 1177.

Constitutionality of automobile and aviation guest statutes. 66 ALR3d 532.

Infant as guest within automobile guest statutes. 66 ALR3d 601.

Liability for automobile accident allegedly caused by driver's blackout, sudden unconsciousness, or the like. 93 ALR3d 326.

Motor vehicle passenger's contributory negligence or assumption of risk where accident resulted from driver's drowsiness, physical defect, or illness. 1 ALR4th 556.

Modern status of choice of law in application of automobile guest statutes. 63 ALR4th 167.

Passenger's liability to vehicular accident victim for harm caused by intoxicated motor vehicle driver. 64 ALR4th 272.

Driving while intoxicated: "choice of evils" defense that driving was necessary to protect life or property. 64 ALR4th 298.

II. OWNER, OPERATOR OR PERSON RESPONSIBLE.

Section applies only to person responsible for manner of operation of vehicle. — This section applies only to such person as may be responsible for the manner of vehicle's operation; it does not apply to the owner unless he is operating the car in person or unless it is under his immediate control or is operated by his servant or agent duly authorized by him. When the vehicle is not being so operated the liability of the owner is governed by common-law principles. Penton v. Favors, 262 Ala. 262, 78 So. 2d 278 (1955).

And does not affect liability of owner for entrusting automobile to another. — This section was not intended to limit the duty of the owner who entrusts to an incompetent driver an automobile or to a competent driver a defective automobile. Such liability depends upon common-law principles. Penton v. Favors, 262 Ala. 262, 78 So. 2d 278 (1955).

III. GUEST.

Section does not undertake to define

"guest." The definition of the term has been left to the court. Harrison v. McCleary, 281 Ala. 87, 199 So. 2d 165 (1967).

And whether one is a "guest" is a question of fact. — Because the term "guest" is not defined in this section, definition of such term falls upon the court. Therefore, it is a question of fact whether one is a guest within the statute. Roe v. Lewis, 416 So. 2d 750 (Ala. 1982).

Unless uncontroverted facts allow only one conclusion. — Where a dispute exists as to what were the respective purposes or conditions for or upon which the transportation was undertaken, relative to the nature and existence, if any, of the benefits conferred upon the respective parties, it is ordinarily a question of fact whether or not the invitee was a guest within the meaning of the statutes. Where, however, reasonable minds can reach but one conclusion from the uncontroverted facts, the question becomes one of law for the court. Wagnon v. Patterson, 260 Ala. 297, 70 So. 2d 244 (1954); Zemczonek v. McElroy, 264 Ala. 258, 86 So. 2d 824 (1956); Harrison v. McCleary, 281 Ala. 87, 199 So. 2d 165 (1967).

General rule is that if the transportation of a rider confers a benefit only on the person to whom the ride is given, and no benefits other than such as are incidental to hospitality, goodwill or the like on the person furnishing the transportation, the rider is a guest; but if his carriage tends to promote the mutual interest of both himself and driver for their common benefit, thus creating a joint business relationship between the motorist and his rider, or where the rider accompanies the driver at the instance of the latter for the purpose of having the rider render a benefit or service to the driver on a trip which is primarily for the attainment of some objective of the driver, the rider is a passenger and not a guest. Harrison v. McCleary, 281 Ala. 87, 199 So. 2d 165 (1967); Westbrook v. Gibbs, 285 Ala. 223, 231 So. 2d 97 (1970).

"Guest" may be invitee or licensee. — Under this section a "guest" may be invited, and called an "invitee," or may be permitted, and called a "licensee." Pickett v. Matthews, 238 Ala. 542, 192 So. 261 (1939).

Evidence in particular case must determine whether person is "guest" or "passenger for hire." Boggs v. Turner, 277 Ala. 157, 168 So.2d 1 (1964).

Identity of persons advantaged is important element. — One important element in determining whether person is guest is the identity of the person or persons advantaged by the carriage. Russell v. Thomas, 278 Ala. 400, 178 So. 2d 556 (1965).

When benefit sufficient to remove case from guest statute. — If the trip is for any benefit to the driver, conferred or anticipated, it is sufficient to take the case out of the guest statute, but a mere incidental benefit to the driver is not sufficient. The benefit to the driver must in some way have induced the driver to extend the offer to the rider, and the benefit must be material and tangible and must flow from the transportation provided. Kemp v. Jackson, 274 Ala. 29, 145 So. 2d 187 (1962); Russell v. Thomas, 278 Ala. 400, 178 So. 2d 556 (1965); Harrison v. McCleary, 281 Ala. 87, 199 So. 2d 165 (1967).

If the excursion is not purely social, any benefit to the driver of the automobile conferred or anticipated or mutual benefit present or anticipated to the driver and the person carried is sufficient to take the case out of the automobile guest statute. Harrison v. McCleary, 281 Ala. 87, 199 So. 2d 165 (1967).

The legislature, when it used the word "guest," did not intend to include persons who are being transported for the benefit of both the passenger and the operator or owner of the car, and in determining whether the transportation is for the mutual benefit of both, not merely the act of transportation must be considered, but also any contract or relationship between the parties to which it was an incident. Sullivan v. Davis, 263 Ala. 685, 83 So. 2d 434 (1955).

Nature of compensation or contract relation. — To take a person riding in an automobile out of the "guest" status, it is not necessary that compensation for the ride be a strict contractual consideration or that an enforceable contract relation relative to the ride should exist between the parties. Russell v. Thomas, 278 Ala. 400, 178 So. 2d 556 (1965).

A multitude of factual situations exists to which this section must be applied. The commercial and social relationships that can exist between the driver of an automobile and his passenger are almost as numerous and varied as human activity itself. At one extreme the court has the "hitchhiker" guest who clearly falls within the purview of the statute. At the other extreme is the passenger who pays the driver to be transported to a particular place and who is unquestionably beyond the scope of the statute. Between these two extremes the dividing line may at times become illusory and shadowy. It is sometimes necessary to enter into a detailed examination of the present and former relations between driver and passenger: implied and expressed arrangements made between them as to the conduct of the particular trip, the purpose of the mission, the benefits accruing to the driver and passenger from the expedition, and any other factors that bring into proper focus the true status of the parties at the time of the accident which gave rise to the legal action. Roe v. Lewis, 416 So. 2d 750 (Ala. 1982).

Compensation is not given where main purpose of trip is joint pleasure of the participants. Russell v. Thomas, 278 Ala. 400, 178 So. 2d 556 (1965).

Where relationship between parties is one of business and the transportation is supplied in the pursuit thereof for their mutual benefit, compensation has been given and the plaintiff is a passenger and not a guest. Russell v. Thomas, 278 Ala. 400, 178 So. 2d 556 (1965).

Guest need not make cash payment for his transportation to be "guest paying for his transportation" so as to be entitled under this section to recover from motorist for injury sustained in accident without proof of gross negligence or willful and wanton conduct, but it is sufficient if a benefit accrues by reason of the transportation. Russell v. Thomas, 278 Ala. 400, 178 So. 2d 556 (1965).

Sharing of expenses does not necessarily make one a paying passenger. — It is a general rule of wide acceptance that the sharing of the cost of operating the car on a trip, when the trip is undertaken for pleasure or social purposes and the invitation is not motivated by, or conditioned on, such contribution, is nothing more than the exchange of social amenities and does not transform into a paying passenger one who without the exchange would be a guest. Wagnon v. Patterson, 260 Ala. 297, 70 So. 2d 244 (1954).

But it may under certain circumstances. — Where the offer of transportation is conditioned on the contribution of the passenger toward the expenses, or where it appears that the agreement for transportation bears one or more of the indicia of a business arrangement, and especially where such arrangement is specifically for transportation, or comprehends a trip of considerable magnitude, or contemplates repeated and more or less regular rides, the person paying for gasoline and oil consumed or other automobile expenses is held to be a passenger and not a guest, and this is true even though the ultimate purpose of the arrangement may be for pleasure. Wagnon v. Patterson, 260 Ala. 297, 70 So. 2d 244 (1954).

And intent of parties is important element. — Each case involving the question of whether the occupant who contributes towards the expense is a passenger or a guest must be decided on its own facts, and the important factor to determine is the intent of the parties. Wagnon v. Patterson, 260 Ala. 297, 70 So. 2d 244 (1954).

Helping pay for gas. — Where plaintiff was injured while a passenger in defendant's car, plaintiff's occasional helping with gas was

mere social courtesy on behalf of friend and therefore, plaintiff was guest and not a paying passenger in defendant's car under this section. Klaber ex rel. Klaber v. Elliott, 533 So. 2d 576 (Ala. 1988).

Consent and ability to consent are major factors in the operation of the guest statute, even though individuals generally give no thought to the statute's effect when they ride in another's car. Walker v. Garris, 368 So. 2d 277 (Ala. 1979).

Nullification of consensual relationship. — In actions under guest statute, misrepresentations on the part of the driver may nullify the consensual relationship between host and guest, just as a "guest's" protests may convert him into a passenger. Walker v. Garris, 368 So. 2d 277 (Ala. 1979).

The relationship between the host and guest is consensual in nature and involves some acceptance by the guest of the relationship and its attendant hazards; and misrepresentations, express or by implication, which operate to induce one to become a rider in the automobile, can nullify the relationship. Roe v. Lewis, 416 So. 2d 750 (Ala. 1982).

The relationship between host and guest is consensual in nature, therefore protests by a guest may vitiate that consent and change his status to that of a passenger. Roe v. Lewis, 416 So. 2d 750 (Ala. 1982).

Where passenger had opportunity to leave driver's car. — Trial court did not err by excluding testimony concerning passenger's protests, as testimony about such protests was irrelevant where passenger had opportunity to remove himself from driver's car and chose not to do so. McDougle v. Shaddrix, 534 So. 2d 228 (Ala. 1988).

Mere complaints by passenger did not constitute sufficient protest to enable passenger to circumvent Alabama's guest statute, since no evidence was presented to trial court to indicate that passenger had become captive in driver's car, where after driver stopped, passenger opened his door, leaned out, and waved to his friends behind and then closed his door and remained in driver's car. McDougle v. Shaddrix, 534 So. 2d 228 (Ala. 1988).

Whether children under 14 are subject to guest statute is to be determined by jury based on individual child's capacity to consent. Walker v. Garris, 368 So. 2d 277 (Ala. 1979).

Trip facilitating employment negotiations. — Where the trip which resulted in injury to nurse was undertaken by defendant and his daughter to facilitate negotiations leading to employment of the nurse for defendant's sick wife, the supreme court could not hold as a matter of law that no tangible benefit flowed to the defendant from the automobile trip, or that such benefit did not induce the defendant to transport the nurse. Sullivan v. Davis, 263 Ala. 685, 83 So. 2d 434 (1955).

Employee riding home in employer's car. — Where employee was injured while riding home from work in employer's station wagon, the court held that employee was not a "guest" within the meaning of this section. Blair v. Greene, 247 Ala. 104, 22 So. 2d 834 (1945).

Son riding in father's car. — Where a father loaned his automobile to his son, the son stood in the shoes of the owner and was not a guest or a passenger while the son's friend drove the automobile. Taylor v. Bass, 279 Ala. 518, 187 So. 2d 560 (1966).

Issue of whether deceased, while riding in his father's car, was a "guest" of the driver within the meaning of this section, so as to entitle the driver to claim the benefit of this section, was a jury question. Richards v. Eaves, 273 Ala. 120, 135 So. 2d 384 (1961).

Friend injured in automobile accident on way to purchase parts to repair owner's brakes was not a guest. Klein v. Harris, 268 Ala. 540, 108 So. 2d 425 (1958).

Cheerleader riding in car of schoolteacher. — Where the present benefits, if any, which were derived by a schoolteacher from driving school cheerleaders to school basketball games were nebulous and intangible and any anticipated future benefits were speculative and dependent on future circumstances, plaintiff cheerleader was a "guest," and this section therefore excluded defendant schoolteacher from liability under a count for simple negligence in an automobile collision in which plaintiff was injured. Boggs v. Turner, 277 Ala. 157, 168 So. 2d 1 (1964).

IV. WILLFUL OR WANTON MISCONDUCT.

Duty owed to guest under this section is not to willfully or wantonly injure or kill him. Harper v. Griffin Lumber Co., 250 Ala. 339, 34 So. 2d 148 (1948); Walker v. Bowling, 261 Ala. 46, 72 So. 2d 841 (1954); English v. Jacobs, 263 Ala. 376, 82 So. 2d 542 (1955).

Willful or wanton misconduct is required in Alabama to hold a driver liable for injury to a guest. United States Fire Ins. Co. v. Watts, 370 F.2d 405 (5th Cir. 1966).

For motorist to be held liable under this section, it must be shown that he acted in a wanton manner resulting in the death of the person. Costarides v. Miller, 374 So. 2d 1335 (Ala. 1979).

A minor is held to an adult standard in determining whether his conduct while operating a motor vehicle is willful or wanton. Gunnells v. Dethrage, 366 So. 2d 1104 (Ala. 1979).

In determining whether a minor has knowledge of the circumstances and the probable consequences of his acts or omissions on the highways, he must be held to the same standard as all other users of the highways. Gunnells v. Dethrage, 366 So. 2d 1104 (Ala. 1979).

"Wantonness" defined. — "Wantonness" is the conscious doing of some act or omission of some duty under knowledge of existing conditions, conscious that from the doing of such act or omission of such duty injury will likely or probably result. Randolph v. Kessler, 275 Ala. 73, 152 So. 2d 138 (1963); Jackson v. Cook, 275 Ala. 151, 153 So. 2d 229 (1963); Lankford v. Mong, 283 Ala. 24, 214 So. 2d 301 (1968); Marshall v. Marshall, 284 Ala. 512, 226 So. 2d 298 (1969); McDougle v. Shaddrix, 534 So. 2d 228 (Ala. 1988).

In wantonness, the party doing the act, or failing to act, is conscious of his conduct and, without having the intent to injure, is conscious from his knowledge of existing circumstances and conditions that his conduct will likely or probably result in injury. Jackson v. Cook, 275 Ala. 151, 153 So. 2d 229 (1963).

An approved definition of wantonness is the conscious failure of one charged with the duty to exercise due care and diligence to prevent an injury after discovery of peril. Or, under circumstances where one is charged with the knowledge of such peril, and conscious that injury will likely, probably or inevitably result from his actions, or his failure to act, to not take the proper precautions to prevent injury. English v. Jacobs, 263 Ala. 376, 82 So. 2d 542 (1955).

In death action under this section, "wantonness" required knowledge by truck driver of peril to deceased and of probable consequences of truck driver's conduct and that, with reckless disregard of such consequences, driver pursued that conduct which proximately caused death, though driver had no intention to inflict injury. Couch v. Hutcherson, 243 Ala. 47, 8 So. 2d 580 (1942). See also Smith v. Roland, 243 Ala. 400, 10 So. 2d 367 (1942); Dean v. Adams, 249 Ala. 319, 30 So. 2d 903 (1947).

Knowledge and consciousness as essential elements of wantonness. — Knowledge and consciousness that injury might likely or probably result are elements which are essential if the issue of wantonness is to be properly submitted to the jury. Marshall v. Marshall, 284 Ala. 512, 226 So. 2d 298 (1969).

Knowledge may be proved circumstantially. — Before a party can be said to be guilty of wanton conduct, it must be shown that, with reckless indifference to the consequences, he consciously and intentionally did some wrongful act or omitted some known duty which produced the injury. But knowledge need not be shown by direct proof. It may be made to appear, like any other fact, by showing circumstances from which the fact or actual knowledge is a legitimate inference. Lankford v. Mong, 283 Ala. 24, 214 So. 2d 301 (1968).

Definition of wantonness must be viewed in light of circumstances of the particular case under review. Marshall v. Marshall, 284 Ala. 512, 226 So. 2d 298 (1969).

And depends upon facts of particular case. — That which constitutes wanton misconduct depends upon the facts in each particular case. Marshall v. Marshall, 284 Ala. 512, 226 So. 2d 298 (1969).

Occurrence witnesses are no more essential to the establishment of wantonness than in the proof of actionable negligence. Richards v. Eaves, 273 Ala. 120, 135 So. 2d 384 (1961).

Falling asleep while driving. — A driver of an automobile is not guilty of wanton or willful misconduct in falling asleep while driving unless it appears that he continued to drive in reckless disregard of premonitory symptoms. Generally speaking, if it appears that the driver of an automobile has been without sleep for a considerable period of time and has experienced symptoms of the approach of sleep, the fact that he continues to drive under such circumstances has been held to manifest a willful and wanton disregard for the safety of others within the meaning of the applicable guest statute. Lankford v. Mong, 283 Ala. 24, 214 So. 2d 301 (1968).

For case holding evidence insufficient to support an inference of wanton conduct, see Richards v. Eaves, 273 Ala. 120, 135 So. 2d 384 (1961).

Wantonness should be submitted to jury unless there is a total lack of evidence from which jury could reasonably infer wantonness. McDougle v. Shaddrix, 534 So. 2d 228 (Ala. 1988).

Issue of wantonness held a jury question. — Under evidence that truck driver started down hill at considerable speed, with heavy load and without brakes, that there was obstruction at base of hill and fill of six feet, all of which was known to truck driver, whether truck driver was guilty of wantonness was for jury. Couch v. Hutcherson, 243 Ala. 47, 8 So. 2d 580 (1942). See also English v. Jacobs, 263 Ala. 376, 82 So. 2d 542 (1955).

Trial court erred when it directed a verdict against passenger's wantonness claim, since there was evidence from which a jury could have concluded that the driver's conduct was wanton where testimony indicated that truck was in driver's unobstructed view for approximately one-quarter of mile, yet she drove in front of truck without regard for present danger, and where testimony indicated that driver drove in front of the truck when it was no more than 50 feet away from her. McDougle v. Shaddrix, 534 So. 2d 228 (Ala. 1988).

Sufficiency of evidence of wantonness on appeal. — In considering the question of the sufficiency of the evidence of wantonness to be submitted to the jury, the supreme court must accept the adduced evidence most favorable to the plaintiff as true, and indulge in such reasonable inferences as the jury was free to draw from the evidence. Randolph v. Kessler, 275 Ala. 73, 152 So. 2d 138 (1963).

§ 32-1-3. When right to use highways may be restricted.

Local authorities may by ordinance or resolution prohibit the operation of vehicles upon any highways or impose restrictions as to the weight of vehicles when operated upon any highway under the jurisdiction of and for the maintenance of which such local authorities are responsible, whenever any said highway by reason of deterioration, rain, snow or other climatic conditions will be seriously damaged or destroyed unless the use of vehicles thereon is prohibited or the permissible weights reduced. Such local authorities enacting any such ordinance or resolution shall erect or cause to be erected and maintained signs designating the provisions of the ordinance or resolution at each end of that portion of any highway affected thereby, and the ordinance or resolution shall not be effective until or unless such signs are erected and maintained. Local authorities may also, by ordinance or resolution, prohibit the operation of trucks or other commercial vehicles or impose limitations as to the weight thereof on designated highways, which prohibitions and limitations shall be designated by appropriate signs.

The highway department in respect to state highways or roads designated as part of the state system of primary roads may prescribe loads and weights lower than the limits prescribed in section 32-9-20 whenever in its or their judgment any road or part thereof, any bridge or culvert shall by reason of deterioration, rain, snow or other climatic conditions be liable to be damaged or destroyed by vehicles. In such event there shall be erected and maintained proper signs designating the provisions of such additional restrictions, such signs to be placed at each end of that portion of highway affected thereby. After such signs have been erected, the operation of any vehicle contrary to its provisions shall constitute a violation of this title, and such violation shall be punishable as provided in this title. (Acts 1927, No. 347, p. 348; Acts 1932, Ex. Sess., No. 58, p. 68; Code 1940, T. 36, §§ 79, 82.)

Collateral references. — 60 C.J.S., Motor Vehicles, § 31.

Power to limit weight of vehicle or load thereon with respect to use of highways. 26 ALR 747, 72 ALR 1004, 75 ALR2d 376.

Construction and operation of statutes or regulations restricting the weight of motor vehicles or their loads. 45 ALR3d 503.

§ 32-1-4. Appearance upon arrest for misdemeanor.

(a) Whenever any person is arrested for a violation of any provisions of this title punishable as a misdemeanor, the arresting officer shall, unless otherwise provided in this section, take the name and address of such person and the license number of his motor vehicle and issue a summons or otherwise notify him in writing to appear at a time and place to be specified in such summons or notice, and such person shall, if he so desire, have a right to an immediate hearing or a hearing within 24 hours at a convenient hour and such hearing to be before a magistrate within the county or city where such offense was committed. Such officer shall thereupon and upon the giving by such person of a sufficient written bond, approved by the arresting officer, to appear at such time and place, forthwith release him from custody.

Any person refusing to give such bond to appear shall be taken immediately by the arresting officer before the nearest or most accessible magistrate.

Any person who willfully violates his written bond to appear, given in accordance with this section, shall be guilty of a misdemeanor regardless of the disposition of the charge upon which he was originally arrested.

(b) The provisions of this section shall not apply to any person arrested and charged with an offense causing or contributing to an accident resulting in injury or death to any person nor to any person charged with driving while under the influence of intoxicating liquor or of narcotic or other drugs nor to any person whom the arresting officer shall have good cause to believe has committed any felony, and the arresting officer shall take such person forthwith before the nearest or most accessible magistrate.

(c) Any officer violating any of the provisions of this section shall be guilty of misconduct in office and shall be subject to removal from office. (Acts 1927, No. 347, p. 348; Code 1940, T. 36, § 52; Acts 1949, No. 517, p. 754, § 16.)

Cross references. — As to traffic infractions and uniform traffic tickets generally, see § 12-12-50 et seq. As to violations of rules of the road, see §§ 32-5-310, 32-5A-8. As to the Alabama uniform traffic ticket and complaint form, see Rule 19, ARJA.

The clear import of this section is that the police have no authority to take a motorist into custody and then require him to go to the local stationhouse when that motorist has committed a misdemeanor traffic violation but is willing to sign the summons to court. Morton v. State, 452 So. 2d 1361 (Ala. Crim. App. 1984); Hays v. City of Jacksonville, 518 So. 2d 892 (Ala. Crim. App. 1987).

This statute requires strict compliance by the arresting officer as is evidenced by the penalty provisions of subsection (c). Morton v. State, 452 So. 2d 1361 (Ala. Crim. App. 1984).

In this section provision is made for hearing before magistrate "within the county or city where such offense was committed." By the terms of this section, it has reference to any of the misdemeanor offenses provided for in this title. Pharr v. Whittle, 237 Ala. 124, 185 So. 895 (1939).

Jurisdiction conferred upon and hearing before magistrate referred to in this section is final jurisdiction, and not merely for a preliminary hearing. The legislative intent is clear to that effect from the language used. Pharr v. Whittle, 237 Ala. 124, 185 So. 895 (1939).

Detention for minor traffic violation. — Except for the exceptions provided by subsection (b) of this section, a person arrested for a misdemeanor traffic violation is not subject to further detention for that offense once the arresting officer has obtained the necessary information and given the motorist the "summons or notice" to appear. Daniels v. State, 416 So. 2d 760 (Ala. Crim. App. 1982); Morton v. State, 452 So. 2d 1361 (Ala. Crim. App. 1984).

Although this section generally forbids police officers from taking persons into custody for violation of minor traffic laws, as a matter of constitutional law, however, any person lawfully arrested for the pettiest misdemeanor may be temporarily placed in custody. Daniels v. State, 416 So. 2d 760 (Ala. Crim. App. 1982).

Detention for speeding not authorized. — Because defendant was charged with speeding only, his detention following the arrest for speeding was not authorized for the purpose of transporting defendant to headquarters in order to take a breath test and the arrest was illegal under the meaning of § 32-5-192(a), and the results of the blood alcohol test were

also inadmissible. McCall v. State, 534 So. 2d 668 (Ala. Crim. App. 1988).

Subject to exceptions of subsection (b), custodian arrest not authorized for improper lane usage. Hays v. City of Jacksonville, 518 So. 2d 892 (Ala. Crim. App. 1987).

Because none of subsection (b) exceptions to the misdemeanor traffic offense arrest provisions of subsection (a) applied to the defendant here, police officer was not authorized to detain her following her arrest for improper lane usage. Her arrest was, therefore, not lawful within the meaning of subsection (a), and the results of her blood alcohol test were inadmissible in evidence. Hays v. City of Jacksonville, 518 So. 2d 892 (Ala. Crim. App. 1987).

Clear language of subsection (b) requires that in order to fall within custodial arrest exception of subsection (a), motorist must be charged with DUI. This is true unless one of the other exceptions would be applicable, such as an accident resulting in personal injury or where the officer had probable cause to believe the motorist had committed a felony. Thus, there must be an actual arrest for DUI based on probable cause to arrest and such must be lawful within the meaning of this section. Sheffield v. State, 522 So. 2d 4 (Ala. Crim. App. 1987).

The defendant's cause must be reversed and remanded as he was arrested for speeding and required to submit to a breath test without being formally charged with DUI until the results of the intoxilizer were available. Sheffield v. State, 522 So. 2d 4 (Ala. Crim. App. 1987).

Noncustodial arrest will not give rise to search incident to arrest. State v. Davis, 477 So. 2d 504 (Ala. Crim. App. 1985).

Arresting officer's conduct held within exception of subsection (b). — See Gaskin v. State, 338 So. 2d 1041 (Ala. Crim. App. 1976).

Arrest held illegal. — From the record, it appears that defendant was arrested only for speeding. The circumstances of the arrest did not meet any of the statutory requirements necessary to justify a custodial arrest. Therefore, the arrest was illegal, and the results of the breath tests were the direct result of the illegal arrest. Therefore, the test results were tainted and should not have been admitted into evidence. McDaniel v. State, 526 So. 2d 642 (Ala. Crim. App. 1988).

Cited in Richardson v. State, 446 So. 2d 662 (Ala. Crim. App. 1983); McElroy v. State, 469 So. 2d 1337 (Ala. Crim. App. 1985).

Collateral references. — 61A C.J.S., Motor Vehicles, §§ 593(1)-593(5).

§ 32-1-5. Depositing driver's license in lieu of bail in certain cases — Procedure.

(a) Whenever any person lawfully possessed of a chauffeur's or driver's license theretofore issued to him by the department of public safety of the state of Alabama, or under the laws of any other state or territory, or the District of Columbia of the United States, shall be arrested and charged with any violation of the provisions of this title for which under the provisions of sections 32-1-4 and 32-5-36 the arresting officer is directed to take a written bond, he shall have the option of depositing his chauffeur's or driver's license so issued to him with the arresting officer or the court, in lieu of any other security which may be required for his appearance in any court in this state in answer to such charge lodged in such court.

(b) If such person arrested elects to deposit his license as provided, the arresting officer or court shall issue such person a receipt for said license upon a form furnished or prescribed by the Alabama department of public safety, and thereafter, said person shall be permitted to operate a motor vehicle upon the highways of this state during the pendency of the case in which the license was deposited, unless his license or privilege is otherwise revoked, suspended or cancelled.

(c) The clerk or judge of the court, in which the charge is lodged, shall immediately forward to the department the license of the driver deposited in lieu of bail if the driver fails to appear in answer to the charge against him. The director of public safety shall upon receipt of a license so forwarded by the court suspend the driver license and driving privilege of the defaulting driver until notified by the court that the charge against such driver has been finally adjudicated. (Acts 1967, Ex. Sess., No. 220, p. 276.)

Code commissioner's note. — Section 32-5-36, referred to in this section, was repealed by Acts 1980, No. 80-434, p. 604, § 15-106, effective May 19, 1980. For the Rules of the Road, see now Chapter 5A of this title.

§ 32-1-6. Same — Violation of traffic ordinance of incorporated municipality.

(a) Whenever any person lawfully possessed of a chauffeur's or driver's license theretofore issued to him by the department of public safety of the state of Alabama, or under the laws of any other state or territory, or the District of Columbia of the United States, shall be arrested and charged with any violation of any traffic ordinance of any incorporated municipality, for which under the provisions of such ordinance the arresting officer is directed to take a written bond, he shall have the option of depositing his chauffeur's or driver's license so issued to him with the arresting officer or the clerk of the district court or municipal court, in lieu of any other security which may be required for his appearance in the district court or municipal court in answer to such charge lodged in such court.

(b) If such person arrested elects to deposit his license, as herein provided, the arresting officer or clerk of the district court or municipal court shall issue such person a receipt for said license upon a form furnished or prescribed by the municipality, and thereafter said person shall be permitted to operate a motor vehicle upon the highways of this state during the pendency of the case in which the license was deposited, unless his license or privilege is otherwise revoked, suspended or cancelled.

(c) The clerk of the court in which the charge is lodged shall immediately forward to the department of public safety of the state of Alabama the license of the driver which was deposited in lieu of bail if the driver fails to appear in answer to the charge against him. The director of public safety shall, upon receipt of a license so forwarded by the clerk, suspend the driver license and driving privilege of the defaulting driver until notified by the court that the charge against such driver has been finally adjudicated. (Acts 1969, No. 736, p. 1310.)

§ 32-1-7. Operation of vehicles on beaches and sand dunes of Gulf of Mexico prohibited; exceptions, penalty, etc.

(a) It shall be unlawful to operate a motor vehicle, motorcycle or motor driven cycle as they are defined by section 32-1-1.1 on the beaches and sand dunes on the Gulf of Mexico along the southern boundary of the state of Alabama off of the public roads, parking places and private driveways. Provided, however, owners of private property, their families, and invited guests may park their motor vehicles on their private property; and provided that motor vehicles engaged in the construction, maintenance or repair of utility facilities may be operated on such beaches and sand dunes to the extent necessary to carry out such construction, repair or maintenance of utility facilities; and provided further that motor vehicles actively engaged in construction projects may be operated on sites for which building permits have been issued by the proper building inspector or authority.

(b) Any person violating the provisions of this section shall be guilty of a Class C misdemeanor. (Acts 1981, No. 81-563, p. 948.)

CHAPTER 2.

DEPARTMENT OF PUBLIC SAFETY.

ARTICLE 1.

GENERAL PROVISIONS.

§ 32-2-1. Creation; headed by director; appointment and term of director.

There is hereby created a department of the state of Alabama which shall be known as the department of public safety and shall be headed by the director of public safety. The governor shall appoint the director, who shall serve at the pleasure of the governor. (Acts 1953, No. 585, p. 828, § 1.)

Cited in Mieth v. Dothard, 418 F. Supp. 1169 (M.D. Ala. 1976).

Collateral references. — 81 C.J.S., States, §§ 66, 68, 77.

§ 32-2-2. Assistant director.

There is hereby created within the department of public safety the position of assistant director of public safety, which position shall be in lieu of that of confidential assistant provided for by section 36-26-10, which shall be filled by appointment by the governor, and the appointed person shall serve at the pleasure of the governor and may be removed by the governor; and the appointment, service and removal of the assistant director shall not be subject to the state merit system regulations.

The duties of the assistant director of the department of public safety shall include direction and coordination of the activities of the department of public safety, subject to and under the control and supervision of the director of public safety. Such assistant director shall receive an annual salary not to exceed that salary fixed by sections 36-6-5 through 36-6-7 to be paid from the funds of the department of public safety in the same manner as other state employees are paid. (Acts 1967, Ex. Sess., No. 175, p. 224.)

§ 32-2-3. Divisions — Creation; enumeration.

The director shall create such divisions within the department of public safety as shall be necessary. Said divisions shall include:

(1) An administrative division;

(2) A highway patrol division;

(3) A driver's license division;

(4) A service division. (Acts 1953, No. 585, p. 828, § 3.)

Cited in Mieth v. Dothard, 418 F. Supp. 1169 (M.D. Ala. 1976).

§ 32-2-4. Same — Chiefs; employees.

The director shall appoint chiefs of said divisions and all other employees subject to the provisions of the Merit System Act, and said chiefs and employees shall hold their positions subject to the provisions of the Merit System Act. (Acts 1953, No. 585, p. 828, § 4.)

Cross references. — As to merit system, see § 36-26-1 et seq.

Height and weight requirements for job of state trooper held violation of equal protection. — The five feet, nine inches and 160 pound height and weight requirements set by the department of public safety for the job of state trooper are not rationally related to the achievement of any legitimate state interest and therefore violate the equal protection clause of the fourteenth amendment to the United States Constitution. Mieth v. Dothard, 418 F. Supp. 1169 (M.D. Ala. 1976), aff'd in part and rev'd in part sub nom. Dothard v. Rawlinson, 433 U.S. 321, 97 S. Ct. 2720, 53 L. Ed. 2d 786 (1977).

§ 32-2-5. What laws director to enforce.

It shall be the duty of the director of the department of public safety, and he shall have power to do all that is necessary to administer and enforce:

(1) All laws contained in this title, as the same may now or hereafter be amended;

(2) All other laws relating or pertaining to the operation or movement of vehicles on the public highways of this state;

(3) Such other laws as the department of public safety has heretofore administered and enforced. (Acts 1953, No. 585, p. 828, § 5.)

Cross references. — As to duty of director of public safety to provide for taking up and impounding livestock or other animals running at large upon state and federal aid highways, see § 3-2-20.

Cited in Mieth v. Dothard, 418 F. Supp. 1169 (M.D. Ala. 1976).

Collateral references. — 81 C.J.S., States, § 66.

§ 32-2-6. Compensation and expenses of officers, employees, etc. — Method of payment generally.

The compensation of the officers, agents and employees provided for by this chapter shall be paid by warrants drawn by the comptroller on the funds appropriated by the legislature therefor as the salaries of state officials and employees are paid, and the necessary expenses and costs of necessary equipment are likewise to be paid by warrant drawn by the comptroller on the funds appropriated by the legislature therefor, and the amount to be expended hereunder shall be limited to the amount appropriated therefor by the legislature and shall be budgeted, allotted and expended pursuant to article 4 of chapter 4 of Title 41 of this Code. (Acts 1953, No. 585, p. 828, § 8; Acts 1955, No. 44, p. 263, § 1.)

Cross references. — As to salaries of public officers and employees generally, see § 36-6-1 et seq.

§ 32-2-7. Same — Controlling civil disturbances; rescue or protective duties.

Whenever any officer, agent or employee of the department of public safety shall be called upon by the governor, or the appointing authority of said department, to perform a duty or duties, or to be present at or on an alert basis at the scene of, or at any marshalling point for movement to such scene, of any public disorder for the control of civil disturbances, the restoration of the public order, or to perform rescue or protective duties at a natural or man-made disaster which shall extend beyond 24 hours, then any law or laws to the contrary notwithstanding, the compensation of such officers, agents or employees of said department, the expenses of subsistence while so engaged at the call of the governor, or of the appointing authority of said department, may be paid out of the general treasury of the state upon the approval of the governor, and not from the regular appropriations provided for the organization, maintenance and upkeep of the department of public safety. Warrants for these purposes shall be issued by the comptroller on vouchers or payrolls, as may be required by the governor, certified by the director of public safety and approved by the governor. (Acts 1969, No. 167, p. 452.)

§ 32-2-8. Fees for copies of records and reports.

Whenever the director of public safety is required or allowed by law to furnish a copy of any record or report in the department's files, the director shall set and collect a fee not to exceed the sum of $5.00 for each record or report, unless a different fee is otherwise prescribed by law. Said fee shall be paid into the state treasury and credited to the state general fund. (Acts 1971, No. 959, p. 1717; Acts 1988, 1st Sp. Sess., No. 88-721, p. 112, § 1.)

The 1988, 1st Sp. Sess., amendment, effective September 13, 1988, substituted "the sum of $5.00 for each record or report" for "the sum of $3.00."

Cross references. — As to responsibilities of county departments relative to child abuse or neglect, see § 26-14-1 et seq.

§ 32-2-8.1. Fee for criminal history records search.

When the director of public safety is allowed by Alabama law to provide a criminal history records search of convictions within the state of Alabama, the director shall set and collect a minimum fee of $20.00 or the actual cost incurred. All fees collected under the provisions of this section shall be deposited in the state treasury to the credit of the state general fund. (Acts 1988, 1st Sp. Sess., No. 88-814, p. 255, § 1.)

Effective date. — The act which added this section became effective September 20, 1988.

§ 32-2-9. Promulgation of rules and regulations.

The director of public safety, with the approval of the governor, may establish and promulgate reasonable rules and regulations not in conflict with the laws of this state concerning operation of motor vehicles and concerning the enforcement of the provisions of this chapter. (Acts 1953, No. 585, p. 828, § 15.)

§ 32-2-10. Insurance for employees.

The state department of public safety is authorized, subject to approval by the governor, to insure its employees in some insurance company or companies authorized to do business in the state of Alabama against personal injury or death caused by accident or violence while discharging their duties as such employees; provided, the amount of insurance to be procured as to any such employee shall not exceed the amount which would be payable to such employee under the workmen's compensation laws of the state of Alabama if such employee were privately employed; except, that such policy may provide additional benefits not to exceed $10,000.00 per employee for the payment of hospital and medical expenses.

The cost of such insurance shall be paid by the state department of public safety out of any funds appropriated to its use in manner provided by law. (Acts 1943, No. 388, p. 606; Acts 1953, No. 722, p. 976.)

Cited in Alabama Farm Bureau Mut. Cas. Ins. Co. v. Smelley, 295 Ala. 346, 329 So. 2d 544 (1976).

ARTICLE 2.

HIGHWAY PATROL.

Cross references. — As to compensation for death or disability of peace officers, see § 36-30-1 et seq.

§ 32-2-20. Establishment and maintenance.

The governor is authorized to establish and maintain a state highway patrol. (Acts 1939, No. 181, p. 300; Code 1940, T. 36, § 71; Acts 1943, No. 446, p. 408; Acts 1953, No. 17, p. 22; Acts 1955, No. 43, p. 260, § 3.)

Cited in Roberts v. State ex rel. Cooper, 253 Ala. 565, 46 So. 2d 5 (1950).

Collateral references. — 60 C.J.S., Motor Vehicles, §§ 101, 136(1), 145, 149, 158. 61A C.J.S., Motor Vehicles, § 593(1). 81 C.J.S., States, §§ 66, 68, 77.

§ 32-2-21. Disposition of costs, fees and mileage otherwise collectible by officers.

No state trooper shall be entitled to any costs, fees or mileage for attending any court, but instead the proper authority shall collect such costs, fees and mileage as may be due such officers for attendance on any court or for any official act and shall promptly turn the same over to the director of public safety, who shall cover the same into the state treasury to the credit of the general fund. (Acts 1953, No. 585, p. 828, § 6.)

§ 32-2-22. Officers have powers of peace officers.

Members of the state highway patrol, when duly appointed, shall have the powers of peace officers in this state and may exercise such powers anywhere within the state. (Acts 1953, No. 585, p. 828, § 7.)

§ 32-2-23. Bonds of officers and members.

Before entering upon the duties of their respective offices, all officers and members of the state highway patrol shall execute to the state of Alabama a bond, to be approved by the governor, in the amount of $2,000.00, for the faithful performance of their duties. (Acts 1943, No. 122, p. 123; Acts 1961, Ex. Sess., No. 208, p. 2190.)

§ 32-2-24. Liabilities under bonds.

The officers and members of the state highway patrol shall be subject to the same liabilities, penalties and damages under their bonds as sheriffs are under their bonds. (Acts 1953, No. 585, p. 828, § 9.)

§ 32-2-25. Arrest fee; when fees and costs not to be paid by county.

In all cases where arrests are made by a state trooper, an arrest fee of $5.00 for such arrest shall be collected by the proper authorities and promptly turned over to the director of public safety, who shall cover the same into the state treasury to the credit of the general fund; provided, that no witness fee, arrest fee, mileage cost or any other fees or costs shall be paid by any county out of its funds to said department and no fine and forfeiture claim shall be issued against the fine and forfeiture fund of any county to or for any such state trooper for or on account of those cases brought in any court or before any grand jury by any such officer wherein no indictment is found, the state fails to convict, or the indictment or complaint abates or is nolle prossed or is withdrawn and filed in such case. (Acts 1953, No. 585, p. 828, § 10; Acts 1955, No. 44, p. 263, § 1; Acts 1961, No. 834, p. 1237.)

§ 32-2-26. Officers to receive badge, pistol, etc., as part of retirement benefits.

Any person who, at the time of his retirement, is employed by the state department of public safety as a state trooper or other law-enforcement officer shall receive, as a part of his retirement benefit, without cost to him, his badge, pistol and such other equipment as the department of public safety may designate. (Acts 1971, No. 2340, p. 3774.)

ARTICLE 3.

STATE TROOPER RESERVE.

§ 32-2-40. Establishment authorized; composition; members to serve without compensation.

The director of the department of public safety is hereby authorized to establish a state trooper reserve of the Alabama state troopers to be composed of such persons who may volunteer to serve as state trooper reserves of the Alabama state troopers. Such service to be without compensation to the individual so volunteering. (Acts 1978, 2nd Ex. Sess., No. 123, p. 1838, § 1.)

§ 32-2-41. Reserve troopers to serve under direction and supervision of director of public safety; privileges and immunities of reserves.

Reserve state troopers serving with the Alabama state troopers shall at all times serve under the direction and supervision of the director of the department of public safety and/or members of the Alabama state troopers. State trooper reserves, while serving under the supervision and direction of the director or a member of the Alabama state troopers, shall have the same protection and immunities afforded regularly employed state troopers, which shall be recognized by all courts having jurisdiction over offenses against the laws of this state. (Acts 1978, 2nd Ex. Sess., No. 123, p. 1838, § 2.)

§ 32-2-42. Determination of fitness of persons to serve.

The director of the department of public safety shall determine the fitness of persons to serve as state trooper reserves. (Acts 1978, 2nd Ex. Sess., No. 123, p. 1838, § 3.)

§ 32-2-43. Duties of members of reserve.

The duties of a state trooper reserve officer shall be limited to assisting the department of public safety in the performance of its regularly constituted duties and shall serve under the immediate supervision of a lawful department of public safety officer. (Acts 1978, 2nd Ex. Sess., No. 123, p. 1838, § 4.)

§ 32-2-44. Authority to carry firearms when summoned to duty.

State trooper reserves shall have the authority to carry firearms when summoned to duty. (Acts 1978, 2nd Ex. Sess., No. 123, p. 1838, § 5.)

CHAPTER 3.

STATE SAFETY COORDINATING COMMITTEE.

§ 32-3-1. Establishment; composition; terms of members.

There is hereby established a committee to be designated the state safety coordinating committee which shall be composed of the governor as chairman thereof, the director of public safety, the director of the state highway department, two members of the senate appointed by the president of the senate, two members of the house appointed by the speaker, the attorney general, the administrator of the state alcoholic beverage control board, the state toxicologist and the chief justice of the Alabama supreme court and a person appointed by the governor for a term of four years from the state at large. The same per diem allowance and travel expenses paid state employees will be paid to the governor's appointee. Thereafter, he shall serve four-year terms. The ex officio members shall serve until the expiration of the terms for which they have been elected. The appointive members shall serve for the terms for which they have been appointed. (Acts 1965, 1st Ex. Sess., No. 92, p. 107, § 1; Acts 1982, 2nd Ex. Sess., No. 82-708, p. 166.)

§ 32-3-2. Time and purpose of meetings.

The state safety coordinating committee shall meet regularly upon call of the governor for the purpose of exploring every facet of the complex problem of traffic safety; to identify major highway and traffic problems; to formulate concrete plans of action to meet those needs; to establish a schedule of priorities for action; and to coordinate the separate programs adopted by traffic officials in all executive branches of state government, as well as those of county and municipal governments, and those of civic, commercial, industrial, labor, fraternal, religious, educational and national organizations in a major effort to promote all aspects of public safety. (Acts 1965, 1st Ex. Sess., No. 92, p. 107, § 2.)

§ 32-3-3. Problems to be specifically studied.

The state safety coordinating committee shall study specifically the problems of interstate and intrastate highway safety; the feasibility and advisability of the adoption of interstate highway safety compacts; the adoption of uniform laws and ordinances, uniform signs, signals and markings; the means of obtaining more uniform enforcement of traffic laws, the use of motor vehicle safety equipment; and the problem of engineering safety control in roads and highways. (Acts 1965, 1st Ex. Sess., No. 92, p. 107, § 3.)

§ 32-3-4. Recommendations of committee.

The state safety coordinating committee shall also from time to time make recommendations to the legislature for the enactment of laws designed to promote improvement in existing programs of highway safety and for the adoption of additional programs or measures as may be considered necessary and advisable to accomplish the objects of the committee. (Acts 1965, 1st Ex. Sess., No. 92, p. 107, § 4.)

§ 32-3-5. Administrative expenses.

The state safety coordinating committee is hereby authorized to expend for payment of administrative expenses heretofore or hereafter incurred in its program any funds appropriated to it by section 32-5-313. (Acts 1965, 1st Ex. Sess., No. 92, p. 107, § 5.)

§ 32-3-6. Allocation of funds — Highway and traffic safety programs.

The state safety coordinating committee is hereby authorized to allocate any funds appropriated to it to the office of the coordinator of highway and traffic safety for expense of highway and traffic safety programs and for participation to secure benefits available under the National Highway Safety Act of 1966, and all subsequent amendments thereto, and similar federal programs of highway and traffic safety. (Acts 1971, No. 957, p. 1716, § 1.)

§ 32-3-7. Same — Department of education or any educational institution for prelicensing driver education and training program.

The state safety coordinating committee is hereby authorized to allocate any funds appropriated to it to the department of education or to any educational institution in Alabama for the sole purpose of instituting and conducting a program of prelicensing driver education and training. All funds so allocated shall be set up in a special fund in the state treasury known as the "driver education and training fund" which shall be used solely for the purpose of carrying out the provisions of this section. (Acts 1973, No. 1137, p. 1921; Acts 1977, No. 501, p. 657.)

CHAPTER 4.

HIGHWAY AND TRAFFIC SAFETY COORDINATION ACT.

§ 32-4-1. Short title.

This chapter shall be known as, and may be cited as, the "Highway and Traffic Safety Coordination Act of 1967." (Acts 1967, No. 270, p. 775, § 1.)

Collateral references. — Highway contract's liability to highway user for highway surface defects. 62 ALR4th 1067.

§ 32-4-2. Declaration of policy; authority of governor.

It is the public policy of this state in every way possible to reduce the number of traffic accidents, deaths, injuries and property damage through the formulation of comprehensive highway and traffic safety programs. The governor, as the chief executive and highest elected official of this state, is hereby invested with the power and authority to act as the chief administrator in the formulation of such programs on highway and traffic safety. (Acts 1967, No. 270, p. 775, § 2.)

§ 32-4-3. Coordinator of highway and traffic safety — Office created; appointment; term of office; duties.

There is hereby created within the executive department of the state government, and immediately under the supervision of the governor, the office of coordinator of highway and traffic safety. The coordinator shall be appointed by the governor, and shall serve at the pleasure of the governor. The coordinator shall advise with and assist the governor in the formulation, coordination and supervision of comprehensive state and local highway and traffic safety programs to reduce traffic accidents, deaths, injuries and property damage within this state. The coordinator, acting under the direction and supervision of the governor, shall also advise the various departments and agencies of state government concerned with highway and traffic safety programs. He shall coordinate and review, cooperatively, the programs developed by the various local political subdivisions, for the purpose of assisting them in the preparation of their highway traffic safety programs to insure that they meet the criteria established for such programs by the appropriate state and federal authorities. (Acts 1967, No. 270, p. 775, § 3.)

§ 32-4-4. Same — Quarters; staff; supplies.

The governor is authorized to provide and designate for the use of the coordinator such space as shall be necessary to quarter the coordinator and his staff. The coordinator is authorized to employ and secure the necessary staff, supplies and materials to carry out the provisions of this chapter, subject to the approval of the governor, under the provisions of the merit system. (Acts 1967, No. 270, p. 775, § 4.)

Cross references. — As to merit system, see § 36-26-1 et seq.

§ 32-4-5. Participation in benefits of National Highway Safety Act of 1966; standards and programs of political subdivisions.

The governor is hereby authorized and granted the power to contract and to exercise any other powers which may be necessary in order to insure that all departments of state government and local political subdivisions participate to the fullest extent possible in the benefits available under the "National Highway Safety Act of 1966" and all subsequent amendments thereto and similar federal programs of highway and traffic safety. The governor is hereby authorized to formulate standards for highway and traffic safety programs for political subdivisions to assure that they meet criteria of the national highway safety bureau, or its successor, and shall institute a reporting system for the local political subdivisions to report the status of their programs to the state. (Acts 1967, No. 270, p. 775, § 5.)

§ 32-4-6. Cooperation with and participation in programs of federal and other agencies.

The governor, acting for and in behalf of the state of Alabama, is authorized to cooperate with, and participate in, the programs of all federal, state, local, public and private agencies and organizations in order to effectuate the purposes of this chapter. (Acts 1967, No. 270, p. 775, § 6.)

§ 32-4-7. Powers of local governing bodies.

The governing authorities of the various counties and municipalities are empowered to contract with the state, federal and other local, public and private agencies and organizations and exercise other necessary powers to participate to the fullest extent possible in the highway and traffic safety programs of this state, the provisions of the "National Highway Safety Act of 1966" and all subsequent amendments thereto and similar federal programs of highway and traffic safety. (Acts 1967, No. 270, p. 775, § 7.)

CHAPTER 5.

REGULATION OF OPERATION OF MOTOR VEHICLES, ETC., GENERALLY.

Cross references. — As to rules of the road generally, see chapter 5A of this title.

Motorist must have been lawfully arrested before any chemical test to determine intoxication conducted in order to authorize the admission into evidence of the test results. Hays v. City of Jacksonville, 518 So. 2d 892 (Ala. Crim. App. 1987).

ARTICLE 1.

GENERAL PROVISIONS.

§ 32-5-1. Powers of local authorities.

(a) Except as herein otherwise provided, local authorities shall have no power to pass, enforce or maintain any ordinance, rule or regulation requiring from any owner or chauffeur or other authorized driver to whom this chapter is applicable, any additional license or permit for the use of the public highways, or excluding any such owner, chauffeur or other authorized driver from the public highway, nor to pass, enforce or maintain any ordinance, rule or regulation regulating motor vehicles or their speed contrary to the provisions of this chapter, nor shall any such law now in force or hereafter enacted have any effect.

(b) Local authorities shall have no power or authority to charge a license or tax upon any motor carrier hauling passengers or any truck hauling freight for hire, when such motor carriers in the usual course of operations enter or pass through any county, municipality or town of this state; provided, that this limitation shall not restrict the right of any municipality to charge a license for the privilege of maintaining or operating a terminal station, depot or waiting room therein.

(c) Local authorities may set aside for a given time a specified public highway for speed contests or races, to be conducted under proper restrictions for the safety of the public. Local authorities may exclude motor vehicles from any cemetery or grounds used for burial of the dead.

(d) Local authorities shall have power to provide by ordinance for the regulation of traffic by means of traffic officers or semaphores or other signaling devices on any portion of the highway where traffic is heavy or continuous and may prohibit other than one-way traffic upon certain highways and may regulate the use of the highways by processions or assemblages.

(e) Local authorities may also regulate or prohibit the parking of vehicles within the limits of their respective municipalities, and may also regulate the speed of vehicles in public parks and shall erect at all entrances to such parks adequate signs giving notice of any such special speed regulations. (Code 1923, § 6269; Acts 1927, No. 347, p. 348; Code 1940, T. 36, § 32.)

Authority to pass speed ordinances. — This section does not prohibit municipal corporations from passing speed ordinances consistent with limits set up by the legislature and punishing violations of such ordinances by appropriate fines. State v. Town of Springville, 220 Ala. 286, 125 So. 387 (1929).

Constitutionality of license and permit provisions. — In City of Montgomery v. Orpheum Taxi Co., 203 Ala. 103, 82 So. 117

(1919), it was held that the provision in § 32, Gen. Acts 1911, pp. 634-650, wherein municipal authorities were forbidden to require "any additional license or permit" as a condition to the use of the streets, etc., in cities, towns or villages, was in conflict with Constitution 1901, § 220, and invalid for the reason that the effect of the provision was, if valid, to clothe chauffeurs operating automobiles for hire with the licensed right to use the streets, etc., of cities, towns and villages "without first obtaining the consent of the proper authorities of such city, town, or village."

Cited in City of Decatur v. Robinson, 251 Ala. 99, 36 So. 2d 673 (1948); Mobile Cab & Baggage Co. v. Armstrong, 259 Ala. 1, 65 So. 2d 192 (1953).

Collateral references. — 61A C.J.S., Motor Vehicles, § 588.

7 Am. Jur. 2d, Automobiles & Highway Traffic, § 13.

Conflict between statutes and local regulations. 21 ALR 1196, 64 ALR 993, 147 ALR 522.

Failure of municipality to adopt, or to enforce, traffic regulations as ground of its liability for damage to property or person. 92 ALR 1495, 161 ALR 1404.

Liability of governmental unit for collision with safety and traffic control devices in traveled way. 7 ALR2d 226.

Public regulation and prohibition of sound amplifiers or loudspeaker broadcasts in streets and other public places. 10 ALR2d 627.

Right of municipality or public to use of subsurface of street or highway for purposes other than sewers, pipes, conduits for wires, and the like. 11 ALR2d 180.

Liability for automobile accident, other than direct collision with pedestrian, as affected by reliance upon or disregard of stop-and-go signal. 2 ALR3d 12.

Liability for collision of automobile with pedestrian at intersection as affected by reliance upon or disregard of stop-and-go signal. 2 ALR3d 155.

Liability for automobile accident at intersection as affected by reliance upon or disregard of "yield" sign or signal. 2 ALR3d 275.

Liability for automobile accident at intersection as affected by reliance upon or disregard of unchanging stop signal or sign. 3 ALR3d 180.

Liability for automobile accident at intersection as affected by reliance upon or disregard of unchanging caution, slow, danger, or like sign or signal. 3 ALR3d 507.

State or municipal towing, impounding, or destruction of motor vehicles parked or abandoned on streets or highways. 32 ALR4th 728.

Validity of routine roadblocks by state or local police for purpose of discovery of vehicular or driving violations. 37 ALR4th 10.

§ 32-5-2. Regulation of use of real property by owner; owner to erect and maintain traffic-control devices.

Nothing in this chapter shall be so construed as to prevent the owner of real property used in public for purposes of vehicular travel by permission of the owner and not as matter of right, from prohibiting such use nor from requiring other or different or additional conditions than those specified in this chapter or otherwise regulating such use as may seem best to such owner. Provided, however, when the owner of real property allows said real property to be used by the public for the purpose of vehicular travel, and/or as a quasi-public parking lot for the use of customers, tenants or employees of said property, the owner of said real property shall erect and maintain all traffic-control devices thereon in strict accordance with the rules and regulations in effect in the local jurisdiction and in conformance with the Alabama Manual on Uniform Traffic-Control Devices and any revisions thereof.

Nothing herein contained, however, shall be construed to compel the state or local governmental jurisdiction to maintain such quasi-public parking areas and lots or to install or maintain any traffic-control device therein and thereon.

The owner of said real property shall be required to meet the requirements of section 32-5-31(a) with respect to local authorities in their respective jurisdictions. (Acts 1927, No. 347, p. 348; Code 1940, T. 36, § 33; Acts 1979, No. 79-673, p. 1188.)

Cited in Shell v. Shell, 48 Ala. App. 668, 267 So. 2d 461 (1972).

§ 32-5-3. Loading from ramps, platforms or other devices.

It shall be unlawful and constitute a misdemeanor for any person to park or place any vehicle upon the public highway opposite or at or near a ramp or any other constructed platform, or any other loading device, and take on or be loaded therefrom.

Any person violating this section upon conviction shall be punished by a fine of not less than $25.00 nor more than $100.00, or by imprisonment in the county jail for not less than 10 days, nor more than 30 days, or by both fine and imprisonment. (Acts 1927, No. 347, p. 348; Code 1940, T. 36, § 4.)

Collateral references. — 60 C.J.S., Motor Vehicles, § 43. 60A C.J.S., Motor Vehicles, § 322.

§ 32-5-4. Unloading logs, lumber, etc., on or near highways.

It shall be unlawful and constitute a misdemeanor for any person to unload from a vehicle of any kind in whole or in part any lumber, logs or any other article upon the highway, or within the limits of the right-of-way of any public highway, or place lumber or logs, or any other article at or near either limit of the road right-of-way which may endanger the safety of life, limb or property of any person passing upon the highway.

Any person violating this section upon conviction shall be punished by a fine of not less than $25.00 nor more than $100.00, or by imprisonment in the county jail for not less than 10 days nor more than 30 days, or by both fine and imprisonment. (Acts 1927, No. 347, p. 348; Code 1940, T. 36, § 4.)

§ 32-5-5. Removal of ramps, platforms and obstructions.

It shall be the duty of the highway director to immediately remove or cause to be removed any ramp or platform extending upon the right-of-way of any public highway and to remove or cause to be removed immediately upon notice any obstruction found upon the roadway likely to endanger life, limb or property and to remove or cause to be removed any obstruction found in the ditches or drains of any public highway, and he shall have the authority to proceed against any person guilty of violating any provision of sections 32-5-3 and 32-5-4 as provided by law. (Acts 1927, No. 347, p. 348; Code 1940, T. 36, § 4.)

Collateral references. — Highway contractor's liability to highway user for highway surface defects. 62 ALR4th 1067.

§§ 32-5-6, 32-5-7. Repealed by Acts 1980, No. 80-434, p. 604, § 15-106, effective May 19, 1980.

§ 32-5-8. School bus specifications and operation.

The state board of education shall adopt minimum standards, not inconsistent with this chapter, to govern the specifications of all new school buses purchased in the future and for the overall operation of all school buses used for the transportation of school children when owned and operated by any school system or privately owned and operated under contract with any school system. (Acts 1949, No. 516, p. 740, § 33.)

Cross references. — As to monthly safety inspections of school buses, see § 16-27-5. As to requirement that school buses be equipped with a seat belt for the driver, see § 16-27-6.

Collateral references. — 60 C.J.S., Motor Vehicles, § 48.

§ 32-5-9. Liability for damage to highway or structure.

(a) Any person driving any vehicle, object or contrivance upon any highway or highway structure shall be liable for all damage which said highway or structure may sustain as a result of any illegal or careless operation, driving or moving of such vehicle, object or contrivance, or as a result of operating, driving or moving any vehicle, object or contrivance weighing in excess of the maximum weight prescribed by law but authorized by a special permit issued as provided in section 32-9-29.

(b) Whenever such driver is not the owner of such vehicle, object or contrivance, but is so operating, driving or moving the same with the express or implied permission of said owner, then said owner and driver shall be jointly and severally liable for any such damage.

(c) Such damage may be recovered in a civil action brought by the authorities in control of such highway or highway structures. (Acts 1949, No. 516, p. 740, § 41.)

Collateral references. — 60A C.J.S., Motor Vehicles, §§ 422, 423.

Liability for damage to highway or bridge caused by size or weight of motor vehicle. 53 ALR3d 1035.

Liability of private owner or occupant of land abutting highway for injuries or damage resulting from tree or limb falling onto highway. 94 ALR3d 1160.

§ 32-5-10. Repealed by Acts 1980, No. 80-434, p. 604, § 15-106, effective May 19, 1980.

§ 32-5-11. Throwing or shooting deadly or dangerous missile into occupied vehicle.

Whoever willfully throws or shoots a rock, stone, brick or piece of iron, steel or other like metal, or any deadly or dangerous missile or fire bomb, into a motor vehicle that is occupied by one or more persons is guilty of a felony and upon conviction shall be imprisoned for not less than one year and a day and shall be fined not less than $500.00.

This section is cumulative. (Acts 1967, No. 429, p. 1099.)

Collateral references. — 60A C.J.S., Motor Vehicles, § 348. 61A C.J.S., Motor Vehicles, §§ 673, 690.

§ 32-5-12. Distress flag for handicapped or paraplegic drivers — Authorized; design.

Handicapped or paraplegic drivers of motor vehicles are authorized when getting into and out of such vehicles, or when in motor vehicle distress, to display a white flag of approximately seven and one-half inches in width and 13 inches in length, with the letter "H" thereon in red color with an irregular one-half inch red border. Said flag shall be of reflective material so as to be readily discernible under darkened conditions and shall be issued under section 32-5-13. (Acts 1961, No. 710, p. 1006, § 1.)

§ 32-5-13. Same — Fee; card authorizing use; replacement flags.

The director of public safety may, upon application and payment of a fee of $1.00, issue to any handicapped person a distress flag as described in section 32-5-12, and a card which shall be applicant's authority to use such flag. This card shall set forth applicant's name, address, date of birth, physical apparatus, if any, needed to operate a motor vehicle and other pertinent facts which the director deems desirable. The card and flag issued to an applicant shall bear corresponding numbers. In the event of loss or destruction of such flag a replacement may be issued upon the payment of the sum of $1.00 by the applicant. The director of public safety shall maintain a list of those persons to whom distress flags and cards have been issued. (Acts 1961, No. 710, p. 1006, § 2.)

§ 32-5-14. Same — Penalty for illegal use.

Any person who is not a handicapped or paraplegic person who uses the distress flag as a distress signal or for any other purpose or any other person who violates any provision of sections 32-5-12 through 32-5-14 shall be guilty of a misdemeanor and upon conviction thereof shall be punished as provided by law. (Acts 1961, No. 710, p. 1006, § 3.)

§ 32-5-15. Repealed by Acts 1980, No. 80-434, p. 604, § 15-106, effective May 19, 1980.

§ 32-5-16. State trooper may close highways.

When it becomes apparent to any state trooper that a road is dangerous for use of motor vehicles on account of weather conditions, high water, damaged roadways or bridges or from any other cause, or when in the opinion of any state trooper a road may be seriously injured by allowing traffic on same, then the state trooper is authorized to close such highway immediately by placing thereon a barricade, lights or other sign stating that the road is closed, and immediately notifying the division engineer or some other official of the highway department. Such road shall remain closed until the hazard has been corrected and the road ordered opened by the highway department. (Acts 1949, No. 516, p. 740, § 40.)

§ 32-5-17. Nuisance of casting light from motor vehicle on real property at night; exceptions; penalty.

(a) It shall be deemed a nuisance and shall be unlawful for any person, or one or more of a group of persons together, between the hours of sunset and sunrise, to willfully throw or cast, or cause to be thrown or cast, in a continuous and repeated manner, the rays of a spotlight, headlight or other artificial light from any motor vehicle or with the aid of any motor vehicle, while the motor vehicle is on any highway or public road and casting said light on any real property. The provisions of this section shall not apply to farmers while checking livestock and repair upon land which they own, lease or rent, nor to employees of a utility company when such employees are acting within the scope of their employment. The commissioner of the department of conservation and natural resources shall be empowered to issue exceptional permits for the purpose of wildlife management, research or education.

(b) Any violation of the provisions of this section shall be a Class B misdemeanor. (Acts 1979, No. 79-709, p. 1262; Acts 1987, No. 87-575, p. 918.)

Cross references. — As to nuisances generally, see §§ 6-5-120 through 6-5-127.

ARTICLE 2.

SIGNS, SIGNALS AND MARKINGS.

§ 32-5-30. Repealed by Acts 1980, No. 80-434, p. 604, § 15-106, effective May 19, 1980.

§ 32-5-31. Local traffic-control devices.

(a) Local authorities in their respective jurisdictions shall place and maintain such traffic-control devices upon highways under their jurisdiction as they may deem necessary to indicate and carry out the provisions of this chapter or local traffic ordinances or to regulate, warn or guide traffic.

(b) Repealed by Acts 1980, No. 80-434, § 15-106. (Acts 1927, No. 347, p. 348; Code 1940, T. 36, § 48; Acts 1949, No. 517, p. 754, § 14; Acts 1976, No. 355, p. 399.)

Cross references. — As to requirement that the owner of real property meet the requirements of subsection (a) of this section with respect to local authorities in their respective jurisdictions, see § 32-5-2. For provisions relating to traffic-control signal legends, see § 32-5A-32.

It was presumed stop signal was authoritatively placed at intersection, and evidence of its presence was therefore admissible in automobile collision case. Harris v. Blythe, 222 Ala. 48, 130 So. 548 (1930).

Cities have authority to set up traffic control devices, and when such traffic signals are set up, they are presumed to be by due authority of the city. Mobile City Lines v. Orr, 253 Ala. 528, 45 So. 2d 766 (1950); Mobile Cab & Baggage Co. v. Armstrong, 259 Ala. 1, 65 So. 2d 192 (1953).

Although it did not appear whether a stop sign was placed on an intersecting street by virtue of city ordinance or by the state highway department, it was assumed that it was placed pursuant to law. Gilbert v. Gwin-McCollum Funeral Home, 268 Ala. 372, 106 So. 2d 646 (1958).

State law prevails in absence of local regulations. — See Gilbert v. Gwin-McCollum Funeral Home, 268 Ala. 372, 106 So. 2d 646 (1958).

Collateral references. — Failure of municipality to adopt, or to enforce, traffic regulations as ground of its liability for damage to property or person. 92 ALR 1495, 161 ALR 1404.

Liability of governmental unit for collision with safety and traffic-control devices in traveled way. 7 ALR2d 226.

Liability for subsequent motor vehicle accident of private person negligently causing malfunctioning, removal, or extinguishment of traffic signal or sign. 64 ALR2d 1364.

Motorist's liability for collision at intersection of ordinary and arterial highways as affected by absence, displacement, or malfunctioning of stop sign or other traffic signal. 74 ALR2d 242.

Liability for automobile accident with pedestrian as affected by reliance upon or disregard of traffic signal. 2 ALR3d 12, 155, 3 ALR3d 557.

Liability for automobile accident at intersection as affected by reliance upon or disregard of "yield" sign or signal. 2 ALR3d 275.

Liability for automobile accident at intersection as affected by reliance upon or disregard of unchanging caution, slow, danger, stop or like sign or signal. 3 ALR3d 180, 507.

Liability of highway authorities arising out of motor vehicle accident allegedly caused by failure to erect or properly maintain traffic control device at intersection. 34 ALR3d 1008.

§§ 32-5-32 through 32-5-37. Repealed by Acts 1980, No. 80-434, p. 604, § 15-106, effective May 19, 1980.

ARTICLE 3.

OPERATION OF VEHICLES GENERALLY.

§ 32-5-50. Repealed by Acts 1980, No. 80-434, p. 604, § 15-106, effective May 19, 1980.

§ 32-5-51. Towing or hauling disabled vehicle.

No provision of this chapter shall prevent a motor vehicle from hauling or towing a disabled vehicle while on the highway to a point for the purpose of making repairs; provided, that such motor vehicle otherwise complies with the requirements of this chapter and is in charge of a responsible driver; a drawbar or other connection between any two such vehicles shall not exceed 15 feet in length, and there shall be displayed at the rear of the last vehicle a red flag or other signal or cloth not less than 12 inches in length and width and lighted as required by section 32-5-240. Any person violating the provisions of this section shall be guilty of a misdemeanor and, upon conviction, shall be punished as provided in section 32-5-311. (Acts 1927, No. 347, p. 348; Code 1940, T. 36, § 81.)

Code commissioner's note. — Section 32-5-311, referred to in this section, was repealed by Acts 1980, No. 80-434, p. 604, § 15-106, effective May 19, 1980. For provision relating to subject matter of repealed section, see § 32-5A-8.

Collateral references. — 60 C.J.S., Motor Vehicles, § 43. 60A C.J.S., Motor Vehicles, §§ 339-341.

Constitutionality and construction of statutes as regards dimensions of motor vehicles, or combinations of motor vehicles. 86 ALR 281.

Validity and construction of statute or ordinance regulating vehicle towing business. 97 ALR3d 495.

§§ 32-5-52, 32-5-53. Repealed by Acts 1980, No. 80-434, p. 604, § 15-106, effective May 19, 1980.

§ 32-5-54. Keep to the right in crossing intersections or railroads.

In crossing an intersection of highways or in the intersection of a highway by a railroad right-of-way, the driver of a vehicle shall at all times cause such vehicle to travel on the right half of the highway unless such right half is obstructed or impassable. (Acts 1949, No. 516, p. 740, § 5.)

Section appears to apply whether another vehicle is present or not. Bentley v. Lawson, 280 Ala. 220, 191 So. 2d 372 (1966).

And requires driving on right half of highway in crossing intersection. — This section is not a statute which forbids a vehicle driver from passing another vehicle traveling in the same direction at a street intersection. It requires driving on the right half of the highway in crossing an intersection without regard to passing another vehicle. Bentley v. Lawson, 280 Ala. 220, 191 So. 2d 372 (1966).

Section enacted in part for benefit of pedestrians. — The draftsman of this section had the pedestrian in mind as well as vehicles, and the section was enacted in part for the benefit of pedestrians. Bentley v. Lawson, 280 Ala. 220, 191 So. 2d 372 (1966).

Violation of section constitutes negligence. — Automobile driver, undertaking to pass truck ahead of him to left within street intersection, is negligent in leaving right half of highway which was not obstructed or impassable. Greer v. Marriott, 27 Ala. App. 108, 167 So. 597, cert. denied, 232 Ala. 194, 167 So. 599 (1936).

No recovery when in pari delicto. — Truck driver, turning left at street intersection without giving hand signal to driver of automobile following truck, and latter driver, undertaking to pass truck within intersection, stood in pari delicto so as to bar recovery by either party in action for resulting damage to automobile. Greer v. Marriott, 27 Ala. App. 108, 167 So. 597, cert. denied, 232 Ala. 194, 167 So. 599 (1936).

Cited in Edger v. Karl Bradley Ford, Inc., 41 Ala. App. 638, 147 So. 2d 858 (1962).

Collateral references. — 60A C.J.S., Motor Vehicles, §§ 281, 356.

What is street intersection within traffic statute or regulations. 31 ALR 488, 78 ALR 1198, 7 ALR3d 1204.

Construction, applicability and effect of traffic regulation prohibiting vehicles from passing one another at intersection of streets. 78 ALR 1206, 53 ALR2d 850.

§§ 32-5-55 through 32-5-63. Repealed by Acts 1980, No. 80-434, p. 604, § 15-106, effective May 19, 1980.

§ 32-5-64. Persons under 16 years of age operating motor vehicles — Prohibited; driver training programs.

Any person under the age of 16 years who shall drive or operate any motor vehicle upon the public highways of this state shall be guilty of a misdemeanor, and shall be dealt with as provided by the juvenile laws of this state; provided, that the provisions of this section shall not apply to any student enrolled in a driver training program approved by the state superintendent of education or the director of public safety while driving or operating a motor vehicle pursuant to the instructional program. However, no student in any driver training program who is under 16 years of age shall drive or operate any motor vehicle unless accompanied by a licensed driver. (Code 1923, § 3329; Acts 1927, No. 347, p. 348; Code 1940, T. 36, § 55; Acts 1949, No. 517, p. 754, § 17.)

Cross references. — As to juvenile proceedings generally, see § 12-15-1 et seq. As to drivers' licenses generally, see § 32-6-1 et seq. As to issuance of licenses to operate motor-driven cycles to persons 14 years of age and older, see § 32-12-22.

Persons under 16 presumed incompetent. — Any person under 16 years of age is conclusively presumed incompetent to drive automobile on public highway, in view of this section. Rush v. McDonnell, 214 Ala. 47, 106 So. 175 (1925); Paschall v. Sharp, 215 Ala. 304, 110 So. 387 (1926); Chiniche v. Smith, 374 So. 2d 872 (Ala. 1979).

What "accompanied" means. — Prohibiting minors under 16 years to operate motor vehicles unless "accompanied" by an adult person means attended by an adult person, exercising supervision over infant in respect to his operation of car. Rush v. McDonnell, 214 Ala. 47, 106 So. 175 (1925).

No necessity of pleading section. — In action for death of plaintiff's son while riding in automobile driven by defendant's 16-year-old son, this section may be relied on, though not pleaded, as general domestic statutes, state and federal, are judicially known by courts and are read into every pleading. Rush v. McDonnell, 214 Ala. 47, 106 So. 175 (1925).

Sufficiency of complaint. — A complaint that alleges injuries from an automobile driven by a minor under 16 years of age and negligence of parent in allowing the minor to drive the automobile states a cause of action. See also Rush v. McDonnell, 214 Ala. 47, 106 So. 175 (1925); Paschall v. Sharp, 215 Ala. 304, 110 So. 387 (1926).

Collateral references. — 60 C.J.S., Motor Vehicles, § 153.

7 Am. Jur. 2d, Automobiles & Highway Traffic, § 107.

§ 32-5-65. Same — Owner of motor vehicle permitting.

Any owner or person in charge of any motor vehicle who permits any child under the age of 16 years to operate such motor vehicle upon the public highways of this state, except as provided by section 32-5-64, shall be guilty of a misdemeanor, and upon conviction shall be punished as provided by section 32-5-311. (Code 1923, § 3330; Acts 1927, No. 347, p. 348; Code 1940, T. 36, § 56; Acts 1949, No. 517, p. 754, § 18.)

Code commissioner's note. — Section 32-5-311, referred to in this section, was repealed by Acts 1980, No. 80-434, p. 604, § 15-106, effective May 19, 1980. For provision relating to subject matter of repealed section, see § 32-5A-8.

Negligence per se to allow person under 16 to drive. — Any person who allows automobile to be operated by person under 16 years of age on public highway, unaccompanied by adult person, is guilty of negligence as matter of law. Rush v. McDonnell, 214 Ala. 47, 106 So. 175 (1925); Paschall v. Sharp, 215 Ala. 304, 110 So. 387 (1926); Chiniche v. Smith, 374 So. 2d 872 (Ala. 1979).

Manifestations of driver's incompetence basic requirement of negligent entrustment action. — The doctrine of negligent entrustment is founded on the primary negligence of the entruster in supplying a motor vehicle to an incompetent driver, with manifestations of the incompetence of the driver as a basic requirement of a negligent entrustment action. Chiniche v. Smith, 374 So. 2d 872 (Ala. 1979).

To establish negligent entrustment it is not necessary that entruster have owned motor vehicle. Chiniche v. Smith, 374 So. 2d 872 (Ala. 1979).

A cause of action lies for a bailee against a negligent entrustor. Keller v. Kiedinger, 389 So. 2d 129 (Ala. 1980).

One who supplies directly or through a third person a chattel for the use of another whom the supplier knows or has reason to know to be likely, because of his youth, inexperience, or otherwise, to use it in a manner involving unreasonable risk of physical harm to himself and others, whom the supplier should expect to share in or be endangered by its use, is subject to liability for physical harm resulting to them. Keller v. Kiedinger, 389 So. 2d 129 (Ala. 1980).

Negligence on the part of the bailee is not a necessary element of negligent entrustment. Keller v. Kiedinger, 389 So. 2d 129 (Ala. 1980).

Contributory negligence will bar the bailee's claim unless the bailee's lack of capacity makes him incapable of contributory negligence, or unless the bailor's entrustment was so reckless as to constitute wanton entrustment. Keller v. Kiedinger, 389 So. 2d 129 (Ala. 1980).

Contributory negligence is a defense to a bailee's claim against his bailor for negligent entrustment. Keller v. Kiedinger, 389 So. 2d 129 (Ala. 1980).

Application of negligent entrustment to bailor. — Where father of 14-year-old bailee brought action to recover against bailor and others for bailee's death on theory of negligent entrustment, it was held that: (a) negligence on the part of the bailee is not a necessary element of negligent entrustment (all past cases to the contrary being overruled on the point); (b) § 390, Restatement (Second) of Torts (1965) is adopted as the law of Alabama; and (c) contributory negligence is a defense to a bailee's claim against his bailor for negligent entrustment. Accordingly, the court found the contributory negligence of the 14-year-old bailee to be the proximate cause of her death which barred recovery against the bailor on negligent entrustment. Keller v. Kiedinger, 389 So. 2d 129 (Ala. 1980).

Person violating section is liable to all persons injured thereby, whether they are injured by being struck by the automobile or suffer injuries while riding in it. Rush v. McDonnell, 214 Ala. 47, 106 So. 175 (1925).

Permission question for jury. — In personal injury action against parent of 14-year-old automobile driver, question whether driver had permission from defendants to operate car at time of injury held for jury. Paschall v. Sharp, 215 Ala. 304, 110 So. 387 (1926).

Collateral references. — 61A C.J.S., Motor Vehicles, § 687.

8 Am. Jur. 2d, Automobiles & Highway Traffic, § 575.

Common-law liability based on entrusting automobile to incompetent, reckless or unlicensed driver. 68 ALR 1015, 100 ALR 926, 168 ALR 1364.

Civil or criminal liability of one in charge of an automobile who permits an unlicensed person to operate it. 137 ALR 475.

Purchasing motor vehicle for, or giving it to, minor or incompetent driver as rendering donor liable for driver's acts. 36 ALR2d 735.

Construction, application, and effect of legislation imputing negligence to one who permits unauthorized or unlicensed person to operate motor vehicle. 69 ALR2d 978.

Negligent entrustment of motor vehicle to unlicensed driver. 55 ALR4th 1100.

§§ 32-5-66 through 32-5-71. Repealed by Acts 1980, No. 80-434, p. 604, § 15-106, effective May 19, 1980.

§ 32-5-72. Limitations of backing.

(a) The driver of a vehicle shall not back the same unless it shall reasonably appear that such a movement can be made with safety and without interfering with other traffic.

(b) The driver of a vehicle shall not back the same upon any shoulder or roadway of any controlled-access highway. (Acts 1975, No. 1203, p. 2382, § 1.)

§ 32-5-73. Repealed by Acts 1980, No. 80-434, p. 604, § 15-106, effective May 19, 1980.

§ 32-5-74. Vehicles transporting explosives.

Any person operating any vehicle transporting any explosive as a cargo or part of a cargo upon a highway shall at all times comply with the provisions of this section.

(1) Said vehicle shall be marked or placarded on each side and the rear with the word "explosives" in letters not less than eight inches high, or there shall be displayed on the rear of such vehicle a red flag not less than 24 inches square marked with the word "danger" in white letters six inches high.

(2) Every said vehicle shall be equipped with not less than two fire extinguishers, filled and ready for immediate use, and placed at a convenient point on the vehicle so used.

(3) The director of public safety is hereby authorized and directed to promulgate such additional regulations governing the transportation of explosives and other dangerous articles by vehicles upon the highways as he shall deem advisable for the protection of the public. (Acts 1949, No. 516, p. 740, § 44.)

Cross references. — As to carrying explosives on passenger conveyances, see § 37-8-180.

Collateral references. — 60 C.J.S., Motor Vehicles, § 56.

Products liability: sufficiency of evidence to support product misuse defense in actions concerning commercial or industrial equipment and machinery. 64 ALR4th 10.

§ 32-5-75. Loads which must be fastened by cables or chains.

Any person operating a motor vehicle on any highway hauling logs, lumber, pulp wood, tar wood, bale cotton or hay or other articles that may shift or drop onto the highway is required to fasten such load with steel cables or chains of sufficient size to prevent the load from shifting or dropping onto the highway. (Acts 1949, No. 516, p. 740, § 45.)

Violation of section is negligence per se. Horn v. Smith, 292 Ala. 503, 296 So. 2d 719 (1974).

But in order to recover for wrongful death, negligence must be shown to be proximate cause of death. Horn v. Smith, 292 Ala. 503, 296 So. 2d 719 (1974).

Cited in Employer's Cas. Co. v. Baxter Fertilizer Co., 338 So. 2d 418 (Ala. Civ. App. 1976); Black Belt Wood Co. v. Sessions, 455 So. 2d 802 (Ala. 1984).

§ 32-5-76. Spilling loads or litter; penalty.

(a) Whoever willfully and knowingly operates, owns or causes to be operated on any public highway, road, street or public right-of-way a motor vehicle so loaded with gravel, rock, slag, bricks, in such manner or in such condition that the contents of the vehicle spill out and cause it to be deposited upon the highway, road, street or public right-of-way is guilty of a Class C misdemeanor and upon conviction shall be fined not more than $500.00, pursuant to section 13A-7-29, the criminal littering statute.

(b) No vehicle shall be driven or moved on any highway unless such vehicle is so constructed or loaded as to prevent any of its load from dropping, sifting, leaking or otherwise escaping therefrom, except that sand may be dropped for the purpose of securing traction, or water or other substance may be sprinkled on a roadway in cleaning or maintaining such roadway.

(c) Whoever willfully and knowingly operates, owns or causes to be operated on a public highway, road, street or public right-of-way, a motor vehicle in such manner or in such condition that litter is caused or allowed to be deposited upon the highway, road or street or public right-of-way, is guilty of a Class C misdemeanor and upon conviction shall be fined not more than $500.00, pursuant to section 13A-7-29, the criminal littering statute. (Acts 1927, No. 347, p. 348; Code 1940, T. 36, § 39; Acts 1949, No. 517, p. 754, § 9; Acts 1971, No. 1419, p. 2423; Acts 1989, No. 89-661, § 1.)

The 1989 amendment, effective May 11, 1989, in subsection (a) deleted "or" following "road," inserted "or public right-of-way," deleted "sawdust, chips, wood products or other like substances" following "bricks," substituted "and causes it to be deposited upon the highway, road, street or public right-of-way is guilty of a Class C misdemeanor" for "and endangers the safety of the persons or property of motorists and pedestrians is guilty of a misdemeanor," and substituted a fine of $500.00 for a fine of $100.00; and added subsection (c).

Instruction upheld. — The trial court properly instructed the jury on the applicability of subsection (b) of this section to defendant who was tried on theory of negligence in loading logs with knowledge that truck had to travel a distance of 60 miles over rough roads. Black Belt Wood Co. v. Sessions, 514 So. 2d 1249 (Ala. 1986).

Cited in Scotch Lumber Co. v. Baugh, 288 Ala. 34, 256 So. 2d 869 (1972).

Collateral references. — 60 C.J.S., Motor Vehicles, § 34. 60A C.J.S., Motor Vehicles, § 260. 61A C.J.S., Motor Vehicles, § 714(4).

7 Am. Jur. 2d, Automobiles & Highway Traffic, § 158.

Public regulation requiring mufflers or similar noise-preventing devices on motor vehicles. 49 ALR2d 1202.

Liability of motor vehicle owner or operator for personal injury or death of passenger or guest occasioned by inhalation of gases or fumes from exhaust. 56 ALR2d 1099.

Effect of violation of safety equipment statute as establishing negligence in automobile accident litigation. 38 ALR3d 530.

§ 32-5-77. Driving on extreme left side of highway restricted; notice to state highway director to erect markers.

(a) Any law to the contrary notwithstanding, the director of the department of public safety is hereby authorized to restrict driving in the extreme left side in any portion of any interstate highway, or of any highway of sufficient width, except for overtaking and passing. He may issue any reasonable rules and regulations necessary to implement this section.

(b) The director of public safety shall give appropriate notice to the state highway director of the locations of any portions of highways designated as restricted pursuant to the provisions of subsection (a) of this section so that appropriate markers or other equipment may be erected by the state highway department. (Acts 1979, No. 79-799, p. 1462.)

Cross references. — As to driving on right side of highway generally, see § 32-5A-80. As to overtaking and passing generally, see §§ 32-5A-81 through 32-5A-92.

Cited in Schrimsher v. Sullivan, 402 So. 2d 935 (Ala. 1981).

ARTICLE 4.

SPEED LIMITS.

§§ 32-5-90, 32-5-91. Repealed by Acts 1980, No. 80-434, p. 604, § 15-106, effective May 19, 1980.

§ 32-5-92. Special speed limitations on bridges.

(a) The highway department or other proper state body upon request from any local authorities shall, or upon its own initiative may, conduct an investigation of any public bridge, causeway or viaduct, and if it shall thereupon find that such structure cannot with safety to itself withstand vehicles traveling at the speed otherwise permissible under this article, the department shall determine and declare the maximum speed of vehicles which such structure can withstand, and shall cause or permit suitable signs stating such maximum speed to be erected and maintained at a distance of 100 feet before each end of such structure. When such public bridge, causeway or viaduct is within a municipality, such suitable signs stating such maximum speed shall be erected within such less distance of 100 feet before each end of such structure as the governing body of such municipality shall so ordain. The findings and determination of the department shall be conclusive evidence of the maximum speed which can with safety to any such structure be maintained thereon.

(b) It shall be unlawful and constitute a misdemeanor to drive any vehicle upon any public bridge, causeway or viaduct at a speed which is greater than the maximum speed which can with safety to such structure be maintained thereon, when such structure is signposted as provided in this section, and any person violating the provisions of this section upon conviction shall be punished by a fine of not more than $100.00 or by imprisonment in the county or municipal jail for not more than 10 days; for a second such conviction within one year thereafter such person shall be punished by a fine of not more than $200.00 or by imprisonment in the county or municipal jail for not more than 20 days or by both such fine and imprisonment; upon a third or subsequent conviction within one year after the first conviction such person shall be punished by fine of not more than $500.00 or by imprisonment at hard labor in the county or municipal jail for not more than six months or by both such fine and imprisonment. (Acts 1927, No. 347, p. 348; Code 1940, T. 36, § 7.)

Collateral references. — 60A C.J.S., Motor Vehicles, § 292.

Construction and application of restrictive covenants to the use of signs. 61 ALR4th 1028.

§ 32-5-93. Speed limit between working signs.

No driver of a motor vehicle upon any highway of the state shall drive such vehicle at a speed in excess of 15 miles per hour between the warning signs placed on the highway during construction or repairs, when signs are placed not more than 1,000 feet from the place where workmen are actually engaged in construction or repair. (Acts 1949, No. 516, p. 740, § 46.)

Cross references. — As to special limits in urban and rural construction zones, see § 32-5A-176.1.

§§ 32-5-94 through 32-5-96. Repealed by Acts 1980, No. 80-434, p. 604, § 15-106, effective May 19, 1980.

§ 32-5-97. Notation of conviction on driver's license.

When any person is convicted by any judge for violation of the provisions of section 32-5-90, the judge trying the case shall note on the back of such person's driver's license in the place indicated, the date of such conviction, the amount of fine or other disposition of the case. (Acts 1953, No. 22, p. 25, § 4.)

Code commissioner's note. — Section 32-5-90, referred to in this section, was repealed by Acts 1980, No. 80-434, p. 604, § 15-106, effective May 19, 1980. For provisions relating to speed restrictions, see now § 32-5A-170 et seq.

ARTICLE 5.

RIGHT-OF-WAY.

§§ 32-5-110 through 32-5-112. Repealed by Acts 1980, No. 80-434, p. 604, § 15-106, effective May 19, 1980.

§ 32-5-113. Duty of driver on approach of authorized emergency vehicles.

(a) Upon the immediate approach of an authorized emergency vehicle equipped with at least one lighted lamp and audible signal as is required by law, the driver of every other vehicle shall immediately drive to a position parallel to, and as close as possible to, the right-hand edge or curb of the roadway clear of any intersection and shall stop and remain in such position until the authorized emergency vehicle has passed, except when otherwise directed by a police officer.

(b) It shall be unlawful for the driver of any vehicle, except when traveling on official business relative to the emergency, to follow an authorized emergency vehicle answering an emergency call closer than 500 feet.

(c) Violations of this section shall be punished as provided in section 32-5-312. (Acts 1927, No. 347, p. 348; Code 1940, T. 36, § 20; Acts 1949, No. 517, p. 754; Acts 1966, Ex. Sess., No. 432, p. 578.)

Section inapplicable where law enforcement agency attempting to stop vehicle. — The legislative intent in construing this section was not to be applicable in situations where a law enforcement agency is attempting to stop a vehicle when they are in hot pursuit. McFerrin v. State, 339 So. 2d 127 (Ala. Crim. App. 1976).

Collateral references. — 7 Am. Jur. 2d, Automobiles & Highway Traffic, §§ 206, 212.

Use or nonuse of flashing light, siren, or other alarm device as affecting liability arising from accident involving police vehicle. 83 ALR2d 409.

§§ 32-5-114, 32-5-115. Repealed by Acts 1980, No. 80-434, p. 604, § 15-106, effective May 19, 1980.

ARTICLE 6.

OVERTAKING AND PASSING.

§§ 32-5-130 through 32-5-135. Repealed by Acts 1980, No. 80-434, p. 604, § 15-106, effective May 19, 1980.

ARTICLE 7.

STOPPING, STANDING AND PARKING.

§§ 32-5-150, 32-5-151. Repealed by Acts 1980, No. 80-434, p. 604, § 15-106, effective May 19, 1980.

§ 32-5-152. Parking in violation of municipal ordinances; presumption as to person committing violation.

No person shall park, cause to be parked or knowingly permit an automobile or other motor vehicle which he owns to be parked, on any street in any municipality in this state in violation of an ordinance of such municipality. The presence of an unattended automobile or other motor vehicle parked on the streets of any municipality in violation of an ordinance of such municipality shall raise a prima facie presumption that the registered owner of the automobile or other motor vehicle committed or authorized the parking violation, and the burden of proof shall be upon the registered owner to show otherwise. (Acts 1953, No. 844, p. 1135.)

Collateral references. — Inference or presumption that owner of motor vehicle was its driver at time of traffic, driving, or parking offense. 49 ALR2d 456.

§ 32-5-152.1. Owner not liable for violation where vehicle leased to another; notice requirement; owner's liability upon failure to maintain vehicle.

(a) The owner of any motor vehicle leased to another shall not be liable for a state, county or municipal traffic or parking violation occurring while said leased vehicle was not in the owner's possession or control, if upon notice of the violation, the owner notifies the clerk of the court in which the case is pending of the name and address of the lessee of the vehicle on the date the violation occurred. Said notice shall be notarized on a form prescribed by the director of the administrative office of courts. If the owner fails to submit the notice, the court in which the case is heard may take such action as the interests of justice require, including finding the owner of the motor vehicle liable for the violation.

(b) After providing the name and address of the lessee, the owner shall not be required to attend a hearing on the offense, unless notified that the offense occurred through a mechanical failure of the vehicle which resulted from the owner's failure to maintain the vehicle.

(c) The owner of any leased vehicle shall be liable for any violation which was caused by the owner's failure to properly maintain the vehicle. The lessee claiming the violation resulted from the owner's failure to properly maintain the vehicle shall notify the clerk of the court in which the case is pending along with the owner of the vehicle of the claim within seven days after receiving notice of the violation or at least ten days prior to the date the case will be heard by the court, whichever is later. (Acts 1981, No. 81-660, p. 1076.)

Collateral references. — 7A Am. Jur. 2d, Automobiles & Highway Traffic, §§ 271-273, 630-745.

Construction and application of statute im-posing liability expressly upon motor vehicle lessor for damage caused by operation of vehi-cle. 41 ALR4th 993.

§§ 32-5-153, 32-5-154. Repealed by Acts 1980, No. 80-434, p. 604, § 15-106, effective May 19, 1980.

ARTICLE 8.

DRIVING UNDER INFLUENCE OF INTOXICATING LIQUOR OR NARCOTIC DRUGS.

Division 1.

General Provisions.

§ 32-5-170. Repealed by Acts 1980, No. 80-434, p. 604, § 15-106, effective May 19, 1980.

§ 32-5-171. Arrest without warrant.

A uniformed police officer, state trooper, county sheriff or his deputy or member of a municipal police force may arrest, at the scene of a traffic accident, any driver of a vehicle involved in the accident if upon personal investigation, including information from eyewitnesses, the officer has reasonable grounds to believe that the person by violating section 32-5A-191 contributed to the accident. He may arrest such a person without a warrant although he did not personally see the violation. (Acts 1971, No. 1942, p. 3137; Acts 1983, 2nd Ex. Sess., No. 83-201, p. 379.)

Blood alcohol test which was given to defendant after accident was result of a lawful arrest, and therefore was not excluded, since officer had necessary probable cause to arrest defendant and direct that blood test be administered where officer noticed a strong odor of alcohol on defendant's breath and defendant staggered as he walked. Caver v. State, 533 So. 2d 734 (Ala. Crim. App. 1988).

Cited in Smoot v. State, 520 So. 2d 182 (Ala. Crim. App. 1987).

Collateral references. — 61A C.J.S., Motor Vehicles, § 593(1).

What amounts to violation of drunken-driving statute in officer's "presence" or "view" so as to permit warrantless arrest. 74 ALR3d 1138.

Horizontal gaze nystagmus test: use in im-paired driving prosecution. 60 ALR4th 1129.

Social host's liability for injuries incurred by third parties as a result of intoxicated guest's negligence. 62 ALR4th 16.

Alcohol-related vehicular homicide: nature and elements of offense. 64 ALR4th 166.

Passenger's liability to vehicular accident victim for harm caused by intoxicated motor vehicle driver. 64 ALR4th 272.

Driving while intoxicated: "choice of evils" defense that driving was necessary to protect life or property. 64 ALR4th 298.

Division 2.

Chemical Tests for Intoxication.

Provisions of division apply to dead persons. — The provisions of this division apply not only to living persons being prosecuted for violating municipal ordinances and the criminal laws of this state but also to dead persons. Lankford v. Redwing Carriers, Inc., 344 So. 2d 515 (Ala. Civ. App.), cert. denied, 344 So. 2d 522 (Ala. 1977).

Evidence of motorist's refusal to submit to chemical test for intoxication is probative on issue of intoxication and should be presented to the jury for their consideration; any circumstances tending to show the refusal was conditioned upon factors other than consciousness of guilt may properly be considered by the jury in determining the weight to attach to the refusal. Hill v. State, 366 So. 2d 318 (Ala. 1979).

In proceeding in which defendant was convicted of first-degree manslaughter of person fatally injured in automobile accident, evidence of defendant's refusal to submit to a chemical test for intoxication was relevant to issue of intoxication; whether defendant's refusal was due to desire for consultation with his physician or attorney or due to fear of bodily harm, rather than due to consciousness of guilt, was best determined by jury. Hill v. State, 366 So. 2d 318 (Ala. 1979).

Officer may prove chemical test designated. — A city ordinance is not required as a proper predicate to demonstrate or prove which chemical analysis test the law enforcement agency designated for use; such information could be supplied by any officer who would be in a position to know which test was authorized, e.g., among others, the officer who administered the test or a superior officer who authorized or designated the test to be administered. Estes v. State, 358 So. 2d 1050 (Ala. Crim. App. 1977).

Cited in Patterson v. State, 344 So. 2d 543 (Ala. Crim. App. 1977); Chatom v. State, 348 So. 2d 828 (Ala. Crim. App. 1976); Commander v. State, 374 So. 2d 910 (Ala. Crim. App. 1978).

Collateral references. — Driving while intoxicated: Duty of law enforcement officer to offer suspect chemical sobriety test under implied consent law. 95 ALR3d 710.

§ 32-5-190. Short title.

This division may be cited as the Alabama Chemical Test for Intoxication Act. (Acts 1969, No. 699, p. 1255, § 4.)

Cited in Maffett v. Roberts, 388 So. 2d 972 (Ala. 1980).

Collateral references. — Validity, construction, and application of statutes directly proscribing driving with blood-alcohol level in excess of established percentage. 54 ALR4th 149.

Snowmobile operation as DWI or DUI. 56 ALR4th 1092.

Cough medicine as "intoxicating liquor" under DUI statute. 65 ALR4th 1238.

§ 32-5-191. "Driving privilege" or "privilege" defined.

Whenever and wherever the words "driving privilege" or "privilege" appear in this division, they shall mean both the driver license of those licensed in Alabama, and the driving privilege of unlicensed residents and the privilege of nonresidents, licensed or not; the purpose of this section being to make unlicensed and nonresident drivers subject to the same penalties as licensed residents. (Acts 1969, No. 699, p. 1255, § 3.)

Defendant's cause must be reversed and remanded as he was arrested for speeding and required to submit to breath test without being formally charged with DUI until the results of the intoxilizer were available.

Sheffield v. State, 522 So. 2d 4 (Ala. Crim. App. 1987).

Sufficient warning. — Where arresting officer testified that he told defendant "that if he refused to take this test, that he would lose or have his driving privileges suspended," his warning was sufficient, since this section specifically provides that "driving privilege" means "driver license." Smith v. Director of Ala. Dep't of Pub. Safety, 531 So. 2d 674 (Ala. Civ. App. 1988).

Cited in Commander v. State, 374 So. 2d 910 (Ala. Crim. App. 1978); Maffett v. Roberts, 388 So. 2d 972 (Ala. 1980).

Collateral references. — Horizontal gaze nystagmus test: use in impaired driving prosecution. 60 ALR4th 1129.

Alcohol-related vehicular homicide: nature and elements of offense. 64 ALR4th 166.

Passenger's liability to vehicular accident victim for harm caused by intoxicated motor vehicle driver. 64 ALR4th 272.

Driving while intoxicated: "choice of evils" defense that driving was necessary to protect life or property. 64 ALR4th 298.

§ 32-5-192. Implied consent; when tests administered; suspension of license or permit to drive, etc., for refusal to submit to test.

(a) Any person who operates a motor vehicle upon the public highways of this state shall be deemed to have given his consent, subject to the provisions of this division, to a chemical test or tests of his blood, breath or urine for the purpose of determining the alcoholic content of his blood if lawfully arrested for any offense arising out of acts alleged to have been committed while the person was driving a motor vehicle on the public highways of this state while under the influence of intoxicating liquor. The test or tests shall be administered at the direction of a law enforcement officer having reasonable grounds to believe the person to have been driving a motor vehicle upon the public highways of this state while under the influence of intoxicating liquor. The law enforcement agency by which such officer is employed shall designate which of the aforesaid tests shall be administered. Such person shall be told that his failure to submit to such a chemical test will result in the suspension of his privilege to operate a motor vehicle for a period of 90 days; provided if such person objects to a blood test, the law enforcement agency shall designate that one of the other aforesaid tests be administered.

(b) Any person who is dead, unconscious or who is otherwise in a condition rendering him incapable of refusal, shall be deemed not to have withdrawn the consent provided by subsection (a) of this section and the test or tests may be administered, subject to the provisions of this division.

(c) If a person under arrest refuses upon the request of a law enforcement officer to submit to a chemical test designated by the law enforcement agency as provided in subsection (a) of this section, none shall be given, but the director of public safety, upon the receipt of a sworn report of the law enforcement officer that he had reasonable grounds to believe the arrested person had been driving a motor vehicle upon the public highways of this state while under the influence of intoxicating liquor and that the person had refused to submit to the test upon the request of the law enforcement officer, shall, on the first refusal, suspend his license or permit to drive, or the privilege of driving a motor vehicle on the highways of this state given to a nonresident; or if the person is a resident without a license or permit to operate a motor vehicle in this state, the director shall deny to the person the issuance of a license or permit, for a period of 90 days, subject to review as hereinafter provided. For a second or subsequent refusal of such test within a five-year period, the director, upon said receipt of a sworn report, shall suspend his license or permit to drive, or the privilege of driving a motor vehicle on the highways of this state given to a nonresident for a period of one year; or if the person is a resident without a license or permit to operate a motor vehicle in this state, the director shall deny to the person the issuance of a license or permit, for a period of one year subject to review as hereinafter provided. If such person is acquitted on the charge of driving a motor vehicle upon the highways of this state while under the influence of intoxicating liquor, then in that event the director of public safety may, in his discretion, reduce said period of suspension.

(d) Upon suspending the license or permit to drive or the privilege of driving a motor vehicle on the highways of this state given to a nonresident or any person, or upon determining that the issuance of a license or permit shall be denied to the person, as hereinbefore in this section directed, the director of public safety or his duly authorized agent shall immediately notify the person in writing and upon his request shall afford him an opportunity for a hearing in the same manner and under the same conditions as is provided in section 32-6-16, for notification and hearings in the cases of suspension of licenses; except, that the scope of such a hearing for the purposes of this section shall cover the issues of whether a law enforcement officer had reasonable grounds to believe the person had been driving a motor vehicle upon the public highways of this state while under the influence of intoxicating liquor, whether the person was placed under arrest, and whether he refused to submit to the test upon request of the officer. Whether the person was informed that his privilege to drive would be suspended or denied if he refused to submit to the test shall not be an issue. The director of public safety shall order that the suspension or determination that there should be a denial of issuance either be rescinded or sustained.

(e) If the suspension or determination that there should be a denial of issuance is sustained by the director of public safety or his authorized agent upon such hearing, the person whose license or permit to drive or nonresident operating privilege has been suspended or to whom a license or permit is denied, under the provisions of this section, shall have the right to file a petition in the appropriate court to review the final order of suspension or denial by the director or his duly authorized agent in the same manner and under the same conditions as is provided in section 32-6-16 in the cases of suspensions and denials.

(f) When it has been finally determined under the procedures of this section that a nonresident's privilege to operate a motor vehicle in this state has been suspended the director shall give information in writing of the action taken to the motor vehicle administrator of the state of the person's residence and of any state in which he has a license. (Acts 1969, No. 699, p. 1255, § 1; Acts 1983, No. 83-620, p. 959, § 1.)

Code commissioner's note. — Acts 1983, No. 83-620, § 2, provides: "The provisions of this act are supplemental to other laws not inconsistent with this act, and such other laws shall not be deemed to be repealed by this act."

Acts 1983, No. 83-620, § 3, provides that the act applies to conduct occurring after July 29, 1983, and that conduct occurring before that date shall be governed by preexisting law.

Section 32-6-16, referred to in this section, was repealed by Acts 1980, No. 80-434, p. 604, § 15-106, effective May 19, 1980. As to cancellation, suspension or revocation of driver's licenses, see now § 32-5A-195.

Chemical Test for Intoxication Act does not provide "right" of refusal. Hill v. State, 366 So. 2d 318 (Ala. 1979).

Chemical Test for Intoxication Act did not grant a person a "right" to refuse to submit to chemical testing so as to preclude admission of evidence of such a refusal. Hill v. State, 366 So. 2d 296 (Ala. Crim. App. 1978), cert. denied, 366 So. 2d 318 (Ala. 1979).

By virtue of implied consent, a person's refusal to submit to a chemical test for intoxication is admissible into evidence. Pace v. City of Montgomery, 455 So. 2d 180 (Ala. Crim. App. 1984).

Compliance with the act is not the exclusive means for admitting blood alcohol test results; these tests may also be admitted under general evidence principles where a proper foundation has been laid. Powell v. State, 515 So. 2d 140 (Ala. Crim. App. 1986).

Rules and regulations of board of health relating to Alabama chemical test for intoxication apply only to individual who actually performs chemical analysis, not to the person who withdraws the blood. These rules did not apply to the registered nurse who took the blood sample. Holifield v. State, 520 So. 2d 240 (Ala. Crim. App. 1987).

This section does not require that on a criminal charge one must be told that he has a right to refuse the chemical test. The failure to inform a nonconsenting motorist of the consequences of his refusal only affects the validity of the revocation of his driver's license. Redus v. State, 398 So. 2d 757 (Ala. Crim. App.), cert. denied, 398 So. 2d 762 (Ala. 1981).

Sufficient warning. — Where arresting officer testified that he told defendant "that if he refused to take this test, that he would lose or have his driving privileges suspended," his warning was sufficient, since § 32-5-191 specifically provides that "driving privilege" means "driver license." Smith v. Director of Ala. Dep't of Pub. Safety, 531 So. 2d 674 (Ala. Civ. App. 1988).

Refusal to submit to chemical test not compelled communication. — In proceeding in which defendant was convicted of first-degree manslaughter of person fatally injured in automobile accident refusal of defendant to submit to a chemical test for intoxication is not a compelled testimonial communication and the admission of evidence of refusal and comment thereon does not violate the accused's privilege against self-incrimination. Hill v. State, 366 So. 2d 318 (Ala. 1979).

In proceeding in which defendant was convicted of first-degree manslaughter of person fatally injured in automobile accident, admission of evidence of an accused's refusal to take a chemical analysis test violates neither the federal or state privilege against self-incrimination. Hill v. State, 366 So. 2d 296 (Ala. Crim. App. 1978), cert. denied, 366 So. 2d 318 (Ala. 1979).

No constitutional right to consult attorney or physician before test decision. — Defendant motorist had no constitutional or statutory right to consult with attorney or physician before deciding whether to agree or refuse to submit to blood alcohol test or breath test, though officer assertedly told defendant that he had a right to talk to anyone he wanted to before he submitted to the test. Hill v. State, 366 So. 2d 296 (Ala. Crim. App. 1978), cert. denied, 366 So. 2d 318 (Ala. 1979).

Suspension set aside where driver not informed of result of refusal. — Suspension of driver license as a result of refusal to submit to a chemical test to determine the state of intoxication where driver has not been informed by arresting officer that such refusal will result in a suspension of his driver license for 45 days should be set aside. Garrison v. Dothard, 366 So. 2d 1129 (Ala. Civ. App. 1979).

Phrase "shall be told" within statute providing that a person shall be told that refusal to take a chemical test for sobriety will result in a suspension of his license, is ordinarily a mandatory directive as opposed to a permissive directive and operates to require that a person be informed of the effect of a refusal to submit to a sobriety test. Garrison v. Dothard, 366 So. 2d 1129 (Ala. Civ. App. 1979).

No issue of failure to advise of refusal consequences applies to administrative hearings. — Statute providing that no issue will be made as to the failure to be advised of the consequences of a refusal to take sobriety test applies only to administrative hearing, and, hence, is not at odds with statute requiring that person be so informed. Garrison v. Dothard, 366 So. 2d 1129 (Ala. Civ. App. 1979).

Proper administration prerequisite applies to admission of results. — Chemical Test for Intoxication Act provision, which related to proper administration of the tests as a prerequisite for admissibility, applied to the admission of the results of chemical analysis as evidence, not to the admission of the refusal to submit to those tests. Hill v. State, 366 So. 2d 296 (Ala. Crim. App. 1978), cert. denied, 366 So. 2d 318 (Ala. 1979).

State trooper who directed blood alcohol test had reasonable grounds to believe that defendant had been driving under influence of alcohol where trooper directed test after his investigation of automobile accident in which defendant was involved and he had discussed accident with two other officers and knew their opinions. Caver v. State, 533 So. 2d 734 (Ala. Crim. App. 1988).

Where the driver actually consents to the test, his arrest is not a condition precedent to its admissibility. Maffett v. Roberts, 388 So. 2d 972 (Ala. 1980).

An arrest for one of the enumerated offenses furnishes the implied consent under the statute. Maffett v. Roberts, 388 So. 2d 972 (Ala. 1980).

Implied consent arises only on lawful arrest. — Under the express terms of Alabama's implied consent statute, any motorist on the public highways automatically gives his implied consent to a test of his blood, among other things, only if he is lawfully arrested. The legislature did not prescribe any additional conditions which would equate implied consent, such as probable cause to arrest. Love v. State, 513 So. 2d 24 (Ala. 1987).

Requirement of a lawful arrest in the "implied consent" statute grants to the motorist a procedural right, and the failure to accord that right renders blood sample illegal for the purpose of its admission as evidence against the motorist who objects to its admission. Love v. State, 513 So. 2d 24 (Ala. 1987).

Because none of the § 32-1-4(b) exceptions to the misdemeanor traffic offense arrest provisions of § 32-1-4(a) applied to the defendant here, police officer was not authorized to detain her following her arrest for improper lane usage. Her arrest was, therefore, not lawful within the meaning of § 32-5-192(a), and the results of her blood alcohol test were inadmissible in evidence. Hays v. City of Jacksonville, 518 So. 2d 892 (Ala. Crim. App. 1987).

Neither the fact that the defendant's improper lane usage may have arisen because she was driving while under the influence, nor the fact that the arresting officer had probable cause to believe she was driving under the influence, authorized her being required to submit to a chemical test for intoxication because she was unlawfully taken into custody and arrested. Hays v. City of Jacksonville, 518 So. 2d 892 (Ala. Crim. App. 1987).

From the record, it appears that defendant

was arrested only for speeding. The circumstances of the arrest did not meet any of the statutory requirements necessary to justify a custodial arrest. Therefore, the arrest was illegal, and the results of the breath tests were the direct result of the illegal arrest. Therefore, the test results were tainted and should not have been admitted into evidence. McDaniel v. State, 526 So. 2d 642 (Ala. Crim. App. 1988).

There are several steps in the process of laying a proper predicate for admission into evidence of results of photoelectric intoximeter test. First, the law enforcement agency of the officer who administers the test must have designated such test as their means of testing those believed to be under the influence of alcohol. This information may be furnished by the officer who administered the test. Secondly, there must be a showing that the test was performed according to methods approved by the state board of health. This may be proved by the introduction of the rules and regulations the officer followed while administering the test and the officer's testimony that he did, in fact, follow those rules when he administered the test in question. Thirdly, there must be a showing that the person administering the test has a valid permit issued by the state board of health for this purpose. Bush v. City of Troy, 474 So. 2d 164 (Ala. Crim. App. 1984), aff'd, 474 So. 2d 168 (Ala. 1985).

Admission of intoximeter test results without showing of periodic inspection not error. — Trial court did not err in admitting the results of the photoelectric intoximeter test into evidence without a showing by the state that the testing equipment had been periodically inspected by an agent of the state board of health. Reed v. State, 492 So. 2d 293 (Ala. 1986).

Where a toxicologist with the state department of forensic sciences, who performed the chemical analysis of the blood sample taken from the defendant, testified that she conducted that analysis in accordance with the rules and regulations of the state health department and not one question was asked her by opposing counsel regarding this, nor was any contradictory evidence offered by defendant, no error was committed in receiving into evidence the chemical analysis of appellant's blood. Holifield v. State, 520 So. 2d 240 (Ala. Crim. App. 1987).

Admission of test results held harmless error. — Where there was ample evidence of defendant's drunkenness while operating a motor vehicle, error, if any, in the trial court's allowing the results of a chemical blood test was harmless error. Powell v. State, 515 So. 2d 140 (Ala. Crim. App. 1986).

But admission of test results error absent testimony that test officially adopted. — Trial court erred in admitting the results of the photoelectric intoximeter test into evidence without testimony that the law enforcement agency administering the test had officially adopted this test method. Reed v. State, 492 So. 2d 293 (Ala. 1986).

Testimony as to periodic inspection not required to lay foundation. — There is no need for the state to offer testimony concerning a periodic inspection of the testing equipment in order to lay the predicate for admissibility of the photoelectric intoximeter test results. Reed v. State, 492 So. 2d 293 (Ala. 1986).

There is no requirement that the state prove that person who checked and calibrated photoelectric intoximeter was certified to do so by the board of health. Bush v. City of Troy, 474 So. 2d 168 (Ala. 1985).

Detention for speeding not authorized. — Because the defendant was charged with speeding only, his detention following the arrest for speeding was not authorized for the purpose of transporting defendant to headquarters in order to take a breath test and the arrest was illegal under the meaning of subsection (a), and the results of the blood alcohol test were also inadmissible. McCall v. State, 534 So. 2d 668 (Ala. Crim. App. 1988).

Defendant's cause must be reversed and remanded as he was arrested for speeding and required to submit to breath test without being formally charged with DUI until the results of the intoxilizer were available. Sheffield v. State, 522 So. 2d 4 (Ala. Crim. App. 1987).

Cited in State v. Rajala, 54 Ala. App. 502, 310 So. 2d 223 (1975); Harvey v. State Dep't of Pub. Safety, 56 Ala. App. 660, 325 So. 2d 170 (1975); United States v. Hughes, 542 F.2d 246 (5th Cir. 1976); Rehling v. Carr, 295 Ala. 366, 330 So. 2d 423 (1976); Bush v. State, 341 So. 2d 965 (Ala. Crim. App. 1976); Lankford v.

Redwing Carriers, Inc., 344 So. 2d 515 (Ala. Civ. App.), cert. denied, 344 So. 2d 522 (Ala. 1977); Commander v. State, 374 So. 2d 910 (Ala. Crim. App. 1978); Webb v. State, 392 So. 2d 1238 (Ala. Crim. App. 1980); Parker v. State, 397 So. 2d 199 (Ala. Crim. App. 1981); Smith v. State, 460 So. 2d 343 (Ala. Crim. App. 1984); Cooper v. State, 474 So. 2d 182 (Ala. Crim App. 1985); Knighten v. State, 507 So. 2d 1015 (Ala. Crim. App. 1986).

Collateral references. — 60 C.J.S., Motor Vehicles, § 164.16. 61 C.J.S., Motor Vehicles, § 518(5). 61A C.J.S., Motor Vehicles, §§ 593(1), 609, 625(1), 633.

Requiring submission to physical examination or test as violation of constitutional rights. 25 ALR2d 1407.

Admissibility in criminal case of evidence that accused refused to submit to scientific test to determine amount of alcohol in system. 87 ALR2d 370.

Suspension or revocation of license for refusal to take sobriety test. 88 ALR2d 1064.

Driving while intoxicated: Duty of law enforcement officer to offer suspect chemical sobriety test under implied consent law. 95 ALR3d 710.

Request before submitting to chemical sobriety test to communicate with counsel as refusal to take test. 97 ALR3d 852.

Request for prior administration of additional test as constituting refusal to submit to chemical sobriety test under implied consent law. 98 ALR3d 572.

Drunk driving: Motorist's right to private sobriety test. 45 ALR4th 11.

Horizontal gaze nystagmus test: use in impaired driving prosecution. 60 ALR4th 1129.

Cough medicine as "intoxicating liquor" under DUI statute. 65 ALR4th 1238.

Sufficiency of showing of physical inability to take tests for driving while intoxicated to justify refusal. 68 ALR4th 776.

§ 32-5-193. Repealed by Acts 1980, No. 80-434, p. 604, § 15-106, effective May 19, 1980.

§ 32-5-194. Which law-enforcement officers may be authorized to make tests.

The state board of health shall not approve the permit required in this division for making tests for any law-enforcement officer other than a member of the state highway patrol, a sheriff or his deputies or a city policeman. (Acts 1969, No. 699, p. 1255, § 5.)

Cited in Commander v. State, 374 So. 2d 910 (Ala. Crim. App. 1978); Maffett v. Roberts, 388 So. 2d 972 (Ala. 1980).

Collateral references. — 61A C.J.S., Motor Vehicles, § 593(1).

Driving while intoxicated: Duty of law enforcement officer to offer suspect chemical sobriety test under implied consent law. 95 ALR3d 710.

ARTICLE 9.

EQUIPMENT.

Division 1.

General Provisions.

§ 32-5-210. Restrictions as to tire equipment.

(a) Every motor carrier, motor vehicle, truck, semitrailer and trailer shall be equipped with pneumatic tires of sufficient traction surface in accordance with the capacity of the motor carrier or motor vehicle, except as otherwise herein provided, the same to be prescribed by the director of public safety.

(1) No person shall operate any vehicle of a type required to be licensed upon the highways of this state except for those tires on the dead axle of a vehicle with a dead axle when one or more of the tires in use on such vehicle is in unsafe operating condition or has a tread depth less than 2/32 inch or .15875 centimeters measured in any two adjacent tread grooves at three equally spaced intervals around the circumference of the tire; provided, that such measurements shall not be made at the locations of any tread wear indicator. A tire shall be considered unsafe if it has any part of the ply or cord exposed, any bump, bulge or separation, any tread or sidewall cracks, cuts or snags in excess of one inch in length and deep enough to expose the body cords, any tire marked "not for highway use," or "for racing purposes only," or "unsafe for highway use" or words of similar import and any tire which has been regrooved or recut below the original groove depth, excepting special tires which have extra undertread rubber for this purpose and are identified as such; provided, that the prohibitions of this section shall not apply to the tires upon the dead axle of a vehicle equipped with such a dead axle.

(2) No person, firm, corporation or organization shall sell or offer for sale tires, or a vehicle equipped with tires, for use upon the highways of this state, which are in unsafe condition or which have a tread depth of less than 2/32 inch or .15875 centimeters measured as specified in subdivision (1) of this subsection.

(b) No tire on a vehicle moved on a highway shall have on its periphery any block, stud, flange, cleat or spike or any other protuberances of any material other than rubber which project beyond the tread of the traction surface of the tire, except that it shall be permissible to use farm machinery with tires having protuberances which will not injure the highway and, except also, that it shall be permissible to use tire chains or metal studded or safety spike tires of reasonable proportions upon any vehicle when required for safety because of snow, rain or other conditions tending to cause a vehicle to slide or skid.

(c) Every solid rubber tire on a vehicle moved on any highway shall have rubber on its entire traction surface of at least four inches and one inch thick above the edge of the flange of the entire periphery.

(d) The department of public safety and local authorities in their respective jurisdictions may, in their discretion, issue special permits authorizing the operation upon a highway of traction engines or tractors having movable tracks with transverse corrugations upon the periphery of such movable tracks or farm tractors or other farm machinery. (Acts 1927, No. 347, p. 348; Code 1940, T. 36, §§ 34, 76; Acts 1966, Ex. Sess., No. 411, p. 557; Acts 1975, No. 931, p. 1861, § 1.)

Collateral references. — 60A C.J.S., Motor Vehicles, §§ 256, 260, 296, 298.

Liability of motor vehicle owner or operator for accident occasioned by blowout or other failure of tire. 24 ALR2d 161.

Liability of motor carrier for injuries to passengers from accident occasioned by blowout or other failure of tire. 44 ALR2d 835.

§ 32-5-211. Flag or light at end of load.

Whenever the load of any vehicle shall extend more than four feet beyond the rear of the bed or body thereof, there shall be displayed at the end of such load in such position as to be clearly visible at all times from the rear of such load a red flag not less than 12 inches both in length and width; except, that between one-half hour after sunset and one-half hour before sunrise there shall be displayed at the end of any such load a red light plainly visible under normal atmospheric conditions at least 200 feet from the rear of such vehicle. Any person violating this section shall be guilty of a misdemeanor and upon conviction shall be punished as provided in section 32-5-311. (Acts 1927, No. 347, p. 348; Code 1940, T. 36, § 77.)

Code commissioner's note. — Section 32-5-311, referred to in this section, was repealed by Acts 1980, No. 80-434, p. 604, § 75-106, effective May 19, 1980. See now § 32-5A-8.

Cross references. — As to required lights on vehicles generally, see § 32-5-240 et seq.

Cited in Deaton, Inc. v. Burroughs, 456 So. 2d 771 (Ala. 1984).

Collateral references. — 60 C.J.S., Motor Vehicles, § 22. 60A C.J.S., Motor Vehicles, § 348.

§ 32-5-212. Brakes.

Every motor vehicle when operated upon a highway shall be equipped with brakes adequate to control the movement of and to stop and to hold such vehicle, including two separate means of applying the brakes, each of which shall be effective to apply the brakes to at least two wheels and so constructed that no part which is liable to failure shall be common to two; except, that a motorcycle need be equipped with only one brake. All such brakes shall be maintained in good working order and shall conform to regulations not inconsistent with this section to be promulgated by the director of public safety. Any person violating this section shall be guilty of a misdemeanor. (Acts 1927, No. 347, p. 348; Code 1940, T. 36, § 35.)

Cross references. — As to brakes on motor-driven cycles, see § 32-12-24.

Driving with defective brakes negligence per se. — Where alleged servant of defendant was driving defendant's automobile with defective brakes over a public street at the time of collision, with plaintiff in violation of this section, driving of automobile was "negligence per se." Harden v. Harden, 29 Ala. App. 411, 197 So. 94 (1940).

Notice of defective brakes. — While this section requires no notice of defective brakes, it would be an unreasonable construction of this section to require an operator or owner to be an insurer of the manufacturing of a brake system. The better rule is to require knowledge of the brakes' defective nature. City of Montgomery v. Bennett, 487 So. 2d 942 (Ala. Civ. App. 1986).

Infliction of injury or damage does not create absolute liability therefor. — An owner or operator of a motor vehicle which inflicts injury or damage as a result of violation of a safe brake statute does not create absolute liability for damages suffered as a result of said violation, and the owner or operator is excused from liability, insofar as liability is based upon the instance of a brake defect, if he did not have notice, actual or constructive, of the brake defect and exercised reasonable care with respect to the inspection and maintenance of said braking system. City of Montgomery v. Bennett, 487 So. 2d 942 (Ala. Civ. App. 1986).

The law does not require that plaintiffs prove that a violation of a rule of the road was the sole cause of injury. The jury must find only that the statutory violation proximately caused the injury. Childers v. Ashburn & Gray, Inc., 398 So. 2d 682 (Ala. 1981).

Allegations. — A charge that defendant placed a vehicle on the highway with defective brakes is embraced within the charge that defendant negligently caused or allowed the vehicle to collide with another vehicle, because operating, or causing to be operated, on a public highway a motor vehicle with defective brakes constitutes negligent operation of the vehicle. Wood Lumber Co. v. Bruce, 275 Ala. 577, 157 So. 2d 3 (1963).

Cited in Al De Ment Chevrolet Co. v. Wilson, 252 Ala. 662, 42 So. 2d 585 (1949); Waddell v. Crescent Motors, Inc., 260 Ala. 124, 69 So. 2d 414 (1953).

Collateral references. — 60 C.J.S., Motor Vehicles, § 26. 60A C.J.S., Motor Vehicles, § 261.

7 Am. Jur. 2d, Automobiles & Highway Traffic, § 151.

Effect of defective brakes on liability for injury. 14 ALR 1339, 63 ALR 398, 170 ALR 611.

Criminal responsibility for injury or death in operation of mechanically defective motor vehicle. 88 ALR2d 1165.

Effect of violation of safety equipment statute as establishing negligence in automobile accident litigation. 38 ALR3d 530.

Liability of owner or operator of motor vehicle for injury, death, or property damage resulting from defective brakes. 40 ALR3d 9.

Failure to set brakes or maintain adequate brakes, as causing accidental runaway of parked motor vehicle. 42 ALR3d 1252.

§ 32-5-213. Horns and warning devices.

(a) Every motor vehicle when operated upon a highway shall be equipped with a horn in good working order capable of emitting a sound audible under normal conditions for a distance of not less than 200 feet.

It shall be unlawful for any vehicle to be equipped with or for any person to use upon a vehicle any siren or for any person at any time to use a horn otherwise than as a reasonable warning or to make any unnecessary or unreasonably loud or harsh sound by means of a horn or other warning device.

(b) Every police and fire department and fire patrol vehicle and every ambulance used for emergency calls shall be equipped with a siren, bell, ululating multi-toned horns or other electronic siren type device approved by the director of public safety.

(c) Any person violating any of the provisions of this section shall be guilty of a misdemeanor. (Acts 1927, No. 347, p. 348; Code 1940, T. 36, § 36; Acts 1966, Ex. Sess., No. 432, p. 578.)

Violation of section constitutes negligence. McGough Bakeries Corp. v. Reynolds, 250 Ala. 592, 35 So. 2d 332 (1948).

Cited in Jones v. State, 33 Ala. App. 451, 34 So. 2d 483 (1948); Long v. State, 33 Ala. App. 463, 36 So. 2d 133 (1948); Smith v. Lilley, 252 Ala. 425, 41 So. 2d 175 (1949).

Collateral references. — 60 C.J.S., Motor Vehicles, § 26. 60A C.J.S., Motor Vehicles, §§ 260, 371, 374, 375.

§ 32-5-214. Mirrors.

Every motor vehicle, operated singly or when towing any other vehicle, shall be equipped with a mirror so located as to reflect to the driver a view of the highway for a distance of at least 200 feet to the rear of such motor vehicle. (Acts 1927, No. 347, p. 348; Code 1940, T. 36, § 37; Acts 1959, No. 292, p. 860.)

Cited in Holman v. Brady, 241 Ala. 487, 3 So. 2d 30 (1941); Jones v. State, 33 Ala. App. 451, 34 So. 2d 483 (1948); Rhodes v. Strickland, 284 Ala. 621, 227 So. 2d 392 (1969); Scotch Lumber Co. v. Baugh, 288 Ala. 34, 256 So. 2d 869 (1972).

Collateral references. — 60A C.J.S., Motor Vehicles, § 260.

Liability for failure to provide motor vehicle with adequate rearview mirror. 27 ALR2d 1040.

Criminal responsibility for injury or death in operation of mechanically defective motor vehicle. 88 ALR2d 1165.

Effect of violation of safety equipment statute as establishing negligence in automobile accident litigation. 38 ALR3d 530.

§ 32-5-215. Windshields must be unobstructed; windshield wipers; tinting.

(a) No person shall drive any motor vehicle with any sign, poster or other nontransparent material upon the front windshield, sidewings or side or rear windows of such vehicle which obstructs the driver's clear view of the highway or any intersecting highway.

(b) The windshield on every motor vehicle shall be equipped with a device for cleaning rain, snow or other moisture from the windshield, which device shall be so constructed as to be controlled or operated by the driver of the vehicle.

(c) Every windshield wiper upon a motor vehicle shall be maintained in good working order.

(d) No person shall operate a motor vehicle which has a windshield, sidewing or rear window which has tinting to the extent or manufactured in such a way that occupants of the vehicle cannot be easily identified or recognized through the sidewing or rear windows from outside the motor vehicle.

(e) The provisions of this section shall not apply to the manufactured tinting of windshields of motor vehicles or to certificates of identification, decals or other papers required by law to be displayed on such windshield or windows. (Acts 1927, No. 347, p. 348; Code 1940, T. 36, § 38; Acts 1949, No. 517, p. 754, § 8; Acts 1983, No. 83-572, p. 877.)

Collateral references. — 60A C.J.S., Motor Vehicles, § 285. 61 C.J.S., Motor Vehicles, § 505(2).

Liability for motor vehicle accident where vision of driver is obscured by smoke, dust, atmospheric condition or unclean windshield. 42 ALR2d 13.

Motor vehicle operator's liability for accident occurring while driving with vision obscured by smoke or steam. 32 ALR4th 933.

§ 32-5-216. Mufflers; prevention of noise, smoke, etc.

(a) Every motor vehicle shall at all times be equipped with a muffler in good working order and in constant operation to prevent excessive or unusual noise and annoying smoke, and no person shall use a muffler cut-out, bypass, a muffler without baffles or similar device upon a motor vehicle on a highway.

(b) The engine and power mechanism of every motor vehicle shall be so equipped and adjusted as to prevent the escape of excessive fumes or smoke. (Acts 1927, No. 347, p. 348; Code 1940, T. 36, § 39; Acts 1949, No. 517, p. 754, § 9.)

Cross references. — As to authority of state air pollution control commission to estab- lish rules and regulations for control of emis- sions from motor vehicles, see § 22-28-12.

§ 32-5-217. Safety belts.

(a) No seat safety belt or anchor shall be sold or installed for use in connection with the operation of a motor vehicle on any highway in this state unless it meets the specifications prescribed by the department of public safety.

(b) The department shall adopt regulations governing approved types of seat safety belts and anchors, but the department shall accept, as approved, all seat safety belts and anchors meeting the specifications of the society of automotive engineers.

(c) Any person who knowingly sells or installs a seat safety belt in violation of the provisions of this section shall be fined not less than $25.00 and not more than $50.00. (Acts 1967, No. 734, p. 1570.)

Cited in Britton v. Doehring, 286 Ala. 498, 242 So. 2d 666 (1970).

Collateral references. — Liability of owner or operator of motor vehicle or aircraft for injury or death allegedly resulting from failure to furnish or require use of seat belt. 49 ALR3d 295.

§ 32-5-218. Safety glazing material in motor vehicles.

(a) On and after January 1, 1968, no person shall sell any new motor vehicle as specified herein, nor shall any new motor vehicle as specified herein be registered thereafter unless such vehicle is equipped with safety glazing material of a type approved by the director wherever glazing material is used in doors, windows and windshields. The foregoing provisions shall apply to all passenger-type motor vehicles, including passenger buses and school buses, but in respect to trucks, including truck tractors, the requirements as to safety glazing material shall apply to all glazing material used in doors, windows and windshields in the drivers' compartments of such vehicles. All replacements made of any glazing material in motor vehicles as described herein shall be made with safety glazing material as herein described.

(b) The term "safety glazing materials" means glazing materials so constructed, treated or combined with other materials as to reduce substantially, in comparison with ordinary sheet glass or plate glass, the likelihood of injury to persons by objects from exterior sources or by these safety glazing materials when they may be cracked or broken.

(c) The director shall compile and publish a list of types of glazing material by name approved by him as meeting the requirements of this section and the commissioner of revenue shall not register after January 1, 1968, any motor vehicle which is subject to the provisions of this section unless it is equipped with an approved type of safety glazing material, and the commissioner of revenue shall thereafter suspend the registration of any motor vehicle so subject to this section which is not so equipped until it is made to conform to the requirements of this section. (Acts 1949, No. 516, p. 740, § 34; Acts 1967, No. 735, p. 1571.)

Collateral references. — 60 C.J.S., Motor Vehicles, §§ 26, 165(7).

§ 32-5-219. Location of television viewers.

No television viewer, screen or other means of visually receiving a television broadcast shall be located in a motor vehicle at any point forward of the back of the driver's seat or in any manner so that the driver of the vehicle can see it while in actual control of the vehicle. (Acts 1949, No. 516, p. 740, § 35.)

§ 32-5-220. Flares or other warning devices — Carrying required by certain vehicles; specifications.

(a) No person shall operate any truck, passenger bus or truck tractor upon any highway outside the corporate limits of municipalities at any time from a half hour after sunset to a half hour before sunrise unless there shall be carried in such vehicle the following equipment, except as provided in subsection (b) of this section:

(1) At least three flares or three red electric lanterns each of which shall be capable of being seen and distinguished at a distance of 500 feet under normal atmospheric conditions at nighttime. Each flare (liquid-burning pot torch) shall be capable of burning for not less than 12 hours in five miles per hour wind velocity and capable of burning in any air velocity from zero to 40 miles per hour. Every such flare shall be substantially constructed so as to withstand reasonable shocks without leaking. Every such flare shall be carried in the vehicle in a metal rack or box. Every such red electric lantern

shall be capable of operating continuously for not less than 12 hours and shall be substantially constructed so as to withstand reasonable shock without breakage.

(2) At least three red-burning fusees unless red electric lanterns are carried. Every fusee shall be made in accordance with specifications of the Bureau of Explosives, New York, and so marked and shall be capable of burning at least 15 minutes.

(3) At least two red cloth flags, not less than 12 inches square, with standards to support same.

(b) No person shall operate at the time and under the conditions stated in subsection (a) of this section any motor vehicle used in the transportation of inflammable liquids in bulk, or transporting compressed inflammable gases unless there shall be carried in such vehicle three red electric lanterns meeting the requirements above stated and there shall not be carried in any said vehicle any flares, fusees or signal produced by a flame.

(c) As an alternative it shall be deemed a compliance with this section in the event a person operating any motor vehicle described in this section shall carry in such vehicle three portable reflector units on standards of a type approved by the department. No portable reflector unit shall be approved unless it is so designed and constructed as to include two reflectors one above the other each of which shall be capable of reflecting red light clearly visible from all distances within 500 feet to 50 feet under normal atmospheric conditions at nighttime when directly in front of lawful upper beams of head lamps. (Acts 1949, No. 516, p. 740, § 42.)

Collateral references. — 60 C.J.S., Motor Vehicles, § 56. 60A C.J.S., Motor Vehicles, § 335(1).

Negligence as contributory negligence of driver or occupant of disabled motor vehicle parked or stopped on highway without flares. 67 ALR2d 30.

§ 32-5-221. Same — Display.

(a) Whenever any truck, passenger bus, truck tractor, trailer, semitrailer or pole trailer is disabled upon the traveled portion of any highway or the shoulder thereof outside of any municipality at any time when lighted lamps are required on vehicles the driver of such vehicle shall display the following warning devices upon the highway during the time the vehicle is so disabled on the highway except as provided in subsection (b) of this section:

(1) A lighted fusee or other flare shall be immediately placed on the roadway at the traffic side of the motor vehicle unless electric lanterns are displayed.

(2) Within the burning period of the fusee or other flare and as promptly as possible three lighted flares (pot torches) or three electric lanterns shall be placed on the roadway as follows: one approximately 100 feet in advance of the vehicle; one at a distance of approximately 100 feet to the rear of the vehicle, each in the center of the lane of traffic occupied by the disabled

vehicle; and one at the traffic side of the vehicle approximately 10 feet rearward or forward thereof.

(b) Whenever any vehicle used in the transportation of inflammable liquid in bulk or transporting compressed inflammable gases is disabled upon a highway at any time or place mentioned in subsection (a) of this section, the driver of such vehicle shall display upon the roadway one red electric lantern to be immediately placed on the roadway at the traffic side of the vehicle and two other red electric lanterns to be placed to the front and rear of the vehicle in the same manner prescribed in subsection (a) above for flares. When a vehicle of a type specified in this subsection is disabled, the use of flares, fusees or any signal produced by flame as warning signals is prohibited.

(c) Whenever any vehicle of a type referred to in this section is disabled upon the traveled portion of a highway or the shoulder thereof, outside of any municipality at any time when the display of fusees, flares or electric lanterns is not required, the driver of such vehicle shall display two red flags upon the roadway in the lane of traffic occupied by the disabled vehicle, one at a distance of approximately 100 feet in advance of the vehicle, and one at a distance of approximately 100 feet to the rear of the vehicle.

(d) In the alternative, it shall be deemed a compliance with this section in the event three portable reflector units on standards of a type approved by the department are displayed at the times and under the conditions specified in this section either during the daytime or at nighttime and such portable reflector units shall be placed on the roadway in the locations prescribed above for the placing of electric lanterns and lighted flares.

(e) The flares, fusees, lanterns and flags to be displayed as required in this section shall conform to the requirements of section 32-5-220. (Acts 1949, No. 516, p. 740, § 43.)

Collateral references. — When is a motor vehicle "disabled" or the like within exception to statute regulating parking or stopping. 15 ALR2d 909.

§ 32-5-222. Child passenger restraints; required for children under six; penalty.

(a) Every person transporting a child under the age of six years in a motor vehicle registered in this state and operated on the roadways, streets, or highways of this state, shall provide for the protection of the child by properly using a child passenger restraint system meeting applicable federal motor vehicle safety standards. Provided that, with respect to a child who is either four or five years of age, the term "child passenger restraint system meeting applicable federal motor vehicle safety standards" shall be deemed to include seat belts installed by the motor vehicle manufacturer, dealer or owner. Provided that in no event shall failure to wear a child passenger restraint system be considered as contributory negligence. Provided that the term "motor vehicle" as used in this section shall not apply to trucks or buses having tonnage rating of one ton or more.

(b) No provision of this section shall be construed as creating any duty, standard of care, right, or liability between parent and child that is not recognized under the laws of the state of Alabama as they presently exist, or may, at any time in the future, be constituted by statute or decision.

(c) Any person violating the provisions of this section may be fined not more than $10.00 for each offense.

(d) The provisions of this section notwithstanding, nothing contained herein shall be deemed a violation of any law which would otherwise nullify or change in any way the provisions or coverage of any insurance contract. (Acts 1982, No. 82-421, p. 663; Acts 1989, No. 89-781, § 1.)

The **1989 amendment,** effective May 11, 1989, substituted "age of six years" for "age of three years" in the first sentence, and inserted the present second sentence.

Division 2.

Lights, Lamps and Reflective Devices.

§ 32-5-240. Required lighting equipment and illuminating devices of vehicles.

(a) *When lighted lamps required.* — Every vehicle upon a highway within this state at any time from a half hour after sunset to a half hour before sunrise and at any other time when there is not sufficient light to render clearly discernible persons and vehicles on the highway at a distance of 500 feet ahead shall display lighted lamps and illuminating devices as hereinafter respectively required for different classes of vehicles, subject to exception with respect to parked vehicles, as hereinafter stated, and the further exception that whenever motor and other vehicles are operated in combination during the time that lights are required, any lamp (except tail lamps) need not be lighted which by reason of its location on a vehicle of the combination, would be obscured by another vehicle of the combination, but this shall not affect the requirement that lighted clearance lamps be displayed on the front of the foremost vehicle required to have clearance lamps, nor that all lights required on the rear of the rearmost vehicle of any combination shall be lighted.

(b) *Head lamps on motor vehicles.*

(1) Every motor vehicle other than a motorcycle or motor-driven cycle shall be equipped with at least two but not more than four head lamps, with at least one but not more than two on each side of the front of the motor vehicle, which head lamps shall comply with the requirements and limitations set forth in section 32-5-242.

(2) Every motorcycle and every motor-driven cycle shall be equipped with at least one and not more than two head lamps which shall comply with the requirements and limitations of section 32-5-242.

(3) Every head lamp, upon every new motor vehicle sold hereafter including every motorcycle and motor-driven cycle, shall be located at a height measured from the center of the head lamp of not more than 54

inches nor less than 24 inches to be measured as set forth in section 32-5-242.

(c) *Tail lamps.*

(1) Every motor vehicle, trailer, semitrailer and pole trailer and any other vehicle which is being drawn at the end of a train of vehicles shall be equipped with at least one tail lamp mounted on the rear, which when lighted as hereinbefore required, shall emit a red light plainly visible from a distance of 500 feet to the rear; provided, that in case of a train of vehicles, only the tail lamp on the rearmost vehicle need actually be seen from the distance specified.

(2) Every tail lamp upon every vehicle shall be located at a height of not more than 60 inches nor less than 20 inches to be measured as set forth in section 32-5-242.

(3) Either a tail lamp or a separate lamp shall be so constructed and placed as to illuminate with a white light the rear registration plate and render it clearly legible from a distance of 50 feet to the rear. Any tail lamp or tail lamps, together with any separate lamp for illuminating the rear registration plate, shall be so wired as to be lighted whenever the head lamps or auxiliary driving lamps are lighted.

(d) *Additional equipment required on certain vehicles.* — In addition to other equipment required in this article the following vehicles shall be equipped as herein stated under the conditions stated in subsection (a) of this section:

(1) On every bus or truck, whatever its size, there shall be the following: on the rear, two red reflectors, one at each side, and one stop light.

(2) On every bus or truck 80 inches or more in overall width, in addition to the requirements in subdivision (1):

a. On the front, two clearance lamps, one at each side.

b. On the rear, two clearance lamps, one on each side.

c. On each side, two side marker lamps, one at or near the front and one at or near the rear.

d. On each side, two reflectors, one at or near the front and one at or near the rear.

(e) *Lamps on other vehicles and equipment.* — All vehicles, including animal-drawn vehicles and including those for which special permits have been issued under authority of section 32-9-29, not hereinbefore specifically required to be equipped with lamps, shall at the time specified in subsection (a) of this section be equipped with at least one lighted lamp or lantern exhibiting a white light visible from a distance of 500 feet to the front of such vehicle and with a lamp or lantern exhibiting a red light visible from a distance of 500 feet to the rear.

(f) *Stop lamps required on new motor vehicles.* — Hereafter, it shall be unlawful for any person to sell any new motor vehicle, including any motorcycle or motor-driven cycle, in this state or for any person to drive such vehicle on the highways unless it is equipped with a stop lamp meeting the requirements of section 32-5-242.

(g) *New motor vehicles to be equipped with reflectors.*

(1) Every new motor vehicle hereafter sold and operated upon a highway, other than a truck tractor, shall carry on the rear, either as a part of the tail lamps or separately, two red reflectors; except, that every motorcycle and every motor-driven cycle shall carry at least one reflector, meeting the requirements of this section; and except, that vehicles of the type mentioned in subsection (d) of this section shall be equipped with reflectors as required in those sections applicable thereto.

(2) Every such reflector shall be mounted on the vehicle at a height not less than 20 inches nor more than 60 inches measured as set forth in subsection (a) of section 32-5-242, and shall be of such size and characteristics and so mounted as to be visible at night from all distances within 300 feet to 50 feet from such vehicle except that visibility from the greater distance is hereinafter required of reflectors on certain types of vehicles.

(3) On every truck tractor:

a. On the front, two clearance lamps, one at each side.

b. On the rear, one stop light.

(4) On every trailer or semitrailer having a gross weight in excess of 3,000 pounds:

a. On the front, two clearance lamps, one at each side.

b. On each side, two side marker lamps, one at or near the front and one at or near the rear.

c. On each side, two reflectors, one at or near the front and one at or near the rear.

d. On the rear, two clearance lamps, one at each side, also two reflectors, one at each side, and one stop light.

(5) On every pole trailer in excess of 3,000 pounds gross weight:

a. On each side, one side marker lamp and one clearance lamp which may be in combination, to show to the front, side and rear.

b. On the rear of the pole trailer or load, two reflectors, one at each side.

(6) On every trailer, semitrailer, or pole trailer weighing 3,000 pounds gross or less: on the rear, two reflectors, one on each side. If any trailer or semitrailer is so loaded or is of such dimensions as to obscure the stop light on the towing vehicle, then such towed vehicle shall also be equipped with one stop light. (Acts 1927, No. 347, p. 348; Code 1940, T. 36, § 40; Acts 1949, No. 517, p. 754, § 10; Acts 1957, No. 414, p. 577.)

Driving with improper lights constitutes a traffic infraction and is a violation of this section. Sly v. State, 387 So. 2d 913 (Ala. Crim. App.), cert. denied, 387 So. 2d 917 (Ala. 1980).

Question for jury. — In prosecution for reckless driving of an automobile, wherein state introduced evidence tending to show that defendant was traveling about 25 miles per hour around curve on left side of road after dark with no lights on his automobile, defendant's guilt was question for jury. Hill v. State, 27 Ala. App. 202, 169 So. 21 (1936).

Purpose of requiring clearance lamps. — See Clift v. Donegan, 237 Ala. 304, 186 So. 476 (1939).

Violation constitutes negligence. — A violation, by either a truck owner or driver, of this section constitutes negligence. Clift v. Donegan, 237 Ala. 304, 186 So. 476 (1939).

Whether violation proximate cause of collision jury question. — Where a wide truck, which did not carry front clearance light on left side as required by statute, collided with left-hand side of an oncoming automobile at night, whether violation of section was a proximate cause of collision was question for jury. Clift v. Donegan, 237 Ala. 304, 186 So. 476 (1939).

Where the record, in an action for negligence wherein the defendant's truck collided with an oncoming car when defendant attempted to pass plaintiff's tractor and trailer, disclosed that plaintiff's tractor had four headlights burning and a lighted flashlight wired to the rear of the trailer, that the roadway was straight for a considerable distance from the place of the collision and that defendant was driving at an improper speed, a question of fact arose for the jury's determination as to whether, even though the plaintiff may have been negligent in failing to have a rear red light on the trailer as required by this section, defendant's conduct was yet the proximate cause of the injury. Lancaster v. Johnson, 34 Ala. App. 637, 42 So. 2d 604 (1949).

Cited in McIntosh v. State, 28 Ala. App. 488, 188 So. 78 (1939); Powers v. State, 49 Ala. App. 690, 275 So. 2d 369 (1973).

Collateral references. — 60 C.J.S., Motor Vehicles, § 26. 60A C.J.S., Motor Vehicles, §§ 263, 285, 301, 340.

7 Am. Jur. 2d, Automobiles & Highway Traffic, §§ 152-156.

Validity and construction of regulations as to lights. 11 ALR 1226, 78 ALR 815.

Driving motor vehicle without lights or with improper lights as affecting liability for collision. 21 ALR2d 7.

Driving motor vehicle without lights or with improper lights as gross negligence or the like warranting recovery by guests under guest statute or similar common-law rule. 21 ALR2d 209.

Negligence or contributory negligence of driver or occupant of motor vehicle parked or stopped on highway without flares. 67 ALR2d 12.

Contributory negligence of driver or occupant of motor vehicle driven, parked or stopped without lights or with defective or inadequate lights. 67 ALR2d 118.

Contributory negligence of driver or occupant of motor vehicle being driven or parked without dimming lights. 67 ALR2d 183.

Criminal responsibility for injury or death in operation of mechanically defective motor vehicle. 88 ALR2d 1165.

Effect of violation of safety equipment statute as establishing negligence in automobile accident litigation. 38 ALR3d 530.

Liability or recovery in automobile negligence action as affected by absence or insufficiency of lights on parked or standing motor vehicle. 61 ALR3d 13.

Liability or recovery in automobile negligence action arising out of collision or upset as affected by operation of vehicle without front lights, or with improper front lights. 62 ALR3d 560.

Liability or recovery in automobile negligence action arising out of collision or upset as affected by operation of vehicle without or with improper taillights or rear reflectors. 62 ALR3d 771.

Liability or recovery in automobile negligence action arising out of collision or upset as affected by operation of vehicle without, or with improper, clearance, load, or similar auxiliary lights. 62 ALR3d 844.

§ 32-5-241. Additional permissible lights on vehicles.

(a) *Spot lamps and auxiliary lamps.*

(1) SPOT LAMPS. — Any motor vehicle may be equipped with not to exceed one spot lamp and every lighted spot lamp shall be so aimed and used upon approaching another vehicle that no part of the high intensity portion of the beam will be directed to the left of the prolongation of the extreme left side of the vehicle nor more than 100 feet ahead of the vehicle.

(2) FOG LAMPS. — Any motor vehicle may be equipped with not to exceed two fog lamps mounted on the front at a height not less than 12 inches nor more than 30 inches above the level surface upon which the vehicle stands and so aimed that when the vehicle is not loaded none of the high intensity portion of the light to the left of the center of the vehicle shall at a distance of 25 feet ahead project higher than a level of four inches below the level of the center of the lamp from which it comes.

(3) AUXILIARY PASSING LAMPS. — Any motor vehicle may be equipped with not to exceed one auxiliary passing lamp mounted on the front at a height not less than 24 inches nor more than 42 inches above the level surface upon which the vehicle stands and every such auxiliary passing lamp shall meet the requirements and limitations set forth in this chapter.

(4) AUXILIARY DRIVING LAMPS. — Any motor vehicle may be equipped with not to exceed one auxiliary driving lamp mounted on the front at a height not less than 16 inches nor more than 42 inches above the level surface upon which the vehicle stands and every auxiliary driving lamp shall meet the requirements and limitations set forth in this chapter.

(b) *Signal lamps and signal devices.*

(1) Any motor vehicle may be equipped and when required under this division shall be equipped with the following signal lamps or devices:

a. A stop lamp on the rear which shall emit a red or yellow light and which shall be actuated upon application of the service (foot) brake and which may but need not be incorporated with a tail lamp.

b. A lamp or lamps or mechanical signal device capable of clearly indicating any intention to turn either to the right or the left and which shall be visible both from the front and rear.

(2) A stop lamp shall be plainly visible and understandable from a distance of 100 feet to the rear both during normal sunlight and at nighttime and a signal lamp or lamps indicating intention to turn shall be visible and understandable during daytime and nighttime from a distance of 100 feet both to the front and rear. When a vehicle is equipped with a stop lamp or other signal lamps, such lamp or lamps shall at all times be maintained in good working condition. No stop lamp or signal lamp shall project a glaring or dazzling light.

(3) All mechanical signal devices shall be self-illuminated when in use at the time mentioned in subsection (a) of section 32-5-240.

(c) *Additional lighting equipment.*

(1) Any motor vehicle may be equipped with not more than two side cowl or fender lamps which shall emit an amber or white light without glare.

(2) Any motor vehicle may be equipped with not more than one running-board courtesy lamp on each side thereof which shall emit a white or amber light without glare.

(3) Any motor vehicle may be equipped with not more than two back-up lamps either separately or in combination with other lamps, but any such back-up lamp shall not be lighted when the motor vehicle is in forward motion.

(d) *Special restriction on lamps.*

(1) Any lighted lamp or illuminated device upon a motor vehicle other than head lamps, spot lamps, auxiliary lamps or flashing front direction signals which projects a beam of light of an intensity greater than 300 candlepower shall be so directed that no part of the beam will strike the level of the roadway on which the vehicle stands at a distance of more than 75 feet from the vehicle.

(2) No person shall drive or move any vehicle or equipment upon any highway with any lamp or device thereon displaying a red light visible from directly in front of the center thereof. This section shall not apply to authorized emergency vehicles.

(3) Any vehicle may be equipped with flashing lamps which may be used for the purpose of warning the operators of other vehicles of the presence of a vehicular traffic hazard requiring the exercise of unusual care in approaching, overtaking or passing, and when so equipped may display such warning in addition to any other warning signals required by this section. The lamps used to display such warning to the front shall be mounted at the same level and as widely spaced laterally as practicable and shall display simultaneously flashing white or amber lights, or any shade of color between white and amber.

The lamps used to display such warning to the rear shall be mounted at the same level and as widely spaced laterally as practicable, and shall show simultaneously flashing amber or red lights, or any shade of color between amber and red. These warning lights shall be visible from a distance of not less than 1,500 feet under normal atmospheric conditions at night.

(4) Flashing lights may be used on motor vehicles as a means of indicating a right or left turn; a stop lamp may pulsate with different intensities provided that it meets at all intensities the provisions of subdivision (2) of subsection (b) of this section; and the warning lights on emergency vehicles may flash. (Acts 1927, No. 347, p. 348; Code 1940, T. 36, § 41; Acts 1949, No. 517, p. 754, § 11; Acts 1961, Ex. Sess., No. 136, p. 2062, § 3; Acts 1965, No. 815, p. 1522.)

Collateral references. — 60A C.J.S., Motor Vehicles, §§ 263, 286.

§ 32-5-242. Requirements as to head lamps and auxiliary driving lamps.

(a) *Visibility distance and mounted height of lamps.*

(1) Whenever requirement is hereinafter declared as to the distance from which certain lamps and devices shall render objects visible or within which such lamps or devices shall be visible, said provisions shall apply during the times stated in section 32-5-240 in respect to a vehicle without load when upon a straight, level, unlighted highway under normal atmospheric conditions unless a different time or condition is expressly stated.

(2) Whenever requirement is hereinafter declared as to the mounted height of lamps or devices it shall mean from the center of such lamp or device to the level ground upon which the vehicle stands when such vehicle is without a load.

(b) *Multiple-beam road-lighting equipment.* — Except as hereinafter provided, the head lamps or the auxiliary driving lamp or the auxiliary passing lamp or combination thereof on motor vehicles other than motorcycles or motor-driven cycles shall be so arranged that the driver may select at will between distributions of light projected to different elevations and such lamps may, in addition, be so arranged that such selection can be made automatically, subject to the following limitations:

(1) There shall be an uppermost distribution of light, or composite beam, so aimed and of such intensity as to reveal persons and vehicles at a distance of at least 350 feet ahead for all conditions of loading.

(2) There shall be a lowermost distribution of light, or composite beam so aimed and of sufficient intensity to reveal persons and vehicles at a distance of at least 100 feet ahead; and on a straight level road under any condition of loading none of the high-intensity portion of the beam shall be directed to strike the eyes of an approaching driver.

(3) Every new motor vehicle, other than a motorcycle or motor-driven cycle, registered hereafter in this state, which has multiple-beam road-lighting equipment shall be equipped with a beam indicator, which shall be lighted whenever the uppermost distribution of light from the head lamps is in use, and shall not otherwise be lighted. Said indicator shall be so designed and located that when lighted it will be readily visible without glare to the driver of the vehicle so equipped.

(c) *Use of multiple-beam road-lighting equipment.* — Whenever a motor vehicle is being operated on a roadway or shoulder adjacent thereto during the times specified in subsection (a) of section 32-5-240 the driver shall use a distribution of light, or composite beam, directed high enough and of sufficient intensity to reveal persons and vehicles at a safe distance in advance of the vehicle, subject to the following requirements and limitations:

(1) Whenever a driver of a vehicle approaches an oncoming vehicle within 500 feet, such driver shall use a distribution of light, or composite beam, so aimed that the glaring rays are not projected into the eyes of the oncoming driver. The lowermost distribution of light or composite beam, specified in subdivision (2) of subsection (b) of this section shall be deemed to avoid glare at all times, regardless of road contour and loading.

(2) Whenever the driver of a vehicle follows another vehicle within 200 feet to the rear, except when engaged in the act of overtaking and passing, such driver shall use a distribution of light permissible under this division other than the uppermost distribution of light specified in subdivision (1) of subsection (b) of this section.

(d) *Single-beam road-lighting equipment.* — Head lamps arranged to provide a single distribution of light not supplemented by auxiliary driving lamps shall be permitted on motor vehicles manufactured and sold one year hereafter in lieu of multiple-beam road-lighting equipment herein specified if the single distribution of light complies with the following requirements and limitations:

(1) The head lamps shall be so aimed that when the vehicle is not loaded none of the high-intensity portion of the light shall, at a distance of 25 feet ahead, project higher than a level of five inches below the level of the center of the lamp from which it comes, and in no case higher than 42 inches above the level on which the vehicle stands at a distance of 75 feet ahead.

(2) The intensity shall be sufficient to reveal persons and vehicles at a distance of at least 200 feet.

(e) *Lighting equipment on motor-driven cycles.* — The head lamp or head lamps upon every motor-driven cycle may be of the single-beam or multiple-beam type but in either event shall comply with the requirements and limitations as follows:

(1) Every said head lamp or head lamps on a motor-driven cycle shall be of sufficient intensity to reveal a person or a vehicle at a distance of not less than 100 feet when the motor-driven cycle is operated at any speed less than 25 miles per hour; at a distance of not less than 200 feet when the motor-driven cycle is operated at a speed of 25 or more miles per hour but less than 35 miles per hour; and at a distance of 300 feet when the motor-driven cycle is operated at a speed of 35 miles or more per hour.

(2) In the event the motor-driven cycle is equipped with a multiple-beam head lamp or head lamps the upper beam shall meet the minimum requirements set forth above and shall not exceed the limitations set forth in subdivision (2) of subsection (b) of this section.

(3) In the event the motor-driven cycle is equipped with a single-beam lamp or lamps, said lamp or lamps shall be so aimed that when the vehicle is loaded none of the high-intensity portion of light, at a distance of 25 feet ahead, shall project higher than the level of the center of the lamp from which it comes.

(f) *Alternate road-lighting equipment.* — Any motor vehicle may be operated under the conditions specified in subsection (a) of section 32-5-240 when equipped with two lighted lamps upon the front thereof capable of revealing persons and objects 75 feet ahead in lieu of lamps required in subsection (b) or subsection (d) of this section; provided, that at no time shall it be operated at a speed in excess of 20 miles per hour.

(g) *Color of clearance lamps, side marker lamps and reflectors.*

(1) Front clearance lamps and those marker lamps and reflectors mounted on the front or on the side near the front of a vehicle shall display or reflect an amber color.

(2) Rear clearance lamps and those marker lamps and reflectors mounted on the rear or on the sides near the rear of a vehicle shall display or reflect a red color.

(3) All lighting devices and reflectors mounted on the rear of any vehicle shall display or reflect a red color, except the stop light or other signal device, which may be red, amber or yellow, and except that the light illuminating the license plate or the light emitted by a back-up lamp shall be white.

(h) *Mounting reflectors, clearance lamps and side marker lamps.*

(1) Reflectors, when required by subsection (d) of section 32-5-240 shall be mounted at a height not less than 24 inches and not higher than 60 inches above the ground on which the vehicle stands; except, that if the highest part of the permanent structure of the vehicle is less than 24 inches

the reflector at such point shall be mounted as high as that part of the permanent structure will permit.

The rear reflectors on a pole trailer may be mounted on each side of the bolster or load.

Any required red reflector on the rear of a vehicle may be incorporated with the tail lamp, but such reflector shall meet all the other reflector requirements of this chapter.

(2) Clearance lamps shall be mounted on the permanent structure of the vehicle in such a manner as to indicate its extreme width and as near the top thereof as practicable. Clearance lamps and side marker lamps may be mounted in combination provided illumination is given as required herein with reference to both.

(i) *Visibility of reflectors, clearance lamps and marker lamps.*

(1) Every reflector upon any vehicle referred to in subsection (d) of section 32-5-240 shall be of such size and characteristics and so maintained as to be readily visible at nighttime from all distances within 500 feet to 50 feet from the vehicle when directly in front of lawful upper beams of head lamps. Reflectors required to be mounted on the sides of the vehicle shall reflect the required color of light to the sides, and those mounted on the rear shall reflect a red color to the rear.

(2) Front and rear clearance lamps shall be capable of being seen and distinguished under normal atmospheric conditions at the times lights are required at a distance of 500 feet from the front and rear, respectively, of the vehicle.

(3) Side marker lamps shall be capable of being seen and distinguished under normal atmospheric conditions at the times lights are required at a distance of 500 feet from the side of the vehicle on which mounted. (Acts 1927, No. 347, p. 348; Code 1940, T. 36, § 42; Acts 1949, No. 517, p. 754, § 12; Acts 1955, No. 273, p. 621, § 1.)

Cited in Clark v. Chitwood, 339 So. 2d 1017 (Ala. 1976); Watson v. State, 533 So. 2d 737 (Ala. Crim. App. 1988).

Collateral references. — 60A C.J.S., Motor Vehicles, § 285.

Liability or recovery in automobile negligence action arising out of collision or upset as affected by operation of vehicle without, or with improper, clearance, load, or similar auxiliary lights. 62 ALR3d 844.

§ 32-5-243. Lighting equipment and warning devices for vehicles engaged in mail service.

Any vehicle in active service transporting United States mail may display two simultaneously flashing lights to be used for the purpose of warning other vehicle operators of its presence and to exercise caution in approaching, overtaking or in passing. Such lights may be flashed continuously or actuated by application of the service brake (foot) while the vehicle is either in motion or parked. Such lamps shall have the following specifications and shall meet the following requirements:

(1) Lamps shall be not less than four inches in diameter and shall be powered by a bulb of not less than 21 candlepower with a reflectorization sufficient to assure visibility for at least 500 feet in front and to the rear of the vehicle under normal atmospheric conditions.

(2) Lamps shall be of double face or two way type.

(3) Lamps shall have amber lens to the front and red lens to the rear.

(4) Lamps shall be mounted on the highest part of the top of the vehicle in such a position that illumination from the lights is visible both to the front and rear for the required distance. Lamps shall be spaced laterally as far apart as body construction will permit but not closer than 30 inches. Between the lamps there shall be mounted a 22-inch by seven-inch sign with the wording "U.S. MAIL" in minimum of four-inch letters and of not less than three quarters of an inch in width of strobe, in black on a white background.

(5) This sign and lamps shall be so installed that the sign can be easily lowered and the lamps turned off when the vehicle is not actually engaged in the United States mail service.

(6) Any vehicle in active service transporting United States mail may, as an option to the foregoing, display a flashing red light not less than four inches in diameter with the letters "STOP" printed thereon and a uniform sign not less than 14 inches in diameter approved by the department of public safety with the words printed thereon "U.S. MAIL, WATCH FOR STOPS," which sign and light is to be attached to the rear of such vehicle.

(7) In addition to the above lighting equipment the department of public safety is hereby granted the authority to prescribe rules and regulations for the use of amber colored strobe lights or any other lighting device on mail delivery vehicles. In prescribing said rules and regulations the department of public safety shall seek the advice of the U.S. postal service. (Acts 1961, Ex. Sess., No. 136, p. 2062, § 1; Acts 1989, No. 89-865.)

The 1989 amendment, effective May 17, 1989, added subdivision (7) of this section.

§ 32-5-244. Lights on parked vehicles.

(a) Whenever a vehicle is lawfully parked upon a street or highway during the hours between a half hour after sunset and a half hour before sunrise where there is sufficient light to reveal any person or object within a distance of 500 feet upon such street or highway no lights need to be displayed upon such parked vehicle.

(b) Whenever a vehicle is parked or stopped upon a roadway or shoulder adjacent thereto, whether attended or unattended, during the hours between a half hour after sunset and half hour before sunrise and there is not sufficient light to reveal any person or object within a distance of 500 feet upon such highway, such vehicle so parked or stopped shall be equipped with one or more lamps which shall exhibit a white or amber light on the roadway side visible from a distance of 500 feet to the front of such vehicle and a red light visible from a distance of 500 feet to the rear. The foregoing provisions shall not apply to a motor-driven cycle.

(c) Any lighted headlamps upon a parked vehicle shall be depressed or dimmed. (Acts 1927, No. 347, p. 348; Code 1940, T. 36, § 46; Acts 1949, No. 517, p. 754, § 13; Acts 1959, No. 354, p. 944.)

Violation negligence per se. — The duty to display lights exists although the car may be otherwise properly parked. A violation of this section is negligence per se. McBride v. Baggett Transp. Co., 250 Ala. 488, 35 So. 2d 101 (1948).

Subsection (a) of section prescribes too vague a standard of visibility as to whether a city street light illuminates a "person or object." Without some specification as to the size, reflectivity or luminosity of either a person (child or adult) or object, large or small, there is much to be desired. Moreover, the court could take judicial notice that this section is unenforced in cities. Sims v. Greniewicki, 43 Ala. App. 159, 184 So. 2d 157 (1966).

Section applies to enforced temporary stoppage. — Enforced temporary stoppage of motor vehicle is subject to provisions of this section. Newell Contracting Co. v. Berry, 223 Ala. 111, 134 So. 868 (1931).

Sufficiency of allegation. — Allegation that defendant unlawfully parked truck on "Jackson highway" without lights sufficiently averred that highway was public road within this section. Newell Contracting Co. v. Berry, 223 Ala. 111, 134 So. 868 (1931).

Complaint sufficiently showed violation of this section without alleging there was insufficient light to reveal person within distance of 200 feet on highway. Newell Contracting Co. v. Berry, 223 Ala. 111, 134 So. 868 (1931).

A complaint alleging that plaintiff driving an automobile at night ran into defendants' truck parked on highway without proper lights as required by this section was not demurrable [now subject to motion to dismiss] on ground that the allegation as to absence of "proper" lights was a mere conclusion and did not apprise defendants of the exact nature of their breach of duty. Claude Jones & Son v. Lair, 245 Ala. 441, 17 So. 2d 577 (1944); McBride v. Baggett Transp. Co., 250 Ala. 488, 35 So. 2d 101 (1948).

Plaintiff must allege with certainty place

of injury. — In action by motorist who ran into unlighted parked truck, plaintiff had duty to allege with sufficient certainty place of injury so as to enable defendant to prepare defense. Newell Contracting Co. v. Berry, 223 Ala. 109, 134 So. 870 (1931).

Presumption. — Facts surrounding parking of defendant's truck were presumed peculiarly known to defendant, and, defendant not having produced them, presumption as regards violation of this section was indulged against defendant. Newell Contracting Co. v. Berry, 223 Ala. 109, 134 So. 870 (1931).

Violation of section jury question. — Whether defendant parked truck on highway at night without lights, in violation of this section, held for jury on conflicting evidence. Newell Contracting Co. v. Berry, 223 Ala. 111, 134 So. 868 (1931).

Instruction using word "leaving" instead of parking or stopping was not error. McBride v. Baggett Transp. Co., 250 Ala. 488, 35 So. 2d 101 (1948).

As to instructions under this section, see also Chastain v. Brown, 263 Ala. 440, 82 So. 2d 904 (1955).

Cited in Brown v. Ace Motor Co., 30 Ala. App. 479, 8 So. 2d 585 (1942); Cosby v. Flowers, 249 Ala. 227, 30 So. 2d 694 (1947); Robins Transf. Co. v. Lewis, 261 Ala. 427, 74 So. 2d 247 (1954); Burress v. Dupree, 287 Ala. 524, 253 So. 2d 31 (1971); Aycock v. Martinez, 432 So. 2d 1274 (Ala. 1983).

Collateral references. — 60A C.J.S., Motor Vehicles, §§ 335(1)-335(4).

7 Am. Jur. 2d, Automobiles & Highway Traffic, §§ 152-156.

Negligence or contributory negligence of driver or occupant of motor vehicle parked or stopped on highway without flares. 67 ALR2d 12.

Liability or recovery in automobile negligence action as affected by motor vehicle's being driven or parked without dimming lights. 63 ALR3d 824.

§ 32-5-245. Reflectors or similar warning devices on horse-drawn wagons and other vehicles.

It shall be unlawful for any person to operate a horse-drawn wagon, buggy, carriage or other vehicle upon any public highway, road or street between sunset and sunrise unless there is affixed to the rear of such vehicle at least two red reflectors or similar warning devices, one on each corner, and to the front of such vehicle one amber reflector or similar warning device on the left-hand front of said vehicle. Any person who violates this section is guilty of a misdemeanor and, upon conviction, shall be punished as prescribed by law.

All laws or parts of laws which conflict with this section are repealed, but this section does not repeal the provisions of subsection (e) of section 32-5-240. (Acts 1951, No. 131, p. 357.)

Collateral references. — 61 C.J.S., Motor Vehicles, § 527(20).

§ 32-5-246. Reflective devices for slow-moving vehicles — Required; design.

When operated, propelled, driven, towed, pushed or otherwise moving over, along or across any highway in this state, every vehicle which has a maximum potential speed of 25 miles an hour, implement of husbandry, farm tractor or special mobile equipment shall be identified with a reflective device as follows:

(1) An equilateral triangle in shape at least 16 inches wide at the base and at least 14 inches in height, with a bright red border, at least one and three-quarter inches wide of highly reflective beaded material;

(2) A center triangle, at least $12^{1}/_4$ inches on each side of yellow-orange fluorescent material. (Acts 1971, No. 1186, p. 2048, § 1.)

Collateral references. — 60 C.J.S., Motor Vehicles, §§ 26, 192. 61 C.J.S., Motor Vehicles, § 469. 61A C.J.S., Motor Vehicles, § 608.

§ 32-5-247. Same — Mounting.

The device shall be mounted on the rear of the vehicle, implement or mobile equipment broad base down, not less than three feet nor more than five feet above the ground, measuring to the lowest portion of the device and as near the center of the vehicle, implement or mobile equipment as practicable. (Acts 1971, No. 1186, p. 2048, § 2.)

§ 32-5-248. Same — Restrictions on use.

The use of such device is restricted to use on slow-moving vehicles specified in sections 32-5-246 through 32-5-251 and the use of such reflective device on any other type vehicle or stationary object is prohibited. (Acts 1971, No. 1186, p. 2048, § 3.)

§ 32-5-249. Same — Bicycles or ridden animals.

The provisions of sections 32-5-246 through 32-5-251 shall not apply to bicycles or to ridden animals. (Acts 1971, No. 1186, p. 2048, § 4.)

§ 32-5-250. Same — Other provisions not repealed, etc.

Nothing in sections 32-5-246 through 32-5-251 shall repeal or amend any other provision of the laws of Alabama governing lights or reflectors required to be mounted on vehicles. (Acts 1971, No. 1186, p. 2048, § 5.)

§ 32-5-251. Same — Violations.

Any person violating any provisions of sections 32-5-246 through 32-5-251 shall be guilty of a misdemeanor and shall upon conviction be punished by a fine of not less than $5.00 nor more than $100.00 or by imprisonment in the county jail for not more than 30 days or by both such fine and imprisonment. (Acts 1971, No. 1186, p. 2048, § 6.)

§ 32-5-252. Approval of lighting devices; prohibited lamps and devices; regulations; lists of approved devices to be published.

(a) No person shall have for sale, or offer for sale for use upon or as a part of the equipment of a motor vehicle, trailer or semitrailer, or use upon any such vehicle any head lamp, auxiliary or fog lamp, rear lamp, signal lamp or reflector, which reflector is required hereunder, or parts of any of the foregoing which tend to change the original design or performance, unless of a type which has been submitted to the director and approved by him. The foregoing provisions of this section shall not apply to equipment in actual use when this section is adopted or replacement parts therefor.

(b) No person shall have for sale, sell or offer for sale for use upon or as a part of the equipment of a motor vehicle, trailer or semitrailer any lamp or device mentioned in this section which has been approved by the director unless such lamp or device bears thereon the trademark or name under which it is approved so as to be legible when installed.

(c) No person shall use upon any motor vehicle, trailer or semitrailer any lamps mentioned in this section unless said lamps are mounted, adjusted and aimed in accordance with instructions of the director.

(d) The director is hereby authorized to approve or disapprove lighting devices and to issue and enforce regulations establishing standards and specifications for the approval of such lighting devices, their installation, adjustment and aiming and adjustment when in use on motor vehicles. Such regulations shall correlate with and, so far as practicable, conform to the then current standards and specifications of the society of automotive engineers applicable to such equipment.

(e) The director is hereby required to approve or disapprove any lighting device, of a type on which approval is specifically required in this chapter, within a reasonable time after such device has been submitted.

(f) The director is further authorized to set up the procedure which shall be followed when any device is submitted for approval.

(g) The director, upon approving any such lamp or device, shall issue to the applicant a certificate of approval together with any instructions determined by him.

(h) The director shall publish lists of all lamps and devices by name and type which have been approved by him. (Acts 1927, No. 347, p. 348; Code 1940, T. 36, § 44; Acts 1955, No. 273, p. 621, § 2.)

§ 32-5-253. Enforcement of provisions.

When the director has reason to believe that an approved lighting device being sold commercially does not comply with the requirements of this division, he may, after giving 30 days' previous notice to the person holding the certificate of approval for such device in this state, conduct a hearing upon the question of compliance of the approved device. After such hearing, the director shall determine whether the approved lighting device meets the requirements of this division. If the device does not meet the requirements of this division he shall give notice to the person holding the certificate of approval for such device in this state.

If at the expiration of 90 days after such notice the person holding the certificate of approval for such device has failed to satisfy the director that the approved device as thereafter to be sold meets the requirements of this division, the director shall suspend or revoke the approval issued therefor until or unless such device is resubmitted to and retested by an authorized testing agency and is found to meet the requirements of this division, and may require that all such devices sold since the notification following the hearing be replaced with devices that do comply with the requirements of this division. The director may at the time of the retest purchase in the open market and submit to the testing agency one or more sets of such approved devices, and if such device upon such retest fails to meet the requirements of this division, the director may refuse to renew the certificate of approval of such device. (Acts 1927, No. 347, p. 348; Code 1940, T. 36, § 45; Acts 1955, No. 273, p. 621, § 3.)

Collateral references. — 61A C.J.S., Motor Vehicles, § 608.

ARTICLE 10.

PEDESTRIANS.

§§ 32-5-270 through 32-5-276. Repealed by Acts 1980, No. 80-434, p. 604, § 15-106, effective May 19, 1980.

ARTICLE 11.

BICYCLES.

§§ 32-5-290 through 32-5-296. Repealed by Acts 1980, No. 80-434, p. 604, § 15-106, effective May 19, 1980.

ARTICLE 12.

VIOLATIONS; PENALTIES.

§ 32-5-310. Enforcement of chapter; arrest procedure; bail bond.

Any peace officer, including state troopers, sheriffs and their deputies, constables and their deputies, police officers and marshals of cities or incorporated towns, county police or patrols, state or county license inspectors and their deputies, and special officers appointed by any agency of the state of Alabama for the enforcement of its laws relating to motor vehicles, now existing or hereafter enacted, shall be authorized, and it is hereby made the duty of each of them to enforce the provisions of this chapter and to make arrests for any violation or violations thereof, without warrant if the offense be committed in his presence, and with warrant if he does not observe the commission of the offense. If the arrest be made without warrant, the accused may elect to be immediately taken before the nearest court having jurisdiction, whereupon it shall be the duty of the officer to so take him. If the accused elects not to be so taken, then it shall be the duty of the officer to require of the accused a bail bond in a sum not to exceed $300.00, conditioned that the accused binds himself to appear in the nearest court having jurisdiction at the time fixed in the bond. In case the arrested person fails to appear on the day fixed, the bond shall be forfeited in the manner as is provided for the forfeiture of bonds in other cases. No officer shall be permitted to take a cash bond. The officer making the arrest and taking the bond shall report the same to the court having jurisdiction within 18 hours after taking such bond. (Acts 1949, No. 516, p. 740, § 49.)

Cross references. — As to jurisdiction of misdemeanor prosecutions for traffic infractions and use of uniform traffic ticket generally, see § 12-12-51.

The right that one has to make his own bond for a traffic violation cannot within reason be said to extend to one who having committed a traffic violation is reasonably believed to be concealing his identity, so that his bond would be worthless. Mitchell v. State, 391 So. 2d 1069 (Ala. Crim. App. 1980).

Cited in Sly v. State, 387 So. 2d 913 (Ala. Crim. App. 1980).

§ 32-5-311. Repealed by Acts 1980, No. 80-434, p. 604, § 15-106, effective May 19, 1980.

§ 32-5-312. Penalties for violations of certain sections.

Any person who violates sections 32-5-55 through 32-5-59, 32-5-62, 32-5-63, 32-5-112 through 32-5-114, 32-5-130 through 32-5-133 and 32-5-150 through 32-5-153, or any part or parts thereof shall be guilty of a misdemeanor and, upon conviction, shall be punished by imprisonment in the county or municipal jail for not more than 10 days or by a fine of not more than $100.00; for a second such conviction within one year thereafter such person shall be punished by a fine of not less than $100.00 nor more than $200.00 or by imprisonment in the county or municipal jail for not more than 20 days or by both such fine and imprisonment; upon a third or subsequent conviction within one year after the first conviction such person shall be punished by a fine of not less than $250.00 nor more than $500.00 or by imprisonment in the county or municipal jail for not more than six months or by both such fine and imprisonment. The court shall revoke the driver's license of such person upon the third conviction. (Acts 1927, No. 347, p. 348; Code 1940, T. 36, § 30.)

Code commissioner's note. — Sections 32-5-55 through 32-5-59, 32-5-62, 32-5-63, 32-5-112, 32-5-114, 32-5-130 through 32-5-133, 32-5-150, 32-5-151 and 32-5-153 were repealed by Acts 1980, No. 80-434, p. 604, § 15-106, effective May 19, 1980. See now Chapter 5A of this title.

Collateral references. — 61A C.J.S., Motor Vehicles, §§ 588-714(4).

§ 32-5-313. Additional penalty for traffic infraction; driver education and training fund.

In addition to all other fines, fees, costs and punishments now prescribed by law there shall be imposed or assessed an additional penalty of $2.00 upon conviction by any judge in any court of the state of any offense involving a traffic infraction; or upon conviction of a traffic infraction prescribed by any county or municipal ordinance.

All penalties collected under this section shall be forwarded by the officer of the court who collects the same to the state treasurer, within 30 days after the penalty or forfeiture is collected. All amounts so received shall be credited to special funds to be designated the "driver education and training fund" and the "Alabama traffic safety center fund," and of the amounts so received, an amount equal to 50 percent thereof is hereby appropriated to the state department of education for the sole purpose of instituting and conducting a program of prelicensing driver education and training; an amount equal to 17$\frac{1}{2}$ percent thereof is hereby appropriated to the state department of education for the sole purpose of instituting and conducting a program of truck driver education and training; provided, however, that these funds shall be expended only by institutions under the control of the state board of education; an amount equal to 22$\frac{1}{2}$ percent thereof is hereby appropriated to the Alabama traffic safety center fund for the sole purpose of conducting programs in traffic safety, motorcycle safety and boating safety by the center; and the remaining 10 percent is hereby appropriated to the state safety coordinating committee for payment of administrative expenses incurred in its programs. (Acts 1964, 1st Ex. Sess., No. 244, p. 335; Acts 1983, No. 83-724, p. 1179; Acts 1987, No. 87-638, p. 1142; Acts 1988, No. 88-658, p. 1055.)

The 1988 amendment, which is retroactively effective to August 8, 1987, deleted "and" preceding "safety center fund" in the third sentence, inserted "provided, however, that these funds shall be expended only by institutions under the control of the state board of education;" following "truck driver education and training"; deleted "provided however that these funds shall be expended by institutions under the control of the state board of education" preceding "the remaining 10 percent," and inserted "and" preceding "the remaining 10 percent."

OPINIONS OF THE SUPREME COURT CLERK

Cited in Op. No. 18, 364 So. 2d 672 (Ala. 1978).

§§ 32-5-314, 32-5-315. Repealed by Acts 1980, No. 80-434, p. 604, § 15-106, effective May 19, 1980.

§ 32-5-316. Courts may prohibit operation of motor vehicles by persons convicted of violation of automobile laws.

Whenever a defendant is convicted by any court of competent jurisdiction of operating a motor vehicle in violation of any criminal statute or ordinance, the court trying the case, in its discretion, may, in addition to the other punishment fixed by law, enter an order forbidding such person to drive a motor vehicle upon any street or highway in the state of Alabama for a period to be specified by the court, or perpetually, as the court may determine. Any person driving a motor vehicle in violation of such an order of court shall be guilty of a misdemeanor. Any defendant against whom such an order has been entered shall have the same right of appeal and supersedeas as is now granted him with reference to the sentence of the court imposing punishment fixed by law, and the appellate court shall have the right to modify or annul the order forbidding the operation by the defendant of motor vehicles, as in the opinion of the appellate court the facts may justify or require. (Code 1923, § 3340; Acts 1927, No. 347, p. 348; Code 1940, T. 36, § 54.)

Cross references. — As to driving after driver's license has been cancelled, suspended or revoked, see § 32-6-19.

Collateral references. — 61A C.J.S., Motor Vehicles, §§ 588, 639(2).

7 Am. Jur. 2d, Automobiles & Highway Traffic, §§ 88, 89.

Validity of statute or ordinance relating to revocation of license. 71 ALR 616, 108 ALR 1162, 125 ALR 1459.

Necessity of notice and hearing before revocation or suspension of motor vehicle driver's license. 60 ALR3d 350.

CHAPTER 5A.

RULES OF THE ROAD.

Cited in Shoemaker v. Money, 409 So. 2d 847 (Ala. Civ. App. 1981).

Collateral references. — Entrapment to commit traffic offense. 34 ALR4th 1167.

Article 1.

General Provisions.

Cross references. — For other general provisions as to operation of motor vehicles, see § 32-5-1 et seq. For other provisions as to violations and penalties in the operation of motor vehicles, see § 32-5-310 et seq.

§ 32-5A-1. Short title.

This chapter may be cited as the Alabama Rules of the Road Act. (Acts 1980, No. 80-434, p. 604, § 15-103.)

Cited in Smith v. State, 460 So. 2d 343 (Ala. Crim. App. 1984).

§ 32-5A-2. Provisions of chapter refer to vehicles upon highways; exceptions.

The provisions of this chapter relating to the operation of vehicles refer exclusively to the operation of vehicles upon highways except:

(1) Where a different place is specifically referred to in a given section.

(2) The provisions of sections 32-7-37, 32-7-5, 32-7-12, 32-10-1 through 32-10-12, as they now exist or may hereafter be amended, and any other statutes of this state relating to accidents and accident reports, and also sections 32-5A-190 through 32-5A-195 shall apply upon highways and elsewhere throughout the state. (Acts 1980, No. 80-434, p. 604, § 1-101.)

Commentary

There was no prior Alabama statute comparable to this section. The adoption of this section changes the former Alabama statutes on driving under the influence of alcohol or any controlled substance (section 32-5-170) which formerly applied only on highways but now applies on highways and elsewhere throughout the state. See section 32-5A-191.

§ 32-5A-3. Required obedience to traffic laws.

It is unlawful and, unless otherwise declared in this chapter with respect to particular offenses, it is a misdemeanor for any person to do any act forbidden or fail to perform any act required in this chapter. (Acts 1980, No. 80-434, p. 604, § 1-102.)

Commentary

Previously, various penalties were specified in various sections of the Alabama Code, such as section 32-1-1 et seq. In order to simplify the rules of the road, this section, in conjunction with sections 32-5A-8 and 32-5A-9, provides for a uniform approach to the penalties problem, except where another penalty is specifically set out in an individual section.

Cited in Wright v. State, 494 So. 2d 177 (Ala. Crim. App. 1986).

§ 32-5A-4. Obedience to police officers and firemen.

No person shall willfully fail or refuse to comply with any lawful order or direction of any police officer or fireman invested by law with authority to direct, control or regulate traffic. (Acts 1980, No. 80-434, p. 604, § 1-103.)

Commentary

Similar to section 32-5-15, except the former statute did not include firemen. See also sections 13A-10-5 and 13A-10-6.

I. General Consideration.
II. Decisions Under Prior Law.

I. GENERAL CONSIDERATION.

Collateral references. — 61 C.J.S., Motor Vehicles, §§ 342, 490(3).

II. DECISIONS UNDER PRIOR LAW.

Editor's note. — The cases below were decided under similar provisions of prior law.

Section was enacted as traffic control measure and as a comprehensive amendment to that body of law commonly known as "Rules of the Road." Coughlin v. State, 56 Ala. App. 225, 320 So. 2d 739 (1975).

For order of police officer to be "lawful," such order must be directly related to the direction, control and regulation of traffic. Coughlin v. State, 56 Ala. App. 225, 320 So. 2d 739 (1975); Sly v. State, 387 So. 2d 913 (Ala. Crim. App.), cert. denied, 387 So. 2d 917 (Ala. 1980).

A request to inspect the operating license of one driving an automobile is "directly related to the direction, control and regulation of traffic." Sly v. State, 387 So. 2d 913 (Ala. Crim. App.), cert. denied, 387 So. 2d 917 (Ala. 1980).

A trooper's "request" to see a driver's license constitutes a lawful order. Sly v. State, 387 So. 2d 913 (Ala. Crim. App.), cert. denied, 387 So. 2d 917 (Ala. 1980).

No unbridled power to arrest for refusal to obey "any" order. — Former section was not intended to give police officers unbridled power to arrest for refusal to obey any order they might choose to direct at a citizen. Coughlin v. State, 56 Ala. App. 225, 320 So. 2d 739 (1975); Sly v. State, 387 So. 2d 913 (Ala. Crim. App.), cert. denied, 387 So. 2d 917 (Ala. 1980).

§ 32-5A-5. Persons riding animals or driving animal-drawn vehicles.

Every person riding an animal or driving any animal-drawn vehicle upon a roadway shall be granted all of the rights and shall be subject to all of the duties applicable to the driver of a vehicle by this chapter, except those provisions of this chapter, which by their very nature can have no application. (Acts 1980, No. 80-434, p. 604, § 1-104.)

Commentary

Rewording of former section 32-5-10.

Collateral references. — 60 C.J.S., Motor Vehicles, § 22. 60A C.J.S., Motor Vehicles, § 381(1).

§ 32-5A-6. Persons working on highways; exceptions.

Unless specifically made applicable, the provisions of this chapter except sections 32-5A-190, 32-5A-191 and 32-5A-194 shall not apply to persons, teams, motor vehicles and other equipment while actually engaged in work upon the surface of a highway but shall apply to such persons and vehicles when traveling to or from such work. (Acts 1980, No. 80-434, p. 604, § 1-105.)

Commentary

No comparable Alabama statute previously existed.

§ 32-5A-7. Authorized emergency vehicles.

(a) The driver of an authorized emergency vehicle, when responding to an emergency call or when in the pursuit of an actual or suspected violator of the law or when responding to but not upon returning from a fire alarm, may exercise the privileges set forth in this section, but subject to the conditions herein stated.

(b) The driver of an authorized emergency vehicle may:

(1) Park or stand, irrespective of the provisions of this chapter;

(2) Proceed past a red or stop signal or stop sign, but only after slowing down as may be necessary for safe operation;

(3) Exceed the maximum speed limits so long as he does not endanger life or property;

(4) Disregard regulations governing direction of movement or turning in specified directions.

(c) The exemptions herein granted to an authorized emergency vehicle shall apply only when such vehicle is making use of an audible signal meeting the requirements of section 32-5-213 and visual requirements of any laws of this state requiring visual signals on emergency vehicles.

(d) The foregoing provisions shall not relieve the driver of an authorized emergency vehicle from the duty to drive with due regard for the safety of all persons, nor shall such provisions protect the driver from the consequences of his reckless disregard for the safety of others. (Acts 1980, No. 80-434, p. 604, § 1-106.)

Commentary

This section is designed to elaborate upon the matters covered briefly in former section 32-5-96. Subsection (c) varies somewhat from the UVC text, in order to accommodate prior Alabama law. The term "authorized emergency vehicle" is defined in section 32-1-1.1(3).

Ambulances. — Though drivers of ambulance must at all times exercise due care for protection of others, they were exempted by former statute from the general regulatory rules as to speed limitations when traveling in emergencies. Echols v. Vinson, 220 Ala. 229, 124 So. 510 (1929) (decided under prior law).

Failure to operate emergency vehicle with due regard for safety of others. — Deputy sheriff guilty of manslaughter where his conduct, in failing to operate emergency vehicle with due regard for the safety of all persons, and in failing to sufficiently slow down for the intersection, constituted a gross deviation from the standard of care that a reasonable person would observe in the situation. Poole v. State, 497 So. 2d 530 (Ala. Crim. App. 1985), rev'd on other grounds, 497 So. 2d 537 (Ala. 1986).

Mere fact that a police officer exceeds the maximum speed limit during a pursuit does not present a genuine issue of material fact as to the liability of that officer for negligence. Doran v. City of Madison, 519 So. 2d 1308 (Ala. 1988).

Motorcycle policeman involved in collision on way home to dinner was held not to have been performing official duty requiring unusual speed, nor relieved of duty of due care. Swift & Co. v. Payne, 223 Ala. 25, 134 So. 626 (1931) (decided under prior law).

In an action for the wrongful death of a minor struck and killed by a state trooper's vehicle during a high-speed chase, there was at least a scintilla of evidence presented from which the jury could have determined that the state trooper's conduct was wanton, where he acknowledged that he did not turn on his blue light, siren, or emergency flashers in accordance with this section, he testified that when he saw the bicycle reflectors ahead of him, he was traveling in excess of 80 miles per hour and believed himself in a hazardous and perilous situation, and after observing the reflectors, he changed lanes and applied his brakes after the reflection appeared to be moving to the left or into the lefthand lane and at a certain point he felt that he had passed whatever object the reflectors were on, he started letting up off his brakes. Smith v. Bradford, 475 So. 2d 526 (Ala. 1985).

In an action for the wrongful death of a minor who while riding on his bicycle was struck by a state trooper car, the court erred in admitting into evidence testimony as to the state trooper's training and instruction in "catch-up" driving, which involves catching up to a speed violator without the use of the trooper car's blue lights or siren until the trooper is close enough to identify a violator's tag and vehicle, when that driving practice is directly contrary to subsection (c) of this section. Smith v. Bradford, 512 So. 2d 50 (Ala. 1987).

Cited in Doran v. City of Decatur, 510 So. 2d 813 (Ala. 1987).

Collateral references. — 61 C.J.S., Motor Vehicles, § 516(25). 61A C.J.S., Motor Vehicles, § 643.

7 Am. Jur. 2d, Automobiles & Highway Traffic, §§ 171, 172.

Ambulances as subject to speed regulations. 9 ALR 368.

Validity of statute or ordinance giving right-of-way in streets or highways to certain classes of vehicles. 38 ALR 24.

Liability of operator of ambulance service for personal injuries to person being transported. 68 ALR4th 14.

§ 32-5A-8. Violations as misdemeanor; penalties.

(a) It is a misdemeanor for any person to violate any of the provisions of this chapter or of Title 32, unless such violation is by this chapter or other law of this state declared to be a felony.

(b) Every person convicted of a misdemeanor for a violation of any of the provisions of this chapter for which another penalty is not provided, shall for a first conviction thereof be punished by a fine of not more than $100.00 or by imprisonment for not more than 10 days; for conviction of a second offense committed within one year after the date of the first offense, such person shall be punished by a fine of not more than $200.00 or by imprisonment for not more than 30 days or by both such fine and imprisonment; for conviction of a third or subsequent offense committed within one year after the date of the first offense, such person shall be punished by a fine of not more than $500.00 or by imprisonment for not more than three months or by both such fine and imprisonment. (Acts 1980, No. 80-434, p. 604, § 14-101.)

Commentary

This section is based upon Uniform Vehicle Code section 17-101(a), (b); subsection (c) thereof not having been included here because it is not applicable. Subsection (a) is identical verbatim to former section 32-5-311(a). Subsection (b) is substantially the same as former section 32-5-311(b), except for some very minor variations in punishments for second and third offenses. This section also replaces the general penalty provisions of sections 32-5-312, 32-12-27 and 32-12-44. The penalties herein have been drafted to be consistent with the Alabama Criminal Code (Title 13A).

Detention for minor traffic offense. — Except for the exceptions provided by § 32-1-4(b), a person arrested for a misdemeanor traffic violation is not subject to further detention for that offense once the arresting officer has obtained the necessary information and given the motorist the summons or notice to appear. Morton v. State, 452 So. 2d 1361 (Ala. Crim. App. 1984).

Subject to exceptions of § 32-1-4(b), custodial arrest not authorized for improper lane usage. Hays v. City of Jacksonville, 518 So. 2d 892 (Ala. Crim. App. 1987).

A person who is subject only to a noncustodial arrest may not have his property seized on the basis of that same arrest. Absent some extenuating circumstances, such a sei-zure would be unreasonable and in violation of the fourth amendment. Morton v. State, 452 So. 2d 1361 (Ala. Crim. App. 1984).

Court-imposed fine of $50.00 over normal fine unconstitutional. — Traffic fine of $50 over the normal fine where a radar detector is in the automobile may not be imposed by court order, even though such fine is within the statutory limits of this section, in that such judicial action creates an additional fine which, under Ala. Const. Art. III (1901), can be enacted only by the legislature. Ellis v. State, 502 So. 2d 694 (Ala. 1986).

Cited in Watson v. State, 533 So. 2d 737 (Ala. Crim. App. 1988).

Collateral references. — 61A C.J.S., Motor Vehicles, §§ 588-714(4).

§ 32-5A-9. Penalty for felony.

Any person who is convicted of a violation of any of the provisions of this chapter herein or by the laws of this state declared to constitute a felony shall be punished by imprisonment for not less than one year nor more than 10 years, or by a fine of not more than $5,000.00, or by both such fine and imprisonment. (Acts 1980, No. 80-434, p. 604, § 14-102.)

Commentary

There was no prior comparable Alabama statute. This section is based upon Uniform Vehicle Code § 17-102, and its inclusion was deemed desirable for the sake of uniformity. The penalty provided herein has been drafted to be consistent with the penalty for a Class C felony under the Alabama Criminal Code (Title 13A).

§ 32-5A-10. Disposition of fines and forfeitures.

(a) All fines and forfeitures collected upon conviction or upon forfeiture of bail of any person charged with a violation of any of the provisions of this chapter constituting a misdemeanor shall be, within 30 days after such fine or forfeiture is collected, distributed as provided in chapter 19, Title 12.

(b) Failure, refusal or neglect on the part of any judicial or other officer or employee receiving or having custody of any such fine or forfeiture to comply with the foregoing provisions of this section shall constitute misconduct in office and shall be grounds for removal therefrom. (Acts 1980, No. 80-434, p. 604, § 14-103.)

Commentary

This section is based upon Uniform Vehicle Code § 17-103, and replaces sections 32-5-314 and 32-5-315. Distribution of the fines is to be in accordance with the provisions of Act No. 1205, p. 2384, s. 400, 1975 Regular Session (see chapter 19, Title 12). The section varies somewhat from the UVC model in that some of the provisions of the prior Alabama law are retained, particularly the requirement that moneys be remitted within 30 days, and, in keeping with former practice, no special highway improvement or similar fund is established with the moneys.

As to constitutionality of former similar section, see Bennett v. Cottingham, 290 F. Supp. 759 (N.D. Ala. 1968), aff'd, 393 U.S. 317, 89 S. Ct. 554, 21 L. Ed. 2d 513 (1969).

As to applicability of former section throughout state in all counties, see Cherokee County v. Cunningham, 260 Ala. 1, 68 So. 2d 507 (1953).

Collateral references. — 61A C.J.S., Motor Vehicles, §§ 588-714.

§ 32-5A-11. Uniformity of interpretation.

This chapter shall be so interpreted and construed as to effectuate its general purpose to make uniform the law of various jurisdictions. (Acts 1980, No. 80-434, p. 604, § 15-101.)

Commentary

Sections 32-5A-1 and 32-5A-11 through 32-5A-13 are based upon chapter 19 of the Uniform Vehicle Code.

§ 32-5A-12. Chapter not retroactive.

This chapter shall not have a retroactive effect and shall not apply to any traffic accident, to any cause of action arising out of a traffic accident or judgment arising therefrom, or to any violation of the motor vehicle laws of this state, occurring prior to August 17, 1980. (Acts 1980, No. 80-434, p. 604, § 15-104.)

Increased penalty because of prior conviction before enactment of statute does not constitute retroactive application. Shoemaker v. Atchison, 406 So. 2d 986 (Ala. Civ. App. 1981).

§ 32-5A-13. Provisions cumulative; laws not repealed.

The provisions of this chapter are cumulative and shall not be construed to repeal or supersede any laws not inconsistent herewith.

Without limitation of the generality of the preceding sentence of this section, this chapter shall not repeal or supersede sections 32-5-8, 32-5-9, 32-5-11 through 32-5-14, 32-5-16, 32-5-31, 32-5-51, 32-5-54, 32-5-64, 32-5-65, 32-5-72, 32-5-74 through 32-5-76, 32-5-93, 32-5-97, 32-5-113, 32-5-152, 32-5-171, 32-5-190 through 32-5-192, 32-5-194, 32-5-210 through 32-5-253, 32-5-310, 32-5-312, 32-5-313 and 32-5-316, but nothing contained in this sentence shall be construed as implying that any law not specifically listed herein is or is not repealed or superseded by this chapter. (Acts 1980, No. 80-434, p. 604, § 15-107.)

ARTICLE 2.
TRAFFIC SIGNS, SIGNALS AND MARKINGS.

Cross references. — For other provisions as to local traffic-control devices, see § 32-5-31.

§ 32-5A-30. Uniform marking of highways and erection of traffic-control devices.

(a) The highway department is authorized to classify, designate, and mark both interstate and intrastate highways lying within the boundaries of this state.

(b) The highway department shall adopt a manual and specifications for a uniform system of traffic-control devices consistent with the provisions of this chapter and other state laws for use upon highways within this state. Such uniform system shall correlate with and so far as possible conform to the system set forth in the most recent edition of the Manual on Uniform Traffic-

Control Devices for Streets and Highways and other standards issued or endorsed by the federal highway administrator.

(c) No local authority shall place or maintain any traffic-control device upon any highway under the jurisdiction of the highway department except by the latter's permission. (Acts 1980, No. 80-434, p. 604, § 2-100.)

Commentary

This section revises and replaces section 32-5-30 and adds to it, as has been requested by the state highway department, subsection (b), which is based upon § 15-104 of the UVC. The remaining portions of this commentary are taken from the comments following § 15-104. The requirement that a state agency adopt a manual affords maximum flexibility in devising an appropriate and uniform system for traffic-control devices. The highway department might, for instance: adopt the Manual on Uniform Traffic-Control Devices for Streets and Highways; or develop and publish a manual of its own that conforms to that manual and exceeds its minimum specifications or describes the design and application of supplementary traffic-control devices; or adopt the manual and devise a supplementary publication — the two becoming the manual for the state. The manual is the national standard for uniformity among traffic-control devices. It is prepared and sponsored by the American Association of State Highway Officials, Institute of Traffic Engineers, National Committee on Uniform Traffic Laws and Ordinances, National Association of Counties and National League of Cities. Copies of the manual may be obtained from the United States Government Printing Office, Washington, D.C. 20401. Subsection (c), also included at the request of the state highway department, is based upon § 15-105 of the UVC.

Exclusive authority vested with highway department. — Where a contract to construct a highway has been completed and performance accepted by the state, only the highway department is authorized to classify, designate and mark the highways of the state and to provide a uniform system of the same. Evans v. Patterson, 269 Ala. 250, 112 So. 2d 194 (1959) (decided under prior law).

Company road not governed by Manual. — Company road constructed to allow company equipment access for logging operations, which was privately maintained and was used for vehicular traffic by the owner and those having express or implied permission from the owner, was not governed by the provisions and specifications of the Alabama Manual of Uniform Traffic Control Devices, as it was a private road or driveway, and not a highway. Thompson v. Champion Int'l Corp., 500 So. 2d 1048 (Ala. 1986).

Collateral references. — 60 C.J.S., Motor Vehicles, § 35. 60A C.J.S., Motor Vehicles, §§ 354, 360(1)-360(7).

Private citizen's right to complain of rerouting of highway or removal or change of route or directional signs. 97 ALR 192.

Prohibition to control administrative officers in matters relating to highways and streets. 115 ALR 23, 159 ALR 627.

Liability for automobile accident, other than direct collision with pedestrian, as affected by reliance upon or disregard of stop-and-go signal. 2 ALR3d 12.

Liability for collision of automobile with pedestrian at intersection as affected by reliance upon or disregard of stop-and-go signal. 2 ALR3d 155.

Liability for collision of automobile with pedestrian at intersection as affected by reliance upon or disregard of traffic sign or signal other than stop-and-go signal. 3 ALR3d 557.

§ 32-5A-31. Obedience to traffic-control devices; devices presumed to comply with requirements.

(a) The driver of any vehicle shall obey the instructions of any official traffic-control device applicable thereto placed in accordance with law, unless otherwise directed by a police officer, subject to the exceptions granted the driver of an authorized emergency vehicle in this chapter.

(b) No provision of this chapter for which official traffic-control devices are required shall be enforced against an alleged violator if at the time and place of the alleged violation an official device is not in proper position and sufficiently legible to be seen by an ordinarily observant person. Whenever a particular section does not state that official traffic-control devices are required, such section shall be effective even though no devices are erected or in place.

(c) Whenever official traffic-control devices are placed in position approximately conforming to the requirements of this chapter or other law, such devices shall be presumed to have been so placed by the official act or direction of lawful authority, unless the contrary shall be established by competent evidence.

(d) Any official traffic-control device placed pursuant to the provisions of this chapter or other law and purporting to conform to the lawful requirements pertaining to such devices shall be presumed to comply with the requirements of this chapter or other such law, unless the contrary shall be established by competent evidence. (Acts 1980, No. 80-434, p. 604, § 2-101.)

Commentary

Subsections (a) and (b) are only slight modifications of former section 32-5-35. The word "sign" has been replaced by "traffic-control device". Subsections (c) and (d) had no counterpart in the prior statutes.

Collateral references. — 60A C.J.S., Motor Vehicles, § 284(1).

Liability of governmental unit for collision with safety and traffic-control devices in traveled way. 7 ALR2d 226.

Liability of municipality or other governmental unit for failure to cut weeds, brush, or other vegetation obstructing or obscuring view at railroad crossing or a street or highway intersection. 42 ALR2d 817.

Motorist's liability for collision at intersection of ordinary and arterial highways as affected by absence, displacement or malfunctioning of stop sign or other traffic signal. 74 ALR2d 242.

Liability for automobile accident, other than direct collision with pedestrian, as affected by reliance upon or disregard of stop-and-go signal. 2 ALR3d 12.

Liability for accident at street or highway intersection as affected by reliance upon or disregard of traffic sign, signal or marking. 2 ALR3d 12, 55, 275, 3 ALR3d 180, 507.

Liability for automobile accident with pedestrian as affected by reliance upon or disregard of traffic signal. 2 ALR3d 12, 155, 3 ALR3d 557.

Liability for collision of automobile with pedestrian at intersection as affected by reliance upon or disregard of stop-and-go signal. 2 ALR3d 155.

Liability for automobile accident at intersection as affected by reliance upon or disregard of "yield" sign or signal. 2 ALR3d 275.

Liability for automobile accident at intersection as affected by reliance upon or disregard of unchanging caution, slow, danger, stop or like sign or signal. 3 ALR3d 180, 507.

Liability for collision of automobile with pedestrian at intersection as affected by reliance upon or disregard of traffic sign or signal other than stop-and-go signal. 3 ALR3d 557.

Liability of highway authorities arising out of motor vehicle accident allegdly caused by failure to erect or properly maintain traffic control device at intersection. 34 ALR3d 1008.

Governmental liability for failure to post highway deer crossing warning signs. 59 ALR4th 1217.

§ 32-5A-32. Traffic-control signal legend.

Whenever traffic is controlled by traffic-control signals exhibiting different colored lights, or colored lighted arrows, successively one at a time or in combination, only the colors green, red and yellow shall be used, except for special pedestrian signals carrying a word or symbol legend, and said lights shall indicate and apply to drivers of vehicles and pedestrians as follows:

(1) Green indication:

a. Vehicular traffic facing a circular green signal may proceed straight through or turn right or left unless a sign at such place prohibits either such turn. But vehicular traffic, including vehicles turning right or left, shall yield the right-of-way to other vehicles and to pedestrians lawfully within the intersection or an adjacent crosswalk at the time such signal is exhibited.

b. Vehicular traffic facing a green arrow signal, shown alone or in combination with another indication, may cautiously enter the intersection only to make the movement indicated by such arrow, or such other movement as is permitted by other indications shown at the same time. Such vehicular traffic shall yield the right-of-way to pedestrians lawfully within an adjacent crosswalk and to other traffic lawfully using the intersection.

c. Unless otherwise directed by a pedestrian-control signal, as provided in section 32-5A-33, pedestrians facing any green signal, except when the sole green signal is a turn arrow, may proceed across the roadway within any marked or unmarked crosswalk.

(2) Steady yellow indication:

a. Vehicular traffic facing a steady circular yellow or yellow arrow signal is thereby warned that the related green movement is being terminated or that a red indication will be exhibited immediately thereafter.

b. Pedestrians facing a steady circular yellow or yellow arrow signal, unless otherwise directed by a pedestrian-control signal as provided in section 32-5A-33, are thereby advised that there is insufficient time to cross the roadway before a red indication is shown and no pedestrian shall then start to cross the roadway.

(3) Steady red indication:

a. Vehicular traffic facing a steady circular red signal alone shall stop at a clearly marked stop line, but if none, before entering the crosswalk on the near side of the intersection, or if none, then before entering the intersection and shall remain standing until an indication to proceed is shown except as provided in subdivision (3)b.

b. Except when a sign is in place prohibiting a turn, vehicular traffic facing any steady red signal may cautiously enter the intersection to turn right, or to turn left from a one-way street into a one-way street, after stopping as required by subdivision (3)a. Such vehicular traffic shall yield the right of way to pedestrians lawfully within an adjacent crosswalk and to other traffic lawfully using the intersection.

c. Unless otherwise directed by a pedestrian-control signal as provided in section 32-5A-33, pedestrians facing a steady circular red signal alone shall not enter the roadway.

(4) In the event an official traffic-control signal is erected and maintained at a place other than an intersection, the provisions of this section shall be applicable except as to those provisions which by their nature can have no application. Any stop required shall be made at a sign or marking on the pavement indicating where the stop shall be made, but in the absence of any such signal or marking the stop shall be made at the signal. (Acts 1980, No. 80-434, p. 604, § 2-102.)

Commentary

The former statute corresponding to this section was section 32-5-32, which, because of its similarity, appears to have been based on an earlier version of UVC § 11-202. This section is designed to update the statute and to bring about some uniformity in practice among the states thereby improving traffic safety.

Subdivision (1)a. No change contemplated here, except for minor rewording.

Subdivision (1)b. The prior statute did not cover this situation when the green arrow is used alone. The UVC section is accompanied by the recommendation that the display of a turning green arrow alone or with another indication should indicate that during this display the turning movement is not interfered with by oncoming traffic, which simultaneously should face a red signal.

Subdivision (1)c. The prior statute did not take account of the possible presence of a pedestrian control signal.

Subdivision (2)a. and (2)b. Under this subdivision it is not unlawful, as it was under the former statute, for traffic that has lawfully entered the intersection on yellow, to continue across it when the red signal appears. This will bring the law in conformity with driving practices. Also under this subdivision, no pedestrian may start to cross on yellow, a practice that was permitted under the previous statutes. The corresponding UVC section, § 11-202(b), is accompanied by the recommendation that the color yellow be used only before red. If yellow is used following the red, traffic facing the signal has a tendency to start before the green signal appears, causing interference with cross traffic clearing the intersection.

Subdivision (3)a. Former Alabama law made no reference to the stop lines, which are now in current use. Otherwise this provision makes no substantial change in existing law.

Subdivision (3)b. This section is similar to section 32-5-31.

Subdivision (3)c. This subdivision gives a greater measure of safety than the prior statute which permitted pedestrians to cross on red if it can be done "safely".

Subdivision (4). This was the identical language of section 32-5-32(b).

As to applicability of former section, see Mobile Cab & Baggage Co. v. Armstrong, 259 Ala. 1, 65 So. 2d 192 (1953).

Collateral references. — 60A C.J.S., Motor Vehicles, §§ 354, 360(4).

Liability for accident at crossing as affected by reliance upon or disregard of traffic signals. 75 ALR 870.

Motorist's liability for collision at intersection of ordinary and arterial highways as affected by absence, displacement, or malfunctioning of stop sign or other traffic signal. 74 ALR2d 242.

Liability for automobile accident with pedestrian as affected by reliance upon or disregard of traffic signal. 2 ALR3d 12, 155, 3 ALR3d 557.

Liability for automobile accident at intersection as affected by reliance upon or disregard of unchanging caution, slow, danger, stop or like sign or signal. 3 ALR3d 180, 507.

Liability of highway authorities arising out of motor vehicle accident allegedly caused by failure to erect or properly maintain traffic control device at intersection. 34 ALR3d 1008.

§ 32-5A-33. Pedestrian-control signals.

Whenever special pedestrian-control signals exhibiting the words or symbols "walk" or "don't walk" are in place such signals shall indicate as follows:

(1) "Walk". Pedestrians facing such signal may proceed across the roadway in the direction of the signal and shall be given the right of way by the drivers of all vehicles.

(2) "Don't walk". No pedestrian shall start to cross the roadway in the direction of such signal, but any pedestrian who has partially completed his crossing on the walk signal shall proceed to a sidewalk or safety island while the "don't walk" signal is showing.

(3) "Don't walk" (flashing). No pedestrian shall start to cross the roadway in the direction of such signal, but any pedestrian who has partially completed his crossing on the walk signal shall proceed to a sidewalk or safety island while the "don't walk" signal is flashing. (Acts 1980, No. 80-434, p. 604, § 2-103.)

Commentary

The trend is to use the phrase "don't walk" rather than "wait" since the latter can be confused with the word "walk", especially if viewed from a distance or if one's eyesight is poor. Therefore, this minor change has been made from prior law, section 32-5-33.

Subdivision (3) is new.

Nonfacing signal must be obeyed where same signal shows in all directions. — Where pedestrian control signals operated at an intersection of two streets and the pedestrian knew such signals either showed "Walk" or "Don't Walk" in all directions simultaneously, the fact that the signal which the pedestrian observed was nonfacing did not excuse compliance with commands which it signaled. Hanvey v. Thompson, 46 Ala. App. 476, 243 So. 2d 743, rev'd on other grounds, 286 Ala. 614, 243 So. 2d 748 (1971) (decided under prior law).

Collateral references. — 60A C.J.S., Motor Vehicles, §§ 383, 388(2).

Liability for automobile accident, other than direct collision with pedestrian, as affected by reliance upon or disregard of stop-and-go signal. 2 ALR3d 12.

Liability for collision of automobile with pedestrian at intersection as affected by reliance upon or disregard of stop-and-go signal. 2 ALR3d 155.

Liability for collision of automobile with pedestrian at intersection as affected by reliance upon or disregard of traffic sign or signal other than stop-and-go signal. 3 ALR3d 557.

Intersection: duty and liability with respect to giving audible signal at intersection. 21 ALR3d 268.

Pedestrian: duty and liability with respect to giving audible signal upon approaching pedestrian. 24 ALR3d 183.

§ 32-5A-34. Flashing signals.

(a) Whenever an illuminated flashing red or yellow signal is used in a traffic sign or signal it shall require obedience by vehicular traffic as follows:

(1) Flashing red (stop signal). When a red lens is illuminated with rapid intermittent flashes, drivers of vehicles shall stop at a clearly marked stop line, but if none, before entering the crosswalk on the near side of the intersection, or if none, then at the point nearest the intersecting roadway where the driver has a view of approaching traffic on the intersecting roadway before entering the intersection, and the right to proceed shall be subject to the rules applicable after making a stop at a stop sign.

(2) Flashing yellow (caution signal). When a yellow lens is illuminated with rapid intermittent flashes, drivers of vehicles may proceed through the intersection or past such signal only with caution.

(b) This section shall not apply at railroad grade crossings. Conduct of drivers of vehicles approaching railroad grade crossings shall be governed by the rules as set forth in section 32-5A-150. (Acts 1980, No. 80-434, p. 604, § 2-104.)

Commentary

Subsection (a) is nearly identical to former section 32-5-34 and no change of substance is proposed. Subsection (b) has no counterpart in previous state law.

Collateral references. — 60 C.J.S., Motor Vehicles, §§ 26, 35. 60A C.J.S., Motor Vehicles, §§ 360(3), 360(4).

Liability for automobile accident, other than direct collision with pedestrian, as affected by reliance upon or disregard of stop-and-go signal. 2 ALR3d 12.

Liability for accident at street or highway intersection as affected by reliance upon or disregard of traffic sign, signal or marking. 2 ALR3d 12, 55, 275, 3 ALR3d 180, 507.

Liability for collision of automobile with pedestrian at intersection as affected by reli-

ance upon or disregard of stop-and-go signal. 2 ALR3d 155.

Liability for collision of automobile with pedestrian at intersection as affected by reliance upon or disregard of traffic sign or signal other than stop-and-go signal. 3 ALR3d 557.

Intersection: duty and liability with respect to giving audible signal at intersection. 21 ALR3d 268.

Pedestrian: duty and liability with respect to giving audible signal upon approaching pedestrian. 24 ALR3d 183.

§ 32-5A-35. Lane-direction-control signals.

When lane-direction-control signals are placed over the individual lanes of a street or highway, vehicular traffic may travel in any lane over which a green signal is shown, but shall not enter or travel in any lane over which a red signal is shown. (Acts 1980, No. 80-434, p. 604, § 2-105.)

Commentary

There was no comparable provision in existing Alabama law.

Collateral references. — Liability for automobile accident, other than direct collision with pedestrian, as affected by reliance upon or disregard of stop-and-go signal. 2 ALR3d 12.

Liability for collision of automobile with pedestrian at intersection as affected by reliance upon or disregard of stop-and-go signal. 2 ALR3d 155.

Liability for collision of automobile with pedestrian at intersection as affected by reliance upon or disregard of traffic sign or signal other than stop-and-go signal. 3 ALR3d 557.

Intersection: duty and liability with respect to giving audible signal at intersection. 21 ALR3d 268.

§ 32-5A-36. Display of unauthorized signs, signals or markings as public nuisance; signs, markings, etc., to be approved; procedure for approval.

(a) No person shall place, maintain or display upon or in view of any highway any unauthorized sign, signal, marking or device which purports to be or is an imitation of or resembles an official traffic-control device or railroad sign or signal, or which attempts to direct the movement of traffic, or which hides from view or interferes with the effectiveness of an official traffic-control device or any railroad sign or signal.

(b) No person shall place or maintain nor shall any public authority permit upon any highway any traffic sign or signal bearing thereon any commercial advertising.

(c) This section shall not be deemed to prohibit the erection upon private property adjacent to highways of signs giving useful directional information and of a type that cannot be mistaken for official signs.

(d) Every such prohibited sign, signal or marking is hereby declared to be a public nuisance and the authority having jurisdiction over the highway is hereby empowered to remove the same or cause it to be removed without notice.

(e) No person shall use on any designated federal-aid or state system street or highway in this state any traffic regulator sign, signal, marking, or any other device, unless of a type which has been submitted to the highway director for test and examination, and for which a certification of approval has been issued by the highway director, which certification is then in effect as provided by this section.

(f) Any person desiring approval of any traffic sign, signal or any other traffic regulatory device, shall, when required submit to the highway director, one or more sets of each type of device upon which approval is desired, together with the fee as determined by the highway director. The highway director shall, upon notice to the applicant, submit such device to the proper testing agency, for a report as to the compliance of such device with the rules and uniform standard specifications adopted by the state of Alabama highway department. Such devices will also be subject to any road test or other tests as the highway director may deem necessary to determine that each type of device and its component parts conform to the requirements as adopted by the director. The highway director is authorized to refuse approval of any device certified as complying with the specifications and requirements, which he determines will be, in actual use, unsafe or impracticable or would fail to comply with the provisions of this chapter, or such requirements as may be adopted by him.

(g) The highway director shall request the testing agency to submit a report of each type of device to him in duplicate. For those which are found to comply with the specifications and requirements, the report shall include any special adjustments required. Reports of all tests shall be accessible to the public and a copy thereof shall be furnished by the highway director to the applicant for the test.

(h) No manufacturer, jobber, retailer, his agent, or other person shall sell, lease, or offer for sale or hire, any sign, signal or any other traffic regulatory device that does not conform to the provisions of this chapter. (Acts 1980, No. 80-434, p. 604, § 2-106.)

Commentary

The former statute, section 32-5-36 was somewhat more limited with respect to subsection (a), but nearly identical with respect to subsection (b). There were no comparable provisions in prior law with respect to subsections (c) or (d). Subsections (e), (f), (g), and (h) are not found in the UVC counterpart to this section, UVC § 11-205, but are included here because of recent legislation adding these to the former Alabama statute. The general problem of the respective powers of state and local authorities is the concern of chapter 15 of the Uniform Vehicle Code, which has much more detailed and specific provisions than does the existing Alabama law, even when amended by the addition of subsections (e) through (h).

Collateral references. — Liability for automobile accident, other than direct collision with pedestrian, as affected by reliance upon or disregard of stop-and-go signal. 2 ALR3d 12.

Liability for collision of automobile with pedestrian at intersection as affected by reliance upon or disregard of stop-and-go signal. 2 ALR3d 155.

Liability for collision of automobile with pedestrian at intersection as affected by reliance upon or disregard of traffic sign or signal other than stop-and-go signal. 3 ALR3d 557.

Actionable nature of advertising impugning quality or worth of merchandise or products. 42 ALR4th 318.

§ 32-5A-37. Interference with official traffic-control devices or railroad signs or signals.

No person shall, without lawful authority, attempt to or in fact alter, deface, injure, knock down or remove any official traffic-control device or any railroad sign or signal or any inscription, shield or insignia thereon, or any other part thereof. (Acts 1980, No. 80-434, p. 604, § 2-107.)

Commentary

This section amends section 32-5-37, and removes the criminal penalties therein. This offense is now covered in sections 13A-7-21 through 13A-7-23.

ARTICLE 3.

OPERATION AND USE OF VEHICLES GENERALLY.

Cross references. — For other provisions as to the operation and use of motor vehicles generally, see § 32-5-51 et seq.

§ 32-5A-50. Unattended motor vehicle.

No person driving or in charge of a motor vehicle shall permit it to stand unattended without first stopping the engine, locking the ignition, removing the key from the ignition, effectively setting the brake thereon and, when standing upon any grade, turning the front wheels to the curb or side of the highway. (Acts 1980, No. 80-434, p. 604, § 11-101.)

Commentary

Except for a slight clarifying modification in wording, this section is virtually identical to the prior statute, section 32-5-153.

Former section did not require the wheels to touch the curb or the side of the highway; it only required that when the vehicle was standing upon a grade, the wheels had to be turned to the curb, and "to" did not mean touching. Dean v. Mayes, 274 Ala. 88, 145 So. 2d 439 (1962) (decided under prior law).

For acceptable charge under former section as to what constituted "effectively setting the brake," see Dean v. Mayes, 274 Ala. 88, 145 So. 2d 439 (1962).

Collateral references. — 60 C.J.S., Motor Vehicles, § 28(9).

7 Am. Jur. 2d, Automobiles & Highway Traffic, §§ 230-241.

Liability for damage or injury by stranger starting automobile left unattended in street. 26 ALR 912, 158 ALR 1374.

Liability for injury or damage caused by accidental starting up of parked motor vehicle. 16 ALR2d 979.

Construction and effect in civil actions of statute, ordinance, or regulation requiring vehicles to be stopped or parked parallel with, and within certain distance of curb. 17 ALR2d 582.

Liability for damage or injury by stranger starting motor vehicle left parked on street. 51 ALR2d 633.

Failure of motorist to cramp wheels against curb or to shut off engine or to set or maintain adequate brakes as causing accidental runaway of parked motor vehicle. 42 ALR3d 1252, 1283.

Contributory negligence as defense to action for injury or damage caused by accidental starting up of parked vehicle. 43 ALR3d 930.

Liability of motorist who left key in ignition for damage or injury caused by stranger operating the vehicle. 45 ALR3d 787.

Presumption of negligence and application of res ipsa loquitur doctrine in action for injury or damage caused by accidental starting up of parked motor vehicle. 55 ALR3d 1260.

§ 32-5A-51. Limitations on backing.

(a) The driver of a vehicle shall not back the same unless such movement can be made with safety and without interfering with other traffic.

(b) The driver of a vehicle shall not back the same upon any shoulder or roadway of any controlled-access highway. (Acts 1980, No. 80-434, p. 604, § 11-102.)

Commentary

This section is new. There was no provision in Alabama law on backing at the time of enactment.

§ 32-5A-52. Driving upon sidewalk.

No person shall drive any vehicle upon a sidewalk or sidewalk area except upon a permanent or duly authorized temporary driveway. (Acts 1980, No. 80-434, p. 604, § 11-103.)

Commentary

There was no comparable law in the previous Alabama statutes. This section is new.

§ 32-5A-53. Obstruction to driver's view or driving mechanism.

(a) No person shall drive a vehicle when it is loaded, or when there are in the front seat such a number of persons as to obstruct the view of the driver to the front or sides of the vehicle or as to interfere with the driver's control over the driving mechanism of the vehicle.

(b) No passenger in a vehicle shall ride in such position as to interfere with the driver's view ahead or to the sides, or to interfere with his control over the driving mechanism of the vehicle. (Acts 1980, No. 80-434, p. 604, § 11-104.)

Commentary

This section is similar to former section 32-5-6. One significant change, however, has been made in subsection (a). The prior statute limited the number of front seat passengers to a maximum of three persons. This numerical limitation has been deleted in this section to allow greater flexibility. This section, thus, acknowledges that the crucial inquiry is not how many passengers were in the front seat but whether the driver's view was obstructed.

Former section was only violated when passengers were in such a position as to interfere with the driver's view or control. Williams v. Palmer, 277 Ala. 188, 168 So. 2d 220 (1964), holding that under the evidence the court properly refused charge predicated on contributory negligence because of alleged violation of former section.

Collateral references. — 61 C.J.S., Motor Vehicles, §§ 342, 490(3).

Interference by occupant with driver as factor in determining liability between driver and others. 4 ALR2d 147.

Motor vehicle operator's liability for accident occurring while driving with vision obscured by smoke or steam. 32 ALR4th 933.

Passenger's liability to vehicular accident victim for harm caused by intoxicated motor vehicle driver. 64 ALR4th 272.

Driving while intoxicated: "choice of evils" defense that driving was necessary to protect life or property. 64 ALR4th 298.

§ 32-5A-54. Opening and closing vehicle doors.

No person shall open the door of a motor vehicle on the side available to moving traffic unless and until it is reasonably safe to do so, and can be done without interfering with the movement of other traffic, nor shall any person leave a door open on the side of a vehicle available to moving traffic for a period of time longer than necessary to load or unload passengers. (Acts 1980, No. 80-434, p. 604, § 11-105.)

Commentary

This section is new to Alabama. There was no prior comparable statute in this state.

§ 32-5A-55. Riding in house trailers.

No person or persons shall occupy a house trailer while it is being moved upon a public highway. (Acts 1980, No. 80-434, p. 604, § 11-106.)

Commentary

There was no prohibition of this type under previous Alabama law. However, the majority of states have provisions at least this stringent, most of those being patterned upon this section taken from § 11-1106 of the Uniform Vehicle Code.

§ 32-5A-56. Driving on mountain highways.

The driver of a motor vehicle traveling through defiles or canyons or on mountain highways shall hold such motor vehicle under control and as near the right-hand edge of the roadway as reasonably possible and, except when driving entirely to the right of the center of the roadway, shall give audible warning with the horn of such motor vehicle upon approaching any curve where the view is obstructed within a distance of 200 feet along the highway. (Acts 1980, No. 80-434, p. 604, § 11-107.)

Commentary

This section replaces section 32-5-62. That section was based verbatim on the comparable section of the Uniform Vehicle Code, § 11-1107, prior to its revision in 1971. This section, therefore, incorporates the 1971 UVC revision, removing the requirement that a driver entirely on the right side of the roadway use his or her horn.

Charge on failure to blow horn. — For case decided under former section, holding charge predicating motorist's negligence on failure to blow horn if view was obstructed without regard to distance not error in view of evidence, see Bradford v. Carson, 223 Ala. 594, 137 So. 426 (1931).

Jury question. — For case decided under former section holding issue of defendant's negligence in violating former statutes a question for the jury, see Smith v. Tripp, 246 Ala. 421, 20 So. 2d 870 (1944).

Collateral references. — 60A C.J.S., Motor Vehicles, §§ 296, 305, 306.

Duty in operating car at curve or on hill. 57 ALR 589.

Duty and liability with respect to giving audible signal where driver's view ahead obstructed at curve or hill. 16 ALR3d 897.

§ 32-5A-57. Coasting prohibited.

(a) The driver of any motor vehicle when traveling upon a down grade shall not coast with the gears or transmission of such vehicle in neutral or the clutch disengaged.

(b) The driver of a truck or bus when traveling upon a down grade shall not coast with the clutch disengaged. (Acts 1980, No. 80-434, p. 604, § 11-108.)

Commentary

This section is a revision of section 32-5-63. Subsection (a) is nearly identical to the prior statute, except that the phrase "upon any highway" is removed as superfluous, and the phrase "or transmission" is added to take into account vehicles with automatic transmissions. The phrase "or the clutch disengaged", which does not appear in UVC § 11-1108 or the prior Alabama statute is included here as an added measure of safety, and is based upon § 10-1108 of the proposed Pennsylvania rules of the road. Alabama did not previously have a provision comparable to subsection (b).

Collateral references. — 60A C.J.S., Motor Vehicles, § 296.

§ 32-5A-58. Following emergency vehicle prohibited.

The driver of any vehicle other than one on official business shall not follow any authorized emergency vehicle traveling in response to an emergency call closer than 500 feet or stop such vehicle within 500 feet of any authorized emergency vehicle stopped in answer to an emergency call. (Acts 1980, No. 80-434, p. 604, § 11-109.)

Commentary

This section replaces section 32-5-113(b). This section is significantly different insofar as section 32-5-113(b) did not restrict stopping near where the emergency vehicle has stopped. Such action is prohibited under this section. Moreover, this section is broader than UVC § 11-1109 on which it is largely based, for the UVC section is limited in application to fire apparatus.

Collateral references. — 7 Am. Jur. 2d, Automobiles & Highway Traffic, §§ 206, 212. Use or nonuse of flashing light, siren, or other alarm device as affecting liability arising from accident involving police vehicle. 83 ALR2d 409.

§ 32-5A-59. Crossing fire hose.

No vehicle shall be driven over any unprotected hose of a fire department when laid down on any street, private road or driveway to be used at any fire or alarm of fire, without the consent of the fire department official or police officer in command. (Acts 1980, No. 80-434, p. 604, § 11-110.)

Commentary

This section revises section 32-5-73 and varies from both the prior statute and the relevant UVC § 11-1110 in its additional reference to police officers who may be at the scene directing traffic.

§ 32-5A-60. Putting glass, etc., on highway, road, street or public right-of-way prohibited; removal; throwing of litter onto highway, etc., prohibited; penalty.

(a) No person shall throw or deposit upon any highway, road or street or public right-of-way any glass bottle, glass, nails, tacks, wire, cans or any other substance likely to injure any person, animal or vehicle upon such highway.

(b) Any person who drops, or permits to be dropped or thrown, upon any highway any destructive or injurious material shall immediately remove the same or cause it to be removed.

(c) Any person removing a wrecked or damaged vehicle from a highway shall remove any glass or other injurious substance dropped upon the highway from such vehicle.

(d) No person shall throw litter or allow litter to be thrown from a motor vehicle onto or upon any highway, road or street or public right-of-way.

(e) The uniform traffic citation may be used for any violation of this section.

(f) "Litter" as used in this section is the same as defined in section 13A-7-29.

(g) Notwithstanding the provisions of section 32-5A-266, any person violating the provisions of this section shall be guilty of a Class C misdemeanor and upon conviction shall be fined not more than $500.00, pursuant to section 13A-7-29, the criminal littering statute. (Acts 1980, No. 80-434, p. 604, § 11-111; Acts 1989, No. 89-661, § 1.)

The 1989 amendment, effective May 11, 1989, inserted "road or street or public right-of-way" in subsection (a), and added subsections (d) through (g) of this section.

Commentary

This section is identical to the prior statute, section 32-5-7.

§ 32-5A-61. Driver not to proceed where traffic obstructed.

No driver shall enter an intersection or a marked crosswalk or drive onto any railroad grade crossing unless there is sufficient space on the other side of the intersection, crosswalk or railroad grade crossing to accommodate the vehicle he is operating without obstructing the passage of other vehicles, pedestrians or railroad trains notwithstanding any traffic-control signal indication to proceed. (Acts 1980, No. 80-434, p. 604, § 11-112.)

Commentary

There was no comparable Alabama statute at the time this section was enacted.

§ 32-5A-62. Snowmobile operation limited.

(a) No person shall operate a snowmobile on any controlled-access highway.

(b) No person shall operate a snowmobile on any other highway except when crossing the highway at a right angle, when use of the highway by other motor vehicles is impossible because of snow, or when such operation is authorized by the authority having jurisdiction over the highway. (Acts 1980, No. 80-434, p. 604, § 11-113.)

Commentary

There was no comparable Alabama statute as of the time of enactment. While the practical usefulness of this section is limited in Alabama, it was considered desirable to enact this section simply for the purpose of increasing the extent to which Alabama highway laws generally conform to those in other states. Forty-six states have implemented similar statutes.

Collateral references. — Products liability: sufficiency of evidence to support product misuse defense in actions concerning commercial or industrial equipment and machinery. 64 ALR4th 10.

ARTICLE 4.

DRIVING ON AND USE OF ROADWAYS GENERALLY; OVERTAKING AND PASSING.

Cross references. — For other provisions as to the operation and use of motor vehicles generally, see § 32-5-51 et seq.

§ 32-5A-80. Driving on right side of roadway; exceptions.

(a) Upon all roadways of sufficient width a vehicle shall be driven upon the right half of the roadway, except as follows:

(1) When overtaking and passing another vehicle proceeding in the same direction under the rules governing such movement;

(2) When an obstruction exists making it necessary to drive to the left of the center of the highway; provided, any person doing so shall yield the

right-of-way to all vehicles traveling in the proper direction upon the unobstructed portion of the highway within such distance as to constitute an immediate hazard;

(3) Upon a roadway divided into three marked lanes for traffic under the rules applicable thereon; or

(4) Upon a roadway restricted to one-way traffic.

(b) Upon all roadways any vehicle proceeding at less than the normal speed of traffic at the time and place and under the conditions then existing shall be driven in the right-hand lane then available for traffic, or as close as practicable to the right-hand curb or edge of the roadway, except when overtaking and passing another vehicle proceeding in the same direction or when preparing for a left turn at an intersection or into a private road or driveway.

(c) Upon any roadway having four or more lanes for moving traffic and providing for two-way movement of traffic, no vehicle shall be driven to the left of the center line of the roadway, except when authorized by official traffic-control devices designating certain lanes to the left side of the center of the roadway for use by traffic not otherwise permitted to use such lanes, or except as permitted under subsection (a)(2). However, this subsection shall not be construed as prohibiting the crossing of the center line in making a left turn into or from an alley, private road or driveway. (Acts 1980, No. 80-434, p. 604, § 3-101.)

Commentary

This section does not greatly change the prior practice under former section 32-5-55, but serves to update, clarify and elaborate it in several particulars. There were, for example, no previous provisions for dealing with the roadway that may be divided into three marked lanes. With respect to subsection (b), the prior law did not apply on one-way streets and referred to "slow moving vehicle" rather than to one "proceeding at less than normal speed." There was no counterpart in former law for subsection (c).

I. General Consideration.
II. Decisions Under Prior Law.

I. GENERAL CONSIDERATION.

Collateral references. — 7 Am. Jur. 2d, Automobiles & Highway Traffic, § 219.

Failure to look for or discover automobile approaching on wrong side of road as negligence or contributory negligence. 145 ALR 536.

Negligence of motorist as to injury or damage occasioned in colliding with or avoiding collision with vehicle approaching in the wrong lane. 47 ALR2d 6, 119.

Rights, duties and liability with respect to narrow bridge or passage as between motor vehicles approaching from opposite directions. 47 ALR2d 142.

Passing: gross negligence, recklessness, or the like, within "guest" statute, predicated upon conduct in passing cars ahead or position of car on wrong side of the road. 6 ALR3d 832.

II. DECISIONS UNDER PRIOR LAW.

Editor's note. — The cases cited below were decided under similar provisions of prior law.

Purpose of former similar section was to insure that right-of-way was made available for other traffic lawfully using the highway, either oncoming or overtaking. Daniel v. Matthews, 46 Ala. App. 568, 246 So. 2d 457 (1971).

The rules of the road are subject to reasonable ordinances or traffic regulations by municipalities. L. Hammel Dry Goods Co. v. Hinton, 216 Ala. 127, 112 So. 638 (1927). See also, Birmingham Stove & Range Co. v. Vanderford, 217 Ala. 342, 116 So. 334 (1928).

As to right to assume that other drivers will observe rules of road, see L. Hammel Dry Goods Co. v. Hinton, 216 Ala. 127, 112 So. 638 (1927).

Driving on left side of highway. — There was no exception to former statute which permitted a person to drive on the left side of the highway in order to pick up his family. Lewis v. State, 27 Ala. App. 155, 167 So. 608 (1936).

In prosecution for manslaughter by automobile, argument of associate prosecuting attorney and statement of court that motorist could drive on left side of highway to pick up his family was erroneous and prejudicial to accused, whose automobile struck pedestrian in attempting to avoid collision with oncoming automobile which motorist suddenly drove to left side of highway. Lewis v. State, 27 Ala. App. 155, 167 So. 608 (1936).

Driver may be slightly across on his left of actual center imaginary line on unmarked highway in the exercise of due care without being negligent as a matter of law. Luguire Ins. Co. v. McCalla, 244 Ala. 479, 13 So. 2d 865 (1943).

Overtaking another vehicle. — Fact that overtaking car sounded horn or other signal with sufficient intensity and overtaken car turned to right authorized finding that driver of overtaking car had right to assume that his signal was heard and that such movement was for purpose of giving way in his favor, unless it appeared to have been made for some other

purpose under all circumstances. Buffalo Rock Co. v. Davis, 228 Ala. 603, 154 So. 556 (1934).

Charge that driver of overtaken car owed no duty to overtaking car except to use road in usual way until he had been made aware of desire of driver of overtaking car to pass by signal or otherwise was held properly refused under former statute. Buffalo Rock Co. v. Davis, 228 Ala. 603, 154 So. 556 (1934).

One lawfully in a lane of travel is not required to place himself in peril in order to give way to overtaking vehicle being operated in such manner as to be unable to come safely to a stop. Daniel v. Matthews, 46 Ala. App. 568, 246 So. 2d 457 (1971).

A reasonable person does not drive on the wrong side of the road as a car approaches from the opposite direction. Keller v. Kiedinger, 389 So. 2d 129 (Ala. 1980).

Driving on wrong side held not willful misconduct. — As regards first degree manslaughter, fact that defendant was driving automobile on wrong side of road was held not to be willful misconduct, but mere simple negligence, in violation of former similar statute. Curlette v. State, 25 Ala. App. 179, 142 So. 775 (1932).

As to applicability of principles of law relating to contributory negligence of children where a child violated former similar statute and such violation was a proximate cause of his injury, see Alabama Power Co. v. Bowers, 252 Ala. 49, 39 So. 2d 402 (1949).

As to charge on meaning of "obstruction" under former statute, see Luquire Ins. Co. v. McCalla, 244 Ala. 479, 13 So. 2d 865 (1943).

§ 32-5A-81. Passing vehicles proceeding in opposite directions.

Drivers of vehicles proceeding in opposite directions shall pass each other to the right, and upon roadways having width for not more than one line of traffic in each direction each driver shall give to the other at least one-half of the main-traveled portion of the roadway as nearly as possible. (Acts 1980, No. 80-434, p. 604, § 3-102.)

Commentary

This is very similar to former section 32-5-130, and no change in substance has been made.

For case holding defendant's negligence in violating former similar statute a question for jury, see Smith v. Tripp, 246 Ala. 421, 20 So. 2d 870 (1945).

Collateral references. — 60A C.J.S., Motor Vehicles, §§ 306, 318.

7 Am. Jur. 2d, Automobiles & Highway Traffic, § 219.

Liability for collision due to swaying or swinging of motor vehicle or trailer. 1 ALR2d 172.

Liability for accident arising from failure of

motorist to give signal for left turn at intersection, as against oncoming or intersecting motor vehicle. 39 ALR2d 65.

Rights, duties, and liability with respect to narrow bridge or passage as between motor vehicles approaching from opposite directions. 47 ALR2d 142.

Reciprocal rights, duties, and liabilities where motor vehicle proceeding in same direction, cuts back to the right. 48 ALR2d 232.

Passing: gross negligence, recklessness, or the like, within "guest" statute, predicated upon conduct in passing cars ahead or position of car on wrong side of the road. 6 ALR3d 832.

§ 32-5A-82. Overtaking vehicle on left.

The following rules shall govern the overtaking and passing of vehicles proceeding in the same direction, subject to those limitations, exceptions and special rules hereinafter stated:

(1) The driver of a vehicle overtaking another vehicle proceeding in the same direction shall pass to the left thereof at a safe distance and shall not again drive to the right side of the roadway until safely clear of the overtaken vehicle.

(2) Except when overtaking and passing on the right is permitted, the driver of an overtaken vehicle shall give way to the right in favor of the overtaking vehicle on audible signal and shall not increase the speed of his vehicle until completely passed by the overtaking vehicle. (Acts 1980, No. 80-434, p. 604, § 3-103.)

Commentary

Subsection (a) is identical to former section 32-5-131(a), except that "roadway" is used instead of the word "highway", which has a technical meaning set out in section 32-1-1.1(56). Subsection (b) modifies sections 32-5-131(b) and 32-5-133, which were similar but not identical to this subsection.

I. General Consideration.
II. Decisions Under Prior Law.

I. GENERAL CONSIDERATION.

Cited in Shackleford v. Brumley, 437 So. 2d 1044 (Ala. Civ. App. 1983).

Collateral references. — 7 Am. Jur. 2d, Automobiles & Highway Traffic, § 221.

Reciprocal duties of drivers of automobiles or other vehicles proceeding in the same direction. 24 ALR 507, 47 ALR 703, 62 ALR 970, 104 ALR 485.

Rights and liabilities as between drivers of motor vehicles proceeding in same direction, where one or both attempt to pass on left of another vehicle so proceeding. 27 ALR2d 317.

Reciprocal rights, duties, and liabilities where driver of motor vehicle attempts to pass on right of other motor vehicle proceeding in same direction. 38 ALR2d 114.

Duty and liability of overtaken driver with respect to adjusting speed to that of passing vehicle. 39 ALR2d 1260, 91 ALR2d 1260.

Passing: gross negligence, recklessness, or the like, within "guest" statute, predicated upon conduct in passing cars ahead or position of car on wrong side of the road. 6 ALR3d 832.

Duty and liability with respect to giving audible signal before passing. 22 ALR3d 325.

II. DECISIONS UNDER PRIOR LAW.

Editor's note. — The cases cited below were decided under similar provisions of prior law.

As to inapplicability of former section to passing of standing vehicle, see Alabama Power Co. v. Scholz, 283 Ala. 232, 215 So. 2d 447 (1968).

As to inapplicability of former section where there were two lanes for travel in the same direction, see Socier v. Woodard, 264 Ala. 514, 88 So. 2d 783 (1956).

Drivers of motor vehicles proceeding in line have reciprocal duties; the driver of the overtaken vehicle has the duty before turning into another lane to exercise due care that it is safe to do so; the driver of the overtaking vehicle has the duty of giving audible warning, unless in a business district, of his desire to pass. Socier v. Woodard, 264 Ala. 514, 88 So. 2d 783 (1956); Edger v. Karl Bradley Ford, Inc., 41 Ala. App. 638, 147 So. 2d 858 (1962).

Right to assume horn was heard. — Where overtaking car sounded horn or other signal with sufficient intensity and overtaken car turned to right, driver of overtaking car had right to assume that his signal was heard and that such movement was for purpose of giving way in his favor, unless it appeared to have been made for some other purpose under all circumstances. Buffalo Rock Co. v. Davis, 228 Ala. 603, 154 So. 556 (1934).

Provision for benefit of both pedestrians and occupants of vehicles. — Provision that driver of overtaking vehicle not within business district should give audible warning before passing was for benefit of pedestrians as well as persons riding in vehicles. Bentley v. Lawson, 280 Ala. 220, 191 So. 2d 372 (1966).

In order to bar recovery on ground that plaintiff violated former similar section, it was essential that such violation should have contributed to the injury as a proximate cause.

Alabama Power Co. v. Sellers, 283 Ala. 137, 214 So. 2d 833 (1968).

Jury questions. — Where plaintiff, driving a one-ton truck in the right-hand lane for north-bound traffic, attempted to pass defendant's three-quarter-ton truck with trailer attached, it was a jury question whether plaintiff in undertaking to pass defendant exercised due care in sounding his horn and in passing at a safe distance on the left when the evidence was conflicting on both factors. Socier v. Woodard, 264 Ala. 514, 88 So. 2d 783 (1956).

Where overtaking car collided with left side of car being overtaken, damaging right side of overtaking vehicle, question of guilt of driver of overtaking vehicle of reckless driving was for jury. Graham v. State, 40 Ala. App. 471, 115 So. 2d 289 (1959).

For case holding instruction as to sounding of horn proper, see Campbell v. Jackson, 257 Ala. 618, 60 So. 2d 252 (1952).

Instruction held improper. — Charge that driver of overtaken car owed no duty to overtaking car except to use road in usual way until he had been made aware of desire of driver of overtaking car to pass by signal or otherwise was properly refused. Buffalo Rock Co. v. Davis, 228 Ala. 603, 154 So. 556 (1934).

§ 32-5A-83. When passing on right permitted.

(a) The driver of a vehicle may overtake and pass upon the right of another vehicle only under the following conditions:

(1) When the vehicle overtaken is making or about to make a left turn;

(2) Upon a roadway with unobstructed pavement of sufficient width for two or more lines of vehicles moving lawfully in the direction being traveled by the overtaking vehicle.

(b) The driver of a vehicle may overtake and pass another vehicle upon the right only under conditions permitting such movement in safety. Such movement shall not be made by driving off the roadway. (Acts 1980, No. 80-434, p. 604, § 3-104.)

Commentary

Subsection (a) makes no change in the former statute, section 32-5-134(a), except for minor rewording. Subsection (b) is very similar to former section 32-5-134(b), but this provision makes it clear that a driver should not use a paved shoulder to pass.

Collateral references. — 60A C.J.S., Motor Vehicles, §§ 321-328.

Reciprocal rights, duties, and liabilities where driver of motor vehicle attempts to pass on right of other motor vehicle proceeding in same direction. 38 ALR2d 114.

Reciprocal rights, duties and liabilities where motor vehicle proceeding in same direction, cuts back to the right. 48 ALR2d 232.

Passing: gross negligence, recklessness, or the like, within "guest" statute, predicated upon conduct in passing cars ahead or position of car on wrong side of the road. 6 ALR3d 832.

§ 32-5A-84. Limitations on overtaking on left.

No vehicle shall be driven to the left side of the center of the roadway in overtaking and passing another vehicle proceeding in the same direction unless such left side is clearly visible and is free of oncoming traffic for a sufficient distance ahead to permit such overtaking and passing to be completely made without interfering with the operation of any vehicle approaching from the opposite direction or any vehicle overtaken. In every event the overtaking vehicle must return to an authorized lane of travel as soon as practicable and in the event the passing movement involves the use of a lane authorized for vehicles approaching from the opposite direction, before coming within 200 feet of any approaching vehicle. (Acts 1980, No. 80-434, p. 604, § 3-105.)

Commentary

Sections 32-5A-84 and 32-5A-85 are designed to replace and expand section 32-5-132. The first sentence of section 32-5A-84 is nearly identical to section 32-5-132(a), but there was no counterpart in former law for the second sentence. Section 32-5-132(b) previously applied to overtaking and passing only and did not cover the general problem of driving on the left side of the roadway. In lieu of the 500 feet rule of the prior statute, subdivision 32-5A-85(a)(1) uses a safe-distance rule. As for subdivision 32-5A-85(a)(2), the previous law applied only to overtaking and passing and applied only "at" the crossing or intersection, rather than within 100 feet of them. There was no comparable provision under former law corresponding to subdivision 32-5A-85(a)(3) or subsection 32-5A-85(b).

Making turn when not reasonably safe to do so. — It was a question for the jury whether former similar section, prohibiting a driver from passing another at an intersection, was intended to protect one making a left turn when it was not reasonably safe to do so. Winfrey v. Witherspoon's, Inc., 260 Ala. 371, 71 So. 2d 37 (1954).

Contributory negligence of person passing at intersection. — A person attempting to pass a vehicle at an intersection in violation of former similar statute was guilty of contributory negligence and precluded from recovery, where defendant was initially negligent in turning to left at said intersection without giving proper signal. Griffith Freight Lines v. Benson, 234 Ala. 613, 176 So. 370 (1937). See also, Greer v. Marriott, 27 Ala. App. 108, 167 So. 597, cert. denied, 232 Ala. 194, 167 So. 599 (1936).

Proximate cause as jury question. — If the undisputed proof showed a violation of former similar statute, such violation would constitute negligence as a matter of law, but it would still remain a question for the jury as to whether such violation of the statute proximately contributed to the injury. Edger v. Karl

Bradley Ford, Inc., 41 Ala. App. 638, 147 So. 2d 858 (1962).

Collateral references. — 7 Am. Jur. 2d, Automobiles & Highway Traffic, § 221.

Reciprocal duties of drivers of automobiles or other vehicles proceeding in the same direction. 24 ALR 507, 47 ALR 703, 62 ALR 970, 104 ALR 485.

Duty in operating automobile at curve or on hill. 57 ALR 589.

Negligence of motorist colliding with vehicle approaching in wrong lane. 47 ALR2d 6.

Negligence of motorist as to injury or damage occasioned in avoiding collision with vehicle approaching in wrong lane. 47 ALR2d 119.

Applicability of traffic regulation prohibiting vehicle from passing another at street or highway intersection. 53 ALR2d 850.

Construction and application of statutes regulating or forbidding passing on hill by vehicle. 60 ALR2d 211.

Passing: gross negligence, recklessness, or the like, within "guest" statute, predicated upon conduct in passing cars ahead or position of car on wrong side of the road. 6 ALR3d 832.

What is a street or highway intersection within traffic rules. 7 ALR3d 1204.

§ 32-5A-85. Further limitations on driving on left of center of roadway.

(a) No vehicle shall be driven on the left side of the roadway under the following conditions:

(1) When approaching or upon the crest of a grade or a curve in the highway where the driver's view is obstructed within such distance as to create a hazard in the event another vehicle might approach from the opposite direction;

(2) When approaching within 100 feet of or traversing any intersection or railroad grade crossing;

(3) When the view is obstructed upon approaching within 100 feet of any bridge, viaduct or tunnel.

(b) The foregoing limitations shall not apply upon a one-way roadway, nor under the conditions described in section 32-5A-80(a)(2), nor to the driver of a vehicle turning left into or from an alley, private road or driveway. (Acts 1980, No. 80-434, p. 604, § 3-106.)

Making turn when not reasonably safe to do so. — It was a question for the jury as to whether former similar statute, prohibiting a driver from passing another at an intersection, was intended to protect one making a left turn when it was not reasonably safe to do so. Winfrey v. Witherspoon's, Inc., 260 Ala. 371, 71 So. 2d 37 (1954).

Contributory negligence of person passing at intersection. — A person attempting to pass a vehicle at an intersection in violation of former similar statute was guilty of contributory negligence and precluded from recovery, in a case where defendant was initially negligent in turning to left at said intersection without giving proper signal. Griffith Freight Lines v. Benson, 234 Ala. 613, 176 So. 370 (1937); Greer v. Marriott, 27 Ala. App. 108, 167 So. 597, cert. denied, 232 Ala. 194, 167 So. 599 (1936).

Proximate cause as jury question. — If the undisputed proof showed a violation of former similar statute, such violation would constitute negligence as a matter of law, but it would still remain a question for the jury as to whether such violation of the statute proximately contributed to the injury. Edger v. Karl

Bradley Ford, Inc., 41 Ala. App. 638, 147 So. 2d 858 (1962).

Collateral references. — 7 Am. Jur. 2d, Automobiles & Highway Traffic, § 221.

Reciprocal duties of drivers of automobiles or other vehicles proceeding in the same direction. 24 ALR 507, 47 ALR 703, 62 ALR 970, 104 ALR 485.

Duty in operating automobile at curve or on hill. 57 ALR 589.

Negligence of motorist colliding with vehicle approaching in wrong lane. 47 ALR2d 6.

Negligence of motorist as to injury or damage occasioned in avoiding collision with vehicle approaching in wrong lane. 47 ALR2d 119.

Applicability of traffic regulation prohibiting vehicle from passing another at street or highway intersection. 53 ALR2d 850.

Construction and application of statutes regulating or forbidding passing on hill by vehicle. 60 ALR2d 211.

Passing: gross negligence, recklessness, or the like, within "guest" statute, predicated upon conduct in passing cars ahead or position of car on wrong side of the road. 6 ALR3d 832.

What is a street or highway intersection within traffic rules. 7 ALR3d 1204.

§ 32-5A-86. No-passing zones.

(a) The highway department and local authorities are hereby authorized to determine those portions of any highway under their respective jurisdictions where overtaking and passing or driving to the left of the roadway would be especially hazardous and may by appropriate signs or markings on the roadway indicate the beginning and end of such zones and when such signs or markings are in place and clearly visible to an ordinarily observant person every driver of a vehicle shall obey the directions thereof.

(b) Where signs or markings are in place to define a no-passing zone as set forth in subsection (a) no driver shall at any time drive on the left side of the roadway within such no-passing zone or on the left side of any pavement striping designed to mark such no-passing zone throughout its length.

(c) This section does not apply under the conditions described in section 32-5A-80(a)(2), nor to the driver of a vehicle turning left into or from an alley, private road or driveway. (Acts 1980, No. 80-434, p. 604, § 3-107.)

Commentary

This section replaces section 32-5-135 which was similar, except for subsection (c) and the empowering of local authorities to designate no-passing zones within their jurisdictions.

Yellow lines designated no passing zones in this state under former similar statute, which was not adopted for the benefit of pedestrians. Harvey Ragland Co. v. Newton, 268 Ala. 192, 105 So. 2d 110 (1958).

Collateral references. — Construction and application of statute regulating or forbidding passing on hill by vehicle. 60 ALR2d 211.

Passing: gross negligence, recklessness, or the like, within "guest" statute, predicated upon conduct in passing cars ahead or position of car on wrong side of the road. 6 ALR3d 832.

§ 32-5A-87. One-way roadways and rotary traffic islands.

(a) The highway department and local authorities with respect to highways under their respective jurisdictions may designate any highway, roadway, part of a roadway or specific lanes upon which vehicular traffic shall proceed in one direction at all or such times as shall be indicated by official traffic-control devices.

(b) Upon a roadway so designated for one-way traffic, a vehicle shall be driven only in the direction designated at all or such times as shall be indicated by official traffic-control devices.

(c) A vehicle passing around a rotary traffic island shall be driven only to the right of such island. (Acts 1980, No. 80-434, p. 604, § 3-108.)

Commentary

This section replaces section 32-5-66 which was very similar, except that the former statute did not give local authorities specific power to designate one-way routes within their respective jurisdictions. Local authorities are vested with such power under this section.

Collateral references. — 60 C.J.S., Motor Vehicles, § 33.

§ 32-5A-88. Driving on roadways laned for traffic.

Whenever any roadway has been divided into two or more clearly marked lanes for traffic the following rules in addition to all others consistent herewith shall apply:

(1) A vehicle shall be driven as nearly as practicable entirely within a single lane and shall not be moved from such lane until the driver has first ascertained that such movement can be made with safety.

(2) Upon a roadway which is divided into three lanes and provides for two-way movement of traffic, a vehicle shall not be driven in the center lane except when overtaking and passing another vehicle traveling in the same direction when such center lane is clear of traffic within a safe distance, or in preparation for making a left turn or where such center lane is at the time allocated exclusively to traffic moving in the same direction that the vehicle is proceeding and such allocation is designated by official traffic-control devices.

(3) Official traffic-control devices may be erected directing specified traffic to use a designated lane or designating those lanes to be used by traffic moving in a particular direction regardless of the center of the roadway and drivers of vehicles shall obey the direction of every such device.

(4) Official traffic-control devices may be installed prohibiting the changing of lanes on sections of roadway and drivers of vehicles shall obey the directions of every such device. (Acts 1980, No. 80-434, p. 604, § 3-109.)

Commentary

This section replaces section 32-5-67, which was based on an earlier version of the UVC. Very minor changes are made by subdivisions (1) and (2). Subdivision (3) has been updated by referring to "traffic-control devices" rather than "signs", and by permitting lanes to be marked for any "designated traffic" (e.g., bus lanes, car pool lanes, express lanes) and not merely for "slow moving" traffic. Subdivision (4) is new and had no counterpart in the former law.

Drivers of motor vehicle proceeding in lane have reciprocal duties: the driver of the overtaken vehicle has the duty before turning into another lane to exercise due care to be sure that it is safe to do so; the driver of the overtaking vehicle has the duty of giving audible warning, unless in a business district, of his desire to pass. Socier v. Woodward, 264 Ala. 514, 88 So. 2d 783 (1956) (decided under prior law).

Subject to exceptions of § 32-1-4(b), custodial arrest not authorized for improper lane usage. Hays v. City of Jacksonville, 518 So. 2d 892 (Ala. Crim. App. 1987).

Neither the fact that the defendant's improper lane usage may have arisen because she was driving while under the influence, nor the fact that the arresting officer had probable cause to believe she was driving under the influence, authorized her being required to submit to a chemical test for intoxication because she was unlawfully taken into custody and arrested. Hays v. City of Jacksonville, 518 So. 2d 892 (Ala. Crim. App. 1987).

Reasonable man standard. — Where the applicable Rule of the Road requires a judgment to be made on the part of the driver, the reasonable man standard applies and a violation of the statute is not negligence per se. Consolidated Freightways, Inc. v. Pacheco-Rivera, 524 So. 2d 346 (Ala. 1988).

As to reading of former similar section to jury in negligence case, see Pruett v. Marshall, 283 F.2d 436 (5th Cir. 1960).

Collateral references. — 60A C.J.S., Motor Vehicles, § 276.

§ 32-5A-89. Following too closely.

(a) The driver of a motor vehicle shall not follow another more closely than is reasonable and prudent, having due regard for the speed of such vehicles and the traffic upon and the condition of the highway. Except when overtaking and passing another vehicle, the driver of a vehicle shall leave a distance of at least 20 feet for each 10 miles per hour of speed between the vehicle that he is driving and the vehicle that he is following.

(b) The driver of any truck or motor vehicle drawing another vehicle of 25 or more feet in length when traveling upon a roadway outside of a business or residence district and which is following another truck or motor vehicle drawing another vehicle of 25 or more feet in length shall, whenever conditions permit, leave sufficient space, at least 300 feet, so that an overtaking vehicle may enter and occupy such space without danger, except that this shall not prevent a truck or motor vehicle drawing another vehicle of 25 or more feet in length from overtaking and passing any vehicle or combination of vehicles.

(c) Motor vehicles being driven upon any roadway whether a business or residence district in a caravan or motorcade whether or not towing other vehicles shall be so operated as to allow sufficient space between each such vehicle or combination of vehicles so as to enable any other vehicle to enter and occupy such space without danger. This provision shall not apply to funeral processions or to any parade or procession authorized by official permit of the governing body of the city or county having jurisdiction over said highway. (Acts 1980, No. 80-434, p. 604, § 3-110; Acts 1981, No. 81-803, p. 1412, § 1.)

Commentary

This section replaces section 32-5-56. The first sentence of subsection (a) is virtually identical to the prior statute. The second sentence is new. It is not found in the UVC, but was added by the Senate judiciary committee. Subsection (b) represents a compromise between the UVC's suggested safe-distance rule and the former statute, which referred to a specified number of feet. There was no counterpart in the previous law for subsection (c).

I. General Consideration.
II. Decisions Under Prior Law.

I. GENERAL CONSIDERATION.

Collateral references. — 60A C.J.S., Motor Vehicles, §§ 322, 323(1), 323(2).

Tailgating: driver's failure to maintain proper distance from motor vehicle ahead. 85 ALR2d 613.

II. DECISIONS UNDER PRIOR LAW.

Editor's note. — The cases cited below were decided under similar provisions of prior law.

A motorist approaching an intersection is required to have his vehicle under control so that he does not drive into the rear of a vehicle whose driver is obeying traffic signals by waiting for the red light to change. Gribble v. Cox, 349 So. 2d 1141 (Ala. 1977).

Reasonable care in following another vehicle. — The only rule that can govern the interval to be maintained between two automobiles proceeding in the same direction is that of reasonable care under the circumstances. A motorist has a right to follow another motorist at a reasonable and safe distance. Holley v. Josey, 263 Ala. 349, 82 So. 2d 328 (1955).

Prima facie negligence. — One who drives his auto into the rear of another who is stopped in obedience to a traffic light is prima facie guilty of negligence. Gribble v. Cox, 349 So. 2d 1141 (Ala. 1977).

Once the jury determined that defendant's car followed the other car too closely, in violation of former similar section, the defendant's conduct would be treated as negligence

per se. Couch v. Donahue, 259 F.2d 325 (5th Cir. 1958).

Jury question. — Whether defendant's car followed another car more closely than was reasonable and prudent was a question for the jury. The statutory standard is flexible and depends on the circumstances, having due regard to the speed of such vehicle and the traffic upon and condition of such highway. Couch v. Donahue, 259 F.2d 325 (5th Cir. 1958).

§ 32-5A-90. Driving on divided highways.

Whenever any highway has been divided into two or more roadways by leaving an intervening space or by a physical barrier or clearly indicated dividing section so construed as to impede vehicular traffic, every vehicle shall be driven only upon the right-hand roadway unless directed or permitted to use another roadway by official traffic-control devices or police officers. No vehicle shall be driven over, across or within any such dividing space, barrier or section, except through an opening in such physical barrier or dividing section or space or at a cross-over or intersection as established, unless specifically prohibited by public authority. (Acts 1980, No. 80-434, p. 604, § 3-111.)

Commentary

This section is very similar to former section 32-5-68, but updates it in minor respects. For example, this section refers to two or more roadways, whereas the previous statute spoke only of division into two roadways.

Collateral references. — 60 C.J.S., Motor Vehicles, § 35. 60A C.J.S., Motor Vehicles, §§ 278, 318.

§ 32-5A-91. Access onto controlled roadways restricted.

No person shall drive a vehicle onto or from any controlled access roadway except at such entrances and exits as are established by public authority. (Acts 1980, No. 80-434, p. 604, § 3-112.)

Commentary

This is the same as former section 32-5-69, except that the term "controlled-access" replaces "limited access". See definition of "controlled access" in section 32-1-1.1(8).

Collateral references. — 60A C.J.S., Motor Vehicles, § 303(1).

Exiting from expressways should be done only at designated places. — Expressways are designed for fast travel. Exits from

and entrances to expressways are designed and placed for safety of the motorist and free flow of traffic. Exiting therefrom should be done at designated places not only for the safety of the exiting motorists but also for other motorists

as well. Magnusson v. Swan, 291 Ala. 151, 279
So. 2d 422 (1973) (decided under former
§ 32-5-69).

§ 32-5A-92. Restrictions on use of controlled-access roadway.

(a) The highway department by resolution or order entered in its minutes,
and local authorities by ordinance, may regulate or prohibit the use of any
controlled-access roadway (or highway) within their respective jurisdictions
by any class or kind of traffic which is found to be incompatible with the
normal and safe movement of traffic.

(b) The highway department or the local authority adopting any such
prohibition shall erect and maintain official traffic-control devices on the
controlled-access highway on which such prohibitions are applicable and
when in place no person shall disobey the restrictions stated on such devices.
(Acts 1980, No. 80-434, p. 604, § 3-113.)

Commentary

The term "controlled access" replaces "limited access" which appeared in the
prior statute, section 32-5-70. See comment to section 32-5A-91. The previous
statute was limited in the kinds of traffic that could have been excluded from
controlled-access highways. For example, authorities may prohibit funerals,
parades or non-motorized traffic from using such highways. This section provides
the requisite flexibility.

Collateral references. — State and local
government liability for injury or death of
bicyclist due to defect or obstruction in public
bicycle path. 68 ALR4th 204.

ARTICLE 5.

RIGHT-OF-WAY.

Cross references. — For other provisions
as to duty of driver on approach of authorized
emergency vehicle, see § 32-5-113.

§ 32-5A-110. Vehicle approaching or entering intersection.

(a) When two vehicles approach or enter an intersection from different
highways at approximately the same time, the driver of the vehicle on the left
shall yield the right-of-way to the vehicle on the right.

(b) The right-of-way rule declared in subsection (a) is modified at through
highways and otherwise as stated in this chapter. (Acts 1980, No. 80-434, p.
604, § 4-101.)

Commentary

This section replaces two former statutes, sections 32-5-110(a) and 32-5-111 but
without substantial change.

I. General Consideration.
II. Decisions Under Prior Law.

I. GENERAL CONSIDERATION.

Collateral references. — 61A C.J.S., Motor Vehicles, §§ 35, 362(1).

7 Am. Jur. 2d, Automobiles & Highway Traffic, §§ 198-215.

Right-of-way at street or highway intersections. 21 ALR 974, 37 ALR 493, 47 ALR 595.

Right-of-way at street or highway intersections as dependent upon, or independent of, care or negligence. 89 ALR 838, 136 ALR 1497.

Right-of-way as between vehicles as affected by relative distances or time of reaching intersection. 175 ALR 1013.

What amounts to reckless driving of motor vehicle within statute making such a criminal offense. 52 ALR2d 1337.

Custom or practice of drivers of motor vehicles as affecting liability based on violation of law in failing to yield right-of-way. 77 ALR2d 1335.

Yield sign: liability for automobile accidents at intersection as affected by reliance upon or disregard of yield sign or signal. 2 ALR3d 275.

What is a street or highway intersection within traffic rules. 7 ALR3d 1204.

II. DECISIONS UNDER PRIOR LAW.

Editor's note. — The cases cited below were decided under similar provisions of prior law.

Driver with right-of-way is not relieved of general duty of exercising due care not to injure others at the crossing. Smith v. Lawson, 264 Ala. 389, 88 So. 2d 322 (1956).

Even though the defendant's truck may have reached intersection first, it still was incumbent upon him to use such care as an ordinarily prudent person would have done to avoid accident. Osborn v. Grizzard, 251 Ala. 275, 37 So. 2d 201 (1948).

Trier of fact to determine whether driver has right-of-way. — Person entering paved road from minor road, even though such minor road is a public road, does not necessarily have the right-of-way in regard to traffic approaching from his left. Such matter must be deemed a question for the trier of fact under all the evidence as applied to the general law of negligence. Traylor v. Butler, 291 Ala. 560, 284 So. 2d 263 (1973).

And whether he has forfeited right-of-way. — Whether a person has forfeited his right-of-way at any intersection by approaching at an unlawful speed is a question of fact for the jury. Brown v. Standard Casket Mfg. Co., 234 Ala. 512, 175 So. 358 (1937).

Negligence of one entering road as question for jury. — In guest's action for injuries sustained when defendant's school bus, entering highway from settlement road, collided with automobile in which guest was riding on highway, whether bus driver was negligent in running bus into center of highway at blind intersection was a question for the jury. Moore v. Cruit, 238 Ala. 414, 191 So. 252 (1939).

Negligence in failing to observe vehicle having right-of-way and reduce speed. — Counts charging defendant with ordinary and wanton negligence in intersection collision were for the jury where plaintiff with right-of-way, proceeding from a stop, entered intersection first and defendant failed to reduce her speed though she was in a position to observe plaintiff's peril. Smith v. Lawson, 264 Ala. 389, 88 So. 2d 322 (1956).

Negligence of driver not imputed to guest. — In guest's action for injuries, driver's negligence could not be imputed to guest in absence of proof that guest had authority over movements of automobile in any manner. Moore v. Cruit, 238 Ala. 414, 191 So. 252 (1939).

Jury to determine issue of proximate cause. — Plaintiff's violation of former similar statute constituted negligence on the part of plaintiff as a matter of law, but it remained a question for the jury as to whether violation of the statute proximately contributed to the injury. Giles v. Gardner, 287 Ala. 166, 249 So. 2d 824 (1971).

Quoting statute in charge to jury. — The better policy in dealing with the rules of the road in an oral charge is to quote the applicable statute. Giles v. Gardner, 287 Ala. 166, 249 So. 2d 824 (1971).

Instructions held improper. — Requested charge that driver of school bus in approaching and entering junction of two roads where collision took place had right to assume that driver of another motor vehicle would observe the laws and rules of road in approaching junction point on a different and connecting road was properly refused as misleading. Moore v. Cruit, 238 Ala. 414, 191 So. 252 (1939).

Where evidence was conflicting whether automobile and truck which collided entered intersection at approximately same time, charge that if truck did not enter intersection until after automobile had approached and entered, truck no longer had right-of-way, held prejudicial error. White Dairy Co. v. Sims, 230 Ala. 561, 161 So. 812 (1935).

§ 32-5A-111. Vehicle turning left.

The driver of a vehicle intending to turn to the left within an intersection or into an alley, private road or driveway shall yield the right-of-way to any vehicle approaching from the opposite direction which is within the intersection or so close thereto as to constitute an immediate hazard. (Acts 1980, No. 80-434, p. 604, § 4-102.)

Commentary

This is the same language previously found in section 32-5-110(b).

Duty to look for automobiles approaching intersection from right. — The driver is presumed to know that a vehicle approaching a street intersection from the right has the right-of-way and is under the duty of looking to the right for automobiles approaching from that direction. Observation should be made at the first opportunity and at a point where observation will be reasonably efficient for, and conducive to, protection. Smith v. Lawson, 264 Ala. 389, 88 So. 2d 322 (1956) (decided under prior law).

Collateral references. — 60A C.J.S., Motor Vehicles, § 362(4).

Yield sign: liability for automobile accidents at intersection as affected by reliance upon or disregard of yield sign or signal. 2 ALR3d 275.

Accidents arising from merger of traffic on limited access highway with that from service road or ramp. 40 ALR3d 1429.

§ 32-5A-112. Vehicle entering stop or yield intersection; collision as prima facie evidence of failure to yield.

(a) Preferential right-of-way at an intersection may be indicated by stop signs or yield signs as authorized in section 32-5A-113.

(b) Except when directed to proceed by a police officer every driver of a vehicle approaching a stop sign shall stop at a clearly marked stop line, but if none, before entering the crosswalk on the near side of the intersection or, if none, then at the point nearest the intersecting roadway where the driver has a view of approaching traffic on the intersecting roadway before entering it. After having stopped, the driver shall yield the right-of-way to any vehicle in the intersection or approaching on another roadway so closely as to constitute an immediate hazard during the time when such driver is moving across or within the intersection or junction of roadways.

(c) The driver of a vehicle approaching a yield sign shall in obedience to such sign slow down to a speed reasonable for the existing conditions and, if required for safety to stop, shall stop at a clearly marked stop line, but if none, before entering the crosswalk on the near side of the intersection, or, if none, then at the point nearest the intersecting roadway where the driver has a view of approaching traffic on the intersecting roadway before entering it. After slowing or stopping, the driver shall yield the right-of-way to any vehicle in the intersection or approaching on another roadway so closely as to constitute an immediate hazard during the time such driver is moving across or within the intersection or junction of roadways. Provided, however, that if such a driver is involved in a collision with a vehicle in the intersection or junction of roadways after driving past a yield sign without stopping, such collision shall be deemed prima facie evidence of his failure to yield right-of-way. (Acts 1980, No. 80-434, p. 604, § 4-103.)

Commentary

There was no previous law comparable to subsection (a). The same may be said for subsection (c) except that former section 32-5-111 made some provision for limited-access highways. As for subsection (b), the matters therein were covered somewhat, but inadequately by section 32-5-114. The former law lacked detail on the duty to yield and had no general statement as to when the stop, if required, should be made.

Collateral references. — 60 A C.J.S., Motor Vehicles, §§ 359, 360(5), 363(10).

7A Am. Jur. 2d, Automobiles & Highway Traffic, §§ 238, 816-821.

Yield sign: liability for automobile accidents at intersection as affected by reliance upon or disregard of yield sign or signal. 2 ALR3d 275.

§ 32-5A-113. Authority to designate through highways and stop and yield intersections.

The highway department with reference to state highways and local authorities with reference to highways under their jurisdictions may erect and maintain stop signs, yield signs, or other official traffic-control devices to designate through highways, or to designate intersections or other roadway junctions at which vehicular traffic on one or more of the roadways should yield or stop and yield before entering the intersection or junction. (Acts 1980, No. 80-434, p. 604, § 4-104.)

Commentary

This section is based upon UVC § 15-109 and amends section 32-5-114. The prior statute was similar except that it made no provision for yield signs.

As to controlling effect of state law in absence of local regulations, see Gilbert v. Gwin-McCollum Funeral Home, 268 Ala. 372, 106 So. 2d 646 (1958) (decided under prior law).

It was duty of driver on road intersecting highway to obey stop sign. Johnston v. Weissinger, 225 Ala. 425, 143 So. 464 (1932) (decided under prior law).

Presumption that stop sign placed pursuant to law. — Although it did not appear whether a stop sign was placed on an intersecting street by virtue of city ordinance or by the state highway department, it was assumed that it was placed pursuant to law. Gilbert v. Gwin-McCollum Funeral Home, 268 Ala. 372, 106 So. 2d 646 (1958) (decided under prior law).

Collateral references. — 60 C.J.S., Motor Vehicles, § 35.

7 Am. Jur. 2d, Automobiles & Highway Traffic, § 213.

Conflict between statutes and local regulations. 21 ALR 1196, 64 ALR 993, 147 ALR 522.

Rights and duties at intersection of arterial highway and nonfavored highway. 58 ALR 1197, 81 ALR 185.

Right and duty of motorist on through, favored, or arterial street or highway to proceed where lateral view at intersection is obstructed by physical obstacle. 59 ALR2d 1202.

Yield sign: liability for automobile accidents at intersection as affected by reliance upon or disregarding of yield sign or signal. 2 ALR3d 275.

§ 32-5A-114. Vehicles entering highway from private road or roadway.

The driver of a vehicle about to enter or cross a roadway from any place other than another roadway shall yield the right-of-way to all vehicles approaching on the roadway to be entered or crossed. (Acts 1980, No. 80-434, p. 604, § 4-105.)

Commentary

This section amends former section 32-5-112(a) by minor changes in wording but with no substantial alteration.

I. General Consideration.
II. Decisions Under Prior Law.

I. GENERAL CONSIDERATION.

Collateral references. — 60 C.J.S., Motor Vehicles, § 19. 60A C.J.S., Motor Vehicles, §§ 372, 374, 376.

7 Am. Jur. 2d, Automobiles & Highway Traffic, §§ 206, 212.

Right-of-way at street or highway intersections. 21 ALR 974, 37 ALR 493, 47 ALR 595.

Validity of statute or ordinance giving right-of-way in streets or highways to certain classes of vehicles. 38 ALR 24.

Right-of-way at street or highway intersections as dependent upon, or independent of, care or negligence. 89 ALR 838, 136 ALR 1497.

Liability for personal injury or damage resulting from operation of emergency vehicle: Fire. 82 ALR2d 312; Police. 83 ALR2d 383; Ambulance. 84 ALR2d 121.

Yield sign: liability for automobile accidents at intersection as affected by reliance upon or disregard of yield sign or signal. 2 ALR3d 275.

What is a street or highway intersection within traffic rules. 7 ALR3d 1204.

Liability of one fleeing police for injury resulting from collision of police vehicle with another vehicle, person, or object. 51 ALR3d 1226.

II. DECISIONS UNDER PRIOR LAW.

Editor's note. — The cases cited below were decided under similar provisions of prior law.

"Public road" determined by character, not quantum of use. — The designation of a road as a "settlement road" does not necessarily mean it is not also a "public road" as distinguished from a "private road," it being the character rather than the quantum of use that controls, and even though the chief users are a few families having a special need therefor, this does not necessarily stamp it as a "private way." Moore v. Cruit, 238 Ala. 414, 191 So. 252 (1939).

Person entering paved road from minor road, even though such minor road is a public road, does not necessarily have the right-of-way in regard to traffic approaching from his left. Such matter must be deemed a question for the trier of fact under all the evidence as applied to the general law of negligence. Traylor v. Butler, 291 Ala. 560, 284 So. 2d 263 (1973).

Former statute did not require driver to stop his automobile a second time, after once having yielded the right-of-way as required, and if the driver of a vehicle on a through street was not approaching so closely to the intersection as to constitute an immediate hazard when the other driver proceeded into the through highway, the other driver would be favored with the right-of-way after entering the intersection. Wayland Distrib. Co. v. Gay, 287 Ala. 446, 252 So. 2d 414 (1971).

If driver stopped at the entrance to a through highway, and yielded the right-of-way to other vehicles which had entered the intersection from the through highway, or which were approaching so closely on the through highway as to constitute an immediate hazard, although he still was at all times enjoined to exercise due care not to injure others or himself he owed no further statutory duty to stop his automobile in the intersection to allow other vehicles approaching thereto to pass by. Wayland Distrib. Co. v. Gay, 287 Ala. 446, 252 So. 2d 414 (1971).

Negligence and contributory negligence held for jury. — Where bus driver stopped prior to entering through street, but collided in intersection with plaintiff's intestate riding on a motorcycle at a speed of 30 miles per hour in a 25 miles per hour zone, the question as to whether plaintiff's intestate was guilty of contributory negligence which proximately contributed to the collision or whether the collision was due solely to the negligence of the

bus driver was for the jury. Mobile City Lines
v. Hardy, 264 Ala. 247, 86 So. 2d 393 (1956).

§ 32-5A-115. Operation of vehicles on approach of authorized emergency vehicles; signals on emergency vehicles; duty of emergency vehicle driver.

(a) Upon the immediate approach of an authorized emergency vehicle equipped with at least one lighted lamp and audible signal as is required by law, the driver of every other vehicle shall yield the right-of-way and shall immediately drive to a position parallel to, and as close as possible to, the right-hand edge or curb of the roadway clear of any intersection and shall stop and remain in such position until the authorized emergency vehicle has passed, except when otherwise directed by a police officer.

(b) This section shall not operate to relieve the driver of an authorized emergency vehicle from the duty to drive with regard for the safety of all persons using the highways.

(c) Authorized emergency vehicles shall be equipped with at least one lighted lamp exhibiting a colored light as hereinafter provided visible under normal atmospheric conditions from a distance of 500 feet to the front of such vehicle and a siren, exhaust whistle or bell capable of giving an audible signal. The color of the lighted lamp exhibited by police vehicles may be red or blue and the color of the lighted lamp exhibited by fire department and other authorized emergency vehicles, including ambulances, shall be red. No vehicle other than a police vehicle will use a blue light. An amber or yellow light may be installed on any vehicle or class of vehicles designated by the director of public safety, but such light shall serve as a warning or caution light only, and shall not cause other vehicles to yield the right-of-way. This provision shall not operate to relieve the driver of an emergency vehicle from the duty to drive with due regard for the safety of all persons using the highway nor shall it protect the driver of any such vehicle from the consequences of an arbitrary exercise of such right-of-way. (Acts 1980, No. 80-434, p. 604, § 4-106; Acts 1981, No. 81-803, p. 1412, § 1.)

Commentary

Subsection (a) combines former section 32-5-113(a) with the recommended UVC § 11-405(a). Since the former law on emergency signals in Alabama did not conform to the UVC norms, literal compliance at this time is not possible. Subsection (b) is similar to language previously found in the last sentence of former section 32-5-112(b). Subsection (c) is based on the last paragraph of former section 32-5-112(b), and no substantive change has been made.

Failure to turn emergency signals off while stopped at red light. — Summary judgment for ambulance company defendant was proper where plaintiffs were injured when, in attempt to clear path for ambulance, they drove their automobile into intersection against a red light and collided with a truck, since the ambulance operators did not breach their duty of due care by not turning off emergency signals when they came to stop at red light behind plaintiffs' automobile. Tucker v. Pilcher, 531 So. 2d 652 (Ala. 1988).

Cited in Doran v. City of Decatur, 510 So. 2d 813 (Ala. 1987); Doran v. City of Madison, 519 So. 2d 1308 (Ala. 1988).

Collateral references. — 7 Am. Jur. 2d, Automobiles & Highway Traffic, §§ 206, 212.

Use or nonuse of flashing light, siren, or other alarm device as affecting liability arising from accident involving police vehicle. 83 ALR2d 409.

Yield sign: liability for automobile accidents at intersection as affected by reliance upon or disregarding of yield sign or signal. 2 ALR3d 275.

§ 32-5A-116. Highway construction and maintenance.

(a) The driver of a vehicle shall yield the right-of-way to any authorized vehicle or pedestrian actually engaged in work upon a highway within any highway construction or maintenance area indicated by official traffic-control devices.

(b) The driver of a vehicle shall yield the right-of-way to any authorized vehicle obviously and actually engaged in work upon a highway whenever such vehicle displays such flashing lights as may be required or permitted by law or by regulation of the department. (Acts 1980, No. 80-434, p. 604, § 4-107.)

Commentary

There was no counterpart to this provision in previous Alabama law.

Collateral references. — 60 C.J.S., Motor Vehicles, §§ 168-209.

7A Am. Jur. 2d, Automobiles & Highway Traffic, §§ 212-217, 770, 833.

Yield sign: liability for automobile accidents at intersection as affected by reliance upon or disregard of yield sign or signal. 2 ALR3d 275.

ARTICLE 6.

TURNING, STARTING AND STOPPING GENERALLY.

Cross references. — For other provisions as to parking in violation of municipal ordinances, see § 32-5-152.

§ 32-5A-130. Required position and method of turning at intersections.

The driver of a vehicle intending to turn shall do so as follows:

(1) RIGHT TURNS. — Both the approach for a right turn and a right turn shall be made as close as practicable to the right-hand curb or edge of the roadway.

(2) LEFT TURNS. — The driver of a vehicle intending to turn left shall approach the turn in the extreme left-hand lane lawfully available to traffic moving in the direction of travel of such vehicle. Whenever practicable the turn shall be made to the left of the center of the intersection and so as to leave the intersection or other location in the extreme left-hand lane lawfully available to traffic moving in the same direction as such vehicle on the roadway being entered.

(3) The highway department and local authorities in their respective jurisdictions may cause official traffic-control devices to be placed and thereby require and direct that a different course from that specified in this section be traveled by turning vehicles and when such devices are so placed no driver shall turn a vehicle other than as directed and required by such devices. (Acts 1980, No. 80-434, p. 604, § 6-101.)

Commentary

There was a similar corresponding law previously in force, former section 32-5-57. In many aspects the former law and this section are similar, but revision has been made for several reasons. The prior law applied only to turns at intersections, whereas the rules set forth herein are applicable to all turns whether at intersections or elsewhere. The former law had separate provisions for two-way and one-way roadways, and this section represents an attempt to simplify these provisions and make them easier to understand. Also, this section makes use of the terms "traffic-control devices" rather than enumerating them as in the prior law, another simplifying measure. And this section gives the department the power to erect such traffic-control devices, which the earlier statute did not.

As to when noncompliance with statutory provisions is considered wantonness, see Graves v. Wildsmith, 278 Ala. 228, 177 So. 2d 448 (1965) (decided under prior law).

Instruction held erroneous. — Instruction that automobile entering intersection last in point of time must at its peril be conducted, circumstances permitting, so as to allow the other vehicle to safely pass in front, was prejudicially erroneous. Echols v. Vinson, 220 Ala. 229, 124 So. 510 (1929) (decided under prior law).

Collateral references. — 60A C.J.S., Motor Vehicles, § 367(1).

7 Am. Jur. 2d, Automobiles & Highway Traffic, §§ 216-218.

Automobiles: cutting corners as negligence. 6 ALR 321, 115 ALR 1178.

Right of way at street or highway intersections. 21 ALR 974, 37 ALR 493, 47 ALR 595.

Reciprocal duties of drivers of automobiles or other vehicles proceeding in the same direction with respect to turning at intersections. 24 ALR 513, 47 ALR 703, 62 ALR 970, 104 ALR 485.

Right of way at street or highway intersections as dependent upon, or independent of, care or negligence. 89 ALR 838, 136 ALR 1497.

Liability arising from collision between automobile making U-turn and another vehicle. 53 ALR4th 849.

Liability for accident arising from failure of motorist to give signal for left turn at intersection as against motor vehicle proceeding in same direction or intersecting or oncoming motor vehicle. 39 ALR2d 15, 65.

Liability for accident arising from failure of motorist to give signal for left turn between intersections. 39 ALR2d 103.

§ 32-5A-131. Turning on curve or crest of grade prohibited.

(a) The driver of any vehicle shall not turn such vehicle so as to proceed in the opposite direction unless such movement can be made in safety and without interfering with other traffic.

(b) No vehicle shall be turned so as to proceed in the opposite direction upon any curve, or upon the approach to or near the crest of a grade, where such vehicle cannot be seen by the driver of any other vehicle approaching from either direction within 500 feet. (Acts 1980, No. 80-434, p. 604, § 6-102.)

Commentary

Former section 32-5-71 was identical to subsection (b), but there was no prior statute that stated the general principle set forth in subsection (a).

Collateral references. — Duty in operating automobile at curve or on hill. 57 ALR 589.

Parking illegally at or near street corner or intersection as affecting liability for motor vehicle accident. 4 ALR3d 324.

Parked or standing vehicle: liability or re- covery in automobile negligence action as affected by absence or insufficiency of lights on parked or standing vehicle. 61 ALR3d 13.

Automobiles: liability for U-turn collisions. 53 ALR4th 849.

§ 32-5A-132. Starting parked vehicle.

No person shall start a vehicle which is stopped, standing or parked unless and until such movement can be made with reasonable safety. (Acts 1980, No. 80-434, p. 604, § 6-103.)

Commentary

No change is contemplated. This section is identical to former section 32-5-58(a).

I. General Consideration.
II. Decisions Under Prior Law.

I. GENERAL CONSIDERATION.

Collateral references. — 60 C.J.S., Motor Vehicles, § 28(1).

7A Am. Jur. 2d, Automobiles & Highway Traffic, § 282.

Parking illegally at or near street corner or intersection as affecting liability for motor vehicle accident. 4 ALR3d 324.

Parked or standing vehicle: liability or re- covery in automobile negligence action as affected by absence or insufficiency of lights or parked or standing vehicle. 61 ALR3d 13.

II. DECISIONS UNDER PRIOR LAW.

Editor's note. — The cases cited below were decided under similar provisions of prior law.

It was immaterial under former similar statute which vehicle entered intersection first, since it was incumbent upon the driver turning left into the regular course of traffic to make such that the change of direction could be made with reasonable safety. Morris v. Crumpton, 259 Ala. 565, 67 So. 2d 800 (1953).

Violation of former similar statute was negligence as matter of law. Triplett v. Daniel, 255 Ala. 566, 52 So. 2d 184 (1951); Alabama Power Co. v. Sellers, 283 Ala. 137, 214 So. 2d 833 (1968); Giles v. Gardner, 287 Ala. 166, 249 So. 2d 824 (1971).

Proximate cause of accident. — Violation of former similar section by plaintiff or defen- dant was negligence, but was not the basis of a cause of action or defense unless it was a proximate cause of the accident. Winfrey v. Witherspoon's, Inc., 260 Ala. 371, 71 So. 2d 37 (1954).

Evidence sufficient to show turn could not be made with reasonable safety. — See Morris v. Crumpton, 259 Ala. 565, 67 So. 2d 800 (1953).

Submission of count on "wanton injury" to jury held error. — In action for injuries to motorist resulting from collision with truck near intersection when truck driver made left- hand turn without looking in glass to ascertain whether vehicle was immediately following and without signalling his intention, submis- sion of jury count on "wanton injury" was error. Holman v. Brady, 241 Ala. 487, 3 So. 2d 30 (1941).

§ 32-5A-133. Turning movements and required signals.

(a) No person shall turn a vehicle or move right or left upon a roadway unless and until such movement can be made with reasonable safety nor without giving an appropriate signal in the manner hereinafter provided.

(b) A signal of intention to turn right or left when required shall be given continuously during not less than the last 100 feet traveled by the vehicle before turning.

(c) No person shall stop or suddenly decrease the speed of a vehicle without first giving an appropriate signal in the manner provided herein to the driver of any vehicle immediately to the rear when there is opportunity to give such signal.

(d) The signals provided for in section 32-5A-134(b) shall not be flashed on one side only on a disabled vehicle, flashed as a courtesy or "do pass" signal to operators of other vehicles approaching from the rear, nor be flashed on one side only of a parked vehicle except as may be necessary for compliance with this section. (Acts 1980, No. 80-434, p. 604, § 6-104.)

Commentary

Subsection (a) is intended to simplify the previous provision found in former section 32-5-58(b) and also to apply both at intersections and elsewhere. Subsections (b) and (c) are identical to former subsections 32-5-58(c) and 32-5-58(d). However, there was no provision in the prior law similar to that found in subsection (d).

I. General Consideration.
II. Decisions Under Prior Law.

I. GENERAL CONSIDERATION.

Cited in Creel v. Brown, 508 So. 2d 684 (Ala. 1987).

Collateral references. — 60 C.J.S., Motor Vehicles, § 35. 60A C.J.S., Motor Vehicles, §§ 300, 303(2), 365-367(7).

7 Am. Jur. 2d, Automobiles & Highway Traffic, §§ 217, 227-229.

Stopping without proper warning. 24 ALR 508, 47 ALR 703, 62 ALR 970, 104 ALR 485.

Sudden stop or slowing of motor vehicle as negligence. 29 ALR2d 5.

Liability for accident arising from motorist's failure to give signal for right turn. 38 ALR2d 143.

Duty and liability as to signalling following driver to pass or giving him warning of approaching danger. 48 ALR2d 252.

Liability for injury occasioned by backing of motor vehicle in or from public street or highway. 63 ALR2d 5, 108, 184.

Intersection: duty and liability with respect to giving audible signal at intersection. 21 ALR3d 268.

II. DECISIONS UNDER PRIOR LAW.

Editor's note. — Cases cited below were decided under similar provisions of prior law.

Intent of former similar section was to provide that signal had to be given if it appeared that the movement or operation of another's care might reasonably be affected by the stopping, but the section contained no positive rule requiring that the signal always be given. Triplett v. Daniel, 255 Ala. 566, 52 So. 2d 184 (1951).

Drivers of motor vehicles proceeding in line have reciprocal duties: the driver of the overtaken vehicle has the duty before turning into another lane to exercise due care that it is safe to do so; the driver of the overtaking vehicle has the duty of giving audible warning, unless in a business district, of his desire to pass. Socier v. Woodard, 264 Ala. 514, 88 So. 2d 783 (1956).

No divisible duty to determine ability to stop as part of turn. — While the turn signals prescribed by the legislature do not conclusively establish the duties of care required of a driver, they support the conclusion that there is no divisible duty requiring a driver intending to make a left turn to determine that he can stop with safety as part of the turning maneuver, if he has complied with the requirement that he ascertain that a left turn can be made with reasonable safety. Willingham v. Trailways, Inc., 697 F.2d 994 (11th Cir. 1983).

As to extra precaution in making a left-hand turn between intersections, see Tyler v. Drennen, 255 Ala. 377, 51 So. 2d 516 (1951).

Failure to give signal as negligence. — Truck driver, turning left at street intersection without giving hand signal to driver of automobile following truck, was guilty of simple negligence in failing to comply with former similar section. Greer v. Marriott, 27 Ala. App. 108, 167 So. 597, cert. denied, 232 Ala. 194, 167 So. 599 (1936).

Which would bar recovery if proximate cause of collision. — Plaintiff motorist's failure to give statutory signal of intention to stop in public street held proximate cause of collision and resulting damage which barred a recovery by him. Britt v. Daniel, 230 Ala. 79, 159 So. 684 (1935).

Violation of former similar statute by plaintiff or defendant was negligence, but would not be the basis of a cause of action or defense unless it was a proximate cause of the accident. The negligence of plaintiff which was a proximate contributing cause of the collision was a good defense, although defendant was also guilty of primary negligence which was a proximate contributing cause too. When both parties were guilty of simple negligence and each was a proximate contributing cause without more, neither could recover damages from the other. But if one was guilty of negligence after discovery of the danger of the other in respect to causing the accident and when such subsequent negligence was a proximate contributing cause, he was liable for the damage. In all such cases the questions of proximate cause and subsequent negligence were for the decision of the jury. Alabama Power Co. v. Sellers, 283 Ala. 137, 214 So. 2d 833 (1968).

Statutory violation not actionable unless proximate cause of accident. — Violation of turn signal statute is negligence; however such a breach is not actionable unless it was proximate cause of an accident. Cox v. Miller, 361 So. 2d 1044 (Ala. 1978).

Proximate cause a jury question. — Whether or not undisputed violation of statute was proximate cause of injury is question for jury. Triplett v. Daniel, 255 Ala. 566, 52 So. 2d 184 (1951); Winfrey v. Witherspoon's, Inc., 260 Ala. 371, 71 So. 2d 37 (1954); Alabama Power Co. v. Sellers, 283 Ala. 137, 214 So. 2d 833 (1968); Giles v. Gardner, 287 Ala. 166, 249 So. 2d 824 (1971).

A jury question was presented as to whether defendant was guilty of wantonness when he undertook to move from the left lane to the right lane of traffic without first determining he could do so with reasonable safety. Thrasher v. Darnell, 275 Ala. 570, 156 So. 2d 922 (1963).

No recovery when parties in pari delicto. — Truck driver, turning left at street intersection without giving hand signal to driver of automobile following truck, and latter driver, undertaking to pass truck within intersection, being guilty of violations proximately contributing to accident, stood in pari delicto, so as to bar recovery by either party in action for resulting damage to automobile. Greer v. Marriott, 27 Ala. App. 108, 167 So. 597, cert. denied, 232 Ala. 194, 167 So. 599 (1936).

As to applicability of principles of law relating to contributory negligence of children where a child violated former similar section and such violation was a proximate cause of injury, see Alabama Power Co. v. Bowers, 252 Ala. 49, 39 So. 2d 402 (1949).

As to reading of former similar section to jury in negligence case, see Pruett v. Marshall, 283 F.2d 436 (5th Cir. 1960).

§ 32-5A-134. Signals by hand and arm or signal lamps.

(a) Any stop or turn signal when required herein shall be given either by means of the hand and arm or by signal lamps, except as otherwise provided in subsection (b).

(b) Any motor vehicle in use on a highway shall be equipped with, and the required signal shall be given by, signal lamps when the distance from the center of the top of the steering post to the left outside limit of the body, cab or load of such motor vehicle exceeds 24 inches, or when the distance from the center of the top of the steering post to the rear limit of the body or load thereof exceeds 14 feet. The latter measurement shall apply to any single vehicle, also to any combination of vehicles. (Acts 1980, No. 80-434, p. 604, § 6-105.)

Commentary

Subsection (a) is similar to the first phrase of former section 32-5-58(e), and no change in substance has been made. However, subsection (b) imposes a new and broader requirement than the earlier statute which mandated signal lamps only when the vehicle was constructed or loaded so that hand and arm signals would not be visible. In view of the fact that nearly all vehicles do have signal lamps today, amendment of the prior law was made.

Collateral references. — 60A Motor vehicles, §§ 288, 301, 303, 334, 344, 354.

7A Am. Jur. 2d, Automobiles & Highway Traffic, §§ 204, 232-235, 256-259.

Intersection: duty and liability with respect to giving audible signal at intersection. 21 ALR3d 268.

§ 32-5A-135. Method of giving hand and arm signals.

All signals herein required given by hand and arm shall be given from the left side of the vehicle in the following manner and such signals shall indicate as follows:

(1) LEFT TURN. — Hand and arm extended horizontally.

(2) RIGHT TURN. — Hand and arm extended upward.

(3) STOP OR DECREASE SPEED. — Hand and arm extended downward. (Acts 1980, No. 80-434, p. 604, § 6-106.)

Commentary

This section is virtually identical to the prior statute, section 32-5-58(f).

Collateral references. — 60A Motor Vehicles, §§ 303(3), (4), 354, 367(1), (2).

7A Am. Jur. 2d, Automobiles & Highway Traffic, §§ 204, 232-235, 256-259.

Intersection: duty and liability with respect

to giving audible signal at intersection. 21 ALR3d 268.

Pedestrian: duty and liability with respect to giving audible signal upon approaching pedestrian. 24 ALR3d 183.

§ 32-5A-136. Stopping, standing or parking outside of business or residence districts.

(a) Outside a business or residence district no person shall stop, park or leave standing any vehicle, whether attended or unattended, upon the roadway when it is practicable to stop, park or so leave such vehicle off the roadway, but in every event an unobstructed width of the highway opposite a standing vehicle shall be left for the free passage of other vehicles and a clear view of such stopped vehicle shall be available from a distance of 200 feet in each direction upon such highway.

(b) This section, sections 32-5A-137 and 32-5A-138 shall not apply to the driver of any vehicle which is disabled while on the paved or main-traveled portion of a highway in such manner and to such extent that it is impossible to avoid stopping and temporarily leaving such disabled vehicle in such position. And the provisions of this section, sections 32-5A-137 and 32-5A-138 shall not apply to any vehicle nor to the driver of any vehicle engaged in the business of carrying passengers for hire and operating over a fixed route and between regular termini operating under the authority of the interstate commerce commission of the United States or under authority of the Alabama public service commission or any federal, state or municipal authority while stopped on the right-hand side of the highway to pick up or discharge passengers nor to any vehicle nor to the driver thereof engaged in the official delivery of the United States mail when stopped on the right-hand side of the highway for the purpose of picking up or delivering mail, if a clear view of the vehicle may be obtained from a distance of 300 feet in each direction upon such highway. Nothing herein shall be construed to exempt any vehicle from the provisions of section 32-5-244 and said provisions shall remain applicable to vehicles transporting the United States mail, anything in the section to the contrary notwithstanding. (Acts 1980, No. 80-434, p. 604, § 10-101.)

Commentary

This section replaces former section 32-5-150. Subsection (a) does not represent any substantial change except that the prior law specified a width of 15 feet for the passage of other vehicles whereas this subsection requires a sufficient width, whatever that might be. Subsection (b) is carried over from section 32-5-150(c) with only minor changes in wording. The final two sentences of this subsection do not appear in the Uniform Vehicle Code, but it was considered desirable to continue their provision in force.

I. General Consideration.
II. Decisions Under Prior Law.

I. GENERAL CONSIDERATION.

Police officer authorized to move illegally parked vehicle impeding traffic. — Where defendant's vehicle was parked illegally on the shoulder of a public highway during "rush hour" with the driver's door opened partially out in the roadway obstructing traffic, and the vehicle was impeding traffic and posing a danger to other traffic, as well as to defendant and his passenger, who were asleep, any police officer, as defined by § 32-1-1.1(45), was authorized to move such vehicle, or require the driver or other person in charge of the vehicle to move it to a position off the paved or main-traveled part of such highway. Martin v. State, 529 So. 2d 1032 (Ala. Crim. App. 1988).

Collateral references. — 60A C.J.S., Motor Vehicles, § 329. 61 C.J.S., Motor Vehicles, § 493.1. 61A C.J.S., Motor Vehicles, § 684.

7 Am. Jur. 2d, Automobiles & Highway Traffic, §§ 230-232.

Conflict between statutes and local regulations. 21 ALR 1209, 64 ALR 993, 147 ALR 522.

Parking at improper place as affecting liability for automobile accident. 73 ALR 1074.

Stopping vehicle on traveled portion of highway as affecting responsibility for collision between vehicles. 131 ALR 562.

Liability of motorbus carrier for death of or injury to discharged passenger struck by vehicle not within its control. 145 ALR 1206.

When is a motor vehicle "disabled," or the like, within exception to statute regulating parking or stopping. 15 ALR2d 909.

Duties and liabilities between owners or drivers of parked or parking vehicles. 25 ALR2d 1224.

Sudden or unsignalled stop or slowing of motor vehicle as negligence. 29 ALR2d 5.

Liability for injury or damage growing out of pulling out of parked motor vehicle. 29 ALR2d 107.

Parking illegally at or near street corner or intersection as affecting liability for motor vehicle accident. 4 ALR3d 324.

Applicability of last clear chance doctrine to collision between moving and stalled, parked or standing motor vehicle. 34 ALR3d 570.

Parked or standing vehicle: liability or recovery in automobile negligence action as affected by absence or insufficiency of lights on parked or standing vehicle. 61 ALR3d 13.

II. DECISIONS UNDER PRIOR LAW.

Editor's note. — The cases cited below were decided under similar provisions of prior law.

"Park." — To "park" means something more than a mere temporary or momentary stoppage on the road for a necessary purpose. Deamer v. Evans, 278 Ala. 35, 175 So. 2d 466 (1965).

"Parking," with reference to motor vehicles, is a term used to mean the permitting of such vehicles to remain standing on a public highway or street; the voluntary act of leaving a vehicle on the highway when not in use. Deamer v. Evans, 278 Ala. 35, 175 So. 2d 466 (1965).

Vehicle to be left off paved portion if practicable. — Provision of former section requiring parked vehicle to be in clear view, and to leave at least 15 feet upon traveled portion of highway free for other vehicle, did not strike out requirement that vehicle had to be left off the paved portion, if practicable. Winn v. Cadahy Packing Co., 241 Ala. 581, 4 So. 2d 135 (1941); Campbell v. Jackson, 257 Ala. 618, 60 So. 2d 252 (1952).

And proof of parking thereon showed negligence. — Proof that vehicle was stopped or parked on the improved portion of highway, outside of a residence or business district, when it was practicable to have left the vehicle off that portion, was proof of negligence. Campbell v. Jackson, 257 Ala. 618, 60 So. 2d 252 (1952).

To authorize stopping temporarily upon highway under former similar section, stop had to be for a necessary purpose and under conditions rendering it impossible to avoid leaving vehicle on traveled portion of highway or without 15 feet clearance. Capital Motor Lines v. Gillette, 235 Ala. 157, 177 So. 881 (1937).

Momentary stopping for reasonable purpose. — The provisions of former section were not intended to prohibit a momentary stoppage by a motorist on the paved portion of the highway for a normal and reasonable purpose, such as to permit oncoming traffic to pass where the lane of travel in which the motorist had been correctly proceeding was blocked through no fault of his. Deamer v. Evans, 278 Ala. 35, 175 So. 2d 466 (1965); Yelder v. State, 44 Ala. App. 18, 200 So. 2d 659 (1967).

Applicability of statute in cases of blow-outs or other trouble. — Former similar section regulating stopping on highways manifested intent to conserve life and limb by keeping highway open and free of automobiles standing on the pavement, or, at all events, an open zone of 15 feet, and had to be complied with, if reasonably possible, even in case of a blowout or other trouble necessitating temporary stop. Capital Motor Lines v. Gillette, 235 Ala. 157, 177 So. 881 (1937).

Motorist, compelled to stop on highway because of defective condition of automobile, must not leave it standing on main traveled portion of highway, but must get it onto shoulder or side thereof, where he may leave it, if there is clear, unobstructed width of at least 15 feet on main traveled portion of highway opposite vehicle and a clear view thereof for 200 feet in each direction on highway. Brown v. Ace Motor Co., 30 Ala. App. 479, 8 So. 2d 585, cert. denied, 243 Ala. 92, 8 So. 2d 588 (1942).

Scraping frost from windshield. — A car stopped for the purpose of scraping ice or frost from the windshield is not "disabled." Yarbrough v. Hovis, 277 Ala. 516, 172 So. 2d 782 (1965).

Violation not excused because driver at wheel. — Fact that driver is within automobile and at the wheel was no excuse for violation of former similar section. Capital Motor Lines v. Gillette, 235 Ala. 157, 177 So. 881 (1937).

As to allegation in complaint that it was practicable to park off traveled portion, see McBride v. Baggett Transp. Co., 250 Ala. 488, 35 So. 2d 101 (1948).

As to pleading of exception by defendant, see McBride v. Baggett Transp. Co., 250 Ala. 488, 35 So. 2d 101 (1948).

Jury questions. — In action against truck owner for injuries in collision of automobile with parked truck at night, evidence made issue of contributory negligence a jury question. Winn v. Cudahy Packing Co., 241 Ala. 581, 4 So. 2d 135 (1941).

Instruction held improper. — In action against motor carrier and others for passenger's death in bus which was struck by truck while parked on highway, requested instruction that driver of an automobile who finds highway obstructed may stop his automobile on right side of highway for reasonable time until highway is open for him to proceed was properly refused as ignoring duty to keep an open zone of 15 feet for approach of other automobiles. Capital Motor Lines v. Loring, 238 Ala. 260, 189 So. 897 (1939).

In action for injuries sustained in collision between automobile and parked bus, defendant's charge ignoring former similar section on parking was held properly refused. Chambers v. Cox, 222 Ala. 1, 130 So. 416 (1930).

In action against truck owner for injuries in collision of automobile with parked truck, wherein there was evidence that truck could have been parked clear of the pavement, instruction that former similar statute did not prohibit parking if proper lights were burning, unobstructed width of not less than 15 feet was left upon main traveled portion and clear view of vehicle might be obtained was erroneous, as invading the province of the jury. Winn v. Cudahy Packing Co., 241 Ala. 581, 4 So. 2d 135 (1941).

Recovery on theory of concurring negligence. — In passenger's action against bus owner for injuries sustained in collision between bus and truck, when bus driver stopped on highway to see whether he could render assistance to victims of another accident, evidence authorized recovery on theory of concurring negligence of bus driver and truck driver, as against contention that truck driver's negligence was an independent, intervening and efficient cause. Capital Motor Lines v. Gillette, 235 Ala. 157, 177 So. 881 (1937).

§ 32-5A-137. Stopping, standing or parking prohibited in specified places.

(a) Except when necessary to avoid conflict with other traffic, or in compliance with law or the directions of a police officer or official traffic-control device, no person shall:

(1) Stop, stand or park a vehicle:

a. On the roadway side of any vehicle stopped or parked at the edge or curb of a street;

b. On a sidewalk;

c. Within an intersection;

d. On a crosswalk;

e. Between a safety zone and the adjacent curb or within 30 feet of points on the curb immediately opposite the ends of a safety zone, unless a different length is indicated by signs or markings;

f. Alongside or opposite any street excavation or obstruction when stopping, standing or parking would obstruct traffic;

g. Upon any bridge or other elevated structure, upon a highway or within a highway tunnel;

h. On any railroad tracks;

i. At any place where official signs prohibit stopping.

(2) Stand or park a vehicle, whether occupied or not, except momentarily to pick up or discharge a passenger or passengers:

a. In front of a public or private driveway;

b. Within 15 feet of a fire hydrant;

c. Within 20 feet of a crosswalk at an intersection;

d. Within 30 feet upon the approach to any flashing signal, stop sign, yield sign or traffic-control signal located at the side of a roadway;

e. Within 20 feet of the driveway entrance to any fire station and on the side of a street opposite the entrance to any fire station within 75 feet of said entrance (when properly signposted);

f. At any place where official signs prohibit standing.

(3) Park a vehicle, whether occupied or not, except temporarily for the purpose of and while actually engaged in loading or unloading merchandise or passengers:

a. Within 50 feet of the nearest rail or a railroad crossing;

b. At any place where official signs prohibit parking.

(b) No person shall move a vehicle not lawfully under his control into any such prohibited area or away from a curb such a distance as is unlawful. (Acts 1980, No. 80-434, p. 604, § 10-103.)

Commentary

This section revises section 32-5-151. Subsection (a) covers all of the items listed in the prior statute, but changes the previous Alabama law by distinguishing among the kinds of stoppings or standings (paragraphs (1), (2) and (3)). Subsection (b) is unchanged from the former statute.

Violation of statute held not proximate cause of accident. — Where motorist, in alighting from automobile, fell into storm sewer allegedly improperly covered, act of stopping car allegedly in forbidden proximity to fire hydrant or within 25 feet from intersection of curb lines, in violation of city ordinance and this statute prior to amendment, held not proximate cause of injury; hence charges based on ordinance violation were properly refused as misleading and abstract. In such circumstances the city was not entitled to general affirmative charge. City of Birmingham v. Martin, 228 Ala. 318, 153 So. 235 (1934) (decided under former § 32-5-131).

Argument that defendant town's enforcement of section would have prevented accident without merit. — Plaintiffs' argument that had defendant town enforced the rules of the road, which prevent one from parking too near stop signs, the accident would have been prevented, falls of its own weight.

Nichols v. Town of Mt. Vernon, 504 So. 2d 732 (Ala. 1987).

Collateral references. — 61A C.J.S., Motor Vehicles, § 714(1).

7 Am. Jur. 2d, Automobiles & Highway Traffic, §§ 230-241.

Abutting owner's right to control cab stands or parking in street. 33 ALR 355.

Validity of automobile parking regulations. 72 ALR 229, 108 ALR 1152, 130 ALR 316.

Parking at improper place as affecting liability for automobile accident. 73 ALR 1074.

Validity of regulations excluding or limiting automobile traffic in certain streets. 121 ALR 573.

Parking illegally at or near street corner or intersection as affecting liability for motor vehicle accident. 4 ALR3d 324.

Parked or standing vehicle: liability or recovery in automobile negligence action as affected by absence or insufficiency of lights on parked or standing vehicle. 61 ALR3d 13.

§ 32-5A-138. Additional parking regulations.

(a) Except as otherwise provided in this section, every vehicle stopped or parked upon a two-way roadway shall be so stopped or parked with the right-hand wheels parallel to and within 18 inches of the right-hand curb or edge of the roadway.

(b) Except when otherwise provided by local ordinance, every vehicle stopped or parked upon a one-way roadway shall be so stopped or parked parallel to the curb or edge of the roadway, in the direction of authorized traffic movement, with its right-hand wheels within 18 inches of the right-hand curb or edge of the roadway, or its left-hand wheels within 18 inches of the left-hand curb or edge of the roadway.

(c) Local authorities may by ordinance permit angle parking on any roadway, except that angle parking shall not be permitted on any federal-aid or state highway unless the highway department has determined by regulation that the roadway is of sufficient width to permit angle parking without interfering with the free movement of traffic.

(d) The highway department with respect to highways under its jurisdiction may place signs prohibiting or restricting the stopping, standing or parking of vehicles on any highway where in its opinion, as evidenced by regulation, such stopping, standing or parking is dangerous to those using the highway or where the stopping, standing or parking of vehicles would unduly interfere with the free movement of traffic thereon. Such signs shall be official signs and no person shall stop, stand or park any vehicle in violation of the restrictions stated on such signs. (Acts 1980, No. 80-434, p. 604, § 10-104.)

Commentary

This section replaces section 32-5-154, which was substantially similar. Subsections (a) and (b) are different from the prior law only in phraseology, and the final two subsections are unchanged from the prior statute, except for the requirement that determinations of the highway department be evidenced by resolutions or orders entered in its minutes.

Collateral references. — 60 C.J.S., Motor Vehicles, §§ 28(1)-28(9). 60A C.J.S., Motor Vehicles, §§ 329-338(4).

7 Am. Jur. 2d, Automobiles & Highway Traffic, §§ 230-241.

Validity of automobile parking regulations. 72 ALR 229, 108 ALR 1152, 130 ALR 316.

Parking at improper place as affecting liability for automobile accident. 73 ALR 1074.

Parking illegally at or near street corner or intersection as affecting liability for motor vehicle accident. 4 ALR3d 324.

§ 32-5A-139. Officers authorized to remove vehicles.

(a) Whenever any police officer finds a vehicle standing upon a highway in violation of any of the provisions of section 32-5A-136 such officer is hereby authorized to move such vehicle, or require the driver or other person in charge of the vehicle to move the same, to a position off the paved or main-traveled part of such highway.

(b) Any police officer is hereby authorized to remove or cause to be removed to a place of safety any unattended vehicle illegally left standing upon any highway, bridge, causeway, or in any tunnel, in such position or under such circumstances as to obstruct the normal movement of traffic.

(c) Any police officer is hereby authorized to remove or cause to be removed to the nearest garage or other place of safety any vehicle found upon a highway when:

(1) Report has been made that such vehicle has been stolen or taken without the consent of its owner;

(2) The person or persons in charge of such vehicle are unable to provide for its custody or removal;

(3) When the person driving or in control of such vehicle is arrested for an alleged offense for which the officer is required by law to take the person arrested before a proper magistrate without unnecessary delay; or

(4) When a vehicle has been left unattended for 24 hours or more on or adjacent to any public highway and it is determined by the police officer that the vehicle constitutes a hazard to traffic upon the highway. (Acts 1980, No. 80-434, p. 604, § 10-102.)

Commentary

Subsection (a) is substantially identical to former section 32-5-150(b). However, the prior law did not contain provisions comparable to subsections (b) or (c). Subdivision (c)(4) modifies section 32-13-2(a), but the remainder of that statute is unchanged.

The police have an inherent authority to impound vehicles, aside from statutory authority, based on what is called the community caretaking function. That function is explained as follows: In the interests of public safety, automobiles are frequently taken into police custody. To permit the uninterrupted flow of traffic and in some circumstances to preserve evidence, disabled or damaged vehicles will often be removed from the highways or streets at the behest of police engaged solely in caretaking and traffic-control activities. Police will also frequently remove and impound automobiles which violate parking ordinances and which thereby jeopardize both the public safety and the efficient movement of vehicular traffic. The authority of police to seize and remove from the streets vehicles impeding traffic or threatening public safety and convenience is beyond challenge. Morton v. State, 452 So. 2d 1361 (Ala. Crim. App. 1984).

Impoundment of a vehicle is inappropriate when reasonable alternatives exist. To permit a subsequent warrantless inventory search to be accomplished thereby would be improper. Morton v. State, 452 So. 2d 1361 (Ala. Crim. App. 1984).

Where the circumstances that bring the automobile to the attention of the police in the first place are such that the driver, even though arrested is able to make his or her own arrangements for the custody of the vehicle, or if the vehicle can be parked and locked without obstructing traffic or endangering the public, the police should permit the action to be taken rather than impound the car against the will of the driver and then search it. Just cause to arrest the driver is not, alone, enough; there must also be reasonable cause to take his vehicle into custody. Morton v. State, 452 So. 2d 1361 (Ala. Crim. App. 1984).

When a friend or relative is available to move a vehicle for defendant just arrested for a traffic charge, the arresting officer is not justified in calling for an impoundment absent other circumstances. Morton v. State, 452 So. 2d 1361 (Ala. Crim. App. 1984).

Police were not justified in impounding vehicle under color of authority of this section where such car was legally parked upon private property, creating no safety risk to the public, it was not stolen and the driver was able to provide for its custody. Morton v. State, 452 So. 2d 1361 (Ala. Crim. App. 1984).

Police officer authorized to move illegally parked vehicle impeding traffic. — Where defendant's vehicle was parked illegally on the shoulder of a public highway during "rush hour" with the driver's door opened partially out in the roadway obstructing traffic, and the vehicle was impeding traffic and posing a danger to other traffic, as well as to defendant and his passenger, who were asleep, any police officer, as defined by § 32-1-1.1(45), was authorized to move such vehicle, or require the driver or other person in charge of the vehicle to move it to a position off the paved or main-traveled part of such highway. Martin v. State, 529 So. 2d 1032 (Ala. Crim. App. 1988).

Authority of officer finding vehicle on highway. — Former similar statute did not give a peace officer who found a vehicle standing upon a highway in violation thereof the right to send off for a garageman, or to employ wrecker service, to pull the car to some private garage, but he was only authorized to move such vehicle to a position permitted under the statute or to require the driver or person in charge of such vehicle to move the same to such position. Brown v. Ace Motor Co., 30 Ala. App. 479, 8 So. 2d 585, cert. denied, 243 Ala. 92, 8 So. 2d 588 (1942) (decided under prior law).

Vehicle lawfully impounded where defendant stopped and arrested for felony. — Where defendant was stopped on a public roadway, arrested on a felony warrant, and placed under custodial arrest, the vehicle which he was driving was lawfully impounded, pursuant to subdivision (c)(3) of this section, and an inventory search of the vehicle was justified. Ringer v. State, 489 So. 2d 646 (Ala. Crim. App. 1986).

Argument that defendant town's enforcement of section would have prevented accident without merit. — Plaintiffs' argument that had defendant town enforced the rules of the road, which prevent one from parking too near stop signs, the accident would have been prevented, falls of its own weight. Nichols v. Town of Mt. Vernon, 504 So. 2d 732 (Ala. 1987).

Cited in McElroy v. State, 469 So. 2d 1337 (Ala. Crim. App. 1985).

ARTICLE 7.

SPECIAL STOPS REQUIRED.

§ 32-5A-150. Obedience to signal indicating approach of train.

(a) Whenever any person driving a vehicle approaches a railroad grade crossing under any of the circumstances stated in this section, the driver of such vehicle shall stop within 50 feet but not less than 15 feet from the nearest rail of such railroad, and shall not proceed until he can do so safely. The foregoing requirements shall apply when:

(1) A clearly visible electric or mechanical signal device gives warning of the immediate approach of a railroad train;

(2) A crossing gate is lowered or when a human flagman gives or continues to give a signal of the approach or passage of a railroad train;

(3) A railroad train approaching within approximately 1,500 feet of the highway crossing emits a signal audible from such distance and such railroad train, by reason of its speed or nearness to such crossing, is an immediate hazard;

(4) An approaching railroad train is plainly visible and is in hazardous proximity to such crossing.

(b) No person shall drive any vehicle through, around or under any crossing gate or barrier at a railroad crossing while such gate or barrier is closed or is being opened or closed. (Acts 1980, No. 80-434, p. 604, § 7-101.)

Commentary

The former comparable Alabama statute was section 32-5-52(b). It was similar to subsection (a), having been based upon the 1926 version of the UVC. This subsection, unlike the previous statute, clearly indicates that a stop is required if an approaching train is plainly visible and nearby in the absence of some further signal. The previous law also failed to indicate the distance within which such stops should be made. There was no prior counterpart in the Alabama Code to subsection (b).

Former similar statute concerned only with railroad crossings and their dangers. In action for death of bicyclist resulting from collision with an oncoming truck, refusal of a requested charge based on the theory of failure of truck driver to observe a railroad stop sign set up pursuant to statute was not error, since such statute was only concerned with railroad crossing and its dangers and was not intended for the benefit of bicyclist. Francis v. Imperial San. Laundry & Dry Cleaning Co., 241 Ala. 327, 2 So. 2d 388 (1941).

Admissibility of evidence of subsequent repairs or improvements. — Evidence of subsequent repairs or improvements by a defendant altering the scene of an accident may not be admitted in evidence to show negligence on the part of the defendant. Louisville &

N.R.R. v. Williams, 370 F.2d 839 (5th Cir. 1966) (decided under prior law).

The grounds for excluding evidence of repairs made after an accident are not applicable where the person who allegedly made the repairs is not a party to the action. Hence, where the state highway department made subsequent repairs or improvements at a crossing, but was not a party to the action which was brought against the railroad, and the jury was informed, both at the time of admission of such evidence and in the court's final charge, that the evidence was to be considered solely as circumstantial evidence of whether the crossing was a dangerous or hazardous crossing, it was held that the district court had a broad discretion in determining whether the probative value of the evidence was outweighed by the probability that it would be overemphasized by the jury. Louisville & N.R.R. v. Williams, 370 F.2d 839 (5th Cir. 1966) (decided under prior law).

Collateral references. — 60 C.J.S., Motor Vehicles, § 192.

Applicability of statute relating to crossing signals or other precautions at approach to crossing, to car or engine driven on rails by motor power other than steam. 73 ALR 105.

Responsibility for accident as affected by absence, improper location, or insufficiency of signs, warning approaching travelers of presence of crossing. 93 ALR 218.

Liability of municipality or other governmental unit for failure to cut weeds, brush, or other vegetation obstructing view or obscuring view at railroad crossing or at street or highway intersection. 42 ALR2d 817.

Failure of signaling device at crossing to operate, as affecting railroad company's liability. 90 ALR2d 350.

§ 32-5A-151. Certain vehicles must stop at all railroad grade crossings; exceptions.

(a) Except as provided in subsection (b), the driver of any vehicle described in regulations issued pursuant to subsection (c), before crossing at grade any track or tracks of a railroad, shall stop such vehicle within 50 feet but not less than 15 feet from the nearest rail of such railroad and while so stopped shall listen and look in both directions along such track for any approaching train, and for signals indicating the approach of a train and shall not proceed until he can do so safely. After stopping as required herein and upon proceeding when it is safe to do so the driver of any said vehicle shall cross only in such gear of the vehicle that there will be no necessity for manually changing gears while traversing such crossing and the driver shall not manually shift gears while crossing the track or tracks. Nothing contained in this section is intended to abrogate or modify the present Alabama doctrine of "stop, look and listen" obtaining in the courts of Alabama.

(b) This section shall not apply at:

(1) Any railroad grade crossing at which traffic is controlled by a police officer or human flagman;

(2) Any railroad grade crossing at which traffic is regulated by a traffic-control signal;

(3) Any railroad grade crossing protected by crossing gates or any alternately flashing light signal intended to give warning of the approach of a railroad train;

(4) Any railroad grade crossing at which an official traffic control device gives notice that the stopping requirement imposed by this section does not apply.

(c) The highway director shall adopt such regulations as may be necessary describing the vehicles which must comply with the stopping requirements of this section. In formulating such regulations the highway director shall give consideration to the number of passengers carried by the vehicle and the hazardous nature of any substance carried by the vehicle in determining whether such vehicle shall be required to stop. Such regulations shall correlate with and so far as possible conform to the most recent regulation of the United States department of transportation. (Acts 1980, No. 80-434, p. 604, § 7-102.)

Commentary

The stopping distance of within 50 feet of the crossing but not less than 15 feet from the closest rail of the crossing comes from the UVC; there is no mention of these limits either in Alabama case law or the old section 32-5-52.

This section combines the requirements that the driver stop, look and listen at the crossing with the above. The Alabama doctrine of "stop, look and listen" originated in the courts but was expressly preserved by section 32-5-52. (This section also states that nothing contained within it is intended to modify or change the "stop, look and listen" doctrine.)

The requirement that the driver of a manually shifted car not change gears while crossing the tracks is new and not part of the UVC or from the present statute.

The exceptions to the section on stopping and stopping distances are also new without any origins in the present statute or in case law.

While the UVC and present Alabama law allows the highway department to designate particularly dangerous grade crossings, neither serves as a basis for subsection (c). Subsection (c) empowers the department to specify stopping requirements for certain vehicles, dependent upon their nature and the number of passengers carried. This is new, as it relates to the regulation of railroad crossings.

Ordinarily, in Alabama it is contributory negligence, as matter of law, for motorist to fail to stop, look and listen before crossing a railroad. Louisville & N.R.R. v. Williams, 370 F.2d 839 (5th Cir. 1966) (decided under prior law).

Contributory negligence as jury ques- tion. — Under all of the facts and circumstances of the case, if the jury finds that the crossing was an unusually dangerous one, it is for the jury to decide whether the plaintiff driver was guilty of contributory negligence. Louisville & N.R.R. v. Williams, 370 F.2d 839 (5th Cir. 1966) (decided under prior law).

§ 32-5A-152. Moving heavy equipment at railroad grade crossings.

(a) No person shall operate or move any crawler-type tractor, steam shovel, derrick, roller or any equipment or structure having a normal operating speed of 10 or less miles per hour or a vertical body or load clearance of less than one-half inch per foot of the distance between any two adjacent axles or in any event of less than nine inches, measured above the level surface of a roadway, upon or across any tracks at a railroad grade crossing without first complying with this section.

(b) Before making any such crossing the person operating or moving any such vehicle or equipment shall first stop the same not less than 15 feet nor more than 50 feet from the nearest rail of such railroad and while so stopped shall listen and look in both directions along such track for any approaching train and for signals indicating the approach of a train, and shall not proceed until the crossing can be made safely.

(c) No such crossing shall be made when warning is given by automatic signal or crossing gates or a flagman or otherwise of the immediate approach of a railroad train or car. If a flagman is provided by the railroad, movement over the crossing shall be under his direction. (Acts 1980, No. 80-434, p. 604, § 7-103.)

Commentary

This section is identical to the previous statute, section 32-5-53.

§ 32-5A-153. Emerging from alley, driveway or building.

The driver of a vehicle emerging from an alley, building, private road or driveway within a business or residence district shall stop such vehicle immediately prior to driving onto a sidewalk or onto the sidewalk area extending across such alley, building entrance, road or driveway, or in the event there is no sidewalk area, shall stop at the point nearest the street to be entered where the driver has a view of approaching traffic thereon. (Acts 1980, No. 80-434, p. 604, § 7-105.)

Commentary

This section (which is closely related to section 32-5A-113) is a slight modification of former section 32-5-115 and serves to simplify that statute.

Collateral references. — 60A C.J.S., Motor Vehicles, § 359(1).

§ 32-5A-154. Overtaking and passing school bus or church bus.

(a) The driver of a vehicle upon meeting or overtaking from either direction any school bus which has stopped on the highway for the purpose of receiving or discharging any school children or any church bus which has stopped for the purpose of receiving or discharging passengers shall stop the vehicle before reaching such school or church bus when there is in operation on said school or church bus a visual signal as specified in section 32-5A-155 and said driver shall not proceed until such school or church bus resumes motion or is signaled by the school or church bus driver to proceed or the visual signals are no longer actuated.

(b) Every bus used for the transportation of school children shall bear upon the front and rear thereof plainly visible signs containing the words "school bus" in letters not less than eight inches in height, and in addition shall be equipped with visual signs meeting the requirements of section 32-5A-155, which shall be actuated by the driver of said school bus whenever but only whenever such vehicle is stopped for the purpose of receiving or discharging school children.

(c) Every bus used for the transportation of persons to or from church shall bear upon the front and rear thereof plainly visible signs containing the words "church bus" in letters not less than eight inches in height, and in addition may be equipped with visual signs meeting the requirements of section 32-5A-155, which shall be actuated by the driver of said church bus whenever but only whenever such vehicle is stopped for the purpose of receiving or discharging passengers.

(d) The driver of a vehicle upon a controlled-access highway with separate roadways need not stop upon meeting or passing a school or church bus which is on a different roadway or when upon a controlled-access highway and the school or church bus is stopped in a loading zone which is a part of or adjacent to such highway and where pedestrians are not permitted to cross the roadway. (Acts 1980, No. 80-434, p. 604, § 7-106.)

Commentary

Subsection (a) has its counterpart in former section 32-5-60, but several changes have been made. The prior law applied to "a school bus, or other vehicle engaged in transporting school children." This act makes the latter phrase unnecessary by its broad definition of school bus in section 32-1-1.1(58). The prior law did not require the display of a visual signal by the bus nor did it require the driver to remain stopped until the bus resumes motion, ceases to display its signals or its driver signals the other vehicle to proceed. Subsections (b) and (d) had no counterparts in the previous Alabama law. This section incorporates the provisions previously found in section 32-5-61, relating to church buses. Subsection (b) differs from its UVC counterpart, UVC § 11-706(c), in that the UVC provision provides for certain cases in which the school bus driver is prohibited from operating the visual signals. This provision in the Alabama act requires activation of the signals without exception.

§ 32-5A-155. Visual signals on school and church buses.

(a) Every school bus shall, and every church bus may, in addition to any other equipment and distinctive markings required by this chapter, be equipped with signal lamps mounted as high and as widely spaced laterally as practicable, which shall be capable of displaying to the front two alternately flashing red lights located at the same level and to the rear two alternately flashing red lights located at the same level, and these lights shall have sufficient intensity to be visible at 500 feet in normal sunlight.

(b) The alternately flashing lighting described in subsection (a) of this section shall not be used on any vehicle other than a school bus, a church bus or an authorized emergency vehicle. (Acts 1980, No. 80-434, p. 604, § 7-107.)

Commentary

This section is based upon UVC section 12-218(b), (d). While it is not the purpose of this chapter to deal generally with the equipment of vehicles, adoption of this section is necessary to effectuate the operation of the section immediately preceding. There was no prior comparable Alabama statute. As with the immediately preceding section, this section differs from its UVC counterpart in applying to church buses as well as school buses, in order to incorporate the provisions of former section 32-5-61.

The term "authorized emergency vehicle" used in subsection (b) is a term that is broadly defined in section 32-1-1.1(3) to include not only publicly owned fire department and police vehicles and ambulances, but also "such other publicly or privately owned vehicles as are designated by the director of public safety or the chief of police of an incorporated city."

ARTICLE 8.

SPEED RESTRICTIONS.

Cross references. — For other provisions as to speed limits, see § 32-5-92 et seq.

§ 32-5A-170. Reasonable and prudent speed.

No person shall drive a vehicle at a speed greater than is reasonable and prudent under the conditions and having regard to the actual and potential hazards then existing. Consistent with the foregoing, every person shall drive at a safe and appropriate speed when approaching and crossing an intersection or railroad grade crossing, when approaching and going around a curve, when approaching a hill crest, when traveling upon any narrow or winding roadway, and when special hazards exist with respect to pedestrians or other traffic or by reason of weather or highway conditions. (Acts 1980, No. 80-434, p. 604, § 8-101.)

Commentary

The previous Alabama statute, section 32-5-91, was very similar to this section except that this act uses a "reasonable and prudent" approach to cases of railroad grade crossings, curves, hill crests and the like, rather than setting out specificeds. This approach is to be preferred since it is more flexible and because few persons were able to remember all of the complexities of the former law.

I. General Consideration.
II. Decisions Under Prior Law.

I. GENERAL CONSIDERATION.

Collateral references. — 60 C.J.S., Motor Vehicles, §§ 29(1)-30. 60A C.J.S., Motor Vehicles, §§ 290(1)-299.

7 Am. Jur. 2d, Automobiles & Highway Traffic, §§ 180-193.

Speed alone or in connection with other circumstances as gross negligence, wantonness, recklessness, or the like, under automobile guest statute. 6 ALR3d 769.

II. DECISIONS UNDER PRIOR LAW.

Editor's note. — The cases cited below were decided under similar provisions of prior law.

Violation of former speeding statute was misdemeanor. Pippin v. State, 19 Ala. App. 384, 97 So. 615 (1923).

And constituted prima facie negligence. — Fact that defendant was driving automobile at 50 miles per hour was prima facie negligence only under former similar section. Whittaker v. Walker, 223 Ala. 167, 135 So. 185 (1931).

But question of ultimate negligence was for jury. — Former similar section created only a presumption of unlawfulness, and the question of ultimate negligence was for the jury. Chappell v. Boykin, 41 Ala. App. 137, 127 So. 2d 636 (1960), cert. denied, 271 Ala. 697, 127 So. 2d 641 (1961).

Lawfulness of speed dependent on conditions as well as statute. — Former similar statute did not make specified speed an unlawful act under all circumstances at a place stated in the statute; but driving at a speed not exceeding the rate named was prima facie lawful. The statute made it prima facie unlawful to exceed that speed, but whether it was lawful or not depended upon the conditions then existing. Tyler v. Drennen, 255 Ala. 377, 51 So. 2d 516 (1951); Ditsch v. Baggett Transp. Co., 258 Ala. 26, 61 So. 2d 98 (1952); Mobile City Lines v. Hardy, 264 Ala. 247, 86 So. 2d 393 (1956); Brownell-O'Hear Pontiac Co. v. Taylor, 269 Ala. 236, 112 So. 2d 463 (1959).

Standard of care. — The degree of care to be used by the driver of an automobile upon the highways of this state is that which a reasonably careful and prudent man would use under like conditions. Downey v. State, 30 Ala. App. 285, 4 So. 2d 422, rev'd on other grounds, 241 Ala. 514, 4 So. 2d 428 (1941).

Finding of lack of care warranted. — Where a taxicab was proceeding on a through street about midnight and was traveling downgrade on a wet paved roadway at 50 miles an hour toward an important intersection, the jury could find that traveling at such a speed at such place and on such occasion was not an exercise of care which the taxicab driver owed his passengers, even though no precise rate of speed was specifically fixed by former similar statute to cover such situation. Decatur Transit v. Jennings, 253 Ala. 322, 45 So. 2d 13 (1950).

Lawfulness of speed is jury question. — In action arising from automobile accident, question of lawfulness of plaintiff's speed is ordinarily for jury. McCaleb v. Reed, 225 Ala.

564, 144 So. 28 (1932); Streetman v. Bowdon, 239 Ala. 359, 194 So. 831 (1940); Mobile Cab & Baggage Co. v. Akridge, 240 Ala. 355, 199 So. 486 (1940); Decatur Transit v. Jennings, 253 Ala. 322, 45 So. 2d 13 (1950); Seitz v. Heep, 243 Ala. 372, 10 So. 2d 148 (1942).

The question of whether the speed at which one enters an intersection is lawful is one ordinarily for the jury and is flexible to yield to the circumstances of each case. Horton v. Mobile Cab & Baggage Co., 281 Ala. 35, 198 So. 2d 619 (1967).

In a negligence case, where there was no evidence in the record of any signs increasing the maximum lawful speed, the prima facie lawful speed was a maximum of 20 miles per hour; but whether or not that speed, or the speed at which the vehicle was actually traveling, was, in fact, lawful or not, depending upon all of the surrounding circumstances and conditions confronting the driver at the time, was a question for the jury. Wayland Distrib. Co. v. Gay, 287 Ala. 446, 252 So. 2d 414 (1971).

As is question of recklessness. — It is a question for the jury to determine if the defendant was reckless in the operation of his automobile. Pippin v. State, 19 Ala. App. 384, 97 So. 615 (1923).

Introduction of former similar statute in evidence was not reversible error where the trial judge instructed the jury with reference to the speed law. Harris v. State, 36 Ala. App. 620, 61 So. 2d 769 (1952).

§ 32-5A-171. Maximum limits.

Except when a special hazard exists that requires lower speed for compliance with section 32-5A-170, the limits hereinafter specified or established as hereinafter authorized shall be maximum lawful speeds, and no person shall drive a vehicle at a speed in excess of such maximum limits.

(1) No person shall operate a vehicle in excess of 30 miles per hour in any urban district.

(2) No person shall operate a motor vehicle on the highways in this state, other than interstate highways, at a speed in excess of 55 miles per hour at any time unless a different maximum rate of speed is authorized by the governor under authority granted in subdivision (5).

(3) No person shall operate a motor vehicle, on an interstate highway within the state of Alabama, at a speed in excess of 55 miles per hour in urban areas of 50,000 population or more or in excess of 65 miles per hour outside such urban areas unless a different maximum rate of speed is permitted or allowed by the federal highway administration, or unless a different maximum rate of speed is authorized by the governor under authority granted in subdivision (5) hereof.

(4) Notwithstanding any provisions of this section to the contrary, no person shall operate a passenger vehicle, motor truck or passenger bus which carries or transports explosives or flammable liquids, as defined in section 32-1-1.1, or hazardous wastes, as defined in section 22-30-3(5), in this state unless the vehicle, truck or bus prominently displays a current decal, plate or placard which is required by the rules or regulations of the DOT or the PSC which indicates or warns that the vehicle, truck or bus is carrying or transporting such substances. No person shall operate such vehicle, truck or bus at a rate of speed greater than 55 miles per hour at any time unless a different maximum rate of speed is authorized by the governor under authority granted in subdivision (5).

(5) The governor is hereby specifically authorized to prescribe the maximum rate of speed whenever a different rate of speed is required by federal law in order for Alabama to receive federal funds for highway maintenance and construction.

(6) The maximum speed limits set forth in this section may be altered as authorized in sections 32-5A-172 and 32-5A-173. (Acts 1980, No. 80-434, p. 604, § 8-102; Acts 1987, No. 87-408, p. 593.)

Commentary

This section differs substantially from the comparable UVC provision, UVC § 11-801.1 due to legislative revision of the section and it also represents a substantial change from the wording of the earlier law, which was found in sections 32-5-90 and 32-5-91. A basic difference between the prior law and this section is that the former law's speed limits were prima facie limits (with the exception of special speed limits on bridges under section 32-5-92 and the 60/50 limits in section 32-5-90(a)). This means that under prior law it was not usually an offense to exceed the speed limits if the speed could be deemed reasonable and prudent under all the circumstances. Under this section, all speed limits are absolute limits, which should serve to simplify their enforcement. In addition, this section abolishes separate speed limits for business and residence districts.

I. General Consideration.
II. Decisions Under Prior Law.

I. GENERAL CONSIDERATION.

Negligence not established merely by exceeding speed limit. — Merely exceeding the statutory speed limit does not, in itself, establish actionable negligence. Several other requirements are involved, most particularly, the requirement that the jury must find that the statutory violation proximately caused the injury. Odom v. Schofield, 480 So. 2d 1217 (Ala. 1985).

Unconstitutionality of court-imposed fine of $50.00 over normal fine where radar detector in automobile. — Traffic fine of $50.00 over the normal fine where a radar detector is in the automobile may not be imposed by court order, even though such fine is within the statutory limits of § 32-5A-8, in that such judicial action creates an additional fine which, under Ala. Const., art. III (1901), can be enacted only by the legislature. Ellis v. State, 502 So. 2d 694 (Ala. 1986).

Operation of radar detector not illegal. — Even though the operation of a radar detector may aid its operator to evade the traffic laws, nevertheless, his so doing is in and of itself not illegal. Ellis v. State, 502 So. 2d 694 (Ala. 1986).

Testimony of trooper who "clocked" speed by "pacing" held sufficient to go to jury. — Testimony of trooper that he manually "clocked" appellant, using the speedometer of the trooper car by "pacing," that is, remaining a fixed distance behind the car being checked, that his speedometer was verified for accuracy once a month, and that he observed appellant traveling at the rate of 65 miles per hour, was sufficient to support jury findings as to guilt, since drivers are presumed to know that the maximum lawful speed is 55 MPH. Moss v. State, 428 So. 2d 172 (Ala. Crim. App. 1982).

Collateral references. — 7 Am. Jur. 2d, Automobiles & Highway Traffic, §§ 180-193.

Criminal or penal responsibility of public officer or employee for violating speed regulations. 9 ALR 367.

Violation of speed law as affecting violator's right to recover for negligence. 12 ALR 463.

Public officers or employees as bound by speed regulations. 19 ALR 459, 23 ALR 418.

Conflict between statutes and local regulations as to speed. 21 ALR 1187, 64 ALR 993, 147 ALR 522.

Indefiniteness of automobile speed regulations as affecting validity. 29 ALR 1066.

Violation of speed regulations as affecting right to recover for injuries due to collision with streetcar. 28 ALR 228, 46 ALR 1000.

Excuse for exceeding speed limit for automobiles. 29 ALR 883.

Driving at illegal speed as reckless driving within statute making reckless driving a criminal offense. 86 ALR 1281, 52 ALR2d 1337.

Indictment or information which charges offense as to speed in language of statute. 115 ALR 357.

Expert or opinion evidence of speed not based upon view of vehicle. 156 ALR 382.

Speed alone or in connection with other circumstances as gross negligence, wantonness, recklessness, or the like, under automobile guest statute. 6 ALR3d 769.

Definiteness of automobile speed regulations as affecting validity. 6 ALR3d 1326.

Products liability: sufficiency of evidence to support product misuse defense in actions concerning commercial or industrial equipment and machinery. 64 ALR4th 10.

II. DECISIONS UNDER PRIOR LAW.

Editor's note. — The cases cited below were decided under similar provisions of prior law.

Maximum limits not hard and fast. — Former similar section did not make maximum limits a hard and fast rule. Roberts v. McCall, 245 Ala. 359, 17 So. 2d 159 (1944); Frith v. Studdard, 267 Ala. 315, 101 So. 2d 305 (1958); Brownell-O'Hear Pontiac Co. v. Taylor, 269 Ala. 236, 112 So. 2d 463 (1959); Horton v. Mobile Cab & Baggage Co., 281 Ala. 35, 198 So. 2d 619 (1967).

Compliance with statutory limits prima facie lawful. — Compliance with former similar section was prima facie lawful, but speeds exceeding statutory limits may or may not be lawful depending on existing conditions. Fox v. Barthol, 374 So. 2d 294 (Ala. 1979).

But whether the speed at which one enters an intersection is lawful depends upon the conditions then existing. Horton v. Mobile Cab & Baggage Co., 281 Ala. 35, 198 So. 2d 619 (1967).

Speed alone does not import wantonness, and violation of the speed limit does not of itself amount to willful or wanton misconduct. Crocker v. Lee, 261 Ala. 439, 74 So. 2d 429 (1954).

Where driver's view was obstructed at corner by hedgerow or vines on a garden fence, former similar section made his speed limit 15 miles per hour. Roe v. Brown, 249 Ala. 425, 31 So. 2d 599 (1948).

Jury question. — Under former law, there were no specifically defined limits as to speed at which motor vehicles could be driven on the highways of this state; therefore, whether defendant was driving too fast and was guilty of unlawful conduct under statute was a question for the jury. Garner v. State, 34 Ala. App. 551, 41 So. 2d 634 (1949).

§ 32-5A-172. Establishment of state speed zones.

Whenever the director of public safety and the highway director, with the approval of the governor, shall determine upon the basis of an engineering and traffic investigation that any maximum speed hereinbefore set forth is greater or less than is reasonable or safe under the conditions found to exist at any intersection or other place or upon any part of the state highway system, said directors may determine and declare a reasonable and safe maximum limit thereat, which shall be effective when appropriate signs giving notice thereof are erected. Such a maximum speed limit may be declared to be effective at all times or at such times as are indicated upon the said signs; and differing limits may be established for different times of day, different types of vehicles, varying weather conditions, and other factors bearing on safe speeds, which shall be effective when posted upon appropriate fixed or variable signs. (Acts 1980, No. 80-434, p. 604, § 8-103.)

Commentary

This section in minor particulars modifies former section 32-5-94 but does not substantially change prior law. The phrase "prima facie" has been removed and speed limits are made absolute as discussed in the commentary to section 32-5A-171, and this section permits establishment of different speed limits for different kinds of vehicles.

Collateral references. — 60A C.J.S., Motor Vehicles, §§ 290(1), 308(1).
7A Am. Jur. 2d, Automobiles & Highway Traffic, §§ 218-235.

Speed alone or in connection with other circumstances as gross negligence, wantonness, recklessness, or the like, under automobile guest statute. 6 ALR3d 769.

§ 32-5A-173. When local authorities may and shall alter maximum limits.

(a) Whenever local authorities in their respective jurisdictions determine on the basis of an engineering and traffic investigation that the maximum speed permitted under this article is greater or less than is reasonable and safe under the conditions found to exist upon a highway or part of a highway, the local authority may determine and declare a reasonable and safe maximum limit thereon which:

(1) Decreases the limit at intersections;

(2) Increases the limit within an urban district but not to more than the maximum rate of speed that may be prescribed by the governor under subdivision (4) of section 32-5A-171;

(3) Decreases the limit on any street or highway under the jurisdiction and control of any county commission; or

(4) Increases the limit on any street, or highway under the jurisdiction and control of any county commission but not to more than the maximum rate of speed that is prescribed under section 32-5A-171.

(b) Local authorities in their respective jurisdictions shall determine by an engineering and traffic investigation the proper maximum speed for all arterial streets and shall declare a reasonable and safe maximum limit thereon which may be greater or less than the maximum speed permitted under this chapter for an urban district.

(c) Any altered limit established as hereinabove authorized shall be effective at all times or during hours of darkness or at other times as may be determined when appropriate signs giving notice thereof are erected upon such street or highway.

(d) Any alteration of maximum limits on state highways or extensions thereof in a municipality by local authorities shall not be effective until such alteration has been approved by the highway department.

(e) Not more than six such alterations as hereinabove authorized shall be made per mile along a street or highway, except in the case of reduced limits at intersections, and the difference between adjacent limits shall not be more than 10 miles per hour. (Acts 1980, No. 80-434, p. 604, § 8-104; Acts 1985, 2nd Ex. Sess., No. 85-998, p. 366, § 2.)

Commentary

This section replaces section 32-5-91(c) which is considerably less detailed and specific. Again, reference to "prima facie" limits has been removed, and if limits are to be altered on state highways, the approval of the highway department is required. Further, under this section, local authorities cannot alter speed limits without a prior engineering and traffic investigation, which was not formerly required. On the other hand, the prior statute allowed increases by local authorities but not decreases of speed limits. This section permits either, as appropriate, but limits the number of alterations that local authorities can make per mile.

Collateral references. — 60A C.J.S., Motor Vehicles, §§ 290(1), 308(1).
7A Am. Jur. 2d, Automobiles & Highway Traffic, §§ 218-235.

Speed alone or in connection with other circumstances as gross negligence, wantonness, recklessness, or the like, under automobile guest statute. 6 ALR3d 769.

§ 32-5A-174. Minimum speed regulation.

(a) No person shall drive a motor vehicle at such a slow speed as to impede the normal and reasonable movement of traffic except when reduced speed is necessary for safe operation or in compliance with law.

(b) Whenever the director of public safety and the highway director, with the approval of the governor, or local authorities within their respective jurisdictions determine on the basis of an engineering and traffic investigation that slow speeds on any highway or part of a highway consistently impede the normal and reasonable movement of traffic, the said directors or such local authority may determine and declare a minimum speed limit below which no person shall drive a vehicle except when necessary for safe operation or in compliance with law, and that limit shall be effective when posted upon appropriate fixed or variable signs. (Acts 1980, No. 80-434, p. 604, § 8-105.)

Commentary

This section is very similar to former section 32-5-95 which it replaces. Once again, reference to "prima facie" speed limits has been removed. Moreover, this section extends power to establish minimum speeds to local authorities.

Collateral references. — 60A C.J.S., Motor Vehicles, § 290(3).
7 Am. Jur. 2d, Automobiles & Highway Traffic, § 190.
Application and effect, in civil motor vehicle accident case, of "slow speed" traffic statute prohibiting driving at such a slow speed as to create danger, to impede normal traffic movement, or the like. 66 ALR2d 1194.

Speed alone or in connection with other circumstances as gross negligence, wantonness, recklessness, or the like, under automobile guest statute. 6 ALR3d 769.

Indefiniteness of automobile speed regulations as affecting validity. 6 ALR3d 1326.

§ 32-5A-175. Special speed limitation on motor-driven cycles.

No person shall operate any motor-driven cycle at any time from a half hour after sunset to a half hour before sunrise nor at any other time when, due to insufficient light or unfavorable atmospheric conditions, persons and vehicles on the highway are not clearly discernible at a distance of 1,000 feet ahead at a speed greater than 35 miles per hour unless such motor-driven cycle is equipped with a head lamp or lamps which are adequate to reveal a person or vehicle at a distance of 300 feet ahead. (Acts 1980, No. 80-434, p. 604, § 8-106.)

Commentary

Section 32-12-25 has been replaced by this provision. The prior law was similar, except that it applied only to driving at nighttime and required illumination for 200 rather than 300 feet. Moreover, the former statute read literally did not apply to a motor-driven cycle having no head lamp at all.

Collateral references. — 60A C.J.S., Motor Vehicles, § 386. 61 C.J.S., Motor Vehicles, §§ 470(3), 518(33), 526(43), 527(3), 527(18). Speed alone or in connection with other circumstances as gross negligence, wantonness, recklessness, or the like, under automobile guest statute. 6 ALR3d 769.

§ 32-5A-176. Special speed limitation over bridge or elevated structure; conclusive evidence of speed.

(a) No person shall drive a vehicle over any bridge or other elevated structure constituting a part of a highway at a speed which is greater than the maximum speed which can be maintained with safety to such bridge or structure, when such structure is signposted as provided in this section.

(b) The highway department and local authorities on highways under their respective jurisdictions may conduct an investigation of any bridge or other elevated structure constituting a part of a highway, and if it shall thereupon find that such structure cannot with safety to itself withstand vehicles traveling at the speed otherwise permissible under this chapter, the highway department or local authority shall determine and declare the maximum speed of vehicles which such structure can safely withstand, and shall cause or permit suitable signs stating such maximum speed to be erected and maintained before each end of such structure.

(c) Upon the trial of any person charged with a violation of this section, proof of said determination of the maximum speed by said highway department and the existence of said signs shall constitute conclusive evidence of the maximum speed which can be maintained with safety to such bridge or structure. (Acts 1980, No. 80-434, p. 604, § 8-107.)

Commentary

Subsections (a), (b), and (c) replace section 32-5-92. Subsection (a) makes no change in the substance of the prior law. However, subsection (b) expands the authority of that clause to local authorities with respect to bridges within their jurisdictions. The previous statute required posting of signs within 100 feet of the end of the structure, whereas this section simply requires posting "before each end of such structure." Finally, this section makes the posting of signs a prerequisite to the raising of the conclusive presumption in subsection (c). Posting of such signs was not required by former law. This change has been made in the interest of fairness.

Collateral references. — 60A C.J.S., Motor Vehicles, §§ 290(1), 308(1).

7A Am. Jur. 2d, Automobiles & Highway Traffic, §§ 218-235.

Speed alone or in connection with other circumstances as gross negligence, wantonness, recklessness, or the like, under automobile guest statute. 6 ALR3d 769.

§ 32-5A-176.1. Speed limits in urban and rural construction zones; enforcement; violation; rules and procedures.

(a) The state highway department is hereby authorized and empowered to set the speed limits in urban and rural construction zones along state and interstate highways. Such construction zone speed limits shall be posted on the department's standard size speed limit signs at least one hundred feet in advance of the entrance to a construction zone. Law enforcement authorities shall enforce such construction zone speed limits in the same manner that they enforce normal speed limits along state and interstate highways and violators of construction zone speed limits shall be penalized as prescribed by law or ordinance for a normal speed limit offense.

(b) The state highway department is hereby further authorized and empowered to promulgate and implement such administrative rules and procedures as it deems necessary to both carry out the provisions of subsection (a) of this section and to ensure the safety of private and public construction and maintenance personnel working in designated construction zones on state and interstate highways. (Acts 1988, 1st Sp. Sess., No. 88-917, p. 511, §§ 1, 2.)

Effective date. — The act which added this section became effective September 30, 1988.

Cross references. — As to speed limits between construction signs, see § 32-5-93.

§ 32-5A-177. Charging violations; burden of proof in civil actions; arrest for violation of speed laws communicated from officer operating measuring device to another officer; testimony derived from use of speed measuring device.

(a) In every charge of violation of any speed regulation in this article the complaint, also the summons or notice to appear, shall specify the speed at which the defendant is alleged to have driven, also the maximum speed applicable within the district or at the location.

(b) The provision of this article declaring maximum speed limitations shall not be construed to relieve the plaintiff in any action from the burden of proving negligence on the part of the defendant as the proximate cause of an accident.

(c) Any state trooper, upon receiving information relayed to him from a fellow officer stationed on the ground or in the air operating a speed measuring device that a driver of a vehicle has violated the speed laws of this state, may arrest the driver for violation of said laws where reasonable and proper identification of the vehicle and the speed of same has been communicated to the arresting officer.

(d) A witness otherwise qualified to testify shall be competent to give testimony against an accused violator of the motor vehicle laws of this state when such testimony is derived from the use of such speed measuring device used in the calculation of speed, upon showing that the speed measuring device which was used had been tested. However, the operator of any visual average speed computer device shall first be certified as a competent operator of such device by the department.

(e) Any person accused pursuant to the provisions of this section shall be entitled to have the officer actually operating the device appear in court and testify upon oral or written motion. (Acts 1980, No. 80-434, p. 604, § 8-108; Acts 1989, No. 89-828, § 1.)

The 1989 amendment, effective May 17, 1989, added subsections (c) through (e).

Commentary

Subsection (a) is similar to the final sentence of former section 32-5-91(b), but, in accordance with section 32-5A-172, reference to "prima facie" lawful speeds is omitted. There was no statutory counterpart under prior Alabama law to subsection (b).

Testimony of trooper who "clocked" speed by "pacing" held sufficient to go to jury. — Testimony of trooper that he manually "clocked" appellant, using the speedometer of the trooper car by "pacing," that is, remaining a fixed distance behind the car being checked, that his speedometer was verified for accuracy once a month, and that he observed appellant traveling at the rate of 65 miles per hour, was sufficient to support jury findings as to guilt, since drivers are presumed to know that the maximum lawful speed is 55 MPH. Moss v. State, 428 So. 2d 172 (Ala. Crim. App. 1982).

Collateral references. — 60A C.J.S., Motor Vehicles, §§ 290(1), 308(1).

7A Am. Jur. 2d, Automobiles & Highway Traffic, §§ 218-235.

Speed alone or in connection with other circumstances as gross negligence, wantonness, recklessness, or the like, under automobile guest statute. 6 ALR3d 769.

§ 32-5A-178. Racing on highways; penalties.

(a) No person shall drive any vehicle on any highway in any race, speed competition or contest, drag race or acceleration contest, test of physical endurance, exhibition of speed or acceleration, or for the purpose of making a speed record, and no person shall in any manner participate in any such race, competition, contest, test or exhibition.

(b) "Drag race" is defined as the operation of two or more vehicles from a point side by side at accelerating speeds in a competitive attempt to outdistance each other, or the operation of one or more vehicles over a common selected course, from the same point to the same point, for the purpose of comparing the relative speeds or power of acceleration of such vehicle or vehicles within a certain distance or time limit.

(c) "Racing" is defined as the use of one or more vehicles in an attempt to outgain, outdistance or prevent another vehicle from passing, to arrive at a given destination ahead of another vehicle or vehicles, or to test the physical stamina or endurance of drivers over long distance driving routes.

(d) Every person convicted of racing on highways shall be punished upon a first conviction by imprisonment for a period of not less than five days nor more than 90 days, or by fine of not less than $25.00 nor more than $500.00, or by both such fine and imprisonment, and on a second or subsequent conviction shall be punished by imprisonment for not less than 10 days nor more than six months, or by a fine of not less than $50.00 nor more than $500.00, or by both such fine and imprisonment, and the court may prohibit the person so convicted from driving a motor vehicle on the public highways of this state for a period not exceeding six months, and the license of the person shall be suspended for such period by the director of public safety pursuant to section 32-5A-195. (Acts 1980, No. 80-434, p. 604, § 8-109.)

Commentary

There was no statute previously in force in Alabama comparable to this section. This section is based upon UVC § 11-808, which is entitled "racing on highways." However, the language of the UVC would not limit the prohibition of subsection (a) only to highways, despite the title of the section. Therefore, the qualifying phrase "on any highway" is included in this version, pursuant to the amendment of the Senate committee.

Collateral references. — 60A C.J.S., Motor Vehicles, §§ 290(1), 308(1).

7A Am. Jur. 2d, Automobiles & Highway Traffic, §§ 218-235.

Speed alone or in connection with other circumstances as gross negligence, wantonness, recklessness, or the like, under automobile guest statute. 6 ALR3d 769.

ARTICLE 9.

SERIOUS TRAFFIC OFFENSES.

§ 32-5A-190. Reckless driving.

(a) Any person who drives any vehicle carelessly and heedlessly in willful or wanton disregard for the rights or safety of persons or property, or without due caution and circumspection and at a speed or in a manner so as to endanger or be likely to endanger any person or property, shall be guilty of reckless driving.

(b) Every person convicted of reckless driving shall be punished upon a first conviction by imprisonment for a period of not less than five days nor more than 90 days, or by fine of not less than $25.00 nor more than $500.00, or by both such fine and imprisonment, and on a second or subsequent conviction shall be punished by imprisonment for not less than 10 days nor more than six months, or by a fine of not less than $50.00 nor more than $500.00, or by both such fine and imprisonment, and the court may prohibit the person so convicted from driving a motor vehicle on the public highways of this state for a period not exceeding six months, and the license of the person shall be suspended for such period by the director of public safety pursuant to section 32-5A-195.

(c) Neither reckless driving nor any other moving violation under this chapter is a lesser included offense under a charge of driving while under the influence of alcohol or drugs. (Acts 1980, No. 80-434, p. 604, § 9-101.)

Commentary

Section 32-5-50, the prior statute, was based upon an earlier version of the Uniform Vehicle Code but only in minor details differed from this present section derived from UVC § 11-901. Pursuant to an amendment by a senate committee, subsection (a) basically consists of the language formerly found in the first sentence of section 32-5-50. However, under this section, a person can be convicted of reckless driving even if he is not driving on a highway but is, for example, in a parking lot or on school grounds. See also section 32-5A-2. The words "on the highway," found in previous section 32-5-50, have been removed from this section. In keeping with a 1971 amendment to UVC § 11-901, the maximum penalty in all cases has been reduced to $500.00, but this section deviates from the UVC in retaining the final provision which permits the prohibition of the convicted person from driving. Additional language has been inserted to make it clear that the director of public safety shall revoke the driver's license of any person who has been prohibited from driving by sentence of a court pursuant to this section. It will be noted, however, that license suspension is here made subject to the discretion of the court for reasons discussed in the comment to the next section. Subsection (c) is included here to discourage leniency with persons properly charged with the offense of driving under the influence of alcohol or drugs under the next section. No substantive change in the law is intended by subsection (c), which is included for clarification purposes.

I. General Consideration.
II. Decisions Under Prior Law.

I. GENERAL CONSIDERATION.

Constitutional and statutory protections against double jeopardy do not bar accused from being prosecuted for both D.U.I. and reckless driving when both charges arise from the same event. Sporl v. City of Hoover, 467 So. 2d 273 (Ala. Crim. App. 1985).

Lane violation not necessary element of drunken driving. — Since it was unnecessary to prove the lane violation in order to prosecute the defendant for drunken driving, the two offenses were not the "same" for double jeopardy purposes. Wright v. City of Montgomery, 477 So. 2d 492 (Ala. 1985).

Cited in State v. Davis, 477 So. 2d 504 (Ala. Crim. App. 1985).

Collateral references. — 61A C.J.S., Motor Vehicles, §§ 609-624.

7 Am. Jur. 2d, Automobiles & Highway Traffic, §§ 263-271.

What amounts to reckless driving within statute making reckless driving a criminal offense. 86 ALR 1273, 52 ALR2d 1337.

What amounts to reckless driving within statute making such a criminal offense. 52 ALR2d 1337.

Speed, alone or in connection with other circumstances as gross negligence, wantonness, recklessness, or the like, under automobile guest statute. 6 ALR3d 769.

Reckless driving as lesser included offense of driving while intoxicated or similar charge. 10 ALR4th 1252.

Statute prohibiting reckless driving: definiteness and certainty. 52 ALR4th 1161.

II. DECISIONS UNDER PRIOR LAW.

Editor's note. — The cases cited below were decided under similar provisions of prior law.

Former similar section was aimed at negligent driving on highways of this state, without the qualifying adjective "public" highways. Kirk v. State, 35 Ala. App. 405, 47 So. 2d 283 (1950).

Terms "reckless" and "without due caution and circumspection" are synonymous and mean no more than negligence. Kirk v. State, 35 Ala. App. 405, 47 So. 2d 283 (1950); White v. State, 37 Ala. App. 424, 69 So. 2d 874 (1953).

What constitutes wanton conduct. — Positive intent on part of truck driver to bring about collision between truck and automobile is not essential to constitute wanton conduct. Daniel v. Motes, 228 Ala. 454, 153 So. 727 (1934).

There can be no wanton injury without knowledge of conditions making act causing it likely to result in injury and a consciousness of danger, and wantonness does not result from mere negligence in failure to have such knowledge and consciousness. Buffalo Rock Co. v. Davis, 228 Ala. 603, 154 So. 556 (1934).

Sufficiency of affidavit. — Affidavit supporting charge of reckless driving, which followed language of this former similar statute and stated facts constituting offense in ordinary and concise language, and in manner enabling defendant to know and understand what was therein intended, was not demurrable. Terrell v. State, 27 Ala. App. 160, 167 So. 611 (1936).

Affidavit which followed the words of former similar statute was proper in form and substance. Bradford v. State, 35 Ala. App. 407, 47 So. 2d 599 (1950).

Defendant's admissions held inadmissible. — In prosecution under former similar statute, defendant's testimony as witness at trial of another that he was owner of automobile and was riding therein at time was erroneously admitted, absent satisfactory proof that his confessions or admissions were voluntarily made. Monroe v. State, 23 Ala. App. 441, 126 So. 614 (1930).

Evidence of alleged reckless driving of vehicle at another time and place was inadmissible, since each separate act of reckless driving constitutes separate and distinct offense. Gladden v. State, 22 Ala. App. 85, 112 So. 541 (1927).

Evidence of prior conviction. — Where indictment under former statute contained no allegation as to a prior conviction, evidence of such prior conviction was improperly admitted.

Robinson v. State, 36 Ala. App. 676, 62 So. 2d 608 (1953).

Reading statute to jury in action based on negligence. — Where complaint charged simple negligence only, the trial court should not have read to the jury that portion of former similar statute relating to willful or wanton disregard of the rights or safety of others, as such was at least misleading. McGough Bakeries Corp. v. Reynolds, 250 Ala. 592, 35 So. 2d 332 (1948).

Questions for jury — Violation of statute. — Question of whether defendant had violated former similar statute was, under the evidence, question for jury, and overruling defendant's motion to exclude testimony of witness who stated as conclusion that defendant kept going "still driving reckless" was error. Spooney v. State, 217 Ala. 219, 115 So. 308 (1928).

Same — Guilt of reckless driving. — In prosecution for reckless driving of an automobile, wherein state introduced evidence tending to show that defendant was traveling about 25 miles per hour around curve on left side of road after dark with no lights on his automobile, defendant's guilt was a question for the jury. Hill v. State, 27 Ala. App. 202, 169 So. 21 (1936).

Where overtaking car collided with left side of car being overtaken, damaging right side of overtaking vehicle, question of guilt of driver of overtaking vehicle of reckless driving was for jury. Graham v. State, 40 Ala. App. 471, 115 So. 2d 289 (1959).

Same — Guilty of homicide. — Whether motorist who drove into rear of automobile proceeding in same direction and caused the deaths of two occupants therein was guilty of murder in the second degree was for the jury. Hyde v. State, 230 Ala. 243, 160 So. 237 (1935).

Same — Negligence and wanton conduct. — In action against owner of taxicab which ran over boy who was crossing street, conflicting evidence as to driver's negligence and wanton conduct was for the jury. Graham v. Werfel, 229 Ala. 385, 157 So. 201 (1934).

Same — Due caution. — As former similar section was couched in general terms, it could not have been said that there was necessarily an absence of due caution and circumspection in allowing four persons to ride on the front seat. This was a question of fact under all the circumstances. Malbis Bakery Co. v. Collins, 245 Ala. 84, 15 So. 2d 705 (1943).

Same — Whether driver attempted to pass. — Conflict in evidence as to whether driver attempted to pass another automobile going in the same direction was a question of fact solely within the province of the jury to resolve. Kirk v. State, 35 Ala. App. 405, 47 So. 2d 283 (1950).

Evidence held sufficient. — State's testimony that automobile owned by defendant, in which he was riding while it was driven by another, was driven carelessly and heedlessly, in willful or wanton disregard of rights or safety of others, was sufficient to support an inference of guilt. Monroe v. State, 23 Ala. App. 441, 126 So. 614 (1930).

Where two highway patrolmen testified that defendant, while driving, and at a sharp curve in the road, met two automobiles, and that these vehicles had to pull to the extreme right of the road to avoid a collision with defendant, who was at that time driving at a high rate of speed, defendant's conviction would be upheld. Bradford v. State, 35 Ala. App. 407, 47 So. 2d 599 (1950).

For case holding evidence insufficient to support conviction of second degree murder by running automobile over decedent, see Jordan v. State, 229 Ala. 415, 157 So. 485 (1934).

As to assessment by jury of increased fine provided for second or subsequent convictions under former section, see Robinson v. State, 36 Ala. App. 676, 62 So. 2d 608 (1953).

§ 32-5A-191. Driving while under influence of alcohol, controlled substances, etc.

(a) A person shall not drive or be in actual physical control of any vehicle while:

(1) There is 0.10 percent or more by weight of alcohol in his blood;

(2) Under the influence of alcohol;

(3) Under the influence of a controlled substance to a degree which renders him incapable of safely driving;

(4) Under the combined influence of alcohol and a controlled substance to a degree which renders him incapable of safely driving; or

(5) Under the influence of any substance which impairs the mental or physical faculties of such person to a degree which renders him incapable of safely driving.

(b) The fact that any person charged with violating this section is or has been legally entitled to use alcohol or a controlled substance shall not constitute a defense against any charge of violating this section.

(c) Upon first conviction, a person violating this section shall be punished by imprisonment in the county or municipal jail for not more than one year, or by fine of not less than $250.00 nor more than $1,000.00, or by both such fine and imprisonment. In addition, on a first conviction, the director of public safety shall suspend the driving privilege or driver's license of the person so convicted for a period of 90 days. First time offenders convicted of driving while under the influence of alcohol shall also be required to complete a DUI court referral program approved by the state administrative office of courts. Neither reckless driving nor any other traffic infraction is a lesser included offense under a charge of driving while under the influence of alcohol or controlled substances.

(d) On a second conviction within a five-year period, the person convicted of violating this section shall be punished by a fine of not less than $500.00 nor more than $2,500.00 and by imprisonment, which may include hard labor in the county or municipal jail for not more than one year. Said sentence to include a mandatory sentence which is not subject to suspension or probation of imprisonment in the county or municipal jail for not less than 48 consecutive hours or community service for not less than 20 days. In addition the director of public safety shall revoke the driving privileges or driver's license of the person so convicted for a period of one year.

(e) On a third or subsequent conviction within a five-year period, the person convicted of violating this section shall be punished by a fine of not less than $1,000.00 nor more than $5,000.00 and by imprisonment, which may include hard labor, in the county or municipal jail for not less than 60 days nor more than one year, to include a minimum of 60 days which shall be served in the county or municipal jail and which cannot be probated or suspended. In addition, the director of public safety shall revoke the driving privilege or driver's license of the person so convicted for a period of three years.

(f) All fines collected for violation of this section resulting from arrests by state officers shall be paid into the state general fund; all fines so collected for violations resulting from arrests by county or municipal officers shall be disbursed as is otherwise provided for by law.

(g) A person who has been arrested for violating the provisions of this section shall not be released from jail under bond or otherwise, until there is less than the same percent by weight of alcohol in his blood as specified in subsection (a)(1) hereof. (Acts 1980, No. 80-434, p. 604, § 9-102; Acts 1981, No. 81-803, p. 1412, § 1; Acts 1983, No. 83-620, p. 959, § 1; Acts 1984, No. 84-259, p. 431, § 1.)

Commentary

The purpose of this section is not only to bring the law on driving while intoxicated in line with the most recent advances made in other states to achieve something closer to uniform treatment with our sister states, but also to make DUI statutes more enforceable and to do a better job of helping identify the problem of the drinking driver and to keep him off the highway. Under prior law, the proper treatment of one convicted of driving while intoxicated was not at all clear. Under former Alabama law, section 32-6-16(f)(2) the director of public safety was authorized to revoke the license of any driver convicted of "driving a motor vehicle by a person who is an habitual user of narcotic drugs or while intoxicated ...." Prior law made no clear distinction between first and subsequent convictions.

This section replaces former section 32-5-170. There is no direct provision comparable to subsection (a)(1) although the 0.10 percentage standard was employed in former section 32-5-193(a)(3). In subsection (a)(2), the phrase "under the influence of alcohol" replaces the previous use "is intoxicated". See former section 32-5-170. Subsection (a)(3) broadens prior law, which referred only to "narcotic drugs" and then only to "habitual users" thereof. See former sections 32-5-170 and 32-6-16. Subsection (a)(4) had no counterpart in the prior Alabama law. All these changes were thought to be necessitated by the greatly increased use of controlled substances of all varieties in the past several years. There was no previous counterpart for subsection (b). Subsection (e) is simply a carry-over of the final sentence of former section 32-5-170.

In 1983, several amendments were made to this section. Subsection (a)(5) was added in its entirety. The minimum fine charged for a first conviction was increased from $100.00 to $250.00 in subsection (c). Also, under subsection (c) the director of public safety is required to suspend for 90 days the driving privileges or license of a person upon their first conviction under this section.

Subsection (d) was also amended in 1983. The amount of fine on the second conviction was increased from a minimum of $200.00 to $500.00, and the maximum was raised from $1,500.00 to $2,500.00. Moreover, upon a second conviction a mandatory jail sentence was added. Additionally, the revocation of the driver's privileges was increased from 6 months to one year.

Subsection (e), the punishment for a third and subsequent conviction, was added in the 1983 amendment. Subsection (g) was also added during the 1983 amendment.

Code commissioner's note. — Acts 1983, No. 83-620, § 2, provides: "The provisions of this act are supplemental to other laws not inconsistent with this act, and such other laws shall not be deemed to be repealed by this act."

Acts 1983, No. 83-620, § 3, provides that the act applies to conduct occurring after July 29, 1983, and that conduct occurring before that date shall be governed by preexisting law.

I. General Consideration.
II. Decisions Under Prior Law.

I. GENERAL CONSIDERATION.

Constitutionality. — This statute is not vague because the legislature plainly stated in the statute which conduct is prohibited. Subdivision (a)(2) is therefore constitutional and is not void for vagueness. Pace v. City of Montgomery, 455 So. 2d 180 (Ala. Crim. App. 1984).

The phrase "under the influence" does not make this section constitutionally void. The language of the section clearly sets out the standard of guilt. A person is guilty of violating subdivision (a)(2) if he drives a vehicle under the influence of alcohol, regardless of the degree of that influence. This statute is not vague because the legislature plainly stated in the statute which conduct is prohibited. Jemison v. State, 513 So. 2d 47 (Ala. Crim. App. 1987).

The language of the statute clearly sets out the standard of guilt. A person is guilty of violating subdivision (a)(2) if he drives a vehicle under the influence of alcohol, regardless of the degree of that influence. Pace v. City of Montgomery, 455 So. 2d 180 (Ala. Crim. App. 1984).

Subdivisions (a)(1) and (a)(2) state separate and distinct offenses. Nerud v. City of Mountain Brook, 517 So. 2d 652 (Ala. Crim. App. 1987).

Subdivisions (a)(1) and (a)(2) not separate offenses. — The Court of Criminal Appeals erred in holding that subdivisions (a)(1) and (a)(2) of this section constitute two separate offenses. Sisson v. State, 528 So. 2d 1159 (Ala. 1988).

Uniform Traffic Ticket and Complaint unclear as to whether defendant charged under subdivision (a)(1) or (a)(2). — Where the Uniform Traffic Ticket and Complaint (UTTC) charged defendant with driving with a blood-alcohol level of 0.10% or greater, a violation of subdivision (a)(1), and the complaint charged him with driving under the influence of alcohol in violation of subdivision (a)(2), a separate offense, the complaint was still valid since even though the UTTC was unclear as to whether or not the defendant was being charged under subdivision (a)(1) or (a)(2) the UTTC could have supported a charge for either driving under the influence or driving with a blood-alcohol level of .10% or greater. Beals v. State, 533 So. 2d 717 (Ala. Crim. App. 1988).

Reflection of condition at time of arrest. — Where defendant put forth no evidence to indicate why alcohol level reading at 2:44 a.m. did not reflect his condition when he was taken into custody at 1:58 a.m., the court found the test results did, in fact, reflect his condition at the time he was arrested. Buchanan v. City of Auburn, 512 So. 2d 145 (Ala. Crim. App.), overruled on other grounds, Hays v. City of Jacksonville, 518 So. 2d 892 (Ala. 1987).

Test to be used in DUI cases is to look at all of surrounding circumstances to see if there is sufficient evidence to support the conclusion that the defendant was in "actual physical control" of the vehicle. Cagle v. City of Gadsden, 495 So. 2d 1144 (Ala. 1986).

The three-pronged test in Key v. Town of Kinsey, 424 So. 2d 701 (Ala. Crim. App. 1982) is abandoned and in its place is adopted the totality-of-circumstances test. See Cagle v. City of Gadsden, 495 So. 2d 1144 (Ala. 1986).

Specific criminal offense, condemned by this section, must be alleged. Smith v. State, 435 So. 2d 158 (Ala. Crim. App. 1983).

Constitutional and statutory protections against double jeopardy do not bar accused from being prosecuted for both D.U.I. and reckless driving when both charges arise from the same event. Sporl v.

City of Hoover, 467 So. 2d 273 (Ala. Crim. App. 1985).

Lane violation not necessary element of drunken driving. — Since it was unnecessary to prove the lane violation in order to prosecute the defendant for drunken driving, the two offenses were not the "same" for double jeopardy purposes. Wright v. City of Montgomery, 477 So. 2d 492 (Ala. 1985).

The results of a photoelectric intoximeter test may be received into evidence upon one of two lines of proof. The first is, proof that the test was administered in conformity with § 32-5A-194. The second method is proof in accordance with the accepted traditional legal principles. This refers to establishing the foundation or predicate for the introduction of scientific test results. In neither the statutory path nor the traditional path establishing this foundation does the court find a requirement that each batch of chemicals be tested. Bice v. State, 472 So. 2d 440 (Ala. Crim. App. 1985).

Proof required of state. — Where the evidence clearly established that the defendant was driving his vehicle while there was 0.10 percent by weight of alcohol in his blood in violation of subdivision (a)(1) of this section, the state properly proved that he was driving under the influence; the state did not also need to prove that he was incapable of safely driving his vehicle to obtain a conviction under this section. Smith v. State, 470 So. 2d 1365 (Ala. Crim. App. 1985).

Alternative methods of proof. — Although driving "under the influence of alcohol" and driving with ".10% or more by weight of alcohol in one's blood" are but one offense the legislature provided that the offense could be proved by two alternative methods. Sisson v. State, 528 So. 2d 1159 (Ala. 1988).

Plea of nolo contendere which is accepted by the trial court is equivalent to a conviction for the purpose of suspending or revoking a driver's license. Wolfsberger v. Wells, 528 So. 2d 854 (Ala. Civ. App. 1988).

Suspension not mandatory. — This section, requiring suspension of driver license upon first DUI conviction, is not mandatory when driver is not convicted in Alabama and the director pursuant to subsection (e) was not required to suspend plaintiff's license and should have given plaintiff his duly requested hearing as provided by subsection (l). Wolfsberger v. Wells, 528 So. 2d 854 (Ala. Civ. App. 1988).

There is no need for the state to offer testimony concerning a periodic inspection of the testing equipment in order to lay the predicate for admissibility of photoelectric

intoximeter test results. Jones v. State, 513 So. 2d 50 (Ala. Crim. App. 1986).

Nor for operator to personally verify accuracy of the test. — It was not necessary for photoelectric intoximeter test operator to testify that he had determined that the driver had no disease and was taking no medication which would contaminate the test and that he could personally verify the accuracy of the machine used. Jones v. State, 513 So. 2d 50 (Ala. Crim. App. 1986).

Refusal to submit to chemical test for intoxication probative on issue of intoxication. — Even if defendant had only been charged with being in actual physical control of a motor vehicle while under the influence of alcohol, his refusal to submit to a chemical test for intoxication was probative on the issue of intoxication. Martin v. State, 529 So. 2d 1032 (Ala. Crim. App. 1988).

Proper predicate for admission of photoelectric intoximeter test results shown. — Where officer's certification card was admitted into evidence; he testified that he had administered photoelectric intoximeter test hundreds of times before; he further testified that before he used the instrument on the appellant, he checked to insure that it had been tested for accuracy; and he testified that he followed the apparatus procedure card in administering the photoelectric intoximeter test on defendant, the proper predicate was laid for the admission of the test results. Jemison v. State, 513 So. 2d 47 (Ala. Crim. App. 1987).

Laying proper predicate for admission of G.C.I. — Testimony of police officer that when the Montgomery police department sent him to school in order to learn the operations of the gas chromatograph intoximeter (G.C.I.) instrument, he was told that this instrument had been selected and approved by the chief of police for use by the Montgomery department, that he followed a checklist and performed the test according to the methods approved by the state board of health and that he possessed a valid permit, issued by the state board of health, to operate this instrument, satisfied the first and second elements necessary for laying the proper predicate for admission of the G.C.I. test results. Reeves v. City of Montgomery, 466 So. 2d 1041 (Ala. Crim. App. 1985).

Prerequisite for admissibility of Intoxilyzer 5000 test results is satisfied when an officer testifies that he was so certified and a copy of the certification is admitted into evidence. Such testimony satisfies the requirement that there be a showing that the person administering the test has a valid permit for such purposes issued by the state department of health. Kelley v. State, 519 So. 2d 1368 (Ala. Crim. App. 1987).

"Actual physical control" is defined as the exclusive physical power, and present ability, to operate, move, park, or direct whatever use or nonuse is to be made of the motor vehicle at the moment. Davis v. State, 505 So. 2d 1303 (Ala. Crim. App. 1987).

"Actual physical control" is determined by a totality-of-the-circumstances test. Davis v. State, 505 So. 2d 1303 (Ala. Crim. App. 1987).

Proof of actual physical control. — The elements of proof necessary to establish actual physical control were present, where the motor of the vehicle in question was "running hot," the defendant was seen alighting from the vehicle, and he was standing by it and the odor of alcohol on his breath and person and his staggering was noticeable to the arresting officer. Robinson v. City of Abbeville, 494 So. 2d 155 (Ala. Crim. App. 1985), aff'd, 494 So.2d 159 (Ala. 1986).

Elements of offense of being in actual physical control of a vehicle while under the influence of alcohol were met where the arresting officer testified that although there was no ignition key, "the ignition was busted out" and "you had to have a screwdriver or knife or some sort of instrument like that to crank it"; that defendant "was in preparation of getting out from under the steering wheel of the car"; that the car was "boiling over like it was running hot"; and that defendant "was attempting to let the hood up." Robinson v. City of Abbeville, 494 So. 2d 159 (Ala. 1986).

Physical control shown where slumped over wheel with engine running. — Evidence that defendant was found in his truck, stopped on the side of the road, slumped over the steering wheel, with the engine running and the shift in the neutral position, established each element of "actual physical control" under this section. Loftin v. City of Montgomery, 480 So. 2d 603 (Ala. Crim. App. 1985).

Term "driving" is used interchangeably with **"operating"**. Davis v. State, 505 So. 2d 1303 (Ala. Crim. App. 1987).

Term "operating" broader than "driving". — The general rule is that: it seems clearly established that the term "operating," as used in statutes prohibiting the operation of a vehicle while intoxicated, is broader than the term "driving." Davis v. State, 505 So. 2d 1303 (Ala. Crim. App. 1987).

Phrases "under the influence of alcohol" and "is intoxicated" interchangeable. — The Commentary to this section states that "in subsection (a)(2), the phrase 'under the influence of alcohol' replaces the previously used 'is intoxicated.'" This clearly indicates an interchangeability of terms. Horton v. State, 500 So.2d 485 (Ala. Crim. App. 1986).

State need not show that defendant did not have access to alcoholic beverages after accident. — When a driver is found to be intoxicated, it is a question of fact, to be determined from the circumstances of each case, whether the driver's drunken condition existed at the time of the accident or arose in the interim between the accident and the investigation, and thus, the requirement that the state show that defendant did not have access to, or consume, alcoholic beverages after the accident is now removed. State v. Wilson, 529 So. 2d 1061 (Ala. Crim. App. 1988).

Conviction void where ticket and complaint unverified. — Driving under the influence conviction founded upon an unverified uniform traffic ticket and complaint was void and could not be considered by the director as a DUI conviction. Loyd v. Director, Dep't of Pub. Safety, 480 So. 2d 577 (Ala. Civ. App. 1985).

Uniform Traffic Ticket and Complaint sufficient to charge with DUI. — The Uniform Traffic Ticket and Complaint, as presently constituted, when properly filled out, is sufficient to legally charge the offense of driving while under the influence of alcohol. Knight v. City of Gardendale, 500 So. 2d 1257 (Ala. Crim. App. 1986).

Where the Uniform Traffic Ticket and Complaint form indicated under the section entitled "Description of Offense" that defendant was charged with driving under the influence of alcohol, his contention that he was not informed of the violation of any specific offense condemned by this section is without merit. Carroll v. City of Huntsville, 505 So. 2d 389 (Ala. Crim. App.), cert. denied, — U.S. —, 108 S. Ct. 102, 98 L. Ed. 2d 62 (1987).

District attorney's information, charging that the defendant was operating a motor vehicle "while under the influence of intoxicating liquors or narcotic drugs," was not defective in that defendant was specifically charged with a violation under subdivision (a)(4) of this section. Davis v. State, 505 So. 2d 1303 (Ala. Crim. App. 1987).

No discretion as to revocation of license under subsection (d) of this section and § 32-5A-195(j). — Under subsection (d) of this section and § 32-5A-195(j), the director of the department has no discretion as to whether or not he may revoke the driver's license. When the statutory requisites are met, i.e., the driver has been twice convicted of DUI within a five-year period, revocation of his or her driver's license is mandatory. Thus, no prerevocation hearing is provided by the DUI statutes. Bryant v. State Dep't of Pub. Safety, 494 So. 2d 425 (Ala. Civ. App. 1986).

No hearing where license revoked under subsection (d) of this section and § 32-5A-195(j). — Whether an individual whose driver's license is revoked under subsection (d) of this section and § 32-5A-195(j) is entitled to an administrative hearing is a matter of substantive law. That law is that no such hearing is allowed because revocation under the DUI statutes is mandatory. The Alabama Administrative Procedure Act, which is solely limited to procedural matters, has not altered this substantive law. Bryant v. State Dep't of Pub. Safety, 494 So. 2d 425 (Ala. Civ. App. 1986).

Speeding conviction does not bar subsequent prosecution of DUI which occurred at the same time and was the proximate cause for the DUI arrest. Pate v. State, 488 So. 2d 508 (Ala. Crim. App. 1985).

Opinion of officer as to sobriety. — In a DUI case, a police officer is allowed to give his opinion as to the sobriety vel non of the defendant. Grimes v. State, 488 So. 2d 8 (Ala. Crim. App. 1986).

Where defendant was observed drinking from bottle while parked on side of road with his emergency flashers on, police officer's "stop" and subsequent arrest of defendant on DUI grounds was justified. Scurlock v. State, 487 So. 2d 286 (Ala. Crim. App. 1986).

Date of conviction controls as to sentence enhancement. — Even though defendant's first offense was tried after his second offense, the date of conviction, rather than the date of the offense, would control in determining enhancement of sentence pursuant to this section. Loftin v. City of Montgomery, 480 So. 2d 606 (Ala. Crim. App. 1985).

Lack of counsel when previously convicted. — Where defendant was not imprisoned as a result of first two convictions, those two convictions were not void by reason of his being unrepresented by counsel, and could be considered by the director in driver's license revocation proceedings. Loyd v. Director, Dep't of Pub. Safety, 480 So. 2d 577 (Ala. Civ. App. 1985).

Construction giving everyone not previously convicted under new law first offender status is erroneous. — Construction of this new law which in effect "wipes the slate clean" would be in contradiction to obvious legislative purpose to identify problem drinking drivers so as to revoke their licenses for second and subsequent convictions for driving while intoxicated. Such construction would make everyone not previously convicted under the new law a first offender. It is the duty of the court in cases of statutory construction to give effect to legislative intent, and it should look not only to language of statute, but to its purpose and object as well. Shoemaker v. Atchison, 406 So. 2d 986 (Ala. Civ. App. 1981).

Erroneous treatment as second offender held not harmless. — Although sentence fell within the statutory range of punishment applicable to first offenders, where the trial court treated defendant as a second offender without proper proof of that status his sentence could not constitute harmless error. Loftin v. City of Montgomery, 480 So. 2d 606 (Ala. Crim. App. 1985).

Admission of defendant's attorney that defendant had been convicted of two DUI charges before the time of sentencing (in fact, before the same sentencing judge as in the instant case) could be used to prove defendant's prior conviction for enhancement purposes. Loftin v. City of Montgomery, 480 So. 2d 603 (Ala. Crim. App. 1985).

Revocation not barred by court's imposing of punishment as for first offense. — The fact that district court imposed punishment in defendant's third case as if it were his first such offense presented no impediment to the director's nondiscretionary authority to revoke his license for three years if he had actually been convicted of a total of three DUI offenses within a five-year period. Loyd v. Director, Dep't of Pub. Safety, 480 So. 2d 577 (Ala. Civ. App. 1985).

Evidence of past DUI convictions used in prosecution for murder arising out of vehicle accident. — In a prosecution for murder arising out of a vehicle accident, the trial court did not abuse its discretion in admitting into evidence DUI convictions that occurred approximately seven years before the event. Holifield v. State, 520 So. 2d 240 (Ala. Crim. App. 1987).

When a prior misdemeanor conviction is to be used for enhancement purposes under a recidivist statute, the state must establish that the defendant was represented by counsel, or validly waived counsel at the prior proceeding, only if the prior misdemeanor was punishable by more than six months' imprisonment. Bilbrey v. State, 531 So. 2d 27 (Ala. Crim. App. 1987).

Evidence held sufficient. — Although it was a close question, the testimony at trial was sufficient to allow the jury to conclude, by a fair inference drawn from the totality of the circumstances, that defendant who was found slumped over the wheel of his car, which was stuck in a ditch and on fire, was driving under the influence of alcohol. Hose v. State, 489 So. 2d 670 (Ala. Crim. App. 1986).

The state presented sufficient evidence of the crime of driving under the influence of alcohol and the issue of defendant's guilt was properly submitted to the jury where the sheriff observed defendant's automobile stopped in right-hand lane of the highway with the defendant slumped over the driver's seat either unconscious or asleep and the deputy observed a strong odor of alcohol. Beals v. State, 533 So. 2d 717 (Ala. Crim. App. 1988).

Where judge did look at defendant's prior driving record, but defendant was sentenced as first time DUI offender and his sentence was within the range of punishment set out in subsection (c), the argument that his punishment was enhanced by the trial judge's consideration of his five-year driving record was without merit. Aldridge v. State, 485 So. 2d 810 (Ala. Crim. App. 1986).

Erroneous admission of testimony concerning alco-sensor test rendered harmless by other testimony. — In a trial for driving under the influence, the erroneous admission of testimony concerning the alco-sensor test which defendant failed was rendered harmless by other evidence of intoxication which was properly before the trier of fact. Trousdale v. State, 500 So. 2d 1329 (Ala. Crim. App. 1986).

Amendment of complaint on appeal upheld. — The state did not improperly amend its complaint against defendant on appeal from district court, where in district court he was charged by U.T.T.C. (Uniform Traffic Ticket and Complaint) with "driving while under the influence of alcohol" and on appeal to circuit court in the district attorney's complaint charged that defendant "did ... drive or was in actual physical control of a vehicle while under the influence of alcohol, in violation of § 32-5A-191." There was no change in the nature of the prosecution on appeal to the circuit court. Abbott v. State, 494 So. 2d 789 (Ala. Crim. App. 1986).

Complaint held sufficient. — Complaint stating in pertinent part that defendant "did unlawfully operate a motor vehicle upon a public roadway by driving said motor vehicle while under the influence of alcohol, in violation of § 32-5A-191, and contrary to the peace and dignity of the state of Alabama," sufficiently apprised defendant of the particulars of the offense to enable him to prepare a defense. Jemison v. State, 513 So. 2d 47 (Ala. Crim. App. 1987).

Complaint upheld on appeal from district court. — The circuit judge properly refused to dismiss a complaint charging defendant with unlawfully operating or being in actual physical control of a motor vehicle while under the influence of alcohol on trial de novo on appeal of a conviction from the district court on a complaint charging only the unlawful operation of a motor vehicle. Jones v. State, 513 So. 2d 50 (Ala. Crim. App. 1986).

Charge on both subdivisions (a)(1) and (a)(2) upheld. — A jury charge which instructed the jury as to the elements of both subdivisions (a)(1) and (a)(2) of this section, although defendant was only indicted under subdivision (a)(2), was proper, where he was convicted of driving under the influence of alcohol. Jemison v. State, 513 So. 2d 47 (Ala. Crim. App. 1987).

Where the complaint in circuit court only charged a violation of subdivision (a)(2) of this section (driving "under the influence of alcohol") and the circuit judge charged the jury on subdivision (a)(1) (driving where "there is 0.10 percent or more by weight of alcohol in his blood") as well as subdivision (a)(2), there was no fatal variance from the solicitor's complaint, since a finding of 0.10 or more by weight of alcohol in a person's blood creates a statutory presumption that the person was under the influence of alcohol, and the prosecution proved that the defendant's blood alcohol level was .11%. Jones v. State, 513 So. 2d 50 (Ala. Crim. App. 1986).

Where record shows sentence imposed within statutory boundaries for offense, the court of appeals will not overturn the trial court's decision absent a showing of abuse of discretion. Kelley v. State, 519 So. 2d 1368 (Ala. Crim. App. 1987).

Sentence upheld. — Record did not support defendant's contention that the trial court was in error in sentencing him to 90 days' confinement in the municipal jail on the basis of his being a second offender, where there was no indication that the trial court was under the impression that this was the defendant's second offense and defendant's sentence clearly fell within the statutory limits for a first conviction for driving under the influence. Baker v. City of Huntsville, 516 So. 2d 927 (Ala. Crim. App. 1987).

The defendant was properly arrested for driving under the influence (DUI) when during the predawn hours, officers discovered the defendant sitting in the driver's seat of his car parked in the right-hand lane of a four-lane highway, eating chicken, with the engine not running, and moderately intoxicated, and any statement made by the defendant to the police before his arrest for DUI constituted admissible evidence. State v. Wilson, 529 So. 2d 1061 (Ala. Crim. App. 1988).

Cited in Mays v. City of Prattville, 402 So. 2d 1114 (Ala. Crim. App. 1981); Shoemaker v. Money, 409 So. 2d 847 (Ala. Civ. App. 1981); Roberts v. Town of Leighton, 452 So. 2d 916 (Ala. Crim. App. 1984); Dove v. City of Montgomery, 452 So. 2d 1382 (Ala. Crim. App. 1984); Gullatt v. City of Hoover, 459 So. 2d 1006 (Ala. Crim. App. 1984); Smith v. State,

460 So. 2d 343 (Ala. Crim. App. 1984); Hanners v. State, 461 So. 2d 43 (Ala. Crim. App. 1984); Thigpen v. State, 461 So. 2d 46 (Ala. Crim. App. 1984); Harper v. City of Troy, 467 So. 2d 269 (Ala. Crim. App. 1985); Martin v. City of Montgomery, 469 So. 2d 718 (Ala. Crim. App. 1985); Boyd v. City of Montgomery, 472 So. 2d 694 (Ala. Crim. App. 1985); Vickers v. State, 475 So. 2d 660 (Ala. Crim. App. 1985); Shoemaker v. State, 481 So. 2d 409 (Ala. Crim. App. 1985); GMC v. Edwards, 482 So. 2d 1176 (Ala. 1985); Watkins v. City of Florence, 484 So. 2d 1209 (Ala. Crim. App. 1986); Calhoun v. State, 487 So. 2d 265 (Ala. Crim. App. 1986); Smith v. State, 489 So. 2d 638 (Ala. Crim. App. 1986); Reed v. State, 492 So. 2d 293 (Ala. 1986); Fields v. State, 494 So. 2d 477 (Ala. Crim. App. 1986); Brown v. City of Montgomery, 504 So. 2d 748 (Ala. Crim. App. 1987); Hosmer v. City of Mountain Brook, 507 So. 2d 1038 (Ala. Crim. App. 1987); Hays v. City of Jacksonville, 518 So. 2d 892 (Ala. Crim. App. 1987); Jones v. City of Daphne, 519 So. 2d 587 (Ala. Crim. App. 1986); Moon v. City of Montgomery, 536 So. 2d 139 (Ala. Crim. App. 1988).

Collateral references. — 60 C.J.S., Motor Vehicles, § 37. 61A C.J.S., Motor Vehicles, §§ 625(1)-637.

7 Am. Jur. 2d, Automobiles & Highway Traffic, §§ 253-262.

Driving automobile while intoxicated as a substantive criminal offense. 42 ALR 1498, 49 ALR 1392, 68 ALR 1356.

Constitutionality and effect of statute relating to civil liability of person driving automobile while under influence of liquor. 56 ALR 327.

Driving while intoxicated as reckless driving, where driving while intoxicated is made a separate offense. 86 ALR 1274, 52 ALR2d 1337.

Criminal liability based on permitting unlicensed person to operate automobile under statute forbidding driving while intoxicated. 137 ALR 477.

Degree or nature of intoxication for purposes of statute or ordinance making it a criminal offense to operate an automobile while in that condition. 142 ALR 555.

Admissibility, in vehicle accident case, of evidence as to manner in which participant was driving before reaching scene of accident, to show intoxication of driver. 46 ALR2d 9.

What is a "motor vehicle" within statutes making it an offense to drive while intoxicated. 66 ALR2d 1146.

Speed, alone or in connection with other circumstances as gross negligence, wantonness, recklessness, or the like, under automobile guest statute. 6 ALR3d 769.

Right to trial by jury in criminal prosecution for driving while intoxicated or similar offense. 16 ALR3d 1373.

Driving under the influence, or when addicted to the use, of drugs as criminal offense. 17 ALR3d 815.

Homicide by automobile is murder. 21 ALR3d 116.

Applicability, to operation of motor vehicle on private property, of legislation making drunken driving a criminal offense. 29 ALR3d 938.

Intoxication of automobile driver as basis for awarding punitive damages. 65 ALR3d 656.

What constitutes driving, operating, or being in control of motor vehicle for purposes of driving while intoxicated statute or ordinance. 93 ALR3d 7.

Reckless driving as lesser included offense of driving while intoxicated or similar charge. 10 ALR4th 1252.

Validity of routine roadblocks by state or local police for purpose of discovery of vehicular or driving violations. 37 ALR4th 10.

Consumption or destruction of physical evidence due to testing or analysis by prosecution's expert as warranting suppression of evidence or dismissal of case against accused in state court. 40 ALR4th 594.

Snowmobile operation as DWI or DUI. 56 ALR4th 1092.

Alcohol-related vehicular homicide: nature and elements of offense. 64 ALR4th 166.

Passenger's liability to vehicular accident victim for harm caused by intoxicated motor vehicle driver. 64 ALR4th 272.

Driving while intoxicated: "choice of evils" defense that driving was necessary to protect life or property. 64 ALR4th 298.

II. DECISIONS UNDER PRIOR LAW.

Editor's note. — The cases cited below were decided under similar provisions of prior law.

Purpose of former statute. — Purpose of former similar statute was to reduce alarming frequency of automobile accidents resulting in death and injury to persons and property. Hilyer v. Dixon, 373 So. 2d 1123 (Ala. Civ. App.), cert. denied, 373 So. 2d 1125 (Ala. 1979).

Clear purpose of former similar statute was to prohibit the operation of motor vehicles by those whose faculties were so impaired that they presented a danger to the safety of the public as well as to themselves. Leu v. City of Mountain Brook, 386 So. 2d 483 (Ala. Crim. App.), cert. denied, 386 So. 2d 488 (Ala. 1980).

Roadways of military installations are highways within state and subject to its traffic laws. Hilyer v. Dixon, 373 So. 2d 1123 (Ala. Civ. App.), cert. denied, 373 So. 2d 1125 (Ala. 1979).

One who operates a motor vehicle after

ingesting a drug which renders him incapable of safely driving or operating a vehicle has violated state law. Leu v. City of Mountain Brook, 386 So. 2d 483 (Ala. Crim. App.), cert. denied, 386 So. 2d 488 (Ala. 1980).

Degree of intoxication immaterial. — In a prosecution under former similar statute the degree of intoxication was immaterial, but accused, in order to be guilty, must have been driving while intoxicated at the time and place charged. Rainey v. State, 31 Ala. App. 66, 12 So. 2d 106 (1943).

It was not necessary for the prosecution to establish that the degree or extent of intoxication had reached the stage where it would interfere with the proper operation of the vehicle. Evans v. State, 36 Ala. App. 145, 53 So. 2d 764 (1951).

Place of operation was not element of offense under former similar section. O'Reilly v. State, 235 Ala. 328, 179 So. 263 (1938).

Driving while intoxicated did not make driver "trespasser" on highway. — One unlawfully driving a vehicle on a highway while under the influence of intoxicating liquors was not a trespasser in the sense that defendant railway did not owe the driver the duty to exercise reasonable care not to injure him. Chattahoochee Valley Ry. v. Williams, 267 Ala. 464, 103 So. 2d 762 (1958).

Killing of person as result of intoxication unlawful homicide. — Under former similar statute it was unlawful for a person to drive any vehicle upon a public highway while under the influence of liquor or narcotics. If, while under the influence of liquor or narcotics, he drove the vehicle along the public highway and killed a person as a proximate result of such intoxication, the crime of unlawful homicide was complete. But if there is no connection between the driving while intoxicated and the killing, this rule would not apply. Broxton v. State, 27 Ala. App. 298, 171 So. 390 (1936).

Where jury found that motorist, who had picked up young girl hitchhiker, was at time of wreck in which girl received fatal injury under influence of intoxicating liquor, and that such fact proximately caused the girl's death, conviction for second-degree manslaughter was proper. Rombokas v. State, 27 Ala. App. 227, 170 So. 780, cert. denied, 233 Ala. 214, 170 So. 782 (1936).

Availability of defense of contributory negligence. — Contributory negligence as such is not available as defense in criminal prosecution for homicide caused by the gross and reckless misconduct of the accused, although the decedent's behavior is admissible in evidence and may have a material bearing upon the question of the defendant's guilt. If, however, the culpable negligence of the ac-

cused is found to be the cause of the decedent's death, the former is responsible under the criminal law, whether the decedent's failure to use due care contributed to his injury or not. Broxton v. State, 27 Ala. App. 298, 171 So. 390 (1936).

Intoxication in itself does not constitute contributory negligence. — The intoxication of plaintiff driver of automobile would not in itself constitute such contributory negligence as to bar his recovery for injuries received in crossing accident if plaintiff nevertheless exercised the care of a reasonably prudent driver on occasion of collision with railway car. Chattahoochee Valley Ry. v. Williams, 267 Ala. 464, 103 So. 2d 762 (1958).

Effect of guilt of other driver. — In prosecution for driving automobile while intoxicated, fact that driver of other automobile, with which defendant collided, might also be guilty would not exonerate defendant. Holley v. State, 25 Ala. App. 260, 144 So. 535, cert. denied, 225 Ala. 597, 144 So. 537 (1932).

Fact that defendant, charged with driving automobile while intoxicated, was free from negligence in colliding with another automobile would not necessarily establish his innocence. Holley v. State, 25 Ala. App. 260, 144 So. 535 (1932).

Determination of previous conviction. — It was the duty of the court to ascertain from the evidence whether accused had been previously convicted in order to determine the extent of the punishment to be imposed. Upon review it would be presumed that the lower court properly performed its duty in such procedure. Walker v. State, 38 Ala. App. 204, 84 So. 2d 383 (1955).

Complaint upheld. — A charge in complaint that accused drove motor vehicle while under the influence of liquor was equivalent to charging him with being intoxicated. Sexton v. State, 29 Ala. App. 336, 196 So. 742 (1940).

Affidavit held sufficient. — Affidavit filed in district court, charging that defendant drove automobile while intoxicated, and information filed in circuit court, charging that defendant, being under influence of intoxicating liquors, drove vehicle on highway, was held sufficient and not at variance. Holley v. State, 25 Ala. App. 260, 144 So. 535, cert. denied, 225 Ala. 597, 144 So. 537 (1932).

Testimony that defendant was "drinking" was only a conclusion of the witness and did not establish that defendant was intoxicated or under the influence of intoxicants when driving motor vehicle, where no one testified to having seen defendant take a drink. Rainey v. State, 31 Ala. App. 66, 12 So. 2d 106 (1943).

Proof of prior consumption of intoxicat-

ing beverages by driver is logically relevant to prove intoxication at a later time unless such drinking occurred at a time too remote to prove the alleged later intoxication. As to precisely how many hours must elapse before such proof becomes irrelevant because too remote, no hard and fast rule can be laid down. Each case must depend on the circumstances of that case. Chattahoochee Valley Ry. v. Williams, 267 Ala. 464, 103 So. 2d 762 (1958).

Evidence held admissible. — Evidence that defendant drank whiskey either three and one-half or four hours prior to accident, or five and one-half or six hours prior thereto, was admissible. The weight of such evidence was for the jury. Crump v. State, 29 Ala. App. 22, 191 So. 475, cert. denied, 238 Ala. 439, 191 So. 478 (1939).

Evidence held inadmissible. — Where state's evidence showed that accused, while intoxicated, was seen to drive his automobile on the highway, reception of evidence that accused was drinking an hour and a half later, when arrested, was error, since the drinking was not part of the "res gestae." Rainey v. State, 31 Ala. App. 66, 12 So. 2d 106 (1943).

Evidence held sufficient. — See Faulkner v. Gilchrist, 225 Ala. 391, 143 So. 803 (1932).

Evidence held to present question for jury. — Dowdy v. State, 39 Ala. App. 178, 96 So. 2d 687 (1957).

Trial court sitting without jury to weigh conflicting evidence. — In prosecution for driving while intoxicated, it was within exclusive province of trial court, sitting without jury, to weigh conflicting evidence and ascertain truth of issue raised thereby, and court of appeals, not being clearly convinced that to allow conviction to stand would be manifestly wrong or unjust, would not disturb judgment of trial court. Edmondson v. State, 30 Ala. App. 433, 7 So. 2d 508 (1942).

Questions for jury. — When an accident occurred on a public road in which a person was killed by being run over by an automobile and it was shown that the driver had been drinking, it was a question for the jury to say, from all the facts and circumstances surrounding the homicide, whether or not the driver at the time of the accident was under the influence of liquor and, if so, whether that condition was the proximate cause of the homicide. Broxton v. State, 27 Ala. App. 298, 171 So. 390 (1936).

Instruction held improper. — In prosecution for driving automobile while intoxicated, instruction that, in determining defendant's guilt, jury could consider responsibility for collision between automobiles, was properly refused as misleading. Holley v. State, 25 Ala. App. 260, 144 So. 535, cert. denied, 225 Ala. 597, 144 So. 537 (1932).

Error not cured. — Error in refusing to charge that defendant could not be convicted both of driving an automobile while intoxicated and of careless and heedless driving was not cured by trial court's setting aside conviction of careless and heedless driving after conviction on both counts. Landers v. State, 26 Ala. App. 506, 162 So. 550 (1935).

Sentence to hard labor for first offense held error. — Judgment entry in prosecution for driving automobile on public highway while under influence of intoxicating liquors or narcotic drugs, providing for three months additional hard labor, was unauthorized under former section when it affirmatively appeared to be defendant's first violation. McIntosh v. State, 27 Ala. App. 411, 173 So. 617 (1936), modified on other grounds, 234 Ala. 16, 173 So. 619 (1937).

§ 32-5A-192. Homicide by vehicle.

(a) Whoever shall unlawfully and unintentionally cause the death of another person while engaged in the violation of any state law or municipal ordinance applying to the operation or use of a vehicle or to the regulation of traffic shall be guilty of homicide when such violation is the proximate cause of said death.

(b) Any person convicted of homicide by vehicle shall be fined not less than $500.00 nor more than $2,000.00, or shall be imprisoned for a term not less than one year nor more than five years, or may be so fined and so imprisoned. (Acts 1980, No. 80-434, p. 604, § 9-107; Acts 1983, No. 83-620, p. 959, § 1.)

Commentary

Alabama previously had no statute comparable to this section, although this provision or one similar to it appears in the laws of most other states. This section is not a bar to prosecution under article 1 of chapter 6 of Title 13A which is the homicide sections of the Criminal Code.

Code commissioner's note. — Acts 1983, No. 83-620, § 2, provides: "The provisions of this act are supplemental to other laws not inconsistent with this act, and such other laws shall not be deemed to be repealed by this act."

Acts 1983, No. 83-620, § 3, provides that the act applies to conduct occurring after July 29, 1983, and that conduct occurring before that date shall be governed by preexisting law.

Constitutionality. — This section, as it read prior to the 1983 amendment, clearly allowed misdemeanor imprisonment ranging from three months to one year and felony imprisonment from one to five years and was therefore unconstitutional. Whirley v. State, 481 So. 2d 1151 (Ala. Crim. App. 1985); writ quashed, 481 So. 2d 1154 (Ala. 1986).

Vehicular homicide statute does not violate guarantees of Ala. Const., article 1, § 6, because from a reading of the statute a defendant could be reasonably apprised of the accusation against him or her and the possible penal consequences. Newberry v. State, 493 So. 2d 995 (Ala. 1986); Fields v. State, 494 So. 2d 477 (Ala. Crim. App. 1986).

Refusal to submit to a chemical test for intoxication is not a compelled testimonial communication; thus, admission of evidence of such refusal and comment thereon does not violate the accused's privilege against self-incrimination. Gibson v. City of Troy, 481 So. 2d 463 (Ala. Crim. App. 1985).

Subsection (c) does not grant accused person the "right" to refuse to submit to chemical testing. Rather, this acquiescence in refusal is in the posture of avoiding potential violent conflict. Gibson v. City of Troy, 481 So. 2d 463 (Ala. Crim. App. 1985).

Homicide by vehicle is not a lesser included offense of murder. — The crime proscribed in this section cannot, as a matter of law, be a lesser offense included within an indictment for murder under § 13A-6-2. The use of a vehicle is a required element of proof for vehicular homicide, but not for murder under § 13A-6-2. Homicide by vehicle requires that the "murder weapon" be a vehicle. Whirley v. State, 481 So. 2d 1151 (Ala. Crim. App. 1985); writ quashed, 481 So. 2d 1154 (Ala. 1986). Under the facts of the case, vehicular homicide was a lesser included offense of murder by way of application of either subsections (a)(1) or (a)(4) of § 13A-1-9, Jordan v.

State, 486 So. 2d 485 (Ala. 1986), holding however on application for rehearing that the trial court's refusal to charge the jury on vehicular homicide was harmless error where trial court instructed the jury on murder and on the lesser included offenses of manslaughter and criminally negligent homicide, and the jury reached a verdict of guilty on the offense of murder.

Criminally negligent homicide is not a lesser included offense of homicide by vehicle. Sams v. State, 506 So. 2d 1027 (Ala. Crim. App. 1986).

This section did not bar the state from prosecuting defendant for murder under § 13A-6-2 where his car collided with another vehicle resulting in the death of the driver of the other vehicle and a blood test showed defendant's blood alcohol level to be .204 percent. Duncan v. State, 473 So. 2d 1203 (Ala. Crim. App. 1985).

It was not necessary to allege intoxicant involved, and the failure to do so did not mislead defendant or hamper his ability to defend himself, where the indictments averred the statutes violated, i.e., driving while intoxicated or, in the alternative, reckless driving. They adequately informed defendant of which state laws or municipal ordinances applying to the operation of a vehicle he was being accused of violating. Fields v. State, 494 So. 2d 477 (Ala. Crim. App. 1986).

Testimony of police officer as to breathalyzer test result. — Police officer was properly permitted to testify that defendant registered .15 percent on a breathalyzer test, where he testified (1) that the city police department designated or accepted the breathalyzer machine as a machine to measure alcoholic content in the blood; (2) that he followed the rules and regulations of the state board of health in testing defendant; and (3) that he was licensed and authorized to operate the breathalyzer machine, and in addition, produced a valid license issued by the state department of health. Nagem v. City of Phenix City, 488 So. 2d 1379 (Ala. Crim. App. 1986).

Cited in Irby v. State, 455 So. 2d 271 (Ala. Crim. App. 1984).

Collateral references. — 7A Am. Jur. 2d, Automobiles & Highway Traffic, §§ 324-344, 364.

Speed, alone or in connection with other

circumstances as gross negligence, wantonness, recklessness, or the like under automobile guest statute. 6 ALR3d 769.

Alcohol-related vehicular homicide: nature and elements of offense. 64 ALR4th 166.

Passenger's liability to vehicular accident victim for harm caused by intoxicated motor vehicle driver. 64 ALR4th 272.

Driving while intoxicated: "choice of evils" defense that driving was necessary to protect life or property. 64 ALR4th 298.

§ 32-5A-193. Fleeing or attempting to elude police officer.

(a) Any driver of a motor vehicle who willfully fails or refuses to bring his vehicle to a stop, or who otherwise flees or attempts to elude a pursuing police vehicle, when given a visual or audible signal to bring the vehicle to a stop, shall be guilty of a misdemeanor. The signal given by the police officer may be by hand, voice, emergency light or siren.

(b) Every person convicted of fleeing or attempting to elude a police officer shall be punished by imprisonment for not less than 30 days nor more than six months or by a fine of not less than $100.00 nor more than $500.00, or by both such fine and imprisonment. (Acts 1980, No. 80-434, p. 604, § 9-108.)

Commentary

Alabama formerly had no statute comparable to this section, although this provision or one similar to it appears in the laws of other states. This section was added to the Uniform Vehicle Act proposals in 1968.

Cited in Thigpen v. State, 461 So. 2d 46 (Ala. Crim. App. 1984).

Collateral references. — 7A Am. Jur. 2d, Automobiles & Highway Traffic, §§ 357, 359, 362.

Speed, alone or in connection with other circumstances as gross negligence, wantonness, recklessness, or the like, under automobile guest statute. 6 ALR3d 769.

§ 32-5A-194. Chemical tests; admissible as evidence; procedure for valid chemical analyses; permits for individuals performing analyses; persons qualified to withdraw blood; presumptions based on percent of alcohol in blood; refusal to submit; no liability for technician.

(a) Upon the trial of any civil, criminal or quasi-criminal action or proceeding arising out of acts alleged to have been committed by any person while driving or in actual control of a vehicle while under the influence of alcohol or controlled substance, evidence of the amount of alcohol or controlled substance in a person's blood at the alleged time, as determined by a chemical analysis of the person's blood, urine, breath or other bodily substance, shall be admissible. Where such a chemical test is made the following provisions shall apply:

(1) Chemical analyses of the person's blood, urine, breath or other bodily substance to be considered valid under the provisions of this section shall have been performed according to methods approved by the department of forensic sciences and by an individual possessing a valid permit issued by the department of forensic sciences for this purpose. The court trying the

case may take judicial notice of the methods approved by the department of forensic sciences. The department of forensic sciences is authorized to approve satisfactory techniques or methods, to ascertain the qualifications and competence of individuals to conduct such analyses, and to issue permits which shall be subject to termination or revocation at the discretion of the department of forensic sciences. The department of forensic sciences shall not approve the permit required in this section for making tests for any law enforcement officer other than a member of the state highway patrol, a sheriff or his deputies, a city policeman or laboratory personnel employed by the department of forensic sciences.

(2) When a person shall submit to a blood test at the direction of a law enforcement officer under the provisions of section 32-5-192, only a physician or a registered nurse (or other qualified person) may withdraw blood for the purpose of determining the alcoholic content therein. This limitation shall not apply to the taking of breath or urine specimens. If the test given under section 32-5-192 is a chemical test of urine, the person tested shall be given such privacy in the taking of the urine specimen as will insure the accuracy of the specimen and, at the same time, maintain the dignity of the individual involved.

(3) The person tested may at his own expense have a physician, or a qualified technician, registered nurse or other qualified person of his own choosing administer a chemical test or tests in addition to any administered at the discretion of a law enforcement officer. The failure or inability to obtain an additional test by a person shall not preclude the admission of evidence relating to the test or tests taken at the direction of a law enforcement officer.

(4) Upon the written request of the person who shall submit to a chemical test or tests at the request of a law enforcement officer, full information concerning the test or tests shall be made available to him or his attorney.

(5) Percent by weight of alcohol in the blood shall be based upon grams of alcohol per 100 cubic centimeters of blood or grams of alcohol per 210 liters of breath.

(b) Upon the trial of any civil, criminal, or quasi-criminal action or proceeding arising out of acts alleged to have been committed by any person while driving or in actual physical control of a vehicle while under the influence of alcohol, the amount of alcohol in the person's blood at the time alleged as shown by chemical analysis of the person's blood, urine, breath or other bodily substance shall give rise to the following presumptions:

(1) If there were at that time 0.05 percent or less by weight of alcohol in the person's blood, it shall be presumed that the person was not under the influence of alcohol.

(2) If there were at the time in excess of 0.05 percent but less than 0.10 percent by weight of alcohol in the person's blood, such fact shall not give rise to any presumption that the person was or was not under the influence of alcohol, but such fact may be considered with other competent evidence in determining whether the person was under the influence of alcohol.

(3) If there were at that time 0.10 percent or more by weight of alcohol in the person's blood, it shall be presumed that the person was under the influence of alcohol.

(4) The foregoing provisions of this subsection shall not be construed as limiting the introduction of any other competent evidence bearing upon the question whether the person was under the influence of alcohol.

(c) If a person under arrest refuses to submit to a chemical test under the provisions of section 32-5-192, evidence of refusal shall be admissible in any civil, criminal or quasi-criminal action or proceeding arising out of acts alleged to have been committed while the person was driving or in actual physical control of a motor vehicle while under the influence of alcohol or controlled substance.

(d) No physician, registered nurse or duly licensed chemical laboratory technologist or clinical laboratory technician or medical facility shall incur any civil or criminal liability as a result of the proper administering of a blood test when requested in writing by a law enforcement officer to administer such a test. (Acts 1980, No. 80-434, p. 604, § 9-103; Acts 1988, No. 88-660, p. 1058, § 1.)

Commentary

This section makes relatively minor changes in former section 32-5-193. In general, where the previous statute applied only to alcohol, this section refers to controlled substances as well as alcohol. And where the prior statute referred to blood, urine and breath, this section adds to the list "other bodily substances." The major change has simply been a reorganization of the provisions for clarification purposes, following along the pattern of the 1971 amendments to Uniform Vehicle Code section 11-902.1, on an earlier version of which the prior statute had been patterned. The new introductory paragraph was added to the section, according to Traffic Laws Annotated 628 (1972), "to assure the quality and admissibility of chemical tests performed to determine the presence of drugs in addition to alcohol." The third sentence of subsection (a)(2), does not appear in the UVC, but is carried over from section 32-5-193(e). This subsection also differs from the UVC counterpart in making use of the word "direction" rather than the UVC's "request," in order to parallel the language of section 32-5-192. It should be noted, however, that this prior statute allowed a person to object to a blood test and to have another chemical test substituted in its place. Subsection (a)(4) varies from the UVC in requiring the request to be in writing, as did the former statute. Subsection (b) is identical to the prior law, section 32-5-193(a), except that the word "alcohol" replaces the phrase "intoxicating liquor." Subsection (c) is basically the same as former section 32-5-193(h), except for minor changes in wording. Subsection (d) is not a part of the UVC, but carries over the identical provision in the previous statute, section 32-5-193(g).

The 1988 amendment, effective May 13, 1988, substituted "department of forensic sciences" for "state board of health" in the first, third, and fourth sentences, inserted the second sentence, in subdivision (a)(1); and added "or grams of alcohol per 210 liters of breath" in subdivision (a)(5).

Code commissioner's note. — The "department of toxicology and criminal investigation" was changed to the "department of forensic sciences" in subdivision (a)(1). See § 36-18-1 et seq.

I. General Consideration.
II. Decisions Under Prior Law.

I. GENERAL CONSIDERATION.

Photoelectric intoximeter test not necessary for prima facie case. — It is unnecessary for the prosecution to resort to the photoelectric intoximeter (P.E.I.) test in order to make a prima facie case. However, the results of a P.E.I. test are highly prejudicial. Curtis v. City of Sheffield, 502 So. 2d 833 (Ala. 1986).

Police inquiry for taking blood-alcohol test not interrogation. — In the context of an arrest for driving while intoxicated, a police inquiry of whether the suspect will take a blood-alcohol test is not an interrogation within the meaning of Miranda. Boyd v. City of Montgomery, 472 So. 2d 694 (Ala. Crim. App. 1985).

The authorized method of determining the blood alcohol level of a person suspected of driving under the influence of alcohol may be supplied by any officer who would be in a position to know which test was authorized. Harper v. City of Troy, 467 So. 2d 269 (Ala. Crim. App. 1985).

A duly licensed and certified medical laboratory technician was qualified to draw blood samples in accordance with subdivision (a)(2) of this section. Powell v. State, 515 So. 2d 140 (Ala. Crim. App. 1986).

No duty to inform accused of having independent blood alcohol test. — Subdivision (a)(3) of this section places no duty upon any law enforcement agency administering tests to inform or notify the accused that he may have an independent blood alcohol test performed. Harper v. City of Troy, 467 So. 2d 269 (Ala. Crim. App. 1985).

There is no obligation on the part of police authorities to advise a defendant of the existence of this section. Bilbrey v. State, 531 So. 2d 27 (Ala. Crim. App. 1987).

The purpose of allowing an accused to obtain an additional test is to provide him a means of "cross checking" the state's test. This second test is clearly in addition to, and not in lieu of, the test administered by law enforcement officers. Subdivision (a)(3) requires an accused to first submit to a chemical test properly directed by the arresting officer prior to the taking of additional tests at his own request. Gibson v. City of Troy, 481 So. 2d 463 (Ala. Crim. App. 1985).

No right to independent test upon refusal to take authorized test. — Defendant did not have the right to have an independent blood alcohol test administered when he refused to take the blood alcohol test authorized

by the state. Gibson v. City of Troy, 481 So. 2d 463 (Ala. Crim. App. 1985).

Accused must be allowed reasonable opportunity to obtain independent test. — Pursuant to this section, due process requires that when an accused has complied with police requests to submit to a blood alcohol test and subsequently requests an independent blood alcohol test, the accused must be allowed a reasonable opportunity to obtain a timely, independent test at his own expense, and police authorities may not frustrate his attempts to do so. Bilbrey v. State, 531 So. 2d 27 (Ala. Crim. App. 1987).

Prerequisite to taking additional tests. — This section requires an accused to first submit to a chemical test directed by an arresting officer as a prerequisite to the taking of additional tests at his request. Bilbrey v. State, 531 So. 2d 27 (Ala. Crim. App. 1987).

Refusal to transport defendant to a hospital was not unreasonable under the circumstances, for there were no circumstances which showed the conduct of police to be unreasonable, since defendant was allowed access to a telephone and could have arranged to have an independent test conducted, at his own expense, at the place of incarceration. Bilbrey v. State, 531 So. 2d 27 (Ala. Crim. App. 1987).

Where blood is seized only for medical purposes and not in furtherance of a criminal or accident investigation, the arrest requirement of Alabama's Implied Consent Law is not applicable. Veasey v. State, 531 So. 2d 320 (Ala. Crim. App.), cert. denied, 531 So. 2d 323 (Ala. 1988).

Predicate for admission of test results. — There are no Alabama cases which specifically outline all the requisite elements of a predicate for the admission of scientific test results. However, it is generally held that such a predicate must show that the circumstances of the taking of the sample, the identification, maintenance, and transporting of it, and the testing itself are scientifically acceptable and reasonably expected to produce results which are accurate and reliable. Kent v. Singleton, 457 So. 2d 356 (Ala. 1984).

To establish a predicate for admitting the photoelectric intoximeter test results, without reliance on the statute, there should be evidence that (1) the theory underlying the test is valid and generally accepted as such; (2) the intoximeter is a reliable instrument and generally accepted as such; (3) the intoximeter test was administered by a qualified individual who could properly conduct the test and interpret the results; and (4) the instrument used in conducting the test was in good working condition and the test was conducted in such a manner as to secure accurate results. Moore v. State, 442 So. 2d 164 (Ala. Crim. App. 1983).

In a prosecution for an offense arising while the motorist was driving under the influence of intoxicating liquor, in order for a chemical analysis of a person's blood, breath, or urine to be valid and admissible in evidence, a predicate must be laid showing (1) that the motorist was lawfully arrested before being directed to submit to a test, (2) that the law enforcement officer had reasonable grounds to believe that the motorist was driving under the influence, (3) that the test administered was designated by the proper law enforcement agency, § 32-5-192(a), (4) that the test was performed according to methods approved by the state board of health, and (5) by an individual possessing a valid permit issued by the state board of health for this purpose. A party offering results from tests shown to be given in conformity with the statute is relieved of the burden of laying the extensive predicate generally necessary for admission of scientific test results. Boyd v. City of Montgomery, 472 So. 2d 694 (Ala. Crim. App. 1985).

A proper predicate must be laid for the admissibility of evidence of the amount of alcohol found in a person's blood, breath, or urine. Curtis v. City of Sheffield, 502 So. 2d 829 (Ala. Crim. App.), rev'd on other grounds, 502 So. 2d 833 (Ala. 1986).

Showing prerequisite to admission of blood alcohol test results. — While it is unnecessary for prosecution to resort to chemical test in order to make out prima facie case of vehicular homicide, if a party wishes to have results of blood alcohol test admitted into evidence he has two choices; either he must show that tests were taken in conformity with this section, or he must lay proper foundation for their admission under general evidence principles. Admission of blood alcohol test results for which neither of these procedures is followed results in reversible error. Whetstone v. State, 407 So. 2d 854 (Ala. Crim. App. 1981).

In order for the photoelectric intoximeter (P.E.I.) test results to be admitted into evidence, the prosecution must show (1) which test has been designated for use by the law enforcement agency administering the test, and (2) that the test and operator have been approved by the state board of health. Harper v. City of Troy, 467 So. 2d 269 (Ala. Crim. App. 1985).

Introduction of a certified copy of the rules and regulations promulgated by the state board of health, along with testimony of officer that he adhered to these rules and regulations when administering photoelectric intoximeter (P.E.I.) test to defendant and the officer's valid certification permit, issued by the state board of health, held to show that the test and operator were approved by the state board of health. Harper v. City of Troy, 467 So. 2d 269 (Ala. Crim. App. 1985).

Introduction of photoelectric intoximeter (P.E.I.) logbook for the purpose of indicating that the machine had been inspected and performed properly was without error. Harper v. City of Troy, 467 So. 2d 269 (Ala. Crim. App. 1985).

There are several steps in the process of laying a proper predicate for admission into evidence of results of a photoelectric intoximeter test. First, the law enforcement agency of the officer who administers the test must have designated such test as their means of testing those believed to be under the influence of alcohol. This information may be furnished by the officer who administered the test. Secondly, there must be a showing that the test was performed according to methods approved by the state board of health. This may be proved by the introduction of the rules and regulations the officer followed while administering the test and the officer's testimony that he did, in fact, follow those rules when he administered the test in question. Thirdly, there must be a showing that the person administering the test has a valid permit issued by the state board of health for this purpose. Bush v. City of Troy, 474 So. 2d 164 (Ala. Crim. App. 1984), aff'd, 474 So. 2d 168 (Ala. 1985).

The results of a photoelectric intoximeter test may be received into evidence upon one of two lines of proof. The first is, proof that the test was administered in conformity with this section. The second method is proof in accordance with the accepted traditional legal principles. This refers to establishing the foundation or predicate for the introduction of scientific test results. In neither the statutory path nor the traditional path establishing this foundation does the court find a requirement that each batch of chemicals be tested. Bice v. State, 472 So. 2d 440 (Ala. Crim. App. 1985).

In order for photo-electric intoximeter test results to be admissible, the state is required to show, among other things, that the test was performed according to methods approved by the state board of health. Gibson v. City of Troy, 481 So. 2d 463 (Ala. Crim. App. 1985).

Failure to check off a step on photoelectric intoximeter test. — Requirement that there be a showing that the photoelectric intoximeter test was performed according to methods approved by the state board of health was met, although the investigator failed to place a check mark next to step 18 and could not "independently recollect" having done step 18 on this particular test, since it would be absurd to expect any law enforcement officer to "independently recollect" having performed one particular step, during one particular test upon a person, when that officer regularly administers numerous tests during the course of his duties, and the fact that the inspector did not place a check mark beside step 18 did not necessarily indicate that he did not perform the test according to the approved procedures of the state board of health. This was particularly true where he testified that he was sure he performed step 18 because he wrote in the final reading in step 18. Pate v. State, 512 So. 2d 138 (Ala. Crim. App. 1987).

Admission of test results without showing of periodic inspection not error. — Trial court did not err in admitting the results of the photoelectric intoximeter test into evidence without a showing by the state that the testing equipment had been periodically inspected by an agent of the state board of health. Reed v. State, 492 So. 2d 293 (Ala. 1986).

But admission of test results error absent testimony that test officially adopted. — Trial court erred in admitting the results of the photoelectric intoximeter test into evidence without testimony that the law enforcement agency administering the test had officially adopted this test method. Reed v. State, 492 So. 2d 293 (Ala. 1986).

Admission of photoelectric intoximeter test results without proper predicate not harmless error. — In light of conflicting testimony and the great weight often given to results from sophisticated, technical machinery, admission of photoelectric intoximeter test results without prior admission of related documents cannot be said to be harmless error. Curtis v. City of Sheffield, 502 So. 2d 833 (Ala. 1986).

Testimony as to periodic inspection not required to lay foundation. — There is no need for the state to offer testimony concerning a periodic inspection of the testing equipment in order to lay the predicate for admissibility of the photoelectric intoximeter test results. Reed v. State, 492 So. 2d 293 (Ala. 1986).

Where technologist testified that the machine she used measured milligrams of alcohol per deciliter, the trial court could take judicial notice of the fact that since 100 cubic centimeters was equivalent to one deciliter, 246 milligrams per deciliter was equivalent to .246 grams per 100 cubic centimeters, and technologist's finding that defendant's blood-alcohol level was .246 was correct.

Veasey v. State, 531 So. 2d 320 (Ala. Crim. App.), cert. denied, 531 So. 2d 323 (Ala. 1988).

Testimony of police officer as to breathalyzer test result. — Police officer was properly permitted to testify that defendant registered .15 percent on a breathalyzer test, where he testified (1) that the city police department designated or accepted the breathalyzer machine as a machine to measure alcoholic content in the blood; (2) that he followed the rules and regulations of the state board of health in testing defendant; and (3) that he was licensed and authorized to operate the breathalyzer machine, and in addition, produced a valid license issued by the state department of health. Nagem v. City of Phenix City, 488 So. 2d 1379 (Ala. Crim. App. 1986).

The log sheet for a photo-electric intoximeter was properly admitted into evidence as a business record, where such log sheets were notarized copies, which were kept in the custody of the person who notarized the copies, the log sheet was kept with the P.E.I. machine at all times as required, the officer who administered the test had been present on occasions when the machine had been calibrated and the log sheet indicated when the machine had been checked, and the log sheet also contained the name of each person tested, the test number, the date, time, operator's name, and witnesses. Gibson v. City of Troy, 481 So. 2d 463 (Ala. Crim. App. 1985).

Alco-Sensor test not admissible. — The Alco-Sensor test does not determine the "amount of alcohol or controlled substance in a person's blood" and for that reason is not admissible under Alabama's chemical test for intoxication statute. Boyd v. City of Montgomery, 472 So. 2d 694 (Ala. Crim. App. 1985).

Where the admission into evidence of the results of an Alco-Sensor test constitutes error, that error has been considered harmless where the results were cumulative and there was overwhelming evidence against the motorist, and where the test results were offered not for the purpose of establishing the charge against the motorist but rather to establish justification for placing the motorist under arrest and there was ample evidence to justify the arrest. Boyd v. City of Montgomery, 472 So. 2d 694 (Ala. Crim. App. 1985).

Admission of test results harmless error where evidence was ample. — Where there was ample evidence of defendant's drunkenness while operating a motor vehicle, error, if any, in the trial court's allowing the results of a chemical blood test was harmless error. Powell v. State, 515 So. 2d 140 (Ala. Crim. App. 1986).

There is no requirement that the state prove that person who checked and cali-

brated photoelectric intoximeter was certified to do so by the board of health. Bush v. City of Troy, 474 So. 2d 168 (Ala. 1985).

Nothing requires that this section be used as exclusive means for admitting intoxication test results. Whetstone v. State, 407 So. 2d 854 (Ala. Crim. App. 1981).

This section is not an exclusive means for admitting blood alcohol test results. Kent v. Singleton, 457 So. 2d 356 (Ala. 1984).

The mere fact that a blood sample is taken at a hospital does not insure its reliability. Kent v. Singleton, 457 So. 2d 356 (Ala. 1984).

Motorist's breath not protected by fifth amendment. — The Alco-Sensor test was used by the officer in determining whether he had probable cause to arrest the defendant. The officer was not required to inform the defendant of his Miranda rights before giving the field test. In the usual traffic stop, the policeman who lacks probable cause but whose observations lead him reasonably to suspect that a particular person has committed, is committing, or is about to commit a crime, may detain the person briefly in order to investigate his suspicion and "may ask the detainee a moderate number of questions to determine his identity and to try to obtain information confirming or dispelling the officer's suspicions." A motorist's breath is not protected by the Fifth Amendment privilege against self-incrimination. Boyd v. City of Montgomery, 472 So. 2d 694 (Ala. Crim. App. 1985).

The presumption regarding an individual's state of intoxication, as shown from test results, is rebuttable rather than irrebuttable. Stowes v. State, 513 So. 2d 86 (Ala. Crim. App. 1987).

"Presumption" as permissive inference or rebuttable presumption in subdivision (b)(3). — In subdivision (b)(3) of this section, the legislature used the word "presumption" in the sense of a permissive inference or rebuttable presumption. Salazar v. State, 505 So. 2d 1287 (Ala. Crim. App. 1986).

"Presumption" in subdivision (b)(3) not conclusive presumption. — In subdivision (b)(3) of this section, the legislature did not intend to create a so-called "conclusive presumption" since it specifically provided that "any other competent evidence bearing upon the question whether the person was under the influence of alcohol" may be introduced. Salazar v. State, 505 So. 2d 1287 (Ala. Crim. App. 1986).

Instruction of jury on the rebuttable presumption of subdivision (b)(3). — Trial court must adequately instruct the jury on the nature and effect of the rebuttable presumption in subdivision (b)(3) of this section. Without guidance as to the nature of the presumption, there is no way to know whether the jury has properly or improperly reached its verdict. Salazar v. State, 505 So. 2d 1287 (Ala. Crim. App. 1986).

Court should have instructed the jury that they may infer from the blood alcohol evidence that appellant was driving under the influence of intoxicating liquor, but they are not compelled to do so, and are to consider that evidence together with all other competent evidence in the case in determining whether the state proved beyond a reasonable doubt that appellant was under the influence of intoxicating liquor at the time of the fatal collision. The instruction as it stood, without explanation by the trial court as to the statutory presumption's rebuttable nature, was highly prejudicial to appellant and constituted reversible error. Salazar v. State, 505 So. 2d 1287 (Ala. Crim. App. 1986).

Courts may take judicial notice of board of health administrative regulations pertaining to blood alcohol tests. Vizzina v. City of Birmingham, 533 So. 2d 652 (Ala. Crim. App. 1987), aff'd, 533 So. 2d 658 (Ala. 1988).

Evidence sufficient. — Even had the foundation for the admittance of the blood alcohol test results been insufficient, the erroneous admission of the test results would not have required a reversal since it was clear from the record that the trial judge's ruling was not based on the results of the blood test, the trial judge having clearly indicated that the uncontroverted fact that the appellant had been drinking earlier in the day in combination with the uncontroverted fact that the defendant was aware that he was tired and sleepy and continued to drive the automobile formed basis of his ruling. McDaniel v. State, 506 So. 2d 360 (Ala. Crim. App. 1986).

Where the first blood sample taken by the defendant's physician was never in the custody or control of the state, the state relied on the findings of the defendant's own doctor regarding the blood alcohol level of this sample, and it seemed that the defendant could have gained access to a sample of this blood specimen at any time simply by requesting a sample from his own physician, there was no error due to the fact that the defendant was not able to procure the blood sample in the custody of the state. The fact that his own physician did conduct an independent analysis further served to render the defendant's claim meritless. Horton v. State, 500 So. 2d 485 (Ala. Crim. App. 1986).

Where jury was instructed that a blood alcohol level of .10 percent or more raised an irrebuttable presumption that the person was under the influence of alcohol, and other instructions failed to cure the earlier charge by clearly informing the jury that the presumption of intoxication based on the results of the chemical test was rebuttable, defendant's conviction was reversed. Stowes v. State, 513 So. 2d 86 (Ala. Crim. App. 1987).

No variance shown. — Where complaint in circuit court only charged a violation of § 32-5A-191(a)(2) (driving "under the influence of alcohol") and the circuit judge charged the jury on § 32-5A-191(a)(1) (driving where "there is 0.10 percent or more by weight of alcohol in his blood") as well as § 32-5A-191(a)(2), there was no fatal variance from the solicitor's complaint, since a finding of 0.10 percent or more by weight of alcohol in a person's blood creates a statutory presumption that the person was under the influence of alcohol and the prosecution proved that defendant's blood alcohol level was .11%. Jones v. State, 513 So. 2d 50 (Ala. Crim. App. 1986).

Cited in McGough v. Slaughter, 395 So. 2d 972 (Ala. 1981); Fritz v. Salva, 406 So. 2d 884 (Ala. 1981); Slaughter v. State, 424 So. 2d 1365 (Ala. Crim. App. 1982); Swann v. City of Huntsville, 455 So. 2d 944 (Ala. Crim. App. 1984); O'Connor v. City of Montgomery, 462 So. 2d 756 (Ala. Crim. App. 1984); Warden v. State, 468 So. 2d 203 (Ala. Crim. App. 1985); Knighten v. State, 507 So. 2d 1015 (Ala. Crim. App. 1986); Brown v. City of Montgomery, 504 So. 2d 748 (Ala. Crim. App. 1987).

Collateral references. — 61 C.J.S., Motor Vehicles, § 516(4). 61A C.J.S., Motor Vehicles, §§ 625(4), 633(6), 633(11).

Validity of legislation creating presumption of intoxication or the like from presence of specified percentage of alcohol in blood. 46 ALR2d 1176.

Qualification as expert to testify as to findings or results of scientific test to determine alcoholic content of blood. 77 ALR2d 971.

Constitutional right of one charged with intoxication to summon a physician at accused's own expense to make test for alcohol in system. 78 ALR2d 905.

Construction and application of statutes creating presumption or other inference of intoxication from specified percentages of alcohol present in the system. 16 ALR3d 748.

Admissibility in criminal case of blood alcohol test where blood was taken from unconscious driver. 72 ALR3d 325.

Driving while intoxicated: Duty of law enforcement officer to offer suspect chemical sobriety test under implied consent law. 95 ALR3d 710.

Necessity and sufficiency of proof that tests of blood alcohol concentration were conducted in conformance with prescribed methods. 96 ALR3d 745.

Request before submitting to chemical sobriety test to communicate with counsel as refusal to take test. 97 ALR3d 852.

Evidence of automobile passenger's blood-alcohol level as admissible in support of defense that passenger was contributorily negligent or assumed risk of automobile accident. 5 ALR4th 1194.

Reckless driving as lesser included offense of driving while intoxicated or similar charge. 10 ALR4th 1252.

Admissibility in criminal case of blood-alcohol test where blood was taken despite defendant's objection or refusal to submit to test. 14 ALR4th 690.

Consumption or destruction of physical evidence due to testing or analysis by prosecution's expert as warranting suppression of evidence or dismissal of case against accused in state court. 40 ALR4th 594.

Drunk driving: Motorist's right to private sobriety test. 45 ALR4th 11.

Horizontal gaze nystagmus test: use in impaired driving prosecution. 60 ALR4th 1129.

Social host's liability for injuries incurred by third parties as a result of intoxicated guest's negligence. 62 ALR4th 16.

Cough medicine as "intoxicating liquor" under DUI statute. 65 ALR4th 1238.

Sufficiency of showing of physical inability to take tests for driving while intoxicated to justify refusal. 68 ALR4th 776.

II. DECISIONS UNDER PRIOR LAW.

Editor's note. — Cases cited below were decided under similar provisions of prior law.

As to strict construction of former section, see Weaver v. City of Birmingham, 340 So. 2d 99 (Ala. Crim. App. 1976).

Former Chemical Test for Intoxication Act did not provide "right" of refusal. Hill v. State, 366 So. 2d 318 (Ala. 1979).

Chemical Test for Intoxication Act did not grant a person a "right" to refuse to submit to chemical testing so as to preclude admission of evidence of such a refusal. Hill v. State, 366 So. 2d 296 (Ala. Crim. App. 1978), aff'd, 366 So. 2d 318 (Ala. 1979).

Refusal to submit to test not a compelled communication. — In proceeding in which defendant was convicted of first-degree manslaughter of person fatally injured in automobile accident, refusal of defendant to submit to a chemical test for intoxication was not a compelled testimonial communication and admission of evidence of such refusal and comment thereon did not violate the accused's privilege against self-incrimination. Hill v. State, 366 So. 2d 318 (Ala. 1979).

And was admissible. — In proceeding in which defendant was convicted of first-degree manslaughter of person fatally injured in automobile accident, admission of evidence of accused's refusal to take a chemical analysis test did not violate the federal or state privilege against self-incrimination. Hill v. State, 366 So. 2d 296 (Ala. Crim. App. 1978), aff'd, 366 So. 2d 318 (Ala. 1979).

No constitutional right to consult attorney or physician before test decision. — Defendant motorist had no constitutional or statutory right to consult with attorney or physician before deciding whether to agree or refuse to submit to blood alcohol test or breath test, though officer assertedly told defendant that he had a right to talk to anyone he wanted to before he submitted to the test. Hill v. State, 366 So. 2d 296 (Ala. Crim. App. 1978), aff'd, 366 So. 2d 318 (Ala. 1979).

Former section placed no duty upon law-enforcement agency administering test to inform or notify the accused that he could have an independent blood alcohol test performed. Parker v. State, 397 So. 2d 199 (Ala. Crim. App.), cert. denied, 397 So. 2d 203 (Ala. 1981).

In order to establish the validity and admissibility of a chemical analysis, the test must have been performed (1) By an individual possessing a valid permit issued by the state board of health for this purpose and (2) According to methods approved by the state board of health. Estes v. State, 358 So. 2d 1050 (Ala. Crim. App. 1977), cert. denied, 358 So. 2d 1057 (Ala. 1978).

In order to be valid, chemical analysis must have been performed (1) According to methods approved by the state board of health and (2) By an individual possessing a valid permit issued by the state board of health for this purpose. In addition the state must have proven (3) That the particular test method used had been approved and adopted by officials of the law enforcement agency which administered the test, and (4) Where a blood test was involved, that only a physician, registered nurse or duly licensed clinical laboratory technologist or clinical laboratory technician acting at the request of a law-enforcement officer withdrew blood for the purpose of determining the alcoholic content therein. Webb v. State, 378 So. 2d 756 (Ala. Crim. App.), cert. denied, 378 So. 2d 758 (Ala. 1980).

Performance of test according to methods approved by board as condition precedent to admissibility. — A test such as the photo-electric intoximeter, to be admissible in evidence, must have been performed according to methods approved by the state board of health. Such is a condition precedent to its admissibility. Patton v. City of Decatur, 337 So. 2d 321 (Ala. 1976).

If the state was to use the statutory presumptions of intoxication and the jury was to be charged on those presumptions, it was mandatory under the terms of former statute that the chemical analyses of the person's blood, urine or breath, to be considered valid, had been performed according to the methods approved by the state board of health. Commander v. State, 374 So. 2d 910 (Ala. Crim. App. 1978), cert. denied, 374 So. 2d 921 (Ala. 1979); Webb v. State, 378 So. 2d 756 (Ala. Crim. App.), cert. denied, 378 So. 2d 758 (Ala. 1979).

Applicability of proper administration prerequisite to admission of results. — Former Chemical Test for Intoxication Act provision relating to proper administration of the tests as a prerequisite for admissibility applied to the admission of the results of chemical analysis as evidence, not to the admission of the refusal to submit to those tests. Hill v. State, 366 So. 2d 296 (Ala. Crim. App. 1978), aff'd, 366 So. 2d 318 (Ala. 1979).

As to necessity of written standards for performance of tests, see Patton v. City of Decatur, 337 So. 2d 321 (Ala. 1976); Commander v. State, 374 So. 2d 910 (Ala. Crim. App. 1978), cert. denied, 374 So. 2d 921 (Ala. 1979).

There is no rebuttable presumption that a duly licensed operator knew and used approved methods and techniques in administering test. Commander v. State, 374 So. 2d 910 (Ala. Crim. App. 1978), cert. denied, 374 So. 2d 921 (Ala. 1979).

Purpose of restricting persons who may perform test. — The purpose of allowing only physicians, registered nurses or duly licensed clinical laboratory technologists and technicians to withdraw blood samples is to ensure that standardized procedures and equipment are used, thereby preserving the validity of the test, and strict compliance with this requirement was a condition precedent to the admissibility of the results of tests made under former statute. Lankford v. Redwing Carriers, Inc., 344 So. 2d 515 (Ala. Civ. App.), cert. denied, 344 So. 2d 522 (Ala. 1977).

Coroner had no authority under former statute to take a blood sample for the purposes of analysis. Lankford v. Redwing Carriers, Inc., 344 So. 2d 515 (Ala. Civ. App.), cert. denied, 344 So. 2d 522 (Ala. 1977).

Former statute did not authorize deputy county coroner to take a blood sample from a deceased, who died in an automobile accident. Rehling v. Carr, 295 Ala. 366, 330 So. 2d 423 (1976).

Test results not inadmissible. — Photo-electric intoximeter test results were not rendered inadmissible in prosecution for driving a vehicle while intoxicated, even though blood alcohol content was tested using a standard of grams per 100 cubic centimeters rather than weighed in milligrams per 100 cubic centimeters. Bagony v. City of Birmingham, 365 So. 2d 336 (Ala. Crim. App. 1978).

Former statute merely raised a presumption of intoxication and nothing in the statute or Alabama case law required the trial judge to find that intoxication was the sole cause of any resulting harm. Watkins v. United States, 589 F.2d 214 (5th Cir. 1979).

§ 32-5A-194.1. Effect of certification permits issued by state board of health; effect of rules and regulations enacted by state board of health.

All certification permits issued by the state board of health shall remain in effect until their termination date or reissued by the department of forensic sciences. All rules and regulations enacted under the authority of this chapter by the state board of health shall remain in force until rescinded, modified or adopted by the department of forensic sciences. (Acts 1988, No. 88-660, p. 1058, § 2.)

Effective date. — The act which added this section became effective May 13, 1988.

§ 32-5A-195. Cancellation, suspension or revocation of driver's licenses; grounds, procedure, etc.

(a) The director of public safety is hereby authorized to cancel any driver's license upon determining that the licensee was not entitled to the issuance thereof hereunder or that said licensee failed to give the correct or required information in his application. Upon such cancellation the licensee must surrender the license so cancelled. If such licensee refuses to surrender such license, he shall be guilty of a misdemeanor.

(b) The privilege of driving a motor vehicle on the highways of this state given to a nonresident hereunder shall be subject to suspension or revocation by the director of public safety in like manner and for like cause as a driver's license issued hereunder may be suspended or revoked.

(c) The director of public safety is further authorized, upon receiving a record of the conviction in this state of a nonresident driver of a motor vehicle of any offense, to forward a certified copy of such record to the motor vehicle administrator in the state wherein the person so convicted is a resident.

(d) When a nonresident's operating privilege is suspended or revoked, the director of public safety shall forward a certified copy of the record of such action to the motor vehicle administrator in the state wherein such person resides.

(e) The director of public safety is authorized to suspend or revoke the license of any resident of this state or the privilege of a nonresident to drive a motor vehicle in this state upon receiving notice of the conviction of such person in another state of any offense therein which, if committed in this state, would be grounds for the suspension or revocation of the license of a driver.

(f) The director of public safety may give such effect to conduct of a resident in another state as is provided by the laws of this state had such conduct occurred in this state.

(g) Whenever any person is convicted of any offense for which this chapter makes mandatory the revocation of the license of such person by the department, the court in which such conviction is had shall require the surrender to it of any driver's license then held by the person convicted and the court shall thereupon forward the same together with a record of such conviction to the director of public safety.

(h) Every court having jurisdiction over offenses committed under this article or any other law of this state or municipal ordinance adopted by a local authority regulating the operation of motor vehicles on highways, shall forward to the director of public safety within 10 days a record of the conviction of any person in said court for a violation of any said laws other than regulations governing standing or parking, and may recommend the suspension of the driver's license of the person so convicted.

(i) For the purposes of this article the term "conviction" shall mean a final conviction. Also, for the purposes of this article an unvacated forfeiture of bail or collateral deposited to secure a defendant's appearance in court, a plea of nolo contendere accepted by the court, the payment of a fine, a plea of guilty or a finding of guilt of a traffic violation charge, shall be equivalent to a conviction regardless of whether the penalty is rebated, suspended or probated.

(j) The director of public safety shall forthwith revoke the license of any driver upon receiving a record of such driver's conviction of any of the following offenses:

(1) Manslaughter or homicide by vehicle resulting from the operation of a motor vehicle;

(2) Upon a first conviction of driving or being in actual physical control of any vehicle while under the influence of alcohol or under the influence of a controlled substance to a degree which renders him incapable of safely driving or under the combined influence of alcohol and a controlled substance to a degree which renders him incapable of safely driving, such revocation shall take place only when ordered by the court rendering such conviction;

(3) Upon a second or subsequent conviction within a five-year period, of driving or being in actual physical control of any vehicle while under the influence of alcohol or under the influence of a controlled substance to a degree which renders him incapable of safely driving or under the combined influence of alcohol and a controlled substance to a degree which renders him incapable of safely driving;

(4) Any felony in the commission of which a motor vehicle is used;

(5) Failure to stop, render aid, or identify himself as required under the laws of this state in the event of a motor vehicle accident resulting in the death or personal injury of another;

(6) Perjury or the making of a false affidavit or statement under oath to the director of public safety under this article or under any other law relating to the ownership or operation of motor vehicles;

(7) Conviction upon three charges of reckless driving committed within a period of 12 months;

(8) Unauthorized use of a motor vehicle belonging to another which act does not amount to a felony.

(k) The director of public safety is hereby authorized to suspend the license of a driver without preliminary hearing upon a showing by its records or other sufficient evidence that the licensee:

(1) Has committed an offense for which mandatory revocation of license is required upon conviction;

(2) Has been convicted with such frequency of serious offenses against traffic regulations governing the movement of vehicles as to indicate a disrespect for traffic laws and a disregard for the safety of other persons on the highways;

(3) Is an habitually reckless or negligent driver of a motor vehicle, such fact being established by a record of accidents, or by other evidence;

(4) Is incompetent to drive a motor vehicle;

(5) Has permitted an unlawful or fraudulent use of such license;

(6) Has committed an offense in another state which if committed in this state would be grounds for suspension or revocation;

(7) Has been convicted of fleeing or attempting to elude a police officer; or

(8) Has been convicted of racing on the highways.

(*l*) Upon suspending the license of any person as hereinbefore in this section authorized, the director of public safety shall immediately notify the licensee in writing and upon his request shall afford him an opportunity for a hearing as early as practicable, not to exceed 30 days after receipt of such request in the county wherein the licensee resides unless the director of public safety and the licensee agree that such hearing may be held in some other county. Such hearing shall be before the director of public safety or his duly authorized agent. Upon such hearing the director of public safety or his duly authorized agent may administer oaths and may issue subpoenas for the attendance of witnesses in the production of relevant books and papers and may require a reexamination of the licensee. Upon such hearing the director of public safety or his duly authorized agent shall either rescind its order of suspension or, good cause appearing therefor, may continue, modify or extend the suspension of such licensee or revoke such license. If the license has been suspended as a result of the licensee's driving while under the influence of alcohol, the director or his agent conducting the hearing shall take into account, among other relevant factors, the licensee's successful completion of any duly established "highway intoxication seminar", "DWI counterattack course" or similar educational program designed for problem drinking drivers. If the hearing is conducted by a duly authorized agent instead of by the director of public safety himself, the action of such agent must be approved by the director of public safety.

(m) The director of public safety shall not suspend a driver's license or privilege to drive a motor vehicle upon the public highways for a period of more than one year, except as permitted under section 32-6-19.

(n) At the end of the period of suspension a license surrendered to the director of public safety under subsection (o) shall be returned to the licensee.

(o) The director of public safety upon cancelling, suspending or revoking a license shall require that such license be surrendered to and be retained by the director of public safety. Any person whose license has been cancelled, suspended or revoked shall immediately return his license to the director of public safety. If such licensee refuses to surrender such license, he shall be guilty of a misdemeanor.

(p) Any resident or nonresident whose driver's license or privilege to operate a motor vehicle in this state has been suspended or revoked as provided in this section shall not operate a motor vehicle in this state under a license or permit issued by any other jurisdiction or otherwise during such suspension or after such revocation until a new license is obtained when and as permitted under this article.

(q) Any person denied a license or whose license has been cancelled, suspended or revoked by the director of public safety except where such cancellation or revocation is mandatory under the provision of this article shall have the right to file a petition within 30 days thereafter for a hearing in the matter in the district court, circuit court or court of like jurisdiction in the county wherein such person resides, or in the case of cancellation, suspension or revocation of a nonresident's operating privilege in the county in which the main office of the director of public safety is located, and such court is hereby vested with jurisdiction and it shall be its duty to set the matter for hearing upon 30 days' written notice to the director of public safety, and thereupon to take testimony and examine into the facts of the case and to determine whether the petitioner is entitled to a license or is subject to suspension, cancellation or revocation of license under the provisions of this section. (Acts 1980, No. 80-434, p. 604, § 9-106; Acts 1981, No. 81-803, p. 1412, § 1.)

Commentary

This is a total revision of former section 32-6-16. It is necessitated by the provisions of section 32-5A-191. This section makes no major changes except insofar as the treatment of DWI cases is concerned. However, some minor changes have been made to update this section in accordance with the latest version of the Uniform Vehicle Code.

Subsection (a): No changes made.

Subsection (b): No changes made.

Subsection (c): Minor change in wording.

Subsection (d): This is new, and is based upon UVC § 6-202(b).

Subsection (e): No changes made.

Subsection (f): This is new, and is based upon UVC § 6-203(b).

Subsection (g): No change.

Subsection (h): Slight change in wording.

Subsection (i): This changes the prior statutes which referred solely to forfeiture of bail as being equivalent to a conviction. This section is, therefore, broader and more inclusive.

Subsection (j): This is the subsection where change was particularly mandated in light of section 32-5A-191. Subdivision (1) includes the reference to homicide by vehicle, covered by section 32-5A-192. Subdivision (2) is designed around section 32-5A-191, and varies from both the prior Alabama law and the UVC in not making revocation automatic until the second conviction. Subdivision (3) varies from the previous Alabama law in its reference to any "controlled substance." Subdivisions (4), (5) and (6) are unchanged. Subdivision (7) is reworded in light of changes in subsection (i). Subdivision (8) is new and based upon UVC § 6-205(7).

Subsection (k): Some changes have been based upon UVC § 6-206. Subdivision (1) has been changed to require a showing of commission of the offense (for which there may or may not be a pending charge, which was required under prior law). Subdivision (2) is new and based on UVC § 6-206(2). Subdivision (3) has a slight addition of the final phrase, taken from UVC § 6-206(3). However, the UVC here refers to and adopts (later in the same section) a point system for offenses. This was not suggested for adoption, but may be given consideration later whenever a more thorough revision of the licensing statutes is undertaken. Subdivisions (4), (5) and (6) have no change from the previous Alabama law. Subdivisions (7) and (8) are new, being based upon UVC section 6-206(a).

Subsection (l): There is little change here. This section and the former law use 30 days, the UVC § 6-206(c), suggests 20, but no change was deemed necessary. A small change in phraseology appears in the third sentence. The reference to educational programs for problem drinking drivers is new.

Subsection (m): Here the cross-reference to section 32-6-19 has been added, something suggested by a similar reference in UVC § 6-209(a).

Subsection (n): This is simply a repositioning of this provision, in order to parallel the UVC organization. This appears in the UVC as § 6-209(b).

Subsection (o): Small change in wording.

Subsection (p): No change.

Subsection (q): No change except for the provisions relating to hearings regarding nonresidents, who were unprovided for in the prior statute.

I. General Consideration.
II. Decisions Under Prior Law.

I. GENERAL CONSIDERATION.

Cross references. — As to creation of a driver license medical advisory board to advise the director of public safety concerning the medical aspects of driver licensing, see § 32-6-40 et seq.

Constitutionality. — Due process requires that a state seeking to terminate a driver's license afford an opportunity for notice and hearing before the termination becomes effective, except in an emergency situation. Though Alabama law does not currently afford such an opportunity prior to the mandatory revocation taking effect, the statute is not unconstitutional. Mechur v. Director, Dep't of Pub. Safety, 446 So. 2d 48 (Ala. Civ. App. 1984).

The driver convicted of driving intoxicated is presumed to have had a hearing upon the critical issue of whether he was intoxicated. If such hearing was not held as provided by law, there was available a remedy by appeal under statute. Therefore, the only issue remaining is to connect the person whose license is revoked to the record of conviction on which the director bases the revocation. Mistaken identity or some error on the certificate of conviction may be presented to the director and would provide reason not to revoke. Should the director refuse to act in such case, the courts of this state have provided the remedy of mandamus. This additional safeguard provided by the mandamus action is icing on the constitutional cake. Mechur v. Director, Dep't of Pub. Safety, 446 So. 2d 48 (Ala. Civ. App. 1984).

The due process clause clearly applies to the deprivation of a driver's license by the state. Mechur v. Director, Dep't of Pub. Safety, 446 So. 2d 48 (Ala. Civ. App. 1984).

Once licenses are issued their continued

possession may become essential in the pursuit of a livelihood. Taking away of issued licenses thus involves state action that adjudicates important interests of the licensees, and are not to be taken away without that procedural due process required by the fourteenth amendment. Mechur v. Director, Dep't of Pub. Safety, 446 So. 2d 48 (Ala. Civ. App. 1984).

Lack of prerevocation hearing under subsection (j) does not deny due process. — Despite the fact that subsection (j) of this section does not provide for a prerevocation hearing, the statute does not deny due process of law because of its important governmental and public interest to remove as quickly as possible any driver identified to be a life threatening hazard on the road. Bryant v. State Dep't of Pub. Safety, 494 So. 2d 425 (Ala. Civ. App. 1986).

The purpose of this section is not to punish the driver but to protect the public. The fundamental issue presented by the legislative scheme is whether the licensee has been driving on the highway while under the influence of intoxicating liquor. The showing of convictions for doing so establishes the necessity for the immediate removal of his driving privileges. Mechur v. Director, Dep't of Pub. Safety, 446 So. 2d 48 (Ala. Civ. App. 1984).

Construction giving everyone not previously convicted under new law first offender status is erroneous. — Construction of this new law which in effect "wipes the slate clean" would be in contradiction to obvious legislative purpose to identify problem drinking drivers so as to revoke their licenses for second and subsequent convictions for driving while intoxicated. Such construction would make everyone not previously convicted under the new law a first offender. It is the duty of the court in cases of statutory construction to give effect to legislative intent, and it should look not only to language of statute, but to its purpose and object as well. Shoemaker v. Atchison, 406 So. 2d 986 (Ala. Civ. App. 1981).

No discretion as to revocation of license under § 32-5A-191(d) and subsection (j) of this section. — Under § 32-5A-191(d) and subsection (j) of this section, the director of the department has no discretion as to whether or not he may revoke the driver's license. When the statutory requisites are met, i.e., the driver has been twice convicted of DUI within a five-year period, revocation of his or her driver's license is mandatory. Thus, no prerevocation hearing is provided by the DUI statutes. Bryant v. State Dep't of Pub. Safety, 494 So. 2d 425 (Ala. Civ. App. 1986).

No hearing where license revoked under § 32-5A-191(d) and subsection (j) of this section. — Whether an individual whose driver's license is revoked under § 32-5A-191(d) and subsection (j) of this section is entitled to an administrative hearing is a matter of substantive law. That law is that no such hearing is allowed because revocation under the DUI statutes is mandatory. The Alabama Administrative Procedure Act, which is solely limited to procedural matters, has not altered this substantive law. Bryant v. State Dep't of Pub. Safety, 494 So. 2d 425 (Ala. Civ. App. 1986).

Suspension not mandatory. Section 32-5A-191 requiring suspension of driver license upon first DUI conviction not mandatory when driver not convicted in Alabama and the director pursuant to § 32-5A-195(e) was not required to suspend plaintiff's license and should have given plaintiff his duly requested hearing as provided by § 32-5A-195(l). Wolfsberger v. Wells, 528 So. 2d 854 (Ala. Civ. App. 1988).

Subsection (j) seeks to quickly remove any driver identified to be a life-threatening hazard on the road. — One need only consider the overwhelming number of alcohol-related accidents, injuries and deaths that occur each year to recognize the important governmental interest and very strong public interest in promptly removing such persons from the highway. Mechur v. Director, Dep't of Pub. Safety, 446 So. 2d 48 (Ala. Civ. App. 1984).

The proceeding authorized by subsection (q) of this section is a de novo hearing, i.e., the trial court is empowered to have a hearing, to take testimony, to receive evidence, and to make a finding of its own. Chambers v. Director of Dep't of Pub. Safety, 414 So. 2d 131 (Ala. Civ. App. 1982).

Certification of license revocation by custodian of records at department of public safety required. — Computer generated printout from the department of public safety, certified by the clerk of the municipal court and indicating that appellant's driving license was revoked, was inadmissible because caselaw requires certification by the custodian of records at the department of public safety. Brown v. City of Montgomery, 504 So. 2d 748 (Ala. Crim. App.), overruled on other grounds, Zinn v. State, 527 So. 2d 146 (Ala. Crim. App. 1987).

Collateral review by mandamus of a judgment of conviction is permissible if it is alleged that the conviction is invalid or void. Mechur v. Director, Dep't of Pub. Safety, 446 So. 2d 48 (Ala. Civ. App. 1984).

Cited in Wallis v. Director of Dep't of Pub. Safety, 411 So. 2d 811 (Ala. Civ. App. 1982); McReynolds v. State, 441 So. 2d 1016 (Ala.

Crim. App. 1983); Hosmer v. City of Mountain Brook, 507 So. 2d 1038 (Ala. Crim. App. 1987).

Collateral references. — 60 C.J.S., Motor Vehicles, §§ 146, 160, 164.1-164.50.

7 Am. Jur. 2d, Automobiles & Highway Traffic, §§ 109-124.

Validity of statute or ordinance relating to revocation of license. 71 ALR 616, 108 ALR 1162, 125 ALR 1459.

What amounts to conviction or satisfies requirement as to showing of conviction, within statute making conviction a ground for refusing to grant or for cancelling license. 113 ALR 1179.

What amounts to conviction or adjudication of guilt for purposes of refusal, revocation, or suspension of automobile driver's license. 79 ALR2d 866.

Validity, construction, and application of provision for revocation or suspension of driver's license because of conviction of traffic violation in another state. 87 ALR2d 1019.

Conviction or acquittal in previous criminal case as bar to revocation or suspension of driver's license on same factual charges. 96 ALR2d 612.

Statute providing for judicial review of administrative order revoking or suspending automobile driver's license as providing for de novo trial. 97 ALR2d 1367.

Denial, suspension, or cancellation of driver's license because of physical disease or defect. 38 ALR3d 452.

Necessity of notice and hearing before revocation or suspension of motor vehicle driver's license. 60 ALR3d 361.

Sufficiency of notice and hearing before revocation or suspension of motor vehicle driver's license. 60 ALR3d 427.

Suspension of driving privileges for reasons unrelated to the use of or ability to operate a motor vehicle. 86 ALR3d 1251.

Automobiles: validity and construction of legislation authorizing revocation or suspension of operator's license for "habitual," "persistent," or "frequent" violations of traffic regulations. 48 ALR4th 367.

Social host's liability for injuries incurred by third parties as a result of intoxicated guest's negligence. 62 ALR4th 16.

Alcohol-related vehicular homicide: nature and elements of offense. 64 ALR4th 166.

Passenger's liability to vehicular accident victim for harm caused by intoxicated motor vehicle driver. 64 ALR4th 272.

Driving while intoxicated: "choice of evils" defense that driving was necessary to protect life or property. 64 ALR4th 298.

Cough medicine as "intoxicating liquor" under DUI statute. 65 ALR4th 1238.

II. DECISIONS UNDER PRIOR LAW.

Editor's note. — The cases cited below were decided under similar provisions of prior law.

Constitutionality of former section. — Former § 32-6-16 was not unconstitutional for failure to give fair notice of what behavior was proscribed by the state and to provide standards for the department's suspension decisions. Smith v. McGriff, 434 F. Supp. 673 (M.D. Ala. 1976).

Former § 32-6-16, listing various types of behavior which might lead to summary license suspension upon a showing by court records and other sufficient evidence gave a driver adequate notice of the general disabilities or driver inadequacies the state considered in suspending a license. Smith v. McGriff, 434 F. Supp. 673 (M.D. Ala. 1976).

Although former § 32-6-16 did not detail what was meant by "incompetent," that term was somewhat clarified by § 32-6-7. These two provisions, read together, sufficiently informed drivers what infirmities might lead to license suspension. Smith v. McGriff, 434 F. Supp. 673 (M.D. Ala. 1976).

Former § 32-6-16 allowed summary suspension only upon sufficient evidence. That language required, a bona fide emergency situation to exist before pre-hearing license suspension was justified. In that situation, the state's compelling interest in highway safety justified summary suspension of a driver's license; therefore, section did not deny due process of law. Smith v. McGriff, 434 F. Supp. 673 (M.D. Ala. 1976).

Even though former § 32-6-16 itself did not provide standards for determining a driver's competence, the section was not unduly vague, since a licensee had to be informed at the hearing of the standards being applied by the hearing officer, and since the officer had to make a finding based explicity on the evidence and the department's standards. Smith v. McGriff, 434 F. Supp. 673 (M.D. Ala. 1976).

Procedures held unconstitutional. — Procedure of department of public safety in denying notice and hearing prior to suspension of licenses of persons deemed incompetent to drive because of alcoholism or drug abuse where no emergency situation existed was unconstitutional. Smith v. McGriff, 434 F. Supp. 673 (M.D. Ala. 1976).

Procedure of department of public safety in denying notice and hearing prior to suspension of licenses of persons deemed incompetent to drive because of medical reasons where no emergency situation existed was unconstitutional Tolbert v. McGriff, 434 F. Supp. 682 (M.D. Ala. 1976).

Hearing on whether mandatory license

revocation would result in extreme hardship not required by due process. — Where the state determined in an appropriate hearing that a person had been driving while intoxicated, it could refuse to allow that person to operate a motor vehicle on its highways under the mandatory revocation provisions of former section. The state, consistent with due process, could refuse to grant a separate revocation hearing on the issue of whether revoking the person's license would result in extreme hardship. Rader v. Dothard, 434 F. Supp. 688 (D. Ala. 1977).

Required procedure for suspension of licenses. — In view of the state's compelling interest in highway safety, an appropriate official of the department of public safety may temporarily suspend a license without hearing if he has probable cause to believe that the driver presents an immediate threat to the lives of motorists and pedestrians. Tolbert v. McGriff, 434 F. Supp. 682 (M.D. Ala. 1976).

Absent a bona fide emergency situation, a driver must be afforded notice of possible suspension and the reasons therefor, and a hearing in which he or she may present evidence, and call and cross-examine witnesses. Suspension must be stayed pending the hearing. During the hearing the licensee should be made aware of the medical and department standards by which he or she is being evaluated. If after such hearing the director or hearing officer believes the licensee is incompetent to drive, he may suspend the license upon a finding based on the evidence and the department's standards. He must immediately inform the driver of appeals available. Smith v. McGriff, 434 F. Supp. 673 (M.D. Ala. 1976).

Applicability of bail forfeiture provision where bail forfeited in another state. — Statutory provision concerning forfeiture of bail applied where bail was forfeited in another state for an offense which would have been grounds for revocation in this state. Therefore, such an out-of-state bail forfeiture gave the director cause to exercise his revocation power. Goodman v. Director of Dep't of Pub. Safety, 332 So. 2d 396 (Ala. Civ. App. 1976).

As to treatment of forfeiture of bond as conviction for purpose of revoking driver's license, see Director of Dep't of Pub. Safety v. Relford, 51 Ala. App. 456, 286 So. 2d 860 (1973).

Mandatory duty to revoke. — Former statute imposed a mandatory duty upon the director of public safety, upon receiving a record of a person's conviction of driving while intoxicated and after said conviction had become final, to revoke such person's driver's license. State ex rel. Bates v. Savage, 34 Ala.

App. 633, 42 So. 2d 695 (1949); May v. Lingo, 277 Ala. 92, 167 So. 2d 267 (1964); Kelley v. Lingo, 280 Ala. 128, 190 So. 2d 683 (1966); Ex parte State ex rel. Russell, 280 Ala. 448, 194 So. 2d 851 (1967); Rogers v. Russell, 284 Ala. 477, 225 So. 2d 879 (1969); Director of Dep't of Pub. Safety v. Moore, 54 Ala. App. 351, 308 So. 2d 711 (1975); Dothard v. Whitman, 57 Ala. App. 726, 331 So. 2d 735 (1976).

Provision of former statute that the director of public safety should revoke the license of any driver upon receiving a record of such driver's conviction of any felony in the commission of which a motor vehicle was used was mandatory upon the director. State v. Hatfield, 54 Ala. App. 421, 309 So. 2d 461 (1975).

Mandatory revocations purely administrative. — The director's action under former statute was purely administrative so far as mandatory revocations were concerned. May v. Lingo, 277 Ala. 92, 167 So. 2d 267 (1964); Ex parte State ex rel. Russell, 280 Ala. 448, 194 So. 2d 851 (1967); Rogers v. Russell, 284 Ala. 477, 225 So. 2d 879 (1969).

Where the evidence showed that the director properly performed his duty under statute, and the court so stated, and the judgment record was proper upon its face, showing a conviction of driving while intoxicated and payment of a fine therefor, with such record before him, the director was directed by statute to revoke the license. He could do nothing else. He acted solely in an administrative capacity. He had no authority to question nor determine the validity of a record judgment presented to him. Dothard v. Ridgeway, 54 Ala. App. 429, 309 So. 2d 468 (1975).

No discretion on part of director was involved in mandatory revocation of a license under former statute. May v. Lingo, 277 Ala. 92, 167 So. 2d 267 (1964); Ex parte State ex rel. Russell, 280 Ala. 448, 194 So. 2d 851 (1967); Rogers v. Russell, 284 Ala. 477, 225 So. 2d 879 (1969).

No provision for review of mandatory revocation. — There was no provision in former statute for proceeding to review mandatory revocation of driver's privileges. Kelley v. Lingo, 280 Ala. 128, 190 So. 2d 683 (1966); Rogers v. Russell, 284 Ala. 477, 225 So. 2d 879 (1969); Director of Dep't of Pub. Safety v. Relford, 51 Ala. App. 456, 286 So. 2d 860 (1973); Director of Dep't of Pub. Safety v. Moore, 54 Ala. App. 351, 308 So. 2d 711 (1975); State v. Hatfield, 54 Ala. App. 421, 309 So. 2d 461 (1975).

And agreement of counsel could not invest such jurisdiction. — The court being without jurisdiction to entertain an appeal of the mandatory provisions of former statute, no agreement by counsel could invest such jurisdiction, and the fact that felon needed driver's license to follow his occupation and maintain the conditions of his probation was not a fact for consideration in determining the correctness of the director's act of revocation. State v. Hatfield, 54 Ala. App. 421, 309 So. 2d 461 (1975).

Mandamus was only remedy. — Director's mandatory revocation under former statute was an administrative act, from which mandamus was the only remedy. Dothard v. Forbus, 57 Ala. App. 670, 331 So. 2d 685 (1975), cert. denied, 331 So. 2d 689 (Ala. 1976).

Action for review of the revocation of a person's license by the director because of final conviction for driving while intoxicated could not be by appeal or petition for hearing but could be by petition for mandamus. Director of Dep't of Pub. Safety v. Moore, 54 Ala. App. 351, 308 So. 2d 711 (1975).

Where revocation was a mandatory act by the director under former statute, there could be no appeal of or petition for hearing the revocation and any action for review had to be by petition for mandamus. Watson v. Dothard, 357 So. 2d 361 (Ala. Civ. App. 1978).

But not for collateral attack on judgment. — To grant mandamus against the director of the department of public safety, in cases where he had performed his mandatory duty of revoking a driver's license under former statute, upon allegations that the judgment shown by the record was invalid, would have cast upon him the intolerable burden of defending collateral attacks upon judgments of courts throughout the state. Dothard v. Ridgeway, 54 Ala. App. 429, 309 So. 2d 468 (1975).

Trial court had no jurisdiction to issue writ of mandamus to compel director to issue defendant a limited license to drive while conducting the affairs of his employer after his driving privilege had been revoked under mandatory provisions of former statute. Dupree v. Dothard, 341 So. 2d 955 (Ala. Civ. App. 1977).

Action to review mandatory act of director had to be brought in Montgomery county. Kelley v. Lingo, 280 Ala. 128, 190 So. 2d 683 (1966); Ex parte State ex rel. Russell, 280 Ala. 448, 194 So. 2d 851 (1967); Director of Dep't of Pub. Safety v. Relford, 51 Ala. App. 456, 286 So. 2d 860 (1973); Director of Dep't of Pub. Safety v. Moore, 54 Ala. App. 351, 308 So. 2d 711 (1975); Dothard v. Whitman, 57 Ala. App. 726, 331 So. 2d 735 (1976).

Review provided except when revocation mandatory. — Former statute provided for appeal to the circuit court with trial de novo from the order of suspension or revocation, except when revocation of drivers' licenses was mandatory, and for hearings before the director of public safety after suspension when requested. Surber v. Mann, 46 Ala. App. 700, 248 So. 2d 740 (1971).

No administrative hearing allowed on revocation. — Under former statute, no administrative hearing was allowed on a revocation, regardless of its mandatory or discretionary nature. Dothard v. Forbus, 57 Ala. App. 670, 331 So. 2d 685 (1975), cert. denied, 331 So. 2d 689 (Ala. 1976).

Right to administrative hearing restricted to suspensions. — Former statute, taken literally, restricted the right of an administrative hearing to suspensions. Dothard v. Forbus, 57 Ala. App. 670, 331 So. 2d 685 (1975), cert. denied, 331 So. 2d 689 (Ala. 1976).

ARTICLE 10.

PEDESTRIANS' RIGHTS AND DUTIES.

Collateral references. — Who is pedestrian entitled to rights and subject to duties provided by traffic regulations or judicially stated. 35 ALR4th 1117.

§ 32-5A-210. Pedestrian obedience to traffic-control devices and traffic regulations.

(a) A pedestrian shall obey the instructions of any official traffic-control device specifically applicable to him, unless otherwise directed by a police officer.

(b) Pedestrians shall be subject to traffic and pedestrian control signals as provided in sections 32-5A-32 and 32-5A-33.

(c) At all other places, pedestrians shall be accorded the privileges and shall be subject to the restrictions stated in this chapter. (Acts 1980, No. 80-434, p. 604, § 5-101.)

Commentary

There was no former counterpart to subsection (a), but the other subsections are quite similar to the previous section 32-5-270. This section thus represents little change, except in wording, from prior law.

Collateral references. — 60A C.J.S., Motor Vehicles, § 288.

7 Am. Jur. 2d, Automobiles & Highway Traffic, §§ 242-245.

Who is "pedestrian" with respect to rights given, and duties imposed, by traffic rules and regulations. 30 ALR2d 866.

Application of "assured clear distance ahead" or "radius of lights" doctrine to accident involving pedestrian crossing street or highway. 31 ALR2d 1424.

Liability for automobile accident with pedestrian as affected by reliance upon or disregard of traffic signal. 2 ALR3d 12, 155; 3 ALR3d 557.

Admissibility of evidence of habit, customary behavior, or reputation as to care of pedestrian on question of his care at time of collision with motor vehicle giving rise to his injury or death. 28 ALR3d 1293.

Liability of highway authorities arising out of motor vehicle accident allegedly caused by failure to erect or properly maintain traffic control device at intersection. 34 ALR3d 1008.

§ 32-5A-211. Pedestrians' right-of-way in crosswalks.

(a) When traffic-control signals are not in place or not in operation the driver of a vehicle shall yield the right-of-way, slowing down or stopping if need be to so yield, to a pedestrian crossing the roadway within a crosswalk when the pedestrian is upon the half of the roadway upon which the vehicle is traveling, or when the pedestrian is approaching so closely from the opposite half of the roadway as to be in danger.

(b) No pedestrian shall suddenly leave a curb or other place of safety and walk or run into the path of a vehicle which is so close as to constitute an immediate hazard.

(c) Subsection (a) shall not apply under the conditions stated in section 32-5A-212(b).

(d) Whenever any vehicle is stopped at a marked crosswalk or at any unmarked crosswalk at an intersection to permit a pedestrian to cross the roadway, the driver of any other vehicle approaching from the rear shall not overtake and pass such stopped vehicle. (Acts 1980, No. 80-434, p. 604, § 5-102.)

Commentary

This section is very similar, in fact nearly identical, to former section 32-5-271, except for the last six words of subsection (b).

Violation as negligence per se. — The violation of a traffic ordinance or rule of the road constitutes negligence per se. Hendrix v. Miller, 287 Ala. 486, 252 So. 2d 640 (1971) (decided under prior law).

Collateral references. — 60A C.J.S., Motor Vehicles, § 383.

7 Am. Jur. 2d, Automobiles & Highway Traffic, §§ 242-245.

Right-of-way at street or highway intersec-

tions. 21 ALR 976, 37 ALR 493, 47 ALR 595.
Validity, construction and effect of regula-

tions as to the time, place or manner of crossing street by pedestrian. 49 ALR 1406.

§ 32-5A-212. Crossing at other than crosswalks.

(a) Every pedestrian crossing a roadway at any point other than within a marked crosswalk or within an unmarked crosswalk at an intersection shall yield the right-of-way to all vehicles upon the roadway.

(b) Any pedestrian crossing a roadway at a point where a pedestrian tunnel or overhead pedestrian crossing has been provided shall yield the right-of-way to all vehicles upon the roadway.

(c) Between adjacent intersections at which traffic-control signals are in operation pedestrians shall not cross at any place except in a marked crosswalk.

(d) No pedestrian shall cross a roadway intersection diagonally unless authorized by official traffic-control devices; and, when authorized to cross diagonally, pedestrians shall cross only in accordance with the official traffic-control devices pertaining to such crossing movements. (Acts 1980, No. 80-434, p. 604, § 5-103.)

Commentary

Subsections (a), (b), and (c) are the same as former section 32-5-272. However, there was no previous law comparable to subsection (d).

Collateral references. — 61 C.J.S., Motor Vehicles, § 470(2).
7 Am. Jur. 2d, Automobiles & Highway Traffic, §§ 242-245.

Validity, construction and effect of regulations as to the time, place or manner of crossing street by pedestrian. 49 ALR 1406.

§ 32-5A-213. Drivers to exercise care.

Notwithstanding other provisions of this chapter or the provisions of any local ordinance, every driver of a vehicle shall exercise due care to avoid colliding with any pedestrian and shall give warning by sounding the horn when necessary and shall exercise proper precaution upon observing any child or any obviously confused, incapacitated or intoxicated person. (Acts 1980, No. 80-434, p. 604, § 5-104.)

Commentary

This section is similar to prior section 32-5-273 except that unlike the former law, this section makes reference to local ordinances and intoxicated persons.

Due care to be exercised not only at street crossings but between intersections thereof. — It is a well-established general rule that a driver of an automobile owes a duty to pedestrians to look and reasonably care for the

rights of others upon the public highway, not only at street crossings, but between intersections thereof. Mobile City Lines v. Proctor, 272 Ala. 217, 130 So. 2d 388 (1961) (decided under prior law).

§ 32-5A-214. Pedestrians to use right half of crosswalks.

Pedestrians shall move, whenever practicable, upon the right half of crosswalks. (Acts 1980, No. 80-434, p. 604, § 5-105.)

Commentary

This is identical to the previous law, section 32-5-274.

§ 32-5A-215. Pedestrians on roadways.

(a) Where a sidewalk is provided and its use is practicable, it shall be unlawful for any pedestrian to walk along and upon an adjacent roadway.

(b) Where a sidewalk is not available, any pedestrian walking along and upon a highway shall walk only on a shoulder, as far as practicable from the edge of the roadway.

(c) Where neither a sidewalk nor a shoulder is available any pedestrian walking along and upon a highway shall walk as near as practicable to an outside edge of the roadway, and if on a two-way roadway, shall walk only on the left side of the roadway.

(d) Except as otherwise provided in this chapter, any pedestrian upon a roadway shall yield the right-of-way to all vehicles upon the roadway. (Acts 1980, No. 80-434, p. 604, § 5-106.)

Commentary

Subsection (a) is a slight rewording of former section 32-5-275(a) to conform to the UVC. For subsections (b) and (d) there were no counterparts in the previous Alabama statutes. Subsection (c) differs from the former statute, section 32-5-275(b), only in wording with no substantive change. The previous law required walking on the left as a general rule, whereas subsection (c) takes into account those cases where walking on the left may not necessarily mean walking so as to face oncoming traffic.

§ 32-5A-216. Pedestrian soliciting rides or business or fishing.

(a) No person shall stand in a roadway for the purpose of soliciting a ride.

(b) No person shall stand on a highway for the purpose of soliciting employment, business, or contributions from the occupant of any vehicle, nor for the purpose of distributing any article, unless otherwise authorized by official permit of the governing body of the city or county having jurisdiction over said highway.

(c) No person shall stand on or in proximity to a street or highway for the purpose of soliciting the watching or guarding of any vehicle while parked or about to be parked on a street or highway.

(d) No person shall fish from a bridge, viaduct, or trestle, or the approaches thereto, within the state of Alabama, unless otherwise authorized by the governing body of the city or county having jurisdiction over said highway or from the state of Alabama in the case of state highways. The authorizing authority shall erect and maintain appropriate signs giving notice that fishing is allowed. (Acts 1980, No. 80-434, p. 604, § 5-107; Acts 1981, No. 81-803, p. 1412, § 1.)

Commentary

Subsection (a) is nearly identical to the former statute, section 32-5-275(c). Subsections (b) and (c) are new to Alabama law.

§ 32-5A-217. Driving through safety zone prohibited.

No vehicle shall at any time be driven through or within a safety zone. (Acts 1980, No. 80-434, p. 604, § 5-108.)

Commentary

This section corresponds to the prior statute, section 32-5-59, and is nearly identical to it.

Collateral references. — 60A C.J.S., Motor Vehicles, § 389.
7 Am. Jur. 2d, Automobiles & Highway Traffic, § 215.

Validity of safety zone ordinance. 79 ALR 1328.

§ 32-5A-218. Pedestrians' right-of-way on sidewalks.

The driver of a vehicle shall yield the right-of-way to any pedestrian on sidewalk. (Acts 1980, No. 80-434, p. 604, § 5-109.)

Commentary

This provision would amend and broaden that previously found in section 32-5-115. The former law applied only in business or residence districts.

§ 32-5A-219. Pedestrians to yield to authorized emergency vehicles.

(a) Upon the immediate approach of an authorized emergency vehicle making use of an audible signal meeting the requirements of section 32-5-213 and visual signals meeting the requirements of law, or of a police vehicle properly and lawfully making use of an audible signal only, every pedestrian shall yield the right-of-way to the authorized emergency vehicle.

(b) This section shall not relieve the driver of an authorized emergency vehicle from the duty to drive with due regard for the safety of all persons using the highway nor from the duty to exercise due care to avoid colliding with any pedestrian. (Acts 1980, No. 80-434, p. 604, § 5-110.)

Commentary

The former Alabama statute contained no provision of this type. The statute that requires the use of specific visual signals by emergency vehicles, such as would be comparable to Uniform Vehicle Code § 12-218, is contained in section 32-5A-115(c).

§ 32-5A-220. Blind pedestrian right-of-way.

The driver of a vehicle shall yield the right-of-way to any blind pedestrian carrying a clearly visible white cane or accompanied by a guide dog. (Acts 1980, No. 80-434, p. 604, § 5-111.)

Commentary

There was a comparable, although much more detailed provision in the previous law, section 32-5-276. This section serves to simplify the law and, unlike the prior statute, expressly requires the driver to "yield" to a blind pedestrian.

Cross references. — As to duty of drivers to blind or partially blind pedestrians carrying cane or using guide dog, see § 21-7-6.

Collateral references. — 60A C.J.S., Motor Vehicles, § 394.

Liability for injury to pedestrian struck by automobile as affected by his blindness. 62 ALR 578.

§ 32-5A-221. Pedestrians under influence of alcohol or drugs.

A pedestrian who is under the influence of alcohol or any drug to a degree which renders himself a hazard shall not walk or be upon a highway. (Acts 1980, No. 80-434, p. 604, § 5-112.)

Commentary

There was no comparable statute previously in force in Alabama except as may be included under "public intoxication" in section 13A-11-10.

Plaintiff's intestate guilty of contributory negligence where she was on highway in intoxicated state. — Plaintiff's intestate, who was on the highway in an intoxicated state, was guilty of contributory negligence that proximately contributed to her death, as a matter of law. Johnson v. Allstate Ins. Co., 505 So. 2d 362 (Ala. 1987).

Collateral references. — Consumption or destruction of physical evidence due to testing or analysis by prosecution's expert as warranting suppression of evidence or dismissal of case against accused in state court. 40 ALR4th 594.

Motorist's liability for striking person lying in road. 41 ALR4th 303.

§ 32-5A-222. Bridge and railroad signals.

(a) No pedestrian shall enter or remain upon any bridge or approach thereto beyond the bridge signal, gate or barrier after a bridge operation signal indication has been given.

(b) No pedestrian shall pass through, around, over or under any crossing gate or barrier at a railroad grade crossing or bridge while such gate or barrier is closed or is being opened or closed. (Acts 1980, No. 80-434, p. 604, § 5-113.)

Commentary

There was no comparable statute previously in force in Alabama.

ARTICLE 11.

MOTORCYCLES.

Cross references. — For other provision relating to motor-driven cycles, see § 32-12-20 et seq.

§ 32-5A-240. Traffic laws apply to persons operating motorcycles.

Every person operating a motorcycle shall be granted all of the rights and shall be subject to all of the duties applicable to the driver of any other vehicle under this chapter, except as to special regulations in this article and except as to those provisions of this chapter which by their nature can have no application. (Acts 1980, No. 80-434, p. 604, § 13-101.)

Commentary

This section replaces section 32-12-21 but varies only in phraseology.

Collateral references. — Reciprocal duties of driver of automobile and bicyclist or motorcyclist. 172 ALR 736.

§ 32-5A-241. Riding on motorcycles.

(a) A person operating a motorcycle shall ride only upon the permanent and regular seat attached thereto, and such operator shall not carry any other person nor shall any other person ride on a motorcycle unless such motorcycle is designed to carry more than one person, in which event a passenger may ride upon the permanent and regular seat if designed for two persons, or upon another seat firmly attached to the motorcycle at the rear or side of the operator.

(b) A person shall ride upon a motorcycle only while sitting astride the seat, facing forward, with one leg on each side of the motorcycle.

(c) No person shall operate a motorcycle while carrying any package, bundle or other article which prevents him from keeping both hands on the handlebars.

(d) No operator shall carry any person, nor shall any person ride, in a position that will interfere with the operation or control of the motorcycle or the view of the operator. (Acts 1980, No. 80-434, p. 604, § 13-102.)

Commentary

Subsection (a) is very similar to former section 32-12-1 and represents primarily clarifying phraseology. Subsection (b) replaces and clarifies the requirements of the prior statute, section 32-12-23. Subsection (c) requires the motorcyclist to keep both hands on the handlebars; the prior statute, section 32-12-23(e) required only one hand on the handlebars. There was no prior Alabama law comparable to subsection (d) except for the provision generally applicable to all vehicles, section 32-5-6 which has been replaced by section 32-5A-53.

No requirement for rear footrests where motorcycle not designed for passengers. — Where the motorcycle was not designed for passengers, it was not required to be equipped with rear footrests. Gurley ex rel. Gurley v. American Honda Motor Co., 505 So. 2d 358 (Ala. 1987).

Collateral references. — 60A C.J.S., Motor Vehicles, § 379. 61A C.J.S., Motor Vehicles, § 606.

§ 32-5A-242. Operating motorcycles on roadways laned for traffic.

(a) All motorcycles are entitled to full use of a lane and no motor vehicle shall be driven in such a manner as to deprive any motorcycle of the full use of a lane. This subsection shall not apply to motorcycles operated two abreast in a single lane.

(b) The operator of a motorcycle shall not overtake and pass in the same lane occupied by the vehicle being overtaken.

(c) No person shall operate a motorcycle between lanes of traffic or between adjacent lines or rows of vehicles.

(d) Motorcycles shall not be operated more than two abreast in a single lane.

(e) Subsections (b) and (c) shall not apply to police officers in the performance of their official duties. (Acts 1980, No. 80-434, p. 604, § 13-103.)

Commentary

Subsection (a) replaces section 32-12-23(c) which seemed to take nearly an opposite approach by requiring motorcycles to keep to the far right-hand side of the lane. This subsection, based on Uniform Vehicle Code § 11-1303, allows the motorcycle full use of the lane. There were no counterparts in the prior Alabama statutes for subsections (b), (c) and (e). Subsection (d) would appear to be in substantial conformity with former section 32-12-23(d). The draftsmen of the Uniform Vehicle Code section 11-1303(d), on which subsection (d) is based commented that "although permitting the operation of two motorcycles abreast in a single lane is a departure from the general rule in subsection (a) granting each motorcycle the full use of a lane and may reduce each motorcyclist's maneuverability, such operation is customary, improves their visibility at night for other drivers, restricts the ability of other drivers to encroach upon the lane space alongside one motorcycle, and utilizes far less roadway space than riding single file, particularly when many motorcycles are operated in a caravan or motorcade." Traffic Laws Annotated 762 (1972). On a four lane highway, subsection (d) would permit four motorcycles abreast, whereas the previous law restricted the cycles to riding two abreast in this situation. However, motorcyclists, like motorists generally, are subject to the duties imposed by section 32-5A-82 (and the former section 32-5-133) upon drivers whose vehicles are about to be overtaken by another, as well as the general keep-to-the-right rule of section 32-5A-80(b).

Collateral references. — 60A C.J.S., Motor Vehicles, §§ 284(1), 284(3), 342, 379. 61 C.J.S., Motor Vehicles, §§ 490(1), 490(4), 520(2). 61A C.J.S., Motor Vehicles, § 606.

§ 32-5A-243. Clinging to other vehicles.

No person riding upon a motorcycle shall attach himself or the motorcycle to any other vehicle on a roadway. (Acts 1980, No. 80-434, p. 604, § 13-104.)

Commentary

There was no law on this subject previously in Alabama.

§ 32-5A-244. Footrests and handlebars.

(a) Any motorcycle carrying a passenger, other than in a sidecar or enclosed cab, shall be equipped with footrests for such passenger.

(b) No person shall operate any motorcycle with handlebars more than 15 inches in height above that portion of the seat occupied by the operator. (Acts 1980, No. 80-434, p. 604, § 13-105.)

Commentary

There was no prior law on this subject in Alabama.

No requirement for rear footrests where motorcycle not designed for passengers. — Where the motorcycle was not designed for passengers, it was not required to be equipped with rear footrests. Gurley ex rel. Gurley v. American Honda Motor Co., 505 So. 2d 358 (Ala. 1987).

§ 32-5A-245. Headgear and shoes required for motorcycle riders; approval of headgear; responsibility for juvenile riders; sale of helmets.

(a) No person shall operate or ride upon a motorcycle or motor-driven cycle unless he is wearing protective headgear which complies with standards established by section 32-12-41.

(b) No person shall operate or ride upon a motorcycle or motor-driven cycle unless he is wearing shoes.

(c) This section shall not apply to persons riding within an enclosed cab.

(d) The director of public safety is hereby authorized to approve or disapprove protective headgear, and to issue and enforce regulations establishing standards and specifications for the approval thereof. The director of public safety shall publish lists of all protective headgear which have been approved by him.

(e) No person shall knowingly permit or allow any juvenile for whom he or she is a parent or guardian to operate or ride upon a motorcycle or motor-driven cycle while not wearing a protective helmet of the kind authorized by section 32-12-41.

(f) No person shall knowingly permit or allow any juvenile for whom he or she is a parent or guardian to operate or ride upon a motorcycle or motor-driven cycle while not wearing shoes.

(g) No manufacturer, retailer or other person shall sell or offer for sale motorcycle helmets that fail to comply with the standards established by the director of public safety pursuant to this section. (Acts 1980, No. 80-434, p. 604, § 13-106.)

Commentary

This section differs significantly from the previous Alabama laws on this subject, sections 32-12-40 through 32-12-44. Subsection (a) is in substantial conformity with the prior statute, section 32-12-40. There were no previous laws comparable to subsections (b), (c) or (d). Subsection (d) authorizes the director of public safety to set standards for helmets, and, since these may vary from time to time, especially as new materials become available, within the guidelines of the statutory requirements of sections 32-12-41 and 32-12-42. Subsections (e) and (g) are not to be found in the UVC, but are designed to carry over desirable provisions in prior Alabama law, sections 32-12-43 and 32-12-40 respectively. Subsections (d) and (f) and the portions of other subsections relating to the requirement that shoes be worn are to be found neither in the prior Alabama laws nor in the UVC, but were added pursuant to amendments by the senate committee, and represent an additional and desirable safety provision.

Collateral references. — 60 C.J.S., Motor Vehicles, § 43.

Validity of traffic regulations requiring motorcyclists to wear protective headgear. 32 ALR3d 1270.

Failure of motorcyclist to wear protective helmet or other safety equipment as contributory negligence, assumption of risk, or failure to avoid consequences of accident. 40 ALR3d 856.

Products liability: sufficiency of evidence to support product misuse defense in actions concerning commercial or industrial equipment and machinery. 64 ALR4th 10.

ARTICLE 12.

BICYCLES AND PLAY VEHICLES.

§ 32-5A-260. Traffic laws apply to persons riding bicycles.

Every person riding a bicycle upon a roadway shall be granted all of the rights and shall be subject to all of the duties applicable to the driver of a vehicle by this chapter, except as to special regulations in this article and except as to those provisions of this chapter which by their nature can have no application. (Acts 1980, No. 80-434, p. 604, § 12-102.)

Commentary

This section is virtually identical to the prior statute, section 32-5-291, except for changes in reference to other statutes necessitated by this general revision. Thus, no substantive changes have been made.

Collateral references. — Reciprocal duties of driver of automobile and bicyclist or motorcyclist. 172 ALR 736.

§ 32-5A-261. Riding on bicycles.

(a) A person propelling a bicycle shall not ride other than upon or astride a permanent and regular seat attached thereto.

(b) No bicycle shall be used to carry more persons at one time than the number for which it is designed and equipped. (Acts 1980, No. 80-434, p. 604, § 12-103.)

Commentary

This section is identical to former section 32-5-292.

§ 32-5A-262. Clinging to vehicles.

No person riding upon any bicycle, coaster, roller skates, sled or toy vehicle shall attach the same or himself to any vehicle upon a roadway. (Acts 1980, No. 80-434, p. 604, § 12-104.)

Commentary

This section is identical to the prior statute, section 32-5-293.

§ 32-5A-263. Riding on roadways and bicycle paths.

(a) Every person operating a bicycle upon a roadway shall ride as near to the right side of the roadway as practicable, exercising due care when passing a standing vehicle or one proceeding in the same direction.

(b) Persons riding bicycles upon a roadway shall not ride more than two abreast except on paths or parts of roadways set aside for the exclusive use of bicycles.

(c) Wherever a usable path for bicycles has been provided adjacent to a roadway, bicycle riders shall use such path and shall not use the roadway. (Acts 1980, No. 80-434, p. 604, § 12-105.)

Commentary

This section is identical to the previous law, section 32-5-294.

Collateral references. — Reciprocal duties of driver of automobile and bicyclist or motorcyclist. 172 ALR 736.

§ 32-5A-264. Carrying articles.

No person operating a bicycle shall carry any package, bundle or article which prevents the driver from keeping at least one hand upon the handlebars. (Acts 1980, No. 80-434, p. 604, § 12-106.)

Commentary

This section is identical to former section 32-5-295.

§ 32-5A-265. Lamps and other equipment on bicycles.

(a) Every bicycle when in use at nighttime shall be equipped with a lamp on the front which shall emit a white light visible from a distance of at least 500 feet to the front and with a red reflector on the rear of a type approved by the department which shall be visible from all distances from 100 feet to 600 feet to the rear when directly in front of lawful lower beams of head lamps on a motor vehicle. A lamp emitting a red light visible from a distance of 500 feet to the rear may be used in addition to the red reflector.

(b) Every bicycle shall be equipped with a brake which will enable the operator to make the braked wheels skid on dry, level, clean pavement. (Acts 1980, No. 80-434, p. 604, § 12-107.)

Commentary

Subsection (a) is very similar to the prior statute, section 32-5-296(a), except that this section requires greater visibility of the rear reflectors (100 to 600 feet rather than 50 to 300 feet). Subsection (b) is similar to section 32-5-296(b), but is more specific, since the prior law simply required "adequate" brakes whereas this section specifies what properly functioning brakes should be able to do.

§ 32-5A-266. Violations of article as misdemeanor; responsibility of parent or guardian; applicability of article.

(a) It is a misdemeanor for any person to do any act forbidden or fail to perform any act required in this article.

(b) The parent of any child and the guardian of any ward shall not authorize or knowingly permit any such child or ward to violate any of the provisions of this chapter.

(c) These regulations applicable to bicycles shall apply whenever a bicycle is operated upon any highway or upon any path set aside for the exclusive use of bicycles subject to those exceptions stated herein. (Acts 1980, No. 80-434, p. 604, § 12-101.)

Commentary

Except for changes in references to other sections necessitated by the reorganization of the rules of the road, this section is identical to former section 32-5-290.

Collateral references. — 60A C.J.S., Motor Vehicles, §§ 380, 396(5). 61 C.J.S., Motor Vehicles, § 464.

State and local government liability for injury or death of bicyclist due to defect or obstruction in public bicycle path. 68 ALR4th 204.

CHAPTER 6.

LICENSES AND REGISTRATION.

Article 2.

License Tags and Plates.

Division 1.

General Provisions.

Subdivision 1.

Tags Generally.

Subdivision 2.

Licensing, Registration and Taxation on Staggered Basis.

ARTICLE 1.

DRIVERS' LICENSES.

Division 1.

General Provisions.

Cross references. — As to driver training schools generally, see § 32-14-1 et seq.

Provisions applied by analogy to provision setting age minimum for motorcycle license. — Those cases which concern the statutes dealing with licensing of drivers of motor vehicles may be applied by analogy to the statute requiring a person to be at least 14 years of age to obtain a license to operate a motorcycle. Chiniche v. Smith, 374 So. 2d 872 (Ala. 1979).

§ 32-6-1. Required; expiration date; renewal; identification cards for nondrivers.

(a) Every person, except those specifically exempted by statutory enactment, shall procure a driver's license before driving a motor vehicle upon the highways of this state. Every new resident of the state of Alabama shall procure an Alabama driver's license within 30 days after establishing residence in this state.

(b) Each original driver's license issued to a person born in a year ending in an odd number shall expire on the second anniversary of the licensee's birth date occurring in an odd-numbered calendar year after the date on which the

197

application for the license was filed, and each original driver's license issued to a person born in a year ending with an even number shall expire on the second anniversary of the licensee's birth date occurring in an even-numbered calendar year after the date on which the application for the license was filed; provided, that if the license issued would expire in less than 24 months from the date on which the application for the license was filed, the expiration date of such license is hereby extended for an additional period of two years. After the expiration of an original driver's license, all subsequent renewals shall be for a period of four years from the specified expiration date of the immediately preceding license, regardless of when such renewal shall be issued. Every driver's license issued under this article may be renewed at the end of the license period without examination upon application and payment of the fee. For the purpose of renewal of a driver's license, the department of public safety shall mail renewal notices to each licensee at least 30 days prior to the expiration date; the applicant shall apply for a driver's license anytime during a period beginning 30 days before the expiration date of the then current license until one year after the expiration date of said license. Failure to make application for renewal within the specified time shall result in the applicant being required to take, and successfully pass, a written examination and driving test as administered by the department of public safety. If any person's birthday is February 29, the first day of March following shall be regarded as his birthday for the purposes of this section.

(c) The department of public safety shall make available to any resident of this state who does not hold a valid Alabama driver's license a nondriver identification card to be used for identification purposes only. Such nondriver identification card shall be issued only upon application of the nondriver and shall be similar to the driver's license; except, that it shall bear the word "nondriver" in prominent letters on the face of the identification card. Each nondriver identification card shall bear thereon a distinguishing number assigned to the nondriver and a color photograph of the nondriver, as well as the name, birthdate, residence address and a brief description of the nondriver, who for the purpose of identification, shall immediately upon receipt thereof, endorse his or her usual signature in ink upon the card in the space provided thereon, unless a facsimile of the nondriver signature appears thereon. The same degree of proof of identification required of applicants for driver's licenses in this state shall be required of applicants for nondriver identification cards. (Acts 1975, No. 539, p. 1192, §§ 2, 6; Acts 1981, No. 81-154, p. 177.)

Cross references. — As to licensing of school bus drivers, see § 16-27-4. As to prohibition against persons under 16 years of age operating motor vehicles generally, see § 32-5-64. As to license for operation of motor-driven cycles, see § 32-12-22.

Violation of section cannot be pleaded as contributory negligence. — This section requiring a driver's license imposes a duty for the benefit of the public at large, and the individual defendant, therefore, would acquire no new rights by virtue of its enactment, nor would a violation thereof by the plaintiff, although a criminal offense, inure to the benefit of the defendant so as to be pleaded as contributory negligence against the plaintiff in an action for damages arising from an auto collision between them. Lindsey v. Barton, 260

Ala. 419, 70 So. 2d 633 (1954).

And evidence that driver was not licensed as required by statute is inadmissible unless there is some causal relationship between the injuries and the failure to have a license. Upon like reasoning, the rejection of the evidence of the refusal upon application to grant the plaintiff a driver's license was proper. Lindsey v. Barton, 260 Ala. 419, 70 So. 2d 633 (1954).

Minor held to same standard as other highway users. — In determining whether a minor has knowledge of the circumstances and the probable consequences of his acts or omissions on the highways, he must be held to the same standard as all other users of the highways. Gunnells v. Dethrage, 366 So. 2d 1104 (Ala. 1979).

Immunity of county as to handling applications and fees for licenses. — It is evident that the county, through its officials or employees, is merely an agent of the department of public safety for the purpose of collecting and transmitting applications and fees for the issuance of original or renewal driver's licenses. This function is specified by statute and is carried out in accordance with procedures promulgated by the department of public safety. Therefore, the county and its officials and employees enjoy the immunity of this section in carrying out these acts on behalf of the department of public safety. Rutledge v. Baldwin County Comm'n, 495 So. 2d 49 (Ala. 1986).

Collateral references. — 60 C.J.S., Motor Vehicles, §§ 40-145.

7 Am. Jur. 2d, Automobiles & Highway Traffic, §§ 101-105.

Civil rights and liabilities as affected by failure to comply with regulations as to registration of automobile or motorcycle or licensing of operator. 16 ALR 1108, 35 ALR 62, 38 ALR 1038, 43 ALR 1153, 54 ALR 374, 58 ALR 532, 61 ALR 1190, 78 ALR 1028, 87 ALR 1469, 111 ALR 1258, 163 ALR 1375.

Loan of car to unlicensed driver as affecting liability of owner for negligence. 68 ALR 1015, 100 ALR 920, 168 ALR 1364.

Validity of statute or ordinance relating to grant of license or permit to operate automobile. 71 ALR 616, 108 ALR 1162, 125 ALR 1459.

Construction and application of statutes requiring "chauffeurs'" licenses. 105 ALR 69.

Lack of proper automobile registration or operator's license as evidence of operator's negligence. 29 ALR2d 963.

Construction, application, and effect of legislation imputing negligence to one who permits unauthorized or unlicensed person to operate motor vehicle. 69 ALR2d 978.

§ 32-6-2. Persons exempt from securing license.

The following persons when driving a motor vehicle under the following conditions are exempt from a license hereunder:

(1) Any person in the service of the federal government while driving an official motor vehicle in such service;

(2) Any person while driving any road machine, farm tractor or implement of husbandry temporarily driven or moved on a highway;

(3) A nonresident who is at least 16 years of age and who has in his immediate possession a valid driver's license issued in his home state or country;

(4) Any nonresident who is at least 16 years of age whose home state or country does not require the licensing of drivers for a period of not more than 90 days in any calendar year, if the motor vehicle so driven is duly registered in the home state or country of such nonresident. (Acts 1939, No. 181, p. 300; Code 1940, T. 36, § 67.)

Collateral references. — 60 C.J.S., Motor Vehicles, §§ 149, 150.

7 Am. Jur. 2d, Automobiles & Highway Traffic, § 102.

Statute with respect to nonresident operators' or drivers' licenses. 82 ALR 1392.

Validity of minimum age requirements for issuing drivers' licenses. 86 ALR3d 475.

What constitutes farm vehicle, construction equipment, or vehicle temporarily on highway exempt from registration as motor vehicle. 27 ALR4th 843.

§ 32-6-3. Examination prior to application for license or renewal.

(a) Every person who applies for an original driver's license under the provisions of this article shall be given an examination before he makes application to the judge of probate or license commissioner for the issuance of a driver's license. Such person must first apply to the officer, state trooper or duly authorized agent of the director of public safety, or one of them where there is more than one, designated by the director of public safety to conduct examinations for the county of the applicant's residence, and a minor must furnish a certified copy of his birth certificate or a certified statement from the county superintendent of education of the county in which he resides or the superintendent of the school which he attends to prove that he is at least 16 years of age, and he shall immediately be examined.

(b) A person may be examined in a county other than the county designated by the director of public safety by agreement in writing between him and the director of public safety.

(c) The director of public safety shall promulgate reasonable rules and regulations not in conflict with the laws of this state as to the kind of examination or test to be given and the method and manner of giving the same and ascertaining and reporting the results thereof. Reports of all examinations shall be on forms provided by the director of public safety and must show whether or not the applicant passed the examination.

(d) If the applicant passes his examination, he shall then be given a certificate to that effect, on a form provided by the director of public safety by the officer, state trooper or duly authorized agent of the director of public safety conducting the same, and he shall present said certificate to the judge of probate or license commissioner of his county together with his application for a driver's license, and the judge of probate or license commissioner shall attach the certificate to the application and forward the same to the director of public safety along with the application at the time the application is sent to him.

(e) If any person fails to pass the examination given, no certificate shall be given to him, and no application for an original driver's license shall be accepted by a judge of probate or license commissioner unless it is accompanied by a certificate showing that the applicant has passed the examination herein provided for.

(f) A person who secures a renewal of his license in the manner herein provided shall not be required to take such examination unless the director of public safety deems it advisable to require him to take the same. In such cases, where the director of public safety deems it advisable for any reason to require any person who has already been issued a driver's license to take an examination, he shall notify such person in writing by letter sent to the address given by him on his application at least 10 days before the date on which the examination or test is given of the time and place for the county of his residence where the same shall be given. The examination given to such person shall be conducted in the same manner and the result thereof ascertained and reported in the same way as examinations are given to persons applying for an original driver's license.

(g) Failure of any person to appear after notice to take such examination or test, or refusal by any person to take such examination or test, shall be grounds for suspension or revocation of his license by the director of public safety. Any person to whom such examination or test is given who fails to pass such examination or test shall have his license revoked by the director of public safety. (Acts 1939, No. 181, p. 300; Code 1940, T. 36, § 63; Acts 1951, No. 961, p. 1633; Acts 1978, No. 773, p. 1130.)

Immunity of county as to handling applications and fees for licenses. — It is evident that the county, through its officials or employees, is merely an agent of the department of public safety for the purpose of collecting and transmitting applications and fees for the issuance of original or renewal driver's licenses. This function is specified by statute and is carried out in accordance with procedures promulgated by the department of public safety. Therefore, the county and its officials and employees enjoy the immunity of this section in carrying out these acts on behalf of the department of public safety. Rutledge v. Baldwin County Comm'n, 495 So. 2d 49 (Ala. 1986).

Cited in Lindsey v. Barton, 260 Ala. 419, 70 So. 2d 633 (1954).

Collateral references. — 60 C.J.S., Motor Vehicles, § 154.

Validity of minimum age requirements for issuing drivers' licenses. 86 ALR3d 475.

§ 32-6-4. Application for license or identification card; fee; duration; issuance.

(a) Upon the installation of a system for the issuance of drivers' licenses and nondriver identification cards with color photographs of licensees and nondrivers thereon, all such licenses and identification cards and renewals of licenses issued in this state shall be issued in the following manner:

(1) Such person shall apply under oath to the judge of probate or license commissioner of the county of his residence for said driver's license or nondriver identification card or renewal of a license upon a form which shall be provided by the director of public safety.

(2) The judge of probate or license commissioner shall take a color photograph of the licensee with equipment to be furnished by the department of public safety to be attached to each application.

(b) For the purpose of defraying the cost of issuing drivers' licenses or nondriver identification cards with color photographs of the licensee or nondriver thereon, the probate judge or license commissioner shall collect for each license or identification card the sum of $15.00 for a four-year license or an identification card, and the judge of probate or license commissioner shall give the licensee a driver's license or identification card. The nondriver identification card shall bear no expiration date. (Acts 1939, No. 181, p. 300; Code 1940, T. 36, § 60; Acts 1951, No. 961, p. 1633; Acts 1975, No. 539, p. 1192, §§ 4, 5; Acts 1979, No. 79-203, p. 311, § 1; Acts 1980, No. 80-510, p. 789; Acts 1983, 3rd Ex. Sess., No. 83-825, p. 41.)

Collateral references. — 60 C.J.S., Motor Vehicles, §§ 101, 136(1), 145, 149, 158.

§ 32-6-4.1. Nondriver identification cards for retarded persons.

In addition to the drivers' licenses and nondriver identification cards provided for in section 32-6-4 the director of the state department of public safety shall promulgate the necessary rules and regulations for the issuance of special nondriver identification cards for retarded persons with color photographs of such retarded persons thereon. For the purpose of defraying the cost of issuing such identification cards, the judge of probate or license commissioner shall collect for each card the sum of $2.00 for a eight-year card and after retaining a fee of $.25 for each card issued, such judge or commissioner shall remit the remaining $1.75 to the state treasurer for use by the department of public safety according to the same procedures prescribed in section 32-6-5 for reporting collections on drivers' licenses and nondriver identification cards. (Acts 1984, 1st Ex. Sess., No. 84-815, p. 248.)

§ 32-6-5. Reports and compensation of judge of probate; disposition of fees collected.

At the close of business on Monday of each week when any application has been received or temporary instruction permit provided for in this article has been issued, the judge of probate receiving such application or issuing such permit shall prepare a report of the same upon a form which shall be provided by the director of public safety. One copy of such report, together with all applications received and copies of all permits issued, shall be forwarded to the director of public safety and one copy shall be retained by the judge of probate. On the tenth day of every month, the judge of probate shall prepare a report showing the number of applications received and permits issued and the amount of fees received during the previous calendar month; provided, that said report shall be prepared on the twentieth day of October, November and December. One copy of such report shall be forwarded to the director of public safety, one to the comptroller and one to the treasurer, and he shall retain a copy. He shall also at said time deliver to the treasurer the amount of all such fees collected, less $1.50 for each driver license or identification card issued, which sum shall be retained by him. Each $1.50 retained by the probate judge shall be paid into the public highway and traffic fund of the county; except that, in counties where the probate judge is compensated by fees, two fifths of each $1.50 retained by the probate judge shall be for his own use, and no other or further charge shall be made by him for services rendered in taking or receiving applications or issuing permits; provided, that this provision shall not repeal any local statutes nor general statutes of local application contrary to this provision; the remaining three fifths shall be paid into the public highway and traffic fund of the county. All funds remitted to the state treasurer under the provisions of this section shall be deposited to the credit of the general fund and shall be appropriated for public safety use.

(Acts 1939, No. 181, p. 300; Code 1940, T. 36, § 61; Acts 1951, No. 485, p. 868; Acts 1955, No. 43, p. 260; Acts 1963, No. 193, p. 582, § 2; Acts 1975, No. 539, p. 1192, § 7; Acts 1979, No. 79-203, p. 311, § 2.)

§ 32-6-6. Contents of licenses; photo specifications; fee for photo license or card.

Each driver's license issued by the department of public safety, except temporary permits or other special circumstances as determined by the director of the department of public safety, shall bear thereon a distinguishing number assigned to the licensee and a color photograph of the licensee, the name, birthdate, address and a description of the licensee, who, for the purpose of identification and as a condition precedent to the validity of the license, immediately upon receipt thereof, shall endorse his or her usual or regular signature in ink upon the license in the space provided thereon, unless a facsimile of the licensee's signature appears thereon.

Said photo driver's license and photo nondriver identification card as provided in section 32-6-4 shall have a photo core that meets the minimum width and length dimensions specified in ANSI standards X4.13-1971 and ANSI standard CR80, plus or minus 1/4 inch. In addition to all current and existing fees, the public safety department may charge an additional fee to recover the cost of obtaining photo drivers' licenses, photo nondriver identification cards, and terminal support equipment from the supplier. The fee may not exceed $.10 over the actual cost of obtaining the necessary material from the supplier. Revenues collected under this section shall be used by the department for the sole purpose of this program and any excess shall revert to the general fund at the end of each fiscal year. (Acts 1975, No. 539, § 1; Acts 1984, No. 84-305, p. 678.)

Cross references. — As to notation on license of intent of holder to make anatomical gift, see § 22-19-60.

Collateral references. — 60 C.J.S., Motor Vehicles, § 147.

§ 32-6-7. Persons to whom license not to be issued.

A driver's license shall not be issued to the following persons:

(1) Any person less than 16 years of age;

(2) Any person whose driving right or privilege is suspended;

(3) Any person whose driving right or privilege is revoked;

(4) Any person who is an habitual drunkard or addict to the use of narcotic drugs;

(5) Any person adjudged insane or an idiot, imbecile, epileptic or feeble-minded, until restored to competency by judicial judgment, or released from a hospital for the insane or feeble-minded, upon certification by the superintendent or medical director that such person is competent, nor then, unless the director of public safety or examining officer is satisfied such person is competent to drive a motor vehicle with safety to persons and property;

(6) Any person afflicted with or suffering from a physical or mental disability which, in the opinion of the director of public safety or examining officer will prevent such person from exercising reasonable and ordinary control over a motor vehicle. (Acts 1939, No. 181, p. 300; Code 1940, T. 36, § 66; Acts 1945, No. 59, p. 59; Acts 1947, No. 628, p. 483.)

Cross references. — As to creation of a driver license medical advisory board to advise the director of public safety concerning the medical aspects of driver licensing, see § 32-6-40 et seq.

Subdivision (3) does not incorporate extraterritorial revocations. — This code provision has not been amended since 1947, so the legislature necessarily did not have the Driver License Compact in mind when it wrote this provision. Thus, there is no reason to read subdivision (3) as incorporating extraterritorial revocations, which are entirely outside the control of the legislature of this state. Welch v. Alabama Dep't of Pub. Safety, 519 So. 2d 517 (Ala. 1987).

Although former § 32-6-16 did not detail what is meant by "incompetent," that term is somewhat clarified by this section. These two provisions read together sufficiently inform drivers what infirmities may lead to license suspension. Smith v. McGriff, 434 F. Supp. 673 (M.D. Ala. 1976).

Cited in Rutledge v. Baldwin County Comm'n, 495 So. 2d 49 (Ala. 1986).

Collateral references. — 60 C.J.S., Motor Vehicles, §§ 146, 154, 155.

Loan of car to unlicensed driver as affecting liability of owner for negligence. 68 ALR 1015, 100 ALR 920, 168 ALR 1364.

Civil or criminal liability of one in charge of an automobile who permits an unlicensed person to operate it. 137 ALR 475.

Purchasing motor vehicle for, or giving it to, minor or incompetent driver as rendering donor liable for driver's acts. 36 ALR2d 735.

Denial, suspension, or cancellation of driver's license because of physical disease or defect. 38 ALR3d 452.

Validity of minimum age requirements for issuing driver's licenses. 86 ALR3d 475.

Liability for automobile accident allegedly caused by driver's blackout, sudden unconsciousness, or the like. 93 ALR3d 326.

State's liability to one injured by improperly licensed driver. 41 ALR4th 111.

Liability of physician, for injury to or death of third party, due to failure to disclose driving-related impediment. 43 ALR4th 153.

Social host's liability for injuries incurred by third parties as a result of intoxicated guest's negligence. 62 ALR4th 16.

§ 32-6-8. Temporary instruction and learner's licenses.

(a) Any person 16 years of age or older who, except for his lack of instruction in operating a motor vehicle, would otherwise be qualified to obtain a driver's license under this article may apply for a learner's license, and the judge of probate may issue such license upon a form which shall be provided by the director of public safety, entitling the applicant, while having such license in his immediate possession, to drive or operate a motor vehicle upon the highways for a period of four years, but, except when operating a motorcycle, such person must be accompanied by a licensed driver who is actually occupying a seat beside the driver. At the time of applying for such license, the applicant shall pay to the judge of probate a fee of $15.00, and the judge of probate shall give him a learner's license therefor on a form to be provided by the director of public safety. Such temporary instruction license may be renewed only by order of the director of public safety, and in no case shall the original license be renewed or extended more than once. The judge of probate shall not issue the temporary instruction license until the applicant has undergone the same examination that a person applying for a driver's license is required by law to undergo, with the exception of the driving test, and produced a certificate to that effect signed by the proper examining officer.

(b) Any person not less than 15 but under 16 years of age may obtain a learner's license to learn to operate a motor vehicle upon application to the judge of probate of the county in which he or she resides, which license shall entitle such person to operate a motor vehicle when he or she is accompanied by a parent or his or her legal guardian who is duly licensed in this state as a motor vehicle operator or when accompanied by a licensed or certified driving instructor who is actually occupying a seat beside the motor vehicle operator. The application for such a learner's license must be accompanied by a payment of a fee of $15.00, to be distributed as provided in section 32-6-5; and the age of the applicant must be substantiated by the applicant filing with the judge of probate a certified copy of his or her birth certificate. A learner's license issued under this subsection shall be in such form as the director of public safety may prescribe; it shall expire in four years; or when the holder subsequently applies for and receives a driver's license, such driver's license shall be issued for the remainder of the four year life of the learner's license at no additional fee, the certificate thereof shall be prima facie evidence that the license holder was 15 years of age or older on the date of its issuance. Such a license may be suspended or revoked in the same manner and for the same causes as a driver's license and may also be revoked for any violation of the terms and conditions on which it was issued. The judge of probate shall not issue such a license to any person until the applicant has undergone the same examination that a person applying for a driver's license is required by law to undergo, with the exception of the driving test, and has produced a certificate to that effect signed by the proper examining officer. (Acts 1939, No. 181, p. 300; Code 1940, T. 36, § 64; Acts 1951, No. 880, p. 1519; Acts 1959, No. 346, p. 935; Acts 1973, No. 1289, p. 2201; Acts 1988, 1st Sp. Sess., No. 88-729, p. 125, § 1.)

The 1988, 1st Sp. Sess., amendment, effective September 13, 1988, substituted "license" for "permit" throughout the section; in subsection (a) substituted "to drive or operate a motor vehicle upon the highways for a period of four years, but, except when operating a motorcycle" for "to drive a motor vehicle upon the highways for a period of 30 days, but, except while driving a motorcycle" in the first sentence, in the second sentence substituted "a fee of $15.00" for "a fee of $.50," and substituted "learner's license" for "receipt"; and in subsection (b) substituted "learner's license" for "permit" in the first and third sentences, substituted "a fee of $15.00" for "a fee of $.50" in the second sentence, and substituted "it shall ex-

pire in four years; or when the holder subsequently applies for and receives a driver's license, such driver's license shall be issued for the remainder of the four year life of the learner's license at no additional fee" for "it shall expire on the day after the holder thereof becomes 16 years of age and when the holder subsequently applies for a driver's license."

Collateral references. — 60 C.J.S., Motor Vehicles, § 35.

Liability, for personal injury or property damage, for negligence in teaching or supervision of learning driver. 5 ALR3d 271.

Validity of minimum age requirements for issuing drivers' licenses. 86 ALR3d 475.

§ 32-6-9. Possession and display of license.

Every licensee shall have his license in his immediate possession at all times when driving a motor vehicle and shall display the same, upon demand of a judge of any court, a peace officer or a state trooper. However, no person charged with violating this section shall be convicted if he produces in court or the office of the arresting officer a driver's license theretofore issued to him and valid at the time of his arrest. (Acts 1939, No. 181, p. 300; Code 1940, T. 36, § 65.)

State trooper has right to demand driver's license. — Observing a violation of the state traffic and vehicle safety regulations, a state trooper has a statutory right to request and inspect the driver's operating license. The trooper has a right to "request" or "demand" the defendant's driver's license and the driver has a statutory duty to "display the same." Sly v. State, 387 So. 2d 913 (Ala. Crim. App.), cert. denied, 387 So. 2d 917 (Ala. 1980).

Collateral references. — 60 C.J.S., Motor Vehicles, § 157. 61A C.J.S., Motor Vehicles, § 651.

7 Am. Jur. 2d, Automobiles & Highway Traffic, § 98.

Effect of ulterior motive of official in exercising authority to require motorist to exhibit driver's license. 154 ALR 812.

Validity and construction of statute making it a criminal offense for the operator of a motor vehicle not to carry or display his operator's license or the vehicle registration certificate. 6 ALR3d 506.

§ 32-6-10. Reciprocal agreements — Other states.

The director of public safety is hereby empowered to enter into reciprocal agreements, when not in conflict with law, with other states constituting an exchange of rights or privileges in the use of drivers' licenses within this state by people who hold a valid driver's license in another state; provided, that nothing herein contained shall in any way affect the revocation of licenses of another state. The said reciprocal agreement can be annulled on notice issued to either party by the other party thereto within 30 days. No such agreement shall authorize a person who has been a resident of this state for the past 90 days to operate a motor vehicle in this state without a valid driver's license issued by the director of public safety of this state. (Acts 1951, No. 873, p. 1512.)

This section and subsection (c) of section 32-7-9 deal with separate subjects and have no relation to each other. Nowhere in the Motor Vehicle Safety-Responsibility Act, §§ 32-7-1 through 32-7-42, is there any requirement for reciprocal agreements. Thus the Alabama director of public safety, under the authority of subsection (c) of § 32-7-9, could revoke an operator's driver's license or the owner's license plates for failing to comply with the Motor Vehicle Safety-Responsibility Act of Arkansas where no reciprocal agreement existed between Alabama and Arkansas. Limbaugh v. State Dep't of Pub. Safety, 275 Ala. 260, 154 So. 2d 18 (1963).

Collateral references. — 60 C.J.S., Motor Vehicles, § 68.

§ 32-6-11. Same — Authorities in charge of federal military installations.

The director of public safety is hereby authorized to enter into an agreement with the secretary of defense of the United States or the duly authorized authorities of any federal military installation relative to the reciprocal recognition of point values assessed against drivers of motor vehicles for certain offenses against motor vehicle and traffic laws, rules and regulations when such point values are to be used in determining whether to revoke the driving privileges or the driver's license of the offender because he is an habitually reckless or negligent driver or is an habitual violator of traffic laws and regulations. (Acts 1969, No. 569, p. 1054.)

Collateral references. — Regulations establishing a "point system" as regards suspension or revocation of license of operator of motor vehicle. 5 ALR3d 690.

§ 32-6-12. Restricted licenses.

(a) The director of public safety, upon issuing an operator's license, shall have authority whenever the licensee is afflicted with or suffering from a physical disability to impose restrictions suitable to the licensee's driving ability with respect to the type of or special mechanical control devices required on a motor vehicle which the licensee may operate or such other restrictions applicable to the licensee as the director of public safety may determine to be appropriate to assure the safe operation of a motor vehicle by the licensee.

(b) The director of public safety in such case may either issue a special restricted license or may set forth such restrictions upon the usual license form.

(c) The director of public safety may, upon receiving satisfactory evidence of any violation of the restrictions of such license, suspend the same, but the licensee shall be entitled to a hearing as upon a suspension under section 32-5A-195.

(d) It shall be a misdemeanor for any person to operate a motor vehicle in any manner in violation of the restrictions imposed in such a restricted license issued to him. (Acts 1951, No. 876, p. 1514.)

Collateral references. — 60 C.J.S., Motor Vehicles, § 164.46. 61A C.J.S., Motor Vehicles, § 639(1).

§ 32-6-13. Promulgation of rules and regulations.

The director of public safety, with the approval of the governor, shall establish and promulgate reasonable rules and regulations not in conflict with the laws of this state concerning operation of motor vehicles and concerning the enforcement of the provisions of this article. (Acts 1939, No. 181, p. 300; Code 1940, T. 36, § 72.)

Cited in Rutledge v. Baldwin County Comm'n, 495 So. 2d 49 (Ala. 1986).

Collateral references. — 60 C.J.S., Motor Vehicles, §§ 14-57.

§ 32-6-14. Records to be kept by director.

The director of public safety shall file every application for a license received by him and shall maintain suitable indices thereto. The director of public safety shall also file all accident reports and abstracts of court records of convictions received by him under the laws of this state and in connection therewith maintain convenient records or make suitable notations in order that an individual record of each licensee showing the convictions of such licensee and the traffic accidents in which he has been involved shall be readily ascertainable and available for the consideration of the director of public safety upon any application for renewal of license and at other suitable times. (Acts 1939, No. 181, p. 300; Code 1940, T. 36, § 73.)

§ 32-6-15. Duplicate of lost or destroyed license.

(a) In the event any driver's license issued under the provisions of this article is lost or destroyed, the person to whom the same was issued may upon payment of a fee of $5.00 and upon furnishing proof to the director of public safety that the same has been lost or destroyed, secure a duplicate. The second and subsequent duplicates applied for will require the payment of a fee of $15.00 and, upon furnishing proof to the director of public safety that his previously held license or duplicate has been lost or destroyed, secure another duplicate. Application for such duplicate will be made to the director of public safety on forms provided by him. The said fee shall be collected by the director, paid into the state treasury and credited to the department of public safety.

(b) Any person making a false affidavit to the director of public safety for the purpose of obtaining a duplicate driver's license shall be guilty of a misdemeanor and upon conviction shall be punished by imprisonment in the county jail for not more than 30 days or by a fine of not less than $25.00 nor more than $100.00. (Acts 1939, No. 181, p. 300; Code 1940, T. 36, § 74; Acts 1971, No. 1933, p. 3121; Acts 1973, No. 1290, p. 2203; Acts 1988, 1st Sp. Sess., No. 88-728, p. 125, § 1.)

The 1988, 1st Sp. Sess., amendment, effective September 13, 1988, in subsection (a) substituted "a fee of $5.00" for "a fee of $1.50" in the first sentence, and substituted "a fee of $15.00" for "a fee of $4.00" in the second sentence.

Collateral references. — 60 C.J.S., Motor Vehicles, § 156(2).

§ 32-6-16. Repealed by Acts 1980, No. 80-434, p. 604, § 15-106, effective May 19, 1980.

§ 32-6-17. Cancellation, suspension or revocation — Application and fee for reinstatement; additional fees; duplicate license upon reinstatement.

Any person whose driving license has been cancelled, suspended or revoked under the provisions of section 32-5A-195 or any other provision of Alabama law by the director of public safety or by any court of competent jurisdiction shall, upon application for reinstatement of such driving license, pay to the director of public safety a fee of $50.00 for each cancellation, suspension, or revocation action. An additional $50.00 is imposed if the cancelled, suspended, or revoked license is not voluntarily surrendered within 30 days of a cancellation, suspension, or revocation notice. Upon receipt of the reinstatement fee, clearance for relicensing will be provided; the second and any subsequent clearance for relicensing for this action will be provided for a fee of $5.00. Upon reinstatement the licensee is required to obtain a duplicate license with a new photograph and current personal data. Any sums collected by the director under the provisions of this section shall be deposited into the general fund of the state of Alabama and shall not be returned to the applicant for reinstatement of his license, notwithstanding what action the director may take on such person's application for reinstatement of such driving license. (Acts 1971, No. 1597, p. 2743; Acts 1988, 1st Sp. Sess., No. 88-731, p. 134, § 1.)

The 1988, 1st Sp. Sess., amendment, effective September 13, 1988, substituted "a fee of $50.00 for each cancellation, suspension, or revocation action" for "a fee of $25.00" at the end of the first sentence, and inserted the present second through fourth sentences.

Collateral references. — 60 C.J.S., Motor Vehicles, §§ 129, 164.48-164.50.

§ 32-6-18. Penalties — Violations in general; disposition of funds.

(a) Any person of whom a driver's license is required, who drives a motor vehicle on a public highway in this state without first having complied with the provisions of this article or the rules and regulations promulgated hereunder shall be guilty of a misdemeanor, and, upon conviction thereof shall be punished by a fine of not less than $10.00 nor more than $100.00, to be fixed in the discretion of the judge trying the case.

(b) Any person who willfully makes a false statement under oath in an application for driver's license or for a renewal thereof shall be guilty of perjury and shall be punished as now provided by law.

(c) Any person who willfully conceals or withholds a material fact called for in an application for a driver's license or renewal thereof with intent to obtain such license by such fraud shall be guilty of a misdemeanor and, upon conviction thereof, shall be punished by a fine of not more than $100.00 and may be imprisoned at hard labor for the county for not exceeding 12 months, to be fixed in the discretion of the court trying the case.

(d) Any person who violates any provision of this article for which no fixed punishment is prescribed or who violates any rule or regulation promulgated as herein authorized shall be guilty of a misdemeanor and, upon conviction thereof shall be punished by a fine of not more than $100.00.

(e) All fines, penalties or forfeitures imposed under the provisions of this article shall be forwarded immediately upon the collection of the same by the officer of the court who collects the same to the director of public safety, together with a report giving a list and description of each case in which a fine, penalty or forfeiture was collected. Such reports shall be on forms provided by the director of public safety and shall contain such information as the director of public safety may require. All such moneys received by the director of public safety shall be covered by him immediately upon receipt into the state treasury to the credit of the general fund. Any judge who fails to make the reports provided for hereinabove or who fails to remit any fines, penalties or forfeitures collected under the provisions of this article in the manner provided herein shall be guilty of a misdemeanor and, upon conviction, shall be fined not more than $100.00. (Acts 1939, No. 181, p. 300; Acts 1939, No. 377, p. 503; Code 1940, T. 36, § 69; Acts 1943, No. 341, p. 322; Acts 1953, No. 828, p. 1115; Acts 1955, No. 43, p. 260, § 2.)

Cross references. — As to perjury, see § 13A-10-100 et seq.

Cited in Lindsey v. Barton, 260 Ala. 419, 70 So. 2d 633 (1954).

Collateral references. — 61A C.J.S., Motor Vehicles, §§ 588-714(4).

§ 32-6-19. Same — Violation by person whose license or driving privilege has been cancelled, suspended or revoked.

Any person whose driver's or chauffeur's license issued in this or another state or whose driving privilege as a nonresident has been cancelled, suspended or revoked as provided in this article and who drives any motor vehicle upon the highways of this state while such license or privilege is cancelled, suspended or revoked shall be guilty of a misdemeanor and upon conviction shall be punished by a fine of not less than $100.00 nor more than $500.00, and in addition thereto may be imprisoned for not more than 180 days. Also, at the discretion of the director of public safety, such person's license may be revoked for an additional revocation period of six months. (Acts 1939, No. 181, p. 300; Code 1940, T. 36, § 70; Acts 1951, No. 894, p. 1534; Acts 1983, No. 83-620, p. 959, § 1.)

Code commissioner's note. — Acts 1983, No. 83-620, § 2, provides: "The provisions of this act are supplemental to other laws not inconsistent with this act, and such other laws shall not be deemed to be repealed by this act."

Acts 1983, No. 83-620, § 3, provides that the act applies to conduct occurring after July 29, 1983, and that conduct occurring before that date shall be governed by preexisting law.

The statutory language which sets out the penalty for driving with a revoked license is specific and unambiguous. Mor-

ton v. State, 452 So. 2d 1361 (Ala. Crim. App. 1984).

There is no provision for the seizure of property for violation of this section. Morton v. State, 452 So. 2d 1361 (Ala. Crim. App. 1984).

Proof of violation of subsection (c) of section 32-7-37 irrelevant. — Under this section, proof of violation of subsection (c) of § 32-7-37 would be irrelevant. Balentine v. State, 44 Ala. App. 137, 203 So. 2d 703 (1967).

State entitled to retry case for incorrect

receipt of evidence. — Because the reversal of defendants' conviction for driving while license revoked was not based on the sufficiency of the evidence, but rather, on the incorrect receipt of evidence, under the Burks v. United States, 437 U.S. 1, 98 S. Ct. 2141, 57 L. Ed. 2d 1 (1978) rule the state is entitled to retry the respondent. Zinn v. State, 527 So. 2d 148 (Ala. 1988).

Cited in Turner v. State, 38 Ala. App. 73, 77 So. 2d 503 (1954); McGlasker v. Calton, 397 F.

Supp. 525 (M.D. Ala. 1975); Taylor v. City of Decatur, 465 So. 2d 479 (Ala. Crim. App. 1984); Watkins v. City of Florence, 484 So. 2d 1209 (Ala. Crim. App. 1986); Robinson v. City of Abbeville, 494 So. 2d 155 (Ala. Crim. App. 1985).

Collateral references. — 61A C.J.S., Motor Vehicles, § 639(2).

7 Am. Jur. 2d, Automobiles & Highway Traffic, §§ 125-128.

§ 32-6-20. Standards and requirements for equipment, etc.; contracts for lease or purchase of equipment.

After making such studies and examinations as may be necessary, the director of the department of public safety shall prescribe in writing the standards and requirements for the equipment and processes to be used to implement this article, and shall cause the state purchasing agent to solicit public bids based upon said standards and requirements, in conformity with the competitive bid law of the state of Alabama; except, that such contracts may be awarded for a period of a total of five years, instead of one year, and the director of the department of public safety shall, on behalf of the state of Alabama, enter into contracts with the lowest responsible bidders for such services and/or for the lease or purchase of such equipment as might be required for the efficient and economical operation of the system theretofore developed. In addition thereto, the director of the department of public safety shall require of the successful bidder a sufficient performance bond or written warranty to guarantee performance of the contract awarded, and sufficient to protect the interests of the state of Alabama and the licensees. All procurements and subsequent contracts for data processing equipment shall be coordinated with, and approved by, the data systems management division of the Alabama department of finance. (Acts 1975, No. 539, p. 1192, § 3.)

§ 32-6-21. Fee for conducting examination in county of applicant's residence.

(a) Every applicant for an original driver license, temporary instruction and learner's permit, and motor driven cycle operator's license, shall be required to pay a fee of $5.00 to the Alabama department of public safety upon applying to the officer, state trooper or duly authorized agent of the director of public safety, or to one of them where there is more than one designated by the director of public safety, to conduct examinations in the county of the applicant's residence. The $5.00 fee shall be required prior to each examination.

(b) The Alabama department of public safety shall issue proper receipts for said examination fee and shall properly transmit all moneys received by it for deposit in the state general fund. (Acts 1980, No. 80-530, p. 829.)

Collateral references. — 60 C.J.S., Motor
Vehicles, § 158.

Division 2.

Alabama Driver License Compact Act.

§ 32-6-30. Short title.

This division may be cited as the Alabama Driver License Compact Act. (Acts 1966, Ex. Sess., No. 401, p. 540, § 1.)

§ 32-6-31. Terms of compact.

The Driver License Compact is hereby enacted into law and entered into with all other jurisdictions legally joining therein in the form substantially as follows:

Driver License Compact

Article I

Findings and Declaration of Policy

(a) The party states find that:

(1) The safety of their streets and highways is materially affected by the degree of compliance with state and local ordinances relating to the operation of motor vehicles.

(2) Violation of such a law or ordinance is evidence that the violator engages in conduct which is likely to endanger the safety of persons and property.

(3) The continuance in force of a license to drive is predicated upon compliance with laws and ordinances relating to the operation of motor vehicles, in whichever jurisdiction the vehicle is operated.

(b) It is the policy of each of the party states to:

(1) Promote compliance with the laws, ordinances and administrative rules and regulations relating to the operation of motor vehicles by their operators in each of the jurisdictions where such operators drive motor vehicles.

(2) Make the reciprocal recognition of licenses to drive and eligibility therefor more just and equitable by considering the overall compliance with motor vehicle laws, ordinances and administrative rules and regulations as a condition precedent to the continuance or issuance of any license by reason of which the licensee is authorized or permitted to operate a motor vehicle in any of the party states.

Article II

Definitions

As used in this compact:

(a) "State" means a state, territory or possession of the United States, the District of Columbia or the Commonwealth of Puerto Rico.

(b) "Home state" means the state which has issued and has the power to suspend or revoke the use of the license or permit to operate a motor vehicle.

(c) "Conviction" means a conviction of any offense related to the use or operation of a motor vehicle which is prohibited by state law, municipal ordinance or administrative rule or regulation, or a forfeiture of bail, bond or other security deposited to secure appearance by a person charged with having committed any such offense and which conviction or forfeiture is required to be reported to the licensing authority.

Article III

Reports of Conviction

The licensing authority of a party state shall report each conviction of a person from another party state occurring within its jurisdiction to the licensing authority of the home state of the licensee. Such report shall clearly identify the person convicted; describe the violation specifying the section of the statute, code or ordinance violated; identify the court in which action was taken; indicate whether a plea of guilty or not guilty was entered, or the conviction was a result of the forfeiture of bail, bond or other security; and shall include any special findings made in connection therewith.

Article IV

Effect of Conviction

(a) The licensing authority in the home state, for the purposes of suspension, revocation or limitation of the license to operate a motor vehicle, shall give the same effect to the conduct reported, pursuant to article III of this compact, as it would if such conduct had occurred in the home state, in the case of conviction for:

(1) Manslaughter or negligent homicide resulting from the operation of a motor vehicle;

(2) Driving a motor vehicle while under the influence of intoxicating liquor or a narcotic drug, or under the influence of any other drug to a degree which renders the driver incapable of safely driving a motor vehicle;

(3) Any felony in the commission of which a motor vehicle is used;

213

(4) Failure to stop and render aid in the event of a motor vehicle accident resulting in the death or personal injury of another.

(b) As to other convictions, reported pursuant to article III, the licensing authority in the home state shall give such effect to the conduct as is provided by the laws of the home state.

(c) If the laws of a party state do not provide for offenses or violations denominated or described in precisely the words employed in subdivision (a) of this article, such party state shall construe the denomination and description appearing in subdivision (a) hereof as being applicable to and identifying those offenses or violations of a substantially similar nature and the laws of such party state shall contain such provisions as may be necessary to ensure that full force and effect is given to this article.

Article V

Application for New Licenses

Upon application for a license to drive, the licensing authority in a party state shall ascertain whether the applicant has ever held or is the holder of a license to drive issued by any other party state. The licensing authority in the state where application is made shall not issue a license to drive to the applicant if:

(1) The applicant has held such a license, but the same has been suspended by reason, in whole or in part, of a violation and if such suspension period has not terminated.

(2) The applicant has held such a license, but the same has been revoked by reason, in whole or in part, of a violation and if such revocation has not terminated, except that after the expiration of one year from the date the license was revoked, such person may make application for a new license if permitted by law. The licensing authority may refuse to issue a license to any such applicant if, after investigation, the licensing authority determines that it will not be safe to grant to such person the privilege of driving a motor vehicle on the public highways.

(3) The applicant is the holder of a license to drive issued by another party state and currently in force unless the applicant surrenders such license.

Article VI

Applicability of Other Laws

Except as expressly required by provisions of this compact, nothing contained herein shall be construed to affect the right of any party state to apply any of its other laws relating to licenses to drive to any person or circumstances, nor to invalidate or prevent any driver license agreement or other cooperative arrangement between a party state and a nonparty state.

Article VII

Compact Administrator and Interchange of Information

(a) The head of the licensing authority of each party state shall be the administrator of this compact for his state. The administrators, acting jointly, shall have the power to formulate all necessary and proper procedures for the exchange of information under this compact.

(b) The administrator of each party state shall furnish to the administrator of each other party state any information or documents reasonably necessary to facilitate the administration of this compact.

Article VIII

Entry Into Force and Withdrawal

(a) This compact shall enter into force and become effective as to any state when it has enacted the same into law.

(b) Any party state may withdraw from this compact by enacting a statute repealing the same, but no such withdrawal shall take effect until six months after the executive head of the withdrawing state has given notice of the withdrawal to the executive heads of all other party states. No withdrawal shall affect the validity or applicability by the licensing authorities of states remaining party to the compact of any report of conviction occurring prior to the withdrawal.

Article IX

Construction and Severability

This compact shall be liberally construed so as to effectuate the purposes thereof. The provisions of this compact shall be severable and if any phrase, clause, sentence or provision of this compact is declared to be contrary to the Constitution of any party state or of the United States or the applicability thereof to any government, agency, person or circumstance is held invalid, the validity of the remainder of this compact and the applicability thereof to any government, agency, person or circumstance shall not be affected thereby. If this compact shall be held contrary to the Constitution of any state party thereto, the compact shall remain in full force and effect as to the remaining states and in full force and effect as to the state affected as to all severable matters.

(Acts 1966, Ex. Sess., No. 401, p. 540, § 2.)

Forfeiture of bond amounts to conviction. — Pursuant to the provisions of the Driver License Compact as enacted by Alabama, the forfeiture of bail had against appellant in the state of Tennessee amounted to a conviction for driving while intoxicated, and such conviction had to be treated under the provisions of former § 32-6-16 as a conviction requiring a mandatory revocation by the state of Alabama of appellant's driver license. Director of Dep't of Pub. Safety v. Relford, 51 Ala. App. 456, 286 So. 2d 860 (1973).

Exception construed. — An examination of the terms of the compact and the law of this state leads to the conclusion that the exception should be construed as allowing an application and investigation after a year even if a prior revocation has not expired. Welch v. Alabama Dep't of Pub. Safety, 519 So. 2d 517 (Ala. 1987).

Cited in Watson v. Dothard, 357 So. 2d 361 (Ala. Civ. App. 1978); Hilyer v. Dixon, 373 So. 2d 1123 (Ala. Civ. App. 1979).

§ 32-6-32. Licensing authority; duties of director of public safety.

As used in the compact, the term "licensing authority," with reference to this state, shall mean the department of public safety. The director of public safety shall furnish to the appropriate authorities of any other party state any information or documents reasonably necessary to facilitate the administration of articles III, IV and V of the compact. (Acts 1966, Ex. Sess., No. 401, p. 540, § 3.)

Collateral references. — 60 C.J.S., Motor Vehicles, § 97.

§ 32-6-33. Compensation and expenses of compact administrator.

The compact administrator provided for in article VII of the compact shall not be entitled to any additional compensation on account of his service as such administrator, but shall be entitled to expenses incurred in connection with his duties and responsibilities as such administrator, in the same manner as for expenses incurred in connection with any other duties or responsibilities of his office or employment. (Acts 1966, Ex. Sess., No. 401, p. 540, § 4.)

§ 32-6-34. Meaning of term "executive head."

As used in the compact with reference to this state, the term "executive head" shall mean the governor. (Acts 1966, Ex. Sess., No. 401, p. 540, § 5.)

§ 32-6-35. Courts to report suspension, etc., of licenses to director of public safety.

Any court or other agency of this state, or a subdivision thereof, which has jurisdiction to take any action suspending, revoking or otherwise limiting a license to drive, shall report any such action and the adjudication upon which it is based to the director of public safety in the manner and within the time provided by section 32-6-16. (Acts 1966, Ex. Sess., No. 401, p. 540, § 6.)

Code commissioner's note. — Section 32-6-16, referred to in this section, was repealed by Acts 1980, No. 80-434, p. 604, § 15-106, effective May 19, 1980. As to cancellation, suspension or revocation of driver's license, see now § 32-5A-195.

§ 32-6-36. Application of article IV of compact to offenses enumerated in section 32-6-16.

Article IV of the compact, set forth in section 32-6-31, shall apply to those offenses enumerated in section 32-5A-195, and any suspension therefor shall be governed by the provisions of this section. (Acts 1966, Ex. Sess., No. 401, p. 540, § 7.)

Division 3.

Driver License Medical Advisory Board.

§ 32-6-40. Definitions.

For purposes of this division these terms shall have the following meanings:

(1) DIRECTOR. The director of public safety for the state of Alabama.

(2) DEPARTMENT. The state department of public safety.

(3) BOARD. The driver license medical advisory board established under section 32-6-41. (Acts 1979, No. 79-619, p. 1097, § 1.)

Collateral references. — Liability of physician, for injury to or death of third party, due to failure to disclose driving-related impediment. 43 ALR4th 153.

§ 32-6-41. Board created; membership, appointment, expenses, meetings, etc.

(a) There is hereby created within the state department of public safety a driver license medical advisory board for the purposes of advising the director concerning the medical aspects of driver licensure.

(b) The board shall consist of nine members appointed by the director, from a slate of nominees submitted by the Medical Association of the state of Alabama. Each member of the board shall be a physician licensed to practice medicine in this state.

(c) The board shall be appointed initially as follows: three members to serve two-year terms, three members to serve three-year terms, and three members to serve four-year terms; thereafter appointments shall be for four-year terms, and vacancies shall be filled by appointment for the unexpired portion of the term. The director shall designate the chairman of the board annually.

(d) Board members shall serve without compensation but shall be reimbursed for necessary travel expenses incurred in performing their duties as is provided state employees traveling in the service of the state. Such payments shall be made from funds appropriated to the department.

(e) The board shall meet at least annually and may hold such special meetings as are necessary to fulfill its responsibilities described under section

32-6-42. A majority of the board shall constitute a quorum. (Acts 1979, No. 79-619, p. 1097, § 2(a).)

§ 32-6-42. Responsibilities.

The board shall have the following responsibilities: (1) advise the director on medical criteria relating to the safe operation of motor vehicles; (2) recommend to the director procedures and guidelines for licensing individuals with physical or mental impairment; (3) initiate the development of medically acceptable report forms; (4) direct research of medically impaired individuals; (5) recommend a training course for driver examiners in the medical aspects of licensure; (6) spearhead efforts to orient the general physician population as well as the public in the medical aspects of driver licensure; (7) assist in the development of regional driver license medical advisory boards to be constituted similarly to the board established by this division; and (8) evaluate individual problem cases that require more than one opinion or that cannot be screened out in light of guidelines established by the board. The board may formulate such advice from records and reports or may cause a physical examination and written report to be made by a physician of the applicant's choice, licensed to practice in this state, or by one or more members of the board. The individual licensed driver or applicant may cause a written report to be forwarded to the board by a physician of his choice licensed to practice in this state, and such report shall be given due consideration by the board. The board shall exercise its option of interviewing in person any driver or applicant whose ability to operate a motor vehicle safely cannot be ascertained through written reports or records. (Acts 1979, No. 79-619, p. 1097, § 2(b).)

§ 32-6-43. Reports, records, etc., confidential.

Reports or records, received or made by the board or any of its members or by the director's office, pursuant to this division for the purpose of assisting the director in determining whether a person meets the medical, physical or mental standards to be licensed as a driver are for the confidential use of the board and the director's office, and such reports or records shall not be divulged to any other person, federal, state or local government or private entity, or used as evidence in any trial, except that such reports or records may be submitted in proceedings under the provisions of section 32-5A-195. (Acts 1979, No. 79-619, p. 1097, § 3.)

§ 32-6-44. Consideration of opinions, recommendations, etc., by director; driver considered unqualified if refused examination or information.

(a) The director shall give fair consideration to any opinion, reports, records or recommendations of the board or of private physicians licensed to practice in this state and submitting same pursuant to this division; however, all such opinions and reports shall be solely advisory and not binding on the director.

(b) Any person under review who refuses to admit to an examination or consent to provide information, or both, shall as a matter of law be considered unqualified to operate a motor vehicle until such time as the individual complies with the board's requests and the board can make its findings and recommendations to the director. (Acts 1979, No. 79-619, p. 1097, § 4.)

§ 32-6-45. Immunity from civil liability.

No civil or criminal action may be brought against the board, any of its members, the director or director's office or its employees, or any physician licensed to practice in this state, for providing any reports, records, examinations, opinions or recommendations pursuant to the division. In addition, any other person acting in good faith and without negligence or malicious intent in making a report to the director's office pursuant to this division shall have the immunity from civil liability that might otherwise be incurred or imposed. (Acts 1979, No. 79-619, p. 1097, § 5.)

Collateral references. — Liability of physician, for injury to or death of third party, due to failure to disclose driving-related impediment. 43 ALR4th 153.

§ 32-6-46. Closed meetings of board.

Meetings of the board in which reports received for the purpose of determining the medical condition of an applicant are considered as closed sessions, since those reports are confidential under section 32-6-43. (Acts 1979, No. 79-619, p. 1097, § 6.)

§ 32-6-47. Appeal of suspended, revoked, etc., license; no driving while appeal pending.

A person whose driver's license has been cancelled, suspended or revoked or whose application for a driver's license has been denied shall have the right of judicial appeal of such action, as provided under section 32-5A-195. No person shall be allowed to drive in violation of any cancellation, suspension, revocation or denial of application while any such appeal is pending. (Acts 1979, No. 79-619, p. 1097, § 7.)

Cited in Mechur v. Director, Dep't of Pub. Safety, 446 So. 2d 48 (Ala. Civ. App. 1984). Collateral references. — Liability of physician, for injury to or death of third party, due to failure to disclose driving-related impediment. 43 ALR4th 153.

§ 32-6-48. Advice for promulgation of vision standards.

This division shall not prohibit the director from utilizing the Alabama Optometric Association, the Alabama Academy of Ophthalmology or any other group, association or board for advice relating to the promulgation of vision standards for licensing drivers. (Acts 1979, No. 79-619, p. 1097, § 8.)

ARTICLE 1A.

UNIFORM COMMERCIAL DRIVER LICENSE ACT.

(This article is effective October 1, 1990.)

§ 32-6-49.1. (Effective October 1, 1990) Short title.

This article may be cited as the Alabama Uniform Commercial Driver License Act. (Acts 1989, No. 89-878, § 1.)

Effective date. — The act which adds this article becomes effective October 1, 1990.
Cross references. — As to applicability of this article only to offenses committed 60 days after its effective date and thereafter, see § 32-6-49.20.

§ 32-6-49.2. (Effective October 1, 1990) Purpose; construction.

The purpose of this article is to implement the federal Commercial Motor Vehicle Safety Act of 1986 (CMVSA) (Title XII of Pub. Law 99-570) and reduce or prevent commercial motor vehicle accidents, fatalities and injuries by:

(a) Permitting commercial drivers to hold only one license;

(b) Disqualifying commercial drivers who have committed certain serious traffic violations, or other specified offenses;

(c) Strengthening commercial driver licensing and testing standards.

This article is a remedial law which should be liberally construed to promote the public health, safety and welfare. To the extent that this article conflicts with general driver licensing provisions, this article prevails. Where this article is silent, the general driver licensing provisions apply. (Acts 1989, No. 89-878, § 2.)

Effective date. — The act which adds this article becomes effective October 1, 1990.
U.S. Code. — The federal Commercial Motor Vehicle Safety Act of 1986, referred to in this section, is codified as 49 U.S.C. § 2701 et seq.

§ 32-6-49.3. (Effective October 1, 1990) Definitions.

Notwithstanding any other provision of this article, the following definitions shall be applicable unless the context clearly indicates otherwise:

(1) ALCOHOL.

a. Beer, ale, port or stout and other similar fermented beverages (including sake or similar products), of any name or description containing one-half of one percentum or more of alcohol by volume, brewed or produced from malt, wholly or in part, or from any substitute therefor;

b. Wine of not less than one-half of the percentum of alcohol by volume; or

c. Any substance containing any form of alcohol, including but not limited to, ethanol, methanol, propanol and isopropanol.

(2) ALCOHOL CONCENTRATION.

a. The number of grams of alcohol per 100 milliliters of blood; or

b. The number of grams of alcohol per 210 liters of breath; or

c. The number of grams of alcohol per 67 milliliters of urine.

(3) COMMERCIAL DRIVER LICENSE. (CDL) means a license issued in accordance with the requirements of this article to an individual which authorizes the individual to drive a class of commercial motor vehicle.

(4) COMMERCIAL DRIVER LICENSE INFORMATION SYSTEM. (CDLIS) is the information system established pursuant to the CMVSA to serve as a clearinghouse for locating information related to the licensing and identification of commercial motor vehicle drivers.

(5) COMMERCIAL MOTOR VEHICLE. A motor vehicle designed or used to transport passengers or property:

a. If the vehicle has a gross vehicle weight rating of 26,001 or more pounds or such lesser rating as determined by federal regulation;

b. If the vehicle is designed to transport 16 or more passengers, including the driver; or

c. If the vehicle is transporting hazardous materials and is required to be placarded in accordance with federal or state law.

(6) CONTROLLED SUBSTANCE. Any substance so classified under section 102(6) of the Controlled Substances Act (21 U.S.C. 802(6)), and includes all substances listed on Schedules I through V, of 21 C.F.R. part 1308, as they may be revised from time to time.

(7) CONVICTION. An unvacated adjudication of guilt, or a determination that a person has violated or failed to comply with the law in a court of original jurisdiction or an authorized administrative tribunal, an unvacated forfeiture of bail or collateral deposited to secure the person's appearance in court, the payment of a fine or court cost, or violation of a condition of release without bail, or a plea nolo contendere accepted by the court, regardless of whether or not the penalty is rebated, suspended or probated.

(8) DEPARTMENT. The department of public safety.

(9) DIRECTOR. The director of the department of public safety.

(10) DISQUALIFICATION. A withdrawal of the privilege to drive a commercial motor vehicle, pursuant to section 32-5A-195 and this article.

(11) DRIVE. To drive, operate or be in physical control of a motor vehicle.

(12) DRIVER. Any person who drives, operates, or is in physical control of a commercial motor vehicle, or who is required to hold a commercial driver license.

(13) DRIVER LICENSE. A license issued by a state to an individual which authorizes the individual to drive a motor vehicle.

(14) EMPLOYER. Any person, including the United States, a state, or a political subdivision of a state, who owns or leases a commercial motor vehicle, or assigns a person to drive a commercial motor vehicle.

(15) FELONY. Any offense under state or federal law that is punishable by death or imprisonment for a term exceeding one year.

(16) FOREIGN JURISDICTION. Any jurisdiction other than a state, territory, province or possession of the United States.

(17) GROSS VEHICLE WEIGHT RATING. (GVWR) The value specified by the manufacturer(s) as the maximum loaded weight of a single or a combination (articulated) vehicle, or registered gross weight, whichever is greater. The GVWR of a combination (articulated) vehicle (commonly referred to as the "Gross Combination Weight Rating" or GCWR), is the GVWR of the power unit plus the GVWR of the towed unit or units.

(18) HAZARDOUS MATERIALS. Has the meaning as that found in section 103 of the Hazardous Materials Transportation Act (49 App. U.S.C. 1801 et seq.), and as provided by any federal or state law, existing or hereafter enacted.

(19) MOTOR VEHICLE. Every vehicle which is self-propelled, and every vehicle which is propelled by electric power obtained from overhead trolley wires but not operated upon rails, except vehicles moved solely by human power and motorized wheel chairs.

(20) OUT OF SERVICE ORDER. A temporary prohibition against driving a commercial motor vehicle.

(21) SERIOUS TRAFFIC VIOLATION. A conviction when operating a commercial motor vehicle of:

a. Excessive speeding, involving a single charge of any speed 15 miles per hour or more, above the posted speed limit;

b. Reckless driving, as defined under section 32-5A-190, as amended, or any other state or local law, including charges of driving a commercial motor vehicle in willful or wanton or reckless disregard for the safety of persons or property, improper or erratic traffic lane changes, or following the vehicle ahead too closely;

c. A violation of any state or local law related to motor vehicle traffic control, other than a parking violation, arising in connection with a fatal accident; and

d. Any other violation of Title 32, chapter 5A, article 9, as amended, or any state or local law relating to motor vehicle traffic control, other than a parking violation, which the director of the department of public safety determines by regulation to be serious.

(22) STATE. A state of the United States and the District of Columbia;

(23) UNITED STATES. The 50 states and the District of Columbia, or a territory, province or possession thereof. (Acts 1989, No. 89-878, § 3.)

Effective date. — The act which adds this article becomes effective October 1, 1990.

§ 32-6-49.4. (Effective October 1, 1990) Limitation on number of driver licenses.

No person who drives a commercial motor vehicle may have more than one driver license. (Acts 1989, No. 89-878, § 4.)

Effective date. — The act which adds this article becomes effective October 1, 1990.

§ 32-6-49.5. (Effective October 1, 1990) Notification required by driver.

Notification required by driver shall be as follows:

(a) Notification of convictions:

(1) To STATE. Any driver holding a commercial driver license issued by this state, who is convicted of violating any state law or local ordinance relating to motor vehicle traffic control, in any other state or federal, provincial, territorial or municipal laws of Canada, other than parking violations, must notify the department of public safety in the manner specified by the department within 30 days of the date of conviction.

(2) To EMPLOYERS. Any driver holding a commercial driver license issued by this state, who is convicted of violating any state law or local ordinance relating to motor vehicle traffic control in this or any other state, or federal, provincial, territorial or municipal laws of Canada, other than parking violations, must notify his or her employer in writing of the conviction within 30 days of the date of conviction.

(b) Any driver whose commercial driver license is suspended, revoked, or cancelled by any state, or federal, provincial, territorial or municipal laws of Canada, or who loses the privilege to drive a commercial motor vehicle in any such state for any period, including being disqualified from driving a commercial motor vehicle, or who is subject to an out of service order, must notify his or her employer of that fact before the end of the business day following the day the driver received notice of that fact.

(c) Any person who applies to be a commercial motor vehicle driver must provide the employer, at the time of the application, with the following information for the 10 years preceding the date of application:

(1) A list of the names and addresses of the applicant's previous employers for which the applicant was a driver of a commercial motor vehicle;

(2) The dates between which the applicant drove for each employer; and

(3) The reason for leaving that employer.

The applicant must certify that all information furnished is true and complete. An employer may require an applicant to provide additional information. (Acts 1989, No. 89-878, § 5.)

Effective date. — The act which adds this article becomes effective October 1, 1990.

§ 32-6-49.6. (Effective October 1, 1990) Employer's responsibilities.

(a) Each employer must require the applicant to provide the information specified in section 32-6-49.5(c).

(b) No employer may knowingly allow, permit, or authorize a driver to drive a commercial motor vehicle during any period:

(1) In which the driver has had his or her commercial driver license suspended, revoked, or cancelled by any state, is currently disqualified from driving a commercial vehicle, or subject to an out of service order in any state; or

(2) In which the driver has more than one driver license. (Acts 1989, No. 89-878, § 6.)

Effective date. — The act which adds this article becomes effective October 1, 1990.

§ 32-6-49.7. (Effective October I, 1990) Commercial driver license required; exceptions.

(a) Except when driving with a valid automobile license and accompanied by the holder of a commercial driver license valid for the vehicle being driven, no person may drive a commercial motor vehicle on the highways of this state unless the person holds, and is in immediate possession of, a commercial driver license with applicable endorsements valid for the vehicle he or she is driving.

Active duty military or national guard personnel operating government vehicles, farmers operating certain commercial motor vehicles, fire fighters and operators of emergency equipment exempt from licensing provisions of the CMVSA are exempt from this act as detailed in FHWA's "Notice of Final Disposition" published in the Federal Register, September 26, 1988, 53 FR 37313, and as hereafter updated.

Commercial driver license requirements do not apply to drivers of vehicles used for personal use such as recreational vehicles which would otherwise meet the definition of a commercial motor vehicle.

(b) No person may drive a commercial motor vehicle on the highways of this state while his or her driving privilege is suspended, revoked, or cancelled, while subject to a disqualification, or in violation of an out of service order. (Acts 1989, No. 89-878, § 7.)

Effective date. — The act which adds this article becomes effective October 1, 1990.

§ 32-6-49.8. (Effective October 1, 1990) Commercial driver license qualifications; test; waiver of test; limitations on issuance; when holder of Class D license may drive commercial vehicle.

Commercial driver license qualification standards shall be as follows:

(a) *Testing.*

(1) GENERAL. — No person may be issued a commercial driver license unless that person is a resident of this state and has passed a knowledge and skills test for driving a commercial motor vehicle which complies with minimum federal standards established by federal regulation enumerated in 49 C.F.R. part 383, subparts G and H, and has satisfied all other requirements of the CMVSA in addition to other requirements imposed by state law or federal regulation. The tests must be prescribed and conducted by the department.

(2) THIRD PARTY TESTING. — The department may authorize a person, including an agency of this or another state, an employer, a private driver training facility, or other private institution, or a department, agency or instrumentality of local government to administer the skills test specified by this section, provided:

(i) The test is the same which would otherwise be administered by the state;

(ii) The third party has entered into an agreement with this state which complies with requirements of 49 C.F.R. part 383.75; and

(b) *Waiver of skills test.* — The department may waive the skills test specified in this section for a commercial driver license applicant who meets the requirements of 49 C.F.R. part 383.77. In the case of school bus drivers the department shall waive the skills test herein specified.

(c) *Limitations on issuance of license.* — A commercial driver license may not be issued to a person while the person is subject to a disqualification from driving a commercial motor vehicle, or while the person's driver license is suspended, revoked or cancelled in any state or foreign jurisdiction with reciprocity; nor may a commercial driver license be issued to a person who has a commercial driver license issued by any other state unless the person first surrenders all such licenses, which must be returned to the issuing state(s) for cancellation.

(d) The holder of a valid Class D driver license may drive a commercial motor vehicle only when accompanied by the holder of a commercial driver license valid for the type of vehicle driven who occupies a seat beside the individual for the purpose of giving instruction in driving the commercial vehicle. (Acts 1989, No. 89-878, § 8.)

Effective date. — The act which adds this article becomes effective October 1, 1990.

§ 32-6-49.9. (Effective October 1, 1990) Application for commercial driver license; fee; change of name, etc.; license issued by another jurisdiction; false information.

Application for commercial driver license shall be processed as follows:

(a) The application for a commercial driver license or commercial driver instruction permit, must include the following:

(1) The full name and current mailing (and residential, if different) address of the person;

(2) A physical description of the person including sex, height, weight, eye and hair color;

(3) Date of birth;

(4) The applicant's social security number;

(5) The person's signature;

(6) The person's color photograph;

(7) Certifications including those required by 49 C.F.R. part 383.71 (a);

(8) Any other information required by the department; and

(9) A signed consent to release driving record information.

The application must be accompanied by an application fee of $5.00. The application fee costs for school bus drivers shall not be assessed against existing bus drivers nor school boards.

(b) When the holder of a commercial driver license changes his or her name, mailing address, or residence, an application for a duplicate license must be made as provided by law.

(c) No person who has been a resident of this state for 30 days may drive a commercial motor vehicle under the authority of a commercial driver license issued by another jurisdiction.

(d) Any person who knowingly falsifies information or certifications required under subsection (a) of this section is subject to suspension, revocation, or cancellation of his or her commercial driver license for a period of at least 60 consecutive days. (Acts 1989, No. 89-878, § 9.)

Effective date. — The act which adds this article becomes effective October 1, 1990.

§ 32-6-49.10. (Effective October 1, 1990) Information on commercial driver license; classifications, endorsements, etc.; driving record information to be obtained; notification of information system of issuance of license; expiration; renewal; hazardous materials endorsement.

(a) The commercial driver license must be marked "Commercial Driver License" or "CDL," and must be, to the maximum extent practicable, tamper proof. It must include, but not be limited to, the following information:

(1) The name and residential address of the person;

(2) The person's color photograph;

(3) A physical description of the person including sex, height, weight, eye and hair color;

(4) Date of birth; and

(5) The person's social security number and any other number or identifier deemed appropriate by the department;

(6) The person's signature;

(7) The class or type of commercial motor vehicle or vehicles which the person is authorized to drive together with any endorsements or restrictions;

(8) The name of this state; and

(9) The dates between which the license is valid.

(b) Commercial driver licenses may be issued with the following classifications, endorsements, and restrictions; the holder of a valid commercial driver license may drive all vehicles in the class for which that license is issued, and all lesser classes of vehicles including Class D, except motorcycles (Class M). Vehicles which require an endorsement may not be driven unless the proper endorsement appears on the license.

(1) Commercial driver licenses shall be classified as follows:

Class A — Any combination of vehicles with a gross vehicle weight rating (GVWR) of 26,001 pounds or more, provided the GVWR of the vehicle(s) being towed is in excess of 10,000 pounds.

Class B — Any single vehicle with a GVWR of 26,001 pounds or more, and any such vehicle towing a vehicle not in excess of 10,000 pounds.

Class C — Any single vehicle with a GVWR of less than 26,001 pounds or any such vehicle towing a vehicle with a GVWR not in excess of 10,000 pounds comprising:

(i) Vehicles designed to transport 16 or more passengers, including the driver; and

(ii) Vehicles used in the transportation of hazardous materials which requires the vehicle to be placarded under 49 C.F.R., part 172, subpart F.

(2) Endorsements and restrictions shall be coded as follows:

"H" — Authorizes the driver to drive a vehicle transporting hazardous materials.

"K" — Restricts the driver to vehicles not equipped with airbrakes.

"T" — Authorizes driving double and triple trailers.

"P" — Authorizes driving vehicles carrying passengers.

"N" — Authorizes driving tank vehicles.

"X" — Represents a combination of hazardous materials and tank vehicle endorsements.

(c) Before issuing a commercial driver license, the department must obtain driving record information through the commercial driver license information system, the national driver register and from each state in which the person has been licensed.

(d) Within 10 days after issuing a commercial driver license, the department must notify the commercial driver license information system of that fact, providing all information required to ensure identification of the person.

227

(e) A commercial driver license issued pursuant to this article expires as set by existing state law.

(f) Renewal procedures for commercial driver licenses shall be as follows: every person applying for renewal of a commercial driver license must complete the application form required by subsection (a) of this section, providing updated information and required certifications. If the applicant wishes to retain a hazardous materials endorsement, the written test for a hazardous materials endorsement must be taken and passed. (Acts 1989, No. 89-878, § 10.)

Effective date. — The act which adds this article becomes effective October 1, 1990.

§ 32-6-49.11. (Effective October 1, 1990) Disqualification from driving commercial motor vehicle; time period; disqualification for life; updating of records; penalty for failure to report or disclose information.

(a) Any person is disqualified from driving a commercial motor vehicle for a period of not less than one year if convicted of a first violation of:

(1) Driving a commercial motor vehicle under the influence of alcohol, or a controlled substance or any other drug which renders a person incapable of safely driving;

(2) Driving a commercial motor vehicle while the alcohol concentration of the person's blood, urine, or breath is 0.04 or more;

(3) Knowingly and willfully leaving the scene of an accident involving a commercial motor vehicle driven by the person;

(4) Using a commercial motor vehicle in the commission of any felony as defined in this act; and

(5) Refusal to submit to a test to determine the driver's alcohol concentration while driving a commercial motor vehicle.

If any of the above violations occurred while transporting a hazardous material required to be placarded, the person is disqualified for a period of not less than three years.

(b) A person is disqualified for life if convicted of two or more violations of any of the offenses specified in subsection (a), or any combination of those offenses, arising from two or more separate incidents.

(c) The department may issue regulations and promulgate establishing guidelines, including conditions, under which a disqualification for life under subsection (b) may be reduced to a period of not less than 10 years.

(d) A person is disqualified from driving a commercial motor vehicle for life who uses a commercial motor vehicle in the commission of any felony involving the manufacture, distribution, or dispensing of a controlled substance, or possession with intent to manufacture, distribute or dispense a controlled substance.

(e) A person is disqualified from driving a commercial motor vehicle for a period of not less than 60 days if convicted of two serious traffic violations, or

120 days if convicted of three serious traffic violations, committed in a commercial motor vehicle arising from separate incidents occurring within a three-year period.

(f) After suspending, revoking, or canceling a commercial driver license, the department must update its records to reflect that action within 10 days. After suspending, revoking or canceling a nonresident commercial driver's privilege, the department must notify the licensing authority of the state which issued the commercial driver license or commercial driver instruction permit within 10 days.

Any failure to report or disclose required information, either before or after issuance of a commercial driver license shall be a Class C felony and shall, upon conviction thereof, be punished as provided by law. (Acts 1989, No. 89-878, § 11.)

Effective date. — The act which adds this article becomes effective October 1, 1990.

§ 32-6-49.12. (Effective October 1, 1990) Use of alcohol while driving; when placed out of service; when disqualified.

(a) Notwithstanding any other provision of this article, or of existing law, a person may not drive, operate, or be in physical control of a commercial motor vehicle within this state while having any measurable or detectable amount of alcohol in his or her system.

(b) A person who drives, operates, or is in physical control of a commercial motor vehicle within this state while having any measurable or detectable amount of alcohol in his or her system or who refuses to submit to an alcohol test under section 32-6-49.13, must be placed out of service for 24 hours.

(c) Any person who drives a commercial motor vehicle within this state with an alcohol concentration of 0.04 or more must, in addition to any other sanctions which may be imposed under this article, or under federal or state law, or rules or regulations of the department, be disqualified from driving a commercial motor vehicle under section 32-6-49.11. (Acts 1989, No. 89-878, § 12.)

Effective date. — The act which adds this article becomes effective October 1, 1990.

§ 32-6-49.13. (Effective October 1, 1990) Implied consent to take test of blood, breath, etc.; administration of test; refusal to take test; sanctions.

(a) A person who drives a commercial motor vehicle within this state is deemed to have given consent, subject to provisions of section 32-5-192, to take a test or tests of that person's blood, breath, or urine for the purpose of determining that person's alcohol concentration, or the presence of other drugs.

(b) A test or tests may be administered at the direction of a law enforcement officer, who after stopping or detaining the commercial motor vehicle driver, has probable cause to believe that driver was driving a commercial motor vehicle while having alcohol or drugs in his or her system.

(c) A person requested to submit to a test as provided in subsection (a) above must be warned by the law enforcement officer requesting the test, that a refusal to submit to the test will result in that person being immediately placed out of service for a period of 24 hours and being disqualified from operating a commercial motor vehicle for a period of not less than one year under section 32-6-49.12.

(d) If the person refuses testing, or submits to a test which discloses an alcohol concentration of 0.04 or more, the law enforcement officer must submit a sworn report to the department certifying that the test was requested pursuant to subsection (a) and that the person refused to submit to testing, or submitted to a test which disclosed an alcohol concentration of 0.04 or more.

(e) Upon receipt of the sworn report of a law enforcement officer submitted under subsection (d), the department must disqualify the driver from driving a commercial motor vehicle under section 32-6-49.12. (Acts 1989, No. 89-878, § 13.)

Effective date. — The act which adds this article becomes effective October 1, 1990.

§ 32-6-49.14. (Effective October 1, 1990) Report of conviction.

Within 10 days after receiving a report of the conviction of any nonresident holder of a commercial driver license for any violation of state law or local ordinance relating to motor vehicle traffic control, other than parking violations, committed in a commercial motor vehicle, the department must notify the driver licensing authority in the licensing state of the conviction. (Acts 1989, No. 89-878, § 14.)

Effective date. — The act which adds this article becomes effective October 1, 1990.

§ 32-6-49.15. (Effective October 1, 1990) Information regarding driving record.

Notwithstanding any other provision of law to the contrary, the department must furnish full information regarding the driving record of any person:

(a) To the driver license administrator of any other state, or province or territory of Canada, requesting that information;

(b) To any employer or prospective employer upon request and payment of a fee of $5.75; and

(c) To insurers upon request and payment of a fee of $5.75. (Acts 1989, No. 89-878, § 15.)

Effective date. — The act which adds this article becomes effective October 1, 1990.

§ 32-6-49.16. (Effective October 1, 1990) Rulemaking authority.

The director and the department of public safety may adopt any reasonable rules and regulations necessary to carry out the provisions of this article, and may promulgate and enforce such rules and regulations in accordance with the guidelines of the department of transportation. (Acts 1989, No. 89-878, § 16.)

Effective date. — The act which adds this article becomes effective October 1, 1990.

§ 32-6-49.17. (Effective October 1, 1990) Authority to enter into agreements.

The department may enter into or make agreements, arrangements or declarations to carry out the provisions of this article. (Acts 1989, No. 89-878, § 17.)

Effective date. — The act which adds this article becomes effective October 1, 1990.

§ 32-6-49.18. (Effective October 1, 1990) Reciprocity.

(a) Notwithstanding any law to the contrary, a person may drive a commercial motor vehicle in this state if the person has a valid commercial driver license or commercial driver license instruction permit issued by any state or provinces or territories of Canada in accordance with the minimum federal standards for the issuance of commercial motor vehicle driver licenses, if the license is not suspended, revoked or canceled; and if the person is not disqualified from driving a commercial motor vehicle, or subject to an out of service order.

(b) The department must give all out of state convictions full faith and credit and treat them for sanctioning purposes under this article as if they occurred in this state. (Acts 1989, No. 89-878, § 18.)

Effective date. — The act which adds this article becomes effective October 1, 1990.

§ 32-6-49.19. (Effective October 1, 1990) License fees; term of licenses.

For the purpose of defraying the cost of issuing commercial drivers' license, the probate judge or license commissioner shall collect for each Class A commercial driver license the sum of $45.00; the sum of $35.00 for each Class B commercial driver license; the sum of $15.00 for each Class C commercial driver license. These licenses shall be issued for a period of four years. (Acts 1989, No. 89-878, § 19.)

Effective date. — The act which adds this article becomes effective October 1, 1990.

§ 32-6-49.20. (Effective October 1, 1990) Applicability to offenses committed 60 days after effective date and thereafter.

Only offenses committed 60 days after the effective date of this article, and thereafter, shall be affected by the provisions of this article. (Acts 1989, No. 89-878, § 20.)

Effective date. — The act which adds this article becomes effective October 1, 1990.

§ 32-6-49.21. (Effective October 1, 1990) Sanctions, penalties, etc., are cumulative.

All sanctions, penalties, punishment and fines, whether civil or criminal, are cumulative and shall be levied in addition to any and all other laws now provided relating to commercial motor vehicle licensure requirements, except to the extent such laws or sanctions, penalties, punishment and fines are in direct conflict with the provisions of this article, in which event this article shall supersede. (Acts 1989, No. 89-878, § 21.)

Effective date. — The act which adds this article becomes effective October 1, 1990.

§ 32-6-49.22. (Effective October 1, 1990) Penalty.

Any person who violates the provisions of section 32-6-49.4 shall be guilty of a Class B misdemeanor and, upon conviction thereof, shall be sentenced or fined, or both, as provided by law. (Acts 1989, No. 89-878, § 22.)

Effective date. — The act which adds this article becomes effective October 1, 1990.

ARTICLE 2.

LICENSE TAGS AND PLATES.

Division 1.

General Provisions.

Subdivision 1.

Tags Generally.

Cross references. — As to special license tags for rescue squad vehicles, see § 32-11-4. As to license fees for motor vehicles, see § 40-12-240 et seq.

§ 32-6-50. Repealed by Acts 1979, No. 79-797, p. 1455, § 13.

Code commissioner's note. — Acts 1979, No. 79-797, p. 1455, § 13, effective August 9, 1979, repeals this section. However, Acts 1979, No. 79-797, p. 1455, § 1, provides that effective from and after October 1, 1980, the licensing, registration and taxation of motor vehicles shall be on a staggered basis. This section is treated as repealed, although it is not certain which date the legislature intended for the repeal to be effective. See § 32-6-60.

§ 32-6-51. Rear tags required.

Every motor vehicle operator who operates a motor vehicle upon any city street or other public highway of or in this state shall at all times keep attached and plainly visible on the rear end of such motor vehicle a license tag or license plate as prescribed and furnished by the department of revenue at the time the owner or operator purchases his license.

Anyone violating the provisions of this section shall be guilty of a misdemeanor and shall, upon conviction, be punished by fine not exceeding $500.00 and, in addition thereto, shall be prohibited from driving a motor vehicle in Alabama for a period of not less than 60 days nor more than six months. (Acts 1935, No. 512, p. 1100; Acts 1936-37, Ex. Sess., No. 31, p. 28; Code 1940, T. 36, § 75; Acts 1961, Ex. Sess., No. 143, p. 2085, §§ 1, 3.)

Improper tags not covered by section. — Where defendant is charged with violation of the provisions of this section, and the evidence reveals that license tags, improperly affixed but plainly visible, were attached to both the front and the rear of defendant's automobile, no violation of this section results, since the question of possessing improper license tags is covered by other sections and is not here involved. Geeter v. State, 35 Ala. App. 207, 45 So. 2d 167 (1950).

Bill of sale and license tag two methods of proving ownership. — Since there is no motor vehicle title registration law in this state, a tag receipt bearing the number on the license plate and the identification number of the vehicle is an indicium of title and evidence of ownership. A bill of sale and a license tag are two methods of proving ownership and the right to possession of a motor vehicle. Whistenant v. State, 50 Ala. App. 182, 278 So. 2d 183, cert. denied, 50 Ala. App. 198, 278 So. 2d 198 (1973), 291 Ala. 802, 278 So. 2d 198, 414 U.S. 1066, 94 S. Ct. 573, 38 L. Ed. 2d 470 (1973). But see § 32-8-1 et seq.

Violation of section carries sanctions. — There are penalty sanctions for operating automobiles on the public highways without a proper license tag properly mounted on the vehicle. Whistenant v. State, 50 Ala. App. 182, 278 So. 2d 183, cert. denied, 50 Ala. App. 198, 278 So. 2d 198 (1973), 291 Ala. 802, 278 So. 2d 198, 414 U.S. 1066, 94 S. Ct. 573, 38 L. Ed. 2d 470 (1973).

Collateral references. — 60 C.J.S., Motor Vehicles, §§ 107, 108. 61A C.J.S., Motor Vehicles, § 638.

§ 32-6-52. Using license tag of improper classification.

It shall be unlawful for any person to drive or operate any motor vehicle upon the streets or highways of this state, unless the license tag attached to the vehicle is of the proper classification as required by the revenue laws of this state. Any person violating this provision, upon conviction, shall be punished as provided in section 32-5-311. (Acts 1927, No. 347, p. 348; Code 1940, T. 36, § 78; Acts 1949, No. 518, p. 773, § 1.)

Code commissioner's note. — Section 32-5-311, referred to in this section, was repealed by Acts 1980, No. 80-434, p. 604, § 15-106, effective May 19, 1980. See now § 32-5A-8.

Collateral references. — 60 C.J.S., Motor Vehicles, §§ 63, 101, 133-138.

§ 32-6-53. Power of commissioner of revenue to make rules and regulations.

The commissioner of revenue, or his successor in office, by whatsoever name called, shall have full and continuing power to promulgate, from time to time with the approval of the governor, reasonable rules and regulations governing the number, type or kind, size and method of placement and attachment of license tags, stamps, discs, plates or other devices to be attached to motor vehicles as evidence of the licensing and registration thereof; provided, that such power or authority on the part of the commissioner of revenue, or his successor in office, to issue such rules and regulations shall be dependent upon a proclamation by the governor, from time to time as the occasion may require, of an emergency making reasonably necessary the use of such substitutes for the usual tags attached to or placed upon motor vehicles; and provided further, that the power to make such rules and regulations by the commissioner shall continue until the governor has by proclamation ended that particular emergency; it being the intent of the legislature by this section to confer upon the governor the authority to determine when an emergency exists and to determine by proclamation the end thereof; and, provided further, that the effective date of such emergency shall not begin until the governor's proclamation shall have been published for five days in five daily papers in the state of Alabama, and that such emergency shall not terminate until the governor's proclamation ending the same shall likewise have been published for five days in five daily newspapers of the state.

Any person who violates any rule or regulation issued or promulgated by the commissioner or his successor in office, under the authority of this section, shall be guilty of a misdemeanor and, upon conviction thereof, shall be punished as now provided by law. (Acts 1951, No. 535, p. 947.)

Cross references. — As to provision granting to the commissioner of revenue the authority to control, by regulation, the design of license plates, see § 32-6-64.

§ 32-6-54. Tag to show heart and words "Heart of Dixie."

Every license tag or license plate issued by the state of Alabama for use on motor vehicles, in addition to any letters and figures prescribed by the commissioner of revenue, shall also have imprinted thereon a conventionalized representation of a heart and the words "Heart of Dixie." The design of license tags or license plates shall be approved by the commissioner of revenue. (Acts 1951, No. 675, p. 1168, § 1.)

Cross references. — As to provision granting to the commissioner of revenue the power
to regulate the design of license plates, see
§ 32-6-64.

§ 32-6-55. Special tag number for chairman of USS Alabama battleship commission.

The chairman of the USS Alabama battleship commission, which commission was created by sections 41-9-340 through 41-9-358, shall be entitled to
use on the license tags of both his official and private automobiles the insignia
BB-60 which letters and number were the call letters of battleship USS
Alabama during its proud service throughout World War II. Upon compliance
with the state motor vehicle laws relating to registration and licensing of
motor vehicles and upon the payment of the regular license fee for tags, as
provided by law, said chairman shall be issued receipts which shall authorize
him to cause a special plate or tag to be made bearing the said call letters to
be used by him in lieu of any other license number. (Acts 1965, 2nd Ex. Sess.,
No. 98, p. 131.)

§ 32-6-56. Powers of commissioner of revenue as to reciprocal agree- ments with other states, etc., for registration of vehicles on an apportionment or allocation basis.

Notwithstanding any other provisions of this Code, the commissioner of the
department of revenue is hereby authorized and empowered to enter into
reciprocal agreements on behalf of this state with the duly authorized
representatives of any of the states of the United States, the District of
Columbia or a state or province of a foreign country or a territory or
possession of either the United States or of a foreign country providing for the
registration of vehicles on an apportionment or allocation basis.

In exercising the authority granted to him by this section, the commissioner
is expressly authorized and empowered to enter into and to become a member
of the International Registration Plan or such other designation that may,
from time to time, be given to such plan, developed by the American
Association of Motor Vehicle Administrators.

The commissioner is further authorized and empowered to promulgate and
to enforce such rules and regulations as may be necessary to carry out the
provisions of the International Registration Plan or any other agreement
entered into under the authority of this section.

If the commissioner enters into the International Registration Plan or into
any other agreement under the authority of this section, and if the provisions
set forth in said International Registration Plan or other agreements are
different from the provisions prescribed by this Code or any rules or
regulations promulgated by the commissioner pursuant to the authority
granted hereunder to the commissioner, then the agreement provisions shall
prevail.

The provisions of this section shall constitute complete authority for the
registration of vehicles, including the registration of fleet vehicles, upon an

apportionment or allocation basis under the International Registration Plan. (Acts 1978, No. 848, p. 1267.)

Collateral references. — 60 C.J.S., Motor Vehicles, §§ 63, 66.

7 Am. Jur. 2d, Automobiles & Highway Traffic, §§ 50, 73, 80.

§ 32-6-57. Manufacturing specifications for license tags or plates.

(a) Effective January 1, 1987, every license tag or plate issued under the provisions of this section and sections 40-12-273, 40-12-274 shall be manufactured in such a manner as to meet the minimum federal performance standards as set out in Table I of the Society of Automotive Engineers Standard J594e, "Reflex Reflectors," of Federal Standard 108.

(b) The state revenue department shall implement the provisions of this section and sections 40-12-273, 40-12-274 and, for such purpose, is authorized to promulgate rules and regulations and to adopt plans for such tags or plates, and all decals, slogans, stickers, symbols, characters and other attachments, all of which shall be supplied by the department of corrections. (Acts 1984, No. 84-240, p. 363, § 1.)

Code commissioner's note. — Acts 1984, No. 84-240, which added §§ 32-6-57, 40-12-273, and 40-12-274, provides in § 5: "The provisions of this act shall be construed in pari materia with the provisions of existing laws, specifically those provisions of chapter 6 of Title 32, subdivision 2 (§§ 32-6-60 through 32-6-219) and chapter 12 of Title 40 and subdivision 1 (§§ 40-12-240 through 40-12-296) of said chapters 6 and 12, all of the Code of Alabama 1975. The provisions hereof are supplemental to the above-cited provisions of law and shall supersede and repeal only those provisions of law and any other provisions of law which conflict herewith."

§ 32-6-58. Applicants for registration of heavy motor vehicles must furnish proof of paying federal taxes.

(a) All judges of probate, license commissioners, and other officials authorized by law to register motor vehicles and issue motor vehicle license plates and to perform other duties in connection with the issuance of motor vehicle license plates shall refuse to register a motor vehicle having a gross weight of 33,000 pounds or more and shall refuse to issue any motor vehicle license plate for such motor vehicle and shall refuse to transfer any motor vehicle registrations and license plates for such motor vehicles unless the applicant furnishes proof of payment, in the form prescribed by the secretary of the United States treasury, that the federal heavy vehicle excise tax imposed by Title 26, United States Code § 4481, has been paid.

(b) The department of revenue is empowered to adopt such rules and regulations as it may deem necessary for the proper administration of this section. (Acts 1984, 1st Ex. Sess., No. 84-794, p. 203.)

Subdivision 2.

Licensing, Registration and Taxation
on Staggered Basis.

§ 32-6-60. Licensing, registration, etc., staggered — Implementation period.

Effective from and after October 1, 1980, the licensing, registration and ad valorem taxation of motor vehicles in compliance with the laws of the state of Alabama shall be on a staggered basis. Provided, however, the actual distribution of the license plates described in sections 32-6-63 and 32-6-64 shall begin from and after January 1, 1982. For the fiscal year 1981 the license plates used for the previous five years as set out in section 32-6-50, shall continue to be used in the same manner as used in the past five years. An appropriate 1981 tab, disc or other device suitable for attaching to said motor vehicle tag or plate shall be issued upon the payment of the annual license tax prescribed by law for the 1981 fiscal year. While the actual issuance of license plates described in sections 32-6-63 and 32-6-64, on a staggered basis shall not begin until January 1, 1982, the licensing, registration and ad valorem taxation of motor vehicles shall be on a staggered basis effective from and after October 1, 1980.

To implement this subdivision, the licensing, registration and taxation may be for periods less than or greater than 12 months during the conversion year only. However, such proration of fees during the implementation of a staggered registration system shall result in the collection of a total amount of moneys for the taxable year no more nor less than the current annual amounts received.

During the implementation period and thereafter the licensing, registration and taxation for vehicles weighing 12,001 pounds and over shall be prorated on a monthly basis. (Acts 1979, No. 79-797, p. 1455, § 1; Acts 1980, No. 80-631, p. 1091.)

Code commissioner's note. — Section 32-6-50, referred to in this section, was repealed by Acts 1979, No. 79-797, p. 1455, § 13.

For effective date, see the code commissioner's note under § 32-6-50.

§ 32-6-61. Licensing, registration, etc., staggered — Individual's last name determines month; trucks, commercial fleets, etc.; expiration date; proration; exception; reregistration of purchased vehicles.

The staggered system for the licensing, registration and taxation of motor vehicles shall be implemented thusly: The first letter of an individual's last name shall determine the month in which a vehicle owner shall register his vehicle(s), as indicated below:

January	...	A, D
February	...	B
March	...	C, E

April	...	F, G, N
May	...	H, O
June	...	M, I
July	...	P, L
August	...	J, K, R
September	...	Q, S, T
October	...	U, V, W, X, Y, Z, trucks, mobile homes, commercial and fleet vehicles
November	...	Trucks, mobile homes, commercial and fleet vehicles.

After the conversion period all owners of private passenger vehicles and pickup trucks of 12,000 pounds and under shall continue to register their vehicles during the month assigned to the first initial of their last name. All license plates issued on a staggered registration basis shall expire on the last day of the month which precedes the month assigned for the purchase or renewal of license registration.

All license plates issued to motor vehicles for which licensing, registration and taxation are due in October and November shall expire on September 30.

During the implementation period and thereafter all licensing, registration and ad valorem taxation of motor vehicles shall be prorated on a monthly basis, except that the special license tag or plate fees provided by section 32-6-150(a) shall not be prorated.

All persons who acquire a motor vehicle which is located in this state and required to be registered in this state, with exception of licensed motor vehicle dealers who purchase a vehicle for resale, shall within 10 calendar days from date of purchase reregister the vehicle with the probate judge or other county official authorized and required by law to issue license plates, of the county in which the owner resides, if the owner is an individual, or of the county in which said motor vehicle is used or operated if the owner is a firm, corporation or association. The owner shall be issued a new registration receipt and purchase a license plate or validation decal(s) to the appropriate month assigned for renewal; however, no additional fee or ad valorem tax need be paid other than registration issuance fee when renewal month and year remain the same. (Acts 1979, No. 79-797, p. 1455, § 2; Acts 1980, No. 80-631, p. 1091; Acts 1988, 1st Sp. Sess., No. 88-808, p. 248, § 1.)

The 1988, 1st Sp. Sess., amendment, effective September 20, 1988, inserted "except that the special license tag or plate fees provided by section 32-6-150(a) shall not be prorated" at the end of the next-to-last paragraph.

§ 32-6-62. License plates valid for period of years.

The license plates for private passenger automobiles and pickup trucks, such truck being defined as any truck with two axles and a gross weight not exceeding 12,000 pounds, shall be valid for five years and shall be replaced at the end of that period. License plates for all other vehicles shall be valid for one year and shall be replaced at the end of that period. (Acts 1979, No. 79-797, p. 1455, § 3.)

§ 32-6-63. Tabs, stamps, etc., in lieu of license plates; change of residence.

For the years during which the five-year license plates are not issued, in lieu thereof, tabs, stamps or other devices suitable for attaching to a motor vehicle license plate shall be issued. The tab, stamp or device shall indicate the period for which it was issued and shall, when properly affixed to the license plate, evidence payment for the motor vehicle license fees and taxes for the period indicated thereon. Such tab, stamp or device shall be such size as the legislative oversight committee, as provided for in this subdivision, deems appropriate and shall bear a bright reflective background contrasting with the digits or letters printed thereon. The first three letters of the month of expiration shall be printed on the bottom portion of said tab, stamp or device and shall be no less than three inches in width and one inch in height.

Any numbers shown on such tab, stamp or device shall be for accounting purposes only, to be used by the department of revenue, and shall in no way be used for the identification of the vehicle.

A person changing his county of residence shall be required to purchase a license plate indicating his new county of residence upon expiration of the license period covered by his present license plate or validation device and shall turn in his old license plate. (Acts 1979, No. 79-797, p. 1455, § 4.)

§ 32-6-64. License plate design; numbers for county of issuance; board of corrections to supply plates.

The design of license plates, including all emblems, slogans, symbols or characters appearing thereon, shall be by regulation as promulgated by the revenue commissioner, and as otherwise specified by law. However, the face of the license plate to be displayed shall be fully treated with a reflective material which will increase the nighttime visibility and legibility of the plate. There shall also be provided a special license plate for handicapped persons who operate their motor vehicles with hand controls which shall be specially colored red, white and blue. The purchase of these tags shall be optional with the vehicle owner, who shall bear the cost of such plates, and in no way shall the purchase of these tags be construed as mandatory.

Characters on the license plate which designate the county of issuance shall be numeric, and all numerals on said plates shall be no smaller than two and three-fourths inches in height. The following numbering scheme shall be used:

(1) Jefferson county, 1; Mobile county, 2; Montgomery county, 3.

(2) All other counties shall be ranked alphabetically and assigned consecutive numbers beginning with 4 and concluding with 67.

The board of corrections is directed to supply all license plates and revalidation devices required under this subdivision. The amounts charged by the board of corrections for the manufacture of revalidation devices shall not be less than that charged for the manufacture of license plates on a per item basis.

The board of corrections is hereby required to maintain an accurate system of record-keeping which shall trace and account for the handling and distribution of each plate and revalidation device throughout the manufacturing process until such items are distributed to each county.

After the five-year tag has been in use for a period of three years the board of corrections is hereby directed to manufacture all subsequent tags for the remaining two years of such period from a metal of less durability and quality than the metal used in manufacturing the five-year tags. (Acts 1979, No. 79-797, p. 1455, § 5.)

Code commissioner's note. — Acts 1979, No. 79-426, p. 667, effective October 1, 1979, abolished the board of corrections and vested all its rights, duties, power, property, funds, personnel, etc., in the governor, and authorized him to exercise such functions and duties himself or through designated administrators. See §§ 14-1-15 through 14-1-17.

Cross references. — As to power of commissioner of revenue to make rules and regulations governing license tags, see § 32-6-53. As to license tag to show heart and words "Heart of Dixie," see § 32-6-54. As to prerequisite to issuance of license plates, see § 32-8-32. As to prerequisite to assessment for ad valorem taxes, see § 32-8-33.

§ 32-6-65. Uniform registration renewal forms; centralized registration prohibited; late registration penalty; arrest for operating vehicle without current plate, decal, etc.; distribution of penalties.

(a) There shall be one uniform registration renewal form to be used statewide. Such form shall be designed so as to provide for both the transfer of ownership and the registration of the vehicle. The department of revenue, or any other state agency authorized to do so, shall print and issue vehicle registration renewal notices in such a way that they can be processed or read by "optical character reader" machines. All receipts shall be sent to the county agencies charged with handling vehicle registration. All receipts shall be machine prepared. The state and the county shall capture the color of the motor vehicle in their permanent records. This paragraph shall not give the department of revenue authority to centralize vehicle registration. Centralized registration is specifically prohibited and it is the legislative intent that automotive vehicle registration shall remain at the county level.

(b) A penalty of $15.00 shall be assessed by the official charged with issuing motor vehicle licenses for the late registration of a motor vehicle under the system of registration imposed by this subdivision. Licenses shall be renewed at any time during the month of expiration; provided, however, persons renewing licenses within 10 calendar days after the month of expiration shall pay only a $2.00 penalty fee. Persons renewing licenses 20 days after the $2.00 penalty fee time limit shall pay $15.00. Persons renewing licenses after the $15.00 penalty fee shall pay $25.00. It shall be the duty of all sheriffs, police officers, state troopers, license inspectors, deputy license inspectors, field agents of the department of revenue, and other law enforcement officers to arrest any person operating a motor vehicle without the current license plate displaying the proper tab, disc or decal. Persons apprehended, more than

10 days after the month of expiration of the license, upon conviction by a court of competent jurisdiction, shall be fined not less than $25.00.

(c) All penalties assessed by this section shall be distributed in the same manner as motor vehicle licenses and registration fees are distributed as provided in sections 40-12-269 and 40-12-270. Portions of section 40-12-10 as they may conflict with this section, are hereby repealed and superseded. (Acts 1979, No. 79-797, p. 1455, § 6; Acts 1980, No. 80-631, p. 1091.)

Collateral references. — 60 C.J.S., Motor Vehicles, §§ 133-135.

§ 32-6-66. Subdivision construed in pari materia.

It is hereby specifically provided that this subdivision shall be construed in pari materia with sections 32-8-32 and 32-8-33. (Acts 1979, No. 79-797, p. 1455, § 10.)

§ 32-6-67. Legislative oversight committee; members, appointment, clerical assistance, etc.

(a) There is hereby created a legislative committee to oversee the implementation and administration of this subdivision. Such committee shall be composed of three members of the house of representatives, who shall be appointed by the speaker of the house, and serve at his pleasure, and three members of the senate, who shall be appointed by the lieutenant governor, who shall serve at his pleasure, the director of the Alabama criminal justice information center, the director of public safety and the president of the Probate Judges Association. The chairman who shall be picked by the members of the committee from the legislative members on the committee, shall have the authority to call meetings of the committee when he deems it necessary.

(b) Upon the request of the chairman, the secretary of the senate and the clerk of the house shall provide such clerical assistance as may be necessary for the committee's work. (Acts 1979, No. 79-797, p. 1455, § 11.)

Division 2.

Amateur Radio Operators Generally.

§ 32-6-70. Issuance of special tags.

Owners of motor vehicles who are residents of the state of Alabama and who hold valid amateur radio station or citizen's band radio licenses issued by the federal communications commission, upon application, accompanied by proof of ownership of such amateur radio station or citizen's band radio license, complying with the state motor vehicle laws relating to registration and licensing of motor vehicles, and upon the payment of the regular license fee for tags, as provided by law, and the payment of an additional fee of $3.00, shall be issued license plates, as provided by law, for private or pleasure motor vehicles, upon which, in lieu of the numbers as prescribed by law, shall be inscribed the official amateur radio station or citizen's band radio call letters of such applicant as assigned by the federal communications commission. (Acts 1951, No. 359, p. 646, § 1; Acts 1975, No. 787, p. 1574, § 1.)

§ 32-6-71. Rules and regulations.

The state department of revenue shall make such rules and regulations as necessary to insure compliance with all state license laws relating to use and operation of a private or pleasure motor vehicle before issuing special tags to amateur radio operators in lieu of the regular Alabama license plates, and such rules and regulations as necessary to provide for the application for and issuance of such special tags. (Acts 1951, No. 359, p. 646, § 2.)

Collateral references. — Use of citizens band radio to report information about the highway location of a radar speed checkpoint. 87 ALR3d 83.

§ 32-6-72. List to be furnished to sheriff.

The state department of revenue shall, on or before the first day of January of each year, furnish to the sheriff of each county of the state of Alabama an alphabetically arranged list of the names, addresses and license tag letters of each person to whom a license tag is issued under the provisions of this division, and it shall be the duty of the sheriffs of the state to maintain and to keep current such lists for public information and inquiry. (Acts 1951, No. 359, p. 646, § 2.)

§ 32-6-73. Provisions supplemental.

The provisions of this division are supplementative to the motor vehicle licensing laws of the state of Alabama, and nothing herein shall be construed as abridging or repealing such laws. (Acts 1951, No. 359, p. 646, § 4.)

Division 3.

Amateur Radio Operators Licensed by Civil Air Patrol.

§ 32-6-90. Issuance of special tags.

Owners of motor vehicles who are residents of the state of Alabama and who hold a valid amateur radio station license issued by the civil air patrol, upon application, accompanied by proof of ownership of such amateur radio station license, complying with the state motor vehicle laws relating to registration and licensing of motor vehicles, and upon the payment of the regular license fee for tags, as provided by law, and the additional payment of a fee of $1.00, shall be issued license plates, as provided by law, for private or pleasure motor vehicles, upon which, in lieu of the numbers as prescribed by law, shall be inscribed the official civil air patrol call letters of such applicant as assigned by the federal communications commission. (Acts 1953, No. 765, p. 1026, § 1.)

§ 32-6-91. Rules and regulations.

The state department of revenue shall make such rules and regulations as necessary to insure compliance with all state license laws relating to use and operation of a private or pleasure motor vehicle before issuing special tags to amateur radio operators licensed by the civil air patrol in lieu of the regular Alabama license plates, and such rules and regulations as necessary to provide for the application for and issuance of such special tags. (Acts 1953, No. 765, p. 1026, § 2.)

§ 32-6-92. List to be furnished to sheriff.

The state department of revenue shall, on or before the first day of January of each year, furnish to the sheriff of each county of the state of Alabama an alphabetically arranged list of the names, addresses and license tag letters of each person to whom a license tag is issued under the provisions of section 32-6-90, and it shall be the duty of the sheriffs of the state to maintain and to keep current such lists for public information and inquiry. (Acts 1953, No. 765, p. 1026, § 3.)

§ 32-6-93. Provisions supplemental.

The provisions of this division are supplementative to the motor vehicle licensing laws of the state of Alabama, and nothing herein shall be construed as abridging or repealing such laws. (Acts 1953, No. 765, p. 1026, § 4.)

Division 4.

National Guard.

Cross references. — As to exemption of one vehicle of member of national guard from payment of license fees, see §§ 31-2-12, 40-12-244.

§ 32-6-110. Authority and design for distinctive plates or tags.

In recognition of the many and varied patriotic services rendered the state and the citizens thereof by the national guard and air national guard of Alabama, members thereof, including both enlisted and officer personnel, may, upon application and subject to the provisions of this division, be issued annually distinctive motor vehicle license plates or tags identifying these persons with such organizations. The distinctive plates or tags so issued members of these organizations shall be of such color and design as may be agreed upon by the adjutant general and the commissioner of revenue and shall bear the words "National Guard" and need not bear prefixed numbers identifying the county of issuance. The words "Heart of Dixie" need not be placed on such plates or tags. (Acts 1955, No. 308, p. 707, § 1.)

§ 32-6-111. Preparation; issuance; proof to be submitted by applicant; use.

The distinctive license plates provided for in this division shall be prepared by the commissioner of revenue and shall be issued through the judge of probate or license commissioner of the several counties of the state in like manner as are other motor vehicle license plates or tags, and such officers shall be entitled to their regular fees for such service. Applicants for such distinctive plates shall present to the issuing official proof of their membership in the national guard or air national guard of Alabama by means of certificate signed by the commanding officer of such applicant on forms prescribed by the adjutant general of Alabama. The distinctive license plates or tags so issued shall be used only upon and for personally-owned, private, passenger vehicles (to include station wagons and pick-up trucks) registered in the name of the member of the national guard and air national guard making application therefor and, when so issued to such applicant, shall be used upon the vehicle for which issued in lieu of the standard license plates or license tags normally issued for such vehicle. In addition to use of such distinctive license plates or tags on such personally-owned vehicles, such distinctive plates or tags may be used on state-owned vehicles operated by the state military department provided the prefix "S" is placed ahead of the number thereon. Motor vehicles for which so issued shall be registered by the proper official as are other motor vehicles. (Acts 1955, No. 308, p. 707, § 2; Acts 1959, No. 253, p. 816, § 2; Acts 1975, No. 1237, p. 2603, § 1.)

§ 32-6-112. Transferability of plates.

The distinctive license plates issued under this division shall not be transferable as between motor vehicle owners, and in the event the owner of a vehicle bearing such distinctive plates shall sell, trade, exchange or otherwise dispose of same, such plates shall be retained by the owner to whom issued and by him returned to the judge of probate or license commissioner of the county who shall receive and account for same in the manner stated below. In the event such owner shall acquire by purchase, trade, exchange or otherwise a vehicle for which no standard plates have been issued during the current license year, the judge of probate or license commissioner of the county shall, upon being furnished by the owner thereof proper certification of the acquisition of such vehicle and the payment of the motor vehicle license tax due upon such vehicle, authorize the transfer to said vehicle of the distinctive license plates previously purchased by such owner, which plates shall authorize the operation of said vehicle for the remainder of the then current license year. In the further event the owner of such distinctive plates shall acquire by purchase, trade, exchange or otherwise a vehicle for which standard plates have been issued during the current license year, the judge of probate or license commissioner shall, upon proper certification of such owner and upon delivery to such official of the standard plates previously issued for such vehicle, authorize the owner of such newly-acquired vehicle to place the distinctive plates previously purchased by him upon such vehicle and to use same thereon for the remainder of the then current license year. Such notice of transfer of ownership shall be made of record by the judge of probate or the license commissioner.

Any person acquiring by purchase, trade, exchange or otherwise any vehicle formerly bearing such distinctive plates shall be authorized, upon certification of such fact to the judge of probate or license commissioner of the county and the payment of the fee now required by law, to purchase standard replacement plates for such vehicle which shall authorize the operation of such vehicle by the new owner for the remainder of the license year. (Acts 1955, No. 308, p. 707, § 3.)

§ 32-6-113. Licensing year; estimate of number of plates required.

Such distinctive plates or tags shall be prepared and furnished for the licensing year commencing October 1 each year. The adjutant general shall furnish the commissioner of revenue annually with an estimate of the number of such distinctive plates or tags required in each of the several counties of the state. (Acts 1955, No. 308, p. 707, § 4.)

§ 32-6-114. Provisions supplementary.

The provisions of this division are supplementary to the laws of this state pertaining to the licensing of motor vehicles, and nothing herein shall be construed as abridging or repealing any of such laws. (Acts 1955, No. 308, p. 707, § 5.)

Division 5.

Disabled Veterans.

Cross references. — As to exemption of disabled veterans from payment of motor vehicle registration fee, see § 40-12-244.

§ 32-6-130. Design and issuance of special plates; plates nontransferable.

Any veteran, as defined in section 31-5-1, who is a resident of this state and who is suffering a physical disability which requires that any motor vehicle he operates be equipped with special mechanical control devices or whose physical disability exceeds 50 percent, upon application accompanied by such proof of eligibility to the probate judge of the county for the special license plates provided herein, as may be prescribed by the state department of revenue, and upon payment of $5.00, unless exempted from the payment of such fee by law, shall be issued license plates, by such probate judge as provided by law, for private or pleasure motor vehicles, upon which, in lieu of the number now prescribed by law shall be inscribed in legible letters the words, "Disabled Veteran," and an identifying number as prescribed by the state department of revenue. Such plates shall not be transferable. The fee established by this section shall be in lieu of the regular license fee now required by law for motor vehicles and shall be used to defray the cost of issuing the distinctive license plates. (Acts 1963, No. 576, p. 1250, § 1; Acts 1975, No. 1237, p. 2603, § 1; Acts 1975, 4th Ex. Sess., No. 80, p. 2725, § 1; Acts 1978, No. 775, p. 1133.)

§ 32-6-131. Rules and regulations; wrongful acquisition or use.

The commissioner of revenue shall make such reasonable rules and regulations as may be necessary to administer the provisions of this division, including rules and regulations necessary to insure compliance with all state license laws relating to the use and operation of a private or pleasure motor vehicle and to provide for the application for and issuance of such special tags. Whoever wrongfully obtains or secures the issuance of a motor vehicle license tag or plate under this division, or whoever affixes such a tag or plate to a motor vehicle other than the one for which it was issued is guilty of a misdemeanor and shall be punished as prescribed by section 15-18-3. Whoever willfully uses a motor vehicle equipped with such a tag or plate for any unlawful or deceptive purpose is guilty of a felony and shall be imprisoned for not less than two years. (Acts 1963, No. 576, p. 1250, § 2.)

Code commissioner's note. — Section 15-18-3, referred to in this section, was re- pealed by Acts 1977, No. 607, p. 812, § 9901, as amended, effective January 1, 1980.

§ 32-6-132. Provisions supplementary.

The provisions of this division are supplementary to the motor vehicle license laws of the state of Alabama, and nothing herein contained shall be construed as abridging or repealing such laws. (Acts 1963, No. 576, p. 1250, § 3.)

§ 32-6-133. Specifications for design of motor vehicle tags.

The design of motor vehicle tags for disabled veterans shall be as follows:
(1) The tag shall be the standard size.
(2) The left half of the tag shall be colored red with the words "DISABLED VETERAN" printed in capital letters.
(3) The right side shall be blue with the number prescribed by the state department of revenue imprinted thereon.
(4) The motto "HEART OF DIXIE" shall be located conveniently on the top of the tag.
(5) On the bottom portion of the tag shall appear the word, "ALABAMA".
(6) Any additional regulations or design specifications needed to implement the provisions of this section shall be prescribed by the commissioner of revenue. (Acts 1981, 1st Ex. Sess., No. 81-933, p. 82.)

Division 6.

Personalized License Tags or Plates.

Constitution. — For constitutional provision authorizing legislature to provide for use, etc., of personalized license tags for motor vehicles and to provide for disposition of fees received for said tags, see Constitution, Amendment No. 354.

Cross references. — As to license tags and plates generally, see § 32-6-60 et seq. As to license taxes and registration fees for motor vehicles generally, see § 40-12-242 et seq.

§ 32-6-150. Application; fee; issuance generally; Troy State University commemorative tags.

(a) Owners of motor vehicles who are residents of Alabama, upon application to the probate judge or commissioner of licenses complying with the state motor vehicle laws relating to registration and licensing of motor vehicles and payment of the regular license fee for tags or plates as provided by law for private passenger or pleasure motor vehicles, and the payment of an additional annual fee of $50.00, shall be issued personalized license tags or plates upon which, in lieu of the numbers prescribed by law, shall be inscribed such special letters, figures, numbers or other marks, emblems, symbols or badges of distinction or personal prestige or combination thereof as are approved for and assigned to the application by the state department of revenue.

(b) The special marks or badges of distinction shall include distinctive commemorative tags, assigned by the department of revenue for each of those public and private four year colleges or universities participating in such commemorative tag program. The commemorative tags shall be issued, printed and processed in the same manner as other personalized tags are in this chapter. The fee for such commemorative tags shall be the amount provided in subsection (a) herein. Such commemorative tags shall be valid for five years and shall be replaced at the end of the period with conventional tags or other personalized tags. Payment of the required motor vehicle license fees and taxes for the years during which a new vehicle license plate is not issued shall be evidenced as provided for in section 32-6-63. The board of trustees of the respective colleges and universities shall design, or have designed, the commemorative tag subject to approval by the commissioner of revenue and compliance with all laws and regulations.

(c) The Troy State University commemorative tags issued January 1, 1987, through October 31, 1987, shall continue to be valid without payment of the additional fee provided in this section until the expiration date in the year 1992, or until otherwise becoming invalid or expired provided the regular annual license fees continue to be paid each year.

(d) Each college or university desiring a commemorative tag shall pay to the department of revenue such sum as the commissioner may require to cover the cost of production of the tags requested by such college or university

247

before any such production occurs. (Acts 1975, 3rd Ex. Sess., No. 144, p. 387, § 1; Acts 1985, No. 85-411, p. 373; Acts 1988, No. 88-127, p. 181, § 2.)

The 1988 amendment, effective March 29, 1988, in subsection (a) inserted "annual" following "additional," deleted "excepting the Troy State University commemorative tags issued pursuant to subsection (b) hereof for which the additional fee will be a one time payment of $10.00 only" following "$50.00," inserted "personalized" following "shall be issued" and inserted "figures" following "special letters"; rewrote subsection (b) and added subsections (c) and (d).

Code commissioner's note. — Acts 1988, Act No. 88-127 shall be named, and may be cited as, the "Martin-Estes-Campbell Act" of 1988.

Cross references. — For provision that the special license tag or plate fees provided by subsection (a) of this section shall not be prorated, see § 32-6-61.

Collateral references. — 60 C.J.S., Motor Vehicles, §§ 60, 62, 100, 101.

7 Am. Jur. 2d, Automobiles & Highway Traffic, §§ 51, 54.

§ 32-6-151. Promulgation of rules and regulations by department of revenue.

The state department of revenue shall make such rules and regulations as necessary to insure compliance with all state license laws relating to use and operation of a private passenger or pleasure motor vehicle which must be complied with before these tags or plates in lieu of the regular Alabama license tags or plates may be obtained and such rules and regulations as necessary to provide for the application for and issuance of such special tags or plates. (Acts 1975, 3rd Ex. Sess., No. 144, p. 387, § 2.)

§ 32-6-152. Furnishing of lists to sheriffs; maintenance of lists by sheriffs. Repealed by Acts 1988, No. 88-127, p. 181, § 3.

§ 32-6-153. Issuance of identical tags or plates.

No two owners will be issued identical tags or plates for the same year. An owner who has procured special personalized prestige tags or plates shall be entitled to have a tag or plate issued for succeeding years bearing the same inscription provided he applies therefor within the time prescribed by the commissioner of revenue and pays the fee prescribed in section 32-6-150. However, should the holder of a personalized tag or plate fail within the prescribed time to apply for renewal thereof, then a tag or plate of such design may in subsequent years be issued to any other person applying therefor. (Acts 1975, 3rd Ex. Sess., No. 144, p. 387, § 4.)

§ 32-6-154. Transfer of tags or plates.

Any other provision of law to the contrary notwithstanding, when an automobile for which a personalized tag or plate has been issued is sold or otherwise disposed of, the seller must remove the personalized tag or plate from such automobile, and he then may transfer said personalized tag or plate to a newly acquired automobile of the same class upon payment of the regular transfer fee and all other regular fees and taxes due upon the newly acquired automobile; provided, that any automobile from which a personalized tag or plate has been transferred or removed by a former owner shall be registered and licensed by its new owner for operation on the public roads in the same manner as any unlicensed vehicle, except that no ad valorem tax shall be due on such automobile if same was paid for the current year by the former owner. (Acts 1975, 3rd Ex. Sess., No. 144, p. 387, § 5.)

Collateral references. — 60 C.J.S., Motor Vehicles, §§ 123-124.

§ 32-6-155. Operation of motor vehicle bearing tag or plate not issued therefor or transferred thereto.

It shall be unlawful for any person to operate a motor vehicle bearing a personalized license tag or plate not issued for or duly transferred to such vehicle. Any person violating this section shall be guilty of a misdemeanor and, upon conviction, shall be fined not less than $50.00 and not more than $200.00 for each offense. (Acts 1975, 3rd Ex. Sess., No. 144, p. 387, § 6.)

Collateral references. — 7 Am. Jur. 2d, Automobiles & Highway Traffic, §§ 90-92.

§ 32-6-156. Disposition of fees.

The proceeds of any fees collected under this division except for college or university commemorative tag fees, are hereby appropriated for each fiscal year to the board of corrections and may be used to pay salaries and other expenses of the board; provided, however, that the expenditure of the funds so appropriated shall be budgeted and allotted pursuant to article 4 of chapter 4 of Title 41 and limited to the amount appropriated. Any fees collected for college or university commemorative tags shall be distributed to and are hereby appropriated for each fiscal year to the general scholarship funds of the college or university whose tag is purchased for scholarship grants to Alabama resident students only. These fees represent a charitable contribution from the purchaser to the general scholarship fund of that institution. (Acts 1975, 3rd Ex. Sess., No. 144, p. 387, § 7; Acts 1988, No. 88-127, p. 181, § 4.)

The 1988 amendment, effective March 29, 1988, inserted "except for college or university commemorative tag fees" in the first sentence and added the second and third sentences.

Code commissioner's note. — Acts 1988, Act No. 88-127 shall be named, and may be cited as, the "Martin-Estes-Campbell Act" of 1988.

Division 7.

Members of Volunteer Rescue Squads.

§ 32-6-170. "Volunteer rescue squad" defined.

As used in this division, unless the context clearly requires a different meaning, "volunteer rescue squad" means only those persons or organizations who are members of the Alabama Association of Rescue Squads, Inc. (Acts 1977, No. 777, p. 1336, § 1.)

§ 32-6-171. Authorized; distinctive lettering.

Members of volunteer rescue squads may, upon application and subject to the provisions of this division, be issued distinctive motor vehicle license plates or tags identifying these persons with such organizations. The distinctive plates or tags so issued members of these organizations shall bear the letters "R.S." and the proper number stamped thereon. (Acts 1977, No. 777, p. 1336, § 2.)

§ 32-6-172. Preparation; issuance; proof to be submitted by applicant; use.

The distinctive license plates provided for by this division shall be prepared by the commissioner of revenue and shall be issued through the probate judge or license commissioner of the several counties of the state in like manner as are other motor vehicle license plates or tags, and such officers shall be entitled to their regular fees for such service. Applicants for such distinctive plates shall present to the issuing official proof of their membership in a volunteer rescue squad by means of certificate signed by the treasurer of Alabama Association of Rescue Squads, Inc. The distinctive license plates or tags so issued shall be used only upon and for personally-owned, private passenger vehicles (to include station wagons and pick-up trucks) registered in the name of the member of a volunteer rescue squad making application therefor, and when so issued to such applicant shall be used upon the vehicle for which issued in lieu of the standard license plates or license tags normally issued for such vehicle. (Acts 1977, No. 777, p. 1336, § 3.)

§ 32-6-173. Transferability of plates.

The distinctive license plates issued under this division shall not be transferable as between motor vehicle owners, and in the event the owner of a vehicle bearing such distinctive plates shall sell, trade, exchange or otherwise dispose of same, such plates shall be retained by the owner to whom issued and by him returned to the probate judge or license commissioner of the county, who shall receive and account for same in the manner stated below. In the event such owner shall acquire by purchase, trade, exchange or otherwise a vehicle for which no standard plates have been issued during the current license period, the probate judge or license commissioner of the county shall, upon being furnished by the owner thereof proper certification of the acquisition of such vehicle and the payment of the motor vehicle license tax due upon such vehicle, authorize the transfer to said vehicle of the distinctive license plates previously purchased by such owner, which plates shall authorize the operation of said vehicle for the remainder of the then current license period. In the further event the owner of such distinctive plates shall acquire by purchase, trade, exchange or otherwise a vehicle for which standard plates have been issued during the current license year, the probate judge or license commissioner shall, upon proper certification of such owner and upon delivery to such official of the standard plates previously issued for such vehicle, authorize the owner of such newly-acquired vehicle to place the distinctive plates previously purchased by him upon such vehicle and use same thereon for the remainder of the then current license period. Such notice of transfer of ownership shall be made of record by the probate judge or the license commissioner.

Any person acquiring by purchase, trade, exchange or otherwise any vehicle formerly bearing such distinctive plates shall be authorized, upon certification of such fact to the probate judge or license commissioner of the county and the payment of the fee now required by law, to purchase standard replacement plates for such vehicle which shall authorize the operation of such vehicle by the new owner for the remainder of the license period. (Acts 1977, No. 777, p. 1336, § 4.)

§ 32-6-174. Licensing year.

Such distinctive plates or tags shall be prepared and furnished for the licensing year commencing October 1, 1977, and thereafter as is provided by law for the issuance of other license plates. (Acts 1977, No. 777, p. 1336, § 5.)

Division 8.

Shrine Motorcycle Clubs, Corps or Units.

§ 32-6-190. Authorized; distinctive colors and emblem; limitation on number of plates issued one person.

Any member of any Shrine motorcycle club, corps or unit within the state who owns a heavyweight or heavy-duty motorcycle may, upon application as hereinafter prescribed, be issued a distinctive license plate in lieu of the regular motorcycle license plate. Such distinctive motorcycle license plate shall be of a design to be prescribed by the commissioner of revenue; provided, that the colors used in such design shall be yellow, green and red only and the Shrine emblem shall appear prominently on the plate. Only one such distinctive license plate shall be issued to any individual person. (Acts 1978, 2nd Ex. Sess., No. 133, p. 1861, § 1.)

§ 32-6-191. Preparation; issuance; proof of membership to be submitted by applicant; additional fee; restriction on types of motorcycles.

The distinctive license plates provided for in this subdivision shall be prepared by the commissioner of revenue and shall be issued through the judge of probate or license commissioner of the several counties of the state in like manner as are other motor vehicle license plates, and such officers shall be entitled to their regular fees for such service. Applicants for such distinctive plates shall present to the issuing official proof of their membership in a Shrine motorcycle club, corps or unit within the state by means of a certificate signed by the potentate of the Shrine Temple of such applicant, on forms prescribed by the commissioner of revenue. Such applicant shall pay to the issuing officer the regular license tax prescribed by law and an additional fee of $5.00. Upon such payment, the distinctive license plate shall be issued as is herein provided. The distinctive license plates herein provided for shall be issued for heavyweight or heavy-duty motorcycles only. (Acts 1978, 2nd Ex. Sess., No. 133, p. 1861, § 2.)

Division 9.

Temporary License Tags and Registration Certificates.

§ 32-6-210. Definitions.

For purposes of this division, the terms "dealer," "department," "designated agent," "motor vehicle" and "owner" shall have the meanings as defined in section 32-8-2. (Acts 1979, No. 79-817, p. 1516, § 1.)

§ 32-6-211. Issuance of temporary license tag and registration certificate.

Each designated agent shall, upon proper application, issue to the owner of a motor vehicle which is to be permanently licensed in some state other than Alabama a temporary license tag to be affixed to such motor vehicle and a temporary registration certificate. A dealer who has been appointed by the department to perform the duties of a designated agent shall have the authority to issue a temporary license tag and temporary registration certificate only for motor vehicles which are sold by that dealer. (Acts 1979, No. 79-817, p. 1516, § 2.)

§ 32-6-212. Issuance by certain manufacturers, dealers, etc.; bond or balance sheet in lieu thereof.

A manufacturer of a mobile home, trailer coach, travel trailer or house trailer manufactured on a chassis or undercarriage as an integral part thereof drawn by a self-propelled vehicle who has a manufacturing, constructing or assembling plant in this state may make application to the department for authority to issue temporary license tags and temporary registration certificates in connection with such mobile homes, trailer coaches, travel trailers or house trailers manufactured by it in this state and which are to be permanently licensed in some state other than Alabama. A dealer in mobile homes, trailer coaches, travel trailers or house trailers may also make application to the department for authority to issue temporary license tags and temporary registration certificates in connection with such vehicles sold by it which are to be permanently licensed in some state other than the state of Alabama. If approved by the department, such manufacturer or dealer shall enter into a bond with a corporate surety authorized to do business in this state as surety thereon, payable to the state of Alabama in a sum to be determined by the department, but in no event less than $5,000.00, conditioned on the faithful performance of its duties under this division. In lieu of such bond, such manufacturer or dealer may file a condensed balance sheet as of a date not more than three months prior to July 1 each year in a form prescribed by the department and sworn to by such manufacturer or dealer, evidencing a net worth of not less than $25,000.00. Such manufacturer or dealer may perform its duties under this division either personally or through any of its officers or employees. Temporary license tags issued by any such manufacturer or dealer or by designated agents in connection with mobile homes, trailer coaches, travel trailers and house trailers shall be of a color or design distinctive from the temporary license tags issued for other type motor vehicles. (Acts 1979, No. 79-817, p. 1516, § 3.)

§ 32-6-213. Probate judge or county official may issue temporary tags and certificates.

Each judge of probate of this state or other county official in this state authorized and required by law to issue motor vehicle license tags shall have the authority, upon proper request, to issue a temporary license tag and a temporary registration certificate to the owner of a motor vehicle to be licensed in this state when, due to circumstances, a permanent license tag cannot immediately be issued or when, in the judgment of the probate judge or other county official authorized and required by law to issue motor vehicle license tags, just cause exists for the issuance of such temporary license tag and registration certificate. The temporary license tag provided for herein shall be of a color or design distinctive from the temporary license tags prescribed in sections 32-6-211 and 32-6-212. (Acts 1979, No. 79-817, p. 1516, § 4.)

§ 32-6-214. Valid 20 days; renewed, successive tags.

Each temporary license tag and temporary registration certificate issued hereunder shall be valid for 20 days from the date of issuance and shall be used only on the vehicle for which issued. No temporary license tag shall be renewed nor shall successive temporary license tags be issued in connection with the same motor vehicle. Provided, however, that a probate judge or other county official authorized and required by law to issue motor vehicle license tags issuing a temporary license tag under the provisions of section 32-6-213 may issue a temporary license tag for a motor vehicle which has previously received a temporary license tag issued by some other designated agent, manufacturer or dealer and further may issue successive temporary license tags in connection with the same motor vehicle for periods not to exceed a total of 60 days. (Acts 1979, No. 79-817, p. 1516, § 5.)

§ 32-6-215. Fees.

The fee for issuance of each temporary license tag shall be $2.25 which shall be collected by the designated agent or manufacturer or dealer qualifying under section 32-6-212. From each such fee collected, the designated agent, manufacturer or dealer shall remit $1.50 to the department for deposit to the public road and bridge fund of the state of Alabama and shall remit $.75 to the county in which the temporary license tag is issued to be paid into the treasury of the county, provided, that in all counties where the probate judge is reimbursed on a fee basis instead of on a salary basis, then such $.75 shall be paid to the probate judge. (Acts 1979, No. 79-817, p. 1516, § 6.)

§ 32-6-216. Content of license; copies of certificate.

Every designated agent or manufacturer or dealer qualifying under section 32-6-212 issuing a temporary license tag shall insert clearly and indelibly on the face of each temporary license tag the date of issuance and expiration, the make and vehicle identification number of the motor vehicle for which issued and such other information as the department shall require. Upon issuance of a temporary license tag, the designated agent, manufacturer or dealer shall also deliver to the owner a temporary registration certificate upon a form prescribed by the department. The designated agent, manufacturer or dealer shall retain a copy of the temporary registration certificate and shall transmit the original of such certificate to the department, one copy to the judge of probate or other county official authorized and required by law to issue motor vehicle license tags of the county in which the temporary license tag is issued, and one copy to the applicant. (Acts 1979, No. 79-817, p. 1516, § 7.)

§ 32-6-217. Record of tags and certificates; inspection.

Every designated agent or manufacturer or dealer qualifying under section 32-6-212 shall maintain for one year a record of all temporary license tags and temporary registration certificates issued by him and shall maintain such other information pertaining to the issuance of temporary license tags as the department shall require. All such records maintained by the designated agent, manufacturer or dealer shall be available for inspection and examination by duly authorized representatives of the department upon request. (Acts 1979, No. 79-817, p. 1516, § 8.)

§ 32-6-218. Department to design and supply tags, certificates, etc.; make investigation; adopt rules; revoke issuing authority.

The department shall prescribe the design and material of the temporary license tags, temporary registration certificates, application forms and all other notices and forms necessary to carry out the provisions of this division and shall furnish a supply of such materials to designated agents or manufacturers or dealers qualifying under section 32-6-212 upon request. The department may make necessary investigations to procure information required to carry out the provisions of this division, may adopt and enforce reasonable rules and regulations to carry out the provisions hereof, and may, after a hearing, revoke the authority to issue temporary license tags or registration certificates of any dealer or other person appointed by the department to act as a designated agent or any manufacturer or dealer who it finds has failed to faithfully perform his duties under this division. (Acts 1979, No. 79-817, p. 1516, § 9.)

§ 32-6-219. False statements, operating with expired tag, unlawful; penalty.

It shall be unlawful for any owner to make any false statement in making application for issuance of a temporary license tag and temporary registration certificate, or for any designated agent or manufacturer or dealer qualifying under section 32-6-212 to issue a temporary license tag or temporary registration certificate with knowledge of such false statement, or for any person to operate a motor vehicle upon the public roads of this state with a temporary license tag which has expired. Anyone violating the provisions of this section shall be guilty of a misdemeanor and shall be punished, upon conviction, by a fine of not more than $500.00 or by imprisonment for not more than six months, or by both. (Acts 1979, No. 79-817, p. 1516, § 10.)

Division 10.

Handicapped Persons.

§ 32-6-230. "Handicapped individual" and "temporarily handicapped individual" defined.

(a) For purposes of this division the term "handicapped individual" means any person having a permanent mental or physical handicap, which limits mobility to the extent that the individual would have difficulty safely walking alone a distance of 50 feet or more.

(b) For purposes of this division the term "temporarily handicapped individual" means any person having a temporary (for a period up to one year) mental or physical handicap, which limits mobility to the extent that the individual would have difficulty safely walking alone a distance of 50 feet or more. (Acts 1981, No. 81-695, p. 1167, § 1; Acts 1989, No. 89-856, § 2.)

The 1989 amendment, effective October 1, 1989, designated the former section as subsection (a) and added subsection (b).

Code commissioner's note. — Acts 1989,

No. 89-54 designated Acts 1981, No. 81-695 as the Kelly-Naugher Act.

Collateral references. — 7A Am. Jur. 2d, Automobiles and Highway Traffic, §§ 55, 64.

§ 32-6-231. Distinctive decal authorized; medical proof, fees, rules, etc.; temporary identification placard.

Beginning with the implementation of the staggered system of motor vehicle license plate registration, any person who submits to the judge of probate, license commissioner or other issuing authority medical proof satisfactory to the commissioner of revenue that he or she is a handicapped individual, as herein defined, shall be issued a distinctive license plate decal and a special identification placard displaying the international symbol of access thereby designating the driver of the vehicle or the passenger as being a handicapped person. The distinctive license decals and placards provided herein shall be prepared by the commissioner of revenue and shall be issued in the same manner as motor vehicle license plates and the issuing officers shall be entitled to their regular fees for such services. Provided, however, the fee for these distinctive license decals and placards shall not be greater than the regular license tax prescribed by law. The commissioner of revenue is authorized to make any rules or regulations necessary to carry out the provisions of this division. The "temporarily handicapped" driver or "temporarily handicapped individual" without a driver's license or an automobile shall be issued a temporary identification placard for a period valid up to one year upon submission of satisfactory medical proof to the judge of probate, covered under section 32-6-230(b). (Acts 1981, No. 81-695, p. 1167, § 2; Acts 1989, No. 89-856, § 2.)

The 1989 amendment, effective October 1, 1989, added the last sentence.

§ 32-6-232. Unlimited parking periods; exceptions.

The handicapped individuals and "temporarily handicapped individuals" to whom these distinctive license decals and placards are issued shall be allowed to park for unlimited periods in parking zones designated for handicapped persons. Provided, however, that such handicapped persons shall pay parking fees the same as any other person. The provisions of this section shall not apply to zones where stopping, standing, or parking is prohibited to all vehicles or which are reserved for special types of vehicles, nor will these provisions apply where there is a local ordinance prohibiting parking during heavy traffic periods during morning, afternoon, or evening rush hours, or where parking would clearly present a traffic hazard. All parking places for handicapped persons shall comply with ANSI A. 117.1 (1980) standards. (Acts 1981, No. 81-695, p. 1167, § 3; Acts 1989, No. 89-856, § 2.)

The **1989 amendment,** effective October 1, 1989, inserted "and 'temporarily handicapped individuals'" in the first sentence.

Collateral references. — 60 C.J.S., Motor Vehicles, § 124.

§ 32-6-233. Penalty for false representations or misuse of privileges.

Any person who is not a handicapped individual, or "temporarily handicapped individual," as herein defined, and who willfully and falsely represents himself or herself as a handicapped or a "temporarily handicapped" person to obtain the distinctive decals and placards prescribed by this division or misuses or abuses the parking privilege protected by this division, or owns a vehicle bearing the distinctive license decals and is not entitled to do so under the provisions of this division, shall be guilty of a Class B misdemeanor and, upon conviction, shall be punished according to law. (Acts 1981, No. 81-695, p. 1167, § 4; Acts 1989, No. 89-856, § 2.)

The **1989 amendment,** effective October 1, 1989, inserted "or 'temporarily handicapped individuals'", and inserted "or a 'temporarily handicapped'" near the beginning of the section.

§ 32-6-233.1. Unauthorized use of handicapped parking place.

(a) It shall be unlawful for any person who does not have a distinctive handicapped decal or placard, or "temporarily handicapped" placard as provided in section 32-6-231, to park a motor vehicle in a parking place designated for the handicapped at any place of public accommodation, amusement or resort or any other place to which the general public is invited, even though located on private property, and upon conviction thereof, shall be fined $15.00 per occurrence. Such fines shall be paid in the same manner as other municipal fines for driving violations.

(b) Any authorized municipal, county or state law enforcement officer may go onto private property to enforce the provisions of this section.

(c) The provisions of this section shall be held in pari materia with all other provisions of law related to illegal handicapped parking violations; provided, however, that all laws or parts of laws which conflict with the provisions of this section are hereby repealed. (Acts 1985, 2nd Ex. Sess., No. 85-997, p. 365; Acts 1989, No. 89-856, § 2.)

The **1989 amendment,** effective October 1, 1989, inserted "or placard, or 'temporarily handicapped' placard" in the first sentence of subsection (a).

§ 32-6-234. Agreements with other states.

The commissioner of revenue is hereby authorized to enter into reciprocal agreements with other states concerning parking privileges for handicapped and "temporarily handicapped" individuals. (Acts 1981, No. 81-695, p. 1167, § 5; Acts 1989, No. 89-856, § 2.)

The 1989 amendment, effective October 1, 1989, inserted "and 'temporarily handicapped'."

Division 11.

Medal of Honor Recipients and Prisoners of War.

§ 32-6-250. Distinctive plate authorized; no fee required.

A distinctive permanent license plate shall be issued to any resident of the state who is a recipient of the Medal of Honor or who is a duly recognized American prisoner of war, or who is an American who was a duly recognized prisoner of war while serving with a formal American ally force, for use on a private motor vehicle registered in the recipient's name. There shall be no fee or tax for such license plate but no recipient shall receive a plate for more than one vehicle. (Acts 1981, No. 81-699, p. 1176, § 1; Acts 1982, No. 82-571, p. 1063, § 1.)

Collateral references. — 7A Am. Jur. 2d, Automobiles and Highway Traffic, §§ 55, 64.

§ 32-6-251. Distinctive design of tags.

The special plates shall be of the same size as regular motor vehicle license plates, distinguished by the letters MOH to be of a different color scheme and design to any other vehicle tag in this state, or POW to be of the same color scheme as other distinguished military tags in this state, whichever distinctive design applies, the nature of which shall be prescribed by a committee to be appointed by the chief legislative sponsors of this division. (Acts 1981, No. 81-699, p. 1176, § 2.)

§ 32-6-252. Transfer of plates.

Such license plates issued pursuant to this division may be transferred to another vehicle of the same weight class owned by the same person upon application being made therefor and approved by the department. It shall be unlawful for any person to whom such plates have been issued to knowingly permit them to be displayed on any vehicle except the one authorized by the department. (Acts 1981, No. 81-699, p. 1176, § 3.)

Collateral references. — 60 C.J.S., Motor Vehicles, § 124.

§ 32-6-253. Construction of provisions; penalty for violation.

The provisions of this division shall not affect the registration and licensing of motor vehicles as required by other provisions of the Code of Alabama 1975, but shall be cumulative thereto. Any person violating the provisions of this division or any person who (i) fraudulently gives false or fictitious information in any application for a special license plate, as authorized in this division, (ii) conceals a material fact, or (iii) otherwise commits a fraud in any such application or in the use of any special license plate issued shall be guilty of a Class C misdemeanor as defined by the Code of Alabama 1975. (Acts 1981, No. 81-699, p. 1176, § 4.)

§ 32-6-254. Use and transferability; permanence; use by surviving spouse.

The use and transferability of such plates shall be the same as the method used for national guard and air national guard plates as provided in sections 32-6-111 through 32-6-114. Provided, however, said license plates shall be permanent in nature and shall not be reissued each year. A recipient shall be entitled to keep his license plate for life. Provided further, upon the death of any recipient, the surviving spouse shall be entitled to retain said distinctive permanent plate, at no fee or tax, for one private motor vehicle owned by the surviving spouse for the remainder of said spouse's lifetime or until her remarriage. (Acts 1981, No. 81-699, p. 1176, § 5; Acts 1982, No. 82-571, p. 1063, § 1; Acts 1986, No. 86-621, p. 1209.)

§ 32-6-255. Rules and regulations.

The department of revenue shall be empowered to promulgate all necessary rules and regulations necessary to implement this division. (Acts 1981, No. 81-699, p. 1176, § 6.)

Division 12.

Fire Fighters.

§ 32-6-270. "Fire fighter" and "retired volunteer fire fighter" defined.

(a) As used in this division, unless the context clearly requires a different meaning: "Fire fighter" means a current member or members of, or a retired member or members from, a paid, part-paid or volunteer fire department of a city, town, county or other subdivision of the state or of a public corporation organized for the purpose of providing water, water systems, fire protection services or fire protection facilities in the state; and such words shall include the chief, assistant chief, wardens, engineers, captains, firemen and all other officers and employees of such departments who actually engage in fire fighting or in rendering first aid in case of drownings or asphyxiation at the scene of action.

259

(b) As used in this division, the term "retired volunteer fire fighter" means someone that has retired from performing the required duties of a fire fighter on a voluntary basis at a certified volunteer fire department, wherein, those duties were performed for at least 10 years and said person has attained the age of 55 years old. (Acts 1982, No. 82-550, p. 909, § 1; Acts 1989, No. 89-917.)

The **1989 amendment,** effective May 19, 1989, designated the former section as subsection (a); added subsection (b); in subsection (a) inserted "current," and inserted "or a retired member or members from."

§ 32-6-271. Distinctive plate or tag authorized; form.

A fire fighter may, upon application and subject to the provisions of this division be issued a distinctive motor vehicle license plate or tag as identification as a fire fighter. In addition to the proper numbers, words and insignias used on the standard license plate or tag issued for motor vehicles, the distinctive plates or tags so issued fire fighters shall bear a red Maltese cross emblem on each side to the left and right of the regular tag numbers. The words "Fire Fighter" should be centered at the bottom of the tag. (Acts 1982, No. 82-550, p. 909, § 2.)

§ 32-6-272. Preparation and issuance of plates or tags; lists of eligible fire fighters; additional fee; use of plates or tags.

The distinctive license plates here provided for shall be prepared by the commissioner of revenue and shall be issued through the judge of probate or license commissioner of the several counties of the state in like manner as are other motor vehicle license plates or tags and such officers shall be entitled to their regular fees for such service. The chief of each certified volunteer fire department shall submit to the Alabama forestry commission by October 1 of each year a list of certified fire fighters from his department who are eligible for the distinctive license plate or tag. The fire fighters' personnel standards and education committee shall submit to the Alabama forestry commission by October 1 of each year a list of certified fire fighters who are members of paid or part-paid fire departments and who are eligible for such distinctive license plates or tags. The forestry commission shall submit to the probate judge or license commissioner of each county by December 1 of each year a list of the certified fire fighters in the county who are eligible for the distinctive license plate or tag under this division. Applicants for such distinctive plates shall present to the issuing official proof of their identification. If such applicant's name is on the list furnished by the Alabama forestry commission to the probate judge or license commissioner, the fire fighter shall be issued one distinctive license plate or tag upon the payment of the regular license fee for tags, as provided by law, but shall not be required to pay the $3.00 fee. The distinctive license plates or tags so issued shall be used only upon and for personally-owned, private, passenger vehicles (to include station wagons and pick-up trucks) registered in the name of the fire fighter making application therefor, and when so issued to such applicant shall be used upon the vehicle for which issued in lieu of the standard license plates or license tags normally issued for such vehicle. (Acts 1982, No. 82-550, p. 909, § 3; Acts 1986, No. 86-456, p. 833; Acts 1989, No. 89-944.)

The 1989 amendment, in the sixth sentence, substituted "one distinctive license plate or tag" for "the requested number of distinctive license plates or tags," and substituted "but shall not be required to pay the $3.00 fee" for "and the additional payment of a fee of $3.00 for each plate issued"; and deleted the former seventh sentence, which read "Said applicant shall pay the $3.00 fee for each license plate issued in the future, however, in those years which a decal is issued said applicant shall only pay a single $3.00 fee for all decals issued, regardless of the number."

§ 32-6-273. Nontransferability of plates as between motor vehicle owners; transfer of plates to newly acquired vehicle.

The distinctive license plates issued hereunder shall not be transferable as between motor vehicle owners and in the event the owner of a vehicle bearing such distinctive plates shall sell, trade, exchange or otherwise dispose of same such plates shall be retained by the owner to whom issued and by him returned to the judge of probate or license commissioner of the county who shall receive and account for same in the manner stated below. In the event such owner shall acquire by purchase, trade, exchange or otherwise a vehicle for which no standard plates have been issued during the current license period, the judge of probate or license commissioner of the county shall, upon being furnished by the owner thereof proper certification of the acquisition of such vehicle and the payment of the motor vehicle license tax due upon such vehicle, authorize the transfer to said vehicle of the distinctive license plates previously purchased by such owner, which plates shall authorize the operation of said vehicle for the remainder of the then current license period. In the further event the owner of such distinctive plates shall acquire by purchase, trade, exchange or otherwise a vehicle for which standard plates have been issued during the current license year the judge of probate or license commissioner shall, upon proper certification of such owner and upon delivery to such official of the standard plates previously issued for such vehicle, authorize the owner of such newly-acquired vehicle to place the distinctive plates previously purchased by him upon such vehicle and use same thereon for the remainder of the then current license period. Such notice of transfer of ownership shall be made of record by the judge of probate or the license commissioner.

Provided further, that any person acquiring by purchase, trade, exchange or otherwise any vehicle formerly bearing such distinctive plates shall be authorized, upon certification of such fact to the judge of probate or license commissioner of the county and the payment of the fee now required by law, to purchase standard replacement plates for such vehicle which shall authorize the operation of such vehicle by the new owner for the remainder of the license period. (Acts 1982, No. 82-550, p. 909, § 4.)

§ 32-6-274. Plates to be furnished for licensing year commencing January 1, 1984 and thereafter.

Such distinctive plates or tags shall be prepared and furnished for the licensing year commencing January 1, 1984, and thereafter as is provided by law for the issuance of other license plates. (Acts 1982, No. 82-550, p. 909, § 5.)

Division 13.

Retired Military.

§ 32-6-290. "Retired military" defined.

The words "retired military" as used in this division, unless the context clearly requires a different meaning, means only those persons who are nondisability retirees from active duty in the Army, or the Navy, or the Marine Corps, or the Air Force, or the Coast Guard of the United States. (Acts 1987, No. 87-729, p. 1421, § 1.)

§ 32-6-291. Distinctive plate authorized.

Retired military persons, national guard retirees and military reservists with a minimum of 20 years may, upon application and subject to the provisions of this division, be issued distinctive motor vehicle license plates or tags identifying these persons with such retirement. The special license plate as provided for herein shall, in lieu of the number now prescribed by law, be inscribed with the words "United States Armed Forces Retired," and shall designate the branch of service of the retiree as provided for by section 32-6-290, shall be inscribed with an identifying number prescribed by the department of revenue, and shall have imprinted thereon such other letters and figures as provided for by other applicable sections of this article. (Acts 1987, No. 87-729, p. 1421, § 2; Acts 1989, No. 89-858.)

The 1989 amendment, effective May 17, 1989, inserted "national guard retirees and military reservists with a minimum of 20 years" in the first sentence, and added the last sentence.

§ 32-6-292. Procedure for issuance; fees; limitations.

The distinctive license plates provided for by this division shall be prepared by the commissioner of revenue and shall be issued through the probate judge or license commissioner of the several counties of the state in like manner as are other motor vehicle license plates or tags, and such officers shall be entitled to their regular fees for such service. Applicants for such distinctive plates shall present to the issuing official proof of their military retirement by proof satisfactory to the commissioner. When such applicant presents proof satisfactory to the commissioner, the retired military person shall be issued the requested number of distinctive license plates or tags upon the payment of the regular license fee for tags, as provided by law, and the additional payment of a fee of $3.00 for each plate issued. Said applicant shall pay the additional $3.00 fee for each license plate issued in the future, however in those years in which a decal is issued said applicant shall pay the regular license fees for tags, as provided by law. The distinctive license plates or tags so issued shall be used only upon and for personally-owned, private passenger vehicles (to include station wagons and pick-up trucks) registered in the name of the retired military person making application therefor, and when so issued to such applicant shall be used upon the vehicle for which issued in lieu of the standard license plates or license tags normally issued for such vehicle. (Acts 1987, No. 87-729, p. 1421, § 3.)

§ 32-6-293. Plates not transferable; exceptions.

The distinctive license plates issued pursuant to this division shall not be transferable as between motor vehicle owners, and in the event the owner of a vehicle bearing such distinctive plates shall sell, trade, exchange or otherwise dispose of same, such plates shall be retained by the owner to whom issued and by him returned to the probate judge or license commissioner of the county, who shall receive and account for same in the manner stated below. In the event such owner shall acquire by purchase, trade, exchange or otherwise a vehicle for which no standard plates have been issued during the current license period, the probate judge or license commissioner of the county shall, upon being furnished by the owner thereof proper certification of the acquisition of such vehicle and the payment of the motor vehicle license tax due upon such vehicle, authorize the transfer to said vehicle of the distinctive license plates previously purchased by such owner, which plates shall authorize the operation of said vehicle for the remainder of the then current license period. In the further event the owner of such distinctive plates shall acquire by purchase, trade, exchange or otherwise a vehicle for which standard plates have been issued during the current license year, the probate judge or license commissioner shall, upon proper certification of such owner and upon delivery to such official of the standard plates previously issued for such vehicle, authorize the owner of such newly-acquired vehicle to place the distinctive plates previously purchased by him upon such vehicle and use same thereon for the remainder of the then current license period. Such notice of transfer of ownership shall be made of record by the probate judge or the license commissioner.

Any person acquiring by purchase, trade, exchange or otherwise any vehicle formerly bearing such distinctive plates shall be authorized, upon certification of such fact to the probate judge or license commissioner of the county and the payment of the fee now required by law, to purchase standard replacement plates for such vehicle which shall authorize the operation of such vehicle by the new owner for the remainder of the license period. (Acts 1987, No. 87-729, p. 1421, § 4.)

§ 32-6-294. Licensing year.

Such distinctive plates or tags shall be prepared and furnished for the licensing year commencing October 1, in the year following its passage, and thereafter as is provided by law for the issuance of other license plates. (Acts 1987, No. 87-729, p. 1421, § 5.)

§ 32-6-295. Provisions cumulative.

The provisions of this division shall be construed to be cumulative to any laws or parts of laws relating to motor vehicle license plates or distinctive license plates. (Acts 1987, No. 87-729, p. 1421, § 7.)

CHAPTER 7.

MOTOR VEHICLE SAFETY-RESPONSIBILITY ACT.

Purpose of chapter is to require and establish financial responsibility for every owner or operator of a motor vehicle involved in an accident in this state. Mooradian v. Canal Ins. Co., 272 Ala. 373, 130 So. 2d 915 (1961).

This chapter was designed to protect and secure compensation for automobile accident victims. Layfield v. Director of Pub. Safety, 12 Bankr. 846 (Bankr. N.D. Ala. 1981).

Public policy of chapter. — Public policy, as expressed in this chapter, provides that those who are answerable for injuries and damages resulting from their fault in the use and maintenance of an automobile who do not have automobile liability insurance, or who are otherwise unable to financially respond to such damages, are subject to the loss of their driving privileges. State Farm Fire & Cas. Co. v. Lambert, 291 Ala. 645, 285 So. 2d 917 (1973).

When chapter effective. — The terms of this chapter are not effective or do not apply to automobile liability insurance policies until proof of financial responsibility to respond in damages as a result of an accident is required by the director of public safety of the state of Alabama to be filed in his office, so that the operator of the motor vehicle will not have his driver's license and certificate of registration suspended. Mooradian v. Canal Ins. Co., 272 Ala. 373, 130 So. 2d 915 (1961).

Chapter is for protection and benefit of public. American S. Ins. Co. v. Dime Taxi Serv., Inc., 275 Ala. 51, 151 So. 2d 783 (1963).

And is part of policy. — This chapter, and the extent of the liability which it imposes, is as much a part of the policy as if it were written into it, and no private understanding or provisions can alter, modify, limit or abrogate that liability. American S. Ins. Co. v. Dime Taxi Serv., Inc., 275 Ala. 51, 151 So. 2d 783 (1963).

Requirements of chapter may be fulfilled by one or more carriers. — This chapter is only concerned that required coverage is provided, not by what or which carrier. The requirements of coverage may be fulfilled by policies of one or more carriers which together meet the requirements. State Farm Mut. Auto. Ins. Co. v. Auto-Owners Ins. Co., 331 So. 2d 638 (Ala. 1976).

Chapter does not require medical payments coverage. — The Alabama Motor Vehicle Safety-Responsibility Act mandates automobile liability and uninsured motorist coverage only, it does not require medical payments coverage. Alabama Farm Bureau Mut. Cas. Ins. Co. v. Pigott, 393 So. 2d 1379 (Ala. 1981).

Chapter does not provide that judgment against insured is condition precedent to liability thereunder. American S. Ins. Co. v. Dime Taxi Serv., Inc., 275 Ala. 51, 151 So. 2d 783 (1963).

As insurance is against loss from liability imposed for damages. — The significant provisions of this chapter are that the insurance is against loss from liability imposed for damages and does not provide for insurance against final judgment entered against the insured. American S. Ins. Co. v. Dime Taxi Serv., Inc., 275 Ala. 51, 151 So. 2d 783 (1963).

Proof of financial responsibility not required before issuance of driver's license or certificate of registration. — This chapter does not require operators of motor vehicles to furnish evidence of financial responsibility before issuance of a driver's license or certificate of registration is issued. Mooradian v. Canal Ins. Co., 272 Ala. 373, 130 So. 2d 915 (1961).

Nor until vehicle involved in accident. — Proof of financial responsibility is not required until a motor vehicle is involved in an accident. Mooradian v. Canal Ins. Co., 272 Ala. 373, 130 So. 2d 915 (1961).

There was clear basis for excluding government-owned vehicles from Motor Vehicle Safety-Responsibility Act, which was for public protection against the financially irresponsible using the highways. Higgins v. Nationwide Mut. Ins. Co., 50 Ala. App. 691, 282 So. 2d 295, aff'd, 291 Ala. 462, 282 So. 2d 301 (1973).

Cited in Wallace v. Lindsey, 270 Ala. 401, 119 So. 2d 186 (1960); State Farm Mut. Auto. Ins. Co. v. General Mut. Ins. Co., 282 Ala. 212, 210 So. 2d 688 (1968); Billups v. Alabama Farm Bureau Mut. Cas. Ins. Co., 352 So. 2d

1097 (Ala. 1977); Mathis v. Auto-Owners Ins. Co., 387 So. 2d 166 (Ala. 1980).

Collateral references. — Liability of insurer under compulsory statutory vehicle liability policy, to injured third persons, notwithstanding insured's failure to comply with policy conditions, as measured by policy limits or by limits of financial responsibility act. 29 ALR2d 817.

Construction and effect of exclusionary clause in automobile liability policy making policy inapplicable while vehicle is used as "public or livery conveyance." 30 ALR2d 273.

Trailers as affecting automobile insurance. 31 ALR2d 298.

Effect of provisions of liability policy covering hired automobiles but excluding from definition of "insured" the owner of such vehicle or his employee. 32 ALR2d 572.

Construction and application of automatic insurance clause or substitution provision on automobile liability or indemnity policy. 34 ALR2d 936.

Validity of motor vehicle financial responsibility act. 35 ALR2d 1011.

Automobile liability insurance: operator's policies. 88 ALR2d 995.

Liability insurance policy as covering insured's obligation to indemnify, or make contributions to, cotortfeasor. 4 ALR3d 620.

Combining or "stacking" uninsured motorist coverages provided in policies issued by different insurers to same insured. 21 ALR4th 211.

Unlicensed automobile owned by insured as "owned automobile" within language of automobile liability insurance. 21 ALR4th 918.

Combining or "stacking" medical payment provisions of automobile liability policy or policies issued by one or more insurers to one insured. 29 ALR4th 49.

Propriety of automobile insurer's policy of refusing insurance, or requiring advanced rates, because of age, sex, residence, or handicap. 33 ALR4th 523.

What constitutes sufficiently serious personal injury, disability, impairment, or the like to justify recovery of damages outside of no-fault automobile insurance coverage. 33 ALR4th 767.

Right of liability insurer or uninsured motorist insurer to invoke defense based on insured's tort immunity arising out of marital or other close family relationship to injured party. 36 ALR4th 747.

Right of insured, precluded from recovering against owner or operator of uninsured motor vehicle because of governmental immunity, to recover uninsured motorist benefits. 55 ALR4th 806.

§ 32-7-1. Citation of chapter.

This chapter may be cited as the Motor Vehicle Safety-Responsibility Act. (Acts 1951, No. 704, p. 1224, § 43.)

In general. — Deceased insured who purchased underinsured motorist coverage had reason to expect that, under certain circumstances resulting in his injury or death through the fault of an underinsured motorist, he or his legal representative could recover damages from his own insurer according to the limits and conditions of the contract between them, and also had the legal right to expect that these terms and conditions would not conclusively preclude such recovery under any and all circumstances. Thus, under these circumstances, public policy considerations mandated that his policy provide underinsured motorist coverage with minimum limits of $10,000. Smith v. Auto-Owners Ins. Co., 500 So. 2d 1042 (Ala. 1986), decided under law in effect prior to 1984 amendment to § 32-7-23.

Cited in Madison v. Director, Dep't of Pub. Safety, 465 So. 2d 1148 (Ala. Civ. App. 1984).

§ 32-7-2. Definitions.

For the purposes of this chapter, the following terms shall have the meanings respectively ascribed to them in this section, except in those instances where the context clearly indicates a different meaning:

(1) DIRECTOR. The director of public safety of the state of Alabama.

(2) JUDGMENT. Any judgment which shall have become final by expiration without appeal of the time within which an appeal might have been perfected, or by final affirmation on appeal rendered by a court of competent jurisdiction of any state or of the United States, upon a cause of action arising out of the ownership, maintenance or use of any motor vehicle, for damages, including damages for care and loss of services, because of bodily injury to or death of any person, or for damages because of injury to or destruction of property, including the loss of use thereof, or upon a cause of action on an agreement of settlement for such damages.

(3) LICENSE. Any license, temporary instruction permit or temporary license issued under the laws of this state pertaining to the licensing of persons to operate motor vehicles.

(4) MOTOR VEHICLE. Every self-propelled vehicle which is designed for use upon a highway, including trailers and semitrailers designed for use with such vehicles (except traction engines, road rollers, farm tractors, tractor cranes, power shovels and well drillers) and every vehicle which is propelled by electric power obtained from overhead wires but not operated upon rails.

(5) NONRESIDENT. Every person who is not a resident of this state.

(6) NONRESIDENT'S OPERATION PRIVILEGE. The privilege conferred upon a nonresident by the laws of this state pertaining to the operation by him of a motor vehicle or the use of a motor vehicle owned by him in this state.

(7) OPERATOR. Every person who is in actual physical control of a motor vehicle.

(8) OWNER. A person who holds the legal title of a motor vehicle, or in the event a motor vehicle is the subject of an agreement for the conditional sale or lease thereof with the right of purchase upon performance of the conditions stated in the agreement and with an immediate right of

possession vested in the conditional vendee or lessee, or in the event a mortgagor of a vehicle is entitled to possession, then such conditional vendee or lessee or mortgagor shall be deemed the owner for the purposes of this subdivision.

(9) PERSON. Every natural person, firm, copartnership, association or corporation.

(10) PROOF OF FINANCIAL RESPONSIBILITY. Proof of ability to respond in damages for liability, on account of accidents occurring subsequent to the effective date of said proof, arising out of the ownership, maintenance or use of a motor vehicle in the amount of $5,000.00, because of bodily injury to or death of one person in any one accident, and, subject to said limit for one person, in the amount of $10,000.00 because of bodily injury to or death of two or more persons in any one accident, and in the amount of $1,000.00 because of injury to or destruction of property of others in any one accident.

(11) REGISTRATION. Registration certificate or certificates and registration plates issued under the laws of this state pertaining to the registration of motor vehicles.

(12) STATE. Any state, territory or possession of the United States, the District of Columbia or any province of the Dominion of Canada. (Acts 1951, No. 704, p. 1224, § 1.)

Interpretation of "automobile". — For discussion of cases interpreting "automobile" in particular motor vehicle liability policies to mean "motorcycle" and the possible effect of the definition of "motor vehicles" in this section on similar cases, see Canal Ins. Co. v. Stidham, 281 Ala. 493, 205 So. 2d 516 (1967) (holding that "automobile" did not include after- acquired motorcycle).

Registration consists of both certificate and plates. — As the definition of "registration" appears in this section, it must consist of both registration certificate and registration plates, the two terms being used in the definition in the conjunctive. Stroud v. State, 37 Ala. App. 589, 73 So. 2d 103 (1954).

Cited in Prince v. Lowe, 263 Ala. 410, 82 So. 2d 606 (1955); Thompson v. Hartford Accident & Indem. Co., 460 So. 2d 1264 (Ala. 1984).

§ 32-7-3. Administration of chapter; appeal to court.

(a) *Director to administer chapter.* — The director shall administer and enforce the provisions of this chapter and may make rules and regulations necessary for its administration and shall provide for hearings upon the request of persons aggrieved by orders or acts of the director under the provisions of this chapter.

(b) *Appeal to court.* — At any time within 60 days after the rendition of any order or decision by the director under the provisions of this chapter, any party in interest may appeal to the circuit court in and for any county in the state of Alabama wherein any party in interest may reside, or in which any party in interest which is a corporation may have its principal office or place of business, and said appeal may be for the purpose of having the lawfulness of any order, decision or act of the said director inquired into and determined. The court shall determine whether the filing of an appeal shall operate as a stay of any order or decision of the director. Said appeal shall be taken by serving written notice of said appeal upon the director, which said service shall be made by delivering a copy of such notice to the director and filing the original thereof with the clerk of the court to which said appeal is taken and upon giving bond with sureties to be approved by the said clerk of said court, payable to the state of Alabama, conditioned to pay all costs created by said appeal. A copy of such notice must also be served upon all other parties in interest, if there be any, by mailing the same to said parties in interest to such addresses of such parties as such parties shall have left with the director. If such parties shall have left no address with the director, then no service on such parties shall be required. The order of filing and service of said notice is immaterial. The director shall, within 10 days after receipt of said notice, prepare and file with the clerk of said court a true and correct copy of the order or decision appealed from together with a complete transcript of all the proceedings had by him with reference to the order, decision or act appealed from, together with all official forms or documents in the possession of said director pertaining to said order, decision or act. Immediately upon the return of such matter, the court shall fix a day for the hearing of said appeal and shall cause notice to be served upon the director and upon the appellant and also upon any other parties in interest upon whom service was required under the provisions of this section. The trial upon appeal to said circuit court shall be de novo, and said court shall render judgment confirming, modifying or setting aside the order or decision of the director or, in its discretion, may remand the case to the director for proceedings in conformity with the direction of the court. From the judgment of the circuit court either party may appeal to the supreme court of Alabama, as in civil cases. (Acts 1951, No. 704, p. 1224, § 2.)

Section authorizes appeal from mandatory order of revocation of a driver license by the director. Director of Dep't of Pub. Safety v. Relford, 51 Ala. App. 456, 286 So. 2d 860 (1973).

Cited in Ex parte Darnell, 262 Ala. 71, 76 So. 2d 770 (1954); Sullivan v. Cheatham, 264 Ala. 71, 84 So. 2d 374 (1955); Wallace v. Lindsey, 270 Ala. 401, 119 So. 2d 186 (1960);

State Farm Mut. Auto. Ins. Co. v. Hubbard, 272 Ala. 181, 129 So. 2d 669 (1961); Boone v. Director of Dep't of Pub. Safety, 337 So. 2d 6 (Ala. Civ. App. 1976); Stinnett v. Director, Dep't of Pub. Safety, 435 So. 2d 127 (Ala. Civ. App. 1983).

Collateral references. — 60 C.J.S., Motor Vehicles, § 164.34. 61A C.J.S., Motor Vehicles, § 588.

§ 32-7-4. Director to furnish operating record.

The director shall upon request furnish any person an abstract of the operating record of any person subject to the provisions of this chapter, which abstract shall also fully designate the motor vehicle, if any, registered in the name of such person, and, if there shall be no record of any convictions of such person of violating any law relating to the operation of a motor vehicle or any injury or damage caused by such person, the director shall so certify. The director shall collect for such abstract the sum of $5.75. (Acts 1951, No. 704, p. 1224, § 3; Acts 1961, No. 707, p. 999; Acts 1971, No. 1598, p. 2743; Acts 1983, No. 83-722, p. 1177; Acts 1988, 1st Sp. Sess., No. 88-909, p. 486, § 1.)

The 1988, 1st Sp. Sess., amendment, effective September 30, 1988, substituted "the sum of $5.75" for "the sum of $4.00" at the end of the section.

Cited in State ex rel. Attorney Gen. v. Spann, 270 Ala. 396, 118 So. 2d 740 (1959).

§ 32-7-5. Report required following accident.

The operator of every motor vehicle which is in any manner involved in an accident within this state, in which any person is killed or injured or in which damage to the property of any one person, including himself, in excess of $250.00 is sustained, shall within 10 days after such accident report the matter in writing to the director. Such report, the form of which shall be prescribed by the director, shall contain only such information as may be necessary to enable the director to determine whether the requirements for the deposit of security under section 32-7-6 are inapplicable by reason of the existence of insurance or other exceptions specified in this chapter. The director may rely upon the accuracy of the information unless and until he has reason to believe that the information is erroneous. If such operator is physically incapable of making such report, the owner of the motor vehicle involved in such accident shall, within 10 days after learning of the accident, make such report. The operator or the owner shall furnish such additional relevant information as the director shall require. (Acts 1951, No. 704, p. 1224, § 4; Acts 1984, No. 84-301, p. 672, § 1.)

Code commissioner's note. — Acts 1984, No. 84-301, § 6, which amended §§ 32-7-5, 32-7-6, 32-7-16 and 32-7-23 provides: "All laws or parts of laws which conflict with this act are hereby repealed. Nothing in this act should be construed to abrogate the exclusions, terms, conditions or other provisions of any policy of automobile liability insurance which has been approved by the insurance commissioner."

The purpose of the report required by this section is to enable the director of public safety to determine the financial responsibility of the operator of every motor vehicle involved in an accident in this state. Treadway v. Brantley, 437 So. 2d 93 (Ala. 1983).

Insurer not liable to uninsured motorist for malicious prosecution or abuse of process for filing statutorily required form with-

out improper purpose, where the filing of the report resulted in the temporary suspension of her driving privileges and that the suspension of her license was unlawful under § 32-7-7(2) since uninsured motorist was legally parked at the time of the accident. Green v. Alabama Farm Bureau Mut. Cas. Ins. Co., 522 So. 2d 773 (Ala. 1988).

Cited in Sullivan v. Cheatham, 264 Ala. 71, 84 So. 2d 374 (1955); State Farm Mut. Auto. Ins. Co. v. Hubbard, 272 Ala. 181, 129 So. 2d 669 (1961).

Collateral references. — 61A C.J.S., Motor Vehicles, § 674(2).

What constitutes "entering" or "alighting from" vehicle within meaning of insurance policy, or statute mandating insurance coverage. 59 ALR4th 149.

§ 32-7-6. Security required; exceptions; suspension of licenses and registrations.

(a) *Security required unless evidence of insurance; when security determined.* — If 20 days after the receipt of a report of a motor vehicle accident within this state which has resulted in bodily injury or death, or damage to the property of any one person in excess of $250.00, the director does not have on file evidence satisfactory to him that the person who would otherwise be required to file security under subsection (b) of this section has been released from liability, or has been finally adjudicated not to be liable, or has executed a duly acknowledged written agreement providing for the payment of an agreed amount in installments with respect to all claims for injuries or damages resulting from the accident, the director shall determine the amount of security which shall be sufficient in his judgment to satisfy any judgment or judgments for damages resulting from such accident as may be recovered against each operator or owner.

(b) *Suspension.* — The director shall, within 60 days after the receipt of such report of a motor vehicle accident, suspend the license of each operator and all registrations of each owner of a motor vehicle in any manner involved in such accident, and if such operator is a nonresident the privilege of operating a motor vehicle within this state, and if such owner is a nonresident the privilege of the use within this state of any motor vehicle owned by him, unless such operator or owner or both shall deposit security in the sum so determined by the director; provided that notice of such suspension shall be sent by the director to such operator and owner not less than 10 days prior to the effective date of such suspension and shall state the amount required as security. Where erroneous information is given the director with respect to the matters set forth in subdivisions (1), (2) or (3) of subsection (c) of this section, he shall take appropriate action as hereinbefore provided within 60 days after receipt by him of correct information with respect to said matters.

(c) *Exception.* — This section shall not apply under the conditions stated in section 32-7-7 nor:

(1) To such operator or owner if such owner had in effect at the time of such accident an automobile liability policy with respect to the motor vehicle involved in such accident;

(2) To such operator, if not the owner of such motor vehicle, if there was in effect at the time of such accident an automobile liability policy or bond with respect to his operation of motor vehicles not owned by him;

(3) To such operator or owner if the liability of such operator or owner for damages resulting from such accident is, in the judgment of the director, covered by any other form of liability insurance policy or bond; nor

(4) To any person qualifying as a self-insurer under section 32-7-34, or to any person operating a motor vehicle for such self-insurer.

No such policy or bond shall be effective under this section unless issued by an insurance company or surety company authorized to do business in this state; except, that if such motor vehicle was not registered in this state, or was a motor vehicle which was registered elsewhere than in this state at the effective date of the policy or bond, or the most recent renewal thereof, such policy or bond shall not be effective under this section unless the insurance company or surety company, if not authorized to do business in this state, shall execute a power of attorney authorizing the director to accept service on its behalf of notice or process in any action upon such policy or bond arising out of such accident; provided, that every such policy or bond is subject, if the accident has resulted in bodily injury or death, to a limit, exclusive of interest and costs, of not less than $20,000.00 because of bodily injury to or death to one person in any one accident and subject to said limit for one person, to a limit of not less than $40,000.00 because of bodily injury to or death of two or more persons in any one accident, and, if the accident has resulted in injury to or destruction of property, to a limit of not less than $10,000.00 because of injury to or destruction of property of others in any one accident. (Acts 1951, No. 704, p. 1224, § 5; Acts 1965, No. 578, p. 1074; Acts 1984, No. 84-301, p. 672, § 2.)

Code commissioner's note. — Acts 1984, No. 84-301, § 6, which amended §§ 32-7-5, 32-7-6, 32-7-16 and 32-7-23 provides: "All laws or parts of laws which conflict with this act are hereby repealed. Nothing in this act should be construed to abrogate the exclusions, terms, conditions or other provisions of any policy of automobile liability insurance which has been approved by the insurance commissioner."

The policy behind this section is to assure the availability of minimum coverage for each accident, not for each injured person. Criterion Ins. Co. v. Anderson, 347 So. 2d 384 (Ala. 1977).

Drivers' licenses are not to be taken away without the procedural due process required by the fourteenth amendment. Procedural due process will be satisfied by an inquiry limited to a determination of whether there is a reasonable possibility of judgment in the amount claimed being rendered against the licensee. Madison v. Director, Dep't of Pub. Safety, 465 So. 2d 1148 (Ala. Civ. App. 1984).

Proceeding for review of suspension or revocation of driver's license is civil proceeding. Madison v. Director, Dep't of Pub. Safety, 465 So. 2d 1148 (Ala. Civ. App. 1984).

The right to counsel given by the sixth amendment extends only to criminal or quasi-criminal cases. There is no fundamental interest in the ownership of a driver's license. Madison v. Director, Dep't of Pub. Safety, 465 So. 2d 1148 (Ala. Civ. App. 1984).

"Automobile liability policy" means simply an automobile liability policy valid under the laws of Alabama and containing the minimum prescribed limits of liability. State Farm Mut. Auto. Ins. Co. v. Hubbard, 272 Ala. 181, 129 So. 2d 669 (1961).

Not same as "motor vehicle liability policy" provided in section 32-7-22. — The "automobile liability policy" referred to in subsection (c) of this section is not the same as a "motor vehicle liability policy" provided for in § 32-7-22. State Farm Mut. Auto. Ins. Co. v. Hubbard, 272 Ala. 181, 129 So. 2d 669 (1961).

Section does not invest director with discretion to determine who shall be required to post security for a given accident. The purpose of this section is clearly to require and

establish financial responsibility for every owner or operator of a motor vehicle "in any manner involved in an accident." Sullivan v. Cheatham, 264 Ala. 71, 84 So. 2d 374 (1955).

Posting of security mandatory regardless of fault. — The possible or probable existence of civil liability for an automobile accident is not a consideration for determining whether or not a particular owner or driver of an automobile is required to comply with the applicable provisions of this section. Hence, in an accident involving property damage in excess of $50.00 the director is authorized by this section to suspend the license of the driver whose car inflicted the damage for failure to post security after the accident though the driver was not guilty of any negligence. Sullivan v. Cheatham, 264 Ala. 71, 84 So. 2d 374 (1955).

Funds posted by debtor no longer in estate in bankruptcy. — Fund posted by debtor pursuant to this section was no longer property of the estate following entry of a judgment against the debtor since it was "applicable only to the payment of a judgment ... rendered against the person ... on whose behalf the deposit was made ...", pursuant to § 32-7-11. Thus the debtor's complaint for return of such funds as exempt would be denied and the motion for relief from stay filed by judgment creditors would be granted. Marona v. Conradi, 54 Bankr. 65 (Bankr. N.D. Ala. 1985).

Cited in United States Fid. & Guar. Co. v. Dixie Auto. Ins. Co., 292 F. Supp. 554 (N.D. Ala. 1968); Employers Nat'l Ins. Co. v. Holliman, 287 Ala. 123, 248 So. 2d 717 (1971); State Farm Mut. Auto. Ins. Co. v. Martin, 292 Ala. 103, 289 So. 2d 606 (1974); State Farm Auto. Ins. Co. v. Reaves, 292 Ala. 218, 292 So. 2d 95 (1974); Wilbourn v. Allstate Ins. Co., 293 Ala. 466, 305 So. 2d 372 (1974); Lefeve v. State Farm Mut. Auto. Ins. Co., 527 F. Supp. 492 (N.D. Ala. 1981).

Collateral references. — 60 C.J.S., Motor Vehicles, §§ 110, 164.18, 559.

7 Am. Jur. 2d, Automobiles & Highway Traffic, §§ 135-139.

Constitutionality of compulsory liability insurance legislation as condition of use of automobile not operated for hire. 39 ALR 1028, 69 ALR 397.

Compulsory insurance: estoppel of indemnity or liability insurer to assert as against injured person cancellation of policy that was effective against insured. 129 ALR 851.

Cancellation of compulsory automobile insurance. 171 ALR 550, 34 ALR2d 1297.

Joinder of insurer and insured under policy of compulsory indemnity or liability insurance in action by injured third person. 20 ALR2d 1097.

§ 32-7-7. Further exceptions to requirement of security.

The requirements as to security and suspension in section 32-7-6 shall not apply:

(1) To the operator or the owner of a motor vehicle involved in an accident wherein no injury or damage was caused to the person or property of anyone other than such operator or owner;

(2) To the operator or the owner of a motor vehicle legally parked at the time of the accident;

(3) To the owner of a motor vehicle if at the time of the accident the vehicle was being operated without his permission, express or implied, or was parked by a person who had been operating such motor vehicle without such permission; nor

(4) If, prior to the date that the director would otherwise suspend license and registration or nonresident's operating privilege under section 32-7-6, there shall be filed with the director evidence satisfactory to him that the person who would otherwise have to file security has been released from liability or been finally adjudicated not to be liable or has executed a duly acknowledged written agreement providing for the payment of an agreed amount in installments, with respect to all claims for injuries or damages resulting from the accident. (Acts 1951, No. 704, p. 1224, § 6.)

Insurer not liable to uninsured motorist for malicious prosecution or abuse of process for filing statutorily required form without improper purpose, where the filing of the report resulted in the temporary suspension of her driving privileges and that the suspension of her license was unlawful under subdivision (2) since uninsured motorist was legally parked at the time of the accident. Green v. Alabama Farm Bureau Mut. Cas. Ins. Co., 522 So. 2d 773 (Ala. 1988).

§ 32-7-8. Duration of suspension.

The license and registration and nonresident's operating privilege suspended as provided in section 32-7-6 shall remain so suspended and shall not be renewed, nor shall any such license or registration be issued to such person for a period of three years or until:

(1) Such person shall deposit or there shall be deposited on his behalf the security required under section 32-7-6; or

(2) One year shall have elapsed following the date of such suspension and evidence satisfactory to the director has been filed with him that during such period no action for damages arising out of the accident has been instituted; or

(3) Evidence satisfactory to the director has been filed with him of a release from liability, a final adjudication of nonliability or a duly

acknowledged written agreement, in accordance with subdivision (4) of section 32-7-7; provided, that in the event there shall be any default in the payment of any installment under any duly acknowledged written agreement, then, upon notice of such default, the director shall forthwith suspend the license and registration or nonresident's operating privilege of such person defaulting which shall not be restored unless and until:

a. Such person deposits and thereafter maintains security as required under section 32-7-6 in such amount as the director may then determine; or

b. One year shall have elapsed following the date when such security was required, and during such period no action upon such agreement has been instituted in a court in this state. (Acts 1951, No. 704, p. 1224, § 7; Acts 1959, No. 72, p. 478.)

Cross references. — See notes to § 32-7-9.
Collateral references. — 60 C.J.S., Motor Vehicles, § 164.24.

§ 32-7-9. Application to nonresidents, unlicensed drivers, unregistered motor vehicles and accidents in other states.

(a) In case the operator or the owner of a motor vehicle involved in an accident within this state has no license or registration or is a nonresident, he shall not be allowed a license or registration until he has complied with the requirements of this chapter to the same extent that would be necessary if, at the time of the accident, he had held a license and registration.

(b) When a nonresident's operating privilege is suspended pursuant to section 32-7-6 or section 32-7-8, the director shall transmit a certified copy of the record of such action to the official in charge of the issuance of licenses and registration certificates in the state in which such nonresident resides, if the law of such other state provides for action in relation thereto similar to that provided for in subsection (c) of this section.

(c) Upon receipt of such certification that the operating privilege of a resident of this state has been suspended or revoked in any such other state pursuant to a law providing for its suspension or revocation for failure to deposit security for the payment of judgments arising out of a motor vehicle accident, under circumstances which would require the director to suspend a nonresident's operating privilege had the accident occurred in this state, the director shall suspend the license of such resident if he was the operator and all of his registrations if he was the owner of a motor vehicle involved in such accident. Such suspension shall continue until such resident furnishes evidence of his compliance with the law of such other state relating to the deposit of such security. (Acts 1951, No. 704, p. 1224, § 8.)

Section governs failure of resident to comply with financial responsibility laws of another state. — The period of suspension of Alabama driver's license, registration certificate and license plates of an Alabama resident because of his failure to comply with the financial responsibility laws of another state is governed by this section and not in any way by the provisions of § 32-7-8. Render v. Mann, 271 Ala. 558, 126 So. 2d 94 (1961).

Section and section 32-6-10 deal with separate subjects and have no relation to each other. Nowhere in the Motor Vehicle Safety-Responsibility Act is there any requirement for reciprocal agreements. Thus the Alabama director of public safety, under the authority of this section, could revoke an operator's driver's license or the owner's li-cense plates for failing to comply with the Motor Vehicle Safety-Responsibility Act of Arkansas where no reciprocal agreement existed between Alabama and Arkansas. Limbaugh v. State Dep't of Pub. Safety, 275 Ala. 260, 154 So. 2d 18 (1963).

Collateral references. — 61 C.J.S., Motor Vehicles, § 502(4). 61A C.J.S., Motor Vehicles, §§ 559, 561.

§ 32-7-10. Form and amount of security.

The security required under this chapter shall be in such form and in such amount as the director may require but in no case in excess of the limits specified in section 32-7-6 in reference to the acceptable limits of a policy or bond. The person depositing security shall specify in writing the person or persons on whose behalf the deposit is made and, at any time while such deposit is in the custody of the director or state treasurer, the person depositing it may, in writing, amend the specifications of the person or persons on whose behalf the deposit is made to include an additional person or persons; provided, that a single deposit of security shall be applicable only on behalf of persons required to furnish security because of the same accident.

The director may reduce the amount of security ordered in any case within six months after the date of the accident if, in his judgment, the amount ordered is excessive. In case the security originally ordered has been deposited, the excess deposited over the reduced amount ordered shall be returned to the depositor or his personal representative forthwith, notwithstanding the provisions of section 32-7-11. (Acts 1951, No. 704, p. 1224, § 9.)

§ 32-7-11. Custody, disposition and return of security.

Security deposited in compliance with the requirements of this chapter shall be placed by the director in the custody of the state treasurer and shall be applicable only to the payment of a judgment or judgments rendered against the person or persons on whose behalf the deposit was made, for damages arising out of the accident in question in an action at law, begun not later than one year after the date of such accident or within one year after the date of deposit of any security under subdivision (3) of section 32-7-8, or to the payment in settlement agreed to by the depositor of a claim or claims arising out of such accident. Such deposit or any balance thereof shall be returned to the depositor or his personal representative when evidence satisfactory to the director has been filed with him that there has been a release from liability, or a final adjudication of nonliability, or a duly acknowledged agreement, in accordance with subdivision (4) of section 32-7-7, or whenever, after the expiration of one year from the date of the accident or from the date of any security under subdivision (3) of section 32-7-8, the director shall be given reasonable evidence that there is no such action pending and no judgment rendered in such action left unpaid. (Acts 1951, No. 704, p. 1224, § 10.)

Funds posted by debtor no longer in estate in bankruptcy. — Funds posted by debtor pursuant to § 32-7-6 was no longer property of the estate following entry of a judgment against the debtor since it was "applicable only to the payment of a judgment ... rendered against the person ... on whose behalf the deposit was made ...", pursuant to this section. Thus the debtor's complaint for return of such funds as exempt would be denied and the motion for relief from stay filed by judgment creditors would be granted. Marona v. Conradi, 54 Bankr. 65 (Bankr. N.D. Ala. 1985).

Cited in Wallace v. Lindsey, 270 Ala. 401, 119 So. 2d 186 (1960).

§ 32-7-12. Matters not to be evidence in civil actions.

Neither the report required by section 32-7-5, the action taken by the director pursuant to this chapter, the findings, if any, of the director upon which such action is based nor the security filed as provided in this chapter shall be referred to in any way, nor be any evidence of the negligence or due care of either party, at the trial of any action to recover damages. (Acts 1951, No. 704, p. 1224, § 11.)

No conflict with qualification of jurors as to insurance company connections. — There is no conflict in this section and the rule of cases holding that the plaintiff is entitled, upon his seasonable and proper motion, to have the jurors from whom the trial jury is to be selected qualified as to their relation to, or interest in, any insurance company which would be liable, in whole or in part, for any judgment that might be entered against the defendant. Prince v. Lowe, 263 Ala. 410, 82 So. 2d 606 (1955).

Collateral references. — Products liability: admissibility of experimental or test evidence to disprove defect in motor vehicle. 64 ALR4th 125.

§ 32-7-13. Courts to report nonpayment of judgments.

Whenever any person fails within 60 days to satisfy any judgment, upon the written request of the judgment creditor or his attorney, it shall be the duty of the clerk of the court, or of the judge of a court which has no clerk in which any such judgment is rendered within this state, to forward to the director immediately after the expiration of said 60 days a certified copy of such judgment.

If the defendant named in any certified copy of a judgment reported to the director is a nonresident, the commissioner shall transmit a certified copy of the judgment to the official in charge of the issuance of licenses and registration certificates of the state of which the defendant is a resident. (Acts 1951, No. 704, p. 1224, § 12.)

Effect of nonpayment of judgment. — When a judgment debtor in an automobile accident lawsuit fails to respond to the judgment entered against him within 60 days, then he must overcome two hurdles in order to regain his driving privileges. The judgment debtor is required to satisfy the judgment and to give proof of financial responsibility. Layfield v. Director of Pub. Safety, 12 Bankr. 846 (Bankr. N.D. Ala. 1981).

§ 32-7-14. Suspension of license, registration or operating privilege for nonpayment of judgment.

(a) *Suspension for nonpayment of judgment.* — The director upon the receipt of a certified copy of a judgment shall forthwith suspend the license and registration and any nonresident's operating privilege of any person against whom such judgment was rendered, except as hereinafter otherwise provided in this section and in section 32-7-17.

(b) *Exceptions.* — If the judgment creditor consents in writing, in such form as the director may prescribe, that the judgment debtor be allowed license and registration or nonresident's operating privilege, the same may be allowed by the director, in his discretion, for six months from the date of such consent and thereafter until such consent is revoked in writing, notwithstanding default in the payment of such judgment or of any installments thereof prescribed in section 32-7-17; provided, that the judgment debtor furnishes proof of financial responsibility. (Acts 1951, No. 704, p. 1224, § 13.)

Collateral references. — 60 C.J.S., Motor Vehicles, §§ 129, 164.19.

§ 32-7-15. Suspension to continue until judgments paid and proof given.

The license, registration and nonresident's operating privilege shall remain suspended and shall not be renewed, nor shall any such license or registration be thereafter issued in the name of such person, including any such person not previously licensed, unless and until every judgment is stayed, satisfied in full or to the extent hereinafter provided and until the said person gives proof of financial responsibility subject to the exemptions stated in sections 32-7-14 and 32-7-17.

A discharge in bankruptcy following the rendering of any such judgment shall not relieve the judgment debtor from any of the requirements of this section and sections 32-7-13 and 32-7-14. (Acts 1951, No. 704, p. 1224, § 14.)

Section invalid as violative of "fresh start" doctrine. — This section, as it is presently written, makes a discriminatory distinction based exclusively on a debt and contravenes the fresh start of the debtor. It is therefore invalid under the Perez doctrine as codified in 11 U.S.C.A. § 525. Layfield v. Director of Pub. Safety, 12 Bankr. 846 (Bankr. N.D. Ala. 1981).

Cited in American S. Ins. Co. v. Dime Taxi Serv., Inc., 275 Ala. 51, 151 So. 2d 783 (1963); Employers Nat'l Ins. Co. v. Holliman, 287 Ala. 123, 248 So. 2d 717 (1971).

§ 32-7-16. Payments sufficient to satisfy requirements.

Judgments herein referred to shall, for the purpose of this chapter only, be deemed satisfied:

(1) When $20,000.00 has been credited upon any judgment or judgments rendered in excess of that amount because of bodily injury to or death of one person as the result of any one accident;

(2) When, subject to such limit of $20,000.00 because of bodily injury to or death of one person, the sum of $40,000.00 has been credited upon any judgment or judgments rendered in excess of that amount because of bodily injury to or death of two or more persons as the result of any one accident; or

(3) When $10,000.00 has been credited upon any judgment or judgments rendered in excess of that amount because of injury to or destruction of property of others as a result of any one accident.

Payments made in settlement of any claims because of bodily injury, death or property damage arising from a motor vehicle accident shall be credited in reduction of the amounts provided for in this section. (Acts 1951, No. 704, p. 1224, § 15; Acts 1965, No. 579, p. 1077; Acts 1984, No. 84-301, p. 672, § 3.)

Code commissioner's note. — Acts 1984, No. 84-301, § 6, which amended §§ 32-7-5, 32-7-6, 32-7-16 and 32-7-23 provides: "All laws or parts of laws which conflict with this act are hereby repealed. Nothing in this act should be construed to abrogate the exclusions, terms, conditions or other provisions of any policy of automobile liability insurance which has been approved by the insurance commissioner."

§ 32-7-17. Installment payment of judgments.

(a) A judgment debtor, upon due notice to the judgment creditor, may apply to the court in which such judgment was rendered for the privilege of paying such judgment in installments; and the court, in its discretion and without prejudice to any other legal remedies which the judgment creditor may have, may so order and fix the amounts and times of payment of the installments.

(b) The director shall not suspend a license, registration or a nonresident's operating privilege and shall restore any license, registration or nonresident's operating privilege suspended following nonpayment of a judgment when the judgment debtor gives proof of financial responsibility and obtains such an order permitting the payment of such judgment in installments and while the payment of any said installment is not in default.

(c) In the event the judgment debtor fails to pay any installment as specified by such order, then, upon notice of such default, the director shall forthwith suspend the license, registration or nonresident's operating privilege of the judgment debtor until such judgment is satisfied, as provided in this chapter. (Acts 1951, No. 704, p. 1224, § 16.)

§ 32-7-18. Proof of financial responsibility required upon certain convictions.

(a) Whenever the director, under any law of this state, suspends or revokes the license of any person upon receiving record of a conviction or a forfeiture of bail, the director shall also suspend the registration for all motor vehicles registered in the name of such person; except, that he shall not suspend such registration, unless otherwise required by law, if such person has previously given or shall immediately give and thereafter maintain proof of financial responsibility with respect to all motor vehicles registered by such person.

(b) Such license and registration shall remain suspended or revoked and shall not at any time thereafter be renewed nor shall any license be thereafter issued to such person, nor shall any motor vehicle be thereafter registered in the name of such person until permitted under the motor vehicle laws of this state and not then unless and until he shall give and thereafter maintain proof of financial responsibility.

(c) If a person is not licensed, but by final order or judgment is convicted of or forfeits any bail or collateral deposited to secure an appearance for trial for any offense requiring the suspension or revocation of license, or for operating a motor vehicle upon the highways without being licensed to do so, or for operating an unregistered motor vehicle upon the highways, no license shall be thereafter issued to such person and no motor vehicle shall continue to be registered or thereafter be registered in the name of such person until he shall give and thereafter maintain proof of financial responsibility. (Acts 1951, No. 704, p. 1224, § 17.)

Director has no discretion. — In the absence of proof of financial responsibility, the director had no discretion but to suspend registration when the driver's license had been suspended or revoked because of a conviction under former § 32-6-16. Surber v. Mann, 46 Ala. App. 700, 248 So. 2d 740 (1971).

Cited in American S. Ins. Co. v. Dime Taxi Serv., Inc., 275 Ala. 51, 151 So. 2d 783 (1963).

§ 32-7-19. Alternate methods of giving proof; registration of motor vehicle of person required to give proof.

(a) Proof of financial responsibility when required under this chapter with respect to a motor vehicle or with respect to a person who is not the owner of a motor vehicle may be given by filing:

(1) A certificate of insurance as provided in section 32-7-20 or section 32-7-21; or

(2) A bond as provided in section 32-7-26; or

(3) A certificate of deposit of money or securities as provided in section 32-7-27; or

(4) A certificate of self-insurance, as provided in section 32-7-34, supplemented by an agreement by the self-insurer that, with respect to accidents occurring while the certificate is in force, he will pay the same judgments and in the same amounts that an insurer would have been obligated to pay under an owner's motor vehicle liability policy if it had issued such a policy to said self-insurer.

(b) No motor vehicle shall be or continue to be registered in the name of any person required to file proof of financial responsibility unless such proof shall be furnished for such motor vehicle. (Acts 1951, No. 704, p. 1224, § 18.)

Cited in American S. Ins. Co. v. Dime Taxi Serv., Inc., 275 Ala. 51, 151 So. 2d 783 (1963).

§ 32-7-20. Certificate of insurance as proof.

(a) Proof of financial responsibility may be furnished by filing with the director the written certificate of any insurance carrier duly authorized to do business in this state certifying that there is in effect a motor vehicle liability policy for the benefit of the person required to furnish proof of financial responsibility. Such certificate shall give the effective date of such motor vehicle liability policy, which date shall be the same as the effective date of the certificate, and shall designate by explicit description or by appropriate reference all motor vehicles covered thereby, unless the policy is issued to a person who is not the owner of a motor vehicle.

(b) No motor vehicle shall be or continue to be registered in the name of any person required to file proof of financial responsibility unless such motor vehicle is so designated in such a certificate. (Acts 1951, No. 704, p. 1224, § 19.)

Chapter seeks benefit and protection of public. — This chapter, and particularly that part of it which requires a certificate of insurance to be filed to reinstate a license, is for the benefit and protection of the public rather than for the benefit of the person seeking reinstatement of his license. American S. Ins. Co. v. Dime Taxi Serv., Inc., 275 Ala. 51, 151 So. 2d 783 (1963).

Cited in State Farm Mut. Auto. Ins. Co. v. Sharpton, 259 Ala. 386, 66 So. 2d 915 (1953).

§ 32-7-21. Certificate furnished by nonresident as proof.

(a) The nonresident owner of a motor vehicle not registered in this state may give proof of financial responsibility by filing with the director a written certificate or certificates of an insurance carrier authorized to transact business in the state in which the motor vehicle or motor vehicles described in such certificate is registered, or if such nonresident does not own a motor vehicle, then in the state in which the insured resides, provided such certificate otherwise conforms to the provisions of this chapter, and the director shall accept the same upon condition that said insurance carrier complies with the following provisions with respect to the policies so certified:

(1) Said insurance carrier shall execute a power of attorney authorizing the director to accept service on its behalf of notice or process in any action arising out of a motor vehicle accident in this state; and

(2) Said insurance carrier shall agree in writing that such policies shall be deemed to conform with the laws of this state relating to the terms of motor vehicle liability policies issued herein.

(b) If any insurance carrier not authorized to transact business in this state, which has qualified to furnish proof of financial responsibility, defaults in any said undertakings or agreements, the director shall not thereafter accept as proof any certificate of said carrier whether theretofore filed or thereafter tendered as proof so long as such default continues. (Acts 1951, No. 704, p. 1224, § 20.)

Cited in State Farm Mut. Auto Ins. Co. v. Sharpton, 259 Ala. 386, 66 So. 2d 915 (1953).

Collateral references. — 60 C.J.S., Motor Vehicles, § 164.18.

§ 32-7-22. "Motor vehicle liability policy" defined; policy provisions.

(a) A "motor vehicle liability policy," as said term is used in this chapter, shall mean an owner's or an operator's policy of liability insurance, certified as provided in section 32-7-20 or section 32-7-21 as proof of financial responsibility, and issued, except as otherwise provided in section 32-7-21, by an insurance carrier duly authorized to transact business in this state, to or for the benefit of the person named therein as insured.

(b) Such owner's policy of liability insurance:

(1) Shall designate by explicit description or by appropriate reference all motor vehicles with respect to which coverage is thereby to be granted; and

(2) Shall insure the person named therein and any other person, as insured, using any such motor vehicle or motor vehicles with the express or implied permission of such named insured, against loss from the liability imposed by law for damages arising out of the ownership, maintenance or use of such motor vehicle or motor vehicles within the United States of America or the Dominion of Canada, subject to limits exclusive of interest and costs, with respect to each such motor vehicle, as follows: $5,000.00 because of bodily injury to or death of one person in any one accident and, subject to said limit for one person, $10,000.00 because of bodily injury to or death of two or more persons in any one accident; and $1,000.00 because of injury to or destruction of property of others in any one accident.

(c) Such operator's policy of liability insurance shall insure the person named as insured therein against loss from the liability imposed upon him by law for damages arising out of the use by him of any motor vehicle not owned by him, within the same territorial limits and subject to the same limits of liability as are set forth above with respect to an owner's policy of liability insurance.

(d) Such motor vehicle liability policy shall state the name and address of the named insured, the coverage afforded by the policy, the premium charged therefor, the policy period and the limits of liability and shall contain an agreement or be endorsed that insurance is provided thereunder in accordance with the coverage defined in this chapter as respects bodily injury and death or property damage, or both, and is subject to all the provisions of this chapter.

(e) Such motor vehicle liability policy need not insure any liability under any workmen's compensation law nor any liability on account of bodily injury to or death of an employee of the insured while engaged in the employment, other than domestic, of the insured, or while engaged in the operation, maintenance or repair of any such motor vehicle nor any liability for damage to property owned by, rented to, in charge of or transported by the insured.

(f) Every motor vehicle liability policy shall be subject to the following provisions which need not be contained therein:

(1) The liability of the insurance carrier with respect to the insurance required by this chapter shall become absolute whenever injury or damage

covered by said motor vehicle liability policy occurs; said policy may not be cancelled or annulled as to such liability by any agreement between the insurance carrier and the insured after the occurrence of the injury or damage; no statement made by the insured or on his behalf and no violation of said policy shall defeat or void said policy;

(2) The satisfaction by the insured of a judgment for such injury or damage shall not be a condition precedent to the right or duty of the insurance carrier to make payment on account of such injury or damage;

(3) The insurance carrier shall have the right to settle any claim covered by the policy, and if such settlement is made in good faith, the amount thereof shall be deductible from the limits of liability specified in subdivision (2) of subsection (b) of this section;

(4) The policy, the written application therefor, if any, and any rider or endorsement which does not conflict with the provisions of this chapter shall constitute the entire contract between the parties.

(g) Any policy which grants the coverage required for a motor vehicle liability policy may also grant any lawful coverage in excess of or in addition to the coverage specified for a motor vehicle liability policy, and such excess or additional coverage shall not be subject to the provisions of this chapter. With respect to a policy which grants such excess or additional coverage, the term "motor vehicle liability policy" shall apply only to that part of the coverage which is required by this section.

(h) Any motor vehicle liability policy may provide that the insured shall reimburse the insurance carrier for any payment the insurance carrier would not have been obligated to make under the terms of the policy except for the provisions of this chapter.

(i) Any motor vehicle liability policy may provide for the prorating of the insurance thereunder with other valid and collectible insurance.

(j) The requirements for a motor vehicle liability policy may be fulfilled by the policies of one or more insurance carriers which policies together meet such requirements.

(k) Any binder issued pending the issuance of a motor vehicle liability policy shall be deemed to fulfill the requirements for such a policy. (Acts 1951, No. 704, p. 1224, § 21.)

Cross references. — As to difference between "automobile liability policy" in § 32-7-6 and "motor vehicle liability policy" in this section, see notes to § 32-7-6.

Construction of additional coverage without resort to chapter. — Where an insuring agreement applying to newly acquired automobiles provided for coverage additional to the coverage specified and required for a motor liability policy under the provisions of the Motor Vehicle Safety-Responsibility Act, the act, by its very terms, did not apply to the additional coverage and the policy provisions relating to the additional coverage were construed without resort to the act. Canal Ins. Co.

v. Stidham, 281 Ala. 493, 205 So. 2d 516 (1967).

Terms required by section apply only to those policies required to be certified as proof of financial responsibility to permit the vehicle to continue to be registered. Mooradian v. Canal Ins. Co., 272 Ala. 373, 130 So. 2d 915 (1961).

Where the policy involved was not issued to the insured in compliance with the Motor Vehicle Safety-Responsibility Act as proof of financial responsibility, this section was without influence. Mooradian v. Canal Ins. Co., 272 Ala. 373, 130 So. 2d 915 (1961).

Section is unambiguous in mandating

extension of liability insurance coverage to persons using insured vehicle with express or implied permission of the named insured. Billups v. Alabama Farm Bureau Mut. Cas. Ins. Co., 352 So. 2d 1097 (Ala. 1977).

Accordingly, the uninsured motorist coverage must be as broad. Billups v. Alabama Farm Bureau Mut. Cas. Ins. Co., 352 So. 2d 1097 (Ala. 1977).

Insurance policy must afford uninsured motorist coverage to the occupants of an automobile if it was used with the express or implied permission of the named insured. Billups v. Alabama Farm Bureau Mut. Cas. Ins. Co., 352 So. 2d 1097 (Ala. 1977).

Thus, provisions in insurance policies restricting uninsured motorist coverage to occupants of automobile only if automobile was used with express permission of the named insured were repugnant to statutory requirements and therefore void. Billups v. Alabama Farm Bureau Mut. Cas. Ins. Co., 352 So. 2d 1097 (Ala. 1977).

For discussion of the validity of the household exclusion in a policy of liability insurance in light of this section, see Hutcheson v. Alabama Farm Bureau Mut. Cas. Ins. Co., 435 So. 2d 734 (Ala. 1983).

Protection of subdivision (f)(1) runs to third party. — The protection provided by subdivision (f)(1) of this section runs from the insurer to the third party claimant. American S. Ins. Co. v. Dime Taxi Serv., Inc., 275 Ala. 51, 151 So. 2d 783 (1963).

Where loss exceeds limits of one policy, insured may proceed under the other available policies, "stacking" the policies to cover his loss. Dancy v. State Farm Mut. Auto. Ins. Co., 324 F. Supp. 964 (S.D. Ala. 1971).

Proration of loss among insurers. — The general rule as to insurance policies is that where there are pro rata or proportionate clauses in several insurance policies insuring the same property, the insurance is concurrent and each insurer is liable for its proportionate amount. This has also been held to be the rule where there is no provision about proportionate insurance in either policy. State Farm Mut. Auto. Ins. Co. v. General Mut. Ins. Co., 282 Ala. 212, 210 So. 2d 688 (1968).

When a loss is prorated in the ratio which the limits of the policies bear to the total coverage, the burden imposed on each insurer is generally proportional to the benefit which he received, since the size of the premium is most always directly related to the size of the policy. State Farm Mut. Auto. Ins. Co. v. General Mut. Ins. Co., 282 Ala. 212, 210 So. 2d 688 (1968).

Division of liability as set out in Lamb-Weston, Inc. v. Oregon Auto. Ins. Co., 219 Ore. 110, 341 P.2d 110, 346 P.2d 643 (1959), on rehearing, is the rule adopted by the Alabama supreme court. In that case both companies sought proration according to policy limits. One company had insured up to $25,000.00 and the other up to $5,000.00. The court decided that one company should bear five sixths and the other one sixth of the loss. State Farm Mut. Auto. Ins. Co. v. General Mut. Ins. Co., 282 Ala. 212, 210 So. 2d 688 (1968).

Prejudice to insurer as factor in determining reasonableness of delay in giving notice of accident. — In uninsured motorist insurance cases, unlike liability insurance cases, prejudice to the insurer is a factor to be considered, along with the reasons for delay and the length of delay, in determining the overall reasonableness of a delay in giving notice of an accident. In the typical case, the insured must, at a minimum, put on evidence showing the reason for not complying with the insured's notice requirement. This prerequisite satisfied, the insurer may then demonstrate that it was prejudiced by the insured's failure to give timely notice. If the insurer fails to present evidence as to prejudice, then the insured's failure to give notice will be a bar to his recovery. When the insurer puts on evidence of prejudice, however, the reasonableness of the failure to give notice then becomes a question of fact for a jury to decide. State Farm Mut. Auto. Ins. Co. v. Burgess, 474 So. 2d 634 (Ala. 1985).

Cited in State Farm Mut. Auto. Ins. Co. v. Sharpton, 259 Ala. 386, 66 So. 2d 915 (1953); State Farm Mut. Auto. Ins. Co. v. Auto-Owners Ins. Co., 331 So. 2d 638 (Ala. 1976); Trinity Universal Ins. Co. v. Metzger, 360 So. 2d 960 (Ala. 1978).

Collateral references. — 60 C.J.S., Motor Vehicles, §§ 110, 154.

Automobile liability insurance: operator's policies. 88 ALR2d 995.

Policy provision extending coverage to comply with financial responsibility act as applicable to insured's first accident. 8 ALR3d 388.

Temporary automobile insurance pending issuance of policy. 12 ALR3d 1304.

Who is a "named insured" under an automobile insurance policy provision extending or excluding coverage of "named insureds." 91 ALR3d 1280.

Automobile liability insurance: what are accidents or injuries "arising out of ownership, maintenance, or use" of insured vehicle. 15 ALR4th 10.

Combining or "stacking" medical payment provisions of automobile liability policy or policies issued by one or more insurers to different insureds. 25 ALR4th 66.

Construction and application of "automatic

insurance" or "newly acquired vehicle" clause ("replacement," and "blanket," or "fleet" provisions) contained in automobile liability policy. 39 ALR4th 229.

No-fault insurance: general release of tortfeasor by accident victim as affecting automobile insurer's obligation for personal injury protection (PIP) benefits. 39 ALR4th 378.

Construction and application of substitution provision of automobile liability policy. 42 ALR4th 1145.

Self-insurance against liability as other insurance within meaning of liability insurance policy. 46 ALR4th 707.

Consortium claim of spouse, parent or child of accident victim as within extended "per accident" coverage rather than "per person" coverage of automobile liability policy. 46 ALR4th 735.

§ 32-7-23. Uninsured motorist coverage; "uninsured motorist" defined; limitation on recovery.

(a) No automobile liability or motor vehicle liability policy insuring against loss resulting from liability imposed by law for bodily injury or death suffered by any person arising out of the ownership, maintenance or use of a motor vehicle shall be delivered or issued for delivery in this state with respect to any motor vehicle registered or principally garaged in this state unless coverage is provided therein or supplemental thereto, in limits for bodily injury or death set forth in subsection (c) of section 32-7-6, under provisions approved by the commissioner of insurance for the protection of persons insured thereunder who are legally entitled to recover damages from owners or operators of uninsured motor vehicles because of bodily injury, sickness or disease, including death, resulting therefrom; provided, that the named insured shall have the right to reject such coverage; and provided further, that unless the named insured requests such coverage in writing, such coverage need not be provided in or supplemental to a renewal policy where the named insured had rejected the coverage in connection with the policy previously issued to him by the same insurer.

(b) The term "uninsured motor vehicle" shall include, but is not limited to, motor vehicles with respect to which:

(1) Neither the owner nor the operator carries bodily injury liability insurance;

(2) Any applicable policy liability limits for bodily injury are below the minimum required under section 32-7-6;

(3) The insurer becomes insolvent after the policy is issued so there is no insurance applicable to, or at the time of, the accident; and

(4) The sum of the limits of liability under all bodily injury liability bonds and insurance policies available to an injured person after an accident is less than the damages which the injured person is legally entitled to recover.

(c) The recovery by an injured person under the uninsured provisions of any one contract of automobile insurance shall be limited to the primary coverage plus such additional coverage as may be provided for additional vehicles, but not to exceed two additional coverages within such contract. (Acts 1965, No. 866, p. 1614; Acts 1984, No. 84-301, p. 672, § 4.)

Code commissioner's note. — Acts 1984, No. 84-301, § 6, which amended §§ 32-7-5, 32-7-6, 32-7-16 and 32-7-23 provides: "All laws or parts of laws which conflict with this act are hereby repealed. Nothing in this act should be construed to abrogate the exclusions, terms, conditions or other provisions of any policy of automobile liability insurance which has been approved by the insurance commissioner."

I. GENERAL CONSIDERATION.

The legislative purpose in enacting statutes providing for uninsured motorist coverage is to close the gaps inherent in motor vehicle financial responsibility and compulsory insurance legislation. State Farm Mut. Auto. Ins. Co. v. Griffin, 51 Ala. App. 426, 286 So. 2d 302 (1973).

The legislative purpose of this section is that an insured, under every such required coverage for which a premium has been paid, is entitled to collect within the limits of the policy, all damages which he is "legally entitled to recover." United Servs. Auto. Ass'n v. Smith, 57 Ala. App. 506, 329 So. 2d 562 (1976).

The obvious legislative purpose behind the uninsured motorist act was to protect those financially and ethically responsible enough to obtain automobile liability insurance from injuries caused by those not so responsible. State Farm Mut. Auto. Ins. Co. v. Baldwin, 764 F.2d 773 (11th Cir. 1985).

Purpose of section is to provide coverage "for the protection of persons insured thereunder" against injury, including death, caused by the wrongful act of an uninsured motorist. Higgins v. Nationwide Mut. Ins. Co., 291 Ala. 462, 282 So. 2d 301 (1973); State Farm Auto. Ins. Co. v. Reaves, 292 Ala. 218, 292 So. 2d 95 (1974).

It appears from the plain and unambiguous wording of this section that it is the basic purpose of the Uninsured Motorist Act, and thus the public policy of the state, that Alabama citizens purchasing automobile liability insurance be able to obtain for an additional premium the same protection against injury or death at the hands of an uninsured motorist as they would have had if that motorist had obtained for himself a minimum liability coverage required by the Motor Vehicle Safety-Responsibility Act. Higgins v. Nationwide Mut. Ins. Co., 50 Ala. App. 691, 282 So. 2d 295, aff'd, 291 Ala. 462, 282 So. 2d 301 (1973); Criterion Ins. Co. v. Anderson, 347 So. 2d 384 (Ala. 1977); McCullough v. Standard Fire Ins. Co., 404 So. 2d 637 (Ala. 1981).

The purpose of the Uninsured Motorist Act is to provide a method for an insured motorist to protect himself against the deficiencies of the Motor Vehicle Safety-Responsibility Act as such deficiencies became evident. Higgins v. Nationwide Mut. Ins. Co., 50 Ala. App. 691, 282 So. 2d 295, aff'd, 291 Ala. 462, 282 So. 2d 301 (1973).

Uninsured motorist coverage is intended to provide financial recompense to innocent victims who are injured and to dependents of those who are killed because of the wrongful conduct of uninsured motorists. Dale v. Home Ins. Co., 479 So. 2d 1290 (Ala. Civ. App. 1985).

The design of this section is to protect injured persons who can prove that the accident did in fact occur and that they were injured as a proximate result of the negligence of such other motorist who cannot respond in damages for such injuries, including the unknown or hit-and-run driver. State Farm Fire & Cas. Co. v. Lambert, 291 Ala. 645, 285 So. 2d 917 (1973).

The uninsured motorist coverage inures to a person, not to a vehicle. State Farm Mut. Auto. Ins. Co. v. Jackson, 462 So. 2d 346 (Ala. 1984); State Farm Mut. Auto. Ins. Co. v. Jackson, 757 F.2d 1220 (11th Cir. 1985).

Uninsured motorist coverage is intended to provide financial recompense to innocent persons who are injured and to dependents of those who are killed because of the wrongful conduct of uninsured motorists. State Farm Auto. Ins. Co. v. Reaves, 292 Ala 218, 292 So. 2d 95 (1974).

Uninsured motorist coverage is intended, within fixed limits, to provide financial recompense to innocent persons who are damaged through the wrongful conduct of motorists who, because they are uninsured and not financially responsible, cannot be made to respond in damages. State Farm Mut. Auto. Ins. Co. v. Griffin, 51 Ala. App. 426, 286 So. 2d 302 (1973).

The uninsured motorist statutes were created to provide compensation to the innocent injured party within the limits of the policy for actual damages sustained. Rohleder v. Family

Shows, Inc., 435 So. 2d 95 (Ala. Civ. App. 1983).

And is required in all automobile liability policies unless rejected. State Farm Mut. Auto. Ins. Co. v. Martin, 292 Ala. 103, 289 So. 2d 606 (1974).

This section lays down a rule of construction requiring courts to interpret all motor vehicle liability insurance policies as providing the statutory coverage unless an agreement to reject on the part of the named insured is in evidence. Insurance Co. of N. Am. v. Thomas, 337 So. 2d 365 (Ala. Civ. App. 1976).

Section must be construed so as to assure person injured at hand of uninsured motorist that he will be able to recover, from whatever source available, up to the maximum amount of his damages, and the insurer will not be allowed to insert provisions in its policy limiting or restricting recovery by the insured up to the limits of the policy. Alabama Farm Bureau Mut. Cas. Ins. Co. v. Clem, 49 Ala. App. 457, 273 So. 2d 218 (1973).

Section becomes part of every policy as implied term as if it were written out in full in the policy itself. State Farm Auto. Ins. Co. v. Reaves, 292 Ala. 218, 292 So. 2d 95 (1974); State Farm Auto. Ins. Co. v. Baldwin, 470 So. 2d 1230 (Ala. 1985).

If the statutory conditions are present, the courts will infer the existence of minimum uninsured motorist coverage notwithstanding the absence of a provision for such coverage in the insurance policy itself. Insurance Co. of N. Am. v. Thomas, 337 So. 2d 365 (Ala. Civ. App. 1976).

Uninsured motorist coverage is not dependent on the insured person being injured in connection with a vehicle which is covered by the liability insurer against whom recovery is sought under the uninsured motorist provisions. While to have uninsured motorist coverage the person must have some liability coverage under the policy sued on, he need not have liability coverage in all events and for all purposes. State Farm Mut. Auto. Ins. Co. v. Jackson, 462 So. 2d 346 (Ala. 1984); State Farm Mut. Auto. Ins. Co. v. Jackson, 757 F.2d 1220 (11th Cir. 1985).

If a person is insured under the liability coverage provision of a motor vehicle insurance policy and uninsured motorist coverage is not rejected, the uninsured motorist coverage dictated by this section cannot be excluded from the policy as to such an insured person. State Farm Mut. Auto. Ins. Co. v. Jackson, 757 F.2d 1220 (11th Cir. 1985).

Uninsured motorist coverage, like liability coverage, must be supported by an insurable interest in the insured. Alabama

Farm Bureau Mut. Ins. Co. v. Davis, 354 So. 2d 15 (Ala. Civ. App. 1978).

Test of an insurable interest in an automobile liability policy, as well as the uninsured motorist provisions contained in that policy, is whether the named insured would be liable to others for injury to persons or property arising out of the operation of the insured automobile. Alabama Farm Bureau Mut. Ins. Co. v. Davis, 354 So. 2d 15 (Ala. Civ. App. 1978).

Where named insured was the sole obligor on security agreement and note of indebtedness for the purchase price of the automobile, he was also obligated to pay the insurance premiums on the vehicle and held legal title to the automobile and as the owner of the vehicle was potentially liable for its use, he possessed an insurable interest in the car. Alabama Farm Bureau Mut. Ins. Co. v. Davis, 354 So. 2d 15 (Ala. Civ. App. 1978).

Uninsured motorist coverage inures to a person, not a vehicle, and the coverage is not dependent on the insured person being injured in connection with a vehicle which is covered by the liability insurer. St. Paul Ins. Co. v. Henson, 479 So. 2d 1253 (Ala. Civ. App. 1985).

Governing section states what coverage shall include. — Where the inclusion of uninsured motorist coverage is mandatory under this section, unless specifically waived, the governing section states what the coverage shall include. Higgins v. Nationwide Mut. Ins. Co., 291 Ala. 462, 282 So. 2d 301 (1973); State Farm Auto. Ins. Co. v. Reaves, 292 Ala. 218, 292 So. 2d 95 (1974).

"Umbrella policy" not motor vehicle liability policy. — An "umbrella policy," clearly intended as excess insurance to protect against catastrophic judgments and issued as supplementary insurance to existing primary policies themselves sufficient to meet the requirements of the law, is neither an automobile liability nor motor vehicle liability policy within the scope of the uninsured motorist statute, even though one of the primary policies may itself insure automobiles. Trinity Universal Ins. Co. v. Metzger, 360 So. 2d 960 (Ala. 1978).

Before an umbrella policy is issued, a primary policy must be in existence and this primary policy must by law provide uninsured motorist coverage. Trinity Universal Ins. Co. v. Metzger, 360 So. 2d 960 (Ala. 1978).

Underinsured motorist coverage applies where the negligent or wanton tortfeasor has some liability insurance, but does not have enough to fully compensate the victims of his negligence or wantonness. Hardy v. Progressive Ins. Co., 531 So. 2d 885 (Ala. 1988).

Insurance commissioner has authority to approve provisions consistent with section. — This section does give the insurance commissioner authority to approve provisions governing statutory uninsured motorist coverage. Such provisions must be consistent with the statute. Insurance Co. of N. Am. v. Thomas, 337 So. 2d 365 (Ala. Civ. App. 1976).

The coverage spoken to in this section is not mandatory, and the failure to carry the coverage does not violate the public policy of this state. McCullough v. Standard Fire Ins. Co., 404 So. 2d 637 (Ala. 1981).

Prejudice to insurer as factor in determining reasonableness of delay in giving notice of accident. — In uninsured motorist insurance cases, unlike liability insurance cases, prejudice to the insurer is a factor to be considered, along with the reasons for delay and the length of delay, in determining the overall reasonableness of a delay in giving notice of an accident. In the typical case, the insured must, at a minimum, put on evidence showing the reason for not complying with the insured's notice requirement. This prerequisite satisfied, the insurer may then demonstrate that it was prejudiced by the insured's failure to give timely notice. If the insurer fails to present evidence as to prejudice, then the insured's failure to give notice will not be a bar to his recovery. When the insurer puts on evidence of prejudice, however, the reasonableness of the failure to give notice then becomes a question of fact for a jury to decide. State Farm Mut. Auto Ins. Co. v. Burgess, 474 So. 2d 634 (Ala. 1985).

Courts do not favor efforts to restrict coverage. — Alabama courts have viewed any arguments for restricting uninsured motorist coverage with particular disfavor. Thompson v. American States Ins. Co., 687 F. Supp. 559 (M.D. Ala. 1988).

Cited in State Farm Mut. Auto. Ins. Co. v. De La Cruz, 283 Ala. 167, 214 So. 2d 909 (1968); Phoenix Ins. Co. v. Stuart, 289 Ala. 657, 270 So. 2d 792 (1972); James v. Allstate Ins. Co., 331 So. 2d 682 (Ala. 1976); Key v. Robert M. Duke Ins. Agency, 340 So. 2d 781 (Ala. 1976); United States Fid. & Guar. Co. v. Perry, 361 So. 2d 594 (Ala. Civ. App. 1978); Byrd v. Alabama Farm Bureau Mut. Cas. Ins. Co., 366 So. 2d 1108 (Ala. 1979); Thomas v. Liberty Nat'l Life Ins. Co., 368 So. 2d 254 (Ala. 1979); Mathis v. Auto-Owners Ins. Co., 387 So. 2d 166 (Ala. 1980); Commercial Std. Ins. Co. v. Potete, 409 So. 2d 429 (Ala. 1981); O'Hare v. State Farm Mut. Auto. Ins. Co., 432 So. 2d 1294 (Ala. Civ. App. 1982); Hutcheson v. Alabama Farm Bureau Mut. Cas. Ins. Co., 435 So. 2d 734 (Ala. 1983); Jowers v. State Farm Mut. Ins. Co., 485 So. 2d 1190 (Ala. Civ. App. 1986); Smith v. Auto-Owners Ins. Co., 500 So. 2d 1042 (Ala. 1986); Lipscomb v. Reed, 514 So. 2d 949 (Ala. 1987).

Collateral references. — 60 C.J.S., Motor Vehicles, § 110. 61A C.J.S., Motor Vehicles, §§ 563.1-563.26.

Rights and liabilities under "uninsured motorists" coverage. 79 ALR2d 1252.

What constitutes an "uninsured" or "unknown" vehicle or motorist, within uninsured motorist coverage. 26 ALR3d 883.

Uninsured motorist insurance: validity and construction of "other insurance" provisions. 28 ALR3d 551.

Construction of statutory provision governing rejection or waiver of uninsured motorist coverage. 55 ALR3d 216.

Coverage under uninsured motorist clause of injury inflicted intentionally. 72 ALR3d 1161.

Insured's right to bring direct action against insurer for uninsured motorist benefits. 73 ALR3d 632.

Combining or "stacking" uninsured motorist coverages provided in single policy applicable to different vehicles of individual insured. 23 ALR4th 12.

Combining or "stacking" uninsured motorist coverages provided in separate policies issued by same insurer to different insureds. 23 ALR4th 108.

Uninsured and underinsured motorist coverage: Recoverability, under uninsured or underinsured motorist coverage, of deficiencies in compensation afforded injured party by tortfeasor's liability coverage. 24 ALR4th 13.

Right to recover under uninsured or underinsured motorist insurance for injuries attributable to joint tortfeasors, one of whom is insured. 24 ALR4th 63.

Validity, construction, and effect of "consent to sue" clauses in uninsured motorist endorsement of automobile insurance policy. 24 ALR4th 1024.

Combining or "stacking" uninsured motorist coverages provided in separate policies issued by same insurer to same insured. 25 ALR4th 6.

Combining or "stacking" uninsured motorist coverages provided in fleet policy. 25 ALR4th 896.

Applicability of uninsured motorist statutes to self-insurers. 27 ALR4th 1266.

Combining or "stacking" of "no fault" or personal injury protection (PIP) coverages in automobile liability policy or policies. 29 ALR4th 12.

Combining or "stacking" uninsured motorist coverages provided in policies issued by different insurers to different insureds. 28 ALR4th 362.

Uninsured motorist coverage: validity of exclusion of injuries sustained by insured while occupying "owned" vehicle not insured by policy. 30 ALR4th 172.

Right of insurer issuing "uninsured motorist" coverage to intervene in action by insured against uninsured motorist. 35 ALR4th 757.

Right of liability insurer on uninsured motorist insurer to invoke defense based on insured's tort immunity arising out of marital or other close family relationship to injured party. 36 ALR4th 747.

Necessity or permissibility of naming no-fault insurer as defendant where insured automobile owner or operator is not liable for economic losses under no-fault insurance law. 40 ALR4th 858.

Motorist having "no-fault" insurance affording no liability coverage in circumstances as "uninsured" or "underinsured" motorist under damaged party's insurance. 40 ALR4th 1202.

Uninsured motorist insurance: injuries to motorcyclist as within affirmative or exclusionary terms of automobile insurance policy. 46 ALR4th 771.

II. WHO IS COVERED.

Use of broader term "persons insured thereunder" and narrower term "named insured" in the same sentence clearly indicates that the legislature intended to draw a distinction between the two types of insureds and did intend to require uninsured motorist coverage for the broader class "persons insured thereunder." State Farm Auto. Ins. Co. v. Reaves, 292 Ala. 218, 292 So. 2d 95 (1974).

This section does not read "named insured"; by the literal words of the statute, it mandates uninsured motorist coverage for "persons insured thereunder" in the policy. State Farm Auto. Ins. Co. v. Reaves, 292 Ala. 218, 292 So. 2d 95 (1974).

Who is "insured." — Under this section, the classification of "insured" under the uninsured motor vehicle coverage must be as broad as under the bodily injury liability coverage. Sullivan v. State Farm Mut. Auto. Ins. Co., 513 So. 2d 992 (Ala. 1987).

Two distinct classes of insureds exist and mere occupants of a vehicle are not entitled to stack coverage. White v. Georgia Cas. & Sur. Ins. Co., 520 So. 2d 140 (Ala. 1987) (decided prior to 1984 amendment).

Employee who was included in the primary liability part of the insurance policy as one who was "insured thereunder," was entitled to stack coverage under the fleet policy. His wife, who was a passenger in the delivery truck at the time of the accident, was not a person "insured thereunder," according to the insurance policy and was not entitled by statute to stack coverage. She was entitled only to the amount already paid to her under the uninsured motorist provision of the policy. White v. Georgia Cas. & Sur. Ins. Co., 520 So. 2d 140 (Ala. 1987) (decided prior to 1984 amendment).

Innocent injured party is "insured" under this section. — Under uninsured motorist coverage the innocent injured party, not the intentional tort-feasor, is the "insured"; and viewing the matter from the standpoint of the innocent victim, the injury is an "accident." Alabama Farm Bureau Mut. Cas. Ins. Co. v. Mitchell, 373 So. 2d 1129 (Ala. Civ. App. 1979).

An insured, who is precluded because of governmental immunity from suing the owner or negligent operator of an uninsured motor vehicle, is nevertheless "legally entitled to recover damages" under this section, thus making operative the insurer's obligation to compensate the insured according to the insurance policy's uninsured motorist coverage. State Farm Mut. Auto. Ins. Co. v. Baldwin, 764 F.2d 773 (11th Cir. 1985).

An insured, who is precluded because of governmental immunity from suing the owner or negligent operator of an uninsured motor vehicle, is nevertheless "legally entitled to recover damages" under this section. State Farm Auto. Ins. Co. v. Baldwin, 470 So. 2d 1230 (Ala. 1985).

An insurer may assert only those defenses arising from no-fault policy with the insured but not those substantive defenses available to the negligent driver and the United States government, the owner of the uninsured vehicle in question. Thus, the immunity afforded by the Feres doctrine, which provides that no cause of action arises against the United States government or its employees for injuries incurred by a member of the military arising out of and/or in the course of his active military service is not available to an insurer on a no-fault insurance policy. State Farm Mut. Ins. Co. v. Baldwin, 764 F.2d 773 (11th Cir. 1985).

Recovery by guest for host's negligence. — A guest passenger is not entitled to recover under both the liability and the uninsured motorist coverages of his host driver's insurance policy when the negligence of the host driver caused the accident. Sullivan v. State Farm Mut. Auto Ins. Co., 513 So. 2d 992 (Ala. 1987).

A motor vehicle cannot be both insured and uninsured in the same policy. — Neither can a driver be insured as a permissive driver and at the same time be uninsured for purposes of uninsured motorist coverage. O'Hare v. State Farm Mut. Auto. Ins. Co., 432 So. 2d 1300 (Ala. 1983).

"First class" and "second class" insures defined. — Certain insureds are entitled to uninsured motorist coverage independently of any occupancy or use on their part of a vehicle insured under the policy. These insureds are known as "insureds of the first class." Insureds of the second class include mere occupants of the vehicle and permissive users covered under entitled to uninsured motorist coverage solely because of their occupancy or use of an insured vehicle. Therefore, their right to coverage is necessarily tied to and limited by the coverage applicable to such vehicle and is governed by the policy's limits of liability clause. Holloway v. Nationwide Mut. Ins. Co., 376 So. 2d 690 (Ala. 1979).

A class of insureds named in the provisions of an automobile liability policy in this state are provided uninsured motorist coverage regardless of whether that class is specifically named in the policy providing uninsured motorist coverage. Alabama Farm Bureau Mut. Ins. Co. v. Pigott, 393 So. 2d 1379 (Ala. 1981); State Farm Mut. Auto. Ins. Co. v. Jackson, 757 F.2d 1220 (11th Cir. 1985).

Any liability coverage to an "insured of the first class" spawns uninsured coverage which then becomes fixed as to that insured. Once in place the uninsured motorist coverage is in the nature of casualty or health and accident coverage which is conditioned on injury for which an uninsured motorist is legally liable. State Farm Mut. Auto. Ins. Co. v. Jackson, 757 F.2d 1220 (11th Cir. 1985).

Once an automobile liability policy is issued extending coverage to a certain class of insureds under such a clause, uninsured motorist coverage must be offered to cover the same class of insureds. State Farm Mut. Auto. Ins. Co. v. Jackson, 757 F.2d 1220 (11th Cir. 1985).

Unborn child, being a resident of the same household of named insured, is within the class of insureds under the uninsured motorist provisions. Alabama Farm Bureau Mut. Cas. Ins. Co. v. Pigott, 393 So. 2d 1379 (Ala. 1981).

Coverage for protection of persons insured. — This section provides that the coverage is "for the protection of persons insured thereunder" and not for the uninsured motorist. Gulf Am. Fire & Cas. Co. v. Gowan, 283 Ala. 480, 218 So. 2d 688 (1969).

Corporate entity considered a person. — For most purposes, as with the instant policy, the corporate entity is considered to be a "person." Alabama's Uninsured Motorist Statute (UMS) provides uninsured motorist coverage for the "person" and that personal coverage cannot be excluded because the insured person was driving a vehicle which was not covered under the liability portions of the insurance policy at the time of the accident. Thompson v. American States Ins. Co., 687 F. Supp. 559 (M.D. Ala. 1988).

Exclusion of coverage while occupying vehicle not covered under liability portion unenforceable. — Provision in uninsured motorist policy which excluded coverage for the insured while occupying a motor vehicle

owned by the insured but not covered under the liability portion of the policy was in conflict with the Alabama Uninsured Motorist Act and was therefore unenforceable. St. Paul Ins. Co. v. Henson, 479 So. 2d 1253 (Ala. Civ. App. 1985).

Fireman could not claim uninsured motorist benefits under policy covering fire truck upon which he was riding when he was injured in a one-vehicle accident where he was an "insured" under the policy; a "fellow employee" exclusion contained in the liability endorsement of the policy did not mean that the fire truck upon which plaintiff was riding was, at the time of the accident, "uninsured" as to him. Dale v. Home Ins. Co., 479 So. 2d 1290 (Ala. Civ. App. 1985).

III. WHO IS "UNINSURED MOTORIST."

Motorists are "uninsured" when: (1) policy limits are below the statutory minimum, (2) the policy fails to cover the injury involved, (3) the insurer becomes insolvent after the policy is issued so there is no insurance applicable to, or at the time of, the accident and (4) the owner or operator of the vehicle causing the accident is unknown, commonly classified as a "hit-and-run" case. Willbourn v. Allstate Ins. Co., 293 Ala. 466, 305 So. 2d 372 (1974); Criterion Ins. Co. v. Anderson, 347 So. 2d 384 (Ala. 1977).

Definition of "uninsured automobile". — It is reasonable and safe to state that an "uninsured automobile" is ordinarily defined to include motor vehicles with respect to which neither the owner nor the operator carries bodily injury liability insurance, and "hit-and-run" automobiles. Higgins v. Nationwide Mut. Ins. Co., 291 Ala. 462, 282 So. 2d 301 (1973); Criterion Ins. Co. v. Anderson, 347 So. 2d 384 (Ala. 1977); Lefeve v. State Farm Mut. Auto. Ins. Co., 527 F. Supp. 492 (N.D. Ala. 1981).

It is well-settled and common knowledge that a motorist or a vehicle carrying no liability insurance is "uninsured." Wilbourn v. Allstate Ins. Co., 293 Ala. 466, 305 So. 2d 372 (1974); Criterion Ins. Co. v. Anderson, 347 So. 2d 384 (Ala. 1977).

A vehicle, covered by a liability policy with the minimum limits prescribed by this chapter is not an uninsured vehicle as to an injured party even though such limits have been exhausted by payments to others injured in an accident. Criterion Ins. Co. v. Anderson, 347 So. 2d 384 (Ala. 1977).

Definition of an uninsured motor vehicle in policy as including a motor vehicle which is insured for bodily injury liability, but as to which "the sum of the limits of liability under all bonds and policies that apply are less than the damages the insured is legally entitled to recover," was in accord with the statute defining an uninsured motor vehicle. Sullivan v. State Farm Mut. Auto. Ins. Co., 513 So. 2d 992 (Ala. 1987).

IV. LIMITS OF LIABILITY.

For summary of the law from the leading cases of the Alabama supreme court upon the problem of policy exclusions to uninsured motorist coverage, see Gatson v. Integrity Ins. Co., 451 So. 2d 361 (Ala. Civ. App. 1984).

The mandated reciprocal extent of uninsured motorist coverage is determined by the extent of liability coverage for which the parties have contracted in the same policy, once minimal statutory liability coverage is provided, and not by the extent of liability coverage which would have been provided in the policy of the third-party tortfeasor, if the tortfeasor had liability insurance. State Farm Mut. Auto. Ins. Co. v. Jackson, 757 F.2d 1220 (11th Cir. 1985).

Subdivision (b)(4) of this section must be read into every policy in this state providing "uninsured motorist coverage." Hardy v. Progressive Ins. Co., 531 So. 2d 885 (Ala. 1988).

Insurer cannot avoid liability by inserting liability limiting clause. — Where the premiums have been paid for uninsured motorist coverage, an insurer cannot avoid its statutorily imposed liability by its insertion into the policy of a liability limiting clause which restricts the insured from receiving that coverage for which the premium has been paid. State Farm Mut. Auto. Ins. Co. v. Cahoon, 287 Ala. 462, 252 So. 2d 619 (1971); Hogan v. Allstate Ins. Co., 287 Ala. 696, 255 So. 2d 35 (1971).

Where the premiums have been paid for uninsured motorist coverage, the courts cannot permit an insurer to avoid its statutorily imposed liability by its insertion into the policy of a liability limiting clause which restricts the insured from receiving that coverage for which the premium has been paid. Safeco Ins. Co. of Am. v. Jones, 286 Ala. 606, 243 So. 2d 736 (1970).

An insurance company cannot limit liability when persons required by statute to have uninsured motorist coverage, i.e., those insured for liability purposes, are injured. In cases where the statutory mandate is inapplicable, the insurance contract may legally limit liability by providing for a maximum amount recoverable. Gallups v. Aetna Cas. & Sur. Co., 513 F. Supp. 1074 (N.D. Ala. 1981).

Under this section an insurer cannot avoid liability by inserting into a policy a liability limiting clause restricting an insured from recovering actual damages suffered, within the limits of a policy, where premiums have been paid for such uninsured motorist coverage, even though an insured has workmen's compensation benefits available to him. Preferred Risk Mut. Ins. Co. v. Holmes, 287 Ala. 251, 251 So. 2d 213 (1971).

An insurer cannot avoid the liability imposed by the Uninsured Motorist Act by inserting into a policy a liability limiting clause restricting an insured from recovering actual damages suffered, within the limits of a policy, where premiums have been paid for such uninsured motorist coverage, even though an insured has other similar insurance available to him. State Farm Mut. Auto. Ins. Co. v. Cahoon, 287 Ala. 462, 252 So. 2d 619 (1971).

Where the exclusionary clause tended to limit or restrict the recovery of the appellee under the uninsured motorist coverage of his policy, it constituted an invalid infringement of the coverage required by the uninsured motorist statute. Alabama Farm Bureau Mut. Cas. Ins. Co. v. Clem, 49 Ala. App. 457, 273 So. 2d 218 (1973).

The law of this state with respect to uninsured motorist coverage precludes an insurer from collecting a premium for certain coverage, then taking that coverage away by a limiting clause. Great Cent. Ins. Co. v. Edge, 292 Ala. 613, 298 So. 2d 607 (1974).

Regardless of whether limiting provisions of policy are stated in "plain, unmistakable language," cases clearly establish the rule that an insurer cannot avoid liability where an additional premium was collected by the insertion of a liability limiting clause into the policy. Great Cent. Ins. Co. v. Edge, 292 Ala. 613, 298 So. 2d 607 (1974).

Where an exclusion in a policy is more restrictive than the Uninsured Motorist Statute, it is void and unenforceable. State Farm Auto Ins. Co. v. Reaves, 292 Ala. 218, 292 So. 2d 95 (1974).

In the absence of any language in this section authorizing the exclusion, no exclusion for injuries suffered while driving a vehicle "not an owned motor vehicle" (i.e., not listed in that particular policy) may be created by the policy. State Farm Auto. Ins. Co. v. Reaves, 292 Ala. 218, 292 So. 2d 95 (1974).

Provisions in insurance policies restricting uninsured motorist coverage to occupants of automobile only if automobile was used with express permission of the named insured were repugnant to statutory requirements and therefore void. Billups v. Alabama Farm Bureau Mut. Cas. Ins. Co., 352 So. 2d 1097 (Ala. 1977).

Where terms of an insurance policy are

ambiguous, they are to be construed in favor of the insured. Alabama Farm Bureau Mut. Ins. Co. v. Pigott, 393 So. 2d 1379 (Ala. 1981).

Where loss exceeds limit of one policy, insured may proceed under other available policies. State Farm Mut. Auto. Ins. Co. v. Cahoon, 287 Ala. 462, 252 So. 2d 619 (1971); Hogan v. Allstate Ins. Co., 287 Ala. 696, 255 So. 2d 35 (1971).

Where loss exceeds the limits of one policy, this section permits the insured to proceed under other available policies. Safeco Ins. Co. of Am. v. Jones, 286 Ala. 606, 243 So. 2d 736 (1970).

Plain meaning of subsection (c) extends "stacking" of uninsured motorist coverage to all persons who are insureds, whether named insureds or not, and entitles them to recover "the primary coverage plus such additional coverage as may be provided for additional vehicles, but not to exceed two additional coverages with such contract." Travelers Ins. Co. v. Jones, 529 So. 2d 234 (Ala. 1988).

Stacking founded upon section. — Stacking of uninsured motorist coverage is founded upon this section requiring automobile insurers to provide such coverage. United Servs. Auto. Ass'n v. Smith, 57 Ala. App. 506, 329 So. 2d 562 (1976).

Passengers allowed to stack coverage. — Where the plaintiffs passengers in a collision with an uninsured motorist, were obviously "persons injured," and because the policy provided them primary coverage and contained an additional coverage for an additional vehicle "within such contract," then they were entitled to stack coverage under the plain meaning of subsection (c). Travelers Ins. Co. v. Jones, 529 So. 2d 234 (Ala. 1988).

"Other insurance" and "limits of liability" clauses are ineffective to prevent "stacking," being in derogation of the Alabama uninsured motorist statute. General Mut. Ins. Co. v. Gilmore, 294 Ala. 546, 319 So. 2d 675 (1975)

Rationale upon which stacking under multi-vehicle policies has been justified for insured of first class is inapplicable to insureds of the second class. Although an insured of the first class is covered under uninsured motorist policy provisions in whatever vehicle he may be occupying, and insured of the second class is similarly covered only if the particular vehicle he occupies is specifically included under the coverage of some policy. Holloway v. Nationwide Mut. Ins. Co., 376 So. 2d 690 (Ala. 1979).

Statute mandates stacking in case of named or designated insureds as well as relatives living in the same household where such persons are included in the policy's defini-

tion of "insureds" for purposes of liability. These persons are entitled to stack the available coverages because their right to coverage under the primary liability coverages is not limited to their use or occupancy of a vehicle insured under the policy. Holloway v. Nationwide Mut. Ins. Co., 376 So. 2d 690 (Ala. 1979).

Uninsured motorist coverage, not stacking, is mandated for permissive users where liability coverage arises as an incident of use of an insured vehicle. Holloway v. Nationwide Mut. Ins. Co., 376 So. 2d 690 (Ala. 1979).

Primary and secondary insurers. — In action against uninsured motorist, insurer of a nonowned automobile in which the claimant is injured is the primary insurer, and other insurers are secondary and excess carriers up to the amount of damages suffered or policy limits, whichever is greater. Almeida v. State Farm Mut. Ins. Co., 53 Ala. App. 175, 298 So. 2d 260 (1974).

The insured is bound by the provision in his policy which provides that if the insured is injured by an uninsured motorist while in an automobile other than the owned automobile, and such automobile has uninsured motorist insurance available to insured, such coverage shall be primary and coverage provided to the named insured shall be secondary and only as excess over the first. Thus the insured's first right of recovery is against the insurer of the nonowned automobile. Almeida v. State Farm Mut. Ins. Co., 53 Ala. App. 175, 298 So. 2d 260 (1974).

Exclusionary clauses enforced if clear and not in conflict with statutory law, etc. — It is the settled policy in Alabama that exclusionary definitions and clauses in insurance contracts shall be enforced by the courts of this state so long as their meaning is clear and they do not conflict with statutory law or public policy. Lammers v. State Farm Mut. Auto. Ins. Co., 48 Ala. App. 36, 261 So. 2d 757, cert. denied, 288 Ala. 745, 261 So. 2d 766 (1972).

If one is a person insured under the liability coverage of a policy, he cannot be excluded from protection of the uninsured motorist provision of that policy by an exclusion in the uninsured motorist provision. Such attempted exclusion is void because of the uninsured motorist statute. Nationwide Mut. Ins. Co. v. United Servs. Auto. Ass'n, 359 So. 2d 380 (Ala. Civ. App. 1977), cert. denied, 359 So. 2d 383 (Ala. 1978).

But they are not valid as to settlements with insured motorists by virtue of subrogation. — The exclusionary clause contained in the uninsured motorist coverage part of a policy is not valid as to settlements with insured motorists by virtue of the insurance company's subrogation rights. Alabama Farm Bureau Mut. Cas. Ins. Co. v. Clem, 49 Ala. App. 457, 273 So. 2d 218 (1973).

Subrogation rights of insurer with regard to underinsured motorist coverage. — Underinsured motorist coverage provides compensation to the extent of the insured's injury, subject to the insured's policy limits. It is an umbrella coverage that does not require the insurer to pay to its insured the amount of the tortfeasor's bodily injury liability limits, as those limits pertain to the insured. Therefore, the insurer has no right to subrogation insofar as the tortfeasor's limits of liability are concerned. Its right of subrogation would be for sums paid by the insurer in excess of the tortfeasor's limits of liability. Hardy v. Progressive Ins. Co., 531 So. 2d 885 (Ala. 1988).

Uninsured Motorist Coverage Act neither authorizes nor forbids household exclusion contained in "uninsured automobile" coverage, nor does it undertake to define "uninsured motor vehicles." Lammers v. State Farm Mut. Auto. Ins. Co., 48 Ala. App. 36, 261 So. 2d 757, cert. denied, 288 Ala. 745, 261 So. 2d 766 (1972).

The household exclusion from uninsured motorist coverage previously approved in Lammers v. State Farm Mut. Auto. Ins. Co., 48 Ala. App. 36, 261 So. 2d 757, cert. denied, 288 Ala. 745, 261 So. 2d 766 (1972) (annotated in the bound volume), is no longer the law in this state. Alabama Farm Bureau Mut. Cas. Ins. Co. v. Mitchell, 373 So. 2d 1129 (Ala. Civ. App. 1979).

The supreme court of Alabama has consistently upheld the "household exclusion" clause of liability policies, thereby establishing a judicial policy in this state that insurance companies may, by appropriate exclusions and exclusionary definitions, protect themselves from friendly family lawsuits. If the legislature, knowing the judicial policy of the courts of this state with reference to "household exclusion" clauses, had seen fit to make "uninsured motorist" coverage nullify, in practical effect, such "household exclusion" clauses, it surely would have done so when it adopted the Uninsured Motorist Coverage Act. Lammers v. State Farm Mut. Auto. Ins. Co., 48 Ala. App. 36, 261 So. 2d 757, cert. denied, 288 Ala. 745, 261 So. 2d 766 (1972).

Exclusion more restrictive than statute void and unenforceable. — Where an exclusion in a policy is more restrictive than the uninsured motorist statute, it is void and unenforceable. Alabama Farm Bureau Mut. Cas. Ins. Co. v. Mitchell, 373 So. 2d 1129 (Ala. Civ. App. 1979).

Physical contact requirement in "hit-and-run" clause in uninsured motorist provision is in derogation of section and void as against public policy. State Farm Fire & Cas. Co. v. Lambert, 291 Ala. 645, 285 So. 2d 917 (1973).

The physical contact requirement in a "hit-and-run" provision is void as being more restrictive than this section. State Farm Fire & Cas. Co. v. Lambert, 291 Ala. 645, 285 So. 2d 917 (1973).

Absent contrary written agreement, all policies are interpreted as providing minimum uninsured motorist coverage. — This section and cases applying it make clear that existence of minimum uninsured motorist coverage is inferred in every automobile liability policy notwithstanding absence of provision for such coverage in the policy itself. The courts will interpret all motor vehicle liability insurance policies as providing minimum uninsured motorist coverage unless a written agreement rejecting such coverage on part of named insured is in evidence. Commercial Std. Ins. Co. v. Potete, 409 So. 2d 426 (Ala. Civ. App.), rev'd on other grounds, 409 So. 2d 429 (Ala. 1981).

Where automobile insurance policy was renewed after the passage of this section, but no provision was made for uninsured motorist coverage, the amount of coverage is the minimum amount required by the statute, rather than the same as the coverage for bodily injury liability. Cline v. Aetna Ins. Co., 317 F. Supp. 1229 (S.D. Ala. 1970).

Omnibus clause. — Once an automobile liability policy is issued extending coverage to a certain class of insureds under an omnibus clause, under this section uninsured motorist coverage must be offered to cover the same class of insureds. State Farm Auto. Ins. Co. v. Reaves, 292 Ala. 218, 292 So. 2d 95 (1974).

In the type of policy having the usual "omnibus clause," uninsured motorist coverage was intended to be extended to all "persons insured thereunder," without regard to the mentioned exclusion. State Farm Auto. Ins. Co. v. Reaves, 292 Ala. 218, 292 So. 2d 95 (1974).

Arbitration provisions are neither required nor prohibited by this section. Cline v. Aetna Ins. Co., 317 F. Supp. 1229 (S.D. Ala. 1970).

No exclusion of governmentally owned motor vehicles may be created in policy. — In the absence of any language in the act authorizing the exclusion, no exclusion of governmentally owned motor vehicles may be created in the policy, and an attempt to include such in the policy provisions conflicts with the mandate of the act. The act provides such insurance protection for insureds without limitation or restriction as to whether or not the uninsured motor vehicle is governmentally owned or operated, and restricting the act's scope thwarts its purpose. Higgins v. Nationwide Mut. Ins. Co., 291 Ala. 462, 282 So. 2d 301 (1973).

While there may be argument for not including motor vehicles owned by the United States, Canada, a state or political subdivision or agency of any of these in this section, since governmental bodies are likely able to respond in damages, the fact remains that the legislature did not provide this exclusion. It might have undertaken to do so had it desired, but not having done so, it is mandatory that this section, the governing law, be read into the policy contract as it exists. Higgins v. Nationwide Mut. Ins. Co., 291 Ala. 462, 282 So. 2d 301 (1973).

Pedestrian's action against uninsured motorist and own insurer depended on liability. — In negligence action brought by insured pedestrian against uninsured motorist for injury sustained when hit by automobile driven by motorist and against pedestrian's insurers seeking to recover under uninsured motorist provisions of policy, pedestrian's right to recover against his insurers under such provisions depended upon the legal liability of the motorist to him. Barnes v. Tarver, 360 So. 2d 953 (Ala. 1978).

V. PROCEDURE.

"Legally entitled to recover damages" means that the insured must be able to establish fault on the part of the uninsured motorist, which gives rise to damages, and must be able to prove the extent of those damages. State Farm Mut. Auto. Ins. Co. v. Griffin, 51 Ala. App. 426, 286 So. 2d 302 (1973).

Party making claim for uninsured motorist coverage must prove that vehicle which injured him was uninsured. Lefeve v. State Farm Mut. Auto. Ins. Co., 527 F. Supp. 492 (N.D. Ala. 1981).

Section requires minimum coverage. — The only thing required by this section is uninsured motorist protection in the minimum amount of $10,000.00. Cline v. Aetna Ins. Co., 317 F. Supp. 1229 (S.D. Ala. 1970).

This section requires that insurers provide uninsured motorist coverage in the same minimum limits required under the provisions of § 32-7-6(c) for liability policies. Criterion Ins. Co. v. Anderson, 347 So. 2d 384 (Ala. 1977).

The scope of uninsured motorist coverage must be coextensive with liability coverage. Billups v. Alabama Farm Bureau Mut. Cas. Ins. Co., 352 So. 2d 1097 (Ala. 1977).

If the tort-feasor has insurance up to the statutory limits, he is not "uninsured."

Wilbourn v. Allstate Ins. Co., 293 Ala. 466, 305 So. 2d 372 (1974).

Absence of rejection necessary condition to coverage. — The text of this section indicates that the absence of the named insured's rejection of coverage is one necessary condition to a finding of the existence of minimum uninsured motorist coverage. Insurance Co. of N. Am. v. Thomas, 337 So. 2d 365 (Ala. Civ. App. 1976).

Verbal rejection of coverage held invalid. — Insured's purported verbal rejection of uninsured motorist coverage prior to executing the policy, and not evidenced by a writing contained in or coordinate with the policy, is invalid. Insurance Co. of N. Am. v. Thomas, 337 So. 2d 365 (Ala. Civ. App. 1976).

Maximum recovery not limited except by amount of actual loss. — This section sets a minimum amount for recovery, but it does not place a limit on the total amount of recovery so long as that amount does not exceed the amount of actual loss. Safeco Ins. Co. of Am. v. Jones, 286 Ala. 606, 243 So. 2d 736 (1970); State Farm Mut. Auto. Ins. Co. v. Cahoon, 287 Ala. 462, 252 So. 2d 619 (1971); Hogan v. Allstate Ins. Co., 287 Ala. 696, 255 So. 2d 35 (1971).

An insured is not precluded from recovering the aggregate amount of coverage provided for two vehicles so long as the total does not exceed the total of the judgment for the damages recovered even if the premium for the coverage is not separated and identified as to separate automobiles on the face of the policy, since undisputed proof reflected that an additional premium was charged for the extra automobile. Great Cent. Ins. Co. v. Edge, 292 Ala. 613, 298 So. 2d 607 (1974).

And by amount which injured party legally entitled to recover. — Recovery in excess of that amount to which the injured party was legally entitled to recover by virtue of a judgment against the uninsured motorists is not permitted even though this section does not place a limit on the total amount of recovery. Safeco Ins. Co. of Am. v. Jones, 286 Ala. 606, 243 So. 2d 736 (1970).

This section limits recovery of damages to that amount to which the injured party is legally entitled to recover, and that amount is legally settled prior to the claims under the statute and the policies. Safeco Ins. Co. of Am. v. Jones, 286 Ala. 606, 243 So. 2d 736 (1970).

Section permits enforcement of policy provisions by insured directly against insurer without first obtaining a judgment against the uninsured. State Farm Fire & Cas. Co. v. Lambert, 291 Ala. 645, 285 So. 2d 917 (1973).

The imposition of the requirement that the

insured must first bring an action against the uninsured motorist would transfer uninsured motorist coverage into unsatisfied judgment insurance, and this certainly was not the intent of the legislature. State Farm Mut. Auto. Ins. Co. v. Griffin, 51 Ala. App. 426, 286 So. 2d 302 (1973).

Insured need not first secure a judgment against the uninsured motorist as to fault and damages as a condition precedent to bringing an action against the insurer under the uninsured motorist provisions of the policy. State Farm Mut. Auto. Ins. Co. v. Griffin, 51 Ala. App. 426, 286 So. 2d 302 (1973).

Where an insured motorist is entitled to punitive damages from an underinsured motorist, punitive damages may be awarded against the carrier providing the insured motorist with uninsured motorist coverage. Lavender v. State Farm Mut. Auto. Ins. Co., 828 F.2d 1517 (11th Cir. 1987).

Enforcement of "excess" clause of automobile liability policy providing uninsured motorist coverage, so as to thereby provide only excess coverage for plaintiff insureds under policy when injured while occupying a nonowned automobile which was involved in accident in which uninsured motorist was at fault, with primary insurer being uninsured motorist for nonowned vehicle in which plaintiffs were riding, did no violence to the uninsured motorist statute, since secondary coverage may be reached after the exhaustion of primary coverage if the damages exceed the policy limits of the primary coverage. Gaught v. Evans, 361 So. 2d 1027 (Ala. 1978).

Burden of proof. — In a direct action by the insured against the insurer, the insured has the burden of proving in this regard that the other motorist was uninsured, legally liable for damage to the insured and the amount of this liability. State Farm Mut. Auto.

Ins. Co. v. Griffin, 51 Ala. App. 426, 286 So. 2d 302 (1973).

Plaintiff allowed either to join as party defendant his own liability insurer in suit against underinsured motorist or merely give it notice of filing of action against the motorist and of the possibility of a claim under the underinsured motorist coverage at the conclusion of the trial. If the insurer is named as a party, it would have the right, within a reasonable time after service of process, to elect either to participate in the trial (in which case its identity and the reason for its being involved are proper information for the jury), or not to participate in the trial (in which case no mention of it or its potential involvement is permitted by the trial court). Under either election, the insurer would be bound by the factfinder's decisions on the issues of liability and damages. If the insurer is not joined but merely is given notice of the filing of the action, it can decide either to intervene or to stay out of the case. Lowe v. Nationwide Ins. Co., 521 So. 2d 1309 (Ala. 1988).

Insurer has available, in addition to policy defenses, substantive defenses that would have been available to the uninsured motorist. State Farm Mut. Auto. Ins. Co. v. Griffin, 51 Ala. App. 426, 286 So. 2d 302 (1973).

Right of insurer to intervene. — If a judgment by the insured against an uninsured motorist is to be conclusive or even admissible as evidence against the insurer, procedural due process requires the right to intervene by the insurer. Almeida v. State Farm Mut. Ins. Co., 53 Ala. App. 175, 298 So. 2d 260 (1974).

Judgment conclusive against insurer. — A judgment obtained by insured against an uninsured motorist is conclusive as against the insurer. Almeida v. State Farm Mut. Ins. Co., 53 Ala. App. 175, 298 So. 2d 260 (1974).

§ 32-7-24. Notice of cancellation or termination of certified policy.

When an insurance carrier has certified a motor vehicle liability policy under section 32-7-20 or a policy under section 32-7-21, the insurance so certified shall not be cancelled or terminated until at least 10 days after a notice of cancellation or termination of the insurance so certified shall be filed in the office of the director; except, that such a policy subsequently procured and certified shall, on the effective date of its certification, terminate the insurance previously certified with respect to any motor vehicle designated in both certificates. (Acts 1951, No. 704, p. 1224, § 22.)

Cited in American S. Ins. Co. v. Dime Taxi Serv., Inc., 275 Ala. 51, 151 So. 2d 783 (1963). **Collateral references.** — Cancellation of compulsory or "financial responsibility" automobile insurance. 34 ALR2d 1297.

§ 32-7-25. Chapter not to affect other policies.

(a) This chapter shall not be held to apply to or affect policies of automobile insurance against liability which may now or hereafter be required by any other law of this state, and such policies, if they contain an agreement or are endorsed to conform to the requirements of this chapter, may be certified as proof of financial responsibility under this chapter.

(b) This chapter shall not be held to apply to or affect policies insuring solely the insured named in the policy against liability resulting from the maintenance or use by persons in the insured's employ or on his behalf of motor vehicles not owned by the insured. (Acts 1951, No. 704, p. 1224, § 23.)

§ 32-7-26. Bond as proof of financial responsibility.

(a) Proof of financial responsibility may be furnished by a bond of a surety company duly authorized to transact business in this state, or by a bond with at least two individual sureties each owning real estate within this state and together having equities equal in value to at least twice the amount of such bond, which real estate shall be scheduled in the bond and approved both as to title and value by the judge of probate of the county in which such real estate is located. Such bond shall be conditioned for payments in amounts and under the same circumstances as would be required in a motor vehicle liability policy and shall not be cancelable except after 10 days' written notice to the director. The principal and sureties shall execute and deliver an original and one copy of such bond and schedule and, in addition, when the real property or any part thereof listed or described in such schedule shall be located in more than one county, then as many extra copies as there are other counties in which such real property, or any part thereof, shall lie, to the probate judge to whom such bond is presented for approval, who shall endorse upon the original and the copy of such bond the date the same were presented to him; and such probate judge shall immediately file one of such extra copies in the probate office in each other county in which is located any of the real property so scheduled. Any probate judge who approves an extra copy of such bond shall endorse upon such copy the date upon which such extra copy was filed in his office and after recording the same shall return the extra copy thereof to the probate judge from whom he received the same. The latter, after tabulating the total value of the real estate described therein, shall, if he approves the same, endorse upon the original and a copy of such bond the fact and date of his approval and shall forward the bond to the director and deliver the extra copy or copies thereof to the principal. Such bond shall constitute a lien in favor of the state upon the real estate so scheduled of any surety from the time when a copy of such bond is filed in the probate office in and for the county in which such real property so scheduled is located, which lien shall exist in favor of any holder of a judgment against the person who has filed such bond.

(b) If such a judgment rendered against the principal on such bond shall not be satisfied within 60 days after it has become final, the judgment creditor may, for his own use and benefit and at his sole expense, bring an action or actions (in the name of the state) against the company or persons executing such bond, including an action or proceeding to enforce any lien that may exist upon the real estate of a person who has executed such bond. (Acts 1951, No. 704, p. 1224, § 24.)

§ 32-7-27. Money or securities as proof.

(a) Proof of financial responsibility may be evidenced by the certificate of the state treasurer that the person named therein has deposited with him $11,000.00 in cash, or securities such as may legally be purchased by savings banks or for trust funds of a market value of $11,000.00. The state treasurer shall not accept any such deposit and issue a certificate therefor and the director shall not accept such certificate unless accompanied by evidence that there are no unsatisfied judgments of any character against the depositor in the county where the depositor resides.

(b) Such deposit shall be held by the state treasurer to satisfy, in accordance with the provisions of this chapter, any execution on a judgment issued against such person making the deposit, for damages, including damages for care and loss of services, because of bodily injury to or death of any person, or for damages because of injury to or destruction of property, including the loss of use thereof resulting from the ownership, maintenance, use or operation of a motor vehicle after such deposit was made. Money or securities so deposited shall not be subject to attachment or execution unless such attachment or execution shall arise out of an action for damages as aforesaid. (Acts 1951, No. 704, p. 1224, § 25.)

§ 32-7-28. Owner may give proof for others.

Whenever any person required to give proof of financial responsibility under this chapter is or later becomes an operator in the employ of any owner, or is or later becomes a member of the immediate family or household of the owner, the director shall accept proof given by such owner in lieu of proof by such other person to permit such other person to operate a motor vehicle for which the owner has given proof as herein provided. The director shall designate the restrictions imposed by this section on the face of such person's license. (Acts 1951, No. 704, p. 1224, § 26.)

Collateral references. — Misrepresentation by applicant for automobile liability insurance as to ownership of vehicle as material to risk. 33 ALR2d 948.

Consortium claim of spouse, parent or child of accident victim as within extended "per accident" coverage rather than "per person" coverage of automobile liability policy. 46 ALR4th 735.

§ 32-7-29. Substitution of proof.

The director shall consent to the cancellation of any bond or certificate of insurance or the director shall direct and the state treasurer shall return any money or securities to the person entitled thereto upon the substitution and acceptance of other adequate proof of financial responsibility pursuant to this chapter. (Acts 1951, No. 704, p. 1224, § 27.)

Collateral references. — Construction and application of substitution provision of automobile liability policy. 42 ALR4th 1145.

§ 32-7-30. Additional proof may be required.

Whenever any proof of financial responsibility filed under the provisions of this chapter no longer fulfills the purposes for which required, the director shall, for the purpose of this chapter, require other proof as required by this chapter and shall suspend the license and registration or the nonresident's operating privilege pending the filing of such other proof. (Acts 1951, No. 704, p. 1224, § 28.)

§ 32-7-31. Duration of proof; when proof may be cancelled or returned.

(a) The director shall upon request consent to the immediate cancellation of any bond or certificate of insurance, or the director shall direct and the state treasurer shall return to the person entitled thereto any money or securities deposited pursuant to this chapter as proof of financial responsibility, or the director shall waive the requirement of filing proof, in any of the following events:

(1) At any time after three years from the date such proof was required when, during the three-year period preceding the request, the director has not received record of a conviction or a forfeiture of bail which would require or permit the suspension or revocation of the license, registration or nonresident's operating privilege of the person by or for whom such proof was furnished; or

(2) In the event of the death of the person on whose behalf such proof was filed or the permanent incapacity of such person to operate a motor vehicle; or

(3) In the event the person who has given proof surrenders his license and registration to the director.

(b) The director shall not consent to the cancellation of any bond or the return of any money or securities in the event any action for damages upon a liability covered by such proof is then pending or any judgment upon any such liability is then unsatisfied or in the event the person who has filed such bond or deposited such money or securities has within one year immediately preceding such request been involved as an operator or owner in any motor vehicle accident resulting in injury or damage to the person or property of others. An affidavit of the applicant as to the nonexistence of such facts, or that he has been released from all of his liability or has been finally adjudicated not to be liable for such injury or damage shall be sufficient evidence thereof in the absence of evidence to the contrary in the records of the director.

(c) Whenever any person whose proof has been cancelled or returned under subdivision (3) of subsection (a) of this section applies for a license or registration within a period of three years from the date proof was originally required, any such application shall be refused unless the applicant shall reestablish such proof for the remainder of such three-year period. (Acts 1951, No. 704, p. 1224, § 29.)

§ 32-7-32. Transfer of registration to defeat purpose of chapter prohibited.

If an owner's registration has been suspended hereunder, such registration shall not be transferred nor the motor vehicle in respect of which such registration was issued registered in any other name until the director is satisfied that such transfer of registration is proposed in good faith and not for the purpose or with the effect of defeating the purposes of this chapter. Nothing in this section shall in anywise affect the rights of any conditional vendor, chattel mortgagee or lessor of a motor vehicle registered in the name of another as owner who becomes subject to the provisions of this section. (Acts 1951, No. 704, p. 1224, § 30.)

Mere sale not transfer of registration. — A mere sale of the automobile by the appellant of his interest in the automobile cannot be deemed a transfer of the registration of the automobile within the meaning of this section. If a purchaser from the appellant obtained registration plates for the automobile after the sale, such would be the act of the purchaser, not of the appellant. Stroud v. State, 37 Ala. App. 589, 73 So. 2d 103 (1954).

§ 32-7-33. Surrender of license and registration.

Any person whose license or registration shall have been suspended as provided in this chapter, or whose policy of insurance or bond, when required under this chapter, shall have been cancelled or terminated or who shall neglect to furnish other proof upon request of the director shall immediately return his license and registration to the director. If any person shall fail to return to the director the license or registration as provided herein, the director shall forthwith direct any peace officer to secure possession thereof and to return the same to the director. (Acts 1951, No. 704, p. 1224, § 31.)

Collateral references. — 60 C.J.S., Motor Vehicles, § 164.23.

§ 32-7-34. Self-insurers.

(a) Any person in whose name more than 25 motor vehicles are registered may qualify as a self-insurer by obtaining a certificate of self-insurance issued by the director as provided in subsection (b) of this section.

(b) The director may, in his discretion, upon the application of such a person, issue a certificate of self-insurance when he is satisfied that such person is possessed and will continue to be possessed of ability to pay judgments obtained against such person.

(c) Upon not less than five days' notice and a hearing pursuant to such notice, the director may upon reasonable grounds cancel a certificate of self-insurance. Failure to pay any judgment within 30 days after such judgment shall have become final shall constitute a reasonable ground for the cancellation of a certificate of self-insurance. (Acts 1951, No. 704, p. 1224, § 34.)

Collateral references. — 60 C.J.S., Motor Vehicles, §§ 110, 114, 129.

Necessity or permissibility of naming no-fault insurer as defendant where insured automobile owner or operator is not liable for economic losses under no-fault insurance law. 40 ALR4th 858.

Self-insurance against liability as other insurance within meaning of liability insurance policy. 46 ALR4th 707.

§ 32-7-35. Assigned risk plans.

After consultation with insurance companies authorized to issue automobile liability policies in this state, the superintendent of insurance shall approve a reasonable plan or plans for the equitable apportionment among such companies of applicants for such policies and for motor vehicle liability policies who are in good faith entitled to but are unable to procure such policies through ordinary methods. When any such plan has been approved, all such insurance companies shall subscribe thereto and participate therein. Any applicant for any such policy, any person insured under any such plan and any insurance company affected may appeal to the superintendent of insurance from any ruling or decision of the manager or committee designated to operate such plan. Any person aggrieved hereunder by any order or act of the superintendent of insurance may, within 10 days after notice thereof, file a petition in the circuit court of Montgomery county, Alabama for a review thereof. The court shall summarily hear the petition and may enter any appropriate order or judgment. (Acts 1951, No. 704, p. 1224, § 35.)

Cited in State Farm Mut. Auto. Ins. Co. v. General Mut. Ins. Co., 282 Ala. 212, 210 So. 2d 688 (1968).

Collateral references. — 60 C.J.S., Motor Vehicles, § 164.18.

§ 32-7-36. Exceptions.

This chapter shall not apply with respect to any motor vehicle owned by the United States, this state or any political subdivision of this state or any municipality therein; nor, except for sections 32-7-5 and 32-7-28, with respect to any motor vehicle which is subject to the supervision and regulation of the Alabama public service commission which have filed with such commission a bond or insurance policy, the liability under which is not less than that required of the operator of a motor vehicle under the terms of this chapter. Any person, firm, association or corporation licensed and engaged in the business of renting or leasing motor vehicles to be operated on the public highways shall only be required to furnish proof of financial ability to satisfy any judgment or judgments rendered against said person, firm, association or corporation in his or its capacity as owner of the said motor vehicles and shall not be required to furnish proof of its financial ability to satisfy any judgment or judgments rendered against the person to whom the motor vehicle was rented or leased at the time of the accident. (Acts 1951, No. 704, p. 1224, § 33.)

Collateral references. — Application of financial responsibility or compulsory insurance laws to governmental vehicles or their operators. 87 ALR2d 1224.

State regulation of motor vehicle rental ("you-drive") business. 60 ALR4th 784.

§ 32-7-37. Other violations; penalties.

(a) Failure to report an accident as required in section 32-7-5 shall be punished by a fine not in excess of $25.00, and in the event of injury or damage to the person or property of another in such accident, the director shall suspend the license of the person failing to make such report or the nonresident's operating privilege of such person until such report has been filed and for such further period not to exceed 30 days as the director may fix.

(b) Any person who gives information required in a report or otherwise as provided for in section 32-7-5, knowing or having reason to believe that such information is false, or who shall forge or, without authority, sign any evidence of proof of financial responsibility, or who files or offers for filing any such evidence of proof knowing or having reason to believe that it is forged or signed without authority, shall be fined not more than $1,000.00 or imprisoned for not more than one year, or both.

(c) Any person whose license or registration or nonresident's operating privilege has been suspended or revoked under this chapter and who, during such suspension or revocation drives any motor vehicle upon any highway or knowingly permits any motor vehicle owned by such person to be operated by another upon any highway, except as permitted under this chapter, shall be fined not more than $500.00 or imprisoned not exceeding six months, or both.

(d) Any person willfully failing to return license or registration as required in section 32-7-33 shall be fined not more than $500.00 or imprisoned not to exceed 30 days, or both.

(e) Any person who shall violate any provision of this chapter for which no penalty is otherwise provided shall be fined not more than $500.00 or imprisoned not more than 90 days, or both. (Acts 1951, No. 704, p. 1224, § 32.)

When proof of violation of section irrelevant. — Under § 32-6-19, proof of violation of subsection (c) of this section would be irrelevant. Balentine v. State, 44 Ala. App. 137, 203 So. 2d 703 (1967).

Insurer was not liable to uninsured motorist for malicious prosecution or abuse of process for filing statutorily required form without improper purpose, where the filing of the report resulted in the temporary suspension of her driving privileges and that the suspension of her license was unlawful under § 32-7-7(2) since uninsured motorist was legally parked at the time of the accident. Green v. Alabama Farm Bureau Mut. Cas. Ins. Co., 522 So. 2d 773 (Ala. 1988).

§ 32-7-38. Employment of necessary employees.

The director of public safety, subject to the provisions of the merit system, may appoint such clerical assistants, stenographers or employees as may be necessary to discharge the duties imposed by this chapter. The salaries of such clerical assistants, stenographers and employees and all expenses incurred incident to carrying out their duties shall be paid in the same manner as those of other state employees. (Acts 1951, No. 704, p. 1224, § 40.)

§ 32-7-39. Expenses of administering chapter.

The expenses of administering this chapter, not to exceed $100,000.00 per annum, shall be paid out of the funds appropriated to the department of public safety. (Acts 1951, No. 704, p. 1224, § 41.)

§ 32-7-40. Chapter supplemental to other laws.

This chapter shall in no respect be considered as a repeal of the state motor vehicle laws, but shall be construed as supplemental thereto. (Acts 1951, No. 704, p. 1224, § 36.)

§ 32-7-41. Chapter not to prevent other process.

Nothing in this chapter shall be construed as preventing the plaintiff in any civil action from relying for relief upon the other processes provided by law. (Acts 1951, No. 704, p. 1224, § 38.)

§ 32-7-42. Uniformity of interpretation.

This chapter shall be so interpreted and construed as to effectuate its general purpose to make uniform the laws of those states which enact it. (Acts 1951, No. 704, p. 1224, § 39.)

Cited in Madison v. Director, Dep't of Pub. Safety, 465 So. 2d 1148 (Ala. Civ. App. 1984).

CHAPTER 8.

UNIFORM CERTIFICATE OF TITLE AND ANTITHEFT ACT.

Applicability of chapter. — See Whit-
worth v. Dodd, 435 So. 2d 1305 (Ala. Civ. App.
1983).

Cited in State Farm Mut. Auto. Ins. Co. v.
Hartman, 450 So. 2d 152 (Ala. Civ. App. 1984).

ARTICLE 1.

GENERAL PROVISIONS.

Purpose of chapter. — One purpose of this
chapter is to frustrate the possession and
disposition of stolen motor vehicles in the
states. Congress Fin. Corp. v. Funderburk, 416
So. 2d 1059 (Ala. Civ. App. 1982).

Primary objective of Alabama's Uniform
Certificate of Title and Antitheft Act is to
frustrate the possession and disposition of
stolen motor vehicles and parts within the

state. State v. Spurlock, 393 So. 2d 1052 (Ala.
Crim. App. 1981).

**This chapter provides a means for inter-
ested parties to ascertain essential information** concerning title to vehicles. Congress
Fin. Corp. v. Funderburk, 416 So. 2d 1059
(Ala. Civ. App. 1982).

Collateral references. — Liability of state,
in issuing automobile certificate of title, for
failure to discover title defect. 28 ALR4th 184.

§ 32-8-1. Short title.

This chapter may be cited as the Alabama Uniform Certificate of Title and
Antitheft Act. (Acts 1973, No. 765, p. 1147, § 49.)

Purpose. — This chapter was not enacted to
prevent motor vehicle accidents, but to prevent
motor vehicle thefts. The very title states that
it is an antitheft act. The overall plan of this
chapter shows exclusive attention to maintaining records of the identity and ownership of
vehicles. Treadwell Ford, Inc. v. Campbell, 485
So. 2d 312 (Ala. 1986), appeal dismissed, —

U.S. —, 108 S. Ct. 2007, 100 L. Ed. 2d 596
(1988).

**Violation of chapter did not subject in-
surer to liability for negligence.** Treadwell
Ford, Inc. v. Campbell, 485 So. 2d 312 (Ala.
1986), appeal dismissed, — U.S. —, 108 S. Ct.
2007, 100 L. Ed. 2d 596 (1988).

Cited in Ledbetter v. Darwin Dobbs Co., 473
So. 2d 197 (Ala. Civ. App. 1985).

§ 32-8-2. Definitions.

For the purpose of this chapter, the following terms shall have the
meanings respectively ascribed to them in this section, except where the
context clearly indicates a different meaning:

(1) CURRENT ADDRESS. A new address different from the address shown on
the application or on the certificate of title. The owner shall within 30 days
after his address is changed from that shown on the application or on the
certificate of title notify the department of the change of address in the
manner prescribed by the department.

(2) DEALER. A person licensed as an automobile or motor vehicle dealer,
mobile home dealer, or travel trailer dealer and engaged regularly in the
business of buying, selling or exchanging motor vehicles, trailers, semi-

trailers, trucks, tractors or other character of commercial or industrial motor vehicles, mobile homes or travel trailers in this state, and having in this state an established place of business.

(3) DEPARTMENT. The department of revenue of this state.

(4) DESIGNATED AGENT. Each judge of probate, commissioner of licenses, director of revenue or other county official in this state authorized and required by law to issue motor vehicle license tags, who may perform his duties under this chapter personally or through his deputies, or such other persons, as the department may designate; the term shall also mean those "dealers" as herein defined who are appointed by the department as herein provided in section 32-8-34 to perform the duties of "designated agent" for the purposes of this chapter; such "dealers" may perform their duties under this chapter either personally or through any of their officers or employees.

(5) IMPLEMENT OF HUSBANDRY. Every vehicle designed and adapted exclusively for agricultural, horticultural or livestock raising operations or for lifting or carrying an implement of husbandry and in either case not subject to licensing or registration if used upon the highways.

(6) LIEN. Every kind of written lease which is substantially equivalent to an installment sale or which provides for a right of purchase, conditional sale, reservation of title, deed of trust, chattel mortgage, trust receipt, and every written agreement or instrument of whatever kind or character whereby an interest other than absolute title is sought to be held or given on a motor vehicle.

(7) LIENHOLDER. Any person, firm, copartnership, association or corporation holding a lien as herein defined on a motor vehicle.

(8) MANUFACTURER. Any person regularly engaged in the business of manufacturing, constructing, assembling, importing or distributing new motor vehicles, either within or without this state.

(9) MOBILE HOME. A structure, transportable in one or more sections, and which is built on a permanent chassis, and not designed normally to be drawn or pulled on the highway except to change permanent locations, but is designed to be used as a dwelling, with or without a permanent foundation, when connected to the required utilities, including the plumbing, heating, air conditioning and electrical systems, if any contained therein. It may be used as a place of residence, business, profession, trade or for any other purpose, by the owner, lessee, or assigns and may consist of one or more units that can be attached or jointed together.

(10) MOTOR VEHICLE. Such term shall include:

a. Every automobile, motorcycle, mobile trailer, semitrailer, truck, truck tractor, trailer and other device which is self-propelled or drawn, in, upon or by which any person or property is or may be transported or drawn upon a public highway except such as is moved by animal power or used exclusively upon stationary rails or tracks;

b. Every mobile home, trailer coach, travel trailer and house trailer manufactured upon a chassis or undercarriage as an integral part thereof drawn by a self-propelled vehicle.

(11) NEW VEHICLE. A motor vehicle that has never been the subject of a first sale for use.

(12) NONRESIDENT. Every person who is not a resident of this state.

(13) OWNER. A person, other than a lienholder, having the property in or title to a vehicle. The term includes a person entitled to the use and possession of a vehicle subject to a security interest in another person, but excludes a lessee under a lease not intended as security. Under any lease-purchase or installment sales agreement where a governmental agency, either city, county or state, is the lessee or purchaser with a security interest or right to purchase, such lessee or purchaser shall be the owner for purposes of this chapter.

(14) PERSON. Such term shall include every natural person, firm, copartnership, association or corporation.

(15) POLE TRAILER. Every vehicle without motive power designed to be drawn by another vehicle and attached to the towing vehicle by means of a reach or pole, or by being boomed or otherwise secured to the towing vehicle, and ordinarily used for transporting long or irregularly shaped loads such as logs, poles, pipes, boats or structural members capable generally of sustaining themselves as beams between the supporting connections.

(16) SCRAP METAL PROCESSOR. Any person, firm, or corporation engaged in the business of buying scrap vehicles, automotive parts, or other metallic waste by weight to process such material into scrap metal for remelting purposes, who utilizes machinery and equipment for processing and manufacturing ferrous and nonferrous metallic scrap into prepared grades, and whose principal product is metallic scrap.

(17) SCRAP VEHICLE. Any vehicle which has been crushed or flattened by mechanical means or which has been otherwise damaged to the extent that it cannot economically be repaired or made roadworthy.

(18) SECURITY AGREEMENT. A written agreement which reserves or creates a security interest.

(19) SECURITY INTEREST. An interest in a vehicle reserved or created by agreement and which secures payment or performance of an obligation. The term includes the interest of a lessor under a lease intended as security. A security interest is "perfected" when it is valid against third parties generally, subject only to specific statutory exceptions.

(20) SPECIAL MOBILE EQUIPMENT. Every vehicle not designed or used primarily for the transportation of persons or property and only incidentally operated or moved over the highway, including but not limited to: ditch-digging apparatus; well-boring apparatus; road construction and mainte-nance machinery such as asphalt spreaders, bituminous mixers, bucket loaders, tractors other than truck tractors, ditchers, leveling graders, finishing machines, motor graders, road rollers, scarifiers, earth-moving carryalls and scrapers, power shovels and draglines, and self-propelled cranes; and earth-moving equipment. The term does not include house trailers, dump trucks, truck-mounted transit mixers, cranes or shovels or

other vehicles designed for the transportation of persons or property to which machinery has been attached.

(21) STATE. A state, territory or possession of the United States, the District of Columbia, the Commonwealth of Puerto Rico or a province of the Dominion of Canada.

(22) TRAVEL TRAILER. A vehicle without motive power, designed and constructed as a camping vehicle or a temporary dwelling, living or sleeping place and designed to be drawn or pulled on the highway, but not including folding or collapsible camping trailers and mobile homes as defined herein.

(23) USED VEHICLE. A motor vehicle that has been the subject of a first sale for use, whether within this state or elsewhere.

(24) VEHICLE IDENTIFICATION NUMBER. The numbers and letters on a motor vehicle designated by the manufacturer or assigned by the department for the purpose of identifying the motor vehicle. (Acts 1973, No. 765, p. 1147, § 1; Acts 1985, 2nd Ex. Sess., No. 85-939, p. 249; Acts 1987, No. 87-806, p. 1581, § 1; Acts 1989, No. 89-918, § 1.)

The 1989 amendment, effective May 19, 1989, rewrote this section.

Cross references. — As to application of these definitions to temporary license tags and registration certificates, see § 32-6-210.

Definition of a "new vehicle" in subdivision (10) is only for the purposes of the Alabama Uniform Certificate of Title and Antitheft Act, §§ 32-8-1 — 32-8-88; thus, in an action for fraud, the jury could have found that the defendant car dealer falsely represented that the car was new, even though it had never been the subject of a first sale for use. Larry Savage Chevrolet, Inc. v. Richards, 470 So. 2d 1168 (Ala. 1985).

"Owner." — Where law enforcement officials wanted a stolen car forfeited to state, the trial court properly granted title to the car to creditor even though subdivision (12) defines "owner" as a person, other than the lienholder, having property in or title to the vehicle, since the original owner's insurance company never filed a claim to the car, second owner declared bankruptcy, and trustee in bankruptcy relinquished any claim to the car to creditor. State v. Southtrust Bank, 534 So. 2d 270 (Ala. 1988).

Cited in Harwell v. First Nat'l Bank (In re Sewell), 32 Bankr. 116 (Bankr. N.D. Ala. 1983); Southtrust Bank v. Toffel (In re Blackerby), 53 Bankr. 649 (Bankr. N.D. Ala. 1985); Barton v. State, 519 So. 2d 1344 (Ala. 1988).

§ 32-8-3. Powers and duties of department.

(a) The department shall prescribe and provide suitable forms of applications, certificates of title, notices of security interests and all other notices and forms necessary to carry out the provisions of this chapter.

(b) The department may:

(1) Make necessary investigations to procure information required to carry out the provisions of this chapter;

(2) Adopt and enforce reasonable rules and regulations to carry out the provisions of this chapter;

(3) Assign a new identification number to a vehicle if it has none, or its identification number is destroyed or obliterated, or its motor is changed, and shall either issue a new certificate of title showing the new identification number or make an appropriate endorsement on the original certificate;

(4) Revoke the authority of a dealer or other person appointed by the department to act as a designated agent hereunder when it finds that such dealer or other person has failed to faithfully perform his duties under this chapter.

(c) The department shall make available information concerning the status of a title on any vehicle as reflected by the records in a manner prescribed by the department. Such information supplied by the department shall be considered official only if in writing. The department shall charge the fees set forth in section 32-8-6; provided, that no fee shall be charged Alabama law-enforcement agencies or law-enforcement agencies of any other state when such state furnishes like or similar information without charge to the department or to Alabama law-enforcement agencies. (Acts 1973, No. 765, p. 1147, § 26.)

Cited in Kelley v. State, 429 So. 2d 1184 (Ala. Crim. App. 1983).

§ 32-8-4. Protest of actions of department; hearings.

A person aggrieved by an act or omission to act of the department under this chapter is entitled to a hearing. Such person shall within 60 days of such act or omission to act protest in writing the act or omission to act by which he is aggrieved, request the department to take appropriate action to remedy such act or omission to act, state the grounds on which the request is based and request a hearing of the protest. On receipt of such protest the department shall, if it finds the protest justified, comply forthwith with the request. If the department is of the opinion that the written protest is not sufficient to justify compliance with the request, a hearing of the matter shall be set before the department and notice thereof shall be given to the aggrieved person by registered or certified mail, return receipt requested. The hearing may be continued from time to time as deemed to be appropriate by the department. The aggrieved person may make an appearance by written statement, in person or by attorney or agent. The department shall make such rules for the conduct of the hearing as deemed by it to be appropriate and necessary. At the conclusion of the hearing the department shall within 10 days notify the aggrieved person in writing of its determination of the matter. (Acts 1973, No. 765, p. 1147, § 27.)

§ 32-8-5. Court review of department actions.

An aggrieved person who has filed a protest in accordance with the provisions of section 32-8-4, not being satisfied with the determination made by the department, may request review of the matter by the circuit court of the county in which he resides, or in which the vehicle involved is licensed, or in which the act or omission to act occurred. The court review shall be instituted by filing a petition for a hearing of the matter in the circuit court within 30 days after receipt from the department of notice of its determination of the matter. Such court is hereby vested with jurisdiction and it shall be its duty to set the matter for hearing with written notice to the department, and thereupon to take testimony and examine into the facts of the case and determine whether the petitioner is entitled to relief and if so to grant it. Either the state or the aggrieved person may appeal to the Alabama court of civil appeals within 42 days from the entry of a judgment by the circuit court. (Acts 1973, No. 765, p. 1147, § 28.)

§ 32-8-6. Schedule of fees and commissions.

(a) There shall be paid to the department for issuing and processing documents required by this chapter a fee of $15.00 for each of the following transactions:

 (1) Each application for certificate of title;

 (2) Each application for replacement or corrected certificate of title;

 (3) Each application for certificate of title after transfer;

 (4) Each notice of security interest;

 (5) Each assignment by lienholder;

 (6) Each application for ordinary certificate of title upon surrender of a distinctive certificate; or

 (7) Each application for information as to the status of the title of a vehicle.

(b) The designated agents shall add the sum of $1.50 to each document processed for which this fee is charged to be retained as the agent's commission for services rendered, and all other fees collected shall be remitted to the department.

(c) If more than one transaction is involved in any application on a single vehicle and if supported by all required documents, the fee charged by the department and by the designated agent for processing and issuing shall be considered as only one transaction for which the designated agent shall receive and retain $1.50 and shall collect and remit to the department $15.00. (Acts 1973, No. 765, p. 1147, § 31; Acts 1988, 1st Sp. Sess., No. 88-730, p. 127, § 1.)

The 1988, 1st Sp. Sess., amendment, effective December 1, 1988, rewrote subsection (a); in subsection (b) substituted "the sum of $1.50" for "the sum of $.50," substituted "this fee" for "a fee," and substituted "the agent's commis-sion" for "his commission"; and in subsection (c) substituted "retain $1.50" for "retain $.50," and substituted "remit to the department $15.00" for "remit to the department $3.00."

§ 32-8-7. Additional commission fee.

The probate judge or other county official who is authorized and required by law to issue license plates and who is required to process applications for certificate of title by this chapter may collect and retain a $1.50 commission fee for each application processed in addition to the $1.50 designated agent commission fee to further defray the cost of processing and mailing of title applications. (Acts 1973, No. 765, p. 1147, § 32; Acts 1988, 1st Sp. Sess., No. 88-730, p. 127, § 2.)

The 1988, 1st Sp. Sess., amendment, effective December 1, 1988, rewrote this section, which formerly related to the disposition of a portion of certain fees.

§ 32-8-8. Right of inspection for violations.

(a) Any sheriff, deputy sheriff, policeman of an incorporated municipality or duly authorized representative of the department of public safety or department of revenue of this state may enter into the premises of any automobile salvage dealer, junkyard, automobile or other motor vehicle dealer licensed therefor by the state of Alabama or any political subdivision thereof and inspect the identification numbers of all motor vehicles or parts thereof contained on said premises, at any time of the day or night in order to enforce the provisions of this chapter.

(b) Any sheriff, deputy sheriff, policeman of an incorporated municipality or duly authorized commissioned law-enforcement officer of the department of public safety or the department of revenue of this state shall have the power to serve and execute any and all search warrants obtained in accordance with law for the purposes of the provisions of this chapter.

(c) Interference by any person with proper inspection by lawful officers as authorized by this section is a misdemeanor. (Acts 1973, No. 765, p. 1147, § 42.)

Cited in Cotton v. State, 523 So. 2d 467 (Ala. Crim. App. 1986).

§ 32-8-9. Forms and rules.

The department shall provide each designated agent with a supply of forms and the rules and regulations provided for in this chapter, and shall furnish each designated agent with at least five copies thereof. (Acts 1973, No. 765, p. 1147, § 48.)

§ 32-8-10. Enforcement of chapter.

The department is charged with the enforcement of the provisions of this chapter and it is hereby authorized and empowered to call upon any and all law-enforcement agencies and officers of this state for such assistance as it may deem necessary in order to assure such enforcement; and it shall be the duty of such law-enforcement agencies and officers to render such assistance to the department when called upon by it to so do. (Acts 1973, No. 765, p. 1147, § 47.)

§ 32-8-11. Aiding, abetting, etc., in violations.

A person who, whether present or absent, aids, abets, induces, procures or causes the commission of an act which if done directly by him, would be a felony or a misdemeanor under a provision of this chapter, is guilty of the same felony or misdemeanor. (Acts 1973, No. 765, p. 1147, § 43.)

§ 32-8-12. Offenses constituting felonies.

A person is guilty of a felony who, with fraudulent intent:
(1) Alters, forges or counterfeits a certificate of title;
(2) Alters or forges an assignment of a certificate of title, or an assignment or release of a security interest, on a certificate of title or a form the department prescribes;
(3) Has possession of or uses a certificate of title, knowing it has been altered, forged or counterfeited; or
(4) Uses a false or fictitious name or address, or makes a material false statement, or fails to disclose a security interest, or conceals any other material fact, in an application for a certificate of title. (Acts 1973, No. 765, p. 1147, § 44.)

Fraudulent intent must be alleged. — An indictment under this section is defective where it omits the all-important element of fraudulent intent. Felder v. State, 512 So. 2d 817 (Ala. Crim. App. 1987).

Fraudulent intent is a question of fact to be resolved by jury. — Lucas v. State, 406 So. 2d 1070 (Ala. Crim. App. 1981).

Cited in State v. Spurlock, 393 So. 2d 1052 (Ala. Crim. App. 1981); Felder v. State, 515 So. 2d 17 (Ala. Civ. App. 1987).

§ 32-8-13. Offenses constituting misdemeanors.

A person is guilty of a misdemeanor who:
(1) With fraudulent intent, permits another, not entitled thereto, to use or have possession of a certificate of title;
(2) Willfully fails to mail or deliver a certificate of title or application therefor to the department within 10 days after time required by this chapter;
(3) Willfully fails to deliver to his transferee a certificate of title within 10 days after the time required by this chapter; or
(4) Knowingly and willfully commits a fraud in any application for a title or registration; or
(5) Willfully violates any other provision of this chapter, except as otherwise provided in this chapter. (Acts 1973, No. 765, p. 1147, § 45.)

Cited in State v. Spurlock, 393 So. 2d 1052 (Ala. Crim. App. 1981); Treadwell Ford, Inc. v. Campbell, 485 So. 2d 312 (Ala. 1986).

§ 32-8-14. Penalties.

Unless another penalty is provided in this chapter:

(1) FELONIES. — A person convicted of a felony for the violation of a provision of this chapter is punishable by a fine of not less than $500.00 nor more than $5,000.00, or by imprisonment for not less than one year nor more than 10 years, or by both such fine and imprisonment.

(2) MISDEMEANORS. — A person convicted of a misdemeanor for the violation of a provision of this chapter is punishable by a fine of not more than $500.00 or by imprisonment for not more than six months, or by both such fine and imprisonment. (Acts 1973, No. 765, p. 1147, § 46.)

Cited in State v. Spurlock, 393 So. 2d 1052 (Ala. Crim. App. 1981).

ARTICLE 2.

CERTIFICATE OF TITLE.

Collateral references. — Liability of state, in issuing automobile certificate of title, for failure to discover title defect. 28 ALR4th 184.

§ 32-8-30. Certificate required for certain motor vehicles, mobile homes, and travel trailers; cancellation of title to certain mobile homes affixed to realty; reapplication for certificate when mobile home is detached; penalty.

(a) Except as provided in section 32-8-31, every owner of a motor vehicle designated a 1975 year model, and all models subsequent thereto which is in this state and which is required to be registered under the motor vehicle laws of this state and for which no certificate of title has been issued by the department, shall make application to a designated agent as herein defined for a certificate of title to the vehicle.

(b) Except as provided in section 32-8-31, every owner of a mobile home designated a 1990 year model, and all models subsequent thereto which is in this state and for which no certificate of title has been issued by the department, shall make application to a designated agent as herein defined for a certificate of title to the mobile home, or to each unit thereof if the mobile home consists of more than one unit.

(c) If a mobile home is affixed to a parcel of real property and the ownership of mobile home and real property is identical, the owner or owners may obtain from the Alabama department of revenue a cancellation of title to the mobile home by delivering to the department, the following:

(1) The certificate of title to the mobile home, or each separate certificate of title if the mobile home consists of more than one unit;

(2) A certified copy of the deed or other instruments of conveyance to the realty to which the mobile home has become affixed;

(3) An affidavit executed by all who have an ownership interest in the mobile home and the realty to which the mobile home has become affixed to the effect that the mobile home is affixed to the realty described in the deed;

(4) Lien release from lienholder as recorded on the face of the certificate of title.

If a mobile home for which the certificate of title has been cancelled as provided in this subsection is subsequently detached from the realty to which it became affixed, the owner or owners must reapply for a new certificate of title, provide an abstract of land title showing ownership of the mobile home and realty and any changes, if any, since the previous cancellation of the certificate of title, and pay the required fee specified in section 32-8-6, for the mobile home, or if in more than one section, for each component unit.

(d) Except as provided in section 32-8-31, every owner of a travel trailer designated a 1990 year model, and all models subsequent thereto which is in this state and which is required to be registered under the motor vehicle laws of this state and for which no certificate of title has been issued by the department, shall make application to a designated agent as herein defined for a certificate of title to the travel trailer.

(e) Any dealer, acting for himself or another, who sells, trades or otherwise transfers any vehicle required to be titled under this chapter who does not comply with the provisions of this chapter shall be guilty of a misdemeanor and upon conviction shall be fined in a sum not exceeding $500.00. (Acts 1973, No. 765, p. 1147, § 2; Acts 1989, No. 89-918, § 2.)

The 1989 amendment, effective May 19, 1989, redesignated former subsection (b) as subsection (e), and added subsections (b) through (d).

Cited in Eleven Autos. v. State ex rel. Graddick, 384 So. 2d 1129 (Ala. Civ. App. 1980); Harwell v. First Nat'l Bank (In re Sewell), 32 Bankr. 116 (Bankr. N.D. Ala. 1983); Southtrust Bank v. Toffel (In re Blackerby), 53 Bankr. 649 (Bankr. N.D. Ala. 1985); Underwood v. Kensington Mtg. & Fin. Co. (In re Tuders), 77 Bankr. 904 (Bankr. N.D. Ala. 1987).

§ 32-8-31. Exemptions.

No certificate of title need be obtained for:

(1) A vehicle owned by the United States or any agency thereof;

(2) A vehicle owned by a manufacturer or dealer and held for sale, even though incidentally moved on the highway or used for purposes of testing or demonstration, or a vehicle used by a manufacturer solely for testing;

(3) A vehicle owned by a nonresident of this state and not required by law to be registered in this state;

(4) A vehicle regularly engaged in the interstate transportation of persons or property for which a currently effective certificate of title has been issued in another state;

(5) A vehicle moved solely by animal power;

(6) An implement of husbandry;

(7) Special mobile equipment;

(8) A pole trailer;

(9) Mobile homes, travel trailers, and mobile trailers designated 1989 year models and prior year models. (Acts 1973, No. 765, p. 1147, § 3; Acts 1989, No. 89-918, § 3.)

The 1989 amendment, effective May 19, 1989, rewrote subdivision (9).

Cited in General Elec. Credit Corp. v. Humble, 532 F. Supp. 703 (M.D. Ala. 1982); Harwell v. First Nat'l Bank (In re Sewell), 32 Bankr. 116 (Bankr. N.D. Ala. 1983); Underwood v. Kensington Mtg. & Fin. Co. (In re Tuders), 77 Bankr. 904 (Bankr. N.D. Ala. 1987).

§ 32-8-32. Prerequisite to issuance of license plates.

No motor vehicle license (or license plate) may be issued and no motor vehicle license (or license plate) may be transferred for use on a motor vehicle required to be titled under this chapter except on presentation by the owner to the judge of probate or other issuing officer, the copy of an application for a certificate of title to such vehicle, a certificate of title to such vehicle, a duplicate certificate of title to such vehicle where the original is held by a lienholder, or a copy of the application for a replacement certificate of title; provided however, when the owner of a motor vehicle has complied with the provisions of this section in licensing a motor vehicle transferred to him this section shall not apply thereafter to the renewal of such license by such owner of such motor vehicle. (Acts 1973, No. 765, p. 1147, § 33.)

Cross references. — As to staggered system of registration for the annual issuance of motor vehicle licenses, see §§ 32-6-60 through 32-6-67. As to this section being construed in pari materia with subdivision 2 of division 1 of article 2 of chapter 6 of Title 32, see § 32-6-66.

§ 32-8-33. Prerequisite to assessment for ad valorem taxes.

No motor vehicle required to be titled under the provisions of this chapter shall be assessed for ad valorem taxes by a tax assessor, director of revenue or other county official authorized and required by law to assess motor vehicles for ad valorem taxes unless the application therefor is accompanied by a copy of an application for a certificate of title to such vehicle, a certificate of title to such vehicle, a duplicate certificate of title to such vehicle where the original is held by a lienholder, or a copy of an application for a replacement certificate of title; provided, however, when the owner of a motor vehicle has complied with the provisions of this section in licensing a motor vehicle or having the license for a motor vehicle transferred to him this section shall not apply thereafter to the renewal of such license by such owner of such motor vehicle. (Acts 1973, No. 765, p. 1147, § 32A.)

Cross references. — As to staggered system of registration for the annual issuance of motor vehicle licenses, see §§ 32-6-60 through 32-6-67. As to this section being construed in pari materia with subdivision 2 of division 1 of article 2 of chapter 6 of Title 32, see § 32-6-66.

§ 32-8-34. Designated agents of department.

(a) Each judge of probate, commissioner of licenses, director of revenue or other county official in this state authorized and required by law to issue motor vehicle license tags shall by virtue of his office be a designated agent of the department. Such probate judges, commissioners of licenses, directors of revenue or other county officials may perform their duties under this chapter either personally or through any of their deputies.

(b) Every dealer, as defined in this chapter, shall be a designated agent of the department. Such dealers may perform their duties under this chapter either personally or through any of their officers or employees; provided, that such dealer or persons shall enter into a bond with a corporate surety authorized to do business in this state as surety thereon, payable to the state of Alabama in a sum to be determined by the department, but in no event less than $5,000.00, conditioned on the faithful performance of their duties under this chapter. In lieu of such bond, such dealer may file a condensed balance sheet as of a date not more than three months prior to July 1 each year in a form prescribed by the department and sworn to by such dealer, evidencing a net worth of not less than $25,000.00.

(c) The department may appoint other persons as its designated agents; provided, that such appointee shall enter into a bond as provided in the preceding subsection (b); provided, that full-time bonded employees of the department of revenue may serve as designated agents without additional bond. (Acts 1973, No. 765, p. 1147, § 4.)

§ 32-8-35. Application for first certificate.

(a) The application for the first certificate of title of a vehicle in this state shall be made by the owner to a designated agent, on the form the department prescribes, and shall contain:

(1) The name, current residence and mailing address of the owner;

(2) A description of the vehicle including the following data: year, make, model, vehicle identification number, type of body, the number of cylinders and whether new or used;

(3) The date of purchase by applicant, the name and address of the person from whom the vehicle was acquired and the names and addresses of any lienholders in the order of their priority and the dates of their security agreements; and

(4) Such other information as the department may require.

(b) If the application is for a vehicle purchased from a dealer, it shall contain the name and address of any lienholder holding a security interest created or reserved at the time of the sale and the date of his security agreement and must be signed by the dealer as well as the owner, and the designated agent shall promptly mail or deliver the application to the department.

(c) If the application is for a new vehicle, it shall be accompanied by the certified manufacturer's statement of origin showing proper assignments to the applicant. The manufacturer upon the shipment of a motor vehicle into this state shall forthwith furnish the dealer with such a certified statement of origin.

(d) Each application shall contain or be accompanied by the certificate of a designated agent that the vehicle has been physically inspected by him, that the vehicle identification number and descriptive data shown on the application, pursuant to the requirements of subsection (a) (2) of this section, are correct, and that he identified the person signing the application and witnessed the signature.

(e) If the application is for a first certificate of title on a vehicle other than a new vehicle, then the application shall conform with the requirements of this section; except, that in lieu of the manufacturer's statement of origin, the application shall be accompanied by a copy of the notarized bill of sale of said motor vehicle whereby the applicant claims title or in lieu thereof certified copies of the last two years' license tag and tax receipts and such other information as the department may reasonably require to identify the vehicle and to enable the department to determine the ownership of the vehicle and the existence or nonexistence of security interests in it.

(f) If the application refers to a vehicle last previously registered in another state or country, the application shall contain or be accompanied by:

(1) Any certificate of title issued by the other state or country;

(2) Such other information and documents as the department may reasonably require to establish the ownership of the vehicle and the existence or nonexistence of security interests in it; and

(3) The certificate of a designated agent that the vehicle has been physically inspected by him, that the vehicle identification number and descriptive data shown on the application pursuant to subsection (a) (2) of this section are correct and such other proof of the identity of the vehicle as the department may reasonably require.

(g) Every designated agent within this state shall, no later than the next business day after an application is received by him, forward the same to the department by mail, postage prepaid, with such other evidence of title as may have been delivered to him by the applicant, along with the required fee as hereinafter provided. (Acts 1973, No. 765, p. 1147, § 5; Acts 1977, No. 252, p. 329, § 1.)

Inspection. — The required inspection is made by the department of revenue, not the department of safety. A reading of this section shows that the inspection is for the purpose of determining that the vehicle for which new plates are being sought is the one described in the application for a new certificate of title. Treadwell Ford, Inc. v. Campbell, 485 So. 2d 312 (Ala. 1986), appeal dismissed, — U.S. —, 108 S. Ct. 2007, 100 L. Ed. 2d 596 (1988).

Cited in Freeman v. First State Bank, 401 So. 2d 11 (Ala. 1981).

§ 32-8-36. Application for certificate with bond or cash.

If the department is not satisfied as to the ownership of the vehicle or that there are no undisclosed security interests in it, the department may accept the application but shall either:

(1) Withhold issuance of a certificate of title until the applicant presents documents reasonably sufficient to satisfy the department as to the applicant's ownership of the vehicle and that there are no undisclosed security interests on it; or

(2) As a condition of issuing a certificate of title, require the applicant to file with the department a bond in the form prescribed by the department and executed by the applicant, and either accompanied by the deposit of cash with the department or also executed by a person authorized to conduct a surety business in this state. The bond shall be in an amount equal to one and one-half times the value of the vehicle as determined by the department and conditioned to indemnify any prior owner and lienholder and any subsequent purchaser of the vehicle or person acquiring any security interest in it, and their respective successors in interest, against any expense, loss or damage, including reasonable attorney's fees, by reason of the issuance of the certificate of title of the vehicle or on account of any defect in or undisclosed security interest upon the right, title and interest of the applicant in and to the vehicle. Any such interested person has a right of action to recover on the bond for any breach of its conditions, but the aggregate liability of the surety to all persons shall not exceed the amount of the bond. The bond, and any deposit accompanying it, shall be returned at the end of three years or prior thereto if the vehicle is no longer registered in this state and the currently valid certificate of title is surrendered to the department, unless the department has been notified of the pendency of an action to recover on the bond. (Acts 1973, No. 765, p. 1147, § 10.)

§ 32-8-37. Check of vehicle identification number against list of stolen vehicles; issuance of certificate; records.

(a) The department upon receiving an application for certificate of title shall check the vehicle identification number shown in the application against the record of stolen or converted vehicles maintained by it.

(b) The department shall examine each application received and, when satisfied that the applicant is entitled to the issuance of a certificate of title, shall issue a certificate of title to the vehicle on the form prescribed by the department.

(c) The department shall maintain a record of all certificates of title issued pursuant to the provisions of this chapter:

(1) Under a distinctive title number assigned to the vehicle;

(2) Under the vehicle identification number;

(3) Under the name of the owner; and

(4) In the discretion of the department, by any other method the department determines. (Acts 1973, No. 765, p. 1147, § 6.)

§ 32-8-38. Use of duplicate copy of application as permit to operate motor vehicle; return of duplicate and tags upon refusal to issue certificate.

(a) The rules and regulations promulgated by the department shall make suitable provisions for the use by an applicant of the duplicate copy of his application for a certificate of title to serve as a permit for the operation of the motor vehicle described in the application until the department either issues the certificate of title of such motor vehicle or refuses to issue the certificate; and every designated agent receiving an application for the certificate of title, when the provisions of this chapter have been otherwise complied with, shall deliver to the applicant the duplicate copy of his application which shall contain a suitable permit for the purposes mentioned in this subsection. After the certificate of title is issued, the owner's permit copy of the application for this certificate of title shall continue to serve as evidence of ownership and as a permit for the operation of the vehicle.

(b) In the event the department refuses to issue the certificate of title, the applicant shall, immediately upon receiving written notice from the department that such certificate will not be issued for the reason or reasons stated in the notice, deliver or mail to the department by registered or certified mail the duplicate copy of his application containing the permit mentioned in subsection (a) of this section and the current license tag which was issued for the vehicle; and the motor vehicle described in said application shall not be operated on the highways or other public places of this state after the applicant receives notice that the certificate will not be issued unless its operation is subsequently authorized by the department either by the issuance of a new permit or certificate of title. If for any reason the said duplicate copy of the application for certificate of title and the current license tag which were issued for the vehicle in question are not received by the department within 10 calendar days after the department mails written notice to the applicant that it will not issue the certificate of title applied for, the department, or, at the request of the department, any state highway patrolman, sheriff or other peace officer of this state is authorized and empowered to and shall require and compel the surrender of said duplicate copy of the application for certificate of title and the said current license tag; and the department, after it obtains possession of said duplicate copy of application for certificate of title and said current license tag, is authorized to retain same until it is satisfied that said applicant is entitled to receive a certificate of title to the vehicle in question. (Acts 1973, No. 765, p. 1147, § 7; Acts 1985, No. 85-705, p. 1158, § 1.)

§ 32-8-39. Contents and effect of certificate.

(a) Each certificate of title issued by the department shall contain:

(1) The date issued;

(2) The name and current address of the owner;

(3) The names and addresses of any lienholders in the order of priority as shown on the application, or if the application is based on a certificate of title, as shown on the certificate;

(4) The title number;

(5) A description of the vehicle including the following data: year, make, model, vehicle identification number, type of body, number of cylinders, whether new or used and if a new vehicle the date of the first sale of the vehicle for use; and

(6) Any other data the department prescribes.

(b) Unless security is furnished as provided in section 32-8-36, a distinctive certificate of title shall be issued for a vehicle last previously registered in another state or country, the laws of which do not require that lienholders be named on a certificate of title to perfect their security interests. The certificate shall contain the legend, "This vehicle may be subject to an undisclosed lien" and may contain any other information the department prescribes. If no notice of a security interest in the vehicle is received by the department within four months from the issuance of the distinctive certificate of title, the department shall, upon application and surrender of the distinctive certificate, issue a certificate of title in ordinary form.

(c) The certificate of title shall contain forms for assignment and warranty of title by the owner, and for assignment and warranty of title by a dealer, and may contain forms for applications for a certificate of title by a transferee, the naming of a lienholder and the assignment or release of the security interest by a lienholder.

(d) A certificate of title issued by the department is prima facie evidence of the facts appearing on it.

(e) A certificate of title to a vehicle is not subject to garnishment, attachment, execution or other judicial process, but this subsection does not prevent a lawful levy upon the vehicle. (Acts 1973, No. 765, p. 1147, § 8.)

Certificate of title is only prima facie evidence of ownership, which can be contradicted by other evidence. Government Employees Ins. Co. v. Fulmer, 376 So. 2d 748 (Ala. Civ. App. 1979); City Car Sales, Inc. v. McAlpin, 380 So. 2d 865 (Ala. Civ. App. 1979), cert. denied, 380 So. 2d 869 (Ala. 1980); Eleven Autos. v. State ex rel. Graddick, 384 So. 2d 1129 (Ala. Civ. App. 1980).

In an action for detinue plaintiff seller was ruled not to be the rightful owner of a vehicle, despite having possession of legal title, where the court found that the deceased buyer had made modifications to the vehicle, and that the certificate of title was in possession of deceased at the time of death and had been recovered by plaintiff subsequent to the death of the buyer. Williams v. Seamon, 532 So. 2d 1028 (Ala. Civ. App. 1988).

Cited in Congress Fin. Corp. v. Funderburk, 416 So. 2d 1059 (Ala. Civ. App. 1982); Murray v. Dempsey, 521 So. 2d 1345 (Ala. Civ. App. 1988).

Collateral references. — Products liability: admissibility of experimental or test evidence to disprove defect in motor vehicle. 64 ALR4th 125.

§ 32-8-40. Distinctive certificates for certain vehicles.

If the department is not satisfied that there are no undisclosed security interests created before this chapter takes effect in a previously registered vehicle, the department may, in addition to the department's options under section 32-8-36, issue a distinctive certificate of title of the vehicle containing the legend, "This vehicle may be subject to an undisclosed lien" and containing any other information the department prescribes. (Acts 1973, No. 765, p. 1147, § 29.)

§ 32-8-41. Delivery of certificate.

The certificate of title shall be mailed to the first lienholder named in it or, if none, to the owner. (Acts 1973, No. 765, p. 1147, § 9; Acts 1985, No. 85-705, p. 1158, § 2.)

§ 32-8-42. Refusing certificate.

The department shall refuse issuance of certificate of title if any required fee is not paid or if the department has reasonable grounds to believe that:
  (1) The applicant is not the owner of the vehicle;
  (2) The application contains a false or fraudulent statement; or
  (3) The applicant fails to furnish required information or documents or any additional information the department reasonably requires. (Acts 1973, No. 765, p. 1147, § 11.)

§ 32-8-43. Lost, stolen or mutilated certificates.

(a) If a certificate of title is lost, stolen, mutilated or destroyed or becomes illegible, the first lienholder or, if none, the owner or legal representative of the owner named in the certificate, as shown by the records of the department, shall promptly make application for and may obtain a replacement upon furnishing information satisfactory to the department and payment of the fee as hereinafter required. The replacement certificate of title shall contain the legend, "This is a replacement certificate and may be subject to the rights of a person under the original certificate." It shall be mailed to the first lienholder named in it, or, if none, to the owner.

(b) The department shall not issue a new certificate of title to a transferee upon application made on a replacement certificate until 15 days after receipt of the application.

(c) A person recovering an original certificate of title for which a replacement has been issued shall promptly surrender the original certificate to the department. (Acts 1973, No. 765, p. 1147, § 12.)

§ 32-8-44. Transfer of ownership — Generally.

(a) If an owner transfers his interest in a vehicle, other than by the creation of a security interest, he shall, at the time of the delivery of the vehicle, execute an assignment and warranty of title to the transferee in the space provided therefor on the certificate or as the department prescribes, and cause the certificate and assignment to be mailed or delivered to the transferee or to the department.

(b) Except as provided in this section, the transferee shall, promptly after delivery to him of the vehicle, execute the application for a new certificate of title in the space provided therefor on the certificate or as the department prescribes, and cause the certificate and application to be mailed or delivered to a designated agent.

(c) Upon request of the owner or transferee, a lienholder in possession of the certificate of title shall, unless the transfer was a breach of his security agreement, deliver the certificate to the transferee. Upon receipt of the certificate the transferee shall make application to a designated agent for a new certificate. The delivery of the certificate does not affect the rights of the lienholder under his security agreement.

(d) If a security interest is reserved or created at the time of the transfer, the certificate of title shall be retained by or delivered to the person who becomes the lienholder and the parties shall comply with the provisions of section 32-8-62.

(e) Except as provided in section 32-8-45, and as between the parties, a transfer by an owner is not effective until the provisions of this section have been complied with. (Acts 1973, No. 765, p. 1147, § 13.)

Applicability. — This section is applicable only to 1975 or later model vehicles. Eleven Autos. v. State ex rel. Graddick, 384 So. 2d 1129 (Ala. Civ. App. 1980).

This section does not provide an exclusive method of transferring ownership. For example, nondelivery of a certificate of title does not prevent, as between the parties, the passage of title from the seller to the buyer. Likewise, depending upon the circumstances, it appears that a transfer may be effective as to third parties notwithstanding the parties' failure to transfer the certificate of title. To hold otherwise would, in effect, render a certificate of title the absolute evidence of ownership regardless of the circumstances. This section does not mandate such a conclusion. Congress Fin. Corp. v. Funderburk, 416 So. 2d 1059 (Ala. Civ. App. 1982).

This section is not the exclusive method of passing title to an automobile. Ranger Ins. Co. v. Whitlow, 514 So. 2d 1338 (Ala. 1987).

Evidence supported ownership of vehicle although title never transferred. — In a proceeding pursuant to § 20-2-93 where defendant admitted that his mother "sold" the automobile to him for $500, but contended that only $200 was ever paid to mother and that he thus "abandoned his contract" and mother still owned the vehicle and that title to the vehicle was in mother's name and was never transferred to him pursuant to this section, the undisputed fact of a "sale" of the vehicle to defendant, defendant's control and dominion of the vehicle on at least two occasions to make illicit controlled substance transactions, and the lack of any evidence to support the contention that defendant was not the owner of the automobile was sufficient to support the trial court's finding that defendant was the owner of the automobile. Eleven Autos. v. State ex rel. Graddick, 384 So. 2d 1129 (Ala. Civ. App. 1980).

Cited in Murray v. Dempsey, 521 So. 2d 1345 (Ala. Civ. App. 1988).

§ 32-8-45. Same — To or from dealer; records.

(a) If a dealer buys a vehicle and holds it for resale and procures the certificate of title from the owner or the lienholder within 15 days after delivery to him of the vehicle, he need not send the certificate to the department but, upon transferring the vehicle to another person other than by the creation of a security interest, shall promptly execute the assignment and warranty of title by a dealer, showing the names and addresses of the transferee and of any lienholder holding a security interest created or reserved at the time of the resale and the date of his security agreement, in the spaces provided therefor on the certificate or as the department prescribes, and mail or deliver the certificate to a designated agent with the transferee's application for a new certificate.

(b) Every dealer shall maintain for five years a record in the form the department prescribes of every vehicle bought, sold or exchanged by him or received by him for sale or exchange, which shall be open to inspection by representatives of the department and law-enforcement officers during reasonable business hours. (Acts 1973, No. 765, p. 1147, § 14.)

Cross references. — As to transfer of motor vehicle certificate of title to or from an automo- tive dismantler and parts recycler, see § 40-12-420.

§ 32-8-46. Same — By operation of law.

(a) If the interest of an owner in a vehicle passes to another other than by voluntary transfer, the transferee shall, except as hereinafter provided in subsection (b), promptly mail or deliver to a designated agent the last certificate of title, if available, and proof of the transfer, together with his application for a new certificate in the form the department prescribes.

(b) If the interest of the owner is terminated or the vehicle is sold under a security agreement by a lienholder named in the certificate of title, the transferee shall promptly make application to a designated agent for a new certificate in the form the department prescribes. The application shall be accompanied by the last certificate of title and an affidavit made by or on behalf of the lienholder that the vehicle was repossessed and that the interest of the owner was lawfully terminated or sold pursuant to the terms of the security agreement.

If the lienholder succeeds to the interest of the owner and holds the vehicle for resale, he need not secure a new certificate of title but, upon transfer to another person, shall promptly mail or deliver to the transferee the certificate, affidavit and other documents required by the department. The transferee shall promptly make application to a designated agent for a new certificate in the form prescribed by the department.

(c) Notwithstanding anything to the contrary contained in this section, a person holding a certificate of title whose interest in the vehicle has been extinguished or transferred other than by voluntary transfer shall forthwith mail or deliver the certificate to the department upon request of the

321

department; and the delivery of the certificate pursuant to the request of the department does not affect the rights of the person surrendering the certificate; and the action of the department in issuing a new certificate of title as provided herein is not conclusive upon the rights of an owner or lienholder named in the old certificate. (Acts 1973, No. 765, p. 1147, § 15.)

§ 32-8-47. Same — When department to issue new certificate.

(a) The department, upon receipt of a properly assigned certificate of title, with an application for a new certificate of title, the required fee and any other documents required by the department, shall issue a new certificate of title in the name of the transferee as owner and mail it to the first lienholder named in it or, if none, to the owner.

(b) The department, upon receipt of an application for a new certificate of title by a transferee other than by voluntary transfer, with proof of the transfer, the required fee and any other documents required by law, shall issue a new certificate of title in the name of the transferee as owner. If the outstanding certificate of title is not delivered to the department, the department shall make demand therefor from the holder thereof.

(c) A transferor of a vehicle other than a dealer transferring a new vehicle shall deliver to the transferee at the time of the delivery of possession of the vehicle the license plate for the vehicle; provided, that the license plate does not have to be delivered where a provision of law allows such plate to be retained by the owner of the vehicle.

(d) The department shall file every surrendered certificate of title, or a microfilm of every such certificate, for a period of time deemed necessary by it in order to permit the tracing of title of the vehicle designated therein. (Acts 1973, No. 765, p. 1147, § 16.)

§ 32-8-48. Repealed by Acts 1985, No. 85-650, p. 1010, § 1, effective July 1, 1985.

§ 32-8-49. Suspension or revocation of certificates.

(a) The department shall suspend or revoke a certificate of title, upon notice and reasonable opportunity to be heard in accordance with section 32-8-4, when authorized by any other provision of law or if it finds:

(1) The certificate of title was fraudulently procured or erroneously issued; or

(2) The vehicle has been scrapped, dismantled or destroyed.

(b) Suspension or revocation of a certificate of title does not, in itself, affect the validity of a security interest noted on it.

(c) When the department suspends or revokes a certificate of title, the owner or person in possession of it shall, immediately upon receiving notice of the suspension or revocation, mail or deliver the certificate to the department.

(d) Should any person fail to comply with the provisions of subsection (c) of this section the department shall seize and impound the certificate of title which has been revoked. It shall also be the duty of any peace officer, on notification to him by the department of the failure of a person to mail or deliver a revoked certificate of title to the department, to seize and mail or deliver to the department the revoked certificate of title. (Acts 1973, No. 765, p. 1147, § 25.)

Cited in Mobile Dodge, Inc. v. Alford, 487 So. 2d 866 (Ala. 1986).

ARTICLE 3.

SECURITY INTERESTS.

Cross references. — As to secured transactions generally, see § 7-9-101 et seq.

§ 32-8-60. Excepted liens and security interests.

This chapter does not apply to or affect:

(1) A lien given by statute or rule of law to a supplier of services or materials for the vehicle;

(2) A lien given by statute to the United States, this state or any political subdivision of this state;

(3) A security interest in a vehicle created by a manufacturer or dealer who holds the vehicle for sale, but a buyer in the ordinary course of trade from the manufacturer or dealer takes title free of the security interest. (Acts 1973, No. 765, p. 1147, § 18.)

For priority of conflicting security interests in an automobile, see First Dallas County Bank v. GMAC, 425 So. 2d 460 (Ala. Civ. App. 1982), aff'd, 425 So. 2d 464 (Ala. 1983).

Cited in First Dallas County Bank v. GMAC, 425 So. 2d 464 (Ala. 1983).

§ 32-8-61. Perfection of security interests.

(a) Unless excepted by this section, a security interest in a vehicle for which a certificate of title is required by the terms of this chapter is not valid against creditors of the owner or subsequent transferees or lienholders of the vehicle unless perfected as provided in this article.

(b) A security interest is perfected by the delivery to the department of the existing certificate of title, if any, an application for a certificate of title containing the name and address of the lienholder and the date of his security agreement and the required fee. It is perfected as of the time of its creation if the delivery is completed within 20 days thereafter, otherwise, as of the time of the delivery. (Acts 1973, No. 765, p. 1147, § 19; Acts 1977, No. 252, p. 329, § 2; Acts 1981, No. 81-312, p. 399, § 7-11-109(2); Acts 1987, No. 87-412, p. 606.)

Alabama Comment

The amendment to section 32-8-61 consists in deletion of subsection (c) thereof, which is replaced by subsection (2) of section 7-9-103.

Code commissioner's note. — The 1981 act that amended this section also made extensive changes to the U.C.C. Commentary was prepared for that act and the pertinent part for this section is set out above.

Subsection (b) of this section was enacted to protect a lienholder while awaiting issuance of a tardy certificate of title containing information as to lien. Lightfoot v. Harris Trust & Sav. Bank, 357 So. 2d 651 (Ala. Civ. App. 1977), aff'd, 357 So. 2d 654 (Ala. 1978).

Mistaken notation of release of lien did not operate as release. — Bank did not effectively release its lien on a vehicle simply by virtue of its mistakenly so noting on the certificate of title. Under § 32-8-64, the lien is not effectively released until the certificate of title indicating the release of the lien is mailed or delivered to the next lienholder named therein, or, if none, to the owner or any person who delivers to the lienholder an authorization

from the owner to receive the certificate. Southtrust Bank v. Toffel (In re Blackerby), 53 Bankr. 649 (Bankr. N.D. Ala. 1985).

Cited in Lightfoot v. Harris Trust & Sav. Bank, 357 So. 2d 654 (Ala. 1978); Roper v. Hardeman (In re B & M Contractors), 2 Bankr. 110 (Bankr. N.D. Ala. 1979); Harwell v. Warren, 20 Bankr. 1 (Bankr. N.D. Ala. 1980); Whittington v. Reeves, 11 Bankr. 302 (Bankr. N.D. Ala. 1981); Harwell v. First Nat'l Bank (In re Sewell), 32 Bankr. 116 (Bankr. N.D. Ala. 1983).

Collateral references. — Rights of seller of motor vehicle with respect to purchase price or security on failure to comply with statute requiring registration or notation of lien. 58 ALR2d 1358.

Priorities as between vendor's lien and subsequent title or security interest obtained in another state to which vehicle was removed. 42 ALR3d 1168.

§ 32-8-62. Procedure when owner creates security interest.

If an owner creates a security interest in a vehicle:

(1) The owner shall immediately execute the application in the space provided therefor on the certificate of title, or on a separate form the department prescribes to name the lienholder on the certificate showing the name and address of the lienholder and the date of his security agreement, and cause the certificate, application and the required fee to be delivered to the lienholder.

(2) The lienholder shall immediately cause the certificate, application and required fee to be mailed or delivered to the department.

(3) Upon request of the owner or subordinate lienholder, a lienholder in possession of the certificate of title shall either mail or deliver the certificate to the subordinate lienholder for delivery to the department, or, upon receipt from the subordinate lienholder of the owner's application and the required fee, mail or deliver them to the department with the certificate. The delivery of the certificate does not affect the rights of the first lienholder under his security agreement.

(4) Upon receipt of the certificate of title, application and the required fee, the department shall either endorse on the certificate or issue a new certificate containing the name and address of the new lienholder, and mail the certificate to the first lienholder named in it. (Acts 1973, No. 765, p. 1147, § 20.)

Collateral references. — Motor vehicle certificate of title or similar document as, in hands of one other than legal owner, indicia of ownership justifying reliance by subsequent purchaser or mortgagee without actual notice of other interests. 18 ALR2d 813.

§ 32-8-63. Assignment by lienholder.

(a) A lienholder may assign, absolutely or otherwise, his security interest in the vehicle to a person other than the owner without affecting the interest of the owner or the validity of the security interest, but any person without notice of the assignment is protected in dealing with the lienholder as the holder of the security interest and the lienholder remains liable for any obligations as lienholder until the assignee is named as lienholder on the certificate in the manner prescribed by the department.

(b) The department shall file each assignment received by the department with the required fee, and note the assignee as lienholder upon the record of notices of security interests maintained by the department. (Acts 1973, No. 765, p. 1147, § 21.)

§ 32-8-64. Release of security interest.

(a) Upon the satisfaction of a security interest in a vehicle for which the certificate of title is in the possession of the lienholder, he shall, within 10 days after demand execute a release of his security interest, in the space provided therefor on the certificate or as the department prescribes, and mail or deliver the certificate and release to the next lienholder named therein, or, if none, to the owner or any person who delivers to the lienholder an authorization from the owner to receive the certificate. The owner, other than a dealer holding the vehicle for resale, shall promptly cause the certificate and release to be mailed or delivered to the department, which shall release the lienholder's rights on the certificate or issue a new certificate.

(b) Upon the satisfaction of a security interest in a vehicle for which the certificate of title is in the possession of a prior lienholder, the lienholder whose security interest is satisfied shall within 10 days after demand execute a release in the form the department prescribes and deliver the release to the owner or any person who delivers to the lienholder an authorization from the owner to receive it. The lienholder in possession of the certificate of title shall either deliver the certificate to the owner, or the person authorized by him, for delivery to the department, or, upon receipt of the release, mail or deliver it with the certificate to the department which shall release the subordinate lienholder's rights on the certificate or issue a new certificate.

(c) Upon receipt of the releases of security interests mentioned in subsections (a) and (b) of this section, the department shall file each release in the manner prescribed by the department and note the same upon the records of notices of security interests maintained by it. (Acts 1973, No. 765, p. 1147, § 22.)

Mistaken notation of release of lien did not operate as release. — Bank did not effectively release its lien on a vehicle simply by virtue of its mistakenly so noting on the certificate of title. Under this section, the lien is not effectively released until the certificate of title indicating the release of the lien is mailed or delivered to the next lienholder named therein, or, if none, to the owner or any person who delivers to the lienholder an authorization from the owner to receive the certificate. Southtrust Bank v. Toffel (In re Blackerby), 53 Bankr. 649 (Bankr. N.D. Ala. 1985).

§ 32-8-65. Duty of lienholder to disclose information.

A lienholder named in a certificate of title shall, upon written request of the owner or of another lienholder named on the certificate, disclose any pertinent information as to his security agreement and the indebtedness secured by it. (Acts 1973, No. 765, p. 1147, § 23.)

§ 32-8-66. Exclusiveness of procedure.

The method provided in this article of perfecting and giving notice of security interest in motor vehicles required to be titled under the terms of this chapter or titled under the terms hereof, shall be exclusive.

Security interests in motor vehicles required to be titled or which are titled under this chapter, are hereby exempted from the provisions of law which otherwise require the filing or recording of financing statements or of other instruments creating or evidencing security interests.

Security interests in motor vehicles not required to be titled under this chapter or not titled under the terms hereof, which are perfected under any other applicable laws of this state shall not be affected by this chapter but shall continue in all respects to be governed by such other laws of this state. (Acts 1973, No. 765, p. 1147, § 24.)

For priority of conflicting security interests in an automobile, see First Dallas County Bank v. GMAC, 425 So. 2d 460 (Ala. Civ. App. 1982), aff'd, 425 So. 2d 464 (Ala. 1983).

Cited in Southtrust Bank v. Toffel (In re Blackerby), 53 Bankr. 649 (Bankr. N.D. Ala. 1985).

§ 32-8-67. Filing and recording of notices of security interests; examination of record.

(a) The department shall file each notice of security interest received by the department with the required fee and maintain a record of all notices of security interests filed by the department:

(1) Alphabetically, under the name of the owner;

(2) Under the vehicle identification number;

(3) Under the certificate of title number; and

(4) In the discretion of the department, by any other method it determines.

(b) The department before issuing or reissuing a certificate of title shall check the name of the owner and the certificate of title number of the vehicle against the record provided for in subsection (a). (Acts 1973, No. 765, p. 1147, § 30.)

ARTICLE 4.

ANTITHEFT LAWS.

§ 32-8-80. Exceptions from provisions of article.

This article does not apply to the following unless a title certificate has been issued on such vehicles under this chapter:

(1) A vehicle moved solely by animal power;

(2) An implement of husbandry;

(3) Special mobile equipment; and

(4) A self-propelled wheelchair or invalid tricycle. (Acts 1973, No. 765, p. 1147, § 34.)

§ 32-8-81. Unauthorized use of vehicles.

A person not entitled to possession of a vehicle who, without the consent of the owner and with intent to deprive him, temporarily or otherwise, of the vehicle or its possession, takes, uses or drives the vehicle is guilty of a felony. (Acts 1973, No. 765, p. 1147, § 36.)

Cited in State v. Spurlock, 393 So. 2d 1052 (Ala. Crim. App. 1981).

§ 32-8-82. Unauthorized receiving or disposing of vehicles.

A person not entitled to the possession of a vehicle who receives, possesses, conceals, sells or disposes of it, knowing it to be stolen or converted under circumstances constituting a crime, is guilty of a felony. (Acts 1973, No. 765, p. 1147, § 36.)

Cited in State v. Spurlock, 393 So. 2d 1052 (Ala. Crim. App. 1981).

Collateral references. — Receiving property stolen in another state or country as receiving stolen property. 67 ALR2d 752.

§ 32-8-83. Unauthorized damaging or tampering with vehicles.

(a) A person who, willfully and without right to do so, damages a vehicle or damages or removes any of its parts or components is guilty of a misdemeanor.

(b) A person who, without right to do so and with intent to commit a crime, tampers with a vehicle, or goes in or on it, or works or attempts to work any of its parts or components, or sets or attempts to set it in motion is guilty of a misdemeanor. (Acts 1973, No. 765, p. 1147, § 37.)

Cited in State v. Spurlock, 393 So. 2d 1052 (Ala. Crim. App. 1981).

Collateral references. — Validity and construction of statute making it a criminal offense to "tamper" with motor vehicle or contents, or to obscure registration plates. 57 ALR3d 606.

§ 32-8-84. Reports to department of stolen, converted, recovered and unclaimed vehicles; suspension of registration of stolen or converted vehicles.

(a) A peace officer who learns of the theft of a vehicle not since recovered or of the recovery of a vehicle whose theft or conversion he knows or has reason to believe has been reported to the department shall forthwith report the theft or recovery to the department.

(b) An owner or a lienholder may report the theft of a vehicle, or its conversion if a crime, to the department, but the department may disregard the report of a conversion unless a warrant has been issued for the arrest of a person charged with the conversion. A person who has so reported the theft or conversion of a vehicle shall, forthwith after learning of its recovery, report the recovery to the department.

(c) An operator of a place of business for garaging, repairing, parking or storing vehicles for the public, in which a vehicle remains unclaimed for a period of 30 days, shall, within 30 days after the expiration of that period, report the vehicle as unclaimed to the department. Such report shall be on a form prescribed by the department.

A vehicle left by its owner whose name and address are known to the operator or his employee is not considered unclaimed. A person who fails to report a vehicle as unclaimed in accordance with this subsection forfeits all claims and liens for its garaging, repairing, parking or storing and is guilty of a misdemeanor punishable by a fine of not more than $100.00.

(d) The department shall maintain and appropriately index weekly cumulative public records of stolen, converted, recovered and unclaimed vehicles reported to it pursuant to this section. The department may make and distribute weekly lists of such vehicles so reported to it to peace officers upon request without fee and to others for the fee, if any, the department prescribes.

(e) The department may suspend the registration of a vehicle whose theft or conversion is reported to it pursuant to this section; until the department learns of its recovery or that the report of its theft or conversion was erroneous, it shall not issue a certificate of title for the vehicle. (Acts 1973, No. 765, p. 1147, § 38.)

§ 32-8-85. False report of theft or conversion.

A person who knowingly makes a false report of the theft or conversion of a vehicle to a peace officer or to the department is guilty of a misdemeanor. (Acts 1973, No. 765, p. 1147, § 39.)

Cited in State v. Spurlock, 393 So. 2d 1052
(Ala. Crim. App. 1981).

§ 32-8-86. Removed, falsified or unauthorized identification number, registration or license plate; seizure of vehicle, part, etc., when number altered, etc.; disposition of forfeited property.

(a) A person who willfully removes or falsifies an identification number of a vehicle, engine, transmission or other identifiable component part of a vehicle is guilty of a Class A misdemeanor and shall be punished as required by law.

(b) A person who, willfully and with intent to conceal or misrepresent the identity of a vehicle, engine, transmission or other identifiable component part of a vehicle or removes or falsifies an identification number of the same is guilty of a Class C felony and shall be punished as required by law.

(c) A person who buys, receives, possesses, sells or disposes of a vehicle, or an engine, transmission or other identifiable component part of a vehicle, knowing that an identification number of the same has been removed or falsified, is guilty of a Class A misdemeanor and shall be punished as required by law.

(d) A person who buys, receives, possesses, sells or disposes of a vehicle, engine, transmission or other identifiable component part of a vehicle, with knowledge that an identification number of same has been removed or falsified and with intent to conceal or misrepresent the identity of same is guilty of a Class C felony and shall be punished as required by law.

(e) A person who removes a license plate or tag from a vehicle or affixes to a vehicle a license plate or tag not authorized by law for use on it, in either case with intent to conceal or misrepresent the identity of a vehicle or its owner, is guilty of a Class A misdemeanor and shall be punished as required by law.

(f) As used in this section:

(1) IDENTIFICATION NUMBER. Such term includes an identifying number, serial number, engine number or other distinguishing number or mark placed on a vehicle, engine, transmission or other component part of a vehicle, by its manufacturer or by authority of the department or in accordance with the laws of another state or country.

(2) REMOVE. Such term includes deface, cover and destroy.

(3) FALSIFY. Such term includes alter and forge.

(4) IDENTIFIABLE COMPONENT PART. Such term includes any part of a vehicle that an identifying number stamped or placed on it by the manufacturer or other authorized person or any part that can be identified by other means as being a part of a particular vehicle.

(g) An identification number may be placed on a vehicle, engine, transmission, or other identifiable component part of a vehicle, by its manufacturer in the regular course of business or placed or restored on same by authority of the department without violating this section; an identification number so placed or restored is not falsified.

(h) Any vehicle, engine, transmission, or other identifiable component part, wherein the identification number or numbers appear to be altered, or removed may be seized and detained by law enforcement officials for a reasonable period of time for determination of the true identity of the vehicle, engine, transmission, or other component parts. Any item seized by law enforcement officials, wherein ownership cannot be determined shall be contraband and subject to forfeiture.

(i) Any seized item taken or retained under this section shall not be subject to replevin but is deemed to be in the custody of the state, county or municipal law enforcement agency subject only to the orders and judgment of the court having jurisdiction over the forfeiture proceedings.

(j) Any vehicle which has been reported stolen and subsequently recovered by law enforcement officials may be returned to the person claiming ownership upon proper ownership documentation. However, any recovered vehicle wherein ownership is in question shall be returned subject only to the orders of a circuit court having jurisdiction of the matter.

(k) No civil liability shall attach to any law enforcement official acting in good faith under this section.

(*l*) When property is forfeited under this section, the state, county, or municipal law enforcement agency may with approval of a court of competent jurisdiction:

(1) Retain it for official use.

(2) Have it placed in a crusher and destroyed.

(3) Any vehicle which is retained for official use under this section, shall be placed in a crusher and destroyed, upon its becoming unserviceable. (Acts 1973, No. 765, p. 1147, § 40; Acts 1984, 1st Ex. Sess., No. 84-795, p. 203.)

This section makes it a crime to possess a vehicle knowing that an identification number of the vehicle has been removed or falsified; however, the section fails to render such a vehicle contraband and no right is granted therein either to condemn it or for its forfeiture. Tucker Motor Co. v. Davenport, 396 So. 2d 101 (Ala. Civ. App. 1980), cert. denied, 396 So. 2d 105 (Ala. 1981).

This section is obviously penal in nature, for a violation thereof is made a misdemeanor. Penal statutes are to be strictly construed and all doubts concerning their interpretation are to be resolved in favor of the accused. State v. Honda, 387 So. 2d 219 (Ala. Civ. App. 1980).

Statute requires state to attempt to determine true identity of vehicle and thus the true owner. State v. One 1984 Camaro, 521 So. 2d 42 (Ala. Civ. App. 1988).

Once state shows that vehicle has altered numbers presumption arises that vehicle should be forfeited. However, the presumption can be rebutted by proof of original ownership or proof that the alteration is lawful due to a legitimate salvage operation. State v. One 1984 Camaro, 521 So. 2d 42 (Ala. Civ. App. 1988).

A condemnation or forfeiture right does not exist as to vehicles knowingly possessed in violation of this section. Tucker Motor Co. v. Davenport, 396 So. 2d 101 (Ala. Civ. App. 1980), cert. denied, 396 So. 2d 105 (Ala. 1981).

Subsection (c) of this section requires that the defendant possess the vehicle knowing that the vehicle identification number has been falsified. State v. Honda, 387 So. 2d 219 (Ala. Civ. App. 1980).

Cited in State v. Spurlock, 393 So. 2d 1052 (Ala. Crim. App. 1981); State v. Self, 492 So. 2d 319 (Ala. Crim. App. 1986); Barton v. State, 519 So. 2d 1344 (Ala. 1988).

§ 32-8-87. Dismantling, destroying or changing identity of vehicle; certificates of title to be cancelled; salvage certificates; dealer transport license; responsibilities of insurance company upon settlement of claims; "total loss" defined; penalties regarding removal, sale, etc., of vehicle identification numbers, certificates, etc.; restrictions on transfer of salvage vehicles; application for inspection of salvage vehicle; inspection fee; "component parts" defined; "rebuilt" certificate of title.

(a) Each owner of a motor vehicle and each person mentioned as owner in the last certificate of title who scraps, dismantles, destroys or changes the motor vehicle in such a manner that it is not the same motor vehicle described in the certificate of origin or certificate of title, shall as soon as practicable cause the certificate of origin or certificate of title, if any, and any other documents or information required by the department to be mailed or delivered to the department for processing. The department shall, with the consent of any holder of liens noted on the surrendered certificate, enter a cancellation upon its records. Upon cancellation of a certificate of origin or certificate of title in the manner prescribed by this section, the department shall cancel all certificates of origin or certificates of title and all memorandum certificates in that chain of title. A certificate of title for the vehicle shall not again be issued except upon application containing the information the department requires, accompanied by a certificate of inspection in the form and content as specified in this section.

No motor vehicle for which a salvage or junk certificate has been issued by this state or any other state shall be driven or operated on the highways or other public places of this state. However, a vehicle which is in this state and for which a salvage certificate has been issued, and the vehicle is being restored to its operating condition which existed prior to the event which caused the salvage certificate of title to issue, may be moved to and from repair points as necessary by the rebuilder to complete the restoration or may be moved as permitted by the department of revenue for inspection or for any other purpose. A valid Alabama dealer transport (DT) license plate must be displayed on the vehicle during its movement. Any person who violates this subsection shall, upon conviction, be guilty of a Class C misdemeanor and shall be punishable as required by law.

(b) When the frame or engine is removed from a motor vehicle and not immediately replaced by another frame or engine, or when an insurance company has paid money or made other monetary settlement as compensation for a total loss of any motor vehicle, such motor vehicle shall be considered to be salvage. The owner of every motor vehicle in which total loss or salvage has occurred shall, within 72 hours after such total loss or salvage occurs, make application for a salvage certificate of title and forward to the department the certificate of origin or certificate of title to the motor vehicle, whereupon the department shall process the certificate of origin or certificate of title in a

331

manner prescribed by law or regulation. An insurance company which pays money or makes other monetary settlement as compensation for total loss of a motor vehicle shall at the time of payment or monetary settlement obtain such vehicle's certificate of origin or certificate of title and, as soon as practicable after receiving them, shall forward them along with their application for a salvage certificate, to the department for processing. In the event the payment or monetary settlement was made because of the theft of the vehicle, which shall be considered a total loss as defined in this section, the insurance company shall forward the vehicle's properly assigned certificate of origin or certificate of title as provided herein, to the department as soon as practicable after the vehicle is recovered. When a stolen motor vehicle has been reported to the department in compliance with this section and is later recovered, and for which a salvage certificate has been issued, the owner recorded on the salvage certificate shall assign that certificate to the purchaser. Any person who violates this subsection shall, upon conviction, be guilty of a Class C misdemeanor and shall be punishable as required by law.

(c) If an insurance company acquires a motor vehicle in settlement of an insurance claim and holds the vehicle for resale and procures the certificate of origin or certificate of title from the owner or lienholder within 15 days after delivery of the vehicle to the insurance company, and if the vehicle was not a total loss as defined by this section, the insurance company need not send the certificate of origin or certificate of title to the department but, upon transferring the vehicle to another person, other than by the creation of a security interest, the insurance company shall complete an affidavit of acquisition and disposition of the motor vehicle on a form prescribed by the department and deliver the certificate of origin or certificate of title, affidavit and any other documents required by the department to the transferee at the time of delivery of the motor vehicle.

(d) For the purposes of this section, a total loss shall occur when an insurance company or any other person pays or makes other monetary settlement to any person when it is deemed to be uneconomical to repair the damaged vehicle. The compensation for total loss as defined in this subsection shall not include payments by an insurer or other person for medical care, bodily injury, vehicle rental or for anything other than the amount paid for the actual damage to the motor vehicle. A vehicle that has sustained minor damage as a result of theft or vandalism shall not be considered a total loss.

(e) It shall be unlawful for the owner of any junkyard, salvage yard, or motor vehicle dismantler and parts recycler or his agents or employees to have in their possession any motor vehicle which is junk or salvage or a total loss when the manufacturer's vehicle identification number plate(s), authorized replacement vehicle identification number plate(s), or serial plate(s) have been removed, unless previously required to be removed by a statute or law of this state or another jurisdiction. Any person who violates this subsection shall, upon conviction, be guilty of a Class C misdemeanor and shall be punishable as required by law.

(f) It shall be unlawful for any person, firm or corporation to possess, sell or exchange, offer to sell or exchange, or to give away any certificate of origin, certificate of title, salvage certificate of title, manufacturer's identification number plate(s), authorized replacement vehicle identification number plate(s), serial plate(s), or motor vehicle license plate(s) of any motor vehicle which has been scrapped, dismantled or sold as junk or salvage or as a total loss contrary to the provisions of this section, and every officer, agent or employee of any person, firm or corporation, and every person who shall authorize, direct, aid in or consent to the possession, sale or exchange or offer to sell, exchange or give away such certificate of origin, certificate of title, salvage certificate of title, manufacturer's vehicle identification number plate(s), authorized replacement vehicle identification number plate(s), serial plate(s), or motor vehicle license plate(s) contrary to the provisions of this section, shall, upon conviction, be guilty of a Class C misdemeanor and shall be punishable as required by law.

(g) The department is authorized to issue a salvage certificate of title for a fee of $15.00, on a form prescribed by the department which shall provide for assignments of this title. Such salvage certificate of title is to replace a certificate of origin or certificate of title required to be surrendered by this section. The department shall prescribe necessary forms and procedures to comply with the provisions of this subsection.

(h) It shall be unlawful for any person to sign as assignor or for any person to have in his possession a salvage certificate of title which has been signed by the owner as assignor without the name of the assignee and other information called for on the form prescribed by the department. Any person who violates this subsection, upon conviction, shall be guilty of a Class C misdemeanor and shall be punishable as required by law.

(i) Every owner of a salvage or junk motor vehicle who sells or transfers said vehicle shall provide at the time of such sale or transfer a properly executed assignment and warranty of title to the transferee in the space provided therefor on the salvage certificate of title or junk certificate of title or as the department prescribes. Any person who willfully violates this subsection shall, upon conviction, be guilty of a Class C misdemeanor and shall be punishable as required by law.

(j) The department may issue a certificate of title to any motor vehicle for which a salvage certificate has been issued by this or any other state, and such vehicle has, in this state, been completely restored to its operating condition which existed prior to the event which caused the salvage certificate of title to issue, provided that all requirements of this section have been met. However, no certificate of title shall be issued for any motor vehicle for which a "junk" certificate has been issued or for a vehicle which is sold "for parts only."

(k) Every owner of a salvage motor vehicle designated a 1975 year model and all models subsequent thereto which is in this state and which has been restored in this state to its operating condition which existed prior to the event which caused the salvage certificate of title to issue shall make application to the department for an inspection of the vehicle in the form and content as determined by the department. Each application for inspection of a salvage vehicle which has been so restored shall be accompanied by the following:

(1) The outstanding salvage certificate or out-of-state title previously issued for the salvage vehicle;

(2) Notarized bills of sale evidencing acquisition of all major component parts (listing the manufacturer's vehicle identification number of the vehicle from which the parts were removed, if parts contain or should contain the manufacturer's vehicle identification number) used to restore the vehicle and bills of sale evidencing acquisition of all minor component parts. Notarization shall not be required on bills of sale for minor component parts; provided, however, that a notarized bill of sale which lists the manufacturer's vehicle identification number of the vehicle from which the parts were removed, if parts contain or should contain the manufacturer's vehicle identification number shall be required for a transmission;

(3) Evidence that the owner is a licensed motor vehicle rebuilder as defined in section 40-12-390;

(4) The owner shall also provide a written affirmation which states the following:

a. He rebuilt the vehicle or supervised its rebuilders, and what has been done to restore the vehicle to its operating condition which existed prior to the event which caused the salvage certificate to issue;

b. He personally inspected the completed vehicle and it complies with all safety requirements set forth by the state of Alabama and any regulations promulgated thereunder;

c. The identification numbers of the restored vehicle and its parts have not, to the knowledge of the owner, been removed, destroyed, falsified, altered or defaced;

d. The salvage certificate document or out-of-state title certificate attached to the application has not to the knowledge of the owner been forged, falsified, altered or counterfeited;

e. All information contained on the application and its attachments is true and correct to the knowledge of the owner.

(*l*) The application fee for each inspection of a restored vehicle shall be $75.00, payable by certified funds to the department, which must accompany the application.

(1) All such application fees received by the department shall be applied toward the personnel and maintenance costs of the vehicle inspection program and such vehicle inspection program shall be conducted by the Alabama department of revenue, office of investigations and inspections. Upon receipt of the application for inspection, application fee of $75.00, its supporting documents and title fee of $15.00 (payable by certified funds to the department), the department shall require an inspection to be made of the title and the vehicle by qualified agents or law enforcement officers of the Alabama department of revenue.

(2) The inspection and certification shall include an examination of the vehicle and its parts to determine that the identification numbers of the vehicle or its parts have not been removed, falsified, altered, defaced, destroyed, or tampered with, that the vehicle information contained in the application for certificate of title and supporting documents is true and correct and that there are no indications that the vehicle or any of its parts are stolen. Such certification shall not attest to the roadworthiness or safety condition of the vehicle.

(m) Component parts are defined as:

(1) PASSENGER VEHICLES.

a. Major components:

1. Motor or engine.

2. Trunk floor pan or rear section and roof.

3. Frame or any portion thereof (except frame horn), or, in the case of a unitized body, the supporting structure which serves as the frame, except when it is a part of the trunk floor pan, or rear section and roof.

4. Cowl, firewall, or any portion thereof.

5. Roof assembly.

b. Minor components:

1. Each door allowing entrance to or egress from the passenger compartment.

2. Hood.

3. Each front fender or each rear fender when used with a rear section and roof.

4. Deck lid, tailgate or hatchback (whichever is present).

5. Each quarter panel.

6. Each bumper.

7. T-tops, moon roof, or whichever is present.

8. Transmission or trans-axle.

(2) TRUCK, TRUCK TYPE OR BUS TYPE VEHICLES.

a. Major components:

1. Motor or engine.

2. Transmission or trans-axle.

3. Frame or any portion thereof (except frame horn), or, in the case of a unitized body, the supporting structure which serves as the frame.

4. Cab.

5. Cowl or firewall or any portion thereof.

6. Roof assembly.

7. Cargo compartment floor panel or passenger compartment floor pan.

b. Minor components:

1. Each door.

2. Hood.

3. Grill, except on one ton or smaller trucks.

4. Each bumper.

5. Each front fender.

6. Roof panel and rear cab panel.

7. Each rear fender or side panel.

8. Pickup box.

9. Body or bed.

(3) MOTORCYCLE: — COMPONENT PARTS.

a. Engine or motor.

b. Transmission or trans-axle.

c. Frame.

d. Front fork.

e. Crankcase.

(n) A salvage vehicle which has been restored in this state to its operating condition which existed prior to the event which caused the salvage certificate of title to issue shall be issued a certificate of title which shall contain the word "rebuilt." However a passenger vehicle, truck type or bus type vehicle restored with a combination of no more than one major component part, as defined above, and no more than five minor component parts, as defined above; or a combination of no more than six minor component parts, as defined above, shall be issued a certificate of title without "rebuilt" appearing thereon. A motorcycle restored with less than two component parts, as defined above, shall be issued a certificate of title without "rebuilt" appearing thereon. (Acts 1973, No. 765, p. 1147, § 41; Acts 1985, No. 85-650, p. 1010, § 2; Acts 1987, No. 87-806, p. 1581, § 1; Acts 1988, 1st Sp. Sess., No. 88-730, p. 127, § 3; Acts 1989, No. 89-863.)

The 1988, 1st Sp. Sess., amendment, effective December 1, 1988, inserted "or may be moved as permitted by the department of revenue for inspection or for any other purpose" at the end of the second sentence of the second paragraph in subsection (a); substituted "serial plate(s), or motor vehicle license plate(s)" for "serial plate(s), motor vehicle license plate(s)" in subsection (f); substituted "a fee of $15.00" for "a fee of $4.00" in the first sentence of subsection (g); substituted "at the time of such sale or transfer" for "at the time of the delivery of the vehicle" in the first sentence of subsection (i); in paragraph (k)(3)a deleted "personally" preceding "rebuilt" and "supervised"; in subsection (l) divided the first paragraph into two paragraphs, designated the present second paragraph as subdivision (l)(1), designated the former second paragraph as subdivision (l)(2), inserted "application" preceding "fee" in the introductory sentence of subsection (l), and in subdivision (l)(1) substituted "application fees" for "inspection fees" in the first sentence, and rewrote the second sentence.

The 1989 amendment, effective July 1, 1989, rewrote subsection (d); in subdivision (k)(2) inserted "and bills of sale evidencing acquisition of all minor component parts" at the end of the first sentence, and added the last sentence; redesignated former subdivision (k)(3) as subdivision (k)(4); and added present subdivision (k)(3); in subsection (m), deleted paragraph (m)(1)a.2., which read "Transmission or trans-axle", redesignated the former subparagraphs (m)(1)a.3, through (m)(1)a.6. as subparagraphs (m)(1)a.2. through (m)(1)a.5., added subparagraph (m)(1)b.8., deleted former subparagraphs (m)(2)a.6. and (m)(2)a.7., which listed the pickup box and body or bed, redesignated subparagraphs (m)(2)a.8. and (m)(2)a.9. as (m)(2)a.6. and (m)(2)a.7., and added subparagraphs (m)(2)b.8. and (m)(2)b.9.; in subsection (n) substituted "no more than one major component part" for "no more than two major component parts" and "no more than five minor component parts" for "no more than four minor component parts" in the second sentence.

This section is not unconstitutional because it imposes strict liability without a requirement of intent or knowledge. State v. Spurlock, 393 So. 2d 1052 (Ala. Crim. App. 1981).

But is a valid and constitutional exercise of the state's police power. Its designation of the class described is not arbitrary or unreasonable nor does its proscription unequally apply to any member of the class. State v. Spurlock, 393 So. 2d 1052 (Ala. Crim. App. 1981).

This section bears a real and rational relationship to the state's police power and the means adopted thereunder to enforce such are not unreasonable. State v. Spurlock, 393 So. 2d 1052 (Ala. Crim. App. 1981).

The class defined by the statute is reasonable and not arbitrary or capricious. State v. Spurlock, 393 So. 2d 1052 (Ala. Crim. App. 1981).

The statute is equal and nondiscriminating in its application to all members of the class. State v. Spurlock, 393 So. 2d 1052 (Ala. Crim. App. 1981).

The regulations of subsection (c) apply to each member of the group equally. There is no discriminating effect of the statute on any class member. State v. Spurlock, 393 So. 2d 1052 (Ala. Crim. App. 1981).

As to the constitutionality of subsection (c) of this section, see Kelley v. State, 429 So. 2d 1184 (Ala. Crim. App. 1983).

Purpose. — This chapter was not enacted to prevent motor vehicle accidents, but to prevent motor vehicle thefts. The very title states that it is an antitheft act. The overall plan of the act shows exclusive attention to maintaining records of the identity and ownership of vehicles. Treadwell Ford, Inc. v. Campbell, 485 So. 2d 312 (Ala. 1986), appeal dismissed, — U.S. —, 108 S. Ct. 2007, 100 L. Ed. 2d 596 (1988).

Subsection (c) is not a part of the Uniform Motor Vehicle Certificate of Title and Antitheft Act and represents additional matter which Alabama has made a part of its Uniform Act. State v. Spurlock, 393 So. 2d 1052 (Ala. Crim. App. 1981).

This section is unique to Alabama and is not included in the acts of the other nine states which have adopted the Uniform Motor Vehicle Certificate of Title and Antitheft Act. State v. Spurlock, 393 So. 2d 1052 (Ala. Crim. App. 1981).

But was an addition to the Uniform Act. In making it a part of Alabama's Uniform Act, the legislature had the opportunity to conform it to the language of the various penal provisions within the Uniform Act. This omission, when considered in the context of the entire act, makes it clear that it was the intention of the legislature not to include any element of intent, willfulness or knowledge within the terms of subsection (c) of this section. State v. Spurlock, 393 So. 2d 1052 (Ala. Crim. App. 1981).

This section was added to address a problem not covered by the Uniform Act, that being the regulation of those businesses having the capability to easily conceal stolen motor vehicles

and sell or dismantle them and their parts with a minimum of risk and detection. State v. Spurlock, 393 So. 2d 1052 (Ala. Crim. App. 1981).

The legislature intended to exclude any element of intent, willfulness or knowledge from this section and did not intend to criminally punish the owner of one of the enumerated businesses vicariously for the negligent or criminal acts of his agent or employee that fall within the purview of this section. State v. Spurlock, 393 So. 2d 1052 (Ala. Crim. App. 1981).

This section was enacted to protect the public from evils and to prevent junkyards, scrap metal processing plants, and salvage yards throughout the state from becoming conduits of automobile theft rings and strip shops of stolen motor vehicles. State v. Spurlock, 393 So. 2d 1052 (Ala. Crim. App. 1981).

The crime defined in subsection (c) is the possession of a vehicle from which the identification materials have not been removed as required by law and not the possession of a stolen vehicle. State v. Spurlock, 393 So. 2d 1052 (Ala. Crim. App. 1981).

This section is not aimed at penalizing the possession of stolen motor vehicles. It penalizes the failure to remove and to mail or deliver the specified identification materials to the department of revenue as required by § 32-8-48. State v. Spurlock, 393 So. 2d 1052 (Ala. Crim. App. 1981).

This statute was not designed to govern or condemn the possession of stolen property. State v. Spurlock, 393 So. 2d 1052 (Ala. Crim. App. 1981).

Court could reasonably infer that identification numbers were not removed with intent to comply. — While it is true that subsection (a) requires the removal of the identification number plate in certain situations, the appellant failed to recognize that the same statute requires that the identification number plate be mailed or delivered to the department of revenue within 72 hours after the removal. Because this statutory requirement was not satisfied, it was reasonable for the trial judge to infer that the identification numbers were not removed with the intent to comply with the statute. Barton v. State, 519 So. 2d 1344 (Ala. 1988).

Violation of this chapter did not subject insurer to liability for negligence. Treadwell Ford, Inc. v. Campbell, 485 So. 2d 312 (Ala. 1986), appeal dismissed, — U.S. —, 108 S. Ct. 2007, 100 L. Ed. 2d 596 (1988).

Junkyard owner not vicariously liable through doctrine of respondeat superior. — This section does not place vicarious liability upon the junkyard owner for the acts of his agents or employees through the doctrine of respondeat superior. Without either (1) the "authorization, procurement, incitation or moral encouragement," or (2) the "knowledge plus acquiescence" of the principal in the acts of his agent or servant, the owner cannot be held criminally liable. State v. Spurlock, 393 So. 2d 1052 (Ala. Crim. App. 1981).

Junk dealers have been recognized as a separate and distinct class for various purposes. State v. Spurlock, 393 So. 2d 1052 (Ala. Crim. App. 1981).

Cited in State v. One 1984 Camaro, 521 So. 2d 42 (Ala. Civ. App. 1988).

§ 32-8-88. Motor vehicle theft facility prohibited; definitions; seizure and forfeiture of property; disposition of proceeds of forfeiture sale.

(a) For the purposes of this section, the following definitions shall apply:

(1) A theft facility means any area, building, storage lot, field, or any other premises or place where one or more persons are engaged in altering, dismantling, reassembling or in any way concealing or disguising the identity of a stolen motor vehicle; or any area, building storage lot, field, or any other premises or place where there are three or more stolen motor vehicles present or where there are component parts from three or more stolen vehicles present.

(2) For the purpose of this section, "major component part" means one of the following sub-assemblies of a motor vehicle regardless of its actual market value; front end assembly, including fenders, grill, hood, bumper and related parts; engine; transmission; T-Tops; rear clip assembly, including quarter panels and floor panel assembly, doors, tires, tire wheels, frame, and continuous treads and other devices.

(3) "Motor vehicle" includes every device in, upon, or by which any person or property is or may be transported or drawn upon a highway which is self-propelled or which may be connected to and towed by a self-propelled device, and also includes any and all other land based devices which are self-propelled but which are not designed for use upon a highway, including but not limited to farm machinery, bulldozers, and steam shovels.

(b) Any person who shall knowingly own, operate or conduct a theft facility or who knowingly aids and abets another person in owning, operating or conducting a theft facility shall be guilty of a Class C felony and shall be punishable as required by law. In addition to any punishment rendered, each such person convicted shall be subject to the laws regarding restitution of the state.

(c) Upon proper process and hearing as required by the state of Alabama in forfeiture proceedings, including notifying any lien holders, the following property may be seized and held for forfeiture, as described above, when any person is charged with a violation of this section, such forfeiture and sale to take place after conviction:

(1) Any engine, tool, machine, implement, device, chemical, or substance used or designed for altering, dismantling, reassembling or in any other way concealing or disguising the identity of a stolen motor vehicle or any major component part.

(2) Any stolen motor vehicle or major component part found at the site of a theft facility or any motor vehicle or major component part for which there is a probable cause to believe that it is stolen.

(3) A wrecker, car hauler, or any other motor vehicle that is used or has been used to convey or transport a stolen motor vehicle or major component part.

(d) All such proceeds of forfeiture and sale shall be divided equally between the district attorney's fund who proceeded with the forfeiture and sale and the Alabama department of public safety, auto theft division, or its successor.

(e) The records pertaining to a salvage vehicle, junk vehicle, new vehicle, rebuilt vehicle, or the parts of a vehicle, shall be available for inspection by an agent or employee of the department of public safety during normal business hours.

(f) Failure to allow inspection or interference with an agent or employee of the department of public safety inspecting the records of a rebuilder, salvage yard, motor vehicle dealer, reconditioner or salvage sales shall, upon conviction, be guilty of a Class A misdemeanor and shall be punishable as provided by law. (Acts 1985, No. 85-650, p. 1010, § 3.)

CHAPTER 9.

TRUCKS, TRAILERS AND SEMITRAILERS.

ARTICLE 1.

GENERAL PROVISIONS.

§ 32-9-1. Trailers.

Trailers, when used in a truck tractor-semitrailer-trailer combination may be operated on the national system of interstate and defense highways and other highways upon designation by the highway director and final approval by the governor. The highway director shall, as a minimum, designate those highways necessary to cause the state of Alabama to be in compliance with the Federal Surface Transportation Assistance Act of 1982.

Except as provided above, no person shall operate any trailer, as defined in this title, on any highway unless such trailer is operated for the purpose of constructing highways or other facilities of the state or a political subdivision thereof. The highway department is authorized to regulate the movement of such trailers from one job to another by special permits issued in the same manner as permits are issued under section 32-9-29. No trailer or semitrailer of any kind shall be used for the hauling of passengers for hire except as provided by article 2 of this chapter.

The provisions of this article relating to trailers shall not apply to the movement over the highways of trailers manufactured, reconditioned or repaired in this state when reasonably necessary for the delivery of such trailers to the owners or purchasers thereof outside the state; provided, that such movement shall be subject to special permit to be issued by the director of the highway department. Such permits may be issued and may be renewed upon such terms and conditions, in the interest of public safety and the preservation of the highways, as the director of the highway department may in his discretion require, and he may designate the route over which such trailers may be moved and the hours of movement thereof. (Acts 1927, No. 347, p. 348; Acts 1932, Ex. Sess., No. 58, p. 68; Code 1940, T. 36, § 80; Acts 1947, No. 690, p. 526; Acts 1965, 2nd Ex. Sess., No. 138, p. 190; Acts 1985, 2nd Ex. Sess., No. 85-912, p. 188, § 1.)

§ 32-9-2. Towing cotton wagons and module-movers.

The provisions of any other law or the provisions of any administrative rule, regulation or order to the contrary notwithstanding, it shall be lawful to tow cotton wagons and module-movers on the highways of the state during the daylight hours when such wagons or module-movers are being used to haul cotton from the field to the gin and to return them to the farm from the gin, but it shall not be lawful to tow such wagons or module-movers on any interstate or limited-access highway in the state; provided, that no more than two wagons shall be attached to one truck, the width of each wagon or module-mover shall not exceed 10 feet and the overall length of the wagons or module-mover and truck shall not exceed 85 feet. (Acts 1971, No. 2236, p. 3593; Acts 1987, No. 87-562, p. 875, § 1.)

§ 32-9-3. Enforcement of chapter.

Any peace officer, including sheriffs and their deputies, constables and their deputies, police officers and marshals of cities or incorporated towns, county police or patrols, state or county license inspectors and their deputies, state troopers and special officers appointed by any agency of the state of Alabama for the enforcement of its laws relating to motor vehicles, now existing or hereafter enacted, shall be authorized, and it is hereby made the duty of each of them to enforce the provisions of this chapter and to make arrests for any violation or violations thereof, without warrant, if the offense is committed in his presence, and with warrant if he does not observe the commission of the offense. If the arrest is made without warrant, the accused may elect to be immediately taken before the nearest court having jurisdiction, whereupon it shall be the duty of the officer to so take him. If the accused elects not to be so taken, then it shall be the duty of the officer to require of the accused a bail bond in a sum not to exceed $300.00, conditioned that the accused binds himself to appear in the nearest court having jurisdiction at the time fixed in the bond. In case the arrested person fails to appear on the day fixed, the bond shall be forfeited in the manner as is provided for the forfeiture of bonds in other cases. No officer shall be permitted to take a cash bond. The officer making the arrest and taking the bond shall report the same to the court having jurisdiction within 18 hours after taking such bond. (Acts 1932, Ex. Sess., No. 58, p. 68; Code 1940, T. 36, § 86.)

§ 32-9-4. Courts having jurisdiction.

All courts having jurisdiction of misdemeanors punishable by a fine of $500.00 or less and by imprisonment or hard labor, as above provided, shall have concurrent jurisdiction of the trial of all offenses under this chapter committed within their respective territorial jurisdictions. (Acts 1932, Ex. Sess., No. 58, p. 68; Acts 1939, No. 484, p. 687; Code 1940, T. 36, § 84.)

§ 32-9-5. Penalties.

The operation of any truck, semitrailer truck or trailer in violation of any section of this chapter or of the terms of any permit issued under this chapter, shall constitute a misdemeanor, and the owner thereof, if such violation was with his knowledge or consent, and the operator thereof shall, on conviction, be fined not less than $100.00 nor more than $500.00 and may also be imprisoned or sentenced to hard labor for the county for not less than 30 days nor more than 60 days. (Acts 1932, Ex. Sess., No. 58, p. 68; Acts 1939, No. 484, p. 687; Code 1940, T. 36, § 83.)

Imposition of penalty based on extent of truck's weight in excess of legal limit. — The more a truck is overweight, the more it endangers the safety of the public and contributes to the bad repair of our highway system. Thus, the imposition of a penalty based on the extent to which a truck's weight exceeds the maximum legal limit is logical in view of the legislature's purpose in enacting § 32-9-20. Curry v. State, 506 So. 2d 346 (Ala. Crim. App. 1986).

This section does not state that the penalty imposed upon an operator of a truck for the violation of § 32-9-20 should be calculated on the basis of the operator's degree of culpability in violating the truck weight restrictions. In fact, a violation of § 32-9-20 can be committed without regard to the intent or knowledge of the operator of the truck. Curry v. State, 506 So. 2d 346 (Ala. Crim. App. 1986).

Collateral references. — Power to limit weight of vehicle or load thereon with respect to use of highways. 26 ALR 747, 75 ALR2d 376.

Validity of regulation excluding or restricting use of automobiles in certain streets, on basis of weight or size. 121 ALR 586.

Construction and application of statute or ordinance designed to prevent use of vehicles or equipment thereof injurious to the highway. 134 ALR 550.

Interstate commerce clause or federal legislation thereunder as affecting state regulations as to size, dimensions and weight of motor vehicle carriers. 135 ALR 1362.

Violation of regulation governing size or weight of motor vehicles, or combinations of vehicles and loads, on the highway as basis of liability for personal injury, death, or damage to private property. 21 ALR3d 989.

§ 32-9-6. Disposition of fines and forfeitures.

All fines and forfeitures collected upon conviction or upon forfeiture of bail of any person charged with a violation of any of the provisions of this chapter constituting a misdemeanor, shall be, within 30 days after such fine or forfeiture is collected, forwarded to the state treasurer. All amounts received from such fines or forfeitures shall be credited to the state general fund. Failure, refusal or neglect to comply with the provisions of this section shall constitute misconduct in office and shall be ground for removal therefrom. All fines and forfeitures collected by district courts or municipal courts for violation of ordinances, whether for acts constituting violations of the provisions of this chapter or not, shall be paid into the treasury of such municipality in which the same were collected. (Acts 1932, Ex. Sess., No. 58, p. 68; Code 1940, T. 36, § 88; Acts 1943, No. 459, p. 421; Acts 1949, No. 518, p. 773, § 4; Acts 1951, No. 363, p. 658.)

ARTICLE 2.

SIZE AND WEIGHT.

§ 32-9-20. Schedule of restrictions.

It shall be unlawful for any person to drive or move on any highway in this state any vehicle or vehicles of a size or weight except in accordance with the following provisions:

(1) WIDTH. Vehicles and combinations of vehicles, operating on highways with traffic lanes 12 feet or more in width, shall not exceed a total outside width, including any load thereon, of 102 inches, exclusive of mirrors or other safety devices approved by the state highway department. The director of the state highway department may, in his discretion, designate other public highways for use by vehicles and loads with total outside widths not exceeding 102 inches, otherwise; vehicles and combinations of vehicles, operating on highways with traffic lanes less than 12 feet in width, shall not exceed a total outside width, including any load thereon, of 96 inches, exclusive of mirrors or other safety devices approved by the state highway department. No passenger vehicle shall carry any load extending beyond the line of the fenders. No vehicle hauling forest products or culvert pipe on any highway in this state shall have a load exceeding 102 inches in width.

(2) HEIGHT. No vehicle or semitrailer or trailer shall exceed in height 13½ feet, including load.

(3) LENGTH. No vehicle shall exceed in length 40 feet; except, that the length of a truck-semitrailer combination, semitrailers, including load, used in a truck tractor-semitrailer combination, shall not exceed 53 feet and semitrailers and trailers, including load, used in a truck tractor-semitrailer-trailer combination, shall not exceed 28½ feet each. For purposes of enforcement of this subdivision, lengths of semitrailers and trailers refer to the cargo carrying portion of the unit. Truck tractor units used exclusively in combinations transporting motor vehicles may directly carry a portion of the cargo, provided that such combinations are restricted to truck tractor-semitrailer combinations only and provided further that the overall length of these particular combinations shall not exceed 65 feet. No truck tractor-semitrailer combination used exclusively for transporting motor vehicles shall carry any load extending more than three feet beyond the front or four feet beyond the rear of such combination. No other vehicle operated on a highway shall carry any load extending more than a total of five feet beyond both the front and rear, inclusive, of the vehicle.

(4) WEIGHT.

a. The gross weight imposed on the highway by the wheels of any one axle of a vehicle shall not exceed 20,000 pounds, or such other weight, if any, as may be permitted by federal law to keep the state from losing federal funds; provided, that inadequate bridges shall be posted to define load limits.

b. For the purpose of this section, an axle load shall be defined as the total load transmitted to the road by all wheels whose centers are included between two parallel transverse vertical planes 40 inches apart, extending across the full width of the vehicle.

c. Subject to the limit upon the weight imposed upon the highway through any one axle as set forth herein, the total weight with load imposed upon the highway by all the axles of a vehicle or combination of vehicles shall not exceed the gross weight given for the respective distances between the first and last axle of the vehicle or combination of vehicles, measured longitudinally to the nearest foot as set forth in the following table:

COMPUTED GROSS WEIGHT TABLE:

For various spacings of axle groupings

Distance in feet between first and last axles of vehicle or combination of vehicles	Maximum load in pounds on all the axles				
	2 axles	3 axles	4 axles	5 axles	6 axles
8 or less	36,000	42,000	42,000		
9	38,000	42,500	42,500		
10	40,000	43,500	43,500		
11		44,000	44,000		
12		45,000	50,000	50,000	
13		45,500	50,500	50,500	
14		46,500	51,500	51,500	
15		47,000	52,000	52,000	
16		48,000	52,500	58,000	58,000
17		48,500	53,500	58,500	58,500
18		49,500	54,000	59,000	59,000
19		50,000	54,500	60,000	60,000
20		51,000	55,500	60,500	66,000
21		51,500	56,000	61,000	66,500
22		52,500	56,500	61,500	67,000
23		53,000	57,500	62,500	68,000
24		54,000	58,000	63,000	68,500
25		54,500	58,500	63,500	69,000
26		56,000	59,500	64,000	69,500

Distance in feet between first and last axles of vehicle or combination of vehicles	Maximum load in pounds on all the axles				
	2 axles	3 axles	4 axles	5 axles	6 axles
27		57,000	60,000	65,000	70,000
28		59,000	60,500	65,500	71,000
29		60,000	61,500	66,000	71,500
30			62,000	66,500	72,000
31			63,500	67,000	72,500
32			64,500	68,000	73,500
33			65,000	69,000	74,000
34			65,500	70,000	74,500
35			66,500	71,000	75,000
36			67,000	72,000	76,000
37			68,000	73,000	77,000
38			69,000	74,000	78,000
39			70,000	75,000	79,000
40			71,000	76,000	80,000
41			72,000	77,000	81,000
42			73,000	78,000	82,000
43			74,000	79,000	83,000
44 and over			75,000	80,000	84,000

Except as provided by special permits, no vehicle or combination of vehicles exceeding the gross weights specified above shall be permitted to travel on the public highways within the state of Alabama.

No vehicle or combination of vehicles shall be permitted to operate on any portion of the interstate highway system of Alabama that shall have a greater weight than 20,000 pounds carried on any one axle, including all enforcement tolerances, or with a tandem axle weight in excess of 34,000 pounds, including all enforcement tolerances, or with an overall gross weight on a group of two or more consecutive axles produced by application of the following formula:

$$W = 500 \left(\frac{LN + 12N + 36}{N\text{-}1} \right)$$

where W = overall gross weight on any group of two or more consecutive axles to the nearest 500 pounds, L = distance in feet between the extreme of any group of two or more consecutive axles and N = number of axles in group under consideration; except, that two consecutive sets of tandem axles may carry a gross load of 34,000 pounds each, provided the overall distance between the first and last axles of such consecutive sets of tandem axles is 36 feet or more; provided, that such overall gross weight may not exceed 80,000 pounds, including all enforcement tolerances.

Nothing in this section shall be construed as permitting size or weight limits on the national system of interstate and defense highways in this state in excess of those permitted under 23 U.S.C. section 127. If the federal government prescribes or adopts vehicle size or weight limits greater than or less than those now prescribed by 23 U.S.C. section 127 for the national system of interstate and defense highways, the increased or decreased limits shall become effective on the national system of interstate and defense highways in this state. Nothing in this section shall be construed to deny the operation of any vehicle or combination of vehicles that could be lawfully operated upon the highways and roads of this state on January 4, 1975.

d. For purposes of enforcement of subdivision (4) of this section, all scaled weights shall be deemed to have a margin of error of 10 percent of the true gross or axle weights.

e. Dump trucks, dump trailers, concrete mixing trucks, fuel oil, gasoline trucks and trucks designated and constructed for special type work or use shall not be made to conform to the axle spacing requirements of paragraph (4)c of this section; provided, that such vehicle shall be limited to a weight of 20,000 pounds per axle plus scale tolerances; and, provided further, that the maximum gross weight of such vehicles shall not exceed the maximum weight allowed by this section for the appropriate number of axles, irrespective of the distance between axles, plus allowable scale tolerances. All axles shall be brake equipped. Concrete mixing trucks which operate within 50 miles of their home base shall not be required to conform to the requirements of paragraph (4)a of this section; provided, that such vehicles shall be limited to a maximum load of the rated capacity of the concrete mixer, such true gross load not to exceed 66,000 pounds, and all such vehicles shall have at least three axles, each with brake equipped wheels. It shall be a violation if such vehicles named under this subdivision travel upon bridges designated and posted by the highway director as incapable of carrying such load.

f. If the driver of any vehicle can comply with the weight requirements of this section by shifting or equalizing the load on all wheels or axles and does so when requested by the proper authority, said driver shall not be held to be operating in violation of this section.

g. When portable scales are used in the enforcement of the provisions of this section, the axles of any vehicle described or commonly referred to as tandem or triaxle rigs or units (that is, vehicles having two or more axles in addition to a steering axle), the group of tandem or triaxles shall be weighed simultaneously, and the total weight so derived shall be divided by the number of axles weighed in the group to arrive at the per axle weight, except that if any one axle in the group exceeds 20,000 pounds in weight, it shall not exceed the weight of any other axle in the group by more than 50 percent. When portable scales are used to determine the weight of a vehicle pursuant to this section, the operator of the vehicle will be permitted to move the vehicle to the nearest platform scales certified by the department of agriculture and industries and operated by a bonded operator within a distance of 10 highway miles, accompanied by an enforcement officer to verify the accuracy of the portable scales used in determining the vehicle weight. If the weight of the vehicle is shown by the platform scales to be within the legal limits of this section, the operator of the vehicle shall not be held to be in violation of this section.

h. The governing body of a county, by appropriate resolution, may authorize limitations less than those prescribed herein for vehicles operated upon the county highways of such county.

i. The state highway department, for cause, shall have the right to post or limit any road or bridge to weights less than those prescribed by this section. It is the legislative intent and purpose that the provisions of this section be rigidly enforced by the state highway department, the department of public safety and any other authorized law-enforcement officers of the state, any county or city and incorporated towns.

j. Two and three axle vehicles being used exclusively for the purpose of transporting agricultural commodities or products to and from a farm and for agricultural purposes relating to the operation and maintenance of a farm by any farmer, custom harvester or husbandman may not be made to conform to the axle requirements of paragraph (4)a of this section or the gross weight requirements of paragraph (4)c of this section. (Acts 1927, No. 347, p. 348; Acts 1932, Ex. Sess., No. 58, p. 68; Acts 1939, No. 484, p. 687; Code 1940, T. 36, § 89; Acts 1943, No. 179, p. 159; Acts 1947, No. 210, p. 72; Acts 1955, No. 245, p. 560, § 1; Acts 1959, No. 413, p. 1052, § 1; Acts 1961, No. 686, p. 980; Acts 1963, No. 295, p. 762, § 1; Acts 1965, No. 879, p. 1645; Acts 1966, Ex. Sess., No. 334, p. 476; Acts 1975, No. 922, p. 1829, § 1; Acts 1979, No. 79-792, p. 1445, § 1; Acts 1979, No. 79-795, p. 1453; Acts 1985, 2nd Ex. Sess., No. 85-912, p. 188, § 2; Acts 1989, No. 89-631.)

The 1989 amendment, effective May 5, 1989, in the first sentence of subdivision (3) substituted "a truck-semitrailer combination" for "semitrailer trucks," and substituted "53 feet" for "50 feet."

Code commissioner's note. — Acts 1979, No. 79-795, p. 1453, § 2, provides that vehicles previously exempted from the length requirements shall continue to be exempt upon passage of the act.

Section is not unconstitutional as an arbitrary and unreasonable exercise of police power. Department of Pub. Safety v. Freeman Ready-Mix Co., 292 Ala. 380, 295 So. 2d 242, appeal dismissed, 419 U.S. 891, 95 S. Ct. 168, 42 L. Ed. 2d 135 (1974).

The conflicts between § 40-12-248 and this section do not render the truck weight statute so ambiguous as to violate the fair notice requirement of the due process clause. Depart-

ment of Pub. Safety v. Freeman Ready-Mix Co., 292 Ala. 380, 295 So. 2d 242, appeal dismissed, 419 U.S. 891, 95 S. Ct. 168, 42 L. Ed. 2d 135 (1974).

The state, in enforcing the truck weight statute, is carrying out that duty which they are charged by law and their office with performing; this cannot be considered "enacting legislation" in violation of separation of powers. Department of Pub. Safety v. Freeman Ready-Mix Co., 292 Ala. 380, 295 So. 2d 242, appeal dismissed, 419 U.S. 891, 95 S. Ct. 168, 42 L. Ed. 2d 135 (1974).

Truck operators' misplaced reliance on the nonenforcement of the truck weight statute does not deprive them of property without due process of law. Department of Pub. Safety v. Freeman Ready-Mix Co., 292 Ala. 380, 295 So. 2d 242, appeal dismissed, 419 U.S. 891, 95 S. Ct. 168, 42 L. Ed. 2d 135 (1974).

Constitutionality and construction of grandfather clause in paragraph (4)c. — See Tyus v. State, 347 So. 2d 1377 (Ala. Crim. App.), cert. denied, 347 So. 2d 1384 (Ala. 1977).

Limitations of size and weight are subjects within broad range of legislative discretion. Department of Pub. Safety v. Freeman Ready-Mix Co., 292 Ala. 380, 295 So. 2d 242, appeal dismissed, 419 U.S. 891, 95 S. Ct. 168, 42 L. Ed. 2d 135 (1974).

Legislative intent. — The legislature intended that the size and weight of motor vehicles operating on interstate highways in the state of Alabama shall not exceed the provisions set out in Title 23 U.S.C., § 127 which provides to the operator of a motor vehicle a formula to figure the weight allowed on an interstate system, and states the kind of vehicles a state may exempt from the provisions of such section, and allow to operate on an interstate highway. Perry v. State, 441 So. 2d 127 (Ala. Crim. App. 1983).

The formula for figuring weight under Title 27 of U.S.C., § 127 includes all enforcement tolerances; therefore, to add 10 percent allowed by subdivision (4)(d) of this section would violate the weight set out in Title 23 U.S.C., § 127, and result in doing the very thing sought to be prevented by the legislature of the state of Alabama. Perry v. State, 441 So. 2d 127 (Ala. Crim. App. 1983).

Purpose for enacting truck weight laws is for the safety of the public and keeping highways in good condition for the traveling public. State Dep't of Pub. Safety v. Scotch Lumber Co., 293 Ala. 330, 302 So. 2d 844 (1974); Heathcock v. State, 415 So. 2d 1198 (Ala. Crim. App. 1982).

One intention of the legislature in enacting this section was to prevent injury to the roads. Heathcock v. State, 415 So. 2d 1198 (Ala. Crim. App. 1982).

Failure of state to enforce section has not repealed it through nonuse. Department of Pub. Safety v. Freeman Ready-Mix Co., 292 Ala. 380, 295 So. 2d 242, appeal dismissed, 419 U.S. 891, 95 S. Ct. 168, 42 L. Ed. 2d 135 (1974).

Section 40-12-248 does not repeal this section by implication in licensing vehicles of weights in excess of those prescribed in the latter section. Department of Pub. Safety v. Freeman Ready-Mix Co., 292 Ala. 380, 295 So. 2d 242, appeal dismissed, 419 U.S. 891, 95 S. Ct. 168, 42 L. Ed. 2d 135 (1974).

The issuance of a license under § 40-12-248 does not bar the state from constitutionally prosecuting complainants under this section, since it has long been held that a state may tax that which it prohibits. Department of Pub. Safety v. Freeman Ready-Mix Co., 292 Ala.

380, 295 So. 2d 242, appeal dismissed, 419 U.S. 891, 95 S. Ct. 168, 42 L. Ed. 2d 135 (1974).

And it does not specifically authorize weights in excess of the limits set forth in this section. Department of Pub. Safety v. Freeman Ready-Mix Co., 292 Ala. 380, 295 So. 2d 242, appeal dismissed, 419 U.S. 891, 95 S. Ct. 168, 42 L. Ed. 2d 135 (1974).

Imposition of penalty based on extent of truck's weight in excess of legal limit. — The more a truck is overweight, the more it endangers the safety of the public and contributes to the bad repair of our highway system. Thus, the imposition of a penalty based on the extent to which a truck's weight exceeds the maximum legal limit is logical in view of the legislature's purpose in enacting this section. Curry v. State, 506 So. 2d 346 (Ala. Crim. App. 1986).

Section 32-9-5 does not state that the penalty imposed upon an operator of a truck for the violation of this section should be calculated on the basis of the operator's degree of culpability in violating the truck weight restrictions. In fact, a violation of this section can be committed without regard to the intent or knowledge of the operator of the truck. Curry v. State, 506 So. 2d 346 (Ala. Crim. App. 1986).

Operation of vehicle in violation of section criminal regardless of intent. — It being the province of the legislature to determine what shall be permitted or forbidden in the interest of the public and the language of this section being plain and positive and not made to depend upon knowledge or intent, it is clear that the intention of the legislature was to make the commission of the act of operating a vehicle of excessive axle weight criminal without regard to the intent or knowledge of the doer. Leonard v. State, 38 Ala. App. 138, 79 So. 2d 803, cert. denied, 262 Ala. 702, 79 So. 2d 808 (1955).

And it is no defense that accused was agent or employee of another. — It is no defense to a criminal prosecution for operating a vehicle of excessive axle weight that the accused committed the crime in the supposed discharge of his duty as the agent or employee of another person. Leonard v. State, 38 Ala. App. 138, 79 So. 2d 803, cert. denied, 262 Ala. 702, 79 So. 2d 808 (1955).

Evidence held sufficient to sustain conviction of violation of section. — See Leonard v. State, 38 Ala. App. 138, 79 So. 2d 803, cert. denied, 262 Ala. 702, 79 So. 2d 808 (1955).

Insufficient evidence to conclude that violation of section caused accident. — Under the facts, no reasonable factfinder could conclude that the failure of defendant to get a permit and place warning devices on either his pickup or corn chopper to warn approaching motorists of his oversized vehicle, as provided for in this section and § 32-9-29, proximately caused the accident, but could only conclude, as the jury did, that the proximate cause of the accident was plaintiff's decedent's brake failure and his driving his runaway truck in the wrong lane of traffic. Pugh v. Taylor, 507 So. 2d 428 (Ala. 1987).

Cited in Bolden v. City of Mobile, 423 F. Supp. 384 (S.D. Ala. 1976).

Collateral references. — 60 C.J.S., Motor Vehicles, § 32. 60A C.J.S., Motor Vehicles, § 246.

Power to limit weight of vehicle or load thereon with respect to use of highways. 72 ALR 1004, 75 ALR2d 376.

Constitutionality and construction of stat-utes as regards dimensions of motor vehicles, or combinations of motor vehicles. 86 ALR 281.

Validity of regulation excluding or restrict-ing use of automobiles in certain streets, on basis of weight or size. 121 ALR 586.

Construction and application of statute or ordinance designed to prevent use of vehicles or equipment thereof injurious to the highway. 134 ALR 550.

Interstate commerce clause or federal legis-lation thereunder as affecting state regulations as to size, dimensions, and weight of motor vehicle carriers. 135 ALR 1362.

Construction and operation of statutes or regulations restricting the weight of motor vehicles or their loads. 45 ALR3d 503.

§ 32-9-21. Maximum permissible length and width of motor bus.

(a) The term "motor bus," wherever used in this section, means any motor-propelled vehicle used on the highways of this state for the transportation of passengers for hire.

(b) It shall be lawful to drive or operate upon any highway in this state any motor bus which shall not exceed 40 feet in length, and eight and one-half feet in width, but exclusive of detachable wind deflection devices which have been approved by the state highway department, and safety equipment.

(c) Nothing contained in this section shall be construed to change in any way any law affecting the regulation of any motor bus except with respect to the maximum permissible length and width thereof. (Acts 1951, No. 801, p. 1400; Acts 1979, No. 79-792, p. 1445, § 1; Acts 1981, No. 81-402, p. 631.)

Collateral references. — 60 C.J.S., Motor Vehicles, §§ 10, 44(1)-57.

Constitutionality and construction of stat-utes as regards dimensions of motor vehicles, or combinations of motor vehicles. 86 ALR 281.

Validity of regulation excluding or restrict-ing use of automobiles in certain streets, on basis of weight or size. 121 ALR 586.

Construction and application of statute or ordinance designed to prevent use of vehicles or equipment thereof injurious to the highway. 134 ALR 550.

§ 32-9-22. Exemptions — Generally.

(a) There shall be exempt from the provisions of this article trucks, semitrailer trucks or trailers owned by the United States, or any agency thereof, the state of Alabama, or any county or city, or incorporated town; nor shall the provisions of this article apply to implements of husbandry temporarily propelled or moved upon the highways; nor shall the provisions of this article apply to trucks, semitrailer trucks, or trailers used exclusively for carrying 50 bales or less of cotton.

(b) If any truck, semitrailer truck or trailer shall be licensed by any city or incorporated town and the registration plate or plates issued as evidence of said license shall be conspicuously exhibited on said truck, semitrailer truck or trailer, in the manner required by law, the provisions of this article shall not apply to the operation of such vehicles within the limits of the municipality or within the police jurisdiction thereof; provided, that municipalities may provide by ordinance maximum limits with respect to the weight, height, width and length of trucks, semitrailer trucks and trailers within their police jurisdiction; provided, that the maximum limits prescribed shall not be less than those fixed in section 32-9-20 and may impose license taxes on such vehicles and require all such vehicles to have affixed thereto, in some conspicuous place, a registration plate or plates. (Acts 1932, Ex. Sess., No. 58, p. 68; Code 1940, T. 36, § 90; Acts 1947, No. 100, p. 26; Acts 1949, No. 255, p. 377, § 1; Acts 1963, No. 295, p. 762, § 2.)

"Implement of husbandry" is one which is used primarily for and is necessary to the operation of farming. Hester v. State, 40 Ala. App. 126, 108 So. 2d 385 (1959).

An "implement of husbandry" is something necessary for carrying on the business of farming, without which the work could not be done. State Dep't of Pub. Safety v. Scotch Lumber Co., 293 Ala. 330, 302 So. 2d 844 (1974).

Whether a given article is an implement of husbandry depends on the facts of any particular case. Hester v. State, 40 Ala. App. 126, 108 So. 2d 385 (1959).

Although "implements of husbandry" are exempt from width restrictions, this is not a blanket exemption which would apply regardless of the manner in which a motor vehicle was operated on the public highways. The law requires that travelers on public highways, whether in an automobile or on a tractor, use the highway in such a way that they will not injure other travelers. Cordes v. Wooten, 476 So. 2d 89 (Ala. 1985).

Subsection (a) exception not applicable. — Individual who was not on the highway with his corn chopper for a brief period of time or for a short distance, but was intending to travel some 200 miles, which would take approximately six hours, for the purpose of selling his chopper at an auction, as a matter of law did not come within the exception found in subsection (a) of this section. Pugh v. Taylor, 507 So. 2d 428 (Ala. 1987) holding, however, that the trial court's error in submitting that statutory exemption to the jury did not amount to prejudicial error.

Evidence failed to show bulldozer as implement of husbandry. — Hester v. State, 40 Ala. App. 126, 108 So. 2d 385 (1959).

Pulpwood trucks not exempt. — Even though pulpwood trucks are implements of husbandry, they are not exempt from the truck weight law. State Dep't of Pub. Safety v. Scotch Lumber Co., 293 Ala. 330, 302 So. 2d 844 (1974).

Since pulpwood trucks (implements of husbandry) were not temporarily being moved or propelled upon the public highway, they were subject to the provisions of the truck weight law of this state. State Dep't of Pub. Safety v. Scotch Lumber Co., 293 Ala. 330, 302 So. 2d 844 (1974).

The legislature would not necessarily intend to exempt overweight pulpwood trucks traveling unlimited distances on the public highways in three counties from farm to market on a permanent or regular basis. State Dep't of Pub. Safety v. Scotch Lumber Co., 293 Ala. 330, 302 So. 2d 844 (1974).

§ 32-9-23. Same — Milk transporters.

There shall be exempt from the provisions of this article as to weight any truck or semitrailer truck transporting milk for human consumption, for which refrigeration and transit is reasonably necessary in the interest of public health, when moving under refrigeration to or from market from the territory in which such commodity is collected or concentrated. (Acts 1932, Ex. Sess., No. 58, p. 68; Code 1940, T. 36, § 92; Acts 1951, No. 876, p. 1514.)

§ 32-9-24. Same — Farm tractors.

Farm tractors shall be exempt from the restrictions of this article as to width, but, however, shall not exceed nine feet in width. (Acts 1927, No. 347, p. 348; Code 1940, T. 36, § 93.)

§ 32-9-25. Same — Length.

There shall be exempt from the provisions of this article as to length, detachable wind deflection devices which have been approved by the state highway department, loads of poles, logs, lumber, structural steel, piping and timber, and vehicles transporting same. Trucks, trailers and semitrailers which are constructed and used exclusively for the hauling of livestock, shall also be exempt from the restrictions of this article as to length, but, however, shall not exceed 65 feet in length. (Acts 1939, No. 484, p. 687; Code 1940, T. 36, § 94; Acts 1949, No. 607, p. 939; Acts 1979, No. 79-430, p. 677; Acts 1979, No. 79-792, p. 1445, § 1.)

§ 32-9-26. Same — Two to eight wheel, one to four-axle trailer — Transporting agricultural commodities, etc.

Any provision of any other law or the provision of any administrative rule, regulation or order to the contrary notwithstanding, it shall be lawful for any farmer, custom picker or husbandman to operate a two to eight-wheel, one to four-axle trailer on the highways of this state if the trailer is being used exclusively for the purpose of transporting to and from a farm agricultural commodities or products and for agricultural purposes relating to the operation and maintenance of a farm; provided, that the combined weight of the trailer and its load is not in excess of 36,000 pounds, nor more than 10,000 pounds per axle, whichever is less. (Acts 1953, No. 688, p. 940, § 1; Acts 1964, 1st Ex. Sess., No. 140, p. 204; Acts 1987, No. 87-585, p. 955, § 1.)

§ 32-9-27. Same — Same — Size and equipment of such trailers.

All such trailers as described in section 32-9-26 shall be equipped with red reflectors to adequately illuminate the rear of such trailer by placing at least two on the rear and one at each side. No such trailer shall be in excess of 10 feet in width, except that such trailer shall not exceed 102 inches in width when operated or moved on the interstate highway system, and no such trailer, drawbar or other connection, including the vehicle towing such trailer, shall be in excess of overall length of 76 feet. Overhang of round bales of hay on such trailer shall not exceed one foot per side except that the width of the trailer including overhang shall not exceed 102 inches when operated or moved on the interstate highway system. At no time shall there be more than one loaded trailer towed by any vehicle; provided, that two empty farm wagons or trailers with two or more wheels may be towed in tandem when the overall length of the towing vehicle and its tow does not exceed 76 feet altogether. (Acts 1953, No. 688, p. 940, § 2; Acts 1965, No. 866, p. 1641; Acts 1987, No. 87-585, p. 955, § 2.)

§ 32-9-28. Same — Same — Violations.

Any person violating the provisions of sections 32-9-26 and 32-9-27 shall be guilty of a misdemeanor and punished as provided by law. (Acts 1953, No. 688, p. 940, § 3.)

§ 32-9-29. Permits for movement of oversized vehicles or loads.

(a) *Authorized; application; issuance; seasonal, etc., limitations; refusal, revocation or cancellation.*

(1) The director of the highway department or the official of the highway department designated by the director may, in his discretion, upon application and for good cause being shown therefor, issue a permit in writing authorizing the applicant to operate or move upon the state's public roads a vehicle or combination of no more than two vehicles and loads whose weight, width, length or height, or combination thereof, exceeds the maximum limit specified by law; provided, that the load transported by such vehicle or vehicles is of such nature that it is a unit which cannot be readily dismantled or separated; provided however, that bulldozers and similar construction equipment shall not be deemed readily separable for purposes of this chapter; and further provided, that no permit shall be issued to any vehicle whose operation upon the public roads of this state threatens to unduly damage a road or any appurtenances thereto.

(2) Permits may be issued on application to the department to persons, firms or corporations. The director of the highway department shall promulgate reasonable rules and regulations which are necessary or desirable governing the issuance of such permits; provided, that such rules and regulations shall not conflict with the provisions of this title and other provisions of law.

(3) The original copy of every such permit shall be carried in the vehicle itself and shall be open to inspection by any police officer or state trooper or authorized agent of the highway department.

(4) The application for any such permit shall specifically describe the type of permit applied for, as said types of permits are described in subsection (b) of this section, and the application for a single trip permit shall, in addition, describe the points of departure and destination.

(5) The director of the highway department or the official of the highway department designated by the director is authorized to withhold such permit or, if such permit is issued, to establish seasonal or other time limitations within which the vehicles described may be operated on the public road indicated, or otherwise to limit or prescribe conditions of operation of such vehicle, when necessary to assure against undue damage to the road foundation, surfaces or bridge structures, and require such

undertaking or other security as may be deemed necessary to compensate the state for any injury to any roadway or bridge structure.

(6) For just cause, including, but not limited to, repeated and consistent past violations, the director of the highway department or an official of the highway department designated by the director may refuse to issue, or may cancel, suspend or revoke, the permit of an applicant or permittee.

(b) *Duration and limits of permits; bond or insurance requirements.*

(1) ANNUAL. The director of the highway department or the official of the highway department designated by the director may, pursuant to the provisions of this section, issue an annual permit which shall permit the vehicle or combination vehicle and load to be operated on the state highway system of this state for 12 months from the date the permit is issued, even though the vehicle or its load exceeds the maximum limits specified in this article; provided, that an annual permit shall not authorize the operation of a vehicle including all enforcement tolerances:

a. Whose total gross weight exceeds 150,000 pounds; provided, that gross weights over 100,000 pounds shall require advance routing by the highway department;

b. Whose single axle weight exceeds 22,000 pounds;

c. Whose total length exceeds 75 feet; with the exception of mobile homes, whose length limitations, including towing vehicle, shall be 85 feet;

d. Whose total width exceeds 120 inches or whose load width exceeds 144 inches; with the exception of mobile homes, whose width limitation shall be 168 inches; provided, that mobile homes whose width exceeds 144 inches shall require advance route approval by the highway department; or

e. Whose height exceeds 14 feet.

A permit to operate a vehicle which exceeds the statutory limits of height, weight, width or length shall be issued only on condition of payment of an indemnity bond or proof of insurance protection for $300,000.00, said bond or insurance protection conditioned for payment to the highway department to be held in trust for the benefit of the owners of bridges and appurtenances thereof, traffic signals, signs or other highway structures damaged by a vehicle operating under authority of such overheight permit. The liability under the bond or insurance certificate shall be contingent upon proof of negligence or fault on the part of the permittee, his agents or operators.

(2) SINGLE TRIP. The director of the highway department may issue a single trip permit, pursuant to the provisions of this section, to any vehicle.

(c) *Fees.* The director of the highway department may promulgate rules and regulations concerning the issuance of permits and charge a fee for the issuance as follows:

(1) ANNUAL. Charges for the issuance of annual permits shall be as follows:

a. For modular homes, sectional houses, portable buildings, boats and any vehicle or combination of vehicles, $100.00; except, that a vehicle or combination of vehicles having trailer or combination of trailers with sidewalls or roof which has transported modular homes, sectional houses and portable buildings may, after depositing any said load, return unloaded to its point of origin, even though the unloaded vehicles exceed the 55 foot limitation provided for in this article, up to and including 12 feet wide and 75 feet long.

b. For heavy commodities or equipment, overweight, overlength, overheight and overwidth, $100.00. A tractor and trailer (low boy type) may, after depositing a load referred to in this subparagraph, return to its point of origin, even though the unloaded tractor and trailer (low boy type) may exceed the 55 foot limitation provided for in this article up to and including 12 feet wide and 75 feet long.

c. For mobile homes up to and including 14 feet wide and 85 feet long, including towing vehicle, $100.00.

(2) SINGLE TRIP. Charges for the issuance of single trip permits shall be as follows:

a. Mobile homes, modular homes, sectional houses, portable buildings and boats:

1. Up to and including 12 feet wide and 75 feet long, $10.00.

2. Boats in excess of 12 feet wide, $20.00.

3. Mobile homes, modular homes, sectional houses and portable buildings in excess of 12 feet wide and/or 75 feet long, $20.00.

b. Heavy commodities or equipment:

1. Over on any limitations as to length, height or width, $10.00.

2. Over on weight, as follows:

WEIGHT PERMITTED	PERMIT FEE
From 80,001 pounds up to 100,000 pounds	$ 10.00
From 100,001 pounds up to 125,000 pounds	30.00
From 125,001 pounds up to 150,000 pounds	60.00
From 150,001 pounds and over	100.00

c. Miscellaneous:

1. Houses, $20.00.

2. Off-the-road equipment, $10.00.

3. Other oversized vehicles, loads and equipment not herein specified, $20.00.

4. Other overheight loads not herein specified, $10.00.

(d) *Certain vehicles on interstate highways.* Under the provisions of this section, 14 feet-wide vehicles and combination vehicles and load may be issued a permit to travel the interstate highways.

(e) *Violations of federal law, etc.* No permit shall be issued under this section if the issuance of the permit would violate United States law or would cause the state of Alabama to lose federal-aid funds. Notwithstanding any provisions of any statute to the contrary, all permit fees collected in accordance with this section shall be paid to the public road and bridge fund in addition to any sums appropriated therefor to the highway department.

(f) *Farm and agricultural commodities and equipment exempt.* The term "heavy commodities or equipment," as used in this section, is not intended to include farm and agricultural commodities or equipment, and such farm or agricultural commodities and equipment are exempt from the requirement of obtaining permits for movement on the state highway system of Alabama. (Acts 1932, Ex. Sess., No. 58, p. 68; Acts 1939, No. 484, p. 687; Code 1940, T. 36, § 91; Acts 1977, No. 775, p. 1332, §§ 1 through 3; Acts 1977, 1st Ex. Sess., No. 78, p. 1506; Acts 1978, No. 837, p. 1241.)

Insufficient evidence to conclude that violation of section caused accident. — Under the facts, no reasonable factfinder could conclude that the failure of defendant to get a permit and place warning devices on either his pickup or corn chopper to warn approaching motorists of his oversized vehicle, as provided for in § 32-9-20 and this section, proximately caused the accident, but could only conclude, as the jury did, that the proximate cause of the accident was plaintiff's decedent's brake failure and his driving his runaway truck in the wrong lane of traffic. Pugh v. Taylor, 507 So. 2d 428 (Ala. 1987).

Cited in Slayton v. Slayton, 521 So. 2d 928 (Ala. 1988).

Collateral references. — Power to limit weight of vehicle or load thereon with respect to use of highways. 72 ALR 1004, 75 ALR2d 376.

Isolated, occasional, or incidental transportation of person or property for compensation as within contemplation of statute requiring permits or otherwise regulating transportation of person or property on highway. 123 ALR 229.

§ 32-9-29.1. Special permits for movement of certain site-built buildings.

(a) The director of the state highway department or the official of the highway department designated by the director may, at his discretion, upon application and for good cause being shown therefor, issue special permits to the applicant, for movement on or over the public highways, for motor vehicles when used in the transportation of site-built residential buildings or otherwise, which had at one time been affixed to a permanent foundation; provided, however, that this section shall not extend to those motor vehicles used in the transportation of what is commonly referred to as mobile homes, house trailers, prefabricated housing or other factory-built buildings.

The applicants for the permits issued under this section shall state if the route of the movement will cross one or more railroads at grade.

If such a crossing is to be made, the director of the state highway department or the official of the highway department designated will notify the railroad or railroads involved, stating the time and route of the anticipated move.

(b) The fee for the issuance of such permits shall be the same as set forth in section 32-9-29(c). (Acts 1983, No. 83-646, p. 1008.)

§ 32-9-30. Repealed by Acts 1977, No. 775, p. 1332, § 4, effective June 22, 1977.

§ 32-9-31. Measuring and weighing vehicles.

Any officer enumerated in section 32-9-3 having reason to believe that the height, length, width or weight of any truck, semitrailer truck or trailer is in excess of the maximum limits prescribed by section 32-9-20 or permitted by any permit issued under authority of section 32-9-29 is authorized to measure or weigh the same, either by means of portable or stationary scales, and may require such vehicle to be driven to the nearest stationary scales, in the event such scales are within a distance of five miles. All scales used for the weighing of vehicles as provided in this section shall be approved by the weights and measures division of the department of agriculture and industries. Said officer shall require the operator of said truck, semitrailer truck or trailer to unload such portion of load as may be necessary to decrease the gross weight of such vehicle to the maximum gross weight permitted by this title or by the terms of any permit in the possession of such operator and issued under the provisions of section 32-9-29 (which excess load, when unloaded, shall be at the sole risk of the owner) or, at the election of the operator, said officer shall permit said operator to move such vehicle and its load to the nearest incorporated town or the nearest court having jurisdiction, at which place said excess load shall be unloaded. The refusal of any such operator to permit his truck, semitrailer truck or trailer to be measured or weighed, or to proceed to a stationary scales or to unload the excess load shall constitute a violation of this chapter. (Acts 1932, Ex. Sess., No. 58, p. 68; Code 1940, T. 36, § 85; Acts 1949, No. 518, p. 773, § 2.)

State trooper who believed truck was overweight had authority to weigh truck. — Where the bulging of the tires on the defendant's truck indicated to the state trooper that the truck was probably loaded in excess of the legal weight, he had reason to believe the defendant's truck was overweight and had the authority to weigh his truck. Curry v. State, 506 So. 2d 346 (Ala. Crim. App. 1986).

Where all trucks that passed by the weigh station were stopped and weighed unless they were obviously underweight, the stopping and weighing of the defendant's truck did not involve the unconstrained or unbridled discretion of the state trooper and his crew, and thus did not constitute the type of impermissible intrusion contemplated by the fourth amendment. Curry v. State, 506 So. 2d 346 (Ala. Crim. App. 1986).

Collateral references. — Power to limit weight of vehicle or load thereon with respect to use of highways. 72 ALR 1004, 75 ALR2d 376.

Construction and operation of statutes or regulations restricting the weight of motor vehicles or their loads. 45 ALR3d 503.

§ 32-9-32. Scales.

The director of the highway department is authorized to designate, furnish instructions to, prescribe rules and regulations for the conduct of and to supervise official stations for determining the weight of motor vehicles at such points as it may be deemed necessary. Such designated weighing devices shall be checked by the weights and measures division of the department of agriculture and industries and certified to be correct within the tolerances prescribed under the rules and regulations established by the state department of agriculture and industries, and checks shall be made at such points as is deemed necessary by the weights and measures division of the department of agriculture and industries. All stations shall comply with the requirements of the director and shall be available for the use of all officers in the enforcement of this chapter. The expense of weighing such motor vehicles shall be paid out of any funds made available for the use of the state highway patrol. If it is found that any motor vehicle is being operated in violation of this chapter, the expenses of such weighing shall be taxed as part of the costs for the prosecution of such violation. A certificate issued by the chief of the division of weights and measures of the department of agriculture and industries, signed by such official, under oath, and countersigned by the commissioner of agriculture and industries, in which the chief of the division of weights and measures certifies that scales, or weighing devices, have been checked and approved as required under the provisions of this section and section 32-9-31 and found to be correct, within prescribed tolerances, shall be received in any court as prima facie evidence of the fact that the scales or weighing devices designated and identified in such certificate have been checked and approved for accuracy in accordance with the requirements of this section and section 32-9-31; provided, that such certificate must show that the scales or weighing devices were checked for accuracy within a period of four months (120 days) prior to the date on which the motor vehicle was weighed to determine whether such vehicle was being operated in violation of this chapter. (Acts 1932, Ex. Sess., No. 58, p. 68; Code 1940, T. 36, § 87; Acts 1949, No. 518, p. 773, § 3; Acts 1953, No. 827, p. 1114.)

That weigh stations are portable and not permanent does not mean they do not constitute "official stations." Curry v. State, 506 So. 2d 346 (Ala. Crim. App. 1986).

Certificate of accuracy of scales admissible under business records exception to hearsay rule. — Since a certificate of accuracy of scales used to weigh motor vehicles is issued in the regular course of his operations and the certificate is normally issued after an inspection is done, the certificate of accuracy was properly admissible under the business records exception to the hearsay rule. This exception is applicable in criminal cases. Curry v. State, 506 So. 2d 346 (Ala. Crim. App. 1986).

Officer's testimony as to inspection of weighing scales not hearsay. — An officer's testimony as to the inspection of weighing scales by the department of agriculture and industries was not hearsay where the officer testified that he was present and observed the inspection and testing of the scales. Curry v. State, 506 So. 2d 346 (Ala. Crim. App. 1986).

Cited in Leonard v. State, 38 Ala. App. 138, 79 So. 2d 803 (1955); Perry v. State, 441 So. 2d 127 (Ala. Crim. App. 1983).

CHAPTER 10.

MOTOR VEHICLE ACCIDENTS.

Cross references. — As to removing glass, etc., from highway after accident, see § 32-5A-60.

Cited in Hartung v. Graddick, 16 Bankr. 40 (Bankr. S.D. Ala. 1981); Gosnell v. Slaughter, 364 So. 2d 1158 (Ala. 1978).

§ 32-10-1. Accidents involving death or personal injuries.

(a) The driver of any motor vehicle involved in an accident resulting in injury to or the death of any person, or in damage to a motor vehicle or other vehicle which is driven or attended by any person, shall immediately stop such vehicle at the scene of such accident or as close thereto as possible and shall then forthwith return to and in every event shall remain at the scene of the accident until he has fulfilled the requirements of section 32-10-3. Every such stop shall be made without obstructing traffic more than is necessary.

(b) The director shall revoke the driver's license of a person convicted under this section. (Acts 1943, No. 558, p. 548, § 2.)

For case dismissing prosecutions under this section as violative of defendants' civil rights, holding that such prosecutions were in fact a subterfuge and stemmed from their protest of certain stores' discriminatory practices, see McMeans v. Mayor's Court, 247 F. Supp. 606 (M.D. Ala. 1965).

Circumstances requiring operator to stop. — If an injury is inflicted under such circumstances as would ordinarily superinduce the belief in a reasonable person that injury would flow, or had flowed, from the accident or collision, then it is the duty of the operator to stop his vehicle. Touchstone v. State, 42 Ala. App. 141, 155 So. 2d 349 (1963).

Danger to life or bodily harm as defense to prosecution for failure to comply with section. — In a prosecution under this section, if, according to the evidence, the defendant was confronted with danger to life or great bodily harm, it would be unjust and unreasonable to declare that, despite this, he was required to remain at the scene of the accident and go through the formality of complying with each and every requirement of the section. Isom v. State, 37 Ala. App. 416, 69 So. 2d 716 (1954), holding that, in a prosecution for violation of this section, the refusal to give the following charge was error: "I charge you, Gentlemen of the Jury, if you believe from the evidence that the defendant honestly believed he was in danger of bodily harm if he stayed at the scene of the accident, then I charge you he had a right to leave without giving his name and address and you should acquit him."

Leaving the scene of accident. — The failure to fulfill the requirements of this section and § 32-10-2 is what is commonly referred to as the crime of "leaving the scene of an accident." Fretwell v. State, 414 So. 2d 1012 (Ala. Crim. App. 1982).

Evidence of leaving the scene. — Evidence, indicating that defendant who was convicted of leaving the scene of accident had placed his foot on the accelerator is a sufficient basis for a finding that defendant, intoxicated, though he was, voluntarily moved the truck which was idling in shopping center lot, and voluntarily became the driver, though for a short distance only, of the motor vehicle. Fowler v. State, 364 So. 2d 1201 (Ala. Crim. App. 1978).

Indictment not void by miscitation of code section. — An indictment charging defendant with leaving the scence of an accident "in violation of § 13-10-1 of the Code of Alabama . . ." was not rendered void by the miscitation of the code section, and defendant's plea of guilty waived all waivable defects in the indictment. Mann v. State, 473 So. 2d 1225 (Ala. Crim. App. 1985).

Indictment charging damage to "property". — An indictment under this section charged the driver of a motor vehicle with leaving the scene of an accident resulting in injury or death to a person or damage to property. The alternative averment in the indictment, by its use of the broad word "property," included injuries to things beyond the scope of this section. Thus the indictment charged an offense not prohibited by law, and the court erred in overruling a demurrer in this aspect. Echols v. State, 35 Ala. App. 602, 51 So. 2d 260 (1951).

Indictment must identify owner of vehicle. — A demurrer challenged an indictment under this section because of its failure to identify or show the owner of the property alleged to have been damaged. Even had the indictment averred damage to a vehicle, rather than damage to property as it did aver, this ground of the demurrer was meritorious. Echols v. State, 35 Ala. App. 602, 51 So. 2d 260 (1951).

Defendant as bailee. — Where defendant testified that the automobile involved in the hit-and-run accident belonged to his father, who had loaned it to him, assuming this to be true, defendant had a special interest as bailee in the automobile, and as against all other persons, except his father, he was the owner of the car involved in the accident. Rider v. State, 56 Ala. App. 137, 319 So. 2d 756 (1975).

Prior conviction of manslaughter no bar to prosecution. — A plea of autrefois convict averred that the appellant had heretofore been indicted and convicted of manslaughter, which conviction was based on and grew out of the accident for which he was being prosecuted for leaving. The state filed a demurrer to this plea,

which demurrer was properly sustained by the court. Echols v. State, 35 Ala. App. 602, 51 So. 2d 260 (1951).

Indictment charging damage to "automobile". — A demurrer which challenges an indictment under this section because it alleges the accident resulted in "damage to an automobile," rather than "damage to a vehicle" is without merit. Masters v. State, 38 Ala. App. 392, 84 So. 2d 675 (1956).

Questions for jury. — In a prosecution of defendant for violation of this section, the guilt of the defendant was an issue to be determined by the jury where there was a conflict in testimony concerning defendant's ability to stop his car immediately and to notify the authorities concerning the accident. Masters v. State, 38 Ala. App. 392, 84 So. 2d 675 (1956).

Where, according to the testimony of a state witness, defendant was driving the automobile when it struck the bicycle, but on the other hand, defendant claimed the witness was driving at the time of the accident, this conflicting testimony made and presented a jury question. Rider v. State, 56 Ala. App. 137, 319 So. 2d 756 (1975).

Violations may be punished as misdemeanors or felonies. — Upon a grand jury indictment, leaving the scene of an accident in violation of this section may be punished either as a misdemeanor or as a felony. Kennedy v. State, 39 Ala. App. 676, 107 So. 2d 913 (1958).

Collateral references. — 60 C.J.S., Motor Vehicles, § 38. 61A C.J.S., Motor Vehicles, §§ 588-714(4).

Construction and effect of statute in relation to conduct of driver of automobile after happening of an accident. 16 ALR 1425, 66 ALR 1228, 101 ALR 911.

Sufficiency of indictment or information charging failure to stop after accident, give name, etc., or to render assistance. 115 ALR 361.

Failure to comply with statute requiring one involved in automobile accident to stop or report as affecting question as to suspension or tolling statute of limitations. 10 ALR2d 564.

Civil liability of mobile vendor for attracting into street child injured by another's motor vehicle. 84 ALR3d 826.

Liability of owner of motor vehicle for negligence of garageman or mechanic. 8 ALR4th 265.

Governmental liability for failure to post highway deer crossing warning signs. 59 ALR4th 1217.

§ 32-10-2. Duty to give information and render aid.

The driver of any motor vehicle involved in an accident resulting in injury to or the death of any person or damage to any vehicle which is driven or attended by any person shall give his name, address and the registration number of the vehicle he is driving, shall upon request exhibit his driver's license to the person struck or the driver or occupant of or person attending any motor or other vehicle collided with or damaged and shall render to any person injured in such accident reasonable assistance, including the transportation of, or the making of arrangements for the transportation of such person to a physician or hospital for medical or surgical treatment, if it is apparent that such treatment is necessary or if such transportation is requested by the injured person. (Acts 1943, No. 558, p. 548, § 3.)

Constitutionality. — This section commonly known as the "leaving the scene of an accident" statute, does not violate the guarantees of Ala. Const., art. 1, § 6 because, from a reading of the statute, a defendant would be reasonably apprised of the accusation against him or her and the possible penal consequences. Burnett v. State, 494 So. 2d 200 (Ala. Crim. App. 1986).

The sentencing scheme of this section (see § 32-10-6) is constitutional despite its provision that the perpetrator of such offense will be subject to imprisonment in the penitentiary for "not less than one nor more than five years." Thus, the sentencing provisions of this section and § 32-10-6 did not violate the appellant's rights, because from a reading of the statute a defendant could be reasonably apprised of the accusation against him or her and the possible penal consequences. Lyle v. State, 497 So. 2d 834 (Ala. Crim. App. 1986).

Section not strict liability statute. — This section contains no language indicating that this is a strict liability statute, and the issue of the defendant's culpability was an issue which was properly presented to the trial jury. Bettis v. State, 534 So. 2d 1135 (Ala. Crim. App. 1988).

Leaving the scene of accident. — The failure to fulfill the requirements of this section and § 32-10-1 is what is commonly referred to as the crime of "leaving the scene of an accident." Fretwell v. State, 414 So. 2d 1012 (Ala. Crim. App. 1982).

Evidence held sufficient. — Where there was evidence that defendant was very intoxi-

cated when he ran over two children, that he did not stop to render aid, that he returned 10 minutes later only to plead with an eyewitness not to report him to the police, that he also left when he heard the ambulance siren, and that the police had to chase him and eventually stop him with a road block, the evidence was more than sufficient to support a jury's determination that the defendant violated this section. Fretwell v. State, 414 So. 2d 1012 (Ala. Crim. App. 1982).

Duty to render aid in reasonable nonnegligent manner. — This section alters the common law by adding the affirmative duty to render aid, if it is apparent such is necessary, in cases where death or personal injury result from a motor vehicle accident. However, the statute does not, either expressly or impliedly, abrogate the common-law duty to render such aid in a reasonable nonnegligent manner. Feazell v. Campbell, 358 So. 2d 1017 (Ala. 1978).

Cited in Haywood v. State, 43 Ala. App. 358, 190 So. 2d 725 (1966); Collins v. State, 346 So. 2d 43 (Ala. Crim. App. 1977); Fowler v. State, 364 So. 2d 1205 (Ala. Crim. App. 1978).

Collateral references. — 61A C.J.S., Motor Vehicles, §§ 674(1)-683.

Construction and effect of statute in relation to conduct of driver of automobile after happening of an accident. 16 ALR 1228, 101 ALR 911.

Sufficiency of indictment or information charging failure to stop after accident, give name, etc., or to render assistance. 115 ALR 361.

§ 32-10-3. Duty upon striking unattended vehicle.

The driver of any motor vehicle which collides with any motor vehicle or other vehicle which is unattended shall immediately stop and shall then and there either locate and notify the operator or owner of such vehicle of the name and address of the driver and owner of the vehicle striking the unattended vehicle or shall leave in a conspicuous place in or on the vehicle struck a written notice giving the name and address of the driver and/or the owner of the vehicle doing the striking and a statement of the circumstances thereof. (Acts 1943, No. 558, p. 548, § 4.)

Cited in Fowler v. State, 364 So. 2d 1205 (Ala. Crim. App. 1978).
Collateral references. — Construction and effect of statute in relation to conduct of driver of automobile after happening of an accident. 16 ALR 1425, 66 ALR 1228, 101 ALR 911.

§ 32-10-4. Duty upon striking fixtures upon a highway.

The driver of any motor vehicle involved in an accident resulting only in damage to fixtures legally upon or adjacent to a highway shall take reasonable steps to locate and notify the owner or person in charge of such property of such fact and of his name and address and of the registration number of the vehicle he is driving and shall upon request exhibit his driver's license and shall make report of such accident when and as required in section 32-10-5. (Acts 1943, No. 558, p. 548, § 5.)

Cited in Fowler v. State, 364 So. 2d 1205 (Ala. Crim. App. 1978).
Collateral references. — Construction and effect of statute in relation to conduct of driver of automobile after happening of an accident. 16 ALR 1425, 101 ALR 911.

§ 32-10-5. Immediate reports of accidents.

(a) The driver of any motor vehicle involved in an accident resulting in injury to or the death of any person shall immediately by the quickest means of communication give notice of such accident to the local police department if such accident occurs within a municipality; otherwise to the office of the county sheriff or to the state highway patrol.

(b) Every coroner or other official performing like functions upon learning of the death of a person in his jurisdiction as the result of a traffic accident shall immediately notify the nearest office of the director. (Acts 1943, No. 558, p. 548, § 6.)

Collateral references. — 60 C.J.S., Motor Vehicles, §§ 674(2), 676.
Construction and effect of statute in relation to conduct of driver of automobile after happening of an accident. 16 ALR 1228, 101 ALR 911.

Failure to comply with statute requiring one involved in automobile accident to stop or report as affecting question as to suspension or tolling statute of limitations. 10 ALR2d 564.

§ 32-10-6. Penalty for violation of sections 32-10-1 through 32-10-5.

Every person convicted of violating sections 32-10-1 through 32-10-5 or any of the provisions thereof, when such violation involved only damage to property, shall be punished the same as prescribed by law for a Class A misdemeanor; provided, however, that every person convicted of violating such sections, or any provisions thereof, when such violation involved death or personal injury, shall be punished the same as prescribed by law for a Class C felony. (Acts 1945, No. 427, p. 670; Acts 1985, 2nd Ex. Sess., No. 85-918, p. 197.)

Constitutionality. — The sentencing scheme of § 32-10-2 (see this section) is constitutional despite its provision that the perpetrator of such offense will be subject to imprisonment in the penitentiary for "not less than one nor more than five years." Thus, the sentencing provisions of § 32-10-2 and this section did not violate the appellant's rights, because from a reading of the statute a defendant could be reasonably apprised of the accusation against him or her and the possible penal consequences. Lyle v. State, 497 So. 2d 834 (Ala. Crim. App. 1986).

Cited in Newberry v. State, 493 So. 2d 995 (Ala. 1986); Burnett v. State, 494 So. 2d 200 (Ala. Crim. App. 1986).

§ 32-10-7. Written reports of accidents.

Every law-enforcement officer who in the regular course of duty investigates a motor vehicle accident, either at the time of and at the scene of the accident or thereafter by interviewing participants or witnesses, shall, within 24 hours after completing such investigation, forward the necessary completed written report or copy thereof of such accident to the director on the uniform accident report form supplied by the director. (Acts 1943, No. 558, p. 548, § 7; Acts 1951, No. 128, p. 355; Acts 1969, No. 272, p. 603.)

Collateral references. — Admissibility of report of police or other public officer or employee, or portions of report, as to course of or responsibility for accident, injury to person, or damage to property. 69 ALR2d 1148.

Admissibility of police officer's testimony at state trial relating to motorist's admissions made in or for automobile accident report required by law. 46 ALR4th 291.

§ 32-10-8. Accident report forms.

(a) The director shall prepare and upon request supply to police departments, coroners, sheriffs, garages and other suitable agencies or individuals, uniform accident report forms required under this chapter. The required written accident report or citation to be made by persons involved in accidents or charged with a moving violation and by investigating officers shall call for sufficiently detailed information, to disclose with reference to a traffic accident, including but not limited to location of accident, probable cause, injuries to persons, property damage, deaths of persons, registration of vehicles involved including license numbers, name, address, social security number and driver's license number of operator, highway design and maintenance (including lighting, markings and road surface) and names and addresses of witnesses.

(b) Every accident report required to be made in writing shall be made on the uniform accident report form approved and supplied by the director and shall contain all available information required therein. (Acts 1943, No. 558, p. 548, § 8; Acts 1969, No. 272, p. 603; Acts 1980, No. 80-803, p. 1635.)

Cited in Pike Taxi Co. v. Patterson, 258 Ala. 508, 63 So. 2d 599 (1952); Fowler v. State, 364 So. 2d 1205 (Ala. Crim. App. 1978).

Collateral references. — Admissibility of police officer's testimony at state trial relating to motorist's admissions made in or for automobile accident report required by law. 46 ALR4th 291.

§ 32-10-9. Coroners to report.

Every coroner or other official performing like functions shall on or before the tenth day of each month report in writing to the director the death of any person within his jurisdiction during the preceding calendar month as the result of an accident involving a motor vehicle and the circumstances of such accident. (Acts 1943, No. 558, p. 548, § 9.)

§ 32-10-10. Garages to report accident and bullet damage.

The person in charge of any garage or repair shop to which is brought any motor vehicle which shows evidence of having been involved in an accident, of which report must be made as provided in section 32-10-7, or struck by any bullet shall report to the director within 24 hours after such motor vehicle is received, giving the engine number, registration number and the name and address of the owner or operator of such vehicle. (Acts 1943, No. 558, p. 548, § 10.)

§ 32-10-11. Accident reports confidential.

All accident reports made by persons involved in accidents or by garages shall be without prejudice to the individual so reporting and shall be for the confidential use of the director or of other state agencies having use for the records for accident prevention purposes; except, that the director may disclose the identity of a person involved in an accident when such identity is not otherwise known or when such person denies his presence at such accident. No such report shall be used as evidence in any trial, civil or criminal, arising out of an accident; except, that the department shall furnish upon demand of any person who has, or claims to have made such a report, or, upon demand of any court, a certificate showing that a specified accident report has or has not been made to the director solely to prove a compliance or a failure to comply with the requirement that such a report be made to the director. (Acts 1943, No. 558, p. 548, § 11.)

Reports of investigating officers not admissible. — Ordinarily, the reports of investigating officers are not admissible in evidence, as they are deemed hearsay and do not fall within the "business records" exception to that exclusionary rule. Dennis v. Scarborough, 360 So. 2d 278 (Ala. 1978).

Cited in Pike Taxi Co. v. Patterson, 258 Ala. 508, 63 So. 2d 599 (1952).

Collateral references. — Constitutionality,

construction, and effect of statute or regulation relating specifically to divulgence of information acquired by public officers or employees. 165 ALR 1302.

Admissibility of police officer's testimony at state trial relating to motorist's admissions made in or for automobile accident report required by law. 46 ALR4th 291.

§ 32-10-12. Director to tabulate and analyze accident reports and make available to state highway director.

The director shall tabulate and analyze all accident reports and shall publish annually or at more frequent intervals statistical information based thereon as to the number and circumstances of traffic accidents. The director shall make available to the state highway director all accident reports so that he may obtain sufficient detailed information so as to provide data for surveillance of traffic for detection and correction of high or potentially high accident locations. (Acts 1943, No. 558, p. 548, § 12; Acts 1969, No. 272, p. 603.)

CHAPTER 11.

RESCUE SQUADS.

§ 32-11-1. "Rescue squad" defined.

Wherever the term "rescue squad" appears in this chapter, it shall refer to and include only those persons or organizations who are members of the Alabama association of rescue squads. (Acts 1965, 2nd Ex. Sess., No. 74, p. 98, § 4.)

§ 32-11-2. Exemption from license and registration fees and ad valorem taxes.

Motor vehicles owned by volunteer rescue squads incorporated under the laws of Alabama and used exclusively as life saving, rescue or first aid vehicles without profit, and which are not rented, leased or loaned to any private individual, firm or corporation shall be exempt from payment of license and registration fees and all ad valorem taxes otherwise prescribed by law. (Acts 1965, 2nd Ex. Sess., No. 74, p. 98, § 1; Acts 1966, Ex. Sess., No. 422, p. 567.)

§ 32-11-3. Color and lettering of vehicles.

Any vehicle, to come under the provisions of this chapter, shall be painted a distinguishing color and shall display conspicuous letters and figures not less than three inches in height showing the identity of the volunteer rescue squad that owns the vehicle. (Acts 1965, 2nd Ex. Sess., No. 74, p. 98, § 2.)

§ 32-11-4. Special tags.

The treasurer of any rescue squad coming under the provisions of this chapter may apply to the department of revenue, giving the make, type, model, motor number and serial number of the vehicle or vehicles, together with such other information as the department of revenue shall require, which information shall be furnished under oath by such officer; and, if upon examination the same appears regular to the department of revenue, it shall issue to such treasurer the necessary number of tags to be placed on such vehicle, and such tags shall be used on no other vehicle than that for which issued. Such tags shall have the letters "R. S." and proper number stamped thereon. All replacement tags issued for such vehicles shall be similarly stamped or marked. For issuance of such tags and to cover the expense of preparing the same, the treasurer shall pay to the department of revenue the sum of $1.00 for the necessary tags for each vehicle to which this chapter applies. (Acts 1965, 2nd Ex. Sess., No. 74, p. 98, § 3.)

CHAPTER 12.

MOTORCYCLES AND MOTOR-DRIVEN CYCLES.

ARTICLE 1.

GENERAL PROVISIONS.

§ 32-12-1. Repealed by Acts 1980, No. 80-434, p. 604, § 15-106, effective May 19, 1980.

ARTICLE 2.

MOTOR-DRIVEN CYCLES.

Cross references. — As to lighting equipment on motor-driven cycles, see § 32-5-242.

§ 32-12-20. Definition; parent or guardian not to authorize or permit violations.

It is unlawful for any person to do any act forbidden or to fail to perform any act required by this chapter. The parent of any child and the guardian of any ward shall not authorize or knowingly permit any such child or ward to violate any of the provisions of this chapter. As used herein, the term "motor-driven cycle" shall include every motorcycle weighing when fully equipped less than 200 pounds and every bicycle with motor attached and every motor scooter. (Acts 1949, No. 652, p. 1006, § 1.)

Collateral references. — 60 C.J.S., Motor Vehicles, § 14.

Motorcycle as within statute or ordinance in relation to motor cars, motor-driven cars, etc. 48 ALR 1090, 70 ALR 1253.

§ 32-12-21. Repealed by Acts 1980, No. 80-434, p. 604, § 15-106, effective May 19, 1980.

§ 32-12-22. Registration; operator's license generally.

Every person, except a person holding a driver's license issued under authority of chapter 6 of this title, before operating any motor-driven cycle upon a public highway in this state, shall register it with the director of public safety and procure an operator's license. Operators' licenses shall be issued under and be governed by the provisions of chapter 6 of this title; except, that such a license shall be issued to any person 14 years of age and older if such a person can satisfy the director of public safety or an examining officer that he is competent to operate a motor-driven cycle with safety to persons and to property. (Acts 1949, No. 652, p. 1006, § 3.)

Cases concerning driver licensing applicable to motorcycle driver age limits. — Those cases which concern the statutes dealing with licensing of drivers of motor vehicles may be applied by analogy to the statute requiring a person to be at least 14 years of age to obtain a license to operate a motorcycle. Chiniche v. Smith, 374 So. 2d 872 (Ala. 1979).

Collateral references. — 60 C.J.S., Motor Vehicles, §§ 62, 63, 150.

§ 32-12-23. Repealed by Acts 1980, No. 80-434, p. 604, § 15-106, effective May 19, 1980.

§ 32-12-24. Brakes.

(a) Every motor-driven cycle when operated upon the highway shall be equipped with brakes adequate to control the movement of and to stop and hold such vehicle.

(b) The director of public safety is authorized to require an inspection of the brakes of any motor-driven cycle and to disapprove any brakes which he finds are not adequate.

(c) All such brakes shall be maintained in good working order.

(d) The director of public safety may refuse to register or he may suspend or revoke the registration of any motor-driven cycle when he determines that the brakes thereon do not comply with the provisions of this section.

(e) No person shall operate on any highway any motor-driven cycle in the event the director of public safety has disapproved the brake equipment on such cycle or type of cycle.

(f) Every motor-driven cycle when operated upon the highway shall be equipped with at least one brake, which may be operated by hand or foot.

(g) Any person violating this section shall be guilty of a misdemeanor. (Acts 1949, No. 652, p. 1006, § 6.)

Collateral references. — 60 C.J.S., Motor Vehicles, § 26. 60A C.J.S., Motor Vehicles, §§ 258, 261, 350(1). 61 C.J.S., Motor Vehicles, §§ 520(3), 527(18). 61A C.J.S., Motor Vehicles, §§ 609, 640.

§ 32-12-25. Repealed by Acts 1980, No. 80-434, p. 604, § 15-106, effective May 19, 1980.

§ 32-12-26. Revocation of operator's license.

The director of public safety shall be authorized to revoke the license of any operator of a motor-driven cycle convicted of violating any of the provisions of this article. (Acts 1949, No. 652, p. 1006, § 6A.)

Collateral references. — 60 C.J.S., Motor Vehicles, §§ 146, 160, 164.1-164.50.

§ 32-12-27. Penalties.

Any person who violates this article shall be punished by a fine of not more than $500.00 or by imprisonment for not more than six months, or by fine and imprisonment. (Acts 1949, No. 652, p. 1006, § 8.)

ARTICLE 3.

HELMETS.

§ 32-12-40. Repealed by Acts 1980, No. 80-434, p. 604, § 15-106, effective May 19, 1980.

§ 32-12-41. Specifications.

The protective helmet shall meet the following specifications:

(1) DESIGN. — One which is specifically designed for motorcycle riders and motorcycle passenger use.

(2) EXTERIOR SHELL. — A hard exterior shell of nonshatterable material, resistant to impact and penetration.

(3) CRADLE. — A firmly secured shock absorbent cradle for the head designed to support the helmet and maintain separation between the head and outer shell. Materials used in this portion of protective helmet shall be of durable quality and with characteristics that will not undergo appreciable alteration under the influence of aging or of the circumstances of use to which the helmet is normally subjected. Materials commonly known to cause skin irritation or disease shall not be used for these parts of the assembly which come in contact with the skin.

(4) PADDING. — Impact-resistant, absorbent padding or cushioning material of substantial thickness in all areas where the head is in close proximity with or may contact the outer shell.

(5) CHIN STRAP. — A permanently attached adjustable chin strap that will hold the helmet securely in place. A rider must at all times, while a motorized vehicle is in motion, have a chin strap firmly in place on or under the chin.

(6) VISOR. — Not required, but, if the helmet is so equipped, the visor must be flexible or of a snap on type; however, no external projections shall

be more than one-quarter inch above surface of the exterior shell. (Acts 1967, Ex. Sess., No. 171, p. 218, § 2.)

§ 32-12-42. Duties of manufacturers.

The manufacturers of motorcycle helmets for sale in Alabama shall meet the following specifications and comply with the following procedures:

(1) All protective helmets shall be required to meet minimum regulations of the USA standards set forth in Z-90 regulations of 1966.

(2) A manufacturer desiring to secure approval of a protective helmet shall submit to the director of public safety, state of Alabama, Montgomery, Alabama 36104, postage prepaid, a test report certified as required in Z-90 basic standards, together with a sample of the helmet for which approval is sought. The director may contract with the American association of motor vehicle administrators in conducting testing procedures and the giving of approval of helmets submitted.

(3) If, after receipt of the test report from an independent testing laboratory, the director of public safety finds that the helmet meets the requirements, notice of approval of the helmet will be issued.

(4) Each protective helmet approved by the director of public safety shall be labelled on the outside of the helmet above the base of the rear of the helmet with letters or numbers at least one-quarter inch in height, with the manufacturer's trade name and model number or name, which shall be the same as name or number under which the helmet has been approved. (Acts 1967, Ex. Sess., No. 171, p. 218, § 3.)

§ 32-12-43. Repealed by Acts 1980, No. 80-434, p. 604, § 15-106, effective May 19, 1980.

§ 32-12-44. Penalty for violation of article.

Any person or manufacturer who shall violate any provision of this article shall be guilty of a misdemeanor and shall be punished by a fine of not less than $1.00 nor more than $100.00, and may be imprisoned in the county jail or sentenced to hard labor for not more than 180 days, one or both. Each violation of any provision of this article shall constitute a separate offense. (Acts 1967, Ex. Sess., No. 171, p. 218, § 4.)

CHAPTER 13.

ABANDONED MOTOR VEHICLES.

Chapter only applies to what legislature defines as abandoned vehicles. Bryce Hosp. Credit Union, Inc. v. Warrior Dodge, Inc., 50 Ala. App. 15, 276 So. 2d 602, cert. denied, 290 Ala. 362, 276 So. 2d 607 (1973).

It becomes applicable upon abandonment of vehicle. Bryce Hosp. Credit Union, Inc. v. Warrior Dodge, Inc., 50 Ala. App. 15, 276 So. 2d 602, cert. denied, 290 Ala. 362, 276 So. 2d 607 (1973).

But only operates prospectively. — Statutes generally operate prospectively unless the legislature clearly intends to give them retrospective effect. There is no legislative intent evidencing a desire that this chapter should be given retrospective effect, and such effect is not to be given to it. Bryce Hosp. Credit Union, Inc. v. Warrior Dodge, Inc., 50 Ala. App. 15, 276 So. 2d 602, cert. denied, 290 Ala. 362, 276 So. 2d 607 (1973).

There is no conflict between this chapter, section 35-11-110 and section 7-9-310. Bryce Hosp. Credit Union, Inc. v. Warrior Dodge, Inc., 290 Ala. 362, 276 So. 2d 607 (1973).

Cited in State Farm Mut. Auto. Ins. Co. v. Hartman, 450 So. 2d 152 (Ala. Civ. App. 1984).

Collateral references. — State or municipal towing, impounding, or destruction of motor vehicles parked or abandoned on streets or highways. 32 ALR4th 728.

§ 32-13-1. "Abandoned motor vehicle" defined; posted notice.

For the purposes of this chapter, an "abandoned motor vehicle" shall mean a motor vehicle, as defined in section 32-1-1.1:

(1) Which has been left by the owner, or some person acting for the owner, with an automobile dealer, repairman or wrecker service for repair or for some other reason and has not been called for by such owner or other person within a period of 60 days after the time agreed upon and within 60 days after such vehicle is turned over to such dealer, repairman or wrecker service when no time is agreed upon, or within 60 days after the completion of necessary repairs;

(2) Which is left unattended on a public street, road or highway or other public property for a period of at least seven days; or left unattended continuously for at least seven days in a business district or a residence district; or if left unattended in a business district that has at least one posted notice in an open and conspicuous place indicating that there is a time limitation on the length of time a motor vehicle may remain parked in said district and said motor vehicle remains unattended for a period of time in excess of that posted on the notice; or left unattended in a business district or residence district that has at least one posted notice indicating that only authorized motor vehicles may park in that district and the owner

of said motor vehicle or his agent has not received the required authority prior to leaving said motor vehicle unattended; or left unattended on a private road or driveway without the express or implied permission of the owner or lessee of such driveway or their agent. A posted notice when required by this chapter shall meet the following specifications:

(a) The notice must be prominently placed at each driveway access or curb cut allowing vehicular access to the property, within five feet from the public right-of-way line. If there are no curbs or access barriers, the signs must be posted not less than one sign each 25 feet of lot frontage.

(b) The notice must clearly indicate, in not less than two inch high light-reflective letters on a contrasting background, that unauthorized vehicles will be towed away at the owner's expense. The words "Tow Away Zone" must be included on the sign in not less than four inch high letters.

(c) The notice must also provide the name and current telephone number of the person or firm towing or removing the vehicles, if the property owner, lessor or person in control of the property has a written contract with a wrecker service.

(d) The sign structure containing the required notices must be permanently installed with the bottom of the sign not less than four feet above ground level, and be continuously maintained on the property for not less than 24 hours prior to the towing or removal of any vehicles.

(3) Which has been lawfully towed onto the property of another at the written request of a law-enforcement officer and left there for a period of not less than 60 days without anyone having made claim thereto. (Acts 1971, No. 1154, p. 1999, § 1; Acts 1989, No. 89-758, § 1.)

The 1989 amendment, effective May 11, 1989, rewrote subdivision (2).

Use of vehicle by towing and storage service prohibited; compensation for removal. — The Abandoned Motor Vehicle Act does not permit one performing towing and storage service, at the request of a peace officer, the right to retain the vehicle for his own personal use, nor to receive pay except a reasonable fee for the towing and storage from the proceeds of a sale according to the statute. Allstate Ins. Co. v. Reeves, 440 So. 2d 1086 (Ala. Civ. App. 1983).

Collateral references. — Search and seizure: what constitutes abandonment of personal property within rule that search and seizure of abandoned property is not unreasonable — modern cases. 40 ALR4th 381.

§ 32-13-2. Peace officer's responsibility; lien on vehicles removed; removal by property owner, etc.; notice of removal.

(a) Any peace officer who finds a motor vehicle which has been left unattended on a public street, road or highway or other property for a period of at least seven days, shall be authorized to cause such motor vehicle to be removed to the nearest garage or other place of safety.

(b) Any peace officer who under the provisions of this section causes any motor vehicle to be removed to a garage or other place of safety shall be liable for gross negligence only and any person removing such vehicle or other property at the direction of a peace officer in accordance with the provisions of this section shall have a lien on such motor vehicle for a reasonable fee for such removal and for the storage of such motor vehicle.

(c) Any peace officer who under the provisions of this section causes the removal of any motor vehicle to a garage or other place of safety shall within five days give written notice of such removal, which notice shall include a complete description of the motor vehicle serial number and license number thereof, provided such information is available, to both the secretary of state, state of Alabama and the department of public safety, state of Alabama.

(d) The owner or lessee of real property or their agent upon which an abandoned motor vehicle as defined in section 32-13-1 has become abandoned shall be authorized to cause such abandoned motor vehicle to be removed to a secure place. Any owner or lessee of such real property or their agent who shall cause such abandoned motor vehicle to be removed from their real property shall, within 24 hours of such removal, give written notice to the county or municipal law enforcement agency in whose jurisdiction the abandoned motor vehicle was situated. Any person or corporation removing such vehicle or other property at the direction of the owner or lessee of real property or their agent in accordance with the provisions of this section have a lien on such motor vehicle for a reasonable fee for such removal and for storage of such motor vehicle. (Acts 1971, No. 1154, p. 1999, § 2; Acts 1989, No. 89-758, § 2.)

The **1989 amendment,** effective May 11, 1989, added subsection (d) of this section.

Collateral references. — 60 C.J.S., Motor Vehicles, § 43. 61A C.J.S., Motor Vehicles, § 563.

Lien for towing or storage, ordered by public officer, of motor vehicle. 85 ALR3d 199.

§ 32-13-3. Authority to sell; notice; issuance of clear bill of sale.

Any automobile dealer, wrecker service or repair service owner, or any person or firm on whose property a motor vehicle is lawfully towed at the written request of a law-enforcement officer or the owner or lessee of real property or their agent upon which an abandoned motor vehicle as defined in section 32-13-1 has become abandoned, and who shall have an abandoned motor vehicle on his property, may sell the same at public auction. Notice of the date and place of the sale and a description of the vehicle to be sold shall be given by a newspaper publication at least 10 days before the date of the sale in a newspaper of general circulation in the county in which the sale is to be held. In counties in which no newspaper is published, notice shall be given by posting such notice in a conspicuous place at the courthouse. Upon payment of the sales price, the purchaser shall be entitled to and the person making such sale shall issue to him a bill of sale to such abandoned motor vehicle, free and clear of all liens and encumbrances. (Acts 1971, No. 1154, p. 1999, § 3; Acts 1983, No. 83-494, p. 691, § 1; Acts 1989, No. 89-758, § 3.)

The 1989 amendment, effective May 11, 1989, inserted "or the owner or lessee of real property or their agent upon which an abandoned motor vehicle as defined in section 32-13-1 has become abandoned, and" in the first sentence.

Abandoned vehicles may be sold with clear bill of sale. — The legislature, exercising its prerogative, has decided that abandoned vehicles, after the provisions of the chapter have been complied with, may be sold to pay for the cost of repairs, and a bill of sale may be given free and clear of all liens and encumbrances. Bryce Hosp. Credit Union, Inc.

v. Warrior Dodge, Inc., 50 Ala. App. 15, 276 So. 2d 602, cert. denied, 290 Ala. 362, 276 So. 2d 607 (1973).

This section gives an automobile dealer, wrecker service, or repair service owner the authority to sell an abandoned vehicle in order to satisfy a statutory lien he has in the vehicle for its towing and storage. Allstate Ins. Co. v. Reeves, 440 So. 2d 1086 (Ala. Civ. App. 1983).

Collateral references. — What constitutes a "public sale." 4 ALR2d 575.

Garageman's lien as compensation for towing and storage charges. 85 ALR3d 199.

§ 32-13-4. Notice of sale; hearing; appeal.

(a) Any automobile dealer, wrecker service or repair service owner, or any person or firm on whose property a motor vehicle is lawfully towed at the written request of a law-enforcement officer, the owner or lessee of real property or his agent upon which an abandoned motor vehicle as defined in section 32-13-1 has become abandoned, shall give written notice to the owner, secured parties of record, and known lienholders, if any, at least 30 days prior to the date of the sale of the motor vehicle advising of (1) the complete description of the vehicle and the date and place the vehicle was found or taken into possession, (2) the approximate amount owed for the cost of repair, towing and storage, (3) the location of storage of the vehicle, (4) the time and place that a sale of the vehicle will be held, (5) the right of the owner, secured parties or lienholders to contest the right to sell such vehicle by the filing within 10 days before the date of the sale of the vehicle of an application for hearing to be conducted before the judge of the district court or circuit court of the county in which the sale is to be held. The application for hearing shall be on such a form as may be prescribed by the department of court management of the state of Alabama. The notice required by this section shall be deemed to be given when sent by certified mail, postage prepaid, to the address of the owner, secured party of record, and known lienholder shown on any public filing evidencing such ownership, security interest, or lien; or, if none, to any such address ascertained by reasonable effort.

(b) If the name and address of the owner, secured parties or lienholders of the vehicle are unknown or cannot be reasonably ascertained, then the notice required herein shall be given by publication once a week for two successive weeks in a newspaper of general circulation in the county in which the sale is to be held. In counties in which no newspaper is published, notice shall be given by posting such notice in a conspicuous place at the courthouse. The first publication or posting, as the case may be, shall be at least 30 days before the date of sale.

(c) If no application for hearing is made by the owner, secured parties, or lienholders, the vehicle may be sold at the time and place designated in the notice of sale. If application for hearing is made by the owner, secured parties, or lienholders, then all such persons shall be joined as parties and the judge of

374

the district court or circuit court shall conduct a hearing to determine if the vehicle is an abandoned vehicle as defined by this chapter and should be sold in the manner prescribed herein. The vehicle shall not be sold pending the decision by the district or circuit court judge. If the judge shall determine that the vehicle is abandoned and should be sold, the vehicle may be sold after notice of the date and place of the sale is given by newspaper publication as prescribed in section 32-13-3. If the hearing is conducted by the judge of the district court, any person aggrieved by the decision rendered by the judge of the district court may appeal to the circuit court of the judicial circuit wherein the hearing was held by filing notice of appeal in the time and in the manner prescribed by law. (Acts 1971, No. 1154, p. 1999, § 4; Acts 1983, No. 83-494, p. 691, § 1; Acts 1989, No. 89-758, § 3.)

The 1989 amendment, effective May 11, 1989, inserted "the owner or lessee of real property or his agent upon which an abandoned motor vehicle as defined in section 32-13-1 has become abandoned" in the first sentence of subsection (a).

Cited in Allstate Ins. Co. v. Reeves, 440 So. 2d 1086 (Ala. Civ. App. 1983).

Collateral references. — Validity of legislation relating to publication of legal notices. 26 ALR2d 655.

OPINIONS OF THE SUPREME COURT CLERK

Cited in Op. No. 42, 445 So. 2d 905 (Ala. 1984).

§ 32-13-5. Rejection of bids.

The person making the sale shall have the right to reject any and all bids if the amount bid be unreasonably low, and shall have the right to continue the sale from time to time if no bidders are present. (Acts 1971, No. 1154, p. 1999, § 5.)

§ 32-13-6. Deductions from proceeds; filing report of sale.

(a) The person making the sale shall deduct from the proceeds of such sale the reasonable cost of repair, towing and storage and all expenses incurred in connection with such sale, and pay the balance remaining to the register of the circuit court of the county in which such sale is made; provided, that such costs shall in no event exceed the customary charges for like services in the community where the sale is made.

(b) The person making such sale shall promptly file with the register or clerk of the circuit court of the county in which such sale is made a report of the sale, showing the date such abandoned automobile first came into his possession or was abandoned on his premises, the name of the newspaper in which notice of sale was published and the dates of such publication, the time and place of the sale, the amount for which the abandoned motor vehicle was sold, the amounts deducted from such sales price for repair, towing, storage expenses, expense of publication of notice of sale and the amount paid over to the register or clerk of the circuit court. Such report shall contain a statement by the person making such sale, certifying to the correctness of such report under oath.

(c) The clerk or register of the circuit court receiving the report of sale shall deduct from the funds paid with such report a fee of $35.00 in accordance with section 12-19-76. (Acts 1971, No. 1154, p. 1999, § 6.)

Code commissioner's note. — Subsection (c) was added by the code commissioner in order to conform the provisions of this section with the provisions of § 12-19-76, as added by Acts 1976, No. 564, p. 763.

Cross references. — As to fee for report of sales of abandoned motor vehicles, see § 12-19-76.

§ 32-13-7. Disposition of proceeds.

The register or clerk of the circuit court shall retain the remaining balance of the proceeds of such sale for a period of 12 months, and if no claim has been filed against such proceeds by the owner of the abandoned motor vehicle or any interested party, then he shall pay such remaining balance as follows:

(1) If the abandoned motor vehicle came into the possession of the person making such sale other than at the request of a peace officer, the proceeds of the sale shall be divided equally and paid to the general fund of the county in which the sale was made, to the general fund of the municipality, if any, in which the sale was made and to the general fund of the state of Alabama.

(2) If the abandoned motor vehicle came into the possession of the person making such sale at the written request of a police officer of a municipality, the proceeds of sale shall be divided equally and paid to the general fund of the municipality if any, in which the sale was made and to the general fund of the state of Alabama.

(3) If the abandoned motor vehicle came into the possession of the person making such sale at the written request of a county sheriff, the proceeds of sale shall be divided equally and paid to the general fund of the county in which the sale was made, and to the general fund of the state of Alabama.

(4) If the abandoned motor vehicle came into the possession of the person making such sale at the written request of a state trooper or employee of the state of Alabama, the proceeds of sale shall be paid to the general fund of the state of Alabama. (Acts 1971, No. 1154, p. 1999, § 7.)

§ 32-13-8. Chapter cumulative; power of municipality not restricted.

This chapter is cumulative and shall not be construed as limiting or restricting any power or authority any municipality may now have or possess under any other provision of law. (Acts 1971, No. 1154, p. 1999, § 8.)

CHAPTER 14.

DRIVER TRAINING SCHOOLS.

ARTICLE 1.

GENERAL PROVISIONS.

§ 32-14-1. Short title.

This chapter may be cited as the Driver Training School License Act. (Acts 1967, No. 185, p. 547, § 11.)

§ 32-14-2. Definitions.

The following words and phrases when used in this chapter shall, unless the context otherwise requires, have the meanings respectively ascribed to them in this section:

(1) MOTOR VEHICLE. Every vehicle which is self-propelled upon or by which any person or property is or may be transported or drawn upon a public highway, except devices used exclusively upon stationary rails or tracks.

(2) DRIVER TRAINING SCHOOLS. Any person, partnership or corporation giving driving instruction to 10 or more persons per calendar year for the purpose of meeting requirements for licensed driving of motor vehicles in Alabama.

(3) PERSON. Every natural person, firm, copartnership, association, corporation or school.

(4) DEPARTMENT. The state department of education, acting directly or through its duly authorized officers and agents.

(5) SUPERINTENDENT. The superintendent of the state department of education.

(6) DRIVER'S LICENSE EXAMINERS. Examiners appointed by the department of public safety for the purpose of giving driver's license examinations. (Acts 1967, No. 185, p. 547, § 1.)

§ 32-14-3. Rules and regulations.

The superintendent is authorized to prescribe by rule standards for the eligibility, conduct, equipment and operation of driver training schools and instructors and to adopt other reasonable rules and regulations to carry out the provisions of this chapter. (Acts 1967, No. 185, p. 547, § 6.)

§ 32-14-4. Disposition of moneys received.

All moneys received under this chapter shall be deposited with the state treasurer and credited to the state driver education training fund. (Acts 1967, No. 185, p. 547, § 8.)

§ 32-14-5. Exemptions.

This chapter shall not apply to an accredited grade school, high school, junior college or college conducting a driver training course, nor shall it apply to driver improvement schools operated by this state or a municipality thereof. (Acts 1967, No. 185, p. 547, § 10.)

§ 32-14-6. Penalty for violation of chapter.

Any person violating any provision of this chapter shall be guilty of a misdemeanor and upon conviction thereof shall be fined not more than $500.00 or be sentenced to the county jail for not more than six months, or both such fine and imprisonment. (Acts 1967, No. 185, p. 547, § 9.)

ARTICLE 2.

LICENSES.

§ 32-14-20. Required.

No person shall operate a driver training school or engage in the business of giving instruction for hire in the driving of motor vehicles or in the preparation of an applicant for examination given by driver's license examiners for a driver's license or permit, unless a license therefor has been secured from the superintendent. (Acts 1967, No. 185, p. 547, § 2.)

§ 32-14-21. Qualifications — Operation of driving school.

Every person in order to qualify to operate a driving school shall meet the following requirements:

(1) Be of good character.

(2) Maintain an established place of business to the public.

(3) Maintain bodily injury and property damage liability insurance on motor vehicles while used in driving instruction, insuring the liability of the driving school, the driving instructors and any person taking instruction in at least the following amounts: $100,000.00 for bodily injury to or

death of one person in any one accident and, subject to said limit for one person, $200,000.00 for bodily injury to or death of two or more persons in any one accident; and the amount of $20,000.00 for damage to property of others in any one accident. Evidence of such insurance coverage in the form of a certificate from the insurance carrier shall be filed with the superintendent, and such certificate shall stipulate that the insurance shall not be cancelled except upon 10 days' prior written notice to the superintendent. Such insurance shall be written by a company authorized to do business in this state.

(4) Provide a continuous surety company bond in the principal sum of $2,500.00 for the protection of the contractual rights of students in such form as will meet with the approval of the superintendent and written by a company authorized to be in business in this state. However, the aggregate liability of the surety for all breaches of the condition of the bond in no event shall exceed the principal sum of $2,500.00. The surety on any such bond may cancel such bond on giving 30 days' notice thereof in writing to the superintendent and shall be relieved of liability for any breach of any condition of the bond which occurs after the effective date of cancellation.

(5) Have the equipment necessary to the giving of proper instruction in the operation of motor vehicles as prescribed by the state superintendent of education.

(6) Pay to the superintendent an application fee of $25.00. (Acts 1967, No. 185, p. 547, § 3.)

Collateral references. — Liability, for personal injury or property damage, for negligence in teaching or supervision of learning driver. 5 ALR3d 271.

Circumstances under which a student-driver's negligence may properly be imputed to a teacher-passenger. 90 ALR3d 1329.

§ 32-14-22. Same — Instructor for driving school.

Every person in order to qualify as an instructor for a driving school shall meet the following requirements:

(1) Be of good moral character.

(2) Present to the state superintendent of education evidence of credit in driver education and safety from an accredited college or university equivalent to credits in those subjects which are required of instructors in the public schools of Alabama or have a valid Alabama teacher's certificate coded for driver education.

(3) Be physically able to operate safely a motor vehicle and to train others in the operation of motor vehicles.

(4) Provide a certificate of health from a medical doctor stating that he or she is free from contagious disease.

(5) Hold a valid driver's license.

(6) Pay to the superintendent an application fee of $5.00. (Acts 1967, No. 185, p. 547, § 4.)

§ 32-14-23. Issuance, expiration and renewal.

(a) The superintendent shall issue a license certificate to each applicant to conduct a driver training school or to each driver training instructor when the superintendent is satisfied that such person has met the qualifications required under this chapter.

(b) All outstanding licenses issued to any driver training school or driver training instructor pursuant to the provisions of this chapter shall expire as a matter of law at midnight on September 30 of the calendar year for which the license was issued, and must be renewed annually, unless sooner cancelled, suspended or revoked under the provisions of section 32-14-24.

(c) The license of each driver training school and each driver training instructor may be renewed subject to the same conditions as the original license and upon payment of the same fee.

(d) All applications for renewal of a driver training school license or driver training instructor's license shall be on a form prescribed by the superintendent and must be filed with the office of the superintendent not more than 60 days nor less than 10 days preceding the expiration date of the license to be renewed. (Acts 1967, No. 185, p. 547, § 5.)

§ 32-14-24. Cancellation, suspension or revocation of or refusal to renew licenses.

The superintendent may cancel, suspend, revoke or refuse to renew any driver training school or driver training instructor's license:

(1) When the superintendent is satisfied that the licensee fails to meet the requirements to receive or hold a license under this chapter;

(2) Whenever the licensee fails to keep the records required herein;

(3) Whenever the licensee permits fraud or engages in fraudulent practices either with reference to the applicant or the superintendent, or induces or countenances fraud or fraudulent practices on the part of any applicant for a driver's license or permit;

(4) Whenever the licensee fails to comply with any provisions of this chapter or any rule of the superintendent made pursuant thereto;

(5) Whenever the licensee represents himself as an agent or employee of the superintendent or license examiners or uses advertising designed to lead or which would reasonably have the effect of leading persons to believe that such licensee is in fact an employee or representative of the superintendent or license examiners;

(6) Whenever the licensee or any employee or agent of the licensee solicits driver training or instruction in an office of any department of the state having to do with the administration of any law relating to motor vehicles; or

(7) Whenever the licensee or any employee or agent, serving as a driver training instructor, has had his license cancelled, suspended or revoked. (Acts 1967, No. 185, p. 547, § 7.)

CHAPTER 15.

RENTING, HIRING AND USING MOTOR VEHICLES.

Collateral references. — 7 Am. Jur. 2d, Automobiles & Highway Traffic, §§ 298-300.

§ 32-15-1. Fraudulent determination of mileage.

Whoever, with the intent to defraud, shall rent a motor vehicle, the hire of which is determinable either in whole or in part by the distance such motor vehicle travels, knowing that the odometer or other mechanical device attached to such motor vehicle or any part thereof for the purpose of registering the distance that such motor vehicle travels does not correctly register the distance such motor vehicle travels, or who shall knowingly deceive any person or persons hiring any motor vehicle as to the distance such motor vehicle has traveled during the period of hiring and shall make a charge for the use thereof, based either in whole or in part upon such deception, shall, upon conviction, be guilty of a misdemeanor and subject to imprisonment in the county jail for a period of not less than 30 days nor more than 12 months, or be fined not less than $50.00 nor more than $200.00, or be both fined and imprisoned. (Acts 1927, No. 456, p. 507; Code 1940, T. 36, § 96.)

Collateral references. — 61A C.J.S., Motor Vehicles, § 723.

Regulation of business of renting motor vehicles without drivers (drive-it-yourself systems). 7 ALR2d 456.

State regulation of motor vehicle rental ("you-drive") business. 60 ALR4th 784.

§ 32-15-2. Renting to intoxicated person.

Whoever rents a motor vehicle to any person to operate upon any public highway or street, knowing that such person is in an intoxicated condition or under the influence of drugs, shall, upon conviction, be guilty of a misdemeanor and shall be subject to imprisonment in the county jail for a period of not less than 30 days nor more than 12 months, or shall be fined not less than $25.00 nor more than $100.00, or shall be both fined and imprisoned. (Acts 1927, No. 456, p. 507; Code 1940, T. 36, § 97.)

Cited in McGowin v. Howard, 246 Ala. 553, 21 So. 2d 683 (1945).

Collateral references. — 61A C.J.S., Motor Vehicles, § 768.

Regulation of business of renting motor vehicles without drivers (drive-it-yourself systems). 7 ALR2d 456.

Criminal liability in connection with rental of motor vehicles. 38 ALR3d 949.

Rental agency's liability for negligent entrustment of vehicle. 78 ALR3d 1170.

State regulation of motor vehicle rental ("you-drive") business. 60 ALR4th 784.

§ 32-15-3. Person hiring tampering with mileage device.

Whoever, after hiring a motor vehicle from any person or persons under an agreement to pay for the use of such motor vehicle a sum of money determinable either in whole or in part upon the distance such motor vehicle travels during the period for which hired, shall, with the intent to deceive the person or persons letting such motor vehicle or such person's or persons' lawful agent as to the actual distance such motor vehicle traveled during the period for which let, remove or attempt to remove, tamper with or attempt to tamper with, or in any other wise interfere with any odometer or other mechanical device attached to said hired motor vehicle for the purpose of registering the distance such motor vehicle travels, or who shall knowingly aid, abet or assist another in so doing, or shall remove or attempt to remove from such motor vehicle any part thereof upon which is attached such odometer or such other mechanical device, shall, upon conviction, be deemed guilty of a misdemeanor and shall be punished by imprisonment in a county jail for not more than 12 months nor less than 30 days or shall be fined not more than $200.00 nor less than $50.00 or shall be both fined and imprisoned. Any person violating this section may be punished in the county where such motor vehicle is hired or in the county where such odometer or such other mechanical device is removed or attempted to be removed, or tampered with or attempted to be tampered with, or in any other wise interfered with, or in the county where such person knowingly aid, abet or assist another in violating the provisions of this section, or in the county where any part of such motor vehicle upon which is attached such odometer or such other mechanical device is removed or attempted to be removed. (Acts 1927, No. 456, p. 507; Code 1940, T. 36, § 98.)

Collateral references. — 61A C.J.S., Motor Vehicles, § 713.

Construction and application of state statute making it unlawful to tamper with motor

vehicle odometer. 76 ALR3d 981.

State regulation of motor vehicle rental ("you-drive") business. 60 ALR4th 784.

§ 32-15-4. Obtaining possession by trick, false representation, etc.

Whoever, with the intent to deprive or defraud the owner of any motor vehicle, or the person in lawful possession thereof, out of the temporary use, benefit or enjoyment of such motor vehicle, shall obtain the custody of such motor vehicle from the owner thereof, or from such owner's agent, or from any person in lawful possession thereof by some trick or fraudulent or false representation, or any false token or writing, or false personation of another, shall, upon conviction, be deemed guilty of a Class C felony and shall be punished with imprisonment in a state penitentiary for not more than 10 years nor less than one year and one day, or shall be fined not more than $5,000.00 or shall be both fined and imprisoned. (Acts 1927, No. 456, p. 507; Code 1940, T. 36, § 99; Acts 1983, No. 83-564, p. 865, § 1.)

Collateral references. — 60 C.J.S., Motor Vehicles, § 41(2). 60A C.J.S., Motor Vehicles, § 442(6).

State regulation of motor vehicle rental ("you-drive") business. 60 ALR4th 784.

§ 32-15-5. Hiring with intent to defraud.

Whoever, with intent to defraud the owner of any motor vehicle or any person in lawful possession thereof, hires from such owner, or such owner's agents, or any person in lawful possession thereof, any motor vehicle shall, upon conviction, be deemed guilty of a Class C felony and shall be punished by imprisonment in a state penitentiary for not more than 10 years nor less than one year and one day, or shall be fined not more than $5,000.00, or shall be both fined and imprisoned. The refusal to pay the hire of such motor vehicle or absconding without paying or offering to pay such hire shall be prima facie evidence of such fraudulent intent. (Acts 1927, No. 456, p. 507; Code 1940, T. 36, § 100; Acts 1983, No. 83-564, p. 865, § 1.)

Collateral references. — State regulation of motor vehicle rental ("you-drive") business. 60 ALR4th 784.

§ 32-15-6. Failure to redeliver hired vehicle; service of written demand.

Any person who, after hiring, leasing or renting a motor vehicle under an agreement in writing, which provides for return of said vehicle to a particular place, or at a particular time, shall abandon such vehicle, or secrete, convert, sell or attempt to sell the same or any part thereof, or who shall fail to return the vehicle to said place within the time specified, and is thereafter personally served with a written demand, or upon whom written demand is thereafter made by registered mail, to return said vehicle to the place specified in the written agreement within 48 hours from the time of the personal service or service by registered mail of such demand, and who fails, except for causes beyond his control to return said vehicle to the lessor within said period, is guilty of a Class C felony and shall be punished by imprisonment for not more than 10 years or less than one year and one day in a state penitentiary, or shall be fined not more than $5,000.00, or shall be both fined and imprisoned. Service by registered mail shall be deemed to be complete upon deposit in the United States mail of such demand securely wrapped, postpaid and addressed to such person at the address for such person set forth in the written agreement for the hire or use thereof or in the absence of such address to such person's last known place of residence. (Acts 1927, No. 456, p. 507; Code 1940, T. 36, § 101; Acts 1983, No. 83-564, p. 865, § 1.)

Collateral references. — 61A C.J.S., Motor Vehicles, § 764.

State regulation of motor vehicle rental ("you-drive") business. 60 ALR4th 784.

§ 32-15-7. Embezzlement, conversion, etc., of motor vehicle which is subject of larceny.

Whoever embezzles or fraudulently converts to his own use or secretes, with intent to embezzle or fraudulently convert to his own use, any motor vehicle delivered to him, which may be the subject of larceny or any part thereof, shall be deemed guilty of a Class C felony and shall be punished by imprisonment for not more than 10 years or less than one year and one day in a state penitentiary, or shall be fined not more than $5,000.00, or shall be both fined and imprisoned. (Acts 1927, No. 456, p. 507; Code 1940, T. 36, § 102; Acts 1983, No. 83-564, p. 865, § 1.)

Collateral references. — State regulation of motor vehicle rental ("you-drive") business. 60 ALR4th 784.

§ 32-15-8. Permitting another to drive hired car.

Whoever, after hiring a motor vehicle under an agreement not to permit another to operate or drive same, shall, without first securing the consent of the renter thereto, or the renter's duly authorized agent, permit another to operate or drive same shall be guilty of a misdemeanor and shall be punished by imprisonment for not more than six months or shall be fined not more than $200.00, or shall be both fined and imprisoned. (Acts 1927, No. 456, p. 507; Code 1940, T. 36, § 103.)

Collateral references. — 60A C.J.S., Motor Vehicles, § 442(6). 61A C.J.S., Motor Vehicles, § 764.

State regulation of motor vehicle rental ("you-drive") business. 60 ALR4th 784.

CHAPTER 16.

SELLING USED MOTOR VEHICLES.

Collateral references. — 7 Am. Jur. 2d,
Automobiles & Highway Traffic, §§ 29-46.

§ 32-16-1. Definitions.

The terms "dealer" and "vendor" as used in this chapter shall be construed
to include every individual, partnership, corporation or association whose
business in whole or in part is that of selling new or used motor vehicles and
likewise shall be construed to include every agent, representative or
consignee of any such dealer as defined above, as fully as if the same had been
herein expressly set out; except, that no agent, representative or consignee of
such dealer or vendor shall be required to make and file the bond if such
dealer or vendor for whom such agent, representative or consignee acts shall
have fully complied with all of the provisions of this chapter. (Acts 1936-37,
Ex. Sess., No. 220, p. 263; Code 1940, T. 36, § 104.)

Collateral references. — 60 C.J.S., Motor
Vehicles, §§ 41(3), 42(3), 78.

Applicability to automobile dealers of regulations as to certificates of title and bills of
sale. 57 ALR2d 1284.

Rights of seller of motor vehicle with respect
to purchase price or security on failure to
comply with laws concerning transfer of title.
58 ALR2d 1351.

§ 32-16-2. Registration of certain vehicles; bond of certain dealers.

Every dealer in used or secondhand motor vehicles who is a nonresident of
the state of Alabama, or who does not have a permanent place of business in
the state of Alabama, and any person, firm or corporation who brings any
used or secondhand motor vehicle into the state of Alabama for purposes of
sale or resale, except as a trade-in on a new motor vehicle, or another used
car, shall, within 10 days from date of entering of said used or secondhand
motor vehicle into the state of Alabama, register such motor vehicle with the
probate judge of the county in which said secondhand or used motor vehicle is
brought, on a form to be provided by the probate judge, and shall, before said
used or secondhand car is put on a used car lot for sale, or offered for sale, or
sold, execute bond with two good and sufficient sureties or with a surety
company duly authorized to do business in the state of Alabama as surety or
sureties thereon, payable to the said probate judge for the use or benefit of the
purchaser and his vendees, conditioned to pay all loss, damages and expenses
that may be sustained by the purchaser or vendees, that may be occasioned by
reason of any fraudulent misrepresentations or breaches of warranty as to

freedom from liens, quality, condition, use or value of said motor vehicle being so sold. Said bond shall be in the full amount of the sale price of such secondhand or used motor vehicle, but in no event to exceed the sum of $1,000.00, and such bond shall be filed with the probate judge of the county in which such sale is made by the vendor, and such bond shall be approved by said probate judge as to the amount thereof and as to the solvency of the surety or sureties thereon, for which services the vendor shall pay a fee of $1.00 as registration and recording, which said sum shall be held and disposed of as other registration and recording fees are now held and disposed of by him; and the said vendor shall pay over to the probate judge at the time of the registration of said bond the further sum of $5.00, which said sum shall be by the probate judge paid over to the county treasury of the respective counties, less a fee of $.50 to be retained by the probate judge to the credit of county school funds, the same to be distributed and disposed of as provided by law. (Acts 1936-37, Ex. Sess., No. 220, p. 263; Code 1940, T. 36, § 105.)

Constitutionality. — The provisions of this section requiring all persons, including local dealers, who bring used automobiles into Alabama for sale to register each automobile, to file a bond in an amount equal to the value of the used automobile not over $1,000.00 and to pay a $5.00 fee not in any way related to expenses of administering statute are violative of the commerce clause of the federal Constitution. State v. Kimbrough, 30 Ala. App. 235, 3 So. 2d 421, conforming to 241 Ala. 535, 3 So. 2d 424 (1941).

Collateral references. — Validity, construction and application of statutes or ordinances licensing, or otherwise regulating, business of selling motor vehicles. 126 ALR 740, 57 ALR2d 1265.

Constitutionality and construction of statutes or other regulations regarding sale or offer of sale of used automobiles. 134 ALR 647.

Regulation or licensing of business of selling motor vehicles. 57 ALR2d 1265.

§ 32-16-3. Right of action dependent upon compliance.

No action nor the right of action to recover any such secondhand or used motor vehicle, nor any part of the selling price thereof, shall be maintained in the courts of this state by any such dealer or vendor, his successors or assigns, when such vendor or dealer shall have failed to comply with the terms and provisions of this chapter. (Acts 1936-37, Ex. Sess., No. 220, p. 263; Code 1940, T. 36, § 106.)

Collateral references. — 61A C.J.S., Motor Vehicles, § 689.

§ 32-16-4. Penalty.

Any vendor or dealer in used or secondhand motor vehicles who shall violate or fail to observe any of the provisions of this chapter shall be deemed guilty of a misdemeanor and, upon conviction for such violation, shall be punished by a fine of not less than $100.00 nor more than $500.00, and/or by imprisonment for not less than 30 days nor more than six months. The director of public safety and his subordinate officers are hereby authorized and required to enforce, and are charged with the duty of enforcing, the provisions of this chapter. (Acts 1936-37, Ex. Sess., No. 220, p. 263; Acts 1939, No. 621, p. 988, § 1; Code 1940, T. 36, § 107.)

CHAPTER 17.

WARRANTY WORK ON MOTOR VEHICLES.

§ 32-17-1. Compensation by manufacturer, etc., for work performed by dealer or representative.

No manufacturer of motor vehicles, distributor, distributor branch or factory branch or officer, agent or other representative thereof shall fail to compensate adequately and fairly its dealer or representative for labor, parts or expenses incurred by the dealer or representative with regard to factory warranty agreements performed by the dealer or representative. In no event shall said manufacturer of motor vehicles, distributor, distributor branch or factory branch pay to its dealer or representative a labor rate per hour for warranty work less than that charged by said dealer or representative to its retail customer. Conversely, no franchised dealer or representative shall charge its manufacturer, distributor, distributor branch or factory branch a labor rate per hour in excess of the rate charged its retail customers. (Acts 1971, No. 2053, p. 3304, § 1.)

Collateral references. — 60 C.J.S., Motor Vehicles, § 165(1).

Automobile repairman's duty to provide customer with information, estimates, or replaced parts, under automobile repair consumer protection act. 25 ALR4th 506.

§ 32-17-2. Penalty.

Any manufacturer of motor vehicles, distributor, distributor branch or factory branch or officer, agent or other representative thereof, or any dealer or representative of the same, who shall violate any provision of this chapter shall be guilty of a misdemeanor and shall be fined a sum not less than $10.00 nor more than $500.00 for each such violation. (Acts 1971, No. 2053, p. 3304, § 2.)

CHAPTER 17A.

NONORIGINAL EQUIPMENT MANUFACTURER AFTERMARKET CRASH PARTS DISCLOSURE.

Effective date. — The act which added this chapter became effective May 11, 1989.

§ 32-17A-1. Definitions.

As used in this chapter, the following words and phrases shall have the following meanings respectively ascribed to them, unless the context clearly indicates otherwise:

(1) AFTERMARKET CRASH PART. A replacement for any of the nonmechanical sheet metal or plastic parts which generally constitute the exterior of a motor vehicle, including inner and outer panels.

(2) INSTALLER. An individual who performs the work of replacing or repairing parts of a motor vehicle.

(3) INSURER. Includes an insurance company and any person authorized to represent the insurer with respect to a claim and who is acting within the scope of the person's authority.

(4) NONORIGINAL EQUIPMENT MANUFACTURER AFTERMARKET CRASH PART. An aftermarket crash part made by any manufacturer other than the original vehicle manufacturer or his supplier.

(5) REPAIR FACILITY. A motor vehicle dealer, garage, body shop, or other commercial entity which undertakes the repair or replacement of those parts that generally constitute the exterior of a motor vehicle. (Acts 1989, No. 89-662, § 1.)

§ 32-17A-2. Identification of nonoriginal equipment manufacturer aftermarket crash parts manufactured or supplied in this state.

Any nonoriginal equipment manufacturer aftermarket crash part manufactured or supplied for use in this state on or after January 1, 1990, shall have affixed thereto or inscribed thereon the logo, identification number, or name of its manufacturer. Such manufacturer's logo, identification number, or name shall be visible after installation whenever practicable. (Acts 1989, No. 89-662, § 2.)

§ 32-17A-3. Disclosure document.

In all instances where nonoriginal equipment manufacturer aftermarket crash parts are used in preparing an estimate for repairs, the written estimate prepared by the insurer and repair facility shall clearly identify each such part. A disclosure document attached to the estimate shall contain the following information in no smaller than 10 point type:

THIS ESTIMATE HAS BEEN PREPARED BASED ON THE USE OF AFTERMARKET CRASH PARTS SUPPLIED BY A SOURCE OTHER THAN THE MANUFACTURER OF YOUR MOTOR VEHICLE. THE AFTERMARKET CRASH PARTS USED IN THE PREPARATION OF THIS ESTIMATE ARE WARRANTED BY THE MANUFACTURER OR DISTRIBUTOR OF SUCH PARTS RATHER THAN THE MANUFACTURER OF YOUR VEHICLE.

(Acts 1989, No. 89-662, § 3.)

CHAPTER 18.

MUNICIPAL TESTING STATIONS.

Collateral references. — 7 Am. Jur. 2d, Automobiles & Highway Traffic, § 166.

§ 32-18-1. Definitions.

For the purposes of this chapter, the following terms shall have the meanings indicated:

(1) PERSON. Every natural person, firm, copartnership, association or corporation.

(2) OPERATOR. Every person who is in actual physical control of a motor vehicle upon a street, alley or thoroughfare.

(3) MOTOR VEHICLE. Any vehicle propelled by any power other than muscular power, including traction engines, tractor cranes, power shovels, road building machines, road rollers, road sweepers and sand spreaders, which are self-propelled; and trailers, semitrailers and motorcycles. This definition shall not include traction engines, tractor cranes, power shovels, road building machines, road rollers, road sweepers and sand spreaders which are not self-propelled; or tractors used exclusively for agricultural purposes, well drillers, electric trucks with small wheels used in factories, warehouses and railroad stations and operated principally on private property and such vehicles as run only upon rails or tracks; or motor vehicles to the extent of five or more owned by any person having testing equipment and facilities meeting the requirements of the city; or motor vehicles engaged in the business of carrying and transporting passengers or property and subject to the supervision and regulation of the Alabama public service commission.

(4) OWNER. A person who holds the legal title to a motor vehicle, or, in the event a motor vehicle is the subject of an agreement for the conditional sale or lease thereof with the right of purchase upon performance of the conditions stated in the agreement and with an immediate right of possession vested in the conditional vendee or lessee or in the event a mortgagor of a motor vehicle is entitled to possession, then such conditional vendee or lessee or mortgagor shall be deemed the owner for the purpose of this chapter. (Acts 1943, No. 542, p. 522, § 1.)

Collateral references. — 60A C.J.S., Motor Vehicles, §§ 260, 261.

Validity of statutes or ordinances as to inspection of motor vehicles. 106 ALR 795.

§ 32-18-2. City may set up or designate testing stations.

Any city shall have the power to acquire, establish, erect, equip, operate and maintain motor vehicle testing stations therein, to pay for the same out of the proceeds of the collection of fees charged for testing motor vehicles and to make rules and regulations for the purpose of carrying out the provisions of any ordinance adopted under the terms of this chapter. Such city may also designate privately operated stations as official inspecting stations on which such city shall by agreement with the owners or operators of such stations impose the power and authority to conduct such inspections in lieu of or in addition to the stations operated by such city and in accordance with the terms of this chapter and any ordinance adopted under its provisions. (Acts 1943, No. 542, p. 522, § 2.)

§ 32-18-3. Fees.

Such city shall have the power to fix the amount of fees, not exceeding $1.00 per test and not more than $2.00 per annum, for the inspection of any motor vehicle for any and all defects prohibited by law upon and for every restriction and requirement imposed by law with respect to the equipment and maintenance of any such motor vehicle operated upon the streets, alleys or highways of such city. In addition to inspections required by ordinance, any owner or operator may have his motor vehicle inspected as often as he may reasonably desire, between such inspection periods as may be fixed by such city. Such city shall have additional power to set aside all fees so collected by it in a separate fund out of which all costs and expenses in connection with or growing out of the construction, establishment, equipment, operation and maintenance of such stations by it shall be paid. Any surplus remaining in such fund shall be paid into a fund for traffic regulation and enforcement. (Acts 1943, No. 542, p. 522, § 3; Acts 1963, No. 550, p. 1169, § 1.)

§ 32-18-4. Use of streets dependent upon compliance with ordinance.

The right to use the streets, alleys and highways of any city enacting any such ordinance shall be dependent upon compliance with the terms of such ordinance and with the laws of the state relating to motor vehicles and the parking or use thereof on the streets, alleys or highways of such city. (Acts 1943, No. 542, p. 522, § 4.)

Collateral references. — 60 C.J.S., Motor Vehicles, § 10. 60A C.J.S., Motor Vehicles, § 276.

§ 32-18-5. Stickers; control of tests.

The director of public safety of Alabama shall approve the shape, size, color and inscription of a sticker to be placed by any such city so operating or in which are operated motor vehicle testing stations hereunder upon the windshield of any motor vehicle so passing the tests herein provided. No such certificate shall be issued or attached to any motor vehicle until and unless such vehicle shall, upon such inspection, be found to comply with the terms and conditions and requirements imposed by law and the ordinance adopted under this chapter. The director shall also have supervision and control over the type of tests and the facilities therefor in any such motor vehicle testing station, and any such city desiring to establish any such station or to designate any privately owned station shall first procure the approval of such tests and facilities by the director of public safety. (Acts 1943, No. 542, p. 522, § 5.)

Collateral references. — 60 C.J.S., Motor Vehicles, § 26.

§ 32-18-6. City may pay for testing stations from earnings or out of general fund.

Any such city shall have additional powers to pay for any such testing station or stations operated by it and for the equipment, maintenance and operation thereof out of past or future earnings of such station or stations or out of the general fund. (Acts 1943, No. 542, p. 522, § 6.)

§ 32-18-7. Applicable to residents or persons who maintain place of business in city.

Any such city may provide for the inspection of motor vehicles operated upon the streets, alleys or highways thereof when owned or operated by residents or by persons who maintain a place of business in any such city where so operated. (Acts 1943, No. 542, p. 522, § 7; Acts 1963, No. 550, p. 1169, § 2.)

§ 32-18-8. Penalty; seizure of motor vehicle.

Any such city shall have the power to enforce such ordinance by fine, not exceeding $100.00, or imprisonment, not exceeding six months, or both. Each day's violation of such ordinance shall constitute a separate offense. Such fine or imprisonment may be imposed upon either the owner or operator of any such motor vehicle. Such city shall have authority also to seize and impound any motor vehicle which has not been inspected in accordance with the terms of such ordinance and to hold the same until inspection is made as provided by such ordinance. Any expense incurred in the seizure and impounding of such motor vehicle, together with any storage fees, shall be a first lien on the same;

and the city shall have authority to enforce such lien as provided by law. (Acts 1943, No. 542, p. 522, § 8.)

CODE OF ALABAMA
1975

1995 Cumulative Supplement

ANNOTATED

Prepared by

The Editorial Staff of the Publishers

Under the Direction of

D. S. Tussey, R. W. Walter, W. L. Jackson, M. A. Sancilio,
J. H. Runkle, and L. A. Burckell

VOLUME 17A
1989 REPLACEMENT VOLUME

*Including Acts through the 1995 Regular Session and
annotations taken through Southern Reporter,
Second Series, Volume 652, page 1133*

**Place in Pocket of Corresponding Volume of Main Set.
This Supersedes Previous Supplement, Which
May Be Retained for Reference Purposes.**

The Michie Company
Law Publishers
Charlottesville, Virginia
1995

Preface

The general and permanent laws of the State of Alabama, as enacted during the 1995 Regular Session of the Legislature which are contained in the 1995 Cumulative Supplement to certain volumes of the Code and in the 1995 Replacement Volumes of the Code, although operative on their effective dates, will not be adopted and incorporated into the Code of Alabama 1975 until the passage of the annual codification act. The annual codification act is usually passed the year following the current legislative session. As to previous years' codification acts, see Volume 1 of this set.

THIS SUPPLEMENT CONTAINS

Constitutions:

All amendments to the Alabama Constitution of 1901 ratified through September 1, 1995.

All amendments proposed to the Alabama Constitution of 1901 which are subject to referendum and which had not been voted upon as of September 1, 1995.

Statutes:

All laws of a general and permanent nature enacted by the Alabama Legislature through the 1995 Regular Session of the Legislature. Local laws and general laws of local application are not included in this supplement.

Rules of Alabama Supreme Court:

Rules promulgated by the Supreme Court of Alabama through September 1, 1995.

Annotations:

Annotations or constructions of Alabama statutes and the 1901 Constitution of Alabama and amendments thereto by the Alabama Supreme Court, the Alabama Courts of Appeal, the Supreme Court of the United States and other federal courts, taken from the following:

Southern Reporter, Second Series, through volume 652, p. 1133.
Federal Reporter, Third Series, through volume 51, p. 287.
Federal Supplement, through volume 879, p. 1340.
Federal Rules Decisions, through volume 160, p. 274.
Bankruptcy Reporter, through volume 179, p. 985.
Supreme Court Reporter, through volume 115, p. 1731.
Opinions of the Clerk of the Supreme Court of Alabama.

References to:

Corpus Juris Secundum.
American Jurisprudence, Second Edition.
American Law Reports, First Series.
American Law Reports, Second Series.
American Law Reports, Third Series.
American Law Reports, Fourth Series.
American Law Reports, Fifth Series.

Cross references to related provisions of the Code and the Alabama Constitution of 1901.

References to applicable or related federal statutes.

Tables:

Acts of Legislature to 1975 Code.

Index:

A supplement to the general index to the statutes, constitutional amendments and rules contained in this supplement and the bound volumes of the Code of Alabama.

4

User's Guide

In order to assist both the legal profession and the layman in obtaining the maximum benefit from the Code of Alabama, a User's Guide has been included in Volume 1. This guide contains comments and information on the many features found within the Code of Alabama intended to increase the usefulness of this set of laws to the user. See Volume 1 of this set for the complete User's Guide.

CODE OF ALABAMA

1995 Cumulative Supplement

TITLE 32.

MOTOR VEHICLES AND TRAFFIC.

TABLE OF CONTENTS

CHAPTER 1.

GENERAL PROVISIONS.

Cross references. — As to provisions pertaining to motor vehicle lemon law rights, see § 8-20A-1 et seq.

§ 32-1-1.1. Definitions.

Evidence of defendant being on "right-of-way" insufficient. — Where the only testimony the State presented regarding where defendant was standing prior to being arrested was that of the officer, who stated that defendant was on the right-of-way, about six to eight feet from the pavement of highway, the State failed to show that defendant was on the travelled portion of the highway, rather than merely on the right-of-way and such evidence was insufficient to support an arrest for highway intoxication. Stokes v. State, 552 So. 2d 144 (Ala. 1989).

Cited in Garrett v. Alfa Mut. Ins. Co., 584 So. 2d 1327 (Ala. 1991); Dale v. Kelly, 620 So. 2d 632 (Ala. 1993).

Collateral references.

Liability of private landowner for vegetation obscuring view at highway or street intersection. 69 ALR4th 1092.

§ 32-1-2. Liability for injury or death of guest.

I. General Consideration.
III. Guest.
IV. Willful or Wanton Misconduct.

I. GENERAL CONSIDERATION.

Guest passenger statute. — Where driver ran red light as she had glanced back to rear seat of car in conversation and driver could not stop in time to avoid colliding with car, driver's conduct did not rise to the level of "wanton misconduct" to permit guest passenger to recover for injuries. George v. Champion Ins. Co., 591 So. 2d 852 (Ala. 1991).

"Wantonness" defined.

In a case permitting guest passenger to recover for injuries, "wanton misconduct" requires more than some form of inadvertence on the part of the driver; it requires some degree of conscious culpability. George v. Champion Ins. Co., 591 So. 2d 852 (Ala. 1991).

Genuine issue of material fact existed. — Summary judgment entered in favor of driver as to a negligence claim by passenger of driver's against the driver was to be remanded for further proceedings on that claim for genuine issue of material fact existed as to whether the passenger and the driver had a business relationship pursuant to guest statute. Dorman v. Jackson, 623 So. 2d 1056 (Ala. 1993).

Cited in Carter v. Reed, 638 So. 2d 833 (Ala. 1994).

III. GUEST.

Whether one is a guest is a question of fact.

Whether the riders in car were guests or were passengers is a question for the jury, and that question should not be determined by the trial judge as a matter of law. Cash v. Caldwell, 603 So. 2d 1001 (Ala. 1992).

General rule, etc.

If the transportation of a rider confers a benefit only on the person to whom the ride is given, and no benefits other than hospitality, goodwill, or the like are conferred on the person furnishing the transportation, then the rider is a "guest." Dorman v. Jackson, 623 So. 2d 1056 (Ala. 1993).

Passenger is "guest" where benefits received are incidental to good will. — If the only benefits received by a driver are those incidental to good will, then the passenger is a "guest" within the meaning of the statute. Davis v. Davis, 622 So. 2d 901 (Ala. 1993).

Whether children under 14, etc.

In accord with the bound volume. See Fox v. Hollar Co., 576 So. 2d 223 (Ala. 1991).

Grandmother was guest where driver received no benefits. — Grandmother who accompanied driver to doctor's appointment solely out of love and concern for her sick grandchild, and the driver neither sought nor received any "payment" or any benefit from the trip, the grandmother was a "guest," and she thus was not entitled to recover damages in negligence suit against the driver for injuries she sustained in automobile accident. Davis v. Davis, 622 So. 2d 901 (Ala. 1993).

Students sharing transportation to and from school on weekend trips. — Although two students were good friends who were often together in a social manner, they also had an arrangement for transportation that contemplated regular trips of considerable magnitude. A jury, therefore, should determine the status of the passenger, and summary judgment in deceased passenger's father's wrongful death action was incorrect. Sellers v. Sexton, 576 So. 2d 172 (Ala. 1991).

IV. WILLFUL OR WANTON MISCONDUCT.

No evidence of wanton or willful conduct. — Trial court did not err in holding that there was no evidence of wanton or willful conduct on the part of the defendant. Cash v. Caldwell, 603 So. 2d 1001 (Ala. 1992).

Wantonness should be submitted to jury, etc.

Wantonness is a question of fact for the jury, unless there is a total lack of evidence from which the jury could reasonably infer wantonness. Cash v. Caldwell, 603 So. 2d 1001 (Ala. 1992).

Issue of wantonness held a jury question.

Trial court erred in entering summary judgment against passenger's administrator's wantonness claim where there was evidence that driver was operating her car at or near the maximum posted speed limit when she entered a bridge that she should have known had been spread with rock/stone in preparation for bad weather and there was evidence that she knew that the bridge had a wide curve that would obstruct her view of any oncoming traffic. Sellers v. Sexton, 576 So. 2d 172 (Ala. 1991).

Driver not wanton in turning left at intersection. — Where evidence indicated that driver slowed down before crossing the northbound lanes of traffic, and she stated that she merely failed to see the oncoming car, passenger did not show that the driver was wanton in turning left at intersection when crossing the northbound lanes of traffic. Dorman v. Jackson, 623 So. 2d 1056 (Ala. 1993).

§ 32-1-4. Appearance upon arrest for misdemeanor.

Detention for minor traffic violation.

Although this section generally forbids police officers from taking persons charged with the violation of minor traffic offenses into the type of custody traditionally associated with a felony arrest, it does not prohibit the temporary de-

tention or "traffic arrest" of individuals for minor traffic offenses. Pittman v. State, 541 So. 2d 583 (Ala. Crim. App. 1989).

This section does not prohibit the arrest of the traffic offender; it merely provides that, with certain exceptions, that offender shall be subjected only to limited detention or custody. Pittman v. State, 541 So. 2d 583 (Ala. Crim. App. 1989).

Requirement that motorist sit in patrol car. — An officer may require a motorist to sit in a patrol car while the officer completes the uniform traffic ticket and citation. State v. Wahington, 623 So. 2d 392 (Ala. Crim. App. 1993).

Limited detention does not give rise to search of person or car. — The limited detention of requiring motorist to sit in a patrol car while officer completes the uniform traffic ticket and citation does not give rise to a search incident to arrest of either the motorist's person, or the motorist's vehicle. State v. Wahington, 623 So. 2d 392 (Ala. Crim. App. 1993).

Once the traffic offender signs uniform traffic ticket and citation the arresting officer is to forthwith release him from custody; the officer may further detain the driver only if he has probable cause to arrest the driver for some other non-traffic offense. State v. Wahington, 623 So. 2d 392 (Ala. Crim. App. 1993).

No reasonable suspicion to detain defendant after he had signed UTTC. — Trooper clearly established that he had probable cause to stop defendant and effect a non-custodial traffic arrest for the misdemeanor offense of speeding, and it was also clear from both video tape and trooper's testimony that the defendant was willing to and, in fact, did sign the uniform traffic ticket and citation, but the trooper did not have the necessary reasonable suspicion to continue to detain the defendant after the defendant had signed the UTTC based on evidence that the defendant had a temporary license; the car was rented by a third party, the car had a temporary license plate, and the defendant was nervous. State v. Wahington, 623 So. 2d 392 (Ala. Crim. App. 1993).

Running away before signing bond constitutes escape in third degree. — An arresting officer has authority to arrest a violator for a traffic offense and, upon doing so, is under a statutory duty to release the violator only if the violator signs "a bond approved by the arresting officer," agreeing to appear in court; thus, if one runs away before he signs the bond, he can be guilty of escape in the third degree. Vickers v. State, 547 So. 2d 1191 (Ala. 1989).

Arrest was lawful. — Custodial arrest of a traffic offender for further investigation and to search his vehicle was lawful, justified and proper where a trooper smelled marijuana on the offender and the offender admitted to smoking a joint. Pittman v. State, 541 So. 2d 583 (Ala. Crim. App. 1989).

Refusal to sign traffic ticket. — While misdemeanor offense of fleeing or attempting to elude a police officer is one of the "Rules of the Road" and is defined in § 32-5A-193, a custodial arrest is not authorized for this offense alone. A custodial arrest was authorized and justified where the defendant refused to sign the traffic ticket. Gouin v. State, 581 So. 2d 1279 (Ala. Crim. App. 1991).

Motorist could be jailed where motorist arrested for subsequent, separate misdemeanor. — Although the police have no authority to take a motorist into custody and then require him to go to the local stationhouse when that motorist has committed a misdemeanor traffic violation but is willing to sign a summons to court, where the motorist was stopped for a traffic violation, and was then arrested for giving false information to a police officer, a separate nontraffic related misdemeanor, he could be arrested and taken to jail. Hawkins v. State, 585 So. 2d 154 (Ala. 1991).

Cited in Callahan v. State, 557 So. 2d 1292 (Ala. Crim. App. 1989); Sides v. State, 574 So. 2d 856 (Ala. Crim. App. 1990).

CHAPTER 2.

DEPARTMENT OF PUBLIC SAFETY.

9

Sec.
32-2-84. Funds designated for fund in addition
             to money transferred to depart-
             ment.

ARTICLE 4.

CRIMINAL HISTORY INFORMATION.

§ 32-2-60. Definitions.

When used in this article, the following terms have the following meanings, respectively, unless the context clearly indicates a different meaning:

(1) CRIMINAL HISTORY INFORMATION. Information collected and stored in the criminal record repository of the Department of Public Safety reflecting the result of an arrest, detention, or initiation of a criminal proceeding by criminal justice agencies, including, but not limited to, arrest record information, fingerprint cards, correctional induction and release information, identifiable descriptions and notations of arrests, detentions, indictments, or other formal charges. The term shall not include analytical records or investigative reports that contain criminal intelligence information or criminal investigation information.

(2) CRIMINAL JUSTICE AGENCY. Any municipal, county, state or federal agency whose personnel have power of arrest and who perform a law enforcement function. This definition shall also include the Attorney General of the State of Alabama, all federal and state prosecuting attorneys, and all municipal, state, and federal judges.

(3) DEPARTMENT. The Department of Public Safety.

(4) DIRECTOR. The Director of the Department of Public Safety.

(5) PERSON. Any individual, partnership, corporation, association, business, government, governmental subdivision or agency, or any other public or private entity. (Acts 1992, 2nd Ex. Sess., No. 92-676, p. 56, § 1.)

§ 32-2-61. Release of information and fees.

(a) The director may open to any person for inspection, copying, and mechanical reproduction, during the department's regular business hours, criminal history information on any individual, if the individual has given written permission for the release of the information to the requester and if the opening of the information is not forbidden by order of any court of competent jurisdiction or by federal law. Any person requesting criminal history information from the department must present to the department, along with the request, a copy of the required written permission.

(b) The director shall establish and collect a nonrefundable fee for costs incurred by the department in providing the requested criminal history information. The fee shall be $25.00. The proceeds shall be deposited in the State Treasury to the credit of the Public Safety Automated Fingerprint Identification System Fund, which is hereby created. All money deposited in the State Treasury to the credit of the Public Safety Automated Fingerprint

Identification System Fund shall be expended for the department's administrative costs for maintaining and providing the information and for operations and maintenance of the Automated Fingerprint Identification System. No money shall be withdrawn or expended from the fund for any purpose unless the money has been allotted and budgeted in accordance with Article 4 (commencing with Section 41-4-80) of Chapter 4 of Title 41, and only in the amounts and for the purposes provided by the Legislature in the general appropriations bill or other appropriation bills.

(c) Criminal justice agencies and the Alabama Peace Officers Standards and Training Commission requests for criminal history information are hereby exempted from the fee requirements in subsection (b) except when such requests pertain to municipal or county ordinances intended to screen perspective employees of private entities.

(d) Requests for national criminal history record access, authorized by federal law, passing through the criminal record repository of the department to the Federal Bureau of Investigation require the submission of an additional fee as specified by the Federal Bureau of Investigation to cover their costs of processing the request. In addition to the fee specified in subsection (b) the director shall collect a fee and deposit same into the Public Safety Automated Fingerprint Identification System Fund for payment of the fee specified by the Federal Bureau of Investigation for national criminal history record access. (Acts 1992, 2nd Ex. Sess., No. 92-676, p. 56, § 2.)

Cross references. — For provisions as to the Department of Mental Health and Mental Retardation being authorized to use the Department of Public Safety to secure information through the National Crime Information Center, see Article 5 of Chapter 50, Title 22, § 22-50-90 et seq.

§ 32-2-62. Promulgation of procedures and regulations.

In accordance with the Administrative Procedure Act, the director shall promulgate reasonable procedures and regulations for the implementation of this article. (Acts 1992, 2nd Ex. Sess., No. 92-676, p. 56, § 3.)

§ 32-2-63. Unauthorized dissemination of information.

Any person who willfully disseminates information other than the information authorized by this article, is guilty of a Class C misdemeanor and upon conviction thereof shall be punished as prescribed by law. (Acts 1992, 2nd Ex. Sess., No. 92-676, p. 56, § 4.)

ARTICLE 5.

PUBLIC SAFETY MOTOR VEHICLE REPLACEMENT FUND.

Effective date. — The act which added this article became effective July 25, 1995.

§ 32-2-80. Creation; purpose.

There is hereby created in the State Treasury the Public Safety Motor Vehicle Replacement Fund of the Alabama Department of Public Safety. This fund shall assist in providing the necessary funds to replace the Department of Public Safety law enforcement motor vehicles. Vehicles purchased from funds appropriated from the Public Safety Motor Vehicle Replacement Fund shall be used specifically for law enforcement purposes. None of the funds appropriated from this fund may be expended by the department for salaries nor for any purpose other than the purchase of law enforcement vehicles. (Acts 1995, No. 95-389, § 1.)

§ 32-2-81. Funds — Deposit, expenditure, and carry over.

Any funds created from depreciation, equipment replacement allowance, and salvage value for replacement of law enforcement motor vehicles in the department shall be deposited in the Public Safety Motor Vehicle Replacement Fund created pursuant to Section 32-2-80; however the expenditure of any monies appropriated from this fund shall be budgeted and allotted pursuant to the Budget Management Act and Article 4 of Chapter 4 of Title 41. These funds shall not revert at the end of each fiscal year, but shall be carried over to each succeeding fiscal year. (Acts 1995, No. 95-389, § 2.)

§ 32-2-82. Transfer of vehicles; notification of purchase.

The Department of Public Safety may not transfer automotive vehicles from law enforcement personnel nor vehicles designated for law enforcement purposes to other personnel in that department nor shall vehicles be transferred to be used for any other purpose in that department nor transferred to any other state agency. Whenever the Department of Public Safety intends to purchase vehicles, the director shall provide written notification to the Director of Finance, the Chairman of the House Committee on Ways and Means, and the Chairman of the Senate Committee on Finance and Taxation-General Fund at least ten (10) days prior to the purchase. Such notification shall include the number of vehicles, the cost of those vehicles and the designated purpose for those vehicles. (Acts 1995, No. 95-389, § 3.)

§ 32-2-83. Disposal of vehicles.

Any other provisions to the law contrary notwithstanding, the Director of the Department of Public Safety shall be responsible for the disposal of any Department of Public Safety law enforcement vehicle. Such vehicle shall be sold by the director or his designee either at public auction or by a negotiated sale by the Department of Public Safety to any other state department or agency. Any state department or agency may negotiate for the purchase of the vehicle for their use in compliance with state law.

Every proposal to make a sale at public auction shall be advertised for at least two weeks in advance of the date fixed for the auction. Such advertisement shall appear at least once a week for two consecutive weeks in a newspaper of general circulation in the county where the sale is to be made, and a copy of such proposal shall simultaneously be posted on a readily accessible public bulletin board at the main office of the Department of Public Safety. Advertisements for auctions shall state the item or items to be sold, by class and description, where the property is located and the dates, time, and place the property may be inspected. The advertisements shall further state the date, time, and place of auction. All property advertised under the provisions of this section shall be available for inspection during the normal state office hours, and at whatever place advertised for at least 48 hours prior to sale.

All property sold under the provisions of this section shall be paid for by the purchaser or his representative by cashier's check, bank draft, certified check, U.S. currency, or notarized bank letter stating that the holder may purchase surplus property and also stating a maximum amount, at the time of acceptance of bid and award of contract, and said removal shall be not later than seven days after the awarding of the contract.

No officer or employee of the State of Alabama or any of its departments, boards, bureaus, commissions, institutions, corporations, or agencies shall act as agent for any bidder; provided, however, that such officers or employees shall not be excluded from bidding on or purchasing state property at public sale.

Any sale made in violation of the terms of this section shall be null and void, and the person or persons responsible for the violation shall be subject to liquidated damages of not less than $1,000.00 nor more than $10,000.00, which may be recovered for the State of Alabama by the Attorney General by civil action in the circuit court of Montgomery County. Any moneys recovered by the Attorney General under this section shall be deposited into the State General Fund.

All proceeds from sales made under the provisions of this article, whether at public auction or by negotiation, shall be paid into the Public Safety Motor Vehicle Replacement Fund. (Acts 1995, No. 95-389, § 4.)

§ 32-2-84. Funds designated for fund in addition to money transferred to department.

The funds designated by this article to be deposited to the Motor Vehicle Replacement Fund are intended to be in addition to the $3.5 million transferred annually to the Department of Public Safety from the Public Road and Bridge Fund pursuant to Act 91-797. Effective October 1, 1995, funds transferred to the Department of Public Safety pursuant to Act 91-797 shall be expended for the purchase of equipment for traffic law enforcement, as provided by that act. Such equipment shall include motor vehicles and related equipment only. (Acts 1995, No. 95-389, § 5.)

CHAPTER 5.

REGULATION OF OPERATION OF MOTOR VEHICLES, ETC., GENERALLY.

ARTICLE 1.

GENERAL PROVISIONS.

§ 32-5-1. Powers of local authorities.

Collateral references.
Validity of roadblocks by state or local officials for purpose of enforcing fish or game laws.
87 ALR4th 981.
Validity, construction, and effect of statutes
or ordinances forbidding automotive "cruising"

— practice of driving repeatedly through loop of
public roads through city. 87 ALR4th 1110.
Search and seizure: Lawfulness of demand
for driver's license, vehicle registration, or
proof of insurance pursuant to police stop to
assist motorist. 19 ALR5th 884.

§ 32-5-9. Liability for damage to highway or structure.

**Proper measure of damages for the de-
struction of a public bridge** is the value of
the bridge before it collapsed, minus its value
after the accident. Tuscaloosa County v. Jim
Thomas Forestry Consultants, Inc., 613 So. 2d
322 (Ala. 1992).

Cost-benefit analysis had no bearing on
the cost of replacement in the determination of
damages for destruction of bridge. Tuscaloosa
County v. Jim Thomas Forestry Consultants,
Inc., 613 So. 2d 322 (Ala. 1992).

ARTICLE 2.

SIGNS, SIGNALS AND MARKINGS.

§ 32-5-31. Local traffic-control devices.

Collateral references.
Motorist's liability for signaling other vehicle

or pedestrian to proceed, or to pass signaling
vehicle. 14 ALR5th 193.

ARTICLE 3.

OPERATION OF VEHICLES GENERALLY.

§ 32-5-54. Keep to the right in crossing intersections or railroads.

Driver of car held negligent. — Where it
was undisputed that driver of car saw a truck
crossing the highway into the median strip

separating the southbound and northbound
lanes, and although it was foreseeable that
truck would then move out of the median into

14

the inside lane, driver of car switched from the right lane into the left lane and thereby placed himself in danger, the trial court, as factfinder, could have properly found that driver of car acted negligently. Walls v. Forsyth, 611 So. 2d 273 (Ala. 1992).

ARTICLE 8.

DRIVING UNDER INFLUENCE OF INTOXICATING LIQUOR OR NARCOTIC DRUGS.

Division 1.

General Provisions.

§ 32-5-171. Arrest without warrant.

Police officer testimony. — Police officer's testimony was sufficient to show that he arrived upon the scene of a recent accident, even though only one vehicle was involved and even though the damage might have been slight; thus the application of this section was warranted. State v. Adams, 592 So. 2d 639 (Ala. Crim. App. 1991), rev'd on other grounds, 592 So. 2d 641 (Ala. 1991).

Division 2.

Chemical Tests for Intoxication.

Cross references. — As to the Alabama Chemical Testing Training and Equipment Trust Fund Advisory Board, see Article 3 to Title 36, § 36-18-50 et seq.

§ 32-5-192. Implied consent; when tests administered; suspension of license or permit to drive, etc., for refusal to submit to test.

The plain language of this statute refers to alcohol only; the exclusive reference, in this statute, to alcohol means that the statute is applicable to the testing of motorists for the detection of alcohol and nothing else; therefore, it was inapplicable to a drug screen test for different substances. State v. Radford, 557 So. 2d 1285 (Ala. Crim. App. 1989), aff'd, 557 So. 2d 1288 (Ala. 1990).

Section does not limit tests to those admissible pursuant to § 32-5A-194. — This section does not narrowly limit the test to be administered only to such tests as would be admissible pursuant to the statutory predicate of § 32-5A-194. Ex parte Mayo, 652 So. 2d 201 (Ala. 1994).

Admission of test where testing jurisdiction not same as arresting jurisdiction. — Where testing jurisdiction is not the same as arresting jurisdiction, the proper predicate for admission of a chemical test pursuant to this section includes a showing only that the law enforcement agency of the testing jurisdiction has adopted the particular form of test that was in fact used. Mayes v. City of Irondale, 577 So. 2d 556 (Ala. Crim. App. 1990).

Subsection (b) of this section is squarely based upon the consent derived by the application of subsection (a) of this section, where the arrest requirement is found, and the subject's unconsciousness does not eliminate this requirement. Binion v. City of Montgomery, 541 So. 2d 74 (Ala. Crim. App. 1989).

Applicability to Assimilative Crimes Act. — Subsection (a) and § 32-5A-194(a)(1) are clearly procedural and evidentiary in nature for they merely regulate which persons can conduct breath tests in order to ensure the accuracy of the tests for evidentiary purposes, and therefore these provisions did not apply in a federal prosecution under the Assimilative Crimes Act for operating a motor vehicle while under the influence of alcohol on federal military base. United States v. Tyson, 829 F. Supp. 368 (M.D. Ala. 1993).

Strict compliance required for results to be admissible. — Strict compliance with the statute is required for the results of the tests made pursuant to Implied Consent Act to be admissible. Britton v. State, 631 So. 2d 1073 (Ala. Crim. App. 1993).

Compliance with the Act is not the ex-

15

clusive means for admitting blood alcohol test results, etc.

Blood tests performed pursuant to the implied consent law are clearly admissible against a defendant alleged to have committed a criminal act while driving under the influence, see § 32-5A-194(a). However, the implied consent law and § 32-5A-194 are not the exclusive means for admitting intoxication test results; where blood is seized only for medical purposes and not in furtherance of a criminal or accident investigation, the results of a blood alcohol test are admissible under general evidentiary principles. Russo v. State, 610 So. 2d 1206 (Ala. Crim. App. 1992).

The sanction under Alabama law is if a person refuses upon proper request of a law enforcement officer to submit to a chemical test, then such refusal may be placed in evidence at trial and appropriate action may be taken by law enforcement agencies with reference to the party's privilege of driving a motor vehicle upon the public highway. However, this section is clear that a law enforcement agency does not have the right, after refusal by the arrested party, to go forward over their refusal and take a blood sample. Thrower v. State, 539 So. 2d 1127 (Ala. Crim. App. 1988).

No constitutional right to consult attorney, etc.

Although this section does not address the right to counsel, it is established by case law that there is no right to counsel prior to taking a chemical test. Parks v. Director, State Dep't of Pub. Safety, 592 So. 2d 1066 (Ala. Civ. App. 1992).

Statute applicable where officer has probable cause. — The implied consent statute is applicable where the arresting officer has probable cause to believe that the defendant has been driving on a highway even though he does not actually see the defendant drive on the highway. Lunceford v. City of Northport, 555 So. 2d 246 (Ala. Crim. App. 1988), appeal dismissed, 564 So. 2d 1055 (Ala. Crim. App. 1990).

Acquittal in a DUI case. — An acquittal in a DUI case is not synonymous with an unlawful arrest; there could be a lawful arrest even though there is a finding of "not guilty" of the offense charged. Parks v. Director, State Dep't of Pub. Safety, 592 So. 2d 1066 (Ala. Civ. App. 1992).

There may be a lawful arrest even though there is a finding of "not guilty" of the offense charged. Department of Pub. Safety v. Goodwin, 587 So. 2d 404 (Ala. Civ. App. 1991).

Arrest requirement not applicable to tests for medical purposes. — When a test is performed for medical purposes and not as a result of a request by law enforcement officers, there is no requirement that the subject tested

be placed under arrest before the test is conducted. State v. Radford, 557 So. 2d 1285 (Ala. Crim. App. 1989), aff'd, 557 So. 2d 1288 (Ala. 1990).

Since urine drug screen performed by the hospital was ordered in the normal course of the treatment process, the trial court should not have suppressed the evidence obtained as a result of the hospital's routine medical treatment. Ex parte Radford, 557 So. 2d 1288 (Ala. 1990).

How tests may be admitted. — Where a chemical test to determine blood alcohol level is performed pursuant to the implied consent statute, this section, the test results may be admitted either by "showing that the test was administered in conformity with § 32-5A-194" or by laying "the traditional evidentiary foundation used to admit results from scientific tests." Morgan v. City of Vestavia Hills, 628 So. 2d 1047 (Ala. Crim. App. 1993).

Statutory predicate versus scientific test predicate. — Because the statutory predicate is easier to establish than the traditional scientific test predicate, most prosecutors, including the prosecutor in this case, choose to use the statutory predicate. Morgan v. City of Vestavia Hills, 628 So. 2d 1047 (Ala. Crim. App. 1993).

Party offering results relieved of burden of laying extensive predicate. — A party offering results from tests shown to be given in conformity with the statute is relieved of the burden of laying the extensive predicate generally necessary for admission of scientific test results. Britton v. State, 631 So. 2d 1073 (Ala. Crim. App. 1993).

Results of blood-alcohol test should have been suppressed. — Results of a blood-alcohol test performed on a blood sample taken from defendant while in the hospital following an automobile accident should have been suppressed since there was no record that the defendant was arrested prior to the test and defendant did not give his consent. Binion v. City of Montgomery, 541 So. 2d 74 (Ala. Crim. App. 1989).

Limited to public highways. — The implied consent statute is limited to public highways. Lunceford v. City of Northport, 555 So. 2d 246 (Ala. Crim. App. 1988), appeal dismissed, 564 So. 2d 1055 (Ala. Crim. App. 1990).

The implied consent law did not apply because the defendant was arrested for DUI on private property and there was no evidence that he had been driving on highway; consequently, the procedural protections afforded by the Alabama implied consent statute did not apply, and in such a case, the taking of a breath sample was justified on the basis of voluntary consent. Lunceford v. City of Northport, 555 So.

2d 246 (Ala. Crim. App. 1988), appeal dismissed, 564 So. 2d 1055 (Ala. Crim. App. 1990).

An "acquittal" is not synonymous with an "unlawful arrest." Department of Pub. Safety v. Goodwin, 587 So. 2d 404 (Ala. Civ. App. 1991).

Reversible error. — Where lab technician drew the blood sample on direction of doctor, after being directed by police officer, who was at the hospital to obtain a blood sample constituted reversible error under this section.

Thrower v. State, 539 So. 2d 1127 (Ala. Crim. App. 1988).

Cited in Crowe v. Wells, 611 So. 2d 1082 (Ala. Civ. App. 1992); Ex parte Boykin, 643 So. 2d 986 (Ala. 1993).

Collateral references.

Driving while intoxicated: subsequent consent to sobriety test as affecting initial refusal. 28 ALR5th 459.

§ 32-5-194. Which law-enforcement officers may be authorized to make tests.

How test results may be admitted. — Where a chemical test to determine blood alcohol level is performed pursuant to the implied consent statute, § 32-5-192, the test results may be admitted either by "showing that the test was administered in conformity with [this section]" or by laying "the traditional evidentiary foundation used to admit results from scientific tests." Morgan v. City of Vestavia

Hills, 628 So. 2d 1047 (Ala. Crim. App. 1993).

Statutory predicate versus scientific test predicate. — Because the statutory predicate is easier to establish than the traditional scientific test predicate, most prosecutors, including the prosecutor in this case, choose to use the statutory predicate. Morgan v. City of Vestavia Hills, 628 So. 2d 1047 (Ala. Crim. App. 1993).

ARTICLE 9.

EQUIPMENT.

Division 1.

General Provisions.

§ 32-5-212. Brakes.

Test to determine whether operator liable for damages. — There is a two-prong test to determine whether the owner or operator of a motor vehicle operated upon the highways of Alabama is liable for damages caused by defective brakes on the vehicle. First, the owner or operator must lack knowledge, either actual or constructive, of the defective condition. Second, the owner or operator must exercise reasonable care in the inspection and maintenance of the motor vehicle's braking system. Darnell v. Nance's Creek Farms, 903 F.2d 1404 (11th Cir. 1990).

Burden of proof. — Alabama law concerning adequate brakes on a motor vehicle shifts the burden of proof to an owner or operator to show lack of notice and exercise of reasonable care once an injured party has demonstrated a defective braking system proximately caused

the injuries suffered. Darnell v. Nance's Creek Farms, 903 F.2d 1404 (11th Cir. 1990).

Although statutes were not read verbatim, charge was adequate. — In giving a jury charge on § 32-5-215(b) and (c) and this section, the trial judge did not read these statutes verbatim, but he did instruct the jury that the defendants were required by law to maintain adequate brakes, tires, and windshield wipers. The trial judge further instructed the jury that if a party failed to maintain these items and the condition of the vehicle was the proximate cause of damages or injury, then that was negligence. Although the trial judge did not give the requested instructions, the charge was adequate, since proper maintenance of brakes, tires and windshield are within the common knowledge of an average juror. Brown v. Gold Kist, Inc., 540 So. 2d 663 (Ala. 1988).

§ 32-5-215. Windshields must be unobstructed; windshield wipers; tinting.

Subsection (d) of this section is unconstitutional, and the promulgation of Rule 760-X-.17 as proposed by the Alabama Department of Public Safety and approved by a legislative committee on administrative regulation was an unconstitutional usurpation of the legislature's authority to make law. Timmons v. City of Montgomery, 641 So. 2d 1263 (Ala. Crim. App. 1993).

Although statutes were not read verbatim, charge was adequate. — In giving a jury charge on subsections (b) and (c) and § 32-5-212, the trial judge did not read these statutes verbatim, but he did instruct the jury that the defendants were required by law to maintain adequate brakes, tires, and windshield wipers. The trial judge further instructed the jury that if a party failed to maintain these items and the condition of the vehicle was the proximate cause of damages or injury, then that was negligence. Although the trial judge did not give the requested instructions, the charge was adequate, since proper maintenance of brakes, tires and windshield are within the common knowledge of an average juror. Brown v. Gold Kist, Inc., 540 So. 2d 663 (Ala. 1988).

Division 2.

Lights, Lamps and Reflective Devices.

§ 32-5-240. Required lighting equipment and illuminating devices of vehicles.

(a) When lighted headlamps required.

(1) Every vehicle upon a highway within this state, except a parked vehicle, which shall be subject to Section 32-5-244, shall display lighted lamps and illuminating devices required by this section for different classes of vehicles at the following times:

a. From a half hour after sunset to a half hour before sunrise.

b. At any time when the windshield wipers of the vehicle are in use because of rain, sleet, or snow, except when the use is intermittent because of misting rain, sleet, or snow.

c. At any time when there is not sufficient light to render clearly discernible persons and vehicles on the highway at a distance of 500 feet.

(2) Notwithstanding subdivision (1), whenever motor vehicles or other vehicles are operated in combination during a time that lamps and illuminating devices are required to be lighted, any lamp, other than a tail lamp, that, by reason of its location on a vehicle in the combination would be obscured by another vehicle of the combination, need not be lighted. This subdivision shall not affect the requirement that lighted clearance lamps be displayed on the front of the foremost vehicle required to have clearance lamps or that all lamps required on the rear of the rearmost vehicle of any combination shall be lighted.

(b) Head lamps on motor vehicles.

(1) Every motor vehicle, other than a motorcycle or motor-driven cycle, shall be equipped with at least two but not more than four head lamps, with at least one but not more than two on each side of the front of the motor vehicle. The head lamps shall comply with the requirements and limitations of Section 32-5-242.

18

(2) Every motorcycle and every motor-driven cycle shall be equipped with at least one and not more than two head lamps which shall comply with the requirements and limitations of Section 32-5-242.

(3) Every head lamp upon every new motor vehicle sold after January 1, 1950, including every motorcycle and motor-driven cycle, shall be located at a height measured from the center of the head lamp of not more than 54 inches nor less than 24 inches to be measured as set forth in Section 32-5-242.

(c) Tail lamps.

(1) Every motor vehicle, trailer, semitrailer, and pole trailer and any other vehicle which is being drawn at the end of a train of vehicles shall be equipped with at least one tail lamp mounted on the rear which, when lighted as required, emits a red light plainly visible from a distance of 500 feet to the rear. When vehicles are drawn in a train, only the tail lamp on the rearmost vehicle need actually be seen from the distance specified.

(2) Every tail lamp upon every vehicle shall be located at a height of not more than 60 inches nor less than 20 inches to be measured as set forth in Section 32-5-242.

(3) Every motor vehicle shall have a tail lamp or a separate lamp so constructed and placed as to illuminate with a white light the rear registration plate and render it clearly legible from a distance of 50 feet to the rear. Any tail lamp or tail lamps, together with any separate lamp for illuminating the rear registration plate, shall be so wired as to be lighted whenever the head lamps or auxiliary driving lamps are lighted.

(d) Additional equipment required on certain vehicles. In addition to other equipment required in this article, the following vehicles shall be equipped in the following manner:

(1) On every bus or truck, whatever its size, the following shall be on the rear: two red reflectors, one at each side, and one stop light.

(2) On every bus or truck 80 inches or more in overall width, in addition to the requirements in subdivision (1):

a. On the front, two clearance lamps, one at each side.

b. On the rear, two clearance lamps, one on each side.

c. On each side, two side marker lamps, one at or near the front and one at or near the rear.

d. On each side, two reflectors, one at or near the front and one at or near the rear.

(3) On every truck tractor:

a. On the front, two clearance lamps, one at each side.

b. On the rear, one stop light.

(4) On every trailer or semitrailer having a gross weight in excess of 3,000 pounds:

a. On the front, two clearance lamps, one at each side.

b. On each side, two side marker lamps, one at or near the front and one at or near the rear.

c. On each side, two reflectors, one at or near the front and one at or near the rear.

d. On the rear, two clearance lamps, one at each side, also two reflectors, one at each side, and one stop light.

(5) On every pole trailer having a gross weight in excess of 3,000 pounds gross weight:

a. On each side, one side marker lamp and one clearance lamp which may be in combination, to show to the front, side, and rear.

b. On the rear of the pole trailer or load, two reflectors, one at each side.

(6) On every trailer, semitrailer, or pole trailer having a gross weight of 3,000 pounds or less: on the rear, two reflectors, one on each side. If the load or dimensions of any trailer or semitrailer obscures the stop light on the towing vehicle, the towed vehicle shall also be equipped with one stop light.

(e) Lamps on other vehicles and equipment. All vehicles, including animal-drawn vehicles and those for which special permits have been issued under authority of Section 32-9-29, not otherwise specifically required to be equipped with lamps, shall at the times specified in subsection (a) of this section be equipped with at least one lighted lamp or lantern exhibiting a white light visible from a distance of 500 feet to the front of the vehicle and with a lamp or lantern exhibiting a red light visible from a distance of 500 feet to the rear.

(f) Stop lamps required on new motor vehicles. It is unlawful for any person to sell any new motor vehicle, including any motorcycle or motor-driven cycle, in this state or for any person to drive the vehicle on the highways unless it is equipped with a stop lamp meeting the requirements of Section 32-5-242.

(g) New motor vehicles to be equipped with reflectors.

(1) No new motor vehicle first sold on or after January 1, 1950, other than a truck tractor, motorcycle, or motor-driven cycle shall be operated on a highway unless the vehicle carries on the rear, either as a part of the tail lamps or separately, two red reflectors. Every motorcycle and every motor-driven cycle shall carry at least one reflector, meeting the requirements of this section. Vehicles specifically provided for in subsection (d) of this section shall be equipped with reflectors as required by that subsection.

(2) These reflectors shall be mounted on the vehicle at a height not less than 20 inches nor more than 60 inches measured as set forth in subsection (a) of Section 32-5-242, shall be of such size and characteristics, and shall be so mounted as to be visible at night from 300 feet. (Acts 1927, No. 347, p. 348; Code 1940, T. 36, § 40; Acts 1949, No. 517, p. 754, § 10; Acts 1957, No. 414, p. 577; Acts 1993, No. 93-720, p. 1407, § 1.)

The 1993 amendment, effective May 20, 1993, in subsection (a), substituted "headlamps" for "lamps" in the introductory line, added the subdivision (1) designation, and in subdivision (1), rewrote subdivision (1), added paragraphs "a" through "c," and added subdivision (2); in subsection (b), in subdivision (1), divided the former first sentence into the present first and second sentences, and deleted "which" following "motor vehicle" in the present first sentence, and in the present second sentence, added "The," and substituted "of Section 32-5-242" for "set forth in section 32-5-242," substituted "after January 1, 1950" for "hereafter" in subdivision (3); in subsection (c), in subdivision (1), divided the former first sentence into the present first and second sentences, and in the present first sentence, deleted "hereinbefore" preceding "required," substituted "emits" for "shall emit," and deleted "provided, that in" following "rear," and substituted "When vehicles are drawn in a train" for "case of a train of vehicles" in the present second sentence, and in subdivision (3), in the first sentence, substituted "Every motor vehicle shall have" for "Either," and deleted "shall be" following "a separate lamp"; in subsection (d) substituted "in the following manner" for "as herein stated under the conditions stated in subsection (a) of this section" in the introductory paragraph, in subdivision (1), deleted "there shall be" following "size," and inserted "shall be," added subdivisions (3) through (6); in subsection (e), in the second sentence, deleted "including" preceding "those for which special permits," substituted "otherwise" for "hereinbefore," substituted "times" for "time," and substituted the language beginning "to the front of" and ending "500 feet" for "such vehicle"; in subsection (f), added "It is," and substituted "the vehicle" for "such vehicle"; and in subsection (g), in subdivision (1), divided the former first sentence into the present first, second and third sentences, and in the present first sentence, substituted "No new" for "Every new," substituted "first sold on or after January 1, 1950" for "hereafter sold and operated upon a highway," inserted "motorcycle, or motor-driven cycle," substituted "be operated on a highway unless the vehicle carries" for "carry," and deleted "except, that every" following "reflectors,"

in the present second sentence, added "Every," and deleted "and except, that vehicles of the type mentioned" following "section," and in the present third sentence, added "Vehicles specifically provided for," and substituted "by that subsection" for "in those sections applicable thereto," in subdivision (2), substituted "These" for "Every such," inserted "shall be," deleted "and" following "Section 32-5-242," deleted "all distances within" preceding "300 feet," deleted "to 50 feet from such vehicle except that visibility from the greater distance is hereinafter required of reflectors on certain vehicles" following "300 feet," deleted former subdivision (3) which made reference to the requirements of mounting reflectors on truck tractors, deleted former subdivision (4) which made reference to requirements of mounting reflectors on trailers or semitrailers with gross weight of more than 3,000 pounds, deleted former subdivision (5) which made reference to requirements of mounting reflectors on pole trailers in excess of 3,000 pounds gross weight, and deleted former subdivision (6) which made reference to requirements of mounting reflectors on trailers, semitrailers, or pole trailers weighing 3,000 pounds gross or less.

§ 32-5-244. Lights on parked vehicles.

Cited in Carroll v. Deaton, Inc., 555 So. 2d 140 (Ala. 1989).

ARTICLE 12.

VIOLATIONS; PENALTIES.

§ 32-5-313. Moneys collected for disbursement to state drivers' fund to be forwarded to state treasurer; amounts credited to special funds; appropriations.

All moneys collected pursuant to section 12-14-14 and section 12-19-1, et seq., for disbursement to the state drivers' fund shall be forwarded by the officer of the court who collects the same to the state treasurer, no less than once a month and not later than the 15th day of each month. All amounts so received shall be credited to special funds to be designated the "driver education and training fund," "Alabama college system truck driver training consortium fund," the "catastrophic trust fund for special education," and the "Alabama traffic safety center fund," and of the amounts so received, an amount equal to 21 percent thereof is hereby appropriated to the state department of education for the sole purpose of instituting and conducting a program of prelicensing driver education and training; an amount equal to 36 percent thereof is hereby appropriated to the state department of postsecondary education to be distributed equally to the entities comprising the Alabama college system truck driver training consortium on July 29, 1991 for the sole purpose of instituting and conducting programs of truck driver education and training as outlined by the U.S. Department of Transportation with support and recommendations from the transportation industry within such Alabama college system truck driver training consortium provided, however, that these funds shall be expended only by institutions under the control of the state board of education; an amount equal to 10 percent thereof is hereby appropriated to the Alabama traffic safety center fund for the sole purpose of conducting programs in traffic safety, motorcycle safety and boating safety by the center; an amount equal to 3 percent is hereby appropriated to the state safety coordinating committee for payment of administrative expenses incurred in its programs; and the remaining 30 percent is hereby appropriated to the catastrophic trust fund for special education to be administered by the state department of education except that before the above distribution occurs, the amount equivalent to an amount generated by $1.50 of the above increase shall be transferred to the commercial drivers license unit of the department of public safety and is hereby appropriated to the department of public safety for the sole purpose of administering the Commercial Driver License Law. (Acts 1964, 1st Ex. Sess., No. 244, p. 335; Acts 1983, No. 83-724, p. 1179; Acts 1987, No. 87-638, p. 1142; Acts 1988, No. 88-658, p. 1055; Acts 1991, No. 91-433, p. 769, § 1; Acts 1991, 1st Ex. Sess., No. 91-824, p. 224, § 5.)

§ 32-5-316. Courts may prohibit operation of motor vehicles by persons convicted of violation of automobile laws.

Collateral references.
Admissibility, in motor vehicle license sus-

pension proceedings, of evidence obtained by unlawful search and seizure. 23 ALR5th 108.

CHAPTER 5A.

RULES OF THE ROAD.

ARTICLE 1.

GENERAL PROVISIONS.

§ 32-5A-1. Short title.

Issues of negligence and contributory negligence were for jury and not trial court. — Where defendant argued that the plaintiffs had failed to prove any negligence on her part and that plaintiff was himself guilty of contributory negligence, where the plaintiffs countered by arguing that they had proved negligence in defendants failure to follow the "Rules of the Road", that plaintiff had the right to assume that defendant would drive according to the "Rules of the Road," and that the question of plaintiff's alleged contributory negligence was one for the jury to decide, and where the court directed a verdict for defendant, because the evidence presented would not allow the factfinder to "reach but a single conclusion" on the issues of negligence and contributory negligence, and because these issues were ordinarily ones for the jury and not the trial court, the judgment based on the directed verdict was reversed. Lindsay ex rel. Harver v. Cantrell, 649 So. 2d 1277 (Ala. 1994).

§ 32-5A-2. Provisions of chapter refer to vehicles upon highways; exceptions.

Rules of the road do not apply to private parking lots. — Because the statutory definition of the term "highway" excludes private parking lots, the rules of the road do not apply to private parking lots. Dale v. Kelly, 620 So. 2d 632 (Ala. 1993).

§ 32-5A-7. Authorized emergency vehicles.

Collateral references.

Liability for negligence of ambulance attendants, emergency medical technicians, and the like, rendering emergency medical care outside hospital. 16 ALR5th 605.

§ 32-5A-8. Violations as misdemeanor; penalties.

Judge's reasons need not appear when stricter sentence imposed as result of two-tiered system. — Judge's reasons for imposing a more severe sentence upon a defendant after a new trial do not have to affirmatively appear when stricter sentence is imposed as result of two-tiered system of criminal adjudication like the one in this section. Steeley v. State, 567 So.

2d 397 (Ala. Crim. App. 1989), cert. denied, 498 U.S. 1091, 111 S. Ct. 974, 112 L. Ed. 2d 1059 (1991).

No evidence of vindictiveness. — Although trial judge said he questioned whether defendant "really felt he was justified" chal-lenging two speeding tickets, there was no evidence of vindictiveness on part of judge in imposing a stricter sentence on appeal by defendant. Steeley v. State, 567 So. 2d 397 (Ala. Crim. App. 1989), cert. denied, 498 U.S. 1091, 111 S. Ct. 974, 112 L. Ed. 2d 1059 (1991).

ARTICLE 2.

TRAFFIC SIGNS, SIGNALS AND MARKINGS.

§ 32-5A-31. Obedience to traffic-control devices; devices presumed to comply with requirements.

Cited in Truman v. City of Enterprise, 606 So. 2d 1151 (Ala. Crim. App. 1992).

ARTICLE 3.

OPERATION AND USE OF VEHICLES GENERALLY.

§ 32-5A-61. Driver not to proceed where traffic obstructed.

Collateral references. — Liability of private landowner for vegetation obscuring view at highway or street intersection. 69 ALR4th 1092.

ARTICLE 4.

DRIVING ON AND USE OF ROADWAYS GENERALLY; OVERTAKING AND PASSING.

§ 32-5A-88. Driving on roadways laned for traffic.

Driver of car held negligent. — Where it was undisputed that driver of car saw a truck crossing the highway into the median strip separating the southbound and northbound lanes, and although it was foreseeable that truck would then move out of the median into the inside lane, driver of car switched from the right lane into the left lane and thereby placed himself in danger, the trial court, as factfinder, could have properly found that driver of car acted negligently. Walls v. Forsyth, 611 So. 2d 273 (Ala. 1992).

ARTICLE 5.

RIGHT-OF-WAY.

§ 32-5A-110. Vehicle approaching or entering intersection.

I. GENERAL CONSIDERATION.

Cited in Owens v. Lucas, 604 So. 2d 389 (Ala. 1992).

§ 32-5A-113. Authority to designate through highways and stop and yield intersections.

Cited in Owens v. Lucas, 604 So. 2d 389 (Ala. 1992).

ARTICLE 6.

TURNING, STARTING AND STOPPING GENERALLY.

§ 32-5A-133. Turning movements and required signals.

I. GENERAL CONSIDERATION.

Collateral references.
Negligence or contributory negligence of mo-

torist in failing to proceed in accordance with turn signal given. 84 ALR4th 124.

§ 32-5A-139. Officers authorized to remove vehicles.

The police have an inherent authority to impound vehicles.
The police have an inherent authority to impound vehicles, aside from statutory authority, based on what is called the community caretaking function. Cannon v. State, 601 So. 2d 1112 (Ala. Crim. App. 1992).

Parking lot does not fall within defini-

tion of highway. — While this section authorizes a police officer to impound any vehicle found "upon a highway" under certain circumstances, parking lot did not fall within the definition of "highway." Cannon v. State, 601 So. 2d 1112 (Ala. Crim. App. 1992).

Cited in Boyd v. State, 542 So. 2d 1276 (Ala. 1989).

ARTICLE 7.

SPECIAL STOPS REQUIRED.

§ 32-5A-150. Obedience to signal indicating approach of train.

Cited in Gibson v. Norfolk S. Corp., 878 F. Supp. 1455 (N.D. Ala. 1994).

ARTICLE 8.

SPEED RESTRICTIONS.

§ 32-5A-170. Reasonable and prudent speed.

I. GENERAL CONSIDERATION.

Standard of care. — In Alabama, drivers have the duty to travel at a safe and appropriate speed, especially when special hazards exist with respect to pedestrians. Above all, drivers have the duty to take due care to avoid colliding with any pedestrian and shall give warning by sounding the horn of their cars or taking other precautions to warn of the danger of collision.

Hunnicutt v. Walker, 589 So. 2d 726 (Ala. Civ. App. 1991).

Finding of lack of care warranted. — Driver was liable for death of jogger even though jogger crossed the street in front of the car in attempt to avoid the car, instead of moving onto the roadside out of harm's way, because driver failed to warn jogger by signaling with her lights or horn, and there was evidence that driver was traveling faster than

posted limit and did not slow down upon observing jogger and his companions. Hunnicutt
v. Walker, 589 So. 2d 726 (Ala. Civ. App. 1991).

§ 32-5A-171. Maximum limits.

Except when a special hazard exists that requires lower speed for compliance with Section 32-5A-170, the limits hereinafter specified or established as
hereinafter authorized shall be maximum lawful speeds, and no person shall
drive a vehicle at a speed in excess of the maximum limits.

(1) No person shall operate a vehicle in excess of 30 miles per hour in any
urban district.

(2) No person shall operate a motor vehicle in excess of 35 miles per hour
on any unpaved road. For purposes of this chapter the term "unpaved road"
shall mean any highway under the jurisdiction of any county, the surface of
which consists of natural earth, mixed soil, stabilized soil, aggregate,
crushed sea shells, or similar materials without the use of asphalt, cement,
or similar binders.

(3) No person shall operate a motor vehicle on the highways in this state,
other than interstate highways, at a speed in excess of 55 miles per hour at
any time unless a different maximum rate of speed is authorized by the
Governor under authority granted in subdivision (6).

(4) No person shall operate a motor vehicle, on an interstate highway
within the State of Alabama, at a speed in excess of 55 miles per hour in
urban areas of 50,000 population or more or in excess of 65 miles per hour
outside urban areas unless a different maximum rate of speed is permitted
or allowed by the Federal Highway Administration, or unless a different
maximum rate of speed is authorized by the Governor under authority
granted in subdivision (6).

(5) Notwithstanding any provisions of this section to the contrary, no
person shall operate a passenger vehicle, motor truck, or passenger bus
which carries or transports explosives or flammable liquids, as defined in
Section 32-1-1.1, or hazardous wastes, as defined in Section 22-30-3(5), in
this state unless the vehicle, truck, or bus prominently displays a current
decal, plate, or placard which is required by the rules or regulations of the
DOT or the PSC which indicates or warns that the vehicle, truck, or bus is
carrying or transporting such substances. No person shall operate the
vehicle, truck, or bus at a rate of speed greater than 55 miles per hour at any
time unless a different maximum rate of speed is authorized by the Governor
under authority granted in subdivision (6).

(6) The Governor is hereby specifically authorized to prescribe the maximum rate of speed whenever a different rate of speed is required by federal
law in order for Alabama to receive federal funds for highway maintenance
and construction.

(7) The maximum speed limits set forth in this section may be altered as
authorized in Sections 32-5A-172 and 32-5A-173. (Acts 1980, No. 80-434, p.
604, § 8-102; Acts 1987, No. 87-408, p. 593; Acts 1994, No. 94-617, p. 1147,
§ 1.)

The **1994 amendment,** effective December 1, 1994, added subdivision (2) and redesignated the following subdivisions accordingly; in subdivisions (3) and (4), substituted "subdivision (6)" for "subdivision (5)"; substituted "subdivision (6)" for "subdivision (5) hereof" in subdivision (4); and made nonsubstantive changes.

Code Commissioner's note. — In 1994, the Code Commissioner restored the language "such substances. No person shall operate" in the first and second sentences of subdivision (5) to correct an omission made during the drafting of Act No. 94-617.

I. GENERAL CONSIDERATION.

Although the court of appeals did not have before it the district court warrants that were the original charging instruments for the traffic offenses of driving without a license and speeding, the Uniform Traffic Ticket and Complaint (UTTC's) issued for those infractions were sufficient to charge the named offenses. Ex parte State ex rel. Johnson, 636 So. 2d 1266 (Ala. Crim. App. 1994).

§ 32-5A-173. When local authorities may and shall alter maximum limits.

(a) Whenever local authorities in their respective jurisdictions determine on the basis of an engineering and traffic investigation that the maximum speed permitted under this article is greater or less than is reasonable and safe under the conditions found to exist upon a highway or part of a highway, the local authority may determine and declare a reasonable and safe maximum limit thereon which:

(1) Decreases the limit at intersections;

(2) Increases the limit within an urban district but not to more than the maximum rate of speed that may be prescribed by the Governor under subdivision (6) of Section 32-5A-171;

(3) Decreases the limit on any street, unpaved road, or highway under the jurisdiction and control of any county commission; or

(4) Increases the limit on any street, unpaved road, or highway under the jurisdiction and control of any county commission but not to more than the maximum rate of speed that is prescribed under subdivision (3) or by the Governor under subdivision (6) of Section 32-5A-171.

(b) Local authorities in their respective jurisdictions shall determine by an engineering and traffic investigation the proper maximum speed for all arterial streets and shall declare a reasonable and safe maximum limit thereon which may be greater or less than the maximum speed permitted under this chapter for an urban district.

(c) Any altered limit established as hereinabove authorized shall be effective at all times or during hours of darkness or at other times as may be determined when appropriate signs giving notice thereof are erected upon the street or highway.

(d) Any alteration of maximum limits on state highways or extensions thereof in a municipality by local authorities shall not be effective until the alteration has been approved by the highway department.

(e) Not more than six alterations as hereinabove authorized shall be made per mile along a street or highway, except in the case of reduced limits at intersections, and the difference between adjacent limits shall not be more than 10 miles per hour. (Acts 1980, No. 80-434, p. 604, § 8-104; Acts 1985, 2nd Ex. Sess., No. 85-998, p. 366, § 2; Acts 1994, No. 94-617, p. 1147, § 2.)

The 1994 amendment, effective December 1, 1994, in subsection (a), substituted "subdivision (6)" for "subdivision (4)" in subdivision (2); inserted "unpaved road" in subdivisions (3) and (4); inserted "subdivision (3) or by the Governor under subdivision (6) of" in subdivision (4); and made nonsubstantive changes.

Code Commissioner's note. — In 1994, the Code Commissioner deleted "or" following "county commission" in subdivision (3) of subsection (a) to correct a typographical error in the act.

§ 32-5A-178. Racing on highways; penalties.

Conspiracy based on defendants' presence at time and place race expected. — Defendants were correct in their contention that the trial court should have granted their motion for judgment of acquittal because the state's evidence of conspiracy was based solely upon the presence of the defendants at the time and place where a drag race was expected to occur. Greer v. State, 563 So. 2d 39 (Ala. Crim. App. 1990).

ARTICLE 9.

SERIOUS TRAFFIC OFFENSES.

Cross references. — For provisions concerning the Safe Streets Act which relates to the seizure and forfeiture of a motor vehicle driven by a person who is driving while his or her driver's license or privilege has been suspended or revoked, see § 32-5A-200 et seq.

§ 32-5A-190. Reckless driving.

I. GENERAL CONSIDERATION.

DUI and reckless driving. — DUI and reckless driving are separate offenses and a defendant may be convicted of both offenses. Davis v. State, 589 So. 2d 1305 (Ala. Crim. App. 1991).

Reckless driving not a lesser included offense. — It has been generally held that reckless driving is not a lesser included offense of driving while intoxicated or of variations of the latter charge. Davis v. State, 589 So. 2d 1305 (Ala. Crim. App. 1991).

Failure to introduce municipal ordinance necessitated reversal. — Where city failed to introduce municipal ordinance adopting applicable state offenses, even though there was a stipulation waiving the requirement that the city clerk authenticate the adoption of the ordinance, city failed to prove a requisite element of its case; this failure mandated a reversal of petitioner's convictions under this section and § 32-5A-191. Ex parte Woodson, 578 So. 2d 1049 (Ala. 1991).

§ 32-5A-191. Driving while under influence of alcohol, controlled substances, etc.

(a) A person shall not drive or be in actual physical control of any vehicle while:

(1) There is 0.08 percent or more by weight of alcohol in his or her blood;

(2) Under the influence of alcohol;

(3) Under the influence of a controlled substance to a degree which renders him or her incapable of safely driving;

(4) Under the combined influence of alcohol and a controlled substance to a degree which renders him or her incapable of safely driving; or

(5) Under the influence of any substance which impairs the mental or physical faculties of such person to a degree which renders him or her incapable of safely driving.

(b) The fact that any person charged with violating this section is or has been legally entitled to use alcohol or a controlled substance shall not constitute a defense against any charge of violating this section.

28

(c) Upon first conviction, a person violating this section shall be punished by imprisonment in the county or municipal jail for not more than one year, or by fine of not less than five hundred dollars ($500) nor more than two thousand dollars ($2,000), or by both such fine and imprisonment. In addition, on a first conviction, the Director of Public Safety shall suspend the driving privilege or driver's license of the person so convicted for a period of 90 days.

(d) On a second conviction within a five-year period, a person convicted of violating this section shall be punished by a fine of not less than one thousand dollars ($1,000) nor more than five thousand dollars ($5,000) and by imprisonment, which may include hard labor in the county or municipal jail for not more than one year. The sentence shall include a mandatory sentence, which is not subject to suspension or probation, of imprisonment in the county or municipal jail for not less than 48 consecutive hours or community service for not less than 20 days. In addition the Director of Public Safety shall revoke the driving privileges or driver's license of the person so convicted for a period of one year.

(e) On a third conviction within a five-year period, a person convicted of violating this section shall be punished by a fine of not less than two thousand dollars ($2,000) nor more than ten thousand dollars ($10,000) and by imprisonment, which may include hard labor, in the county or municipal jail for not less than 60 days nor more than one year, to include a minimum of 60 days which shall be served in the county or municipal jail and cannot be probated or suspended. In addition, the Director of Public Safety shall revoke the driving privilege or driver's license of the person so convicted for a period of three years.

(f) On a fourth or subsequent conviction within a five-year period, a person convicted of violating this section shall be guilty of a Class C felony and punished by a fine of not less than four thousand dollars ($4,000) nor more than ten thousand dollars ($10,000) and by imprisonment of not less than one year and one day nor more than 10 years. Any term of imprisonment may include hard labor for the county or state, and where imprisonment does not exceed three years confinement may be in the county jail. Where imprisonment does not exceed one year and one day, confinement shall be in the county jail. The minimum sentence shall include a term of imprisonment for at least one year and one day which may be suspended or probated, but only if the defendant enrolls and successfully completes a state certified chemical dependency program recommended by the court referral officer and approved by the sentencing court. Where probation is granted, the sentencing court may, in its discretion, and where monitoring equipment is available, place the defendant on house arrest under electronic surveillance during the probationary term. In addition to the other penalties authorized, the Director of Public Safety shall revoke the driving privilege or driver's license of the person so convicted for a period of five years.

Any law to the contrary notwithstanding, the Alabama habitual felony offender law shall not apply to a conviction of a felony pursuant to this subsection, and a conviction of a felony pursuant to this subsection shall not be a felony conviction for purposes of the enhancement of punishment pursuant to Alabama's habitual felony offender law.

(g) In addition to the penalties provided herein, any person convicted of violating this section shall be referred to the court referral officer for evaluation and referral to appropriate community resources. The defendant shall, at a minimum, be required to complete a DUI or substance abuse court referral program approved by the Administrative Office of Courts and operated in accordance with provisions of the Mandatory Treatment Act of 1990, Sections 12-23-1 to 12-23-19, inclusive. The Department of Public Safety shall not reissue a driver's license to a person convicted under this section without receiving proof that the defendant has successfully completed the required program.

(h) Neither reckless driving nor any other traffic infraction is a lesser included offense under a charge of driving under the influence of alcohol or of a controlled substance.

(i) Except for fines collected for violations of this section charged pursuant to a municipal ordinance, fines collected for violations of this section shall be deposited to the State General Fund; however, beginning October 1, 1995, of any amount collected over $250 for a first conviction, over $500 for a second conviction within five years, over $1,000 for a third conviction within five years and over $2,000 for a fourth or subsequent conviction within five years, the first one hundred dollars ($100) of that additional amount shall be deposited to the Alabama Chemical Testing Training and Equipment Trust Fund after three percent of the one hundred dollars ($100) is deducted for administrative costs, and the remainder shall be deposited to the State General Fund. Fines collected for violations of this section charged pursuant to a municipal ordinance shall be deposited as follows: the first $250 collected for a first conviction, the first $500 collected for a second conviction within five years, the first $1,000 collected for a third conviction within five years and the first $2,000 collected for a fourth or subsequent conviction within five years shall be deposited to the general fund of the municipality; any amounts collected over these amounts shall be deposited to the State General Fund until October 1, 1995; however, beginning October 1, 1995, of any amount collected over these amounts, the first one hundred dollars ($100) of that additional amount shall be deposited to the Alabama Chemical Testing Training and Equipment Trust Fund after three percent of the one hundred dollars ($100) is deducted for administrative costs, and the remainder shall be deposited to the State General Fund.

(j) A person who has been arrested for violating this section shall not be released from jail under bond or otherwise, until there is less than the same percent by weight of alcohol in his or her blood as specified in subsection (a)(1) hereof.

(k) Upon verification that a defendant arrested pursuant to this section is currently on probation from another court of this state as a result of a conviction for any criminal offense, the prosecutor shall provide written or oral notification of the defendant's subsequent arrest and pending prosecution to the court in which the prior conviction occurred. (Acts 1980, No. 80-434, p. 604, § 9-102; Acts 1981, No. 81-803, p. 1412, § 1; Acts 1983, No. 83-620, p. 959, § 1; Acts 1984, No. 84-259, p. 431, § 1; Acts 1994, No. 94-590, p. 1089, § 1; Acts 1995, No. 95-784, § 2.)

The 1994 amendment, effective August 20, 1994, deleted the former last two sentences of subsection (c) relating to first time offenders and lesser included offenses; in subsection (e), in the first sentence, deleted "or subsequent" following "third" and deleted "which" preceding "cannot"; added present subsections (f), (g), (h); rewrote present subsection (i); deleted "the provisions of" following "violating" in present subsection (j); added subsection (k); and made nonsubstantive changes.

The 1995 amendment, effective August 9, 1995, substituted "0.08" for "0.10" in subdivision (a)(1), in the first sentence of subsection (c), substituted "five hundred dollars ($500)" for "two hundred fifty dollars ($250)," and substituted "two thousand dollars ($2,000)" for "one thousand dollars ($1,000)"; in the first sentence of subsection (d), substituted "one thousand dollars ($1,000)" for "five hundred dollars ($500)," and substituted "five thousand dollars ($5,000)" for "two thousand five hundred dollars ($2,500)"; in the first sentence of subsection (e), substituted "two thousand dollars ($2,000)" for "one thousand dollars ($1,000)," and substituted "ten thousand dollars ($10,000)" for "five thousand dollars ($5,000)"; in the first sentence of subsection (f), substituted "four thousand dollars ($4,000)" for "two thousand dollars ($2,000)," and substituted "ten thousand dollars ($10,000)" for "five thousand dollars ($5,000)"; and rewrote subsection (i).

Code Commissioner's note. — Acts 1994, No. 94-590, which amended this section, in § 2 provides: "This act applies to conduct occurring after its effective date. Conduct occurring before the effective date of this act shall be governed by pre-existing law."

Cross references. — As to provisions for alcohol and drug abuse court referral and treatment program, see chapter 12-23. As to provisions relating to the operation of a vessel and other marine devices while under the influence of alcohol or controlled substances, see § 32-5A-191.3. As to the Alabama Chemical Testing Training and Equipment Trust Fund Advisory Board, see Article 3 to Title 36, § 36-18-50 et seq.

I. GENERAL CONSIDERATION.

Legislative intent. — Subsection (a)(5) was added in 1983, some years after the enactment that included subsections (a)(1) through (a)(4), and it would appear that the legislature enacted subsection (a)(5) in order to cover those situations that were not previously covered by this section. Sturgeon v. City of Vestavia Hills, 599 So. 2d 92 (Ala. Crim. App. 1992).

Enactment of subsection (a)(5). — Subsection (a)(5) was enacted to cover those situations in which the defendant's mental and/or physical faculties are impaired by some substance other than alcohol or a controlled substance. Sturgeon v. City of Vestavia Hills, 599 So. 2d 92 (Ala. Crim. App. 1992).

Notification requirements. — The notification requirements of Rule 19, Ala. R. Jud. Adm. must still be complied with before a complaint alleging a violation of either subdivision (a)(1) or subdivision (a)(2) can be amended to charge the other. Hastings v. State, 589 So. 2d 795 (Ala. Crim. App. 1991).

Separate offenses. — DUI and reckless driving are separate offenses and a defendant may be convicted of both offenses. Davis v. State, 589 So. 2d 1305 (Ala. Crim. App. 1991).

Proof of same offense. — Subdivisions (a)(1) and (a)(2) do not constitute separate offenses but are alternative methods of proving the same offense. Hastings v. State, 589 So. 2d 795 (Ala. Crim. App. 1991).

This section defines the single offense of driving under the influence; however, it provides alternative methods of proving that offense. Bartlett v. State, 600 So. 2d 336 (Ala. Crim. App. 1991).

The different subsections are alternative methods of proving the same offense driving under the influence (DUI) and that specific alternative must be alleged and proved. Sturgeon v. City of Vestavia Hills, 599 So. 2d 92 (Ala. Crim. App. 1992).

Complaint sufficient. — A complaint that substantially tracks the language of the statute is sufficient to inform the defendant of the charges against which he must defend. Gentile v. City of Guntersville, 589 So. 2d 809 (Ala. Crim. App. 1991).

Prima facie case. — To establish a prima facie case of driving under the influence under this section, the state must prove beyond a reasonable doubt that defendant drove or was in actual physical control of a motor vehicle while under the influence of alcohol to the extent that it affected his ability to operate his vehicle in a safe manner. Harris v. State, 601 So. 2d 1099 (Ala. Crim. App. 1991), overruled on other grounds, Ex parte Mayo, 652 So. 2d 201 (Ala. 1994).

Court lacked jurisdiction to sentence. — The trial court did not have jurisdiction to sentence defendant on the DUI charge when a guilty plea to the charge had not been entered. Sampson v. State, 605 So. 2d 846 (Ala. Crim. App. 1992).

No double jeopardy where reckless driving charge nol-prossed. — The nol-prossing of appellant's reckless driving charge, which arose from the same facts as his DUI charge, did not act as an acquittal of that charge and could not act as a bar, on double jeopardy grounds, to his subsequent conviction of DUI. Day v. State, 606 So. 2d 206 (Ala. Crim. App. 1992).

Section 32-5A-194(b)(3) makes no distinction between subdivision (a)(1) or (a)(2); therefore, the appellant's argument that § 32-5A-194(b)(3) was applicable only to subdivision (a)(1) failed. Briggs v. City of Huntsville, 545 So. 2d 167 (Ala. Crim. App. 1988), overruled on other grounds, Frazier v. City of Montgomery, 565 So. 2d 1255 (Ala. Crim. App. 1990).

"Under the influence of alcohol." — For purposes of subdivision (a)(2), the phrase "under the influence of alcohol" is to be defined as having consumed such an amount of alcohol as to affect his ability to operate a vehicle in a safe manner. Buckner v. City of Huntsville, 549 So. 2d 451 (Ala. 1989).

When an individual is charged with driving under the influence of alcohol pursuant to subdivision (a)(2) of this section, the jury must be instructed that in order to render a guilty verdict they must find that the driver was so intoxicated as to be unable to operate his vehicle in a safe manner. Woods v. City of Dothan, 594 So. 2d 238 (Ala. Crim. App. 1991).

For purposes of subdivision (a)(2), the phrase "under the influence of alcohol" is to be defined as having consumed such an amount of alcohol as to affect his ability to operate a vehicle in a safe manner. Pitts v. City of Auburn, 552 So. 2d 184 (Ala. Crim. App. 1989).

Jury may infer driver's intoxicated state from driver's intoxicated condition. — A driver's intoxicated condition after an automobile accident is a fact from which the jury may infer that he was driving while in an intoxicated state. Terry v. City of Montgomery, 549 So. 2d 566 (Ala. Crim. App. 1989).

The Youthful Offender Act is clearly applicable to a person charged with driving under the influence of alcohol, provided that the offense "was committed in his minority but was not disposed of in juvenile court." King v. Wooldridge, 547 So. 2d 579 (Ala. 1989).

Offense may be committed on highways and private property. — The offense of driving under the influence (DUI) as defined by this section applies "upon highways and elsewhere

throughout the state," and unlike Alabama's predecessor offense of DWI, the present offense of DUI may be committed on private property. Lunceford v. City of Northport, 555 So. 2d 246 (Ala. Crim. App. 1988), appeal dismissed, 564 So. 2d 1055 (Ala. Crim. App. 1990).

Implied consent law did not apply where offense on private property. — The implied consent law did not apply because the defendant was arrested for DUI on private property, and there was no evidence that he had been driving on a highway; consequently, the procedural protections afforded by the Alabama implied consent statute did not apply to a motorist arrested for DUI on private property and, in such a case, the taking of a breath sample was justified on the basis of voluntary consent. Lunceford v. City of Northport, 555 So. 2d 246 (Ala. Crim. App. 1988), appeal dismissed, 564 So. 2d 1055 (Ala. Crim. App. 1990).

Where Driving Under the Influence (DUI) charge was dismissed on motion of the prosecutor because of a substantial break in the chain of delivery of the blood alcohol sample to the lab, and where from the record of the proceedings there was no indication that the state ever moved the trial court to set aside the order of dismissal and to reinstate the DUI charge, although the state may have requested the trial court to reinstate the DUI charge, no evidence of such a request had been presented to the court. A petitioner seeking a writ of mandamus is responsible for supplying the record necessary to an understanding of the matter set forth in the petition. Ex parte State ex rel. Johnson, 636 So. 2d 1266 (Ala. Crim. App. 1994).

The "one-leg stand test" and the "walk-and-turn test" are not novel scientific tests. Seewar v. Town of Summerdale, 601 So. 2d 198 (Ala. Crim. App. 1992).

Each subsection requires different elements of proof. — Subdivision (a)(1) prohibits driving with a blood-alcohol level of 0.10% or more. Subdivision (a)(2) prohibits driving while "[u]nder the influence of alcohol." Although each subsection requires different elements of proof, the results of a chemical test for intoxication may be introduced in a prosecution under either subsection. Harry v. State, 571 So. 2d 392 (Ala. Crim. App. 1990).

The Intoxilyzer 5000 blood-alcohol test results are circumstantial evidence of being under the influence of alcohol, and the results of a chemical test for intoxication may be introduced in a prosecution under either subdivision (a)(1) or subdivision (a)(2). Harris v. State, 601 So. 2d 1099 (Ala. Crim. App. 1991), overruled on other grounds, Ex parte Mayo, 652 So. 2d 201 (Ala. 1994).

Proof under subdivision (a)(1). — Where

the defendant is charged under subdivision (a)(1) language, the prosecution must prove that the defendant's blood had an alcohol content of .10 percent or more, but need not prove that the defendant's ability to drive was impaired. Frazier v. City of Montgomery, 565 So. 2d 1255 (Ala. Crim. App. 1990).

Proof under subdivision (a)(2). — If the defendant is charged under subdivision (a)(2) language, the prosecution must prove that the defendant was under the influence of alcohol, i.e., that he had consumed alcohol to the extent that it affected his ability to operate his vehicle in a safe manner. Frazier v. City of Montgomery, 565 So. 2d 1255 (Ala. Crim. App. 1990).

Evidence of blood alcohol level under subdivision (a)(2). — In a prosecution under subdivision (a)(2), it is not necessary to introduce evidence of the defendant's blood alcohol level. Suttle v. State, 565 So. 2d 1197 (Ala. Crim. App. 1990).

Municipal ordinance. — If a driving-under-the-influence prosecution is brought under a municipal ordinance, the municipality is required to introduce into evidence the local municipal ordinance in order to make out its case. United States v. Tyson, 829 F. Supp. 368 (M.D. Ala. 1993).

Where no evidence was presented of defendant's blood alcohol level. — Although the Uniform Traffic Ticket and Complaint (UTTC) specifically charged that defendant was driving with a blood alcohol level of .10 percent or more, no evidence was presented at trial of defendant's blood alcohol level. The trial court committed reversible error by failing to grant defendant's motion for a judgment of acquittal. The prosecution failed to present a prima facie case by failing to offer any evidence of defendant's blood alcohol level at the time the complaint was issued. Joyce v. City of Pleasant Grove, 652 So. 2d 336 (Ala. Crim. App. 1994).

Withdrawal of part of charge. — Withdrawing a part of a charge does not constitute an amendment to the Uniform Traffic Ticket and Complaint, provided that nothing new is added and that the charge under the remaining subsection was not restated differently. Hastings v. State, 589 So. 2d 795 (Ala. Crim. App. 1991).

The factors to be weighed in determining whether the defendant was in fact intoxicated at time of the offense are: (1) the testimony of the witnesses, (2) access to alcohol, and (3) the amount of time between the commission of the offense and the observation of the defendant. Sides v. State, 574 So. 2d 856 (Ala. Crim. App.), aff'd, 574 So. 2d 859 (Ala. 1990).

It is the prosecutor's burden to prove that a defendant was under the influence of any substance to the extent that it affected his ability to operate his vehicle in a safe manner. Raper v. State, 584 So. 2d 544 (Ala. Crim. App. 1991).

Although this section does not explicitly require the state to prove a certain degree of alcoholic influence to obtain a conviction, for purposes of this section, the phrase "under the influence of alcohol" is to be defined as having consumed such an amount of alcohol as to affect a person's ability to operate a vehicle in a safe manner. Raper v. State, 584 So. 2d 544 (Ala. Crim. App. 1991).

Evidence of 0.10% blood alcohol content does not create presumption of guilt. — Evidence showing the prescribed measurement — 0.10% blood alcohol content — creates a rebuttable presumption that the measurement accurately reflects the blood alcohol concentration at the time of driving but does not create a presumption of guilt because the state must prove beyond a reasonable doubt that the defendant was driving or operating a motor vehicle with a blood alcohol concentration of 0.10%. Curren v. State, 620 So. 2d 739 (Ala. 1993).

Sufficient complaint. — For purposes of subdivision (a)(5) of this section, the language "having consumed such an amount of any substance as to affect his ability to operate a vehicle in a safe manner" is sufficiently implied by its incorporation into the phrase "under the influence of a substance." Moreover, this element was qualified by the phrase "which impaired his mental or physical facilities [sic]." Based on the above reasoning, it is abundantly clear that the complaint accurately and fairly informed defendant of the offense charged and that it sufficiently stated an offense prohibited by law. Raper v. State, 584 So. 2d 544 (Ala. Crim. App. 1991).

Adequate notice given to the defendant. — Although the complaint failed to specify under which subsection of this section the defendant was charged, where the Alabama Uniform Traffic Ticket and Complaint ("UTTC"), a copy of which was given to the defendant at the time of his arrest, specifically alleged that defendant did drive or was in actual physical control of a vehicle while under the influence of alcohol, in violation of subsection (a)(2), because the UTTC clearly alleged the proper subsection and because both the UTTC and the circuit court complaint charged the defendant with driving or being in actual physical control of a vehicle while under the influence of alcohol, the defendant had notice from the day of his arrest of the specific offense charged. Fields v. City of Alexander City, 597 So. 2d 242 (Ala. Crim. App. 1992).

Defendant's contention that the Uniform

Traffic Ticket and Complaint (UTTC) did not sufficiently inform him of the offense with which he was charged was meritless, where the UTTC charged the defendant with a violation of the "State Code T 32 . . . Section 5A-191A1A2" and in the description of offense portion of the UTTC, the block next to the statement "There Was .10% or More By Weight of Alcohol in His/Her Blood" had been marked. Medley v. State, 630 So. 2d 163 (Ala. Crim. App. 1993).

It is not required that one be actually driving a vehicle in order to be found guilty of violating this section. Adams v. State, 585 So. 2d 161 (Ala. 1991).

Asleep in parked vehicle. — A person may be convicted of DUI who is in actual physical control of his vehicle, but not yet driving; even where he is asleep in his parked vehicle. Adams v. State, 585 So. 2d 156 (Ala. Crim. App. 1990), rev'd on other grounds, Adams v. State, 585 So. 2d 161 (Ala. 1991); Raley v. State, 586 So. 2d 285 (Ala. Crim. App. 1991).

Officer's testimony sufficient and operator's certificate not required for test admission. — Officer's testimony was sufficient; the state was not required to produce an actual operator's certificate in order to establish a proper predicate under Ex parte Bush, 474 So. 2d 168, 170 (Ala. 1985), for the admission into evidence of the test results. Long v. State, 650 So. 2d 621 (Ala. Crim. App. 1994).

Evidence sufficient to show defendant incapable of operating vehicle safely. — Where the police officer testifed that he smelled alcohol on defendant's breath, that defendant's eyes were glassy, that his speech was confused, that defendant had been weaving in his traffic lane, that he failed to stop at a stop sign and a red traffic light, and moreover, the officer testified that in his opinion defendant was not capable of operating a motor vehicle, and coupled with the results of the Intoxylizer 5000 test, evidence was sufficient to establish that defendant was unable to operate his vehicle safely. Hargrove v. City of Rainbow City, 619 So. 2d 944 (Ala. Crim. App. 1993).

Proof of actual physical control. — Adding the words "or was in actual physical control of a vehicle" to the Uniform Traffic Ticket and Complaint does not change the nature of the offense. Gentile v. City of Guntersville, 589 So. 2d 809 (Ala. Crim. App. 1991).

Reckless driving not a lesser included offense. — It has been generally held that reckless driving is not a lesser included offense of driving while intoxicated or of variations of the latter charge. Davis v. State, 589 So. 2d 1305 (Ala. Crim. App. 1991).

Use of circumstantial evidence to prove driver was in "actual physical control." — Defendant was properly convicted under this section where although no one testified that they actually observed the defendant driving the car, there was wealth of circumstantial evidence that the defendant did in fact drive her car onto a wooden rail. McLaney v. City of Montgomery, 570 So. 2d 881 (Ala. Crim. App. 1990).

Requisite specificity present in vehicular homicide indictment where indictment sufficiently averred the violated statutes and also adequately informed appellant of crime for which he was charged and against which he must be prepared to defend. The indictment was not fatally defective for failure to specify whether appellant was charged with vehicular homicide because of his blood alcohol level (subdivision (a)(1)) or because he was driving "under the influence" (subdivision (a)(2)). Beadnell v. State, 574 So. 2d 890 (Ala. Crim. App. 1990).

Opinion of officer as to sobriety.
An investigating officer may give his opinion as to the sobriety of the accused in a DUI case. Terry v. City of Montgomery, 549 So. 2d 566 (Ala. Crim. App. 1989).

An arresting police officer's opinion as to sobriety of defendant at time of arrest is admissible in a prosecution for driving under the influence. Malone v. City of Silverhill, 575 So. 2d 101 (Ala. Crim. App. 1989), rev'd on other grounds, Ex parte Malone, 575 So. 2d 106 (Ala. 1991).

Police officer testimony. — Police officer's testimony was sufficient to show that he arrived upon the scene of a recent accident, even though only one vehicle was involved and even though the damage might have been slight; thus the application of § 32-5-171 was warranted. State v. Adams, 592 So. 2d 639 (Ala. Crim. App. 1991), rev'd on other grounds, 592 So. 2d 641 (Ala. 1991).

State did not need to prove impaired driving ability. — Where the defendant was properly given a test which showed that he had a blood alcohol content of .20%, the State properly relied on the statutory presumption contained in § 32-5A-194(b)(3) as proof that he was under the influence; the Buckner v. City of Huntsville, 549 So. 2d 451 (Ala. 1989), holding that the State must prove impaired driving ability to establish that the accused was "under the influence" applies only when "no test was administered" and the accused was charged under subdivision (a)(2) or when the test results showed a blood alcohol level of the less than .10% and the accused was charged under subdivision (a)(1). Cains v. State, 555 So. 2d 290 (Ala. Crim. App. 1989).

Eyewitness testimony not necessary. — In order to demonstrate that a defendant could not operate a vehicle in a safe manner, eyewitness testimony that the defendant was seen driving in an unsafe or erratic manner was not essential. A conviction for driving under the influence may be based on circumstantial evidence. Rice v. State, 611 So. 2d 1161 (Ala. Crim. App. 1992).

Eyewitness testimony that the defendant was seen driving in an unsafe or erratic manner is not essential, and a conviction may rest upon circumstantial evidence. Long v. State, 650 So. 2d 621 (Ala. Crim. App. 1994).

Evidence obtained after "traffic arrest" admissible. — Although § 32-1-4 generally forbids police officers from taking persons charged with the violation of minor traffic offense into the type of custody traditionally associated with a felony arrest, it does not prohibit the temporary detention or "traffic arrest" of individuals for minor traffic offenses, thus, where defendant was subjected to only limited detention while officer attempted to confirm or dispel his suspicion that the defendant was under the influence, defendant's statements and the results of his blood alcohol test were not fruits of an unlawful arrest and their suppression was not required. Sides v. State, 574 So. 2d 856 (Ala. Crim. App.), aff'd, 574 So. 2d 859 (Ala. 1990).

Error in allowing testimony that defendant in possession of marihuana. — The trial court erred in allowing into evidence the testimony that defendant was in possession of marihuana when he was arrested. The appellant was charged only with driving under the influence of alcohol; he was not charged with driving under the influence of both alcohol and a controlled substance or of driving under the influence of any other substance that impairs the faculties. The probative value of evidence of the appellant's possession of marihuana did not outweigh its potential prejudicial effect. Krumm v. City of Robertsdale, 648 So. 2d 651 (Ala. Crim. App. 1994).

The testimony concerning the field sobriety tests administered to the appellant by deputy was both relevant and material to prosecution for driving under the influence and was therefore correctly received into evidence. Scott v. State, 624 So. 2d 230 (Ala. Crim. App. 1993).

It was not error to allow deputy's testimony concerning the field sobriety tests to be received into evidence absent a showing of the scientific basis for the tests. Scott v. State, 624 So. 2d 230 (Ala. Crim. App. 1993).

The failure to properly fill out the instant Uniform Traffic Ticket and Complaint and cite a city ordinance or adopting ordinance instead of a state statute affected only the lower court's personal jurisdiction. Therefore, the failure to raise the issue in a timely manner waived the defect. Hanson v.

City of Trussville, 539 So. 2d 1082 (Ala. Crim. App. 1988).

Amending complaint over defendant's objection and over consent was not prejudicial. — Where the defendant was originally charged under the Uniform Traffic Ticket and Complaint (U.T.T.C.) old form, with both methods of committing the offense of driving under the influence, where the U.T.T.C. was amended by agreement when the parties stipulated to a violation of subdivision (a)(1) of this section, and where such change was noted on the U.T.T.C. form but the defendant was then charged in circuit court with both subsections of this section, amending the complaint without the defendant's consent and over his objection was not prejudicial; the jury was only instructed on subdivision (a)(1) of this section, the charge of which he had been given notice. McLaughlin v. City of Homewood, 548 So. 2d 580 (Ala. Crim. App. 1988).

Complaint sufficient to apprise defendant of offense. — The complaint against the appellant was not vague or indefinite, nor did it fail to apprise him of the accusation against him where the complaint charged that the appellant did operate or was in actual physical control of a motor vehicle in violation of this section. Rice v. State, 611 So. 2d 1161 (Ala. Crim. App. 1992).

Information not sufficient to apprise defendant of offense. — Information charging defendant with the offense of DUI in violation of this section was clearly not sufficient to apprise defendant of the specific offense with which he was charged since this section covers the offense of driving or being in actual physical control of a vehicle while there is 0.10 percent or more by weight of alcohol in one's blood. Bishop v. State, 555 So. 2d 317 (Ala. Crim. App.), aff'd, 574 So. 2d 859 (Ala. 1990).

Indictment for reckless murder did not need to include phrase. — The indictment was clearly sufficient to charge the appellant with reckless murder. Because the indictment charged the appellant with reckless murder, and not with driving under the influence of a controlled substance, it was not necessary that the indictment include the phrase "to such a degree that she was rendered incapable of safely driving." Chambers v. State, 644 So. 2d 1294 (Ala. Crim. App. 1994).

Defendant was put on notice to defend against result of breath test. — Defendant, who was charged with violating subdivision (a)(2), was put on notice that he would have to defend against the result of a breath test since the Uniform Traffic Ticket and Complaint was properly filled out and was sufficient to legally charge the offense of driving while under the influence of alcohol. Briggs v. City of Huntsville, 545 So. 2d 167 (Ala. Crim. App. 1988), overruled on other grounds, Frazier v. City of Montgomery, 565 So. 2d 1255 (Ala. Crim. App. 1990).

Where the Uniform Traffic Ticket and Complaint, by reference to the subdivision (a)(2) and by describing the offense by tracking the language of (a)(1), charged the appellant under both subdivisions (a)(1) and (a)(2) and in attempting to prove that the appellant was guilty of driving under the influence, the state had the option of proving either that he was "under the influence of alcohol" or that his blood alcohol content was more than .10 percent. Thus, under subsection (a)(2), the appellant may have had to defend against the results of the blood alcohol test if the state had chosen to introduce them into evidence. Sandlin v. State, 575 So. 2d 1221 (Ala. Crim. App. 1990).

Challenge for cause to venire members. — The trial court properly denied the appellant's challenge for cause to venire members although both of these individuals, upon initial inquiry, indicated that they had a strong religious or moral belief against the use of alcohol; upon individual questioning, one juror stated that if the evidence showed that the appellant wasn't really soused, she would not let it affect her thinking; the other juror stated that she did not think that the fact that the appellant had been drinking before his arrest would affect her ability to decide this case based on the law and evidence, but that it could affect her ability based on her strong opposition to alcohol, and upon further inquiry, juror stated that she could be fair and go by the evidence. McInnish v. State, 584 So. 2d 935 (Ala. Crim. App. 1991).

Where the defendant was charged with a violation of subdivision (a)(2), the trial judge erred in charging the jury on subdivision (a)(1); however, that error was harmless because there was no possibility that the jury could have found that defendant was guilty of driving with a blood-alcohol level of 0.10 percent or more without also finding that he was guilty of driving under the influence of alcohol. Collier v. State, 544 So. 2d 986 (Ala. Crim. App. 1988).

Error in instruction as to degree of influence of alcohol. — The trial court erred in instructing the jury that the degree of the influence of alcohol does not have to be so advanced as to interfere with the proper operation of the vehicle. Buckner v. City of Huntsville, 549 So. 2d 451 (Ala. 1989).

Trial court erred to reversal in giving the oral charge to the jury that, "if you're convinced beyond a reasonable doubt that a person's blood content is more than .10, then it's your duty to convict that person regardless of any other evidence"; the charge, as given,

invaded the province of the jury and amounted to a directed verdict of guilt based upon the results of the blood alcohol test alone. Bouleware v. State, 557 So. 2d 1320 (Ala. Crim. App. 1989).

State produced sufficient evidence to create a jury question as to whether defendant had consumed alcohol and whether he had consumed such an amount of alcohol as to impair his ability to safely operate his vehicle, where police officers testified that defendant's driving was "erratic," that they smelled the odor of alcohol on him when he exited his vehicle after it was stopped, and that he was unable to perform a field test when he was requested to do so. Jones v. State, 579 So. 2d 66 (Ala. Crim. App. 1991).

Failure to introduce municipal ordinance necessitated reversal. — Where city failed to introduce municipal ordinance adopting applicable state offenses, even though there was a stipulation waiving the requirement that the city clerk authenticate the adoption of the ordinance, city failed to prove a requisite element of its case; this failure mandated a reversal of petitioner's convictions under § 32-5A-190 and this section. Ex parte Woodson, 578 So. 2d 1049 (Ala. 1991).

Review of dismissal of charges under ARCrP, Rule 15.7(a) not available in misdemeanor cases. — Where city appealed from order of the circuit court suppressing the results of a breath test to determine blood-alcohol content in a prosecution for driving under the influence of alcohol, the appellee's motion to dismiss this appeal was due to be granted. In felony cases, the prosecution's avenue for review of the dismissal of charges for the pretrial suppression of evidence by the circuit court is appeal pursuant to Rule 15.7(a), ARCrP. However, that avenue is not available in misdemeanor cases. City of Huntsville v. Shanes, 645 So. 2d 339 (Ala. Crim. App. 1994).

The Horizontal Gaze Nystagmus test is generally accepted by the scientific community and thus satisfies the Frye test. Malone v. City of Silverhill, 575 So. 2d 101 (Ala. Crim. App. 1989), rev'd on other grounds, Ex parte Malone, 575 So. 2d 106 (Ala. 1991). But see Sides v. State, 574 So. 2d 859 (Ala. 1990) for differing view on test's reliability.

Judgment withheld on admissibility of HGN test results. — Horizontal Gaze Nystagmus test results might not be admissible in future cases even if the state laid the proper predicate. The Alabama supreme court has not been presented with sufficient evidence concerning the test's reliability or acceptance by the scientific community to address that question. Ex parte State, 574 So. 2d 859 (Ala. 1990).

Court erred in receiving officer's testi-

mony concerning HGN test. — Officer whose only specialized training in this area was an eight-hour course on the proper use of the Horizontal Gaze Nystagmus (HGN) test, was, at most, qualified as an expert in giving the test; the state offered no other evidence to demonstrate the reliability of either the HGN test or the scientific principle upon which the HGN test is based, i.e., that alcohol consumption causes nystagmus; therefore, the court erred in receiving officer's testimony concerning the HGN test. Malone v. City of Silverhill, 575 So. 2d 101 (Ala. Crim. App. 1989), rev'd on other grounds, Ex parte Malone, 575 So. 2d 106 (Ala. 1991).

Admission of HGN test reversible error. — Results of Horizontal Gaze Nystagmus (HGN) test were erroneously admitted where officer was allowed to state the results of the HGN test without a showing of either the reliability of the test itself or his training and experience in conducting the test. In consideration of defendant's ability to pass certain field sensory tests and his testimony about driving experience and awards he received for safe driving, it cannot be said that the admission of the HGN test results had no bearing on the jury's verdict of guilty, thus, the test results admission was reversible error. Sides v. State, 574 So. 2d 856 (Ala. Crim. App.), aff'd, 574 So. 2d 859 (Ala. 1990).

Admission of evidence of Horizontal Gaze Nystagmus (HGN) test results, without a proper predicate, was not harmless error; the

proper inquiry was not whether evidence of the defendant's guilt was overwhelming but, instead, whether a substantial right of the defendant had or probably had been adversely affected; overwhelming evidence of guilt does not render prejudicial error harmless under Rule 45, ARAP; the problem created by the improper admission of the HGN evidence was due to the scientific nature of the test and the disproportionate impact it might have had on the jury's decision-making process. Ex parte Malone, 575 So. 2d 106 (Ala. 1990).

New trial where state failed to establish proper foundation for test. — Defendant was entitled to a new trial, where the state failed to establish a proper foundation regarding the scientific reliability of horizontal gaze nystagmus test (HGN) results. Brunson v. State, 580 So. 2d 62 (Ala. Crim. App. 1991).

Cited in Reuther v. City of Leeds, 599 So. 2d 1246 (Ala. Crim. App. 1992); Truman v. City of Enterprise, 606 So. 2d 1151 (Ala. Crim. App. 1992); Scott v. City of Guntersville, 612 So. 2d 1273 (Ala. Crim. App. 1992); United States v. Tyson, 829 F. Supp. 368 (M.D. Ala. 1993).

Collateral references.

Defense of necessity, duress, or coercion in prosecution for violation of state narcotics laws. 1 ALR5th 938.

Search and seizure: Lawfulness of demand for driver's license, vehicle registration, or proof of insurance pursuant to police stop to assist motorist. 19 ALR5th 884.

§ 32-5A-191.1. Additional fines on persons convicted of offenses involving driving under the influence.

(a) Beginning October 1, 1993, in addition to all fines, fees, costs, and punishments prescribed by law, there shall be imposed or assessed an additional fine of $100 on any conviction in any court of the state for the offense of driving under the influence as defined in Section 32-5A-191.

(b) No later than 30 days after collection, proceeds from the additional fines collected under this section shall be forwarded by the officer of the court who collects the fines to the State Treasurer after five percent of the fine is deducted for administrative costs. All amounts received by the State Treasurer shall be credited to the Impaired Drivers Trust Fund created in the State Treasury by Sections 16-38A-1 to 16-38A-4, inclusive. (Acts 1993, No. 93-323, p. 492, § 1.)

Effective date. — The act which added this section became effective May 5, 1993.

§ 32-5A-191.2. Administration and disposition of moneys in Impaired Drivers Trust Fund.

(a) Beginning October 1, 1994, moneys in the Impaired Drivers Trust Fund shall be distributed to the Division of Rehabilitation Services in the State Department of Education for the following purposes:

(1) As a payer of last resort for the costs of care provided in this state for citizens of this state who have survived neuro-trauma with head or spinal cord injuries. Expenditures for spinal cord injury and head injury care shall be made by the Division of Rehabilitation Services according to criteria established by the Impaired Drivers Trust Fund Advisory Board. Expenditures may include but need not be limited to, post acute medical care, rehabilitation therapies, medication, attendant care, home accessibility modification, and equipment necessary for activities of daily living.

(2) Public information, prevention education, and research coordinated by the Alabama Head Injury Foundation.

(b) The Division of Rehabilitation Services shall issue a report to the Legislature on the first day of the Regular Session of each year, summarizing the activities supported by the moneys from the additional fines levied in this section and Section 32-5A-191.1. (Acts 1993, No. 93-323, p. 492, § 2.)

Effective date. — The act which added this section became effective May 5, 1993.

§ 32-5A-191.3. Operation of vessel and other marine devices while under influence of alcohol or controlled substances.

(a) A person shall not drive or be in actual physical control of any vessel, or manipulate any water skis, aquaplane, or any other marine transportation device on the waters of this state, as the waters are defined in Section 33-5-3, while:

(1) There is 0.10 percent or more by weight of alcohol in the blood;

(2) Under the influence of alcohol;

(3) Under the influence of a controlled substance to a degree which renders the person incapable of safely driving;

(4) Under the combined influence of alcohol and a controlled substance to a degree which renders the person incapable of safely driving; or

(5) Under the influence of any substance which impairs the mental or physical faculties of the person to a degree which renders the person incapable of safely driving.

(b) In the case of a vessel or other marine device described in subsection (a), only where the law enforcement officer of the Department of Conservation and Natural Resources has prior to stopping a vessel probable cause to believe that the operator of the vessel is driving under the influence of alcohol or under the influence of a controlled substance in violation of this section, the law enforcement officer is authorized to administer and may test the operator, at the scene, by using a field breathalyzer or other approved device, as a screening device, to determine if the operator may be operating a vessel or device in violation of subsection (a). Refusal to submit to a field breathalyzer test or other approved testing device shall result in the same punishment as provided in subsection (c) of Section 32-5-192 for operators of motor vehicles on the state highways. No field breathalyzer test shall be administered where the operator is stopped for violations other than under this section.

(c) The fact that any person charged with violating this section is or has been legally entitled to use alcohol or a controlled substance shall not constitute a defense against any charge of violating this section.

(d) Upon first conviction, a person violating this section shall be punished by imprisonment in the county or municipal jail for not more than one year, or by fine of not less than two hundred fifty dollars ($250) nor more than one thousand dollars ($1,000), or by both fine and imprisonment. In addition, on a first conviction, the Commissioner of Conservation and Natural Resources shall suspend the vessel operating privilege or boater safety certification of the person so convicted for a period of 90 days. First time offenders convicted of driving or operating a vessel while under the influence of alcohol shall also be required to complete a DUI court referral program approved by the State Administrative Office of Courts. Neither reckless or careless operation of a vessel, nor any other boating or water safety infraction is a lesser included offense under a charge of operating a vessel while under the influence of alcohol or controlled substances.

(e) On a second conviction within a five-year period, the person convicted of violating this section shall be punished by a fine of not less than five hundred dollars ($500) nor more than two thousand five hundred dollars ($2,500) and by imprisonment, which may include hard labor in the county or municipal jail for not more than one year. The sentence shall include a mandatory sentence which is not subject to suspension or probation of imprisonment in the county or municipal jail for not less than 48 consecutive hours or community service for not less than 20 days. In addition, the Commission of Conservation and Natural Resources shall revoke the vessel operating privileges or boater safety certification of the person so convicted for a period of one year.

(f) On a third or subsequent conviction within a five-year period, the person convicted of violating this section shall be punished by a fine of not less than one thousand dollars ($1,000) nor more than five thousand dollars ($5,000) and by imprisonment, which may include hard labor, in the county or municipal jail for not less than 60 days nor more than one year, to include a minimum of 60 days which shall be served in the county or municipal jail and which cannot be probated or suspended. In addition, the Commissioner of Conservation and Natural Resources shall revoke the vessel operating privilege or boater safety certification of the person so convicted for a period of three years.

(g) All fines collected for violation of this section as to vessels or other marine devices on the waters of this state shall be paid into the State Water Safety Fund.

(h) A person who has been arrested for violating this section shall not be released from jail under bond or otherwise, until there is less than the same percent by weight of alcohol in the person's blood as specified in subdivision (1) of subsection (a).

(i) "Vessel," for the purposes of this section, shall mean any vessel as defined in Section 33-5-3, operated on the waters of this state, as defined in Section 33-5-3.

(j) No provision of this section shall be construed to assess points for DUI convictions under motor vehicle convictions for driving under the influence. (Acts 1994, No. 94-652, p. 1243, § 2.)

Code Commissioner's note. — Section 32-5A-191 was amended by both Acts 94-590 and 94-652. Act 94-590 amended the section to make a fourth and subsequent conviction within a five-year period for operating a vehicle under the influence a felony, effective August 20, 1994. Act 94-652 amended the section to include within the existing penalty provisions for operating a vehicle under the influence operating a vessel under the influence, but did not address the penalty for a fourth and subsequent conviction. That change was effective on April 28, 1994. There is no substantive conflict between the two acts and no indication of any legislative intent to either undo the changes made by Act 94-590 in the enactment of Act 94-652 or make the changes applicable to a fourth or subsequent conviction for operating a vessel under the influence. To give full effect to both Acts, and the apparent intent of the Legislature, the amendments to Section 32-5A-191 made by Act 94-652 have been codified as a new Section 32-5A-191.3, relating only to penalties

for operating a vessel under the influence. Those penalties would be the same as those in effect for operating a vehicle under the influence prior to the enactment of Act 94-652, without the changes made by Act 94-590 that became effective August 20, 1994, after the enactment of Act 94-652. The amendments to Section 32-5A-191 made by Act 94-590 have been incorporated into that section as set forth above and are applicable only to operating a vehicle under the influence.

Additionally, in subsection (b), the citation to subsection (c) of Section 32-5-192 is substituted for Section 32-5A-192(c) as it appears in the act to reflect the code section in which punishment for refusal to submit to a field breathalyzer test or other approved testing device for operators of motor vehicles on the state highways is located.

Cross references. — For provisions relating to the Alabama Boating Safety Reform Act, see Article 2 of Chapter 5, Title 33, § 33-5-50 et seq.

§ 32-5A-192. Homicide by vehicle or vessel.

(a) Whoever shall unlawfully and unintentionally cause the death of another person while engaged in the violation of any state law or municipal ordinance applying to the operation or use of a vehicle, or vessel, as defined in Section 33-5-3, or to the regulation of traffic or boating, shall be guilty of homicide when the violation is the proximate cause of the death.

(b) Any person convicted of homicide by vehicle or vessel shall be fined not less than five hundred dollars ($500) nor more than two thousand dollars ($2,000), or shall be imprisoned for a term not less than one year nor more than five years, or may be so fined and so imprisoned. All fines collected for violation of this section relating to vessels shall be paid into the State Water Safety Fund. (Acts 1980, No. 80-434, p. 604, § 9-107; Acts 1983, No. 83-620, p. 959, § 1; Acts 1994, No. 94-652, p. 1243, § 3.)

The 1994 amendment, effective April 28, 1994, inserted "or vessel, as defined in Section 33-5-3" and "or boating" in subsection (a), in subsection (b), inserted "or vessel" in the first sentence and added the second sentence, and made nonsubstantive changes.

Vehicular homicide may constitute a lesser included offense of universal malice murder. — In determining whether vehicular

homicide constitutes a lesser included offense of murder either of two tests should be employed. Test 1: Can all or fewer than all of the facts establishing the commission of murder also establish the commission of vehicular homicide? Test 2: Do the murder and vehicular homicide statutes differ under these facts only in that vehicular homicide contemplates a less serious injury or risk of injury or requires a

40

lesser kind of culpability. Black v. State, 586 So. 2d 968 (Ala. Crim. App.), writ denied, 586 So. 2d 970 (Ala. 1991).

Because vehicular homicide is the next lesser included offense under manslaughter, under the circumstances presented, the failure to instruct on vehicular homicide cannot be harmless error. Ex parte Long, 600 So. 2d 982 (Ala. 1992).

Requisite specificity present in vehicular homicide indictment where indictment sufficiently averred the violated statutes and also adequately informed appellant of crime for which he was charged and against which he must be prepared to defend. The indictment was not fatally defective for failure to specify whether appellant was charged with vehicular homicide because of his blood alcohol level (§ 32-5A-191(a)(1)) or because he was driving "under the influence" (§ 32-5A-191(a)(2)). Beadnell v. State, 574 So. 2d 890 (Ala. Crim. App. 1990).

Ex-girlfriend's testimony concerning diet pills was irrelevant and inflammatory. — Where there was evidence presented at trial that the appellant occasionally took diet pills while he was driving his truck, where the state argued that defendant's ex-girlfriend's testimony was relevant in that since diet pills made her nervous, one could infer that they made everybody nervous, and where he further argued that being nervous would impair one's ability to safely operate a motor vehicle, and therefore, this testimony was an integral part of the state's case in proving whether the defendant had violated a statute by running a red light, the court rejected the state's argument; it was not reasonable to infer that because diet pills make witness nervous, they make everybody nervous; thus, witness' testimony was irrelevant because it neither proved or disproved the main inquiry of the case; moreover, her testimony was unduly inflammatory in that it interjected the issue of driving under the influence of drugs into the trial even though the appellant was not charged in the indictment with that offense. Turner v. State, 584 So. 2d 864 (Ala. Crim. App. 1990).

Cited in Kitsos v. State, 574 So. 2d 979 (Ala. Crim. App. 1990).

§ 32-5A-193. Fleeing or attempting to elude police officer.

Duty to advise defendant regarding possible sentencing. — The defendant must be advised on the record of the maximum and minimum possible sentences of the offenses for which he is charged. This is an absolute constitutional prerequisite before a guilty plea can be accepted. Sampson v. State, 605 So. 2d 846 (Ala. Crim. App. 1992).

Advising defendant of maximum and minimum sentence is a jurisdictional matter, so that failure to so inform the defendant can be raised for the first time on appeal. Sampson v. State, 605 So. 2d 846 (Ala. Crim. App. 1992).

Custodial arrest not authorized for offense alone. — While misdemeanor offense of fleeing or attempting to elude a police officer is one of the "Rules of the Road" and is defined in this section, a custodial arrest is not authorized for this offense alone. A custodial arrest was authorized and justified where defendant refused to sign the traffic ticket. Gouin v. State, 581 So. 2d 1279 (Ala. Crim. App. 1991).

Where the court of appeals did not have before it the district court warrant that was the original charging instrument for the traffic offense of attempting to elude a police officer, and where the Uniform Traffic Ticket and Complaint (UTTC) issued for that offense, which recited that defendant did unlawfully operate a motor vehicle by attempting to elude, was not sufficient to charge the offense set out in this section, although the UTTC was not alone sufficient to charge the offense defined in this section, trooper's affidavit, which was attached to all of the original district court warrants, cured any deficiency and gave defendant notice of the exact charge against which he was required to defend. Ex parte State ex rel. Johnson, 636 So. 2d 1266 (Ala. Crim. App. 1994).

§ 32-5A-194. Chemical tests; admissible as evidence; procedure for valid chemical analyses; permits for individuals performing analyses; persons qualified to withdraw blood; presumptions based on percent of alcohol in blood; refusal to submit; no liability for technician.

(a) Upon the trial of any civil, criminal or quasi-criminal action or proceeding arising out of acts alleged to have been committed by any person while driving or in actual control of a vehicle while under the influence of alcohol or controlled substance, evidence of the amount of alcohol or controlled substance in a person's blood at the alleged time, as determined by a chemical analysis of the person's blood, urine, breath or other bodily substance, shall be admissible. Where such a chemical test is made the following provisions shall apply:

(1) Chemical analyses of the person's blood, urine, breath or other bodily substance to be considered valid under the provisions of this section shall have been performed according to methods approved by the Department of Forensic Sciences and by an individual possessing a valid permit issued by the Department of Forensic Sciences for this purpose. The court trying the case may take judicial notice of the methods approved by the Department of Forensic Sciences. The Department of Forensic Sciences is authorized to approve satisfactory techniques or methods, to ascertain the qualifications and competence of individuals to conduct such analyses, and to issue permits which shall be subject to termination or revocation at the discretion of the Department of Forensic Sciences. The Department of Forensic Sciences shall not approve the permit required in this section for making tests for any law enforcement officer other than a member of the State Highway Patrol, a sheriff or his deputies, a city policeman or laboratory personnel employed by the Department of Forensic Sciences.

(2) When a person shall submit to a blood test at the direction of a law enforcement officer under the provisions of Section 32-5-192, only a physician or a registered nurse (or other qualified person) may withdraw blood for the purpose of determining the alcoholic content therein. This limitation shall not apply to the taking of breath or urine specimens. If the test given under Section 32-5-192 is a chemical test of urine, the person tested shall be given such privacy in the taking of the urine specimen as will insure the accuracy of the specimen and, at the same time, maintain the dignity of the individual involved.

(3) The person tested may at his own expense have a physician, or a qualified technician, registered nurse or other qualified person of his own choosing administer a chemical test or tests in addition to any administered at the discretion of a law enforcement officer. The failure or inability to obtain an additional test by a person shall not preclude the admission of evidence relating to the test or tests taken at the direction of a law enforcement officer.

(4) Upon the written request of the person who shall submit to a chemical test or tests at the request of a law enforcement officer, full information concerning the test or tests shall be made available to him or his attorney.

(5) Percent by weight of alcohol in the blood shall be based upon grams of alcohol per 100 cubic centimeters of blood or grams of alcohol per 210 liters of breath.

(b) Upon the trial of any civil, criminal, or quasi-criminal action or proceeding arising out of acts alleged to have been committed by any person while driving or in actual physical control of a vehicle while under the influence of alcohol, the amount of alcohol in the person's blood at the time alleged as shown by chemical analysis of the person's blood, urine, breath or other bodily substance shall give rise to the following presumptions:

(1) If there were at that time 0.05 percent or less by weight of alcohol in the person's blood, it shall be presumed that the person was not under the influence of alcohol.

(2) If there were at the time in excess of 0.05 percent but less than 0.08 percent by weight of alcohol in the person's blood, such fact shall not give rise to any presumption that the person was or was not under the influence of alcohol, but such fact may be considered with other competent evidence in determining whether the person was under the influence of alcohol.

(3) If there were at that time 0.08 percent or more by weight of alcohol in the person's blood, it shall be presumed that the person was under the influence of alcohol.

(4) The foregoing provisions of this subsection shall not be construed as limiting the introduction of any other competent evidence bearing upon the question whether the person was under the influence of alcohol.

(c) If a person under arrest refuses to submit to a chemical test under the provisions of Section 32-5-192, evidence of refusal shall be admissible in any civil, criminal or quasi-criminal action or proceeding arising out of acts alleged to have been committed while the person was driving or in actual physical control of a motor vehicle while under the influence of alcohol or controlled substance.

(d) No physician, registered nurse or duly licensed chemical laboratory technologist or clinical laboratory technician or medical facility shall incur any civil or criminal liability as a result of the proper administering of a blood test when requested in writing by a law enforcement officer to administer such a test. (Acts 1980, No. 80-434, p. 604, § 9-103; Acts 1988, No. 88-660, p. 1058, § 1; Acts 1995, No. 95-784, § 2.)

The 1995 amendment, effective August 9, 1995, substituted "0.08" for "0.10" in subdivisions (b)(2) and (b)(3).

Cross references. — For this section being commented on by new Rule 901, Alabama Rules of Evidence, effective January 1, 1996, see the Advisory Committee's Notes to new Rule 901 in the 1995 Cumulative Supplement to Volume 23.

I. GENERAL CONSIDERATION.

Subdivision (b)(3) makes no distinction between § 32-5A-191(a)(1) or (a)(2); therefore, the appellant's argument that subdivision (b)(3) of this section was applicable only to § 32-5A-191(a)(1) failed. Briggs v. City of Huntsville, 545 So. 2d 167 (Ala. Crim. App. 1988), overruled on other grounds, Frazier v. City of Montgomery, 565 So. 2d 1255 (Ala. Crim. App. 1990).

Not limited to acts on public highway. — This section is not limited to acts committed upon public highways. Lunceford v. City of Northport, 555 So. 2d 246 (Ala. Crim. App. 1988), appeal dismissed, 564 So. 2d 1055 (Ala. Crim. App. 1990).

Applicability to Assimilative Crimes Act. — Subdivision (a)(1) and § 32-5-192(a) are clearly procedural and evidentiary in nature for they merely regulate which persons can conduct breath tests in order to ensure the accuracy of the tests for evidentiary purposes, and therefore these provisions did not apply in a federal prosecution under the Assimilative Crimes Act for operating a motor vehicle while under the influence of alcohol on federal military base. United States v. Tyson, 829 F. Supp. 368 (M.D. Ala. 1993).

Test of blood plasma not contemplated by this section. — This section does not provide for the admissibility of tests measuring the alcohol content of blood plasma. However, because a second blood test was administered that conformed to the statute any error in the introduction of the "blood plasma" test was, at most, harmless. Stone v. State, 641 So. 2d 293 (Ala. Crim. App. 1993).

Accused must be allowed reasonable opportunity to obtain independent test.

Where a defendant makes a timely request, where the blood alcohol content of that sample is a material element of the charge, and where the defendant would be prejudiced by the denial of his motion for production of the blood sample for independent testing, due process requires that the state produce a sample of his blood for independent testing of its blood alcohol content. Ex parte Harwell, 639 So. 2d 1335 (Ala. 1993).

Refusal admissible only when refusal given by person under arrest. — The evidence of refusal shall be admissible in a criminal action only when the refusal is given by the person under arrest. This statute does not envision that a parent's refusal for a child to submit to a chemical test (or any party's refusal on another's behalf) shall be given the same inference as that of the person under arrest. Ex parte Hanks, 562 So. 2d 540 (Ala. 1989).

Police transportation to private sobriety test. — When a motorist who has been charged with an alcohol-related traffic offense has cooperated fully with the police and subsequently makes telephone arrangements for the administration of a private sobriety test, he is entitled to police transportation to the test site so that the test may be administered. Lockard v. Town of Killen, 565 So. 2d 679 (Ala. Crim. App. 1990).

Where blood is seized only for medical purposes, etc.

The results of blood seized only for medical purposes and not in furtherance of a criminal or accident investigation are generally admissible where the state shows that the circumstances of the taking of the sample, the identification, maintenance, and transporting of it, and the testing itself are scientifically acceptable and reasonably expected to produce results which are accurate and reliable. Davis v. State, 593 So. 2d 145 (Ala. Crim. App. 1991).

Due process requires state to carefully control tests. — Because driving with a blood alcohol content of .10 percent or more is per se illegal, and because the state administers the tests that provide evidence of blood alcohol content, due process requires the state to carefully control the tests it administers to supply proof of blood alcohol content. Ex parte Mayo, 652 So. 2d 201 (Ala. 1994).

Predicate for admission of test results.

The requisite foundation for the admissibility of test results indicating one's blood alcohol content pursuant to this section may be established by showing, first, that the law enforcement agency has adopted the particular form of testing that was in fact used. Second, there must be a showing that the test was performed according to methods approved by the State Board of Health. This may be proved by the introduction of the rules and regulations the officer followed while administering the test and the officer's testimony that he did, in fact, follow those rules when he administered the test in question. Third, there must be a showing that the person administering the test has a valid permit issued by the State Board of Health for that purpose. Seewar v. Town of Summerdale, 601 So. 2d 198 (Ala. Crim. App. 1992).

When statutory predicate not established, tests may be admitted under traditional evidentiary rules. — When the statutory predicate for admission is not established, the results of a chemical test for intoxication may still be admitted if the prosecution establishes a sufficient predicate under traditional evidentiary rules for the admission of scientific test results. Ex parte Mayo, 652 So. 2d 201 (Ala. 1994).

Moore v. State predicate for admission of tests where section requirements not met. — The Moore v. State, 442 So. 2d 164, 167 (Ala. Cr. App. 1983) predicate, substituting the I-5000 for the photoelectric intoximeter (P.E.I.), is appropriate for admission of breath tests where the requirements of this section are not met. Ex parte Mayo, 652 So. 2d 201 (Ala. 1994).

Test results were admissible where results admitted under general evidence principles. — Defendant's blood alcohol content test results were correctly received into evidence even though coroner ordered the blood test and he was not a law enforcement officer which this section requires since blood drawn and tested in duplicate by licensed medical technologists in a licensed hospital was scientifically acceptable and reasonable and any results from tests were accurate and reliable. Nelson v. State, 551 So. 2d 1152 (Ala. Crim. App. 1989).

Blood tests were correctly received into evidence because general evidentiary principles had been satisfied where a medical technologist, testified that she drew three vials of blood from the appellant after obtaining his permission and where she gave one vial to a police officer who delivered it to the Alabama Department of Forensic Sciences in Birmingham where it was tested for the presence of alcohol. Scott v. City of Guntersville, 612 So. 2d 1273 (Ala. Crim. App. 1992).

Failure to require use of simulator on I-5000 at each breath test. — There was no clear abuse of discretion by the Department of Forensic Sciences when it failed to require use of a simulator on the I-5000 at each breath test and to require two breath tests. However, the failure to verify the accuracy and reliability of the I-5000 at each individual breath test made the monthly inspection more critical. Ex parte Mayo, 652 So. 2d 201 (Ala. 1994).

Admission of blood seized only for medical evidence. — Blood tests performed pursuant to the implied consent law, § 32-5-192, are clearly admissible against a defendant alleged to have committed a criminal act while driving under the influence. However, the implied consent law and this section are not the exclusive means for admitting intoxication test results; where blood is seized only for medical purposes and not in furtherance of a criminal or accident investigation, the results of a blood alcohol test are admissible under general evidentiary principles. Russo v. State, 610 So. 2d 1206 (Ala. Crim. App. 1992).

Department of Forensic Sciences' permit not required. — Subsection (a) of this section clearly relates to tests performed under the implied consent law, § 32-5-192; however, where the state sought to introduce the results of a blood test under general evidentiary principles, it was not required that the persons involved in the testing process have a permit issued by the Department of Forensic Sciences. Russo v. State, 610 So. 2d 1206 (Ala. Crim. App. 1992).

Court erroneously held that state was not required to prove machine accurate and inspected. — Where there was evidence that, before and after a breath test, the I-5000 sets itself to zero, and doctor explained that this was not an internal check for calibration or accuracy, but only the setting of a baseline to adjust for the presence of any alcohol in the air of the room, the Court of Criminal Appeals in Harris v. State, 601 So. 2d 1099 (Ala. Cr. App. 1991), erroneously held that the state was not required to prove that the machine used for testing had been previously determined to be accurate and had been periodically inspected. The court incorrectly concluded that the I-5000 internally checked itself for accuracy. Ex parte Mayo, 652 So. 2d 201 (Ala. 1994).

Results admissible where licensed technologists tested blood in duplicate. — Although defendant argued that the State failed to lay the requisite foundation to show that the method of testing used was an approved, satisfactory technique as mandated by this section, defendant's blood alcohol test results were correctly received into evidence since the state either had to show that the test was taken in conformity with this section, or lay the requisite foundation for the admission of the test under general evidence principles and it was apparent that the test results were admitted under general evidence principles. Nelson v. State, 551 So. 2d 1152 (Ala. Crim. App. 1989).

Results of a police-administered intoxilyzer test would have to be suppressed upon retrial after reversal of the conviction of a motorist who was prevented by the police from obtaining an independent blood test and from attacking the accuracy of his intoxilyzer test. Lockard v. Town of Killen, 565 So. 2d 679 (Ala. Crim. App. 1990).

Proof of officer's expertise to conduct intoxilyzer test. — The department of forensic sciences is statutorily authorized to determine whether an individual is qualified and competent to conduct intoxilyzer tests, thus, where testing officer was shown to have a valid permit from the department of forensic sciences, it was proper for him to conduct the test. No further expertise by the officer as required. Stubstad v. City of Orange Beach, 575 So. 2d 1240 (Ala. Crim. App. 1991).

Nonexclusive means for admitting intoxication test results. — There is no requirement that this section be exclusive means for admitting intoxication test results. Davis v. State, 593 So. 2d 145 (Ala. Crim. App. 1991).

Presumption that defendant was intoxicated because of blood alcohol content does not apply. — The statutory rebuttable presumption that the defendant was intoxicated if his blood alcohol content was shown to be 0.10% does not apply to a prosecution for driving with 0.10% or greater blood alcohol content. Curren v. State, 620 So. 2d 739 (Ala. 1993).

State did not need to prove impaired driving ability. — Where the defendant was properly given a test which showed that he had a blood alcohol content of .20%, the state properly relied on the statutory presumption contained in subdivision (b)(3) as proof that he was under the influence; Buckner v. City of Huntsville, 549 So. 2d 451 (Ala. 1989), which holds that the state must prove impaired driving ability to establish that the accused was "under the influence," applies when no test is administered and the accused is charged under § 32-5A-191(a)(2) or when the test results showed a blood alcohol level of less than .10% and the accused was charged under § 32-5A-191(a)(1). Cains v. State, 555 So. 2d 290 (Ala. Crim. App. 1989).

"Presumption" in subdivision (b)(3) not conclusive presumption.

In accord with the bound volume. See Sides v. State, 574 So. 2d 856 (Ala. Crim. App.), aff'd, 574 So. 2d 859 (Ala. 1990).

Instructions properly given under subdivisions (b)(2) and (b)(3) of this section where it cannot be said that the instructions were clearly unrelated to the factual situation of this case, since there was testimony as to appellant's blood alcohol level two hours after the collision and also testimony that alcohol dissipates from the blood system over time. Kitsos v. State, 574 So. 2d 979 (Ala. Crim. App. 1990).

Judicial notice of methods refers only to rules properly promulgated. — Where deputy director of Department of Forensic Sciences (DFS) in charge of blood alcohol testing testified that there were written protocols for inspecting the I-5000's, but no such protocols were introduced, although subdivision (a)(1) states that "the court trying the case may take judicial notice of the methods approved by the DFS," the court was unaware of how it could obtain copies of internal written protocols that were not introduced at trial. This provision refers only to rules properly promulgated in accordance with the Administrative Procedure Act, § 41-22-1 et seq. Ex parte Mayo, 652 So. 2d 201 (Ala. 1994).

Rules of Department of Public Health did not meet requirement of subdivision (a)(1). — The rules found in the Alabama Administrative Code at Rule 420-1-.01 of the Rules of the Alabama State Board of Health/the Alabama Department of Public Health do not meet the requirement of subdivision (a)(1) that chemical analyses "shall have been performed according to methods approved by the Department of Forensic Sciences (DFS)." At a minimum, DFS should adopt these rules as its own and should adopt particularized rules to ensure that the Intoxilyzer 5000 machines are effectively inspected for accuracy and reliability. Ex parte Mayo, 652 So. 2d 201 (Ala. 1994).

Problem with rules did not prevent admission of chemical analysis. — Although the rules found in the Alabama Administrative Code of Rule 420-1-1-.01 did not meet the requirement of subdivision (a)(1), this problem with the rules was not sufficient of itself to prevent admission of a result of chemical analysis pursuant to this section. Thus, the court would not imply that tests of blood, urine, or other bodily substances could not be admitted under Rule 420-1-1-.02 until Department of Forensic Sciences adopted that rule as its own. Ex parte Mayo, 652 So. 2d 201 (Ala. 1994).

Effect of problem with rules on cases before and after ruling. — Where Supreme Court held that rules found in Alabama Administrative Code at Rule 420-1-1-.01 did not meet the requirements of subdivision (a)(1), this ruling would not apply to any other case already tried, unless the defendant in that case made a similar showing and objected to admission of the evidence of the test on the ground that the statute did not make the evidence admissible. In cases arising afterwards but before the Department of Forensic Sciences adopted appropriate rules, if a defendant made a sufficient objection to a breath test result, the prosecuting authority might have to lay a general evidentiary predicate to make evidence of the test admissible. Ex parte Mayo, 652 So. 2d 201 (Ala. 1994).

Driver was negligent as matter of law. — Driver of truck, who was in a collision with a train, was negligent as a matter of law because he was intoxicated at the time of the accident, as he had been drinking the day of the accident and that his blood alcohol level was .162 percent. Borden v. CSX Transp., Inc., 843 F. Supp. 1410 (M.D. Ala. 1993).

Cited in Terry v. City of Montgomery, 549 So. 2d 566 (Ala. Crim. App. 1989); Carroll v. Deaton, Inc., 555 So. 2d 140 (Ala. 1989).

Collateral references.

Horseback riding or operation of horse-drawn vehicle within drunk driving statute. 71 ALR4th 1129.

Challenges to use of breath tests for drunk drivers based on claim that partition or conversion ratio between measured breath alcohol and actual blood alcohol is inaccurate. 90 ALR4th 155.

§ 32-5A-195. Cancellation, suspension or revocation of driver's license; grounds, procedure, etc.

(a) The Director of Public Safety is hereby authorized to cancel any driver's license upon determining that the licensee was not entitled to the issuance thereof hereunder or that said licensee failed to give the correct or required information in his application. Upon such cancellation the licensee must surrender the license so cancelled. If such licensee refuses to surrender such license, he shall be guilty of a misdemeanor.

(b) The privilege of driving a motor vehicle on the highways of this state given to a nonresident hereunder shall be subject to suspension or revocation by the Director of Public Safety in like manner and for like cause as a driver's license issued hereunder may be suspended or revoked.

(c) The Director of Public Safety is further authorized, upon receiving a record of the conviction in this state of a nonresident driver of a motor vehicle of any offense, to forward a certified copy of such record to the Motor Vehicle Administrator in the state wherein the person so convicted is a resident.

(d) When a nonresident's operating privilege is suspended or revoked, the Director of Public Safety shall forward a certified copy of the record of such action to the motor vehicle administrator in the state wherein such person resides.

(e) The Director of Public Safety is authorized to suspend or revoke the license of any resident of this state or the privilege of a nonresident to drive a motor vehicle in this state upon receiving notice of the conviction of such person in another state of any offense therein which, if committed in this state, would be grounds for the suspension or revocation of the license of a driver.

(f) The Director of Public Safety may give such effect to conduct of a resident in another state as is provided by the laws of this state had such conduct occurred in this state.

(g) Whenever any person is convicted of any offense for which this chapter makes mandatory the revocation of the license of such person by the department, the court in which such conviction is had shall require the surrender to it of any driver's license then held by the person convicted and the court shall thereupon forward the same together with a record of such conviction to the Director of Public Safety.

(h) Every court having jurisdiction over offenses committed under this article or any other law of this state or municipal ordinance adopted by a local authority regulating the operation of motor vehicles on highways, shall forward to the Director of Public Safety within 10 days a record of the conviction of any person in said court for a violation of any said laws other than regulations governing standing or parking, and may recommend the suspension of the driver's license of the person so convicted.

(i) For the purposes of this article the term "conviction" shall mean a final conviction. Also, for the purposes of this article an unvacated forfeiture of bail or collateral deposited to secure a defendant's appearance in court, a plea of nolo contendere accepted by the court, the payment of a fine, a plea of guilty or a finding of guilt of a traffic violation charge, shall be equivalent to a conviction regardless of whether the penalty is rebated, suspended or probated.

(j) The Director of Public Safety shall forthwith revoke the license of any driver upon receiving a record of such driver's conviction of any of the following offenses:

(1) Manslaughter or homicide by vehicle resulting from the operation of a motor vehicle;

(2) Upon a first conviction of driving or being in actual physical control of any vehicle while under the influence of alcohol or under the influence of a controlled substance to a degree which renders him incapable of safely driving or under the combined influence of alcohol and a controlled substance to a degree which renders him incapable of safely driving, such revocation shall take place only when ordered by the court rendering such conviction;

47

(3) Upon a second or subsequent conviction within a five-year period, of driving or being in actual physical control of any vehicle while under the influence of alcohol or under the influence of a controlled substance to a degree which renders him incapable of safely driving or under the combined influence of alcohol and a controlled substance to a degree which renders him incapable of safely driving;

(4) Any felony in the commission of which a motor vehicle is used;

(5) Failure to stop, render aid, or identify himself as required under the laws of this state in the event of a motor vehicle accident resulting in the death or personal injury of another;

(6) Perjury or the making of a false affidavit or statement under oath to the Director of Public Safety under this article or under any other law relating to the ownership or operation of motor vehicles;

(7) Conviction upon three charges of reckless driving committed within a period of 12 months;

(8) Unauthorized use of a motor vehicle belonging to another which act does not amount to a felony.

(k) The Director of Public Safety is hereby authorized to suspend the license of a driver without preliminary hearing upon a showing by its records or other sufficient evidence that the licensee:

(1) Has committed an offense for which mandatory revocation of license is required upon conviction;

(2) Has been convicted with such frequency of serious offenses against traffic regulations governing the movement of vehicles as to indicate a disrespect for traffic laws and a disregard for the safety of other persons on the highways;

(3) Is an habitually reckless or negligent driver of a motor vehicle, such fact being established by a record of accidents, or by other evidence;

(4) Is incompetent to drive a motor vehicle;

(5) Has permitted an unlawful or fraudulent use of such license;

(6) Has committed an offense in another state which if committed in this state would be grounds for suspension or revocation;

(7) Has been convicted of fleeing or attempting to elude a police officer; or

(8) Has been convicted of racing on the highways.

(*l*) Upon suspending the license of any person as hereinbefore in this section authorized, the Director of Public Safety shall immediately notify the licensee in writing and upon his request shall afford him an opportunity for a hearing as early as practicable, not to exceed 30 days after receipt of such request in the county wherein the licensee resides unless the Director of Public Safety and the licensee agree that such hearing may be held in some other county. Such hearing shall be before the Director of Public Safety or his duly authorized agent. Upon such hearing the Director of Public Safety or his duly authorized agent may administer oaths and may issue subpoenas for the attendance of witnesses in the production of relevant books and papers and may require a reexamination of the licensee. Upon such hearing the Director of Public Safety or his duly authorized agent shall either rescind its order of suspension or, good cause appearing therefor, may continue, modify or extend the suspension of such licensee or revoke such license. If the license has been suspended as a result of the licensee's driving while under the influence of alcohol, the director or his agent conducting the hearing shall take into account, among other relevant factors, the licensee's successful completion of any duly established "highway intoxication seminar", "DWI counterattack course" or similar educational program designed for problem drinking drivers. If the hearing is conducted by a duly authorized agent instead of by the Director of Public Safety himself, the action of such agent must be approved by the Director of Public Safety.

(m) The Director of Public Safety shall not suspend a driver's license or privilege to drive a motor vehicle upon the public highways for a period of more than one year, except as permitted under Section 32-6-19.

(n) At the end of the period of suspension a license surrendered to the Director of Public Safety under subsection (o) shall be returned to the licensee.

(o) The Director of Public Safety upon cancelling, suspending or revoking a license shall require that such license be surrendered to and be retained by the Director of Public Safety. Any person whose license has been cancelled, suspended or revoked shall immediately return his license to the Director of Public Safety. If such licensee refuses to surrender such license, he shall be guilty of a misdemeanor.

(p) Any resident or nonresident whose driver's license or privilege to operate a motor vehicle in this state has been suspended or revoked as provided in this section shall not operate a motor vehicle in this state under a license or permit issued by any other jurisdiction or otherwise during such suspension or after such revocation until a new license is obtained when and as permitted under this article.

(q) Any person denied a license or whose license has been cancelled, suspended or revoked by the Director of Public Safety except where such cancellation or revocation is mandatory under the provisions of this article shall have the right to file a petition within 30 days thereafter for a hearing in the matter in the circuit court in the county wherein such person resides, or in the case of cancellation, suspension or revocation of a nonresident's operating privilege in the county in which the main office of the Director of Public Safety is located, and such court is hereby vested with jurisdiction and it shall be its duty to set the matter for hearing upon 30 days' written notice to the Director of Public Safety, and thereupon to take testimony and examine into the facts of the case and to determine whether the petitioner is entitled to a license or is subject to suspension, cancellation or revocation of license under the provisions of this section. (Acts 1980, No. 80-434, p. 604, § 9-106; Acts 1981, No. 81-803, p. 1412, § 1; Acts 1993, No. 93-622, p. 1040, § 1.)

The **1993 amendment,** effective May 13, 1993, substituted "a hearing in the matter in the circuit court" for "a hearing in the matter in the district court, circuit court or court of like jurisdiction" near the middle of subsection (q).

I. GENERAL CONSIDERATION.

Duty to revoke is not mandatory, and county was proper venue. — Under subsection (q), an Alabama resident whose license has been revoked may file a petition for a hearing in the circuit court of the county where the licensee resides if the revocation is not mandatory. The director of public safety is "authorized" to revoke an Alabama driver's license upon notice of a conviction of an offense that would support a revocation if committed in Alabama pursuant to subsection (e). That code section does not create a mandatory duty. Therefore, county was the proper venue for the filing of driver's petition. Alabama Dep't of Pub. Safety v. Bell, 646 So. 2d 137 (Ala. Civ. App. 1994).

Director bears burden of proof of out-of-state conviction. — Where the authority for an administrative agency to revoke or suspend an operator's license for an out-of-state conviction is derived from a statutory provision, the administrative agency has the burden of proving that the licensee was convicted in another state of a motor traffic violation; thus, the trial court did not err in holding that the director had the burden of proof in a driver's license suspension action. Director, Dep't of Pub. Safety v. Irvine, 603 So. 2d 1074 (Ala. Civ. App. 1992).

Director is not required to have personal knowledge of recommendations. — This section does not require that the director of public safety have personal knowledge of each and every recommendation to grant his approval of such; it is sufficient that approval be made by a "field officer" to whom such authority has been delegated. Wolfsberger v. Wells, 558 So. 2d 927 (Ala. Civ. App. 1989).

Revocation appropriate although officer did not inquire whether program completed successfully. — Even though hearing officer did not inquire as to whether the alcohol awareness program was successfully completed, the decision to revoke his license was appropriate; the hearing officer testified that, when making a determination that the defendant's license be suspended, he took into consideration the fact that the defendant had participated in an alcohol awareness program. Wolfsberger v. Wells, 558 So. 2d 927 (Ala. Civ. App. 1989).

Drivers were allowed nonjury review in both district and circuit courts. — Drivers, whose licenses were suspended as a result of their refusal to submit to breath tests, were allowed nonjury review in both district and circuit courts; there was no district court record, and since the court of civil appeals did not have the benefit of briefs from the drivers, there was no issue before the court as to whether an appeal or review would lie from subsection (q). Ex parte Dep't of Pub. Safety, 560 So. 2d 765 (Ala. Civ. App. 1990).

A conviction for "pedestrian under the influence" is not a conviction for a moving violation or a driving violation concerning the operation of a motor vehicle on a highway; accordingly, the record of the petitioner's conviction for "pedestrian under the influence" should not have been forwarded to the Department of Public Safety for it to maintain a record thereof; the Department cannot properly maintain on the petitioner's driving record his conviction for "pedestrian under the influence," and the department cannot maintain a notation on the petitioner's driving record concerning a DUI-liquors charge. Ex Parte Wright, 586 So. 2d 901 (Ala. 1991).

Georgia nolo contendere plea could be used to enhance revocation time. — The trial court erred by holding that Georgia nolo contendere plea could not be used by the Department of Public Safety to enhance the period of time for revocation, and therefore, the judgment had to be reversed. Alabama Dep't of Pub. Safety v. Bell, 646 So. 2d 137 (Ala. Civ. App. 1994).

Error not to permit questioning of motorist as an adverse witness. — In a suspension case, where director sought to call motorist as an adverse witness pursuant to ARCP, Rule 43(b), ostensibly to prove Georgia conviction, the trial court's refusal to permit such questioning prejudicially and substantially affected the rights of the director, since motorist's answers may have established the director's case prima facie. Director, Dep't of Pub. Safety v. Irvine, 603 So. 2d 1074 (Ala. Civ. App. 1992).

Collateral references.

Validity and application of statute or regulation authorizing revocation or suspension of driver's license for reason unrelated to use of, or ability to operate, motor vehicle. 18 ALR5th 542.

Admissibility, in motor vehicle license suspension proceedings, of evidence obtained by unlawful search and seizure. 23 ALR5th 108.

ARTICLE 9A.

SAFE STREETS ACT.

Effective date. — The act which added this article became effective July 31, 1995.

§ 32-5A-200. Short title.

This article may be cited as the "Safe Streets Act of 1995." (Acts 1995, No. 95-580, § 1.)

§ 32-5A-201. Legislative findings.

The Legislature finds and declares all of the following:

(1) Driving a motor vehicle on the public streets and highways is a privilege, not a right.

(2) Of all drivers involved in fatal accidents, a driver with a suspended license is more likely to be involved in a fatal accident than a properly licensed driver.

(3) Alabamians who comply with the law are frequently victims of traffic accidents caused by unlicensed drivers. These innocent victims suffer considerable pain and property loss at the hands of people who flaunt the law.

(4) A large number of persons whose driving privilege has been suspended or revoked continue to drive regardless of the law.

(5) It is necessary and appropriate to take additional steps to prevent unlicensed drivers from driving, including the civil forfeiture of vehicles used by unlicensed drivers. The state has a critical interest in enforcing its traffic laws and in keeping unlicensed drivers from illegally driving. Seizing the vehicles used by unlicensed drivers serves a significant governmental and public interest, namely the protection of the health, safety, and welfare of Alabamians from the harm of unlicensed drivers, who are involved in a disproportionate number of traffic incidents, and the avoidance of the associated destruction and damage to lives and property.

(6) The Safe Streets Act of 1995 is consistent with the due process requirements of the United States Constitution and the holding of the Supreme Court of the United States in Calero-Toledo v. Pearson Yacht Leasing Co., 40 L.Ed. 2d 452. (Acts 1995, No. 95-580, § 2.)

§ 32-5A-202. Definitions.

For the purposes of this article, the following words shall have the following meanings:

(1) IMPOUNDING AGENCY. The law enforcement agency which impounded the vehicle driven by a person without a valid driver's license.

(2) LEGAL OWNER. A lienholder, person with a security interest in a motor vehicle, a lessor of a motor vehicle, assignee of the lessor, or a person who is the registered owner of the motor vehicle. (Acts 1995, No. 95-580, § 3.)

§ 32-5A-203. Seizure and forfeiture of vehicle driven by person driving while license suspended or revoked.

(a) Notwithstanding any other provision of law, and except as otherwise provided in this section, a motor vehicle is subject to forfeiture as a nuisance if it is driven on a highway of this state and all of the following conditions exist:

(1) The motor vehicle is registered in the name of the driver.

(2) The motor vehicle is driven by a person whose license or license privilege is suspended or revoked at the time he or she was stopped for having been previously convicted of driving under the influence of alcohol or a controlled substance, as defined in Section 32-5A-191.

(b) A law enforcement officer may not stop a vehicle for the purpose of determining whether the driver is properly licensed under this article.

(c)(1) If a driver is unable to produce a valid driver's license on the demand of a law enforcement officer, the vehicle shall be impounded regardless of ownership, unless the peace officer is reasonably able, by other means, to verify that the driver is properly licensed. Prior to impounding a vehicle, a law enforcement officer shall make a reasonable attempt to verify the license status of a driver who claims to be properly licensed, but who is unable to produce the license on demand of the law enforcement officer.

(2) A law enforcement officer shall not impound a vehicle pursuant to this subsection if the license of the driver expired within the preceding 90 days and the driver would otherwise have been properly licensed.

(3) A registered or legal owner of record including the holder of any lien or encumbrance on the vehicle at the time of impoundment may request a hearing to determine the validity of the impoundment pursuant to subsection (o).

(4) If the driver of a vehicle impounded pursuant to this subsection was not a registered owner of the vehicle at the time of impoundment, or if the driver of the vehicle was a registered owner of the vehicle at the time of impoundment, but the driver does not have a previous conviction for a violation of Section 32-5A-191, the vehicle shall be released and is not subject to forfeiture.

(d) A vehicle impounded pursuant to subsection (c) shall be released if:

(1) On the first violation of this article, the driver presents his or her valid driver's license, including a valid temporary Alabama driver's license or permit, to the impounding agency. The vehicle shall then be released to a registered owner of record at the time of impoundment, or an agent of the owner authorized in writing, upon payment of towing and normal and customary storage charges related to the impoundment, providing that the person claiming the vehicle is properly licensed and the vehicle is properly registered.

(2) On the second violation of this article and if the driver does not have a valid driver's license, and the driver presents a signed statement or affidavit that the loss of the vehicle will cause an economic or personal hardship to his or her household. The vehicle shall then be released to a registered owner of record at the time of impoundment, or an agent of the owner authorized in writing, upon payment of towing and normal and customary storage charges related to the impoundment, providing that the person claiming the vehicle is properly licensed or has a person who is properly licensed to drive the vehicle, and the vehicle is properly registered.

(e) On a third violation of this article, the vehicle shall remain in the custody of the impounding law enforcement agency unless the driver requests a hearing pursuant to subsection (c) and there is a favorable ruling for the driver.

(f)(1) The impounding agency, in the case of a vehicle that has not been redeemed pursuant to subsection (d), or has not been otherwise released, shall promptly ascertain from the Department of Revenue the names and addresses of all legal and registered owners of the vehicle.

(2) The impounding agency, within ten working days of impoundment, shall send a notice by certified mail, return receipt requested, to all legal owners of the vehicle, and to any holder of a lien or encumbrance on the vehicle, at the addresses obtained from the Department of Revenue informing them that the vehicle is subject to forfeiture and will be sold or otherwise disposed of pursuant to this section. The notice shall also include instructions for filing a claim with the district attorney of the judicial circuit wherein the vehicle was impounded, and the time limits for filing a claim. The notice shall also inform any legal owner of its right to conduct the sale pursuant to subsection (h). If a registered owner was personally served at the time of impoundment with a notice containing all the information required to be provided by this subdivision, no further notice is required to be sent to a registered owner. However, a notice shall be sent to the legal owners of the vehicle, if any.

(3) If no claims are filed and served within 30 days after the mailing of notice in subdivision (2), or if no claims are filed and served within 10 days of personal service of the notice specified in subdivision (2), when no other mailed notice is required pursuant to subdivision (2), the district attorney shall prepare a written declaration of forfeiture of the vehicle to the state. A written declaration of forfeiture signed by the district attorney under this subdivision shall be deemed to provide good and sufficient title to the forfeited vehicle. A copy of the declaration shall be provided on request to the person informing of the pending forfeiture pursuant to subdivision (2). A claim that is filed and is later withdrawn by the claimant shall be deemed not to have been filed.

(4) If a claim is timely filed and served, then the district attorney shall file a petition of forfeiture with the appropriate court within 10 days of the receipt of the claim. The district attorney shall establish an expedited hearing date in accordance with instructions from the court, and the court shall hear the matter within five working days. The court filing fee shall be paid by the claimant, but shall be reimbursed by the impounding agency if the claimant prevails. To the extent practicable, the civil and criminal cases shall be heard at the same time in an expedited, consolidated proceeding.

(5) The burden of proof in the civil case shall be on the prosecuting agency by a preponderance of the evidence. All questions that may arise shall be decided and all other proceedings shall be conducted as in an ordinary civil action. A judgment of forfeiture does not require as a condition precedent to the conviction of a defendant of an offense which made the vehicle subject to forfeiture. The filing of a claim within the time limits specified in subdivision

(3) is a jurisdictional prerequisite for the availing of the action authorized by subdivision (3).

(6) All rights, title, and interest in the vehicle shall vest in the state upon commission of the act giving rise to the forfeiture. However, when the certificate of title discloses lienholders, the impounding authority shall notify each lienholder of the seizure within 10 days of the seizure. If the total amount of a valid lien equals or exceeds the value of the vehicle seized, the vehicle shall be made available to the lienholder in order of priority upon payment by the lienholder of all costs of towing and storage to the impounding agency. The lienholder shall not dispose of the vehicle until and unless a verdict of guilty has been entered against the driver of the vehicle.

(g) Any vehicle impounded that is not redeemed pursuant to subsection (d) and is subsequently forfeited pursuant to this section shall be sold after an order of forfeiture is issued by a court pursuant to subsection (f).

(h) Any legal owner who in the regular course of business conducts sales of repossessed or surrendered motor vehicles may take possession and conduct the sale of the forfeited vehicle if it notifies the agency impounding the vehicle of its intent to conduct the sale within 15 days of the mailing of the notice pursuant to subsection (f). The sale of the vehicle after forfeiture pursuant to this subsection may be conducted at the time, in the manner, and on the notice usually given by the legal owner for the sale of repossessed or surrendered vehicles. The proceeds of any sale conducted by the legal owner shall be disposed of as provided in subsection (j).

(i) If the legal owner does not notify the agency impounding the vehicle of its intent to conduct the sale as provided in subsection (h), the agency shall offer the forfeited vehicle for sale at public auction within 60 days of receiving title to the vehicle. Low value vehicles shall be disposed of pursuant to subsection (l).

(j) The proceeds of a sale of a forfeited vehicle shall be disposed of in the following priority:

(1) To satisfy the towing and storage costs following impoundment, the costs of providing notice pursuant to subsection (f), the costs of sale, and the unfunded costs of judicial proceedings, if any.

(2) To the legal owner in an amount to satisfy the indebtedness owed to the legal owner remaining as of the date of sale, including accrued interest or finance charges and delinquency charges, providing that the principal indebtedness was incurred prior to the date of impoundment. The proceeds of the sale payable under this subdivision shall be paid to the holder of the first priority lien or first priority encumbrance on the vehicle.

(3) To the holder of any subordinate lien or encumbrance on the vehicle, other than a registered or legal owner, to satisfy any indebtedness so secured if written notification of demand is received before distribution of the proceeds is completed. The holder of a subordinate lien or encumbrance, if requested, shall furnish reasonable proof of its interest and, unless it does so upon request, is not entitled to distribution pursuant to this section.

(4) To any other person, other than a registered or legal owner, who can reasonably establish an interest in the vehicle, if written notification is received before distribution of the proceeds is completed.

(5) Of the remaining proceeds, funds shall be made available to pay any local agency and court costs that are reasonably related to the implementation of this section, that remain unsatisfied.

(6) Of the remaining proceeds, half shall be transferred to the State Treasurer for deposit in the General Fund for the benefit of the Department of Public Safety and half shall be transferred to the general fund of the municipality or county of the impounding agency. A portion of the local funds may be used to establish a reward fund for persons coming forward with information leading to the arrest and conviction of hit and run drivers and to publicize the availability of the reward fund.

(k) The person conducting the sale shall disburse the proceeds of the sale as provided in subsection (j) and shall provide a written accounting regarding the disposition to the impounding agency and, on request, to any person entitled to claiming a share of the proceeds, within 15 days after the sale is conducted.

(l) If the vehicle to be sold pursuant to this section is not of the type that can readily be sold to the public generally, the vehicle shall be conveyed to a licensed dismantler or donated to a public institution. License plates shall be removed from any vehicle conveyed to a dismantler pursuant to this subsection.

(m) No vehicle shall be sold pursuant to this section if the impounding agency determines the vehicle to have been stolen. In this event, the vehicle may be claimed by the registered owner at any time after impoundment, providing the vehicle registration is current and the registered owner has no outstanding traffic violations. If the identity of the legal and registered owners of the vehicle cannot be reasonably ascertained, the vehicle may be sold.

(n) Any owner of a vehicle who suffers any loss due to the impoundment or forfeiture of any vehicle pursuant to this section may recover the amount of the loss from the unlicensed, suspended, or revoked driver.

(o)(1) The impounding agency, if requested to do so, shall not later than 15 days after the date the vehicle was impounded provide the opportunity for a post-storage hearing to determine the validity of the storage to the persons who were the registered and legal owners of the vehicle at the time of impoundment, except that the hearing shall be requested within three days after the date the vehicle was impounded if personal service was provided to a registered owner pursuant to subdivision (2) of subsection (f) and no mailed notice is required.

(2) The post-storage hearing shall be conducted not later than two days after the date it was requested and it shall be conducted in the office or post headquarters of the law enforcement agency that seized the vehicle. The impounding agency may authorize its own officer or employee or request the municipal or district court, where appropriate, to conduct the hearing if the hearing officer is not the same person who directed the storage of the vehicle. Failure of either the registered or legal owner to request a hearing as

provided in subdivision (1) or to attend a scheduled hearing shall satisfy the post-storage hearing requirement.

(3) The agency employing the person who directed the storage is responsible for the costs incurred for towing and storage if it is determined that the driver at the time of impoundment had a valid driver's license.

(p) As used in this section, "days" means workdays not including weekends and holidays.

(q) Charges for towing and storage for any vehicle impounded pursuant to this section shall not exceed the normal towing and storage rates for other vehicle towing and storage conducted by the impounding agency in the normal course of business.

(r) The Administrative Office of Courts shall prescribe and distribute standard forms and procedures for implementation of this section to be used by all courts and law enforcement agencies throughout the state.

(s) The impounding agency may act as the agent of the state in carrying out this section.

(t) No vehicle shall be impounded pursuant to this section if the driver has a valid license but the license is for a class of vehicle other than the vehicle operated by the driver. (Acts 1995, No. 95-580, § 4.)

Code Commissioner's note. — In 1995, the Code Commissioner inserted "subsection" for "subdivision" in subdivisions (2) and (4) of subsection (c) to correctly reference the appropriate langauge. The Code Commissioner inserted "(c)" for "(d)" in subsection (e) to reference the apparent intended subsection. The Code Commissioner inserted "subdivision (2)" for "paragraph (2)" in the last sentence of subdivision (3) of subsection (f) for the same reason. The Code Commissioner inserted "exceeds" for "exceed" in subdivision (6) of subsection (f) for grammatical purposes. The Code Commissioner inserted "subdivision" for "subparagraph" at the end of subdivision (2) of subsection (j) to correctly reference the appropriate language. The Code Commissioner inserted "is" prior to "received before distribution" in subdivision (4) of subsection (j) for clarity.

§ 32-5A-204. Court to inform defendant convicted of violating § 32-5A-191 that vehicle subject to forfeiture if driven on highway.

Upon conviction of a violation of Section 32-5A-191, the court shall inform the defendant that a motor vehicle is subject to forfeiture as a nuisance if it is driven on a highway in this state by a driver whose driver's license or driving privilege has been suspended or revoked because of a conviction for a violation of Section 32-5A-191. (Acts 1995, No. 95-580, § 5.)

§ 32-5A-205. Enactment of ordinance which provides for administrative sanctions involving impoundment of vehicles.

Nothing in this article shall be deemed either to authorize a municipality to enact an ordinance, or to preempt or preclude a municipality from enacting an ordinance, that provides for administrative sanctions involving impoundment of vehicles used in the commission of the offense of driving with a suspended or revoked license or without a license. (Acts 1995, No. 95-580, § 6.)

ARTICLE 10.

PEDESTRIANS' RIGHTS AND DUTIES.

§ 32-5A-212. Crossing at other than crosswalks.

Instruction that subsection (a) casts upon motorist duty to yield right-of-way. — Trial court did not err in refusing the plaintiff's request that the jury be instructed on the "rule of the road" set out in subsection (a), where the plaintiffs took the position that subsection (a), by negative implication, casts upon a motorist a duty to yield the right-of-way to a pedestrian crossing a road within an unmarked crosswalk at an intersection. The trial court was apparently not asked to, and did not, specifically instruct the jury on the rule set out in § 32-5A-211(a) and that section deals with a motorist's duty with respect to a pedestrian crossing a road within a crosswalk. The instruction requested by the plaintiffs would have constituted nothing more than a statement of an abstract legal principle that was not applicable to any material issue in the case. Crittenden v. Bright, 652 So. 2d 236 (Ala. 1994).

§ 32-5A-213. Drivers to exercise care.

Standard of care. — Drivers have the duty to travel at a safe and appropriate speed, especially when special hazards exist with respect to pedestrians. Above all, drivers have the duty to take due care to avoid colliding with any pedestrian and shall give warning by sounding the horn of their cars or taking other precautions to warn of the danger of collision. Hunnicutt v. Walker, 589 So. 2d 726 (Ala. Civ. App. 1991).

Collateral references.

Motorist's liability for signaling other vehicle or pedestrian to proceed, or to pass signaling vehicle. 14 ALR5th 193.

§ 32-5A-215. Pedestrians on roadways.

Charge was prejudicial error. — Because the trial court's instructions, regarding a pedestrian's responsibility in crossing a road at a place other than at a marked crosswalk, precluded the jury from finding that plaintiff did not violate a rule of the road, the charge was prejudicial error. Okafor v. Sanford, 544 So. 2d 869 (Ala. 1989).

§ 32-5A-221. Pedestrians under influence of alcohol or drugs.

Editor's note. — The citation to Johnson v. Allstate Ins. Co., 505 So. 2d (Ala. 1987) in the bound volume is incorrect. The citation should be Snow v. Parrish, 505 So. 2d 368 (1987).

Evidence insufficient to show highway intoxication. — Where the only testimony the State presented regarding where defendant was standing prior to being arrested was that of the officer, who stated that defendant was on the right-of-way, about six to eight feet from the pavement of highway the State failed to show that defendant was on the travelled portion of the highway, rather than merely on the right-of-way and the evidence was insufficient to support an arrest for highway intoxication. Stokes v. State, 552 So. 2d 144 (Ala. 1989).

ARTICLE 11.

MOTORCYCLES.

§ 32-5A-245. Headgear and shoes required for motorcycle riders; approval of headgear; responsibility for juvenile riders; sale of helmets.

Collateral references.

Motorcyclist's failure to wear helmet or other protective equipment as affecting recovery for personal injury or death. 85 ALR4th 365.

ARTICLE 12.

BICYCLES AND PLAY VEHICLES.

§ 32-5A-260. Traffic laws apply to persons riding bicycles.

Collateral references.
Operation of bicycle within drunk driving
statute. 73 ALR4th 1139.

ARTICLE 13.

BICYCLE SAFETY.

Effective date. — The act which added this
article became effective September 17, 1995.

§ 32-5A-280. Short title.

This article shall be known and may be cited as the "Brad Hudson-Alabama Bicycle Safety Act of 1995." (Acts 1995, No. 95-198, § 1.)

§ 32-5A-281. Definitions.

As used in this article, the following words shall have the following meanings:

(1) BICYCLE. A human-powered vehicle with two wheels in tandem design to transport by the act of pedaling one or more persons seated on one or more saddle seats on its frame. "Bicycle" includes, but is not limited to, a human-powered vehicle designed to transport by the act of pedaling which has more than two wheels when the vehicle is used on a public roadway, public bicycle path, or other public road or right-of-way, but does not include a tricycle.

(2) OPERATOR. A person who travels on a bicycle seated on a saddle seat from which that person is intended to and can pedal the bicycle.

(3) OTHER PUBLIC RIGHT-OF-WAY. Any right-of-way other than a public roadway or public bicycle path that is under the jurisdiction and control of the state or a local political subdivision thereof.

(4) PASSENGER. Any person who travels on a bicycle in any manner except as an operator.

(5) PROTECTIVE BICYCLE HELMET. A piece of headgear which meets or exceeds the impact standard for protective bicycle helmets set by the American National Standards Institute (ANSI) or the Snell Memorial Foundation, or which is otherwise approved by the Alabama Department of Public Safety.

(6) PUBLIC BICYCLE PATH. A right-of-way under the jurisdiction and control of the state, or a local political subdivision thereof, for use primarily by bicyclists and pedestrians.

(7) PUBLIC ROADWAY. A right-of-way under the jurisdiction and control of the state or a local political subdivision thereof for use primarily by motor vehicular traffic.

(8) RESTRAINING SEAT. A seat separate from the saddle seat of the operator of the bicycle or a bicycle trailer or similar product that is fastened securely to the frame of the bicycle and is adequately equipped to restrain the passenger in the seat and protect the passenger from the moving parts of the bicycle.

(9) TRICYCLE. A three-wheeled human-powered vehicle designed for use by a child under the age of six. (Acts 1995, No. 95-198, § 2.)

§ 32-5A-282. Purpose.

The purpose of this article is to reduce the incidence of disability and death resulting from injuries incurred in bicycling accidents by requiring that, while riding on a bicycle on public roadways, public bicycle paths, or other public rights-of-way, all operators and passengers who are under 16 years of age to wear approved protective bicycle helmets, and by requiring that all bicycle passengers who weigh less than 40 pounds or are less than 40 inches in height be seated in separate restraining seats. (Acts 1995, No. 95-198, § 3.)

§ 32-5A-283. Unlawful for person to use bicycle under certain conditions.

It is unlawful for any person to use a bicycle on a public roadway, public bicycle path, other public rights-of-way, state, city, or county public park under any one of the following conditions:

(1) For any person under the age of 16 years to operate or be a passenger on a bicycle unless at all times the person wears a protective bicycle helmet of good fit, fastened securely upon the head with the straps of the helmet.

(2) For any person to operate a bicycle with a passenger who weighs less than 40 pounds or is less than 40 inches in height unless the passenger is properly seated in and adequately secured in a restraining seat.

(3) For any parent or legal guardian of a person under the age of 16 years to knowingly permit the person to operate or be a passenger on a bicycle in violation of subdivision (1) or (2). (Acts 1995, No. 95-198, § 4.)

Code Commissioner's note. — In 1995, the Code Commissioner deleted "of this section" following "subdivision (1) or (2)" in subdivision (3) because the language was surplusage.

§ 32-5A-284. Duties of person regularly engaged in business of renting bicyles.

(a) A person regularly engaged in the business of renting bicycles shall require each person seeking to rent a bicycle to provide his or her signature either on the rental form or on a separate form indicating both of the following:

(1) Receipt of a written explanation of the provisions of this article and the penalties for violations.

(2) A statement concerning whether a person under the age of 16 years will operate the bicycle in an area where the use of a helmet is required.

(b) A person regularly engaged in the business of renting bicycles shall provide a helmet to any person who will operate the bicycle in an area requiring a helmet, if the person does not already have a helmet in his or her possession. A reasonable fee may be charged for the helmet rental.

(c) A person regularly engaged in the business of selling or renting bicycles who complies with this article shall not be liable in a civil action for damages for any physical injuries sustained by a bicycle operator or passenger as a result of the operator's or passenger's failure to wear a helmet or to wear a properly fitted or fastened helmet in violation of this article. (Acts 1995, No. 95-198, § 5.)

§ 32-5A-285. Statewide bicycle safety education program; manner violations handled.

It is the legislative intent to implement an effective statewide bicycle safety education program to reduce disability and death resulting from improper or unsafe bicycle operation. Violations of Section 32-5A-283 shall be handled in the following manner:

(1) On the first offense, the police officer shall counsel and provide written information to the child relative to bicycle helmet safety. The officer shall instruct the child to deliver the written information to the parent.

(2) On the second offense, the police officer shall counsel the child and provide written information on bicycle helmet safety. A warning citation shall be issued to the child to give to the parent. The citation shall instruct the parent or guardian to contact the police department for further information about the law and where to obtain a bicycle helmet.

(3) Beginning on July 1, 1996, upon a third offense, the police officer shall counsel the child, confiscate the bicycle, and take the child to his or her residence. The officer shall then return the bicycle and give a warning ticket to the parent or guardian. If the parent or guardian is unavailable, the ticket shall be left at the residence with instructions to the parent or guardian to pick up the bicycle at the police department.

(4) Beginning on July 1, 1996, upon a fourth offense, the police officer shall confiscate the bicycle, take the child to his or her residence, whereupon a citation for fifty dollars ($50) will be issued to the parent or guardian of the child. No court costs nor fees may be added to the fine or penalty. The fine or penalty shall be waived or suspended if the operator or passenger presents by the court date, proof of purchase or evidence of having provided a protective bicycle helmet or restraining seat and intends to use or causes to be used or intends to cause to be used the helmet as provided by law.

(5) Any fine or penalty monies shall be earmarked and used separately by the local school system for the purpose of safety education or the local municipality for the purchase of helmets for the financially disadvantaged.

(6) The Traffic Safety Center of the University of Montevallo, in conjunction with the Child Safety Institute at Children's Hospital of Alabama, shall furnish all materials, handouts, brochures, and other information related to bicycle safety used by police departments. (Acts 1995, No. 95-198, § 6.)

§ 32-5A-286. Establishment of more comprehensive bicycle safety program by ordinance.

A municipality may establish a more comprehensive bicycle safety program than that imposed by this article by local ordinance. (Acts 1995, No. 95-198, § 7.)

CHAPTER 5B.

ALABAMA SAFETY BELT ACT OF 1991.

Code Commissioner's note. — Acts 1991, No. 91-255, which enacted this chapter, provides in § 8:

"The period from the effective date of this act [July 18, 1991] until twelve months thereafter shall be a warning period in which persons who violate the provisions of this act shall be issued a verbal warning or warning citation by the proper law enforcement officer, but no monetary fine shall be assessed against the offender. At the conclusion of the said warning period, all provisions of this act shall be in full force and effect."

§ 32-5B-1. Title.

This chapter shall be known and may be cited as the "Alabama Safety Belt Use Act of 1991." (Acts 1991, No. 91-255, p. 483, § 1.)

§ 32-5B-2. Definition of "passenger car."

For purposes of this chapter, the term "passenger car" means a motor vehicle with motive power designed for carrying 10 or fewer passengers. Such term does not include a motorcycle or a trailer. (Acts 1991, No. 91-255, p. 483, § 2.)

§ 32-5B-3. Legislative findings.

The legislature finds that it is the policy of the state of Alabama that all precautionary measures be taken to save the lives of the state's citizens from vehicle accidents and thereby, to preserve the most valuable resource of the state. (Acts 1991, No. 91-255, p. 483, § 3.)

§ 32-5B-4. Requirement of front seat occupants of passenger cars to wear safety belts; exemptions of certain persons.

(a) Each front seat occupant of a passenger car manufactured with safety belts in compliance with Federal Motor Vehicle Safety Standard No. 208 shall

61

have a safety belt properly fastened about his body at all times when the vehicle is in motion.

(b) The provisions of subsection (a) shall not apply to:

(1) A child passenger under the purview of section 32-5-222, who is required to use a child passenger restraint system or a seat belt pursuant to section 32-5-222.

(2) An occupant of a passenger car who possesses a written statement from a licensed physician that he is unable for medical reasons to wear a safety belt.

(3) A rural letter carrier of the United States Postal Service while performing his duties as a rural letter carrier.

(4) A driver or passenger delivering newspapers or mail from house to house.

(5) Passengers in a passenger car with model year prior to 1965.

(6) Passengers in motor vehicles which normally operate in reverse. (Acts 1991, No. 91-255, p. 483, § 4.)

§ 32-5B-5. Penalty for violations of chapter.

Any person violating the provisions of this chapter may be fined up to $25.00. The violation of the provisions of this chapter shall not constitute probable cause for search of the vehicle involved. (Acts 1991, No. 91-255, p. 483, § 5.)

§ 32-5B-6. Violation of chapter does not cause issuance of citation or warrant; exception.

Notwithstanding any provision of law to the contrary, no citation or warrant for arrest shall be issued for a violation of this chapter unless a person is stopped by a law enforcement officer for a separate violation of law and is issued a citation or warrant for arrest for the separate violation of law. (Acts 1991, No. 91-255, p. 483, § 6.)

§ 32-5B-7. Failure to wear safety belt; not evidence of contributory negligence; liability of insurer not limited; driving record of individual charged.

Failure to wear a safety belt in violation of this chapter shall not be considered evidence of contributory negligence and shall not limit the liability of an insurer, nor shall the conviction be entered on the driving record of any individual charged under the provisions of this chapter. (Acts 1991, No. 91-255, p. 483, § 7.)

CHAPTER 6.

LICENSES AND REGISTRATION.

ARTICLE 1.

DRIVERS' LICENSES.

Division 1.

General Provisions.

§ 32-6-1. Required; expiration date; renewal; identification cards for nondrivers.

(a) Every person, except those specifically exempted by statutory enactment, shall procure a driver's license before driving a motor vehicle upon the highways of this state. Every new resident of the State of Alabama shall procure an Alabama driver's license within 30 days after establishing residence in this state.

(b) Each original driver's license issued to a person born in a year ending in an odd number shall expire on the second anniversary of the licensee's birth date occurring in an odd-numbered calendar year after the date on which the application for the license was filed, and each original driver's license issued to a person born in a year ending with an even number shall expire on the second anniversary of the licensee's birth date occurring in an even-numbered calendar year after the date on which the application for the license was filed; provided, that if the license issued would expire in less than 24 months from the date on which the application for the license was filed, the expiration date of such license is hereby extended for an additional period of two years. After the expiration of an original driver's license, all subsequent renewals shall be for a period of four years from the specified expiration date of the immediately preceding license, regardless of when such renewal shall be issued. Every driver's license issued under this article may be renewed at the end of the license period without examination upon application and payment of the fee. For the purpose of renewal of a driver's license, the department of public safety shall mail renewal notices to each licensee 30 days after expiration date if the driver's license has not been renewed. A grace period of 60 days after expiration date of a driver's license shall exist for the purpose of driver's license renewal and the driver's license shall be valid for this time period. The applicant shall apply for a driver's license anytime during a period beginning 30 days before the expiration date of the then current license until one year after the expiration date of said license. Failure to make application for renewal within the specified time shall result in the applicant being required to take, and successfully pass, a written examination and driving test as administered by the Department of Public Safety. If any person's birthday is February 29, the first day of March following shall be regarded as his birthday for the purposes of this section.

(c) The Department of Public Safety shall make available to any resident of this state who does not hold a valid Alabama driver's license a nondriver identification card to be used for identification purposes only. Such nondriver identification card shall be issued only upon application of the nondriver and shall be similar to the driver's license; except, that it shall bear the word "nondriver" in prominent letters on the face of the identification card. Each nondriver identification card shall bear thereon a distinguishing number assigned to the nondriver and a color photograph of the nondriver, as well as the name, birth date, residence address and a brief description of the nondriver, who for the purpose of identification, shall immediately upon receipt thereof, endorse his or her usual signature in ink upon the card in the space provided thereon, unless a facsimile of the nondriver signature appears thereon. The same degree of proof of identification required of applicants for driver's licenses in this state shall be required of applicants for nondriver identification cards. (Acts 1975, No. 539, p. 1192, §§ 2, 6; Acts 1981, No. 81-154, p. 177; Acts 1992, 2nd Ex. Sess., No. 92-678, p. 59, § 1.)

Although the court of appeals did not have before it the district court warrants that were the original charging instruments for the traffic offenses of driving without a license and speeding, the Uniform Traffic Ticket and Complaint (UTTC's) issued for those infractions were sufficient to charge the named offenses. Ex parte State ex rel. Johnson, 636 So. 2d 1266 (Ala. Crim. App. 1994).

§ 32-6-3. Examination prior to application for license or renewal.

(a) Every person who applies for an original driver's license under this article shall be given an examination before making application to the judge of probate or license commissioner for the issuance of a driver's license. The person shall first apply to the officer, state trooper, or duly authorized agent of the Director of Public Safety, or one of them where there is more than one, designated by the Director of Public Safety to conduct examinations. A minor shall furnish a certified copy of his or her birth certificate or a certified statement from the county superintendent of education of the county in which the minor resides or from the superintendent of the school which the minor attends proving that the minor is at least 16 years of age. Upon satisfying this requirement, the minor shall immediately be examined.

(b) The Director of Public Safety shall promulgate reasonable rules and regulations not in conflict with the laws of this state as to the kind of examination or test to be given and the method and manner of giving the examination and ascertaining and reporting the results of the examination. Reports of all examinations shall be on forms provided by the Director of Public Safety and shall indicate if the applicant passed the examination.

(c) If the applicant passes the examination, the applicant shall be given a certificate to that effect, on a form provided by the Director of Public Safety, by the officer, state trooper, or duly authorized agent of the Director of Public Safety conducting the examination. The applicant shall present the certificate to the judge of probate or license commissioner of his or her county together with the application for a driver's license. The judge of probate or license commissioner shall attach the certificate to the application and forward the application and certificate to the Director of Public Safety.

(d) If a person fails to pass the examination, no certificate shall be given to the person. No application for an original driver's license shall be accepted by a judge of probate or license commissioner unless it is accompanied by a certificate showing that the applicant has passed the examination.

(e) A person who secures a renewal of a license in the manner provided by law shall not be required to take the examination unless the Director of Public Safety deems it advisable to require the person to take the examination. If the Director of Public Safety deems it advisable, the director shall notify the person in writing by letter sent to the address given on the application of the person at least 10 days before the date on which the examination or test is given of the time and place of the examination. The examination given to such a person shall be conducted in the same manner and the result of the examination ascertained and reported in the same way as examinations are given to persons applying for an original driver's license.

(f) Failure of a person to appear after notice to take such an examination or test, or refusal by a person to take the examination or test, shall be grounds for suspension or revocation of the license of the person by the Director of Public Safety. A person to whom such an examination or test is given who fails to pass the examination or test shall have his or her license revoked by the Director of

Public Safety. (Acts 1939, No. 181, p. 300; Code 1940, T. 36, § 63; Acts 1951, No. 961, p. 1633; Acts 1978, No. 773, p. 1130; Acts 1995, No. 95-191, § 1.)

The 1995 amendment, effective June 15, 1995, rewrote present subsections (a) through (f); and deleted former subsection (b) which related to a person taking a driver's license examination in a county other than the county of residence.

§ 32-6-4. Application for license or identification card; issuance; fee; duration.

(a) Upon the installation of a system for the issuance of drivers' licenses and nondriver identification cards with color photographs of licensees and nondrivers thereon, all licenses and identification cards and renewals of licenses issued in this state shall be issued in the following manner:

(1) The person shall apply under oath to the judge of probate or license commissioner of the county of his or her residence for the driver's license or nondriver identification card or renewal of a license upon a form which shall be provided by the Director of Public Safety.

(2) The judge of probate or license commissioner shall take a color photograph of the licensee with equipment to be furnished by the Department of Public Safety to be attached to each application.

(b) For the purpose of defraying the cost of issuing drivers' licenses or nondriver identification cards with color photographs of the licensee or nondriver thereon, except as provided in Section 32-6-4.1, the judge of probate or license commissioner shall collect for each license or identification card the sum of $20 for a four-year license or an identification card, and the judge of probate or license commissioner shall give the licensee a driver's license or identification card. Except as provided by rules and regulations of the Director of Public Safety, the nondriver identification card shall bear no expiration date for any person 62 years of age or older. (Acts 1939, No. 181, p. 300; Code 1940, T. 36, § 60; Acts 1951, No. 961, p. 1633; Acts 1975, No. 539, p. 1192, §§ 4, 5; Acts 1979, No. 79-203, p. 311, § 1; Acts 1980, No. 80-510, p. 789; Acts 1983, 3rd Ex. Sess., No. 83-825, p. 41; Acts 1993, No. 93-769, p. 1538, § 1; Acts 1995, No. 95-522, § 1.)

The 1993 amendment, effective July 1, 1993, deleted "such" following "all" in subsection (a), in subdivision (1) substituted "The person" for "Such person," inserted "or her," and substituted "the driver's" for "said driver's"; in the first sentence of subsection (b) substituted "the judge of probate" for "the probate judge," and substituted "$20" for "$15.00."

The 1995 amendment, effective September 29, 1995, in subsection (b), inserted "except as provided in Section 32-6-4.1" in the first sentence, and in the second sentence, added "Except as provided by rules and regulations of the Director of Public Safety" and added "for any person 62 years of age or older."

§ 32-6-4.1. Special nondriver identification cards — Issuance; fees; expiration.

In addition to the drivers' licenses and nondriver identification cards provided for in Section 32-6-4, the Director of the State Department of Public Safety shall promulgate the necessary rules and regulations for the issuance of special nondriver identification cards. The judge of probate or license commissioner may charge only the cost to the Department of Public Safety and the county fee, if any, for the issuance of a nondriver identification card for any person 62 years of age or older. A mentally or physically disabled or legally blind person who is incapable of obtaining a driver's license shall not be charged a fee, except the county fee for the issuance of a nondriver identification card nor shall the card have an expiration date, except as provided by rules and regulations of the Director of the Department of Public Safety. (Acts 1984, 1st Ex. Sess., No. 84-815, p. 248; Acts 1995, No. 95-522, § 1.)

The 1995 amendment, effective September 29, 1995, rewrote this section.
Code Commissioner's note. — In 1995, the Code Commissioner added a comma in the first sentence after "Section 32-6-4" for grammatical purposes.

§ 32-6-4.2. Nondriver identification cards — Expiration; renewal, suspension, and revocation; fraudulent use or misuse.

(a) Each nondriver identification card issued to any person, except cards issued pursuant to Section 32-6-4.1, who is less than 62 years of age shall expire eight years from the date of issuance or as otherwise provided by the rules and regulations of the Director of the Department of Public Safety.

(b) Each nondriver identification card issued to any person who is 62 years of age or older or to any person pursuant to Section 32-6-4.1 shall expire as provided by the rules and regulations of the Director of the Department of Public Safety.

(c) Each nondriver identification card may be subject to renewal, reissue, suspension, or revocation by rules and regulations of the Director of the Department of Public Safety, or as otherwise provided by law.

(d) The Director of the Department of Public Safety may adopt and enforce reasonable rules and regulations relating to the fraudulent use, misuse, or abuse of the privilege of using a nondriver identification card, or for purposes of obtaining current information or recent photograph at least every eight years. (Acts 1995, No. 95-522, §§ 2-5.)

Effective date. — The act which added this section became effective September 29, 1995.
Code Commissioner's note. — In 1995, the Code Commissioner substituted "of" for "or" before "age" in subsection (a) to convey the apparent intent of the subsection.

§ 32-6-5. Reports and compensation of judge of probate; disposition of fees collected.

At the close of business on Monday of each week when any application has been received or temporary instruction permit provided for in this article has been issued, the judge of probate receiving the application or issuing the permit shall prepare a report of the same upon a form which shall be provided by the director of public safety. One copy of the report, together with all applications received and copies of all permits issued, shall be forwarded to the director of public safety and one copy shall be retained by the judge of probate. On the tenth day of every month, the judge of probate shall prepare a report showing the number of applications received and permits issued and the amount of fees received during the previous calendar month; provided, that the report shall be prepared on the twentieth day of October, November, and December. One copy of the report shall be forwarded to the director of public safety, one to the comptroller, and one to the treasurer, and the judge of probate shall retain a copy. The judge of probate shall also at that time deliver to the treasurer the amount of all the fees collected, less $1.50 for each driver license or identification card issued, which sum shall be retained by him or her. Except in counties where the judge of probate is compensated by fees, each $1.50 retained by the judge of probate shall be paid into the public highway and traffic fund of the county. In counties where the judge of probate is compensated by fees, two fifths of each $1.50 retained by the judge of probate shall be for his or her own use, and no other or further charge shall be made by him or her for services rendered in taking or receiving applications or issuing permits, and the remaining three fifths shall be paid into the public highway and traffic fund of the county. This section, providing for the allocation of the $1.50 retained by the judge of probate in counties where the judge of probate is compensated by fees, shall not repeal any local statutes or general statutes of local application providing for a different allocation of the $1.50. The funds remitted to the state treasurer under this section, except for that portion representing $5 for each license or card issued, shall be deposited to the credit of the general fund and shall be appropriated for public safety use. From the funds remitted to the state treasurer, the portion representing $5 shall be deposited into the Public Safety Law Enforcement Fund which is hereby created within the State Treasury. All money deposited in the State Treasury to the credit of the Public Safety Law Enforcement Fund shall be expended for law enforcement purposes. No money shall be withdrawn or expended from the fund for any law enforcement purpose unless the money has been allotted and budgeted in accordance with Article 4 (commencing with Section 41-4-80) of Chapter 4 of Title 41, and only in the amounts and for the law enforcement purposes provided by the Legislature in the general appropriations bill. (Acts 1939, No. 181, p. 300; Code 1940, T. 36, § 61; Acts 1951, No. 485, p. 868; Acts 1955, No. 43, p. 260; Acts 1963, No. 193, p. 582, § 2; Acts 1975, No. 539, p. 1192, § 7; Acts 1979, No. 79-203, p. 311, § 2; Acts 1993, No. 93-769, p. 1538, § 1.)

The 1993 amendment, effective July 1, 1993, substituted "the" for "such" throughout the section, substituted "the judge of probate" for "the probate judge" throughout the section, substituted "the report" for "said report" in the third sentence, substituted "the judge of probate" for "he" in the fourth sentence, in the fifth sentence substituted "The judge of probate" for "He," substituted "that" for "said," and inserted "or her," divided the former sixth sentence into the present sixth and seventh sentences, in the present sixth sentence added "Except in counties where the judge of probate is compensated by fees," and deleted "except, that" following "the county," in the seventh sentence inserted "or her" in two places, and substituted "and" for "provided, that this provision shall not repeal any local statutes nor general statutes of local application contrary to this provision," added the present eighth sentence, in the ninth sentence substituted "The funds" for "All funds," deleted "the provisions of" preceding "this section," and inserted "except for that portion representing $5 for each license or card issued," and added the tenth, eleventh, and last sentences.

§ 32-6-7.1. Persons with physical disabilities or impairments.

(a) Any person with physical disabilities, a record of an impairment, or regarded as having an impairment shall be subject to the same laws, rules, and regulations set forth by the Department of Public Safety relating to the licensure of an individual to operate a motor vehicle.

(b) Notwithstanding any law, rule, or regulation, the State Department of Public Safety shall not refuse to issue any permit or license for the operation of a motor vehicle, or the renewal of either, on the grounds of physical appearance, speculations or generalizations that the individual's physical impairment would impede that person's ability to operate a motor vehicle in a safe manner without probable cause to believe the person's ability to operate a motor vehicle in a safe manner is in fact impaired.

(c) If the department refuses to issue a permit or license or arbitrarily questions the person's abilities based on physical appearance or speculated inability to operate a motor vehicle in a safe manner, the person shall have a right to an impartial hearing before the Director of Public Safety or his or her designee. At the hearing, the person shall have the right to be represented by counsel and to present witnesses including, but not limited to, a physician of choice. The person may appeal any decision to the circuit court of competent jurisdiction for a trial de novo.

(d) This section shall be interpreted to be consistent with and to further the purposes and policies of Section 504 of the Rehabilitation Act of 1973, as amended, 34 CFR part 104 and P.L. 101-336, The Americans with Disabilities Act of 1990, together with implementing regulations and subsequent amendments to the laws and regulations. (Acts 1993, No. 93-749, p. 1486, §§ 1-4.)

Effective date. — The act which added this section became effective May 25, 1993.

§ 32-6-8. Temporary instruction and learner's licenses.

(a) Any person 16 years of age or older who, except for his lack of instruction in operating a motor vehicle, would otherwise be qualified to obtain a driver's license under this article may apply for a learner's license, and the judge of probate may issue the license upon a form which shall be provided by the Director of Public Safety, entitling the applicant, while having the license in his or her immediate possession, to drive or operate a motor vehicle upon the highways for a period of four years, except when operating a motorcycle, the person shall be accompanied by a licensed driver who is actually occupying a seat beside the driver. At the time of applying for the license, the applicant shall pay to the judge of probate a fee of $20, and the judge of probate shall give the applicant a learner's license therefor on a form to be provided by the Director of Public Safety. The temporary instruction license may be renewed only by order of the Director of Public Safety, and in no case shall the original license be renewed or extended more than once. The judge of probate shall not issue the temporary instruction license until the applicant has undergone the same examination that a person applying for a driver's license is required by law to undergo, with the exception of the driving test, and produced a certificate to that effect signed by the proper examining officer.

(b) Any person not less than 15 but under 16 years of age may obtain a learner's license to learn to operate a motor vehicle upon application to the judge of probate of the county in which he or she resides, which license shall entitle the person to operate a motor vehicle when he or she is accompanied by a parent or his or her legal guardian who is duly licensed in this state as a motor vehicle operator or when accompanied by a licensed or certified driving instructor who is actually occupying a seat beside the motor vehicle operator. The application for the learner's license must be accompanied by a payment of a fee of $20, to be distributed as provided in Section 32-6-5. The age of the applicant shall be substantiated by the applicant filing with the judge of probate a certified copy of his or her birth certificate. A learner's license issued under this subsection shall be in such form as the Director of Public Safety may prescribe; it shall expire in four years; or when the holder subsequently applies for and receives a driver's license. The driver's license shall be issued for the remainder of the four year life of the learner's license at no additional fee, the certificate thereof shall be prima facie evidence that the license holder was 15 years of age or older on the date of its issuance. The license may be suspended or revoked in the same manner and for the same causes as a driver's license and may also be revoked for any violation of the terms and conditions on which it was issued. The judge of probate shall not issue such a license to any person until the applicant has undergone the same examination that a person applying for a driver's license is required by law to undergo, with the exception of the driving test, and has produced a certificate to that effect signed by the proper examining officer. (Acts 1939, No. 181, p. 300; Code 1940, T. 36, § 64; Acts 1951, No. 880, p. 1519; Acts 1959, No. 346, p. 935; Acts 1973, No. 1289, p. 2201; Acts 1988, 1st Sp. Sess., No. 88-729, p. 125, § 1; Acts 1993, No. 93-769, p. 1538, § 1.)

The 1993 amendment, effective July 1, 1993, substituted "the" for "such" throughout the section, in subsection (a), in the first sentence inserted "or her," deleted "but" following "four years," and substituted "person shall" for "person must," in the second sentence substituted "$20" for "$15.00," and substituted "the applicant" for "him"; in subsection (b), substituted "the" for "such a" in two places, divided the former second sentence into the present second and third sentences, in the present second sentence substituted "$20" for "$15.00," and deleted "and" following "32-6-5," in the third sentence substituted "shall" for "must," and divided the former fourth sentence into the present fourth and fifth sentences.

§ 32-6-14. Records to be kept by director.

A conviction for "pedestrian under the influence" is not a conviction for a moving violation or a driving violation concerning the operation of a motor vehicle on a highway; accordingly, the record of the petitioner's conviction for "pedestrian under the influence" should not have been forwarded to the Department of Public Safety for it to maintain a record thereof; the department cannot properly maintain on the petitioner's driving record his conviction for "pedestrian under the influence"; and the department cannot maintain a notation on the petitioner's driving record concerning a DUI-liquors charge. Ex Parte Wright, 586 So. 2d 901 (Ala. 1991).

§ 32-6-19. Penalties — Violation by person whose license or driving privilege has been cancelled, suspended or revoked.

Cross references. — For provisions concerning the Safe Streets Act which relates to the seizure and forfeiture of a motor vehicle driven by a person who is driving while his or her driver's license or privilege has been suspended or revoked, see § 32-5A-200 et seq.

"Cancellation" versus "revocation" of license in indictment. — In a prosecution under this section for driving with a cancelled, revoked, or suspended driver's license, the prosecution must allege and prove the specific alternative by which the defendant's license or privilege to drive was terminated. Ex parte City of Dothan, 603 So. 2d 1121 (Ala. 1992).

Prosecution allowed to amend pursuant to ARCrP, Rule 13.5. — Where the proof shows that the prosecution has made a prima facie case that the defendant did, in fact, violate the provisions of this section, but there is a variance between the allegations in the charge and the proof, the prosecution can timely move to amend the charge, as provided for in ARCrP, Rule 13.5. Ex parte City of Dothan, 603 So. 2d 1121 (Ala. 1992).

Duty to advise defendant regarding possible sentencing. — The defendant must be advised on the record of the maximum and minimum possible sentences of the offenses for which he is charged. This is an absolute constitutional prerequisite before a guilty plea can be accepted. Sampson v. State, 605 So. 2d 846 (Ala. Crim. App. 1992).

Advising defendant of maximum and minimum sentence is a jurisdictional matter, so that failure to so inform the defendant can be raised for the first time on appeal. Sampson v. State, 605 So. 2d 846 (Ala. Crim. App. 1992).

Circumstantial evidence may be used to show that the defendant was driving in order to convict the defendant under this section. McLaney v. City of Montgomery, 570 So. 2d 881 (Ala. Crim. App. 1990).

Where none of computer printouts showed license status and affidavits were inadmissible. — Where prosecution admitted that none of the computer printouts showed appellant's driver's license status on the date of arrest, where the prosecution argued that it supplied that information through the affidavits of the Supervisor and/or Deputy Custodian of Records, Driver License Division, Department of Public Safety, and each affidavit stated that the custodian had examined the driver's license record of the appellant, and that on the days in question, the appellant's license was "revoked," the computer printouts provided no evidence of when the appellant's license had been revoked, and the affidavits introduced to establish that date were inadmissible hearsay not shown to come within any exception to the hearsay rule. Furthermore, even if the proponent of the affidavits had surmounted the hearsay objection, which they did not, there was no warrant for resorting to the secondary evidence of affidavits concerning the appellant's driving record because the original record was available. Jordan v. City of Huntsville, 650 So. 2d 591 (Ala. Crim. App. 1994).

§ 32-6-21. Examination fee.

(a) Every applicant for an original driver license, temporary instruction and learner's permit, and motor driven cycle operator's license, shall pay an examination fee of five dollars ($5) to the Alabama Department of Public Safety upon applying to the officer, state trooper, or duly authorized agent of the Director of Public Safety, or to one of them where there is more than one designated by the Director of Public Safety. The five dollars ($5) fee shall be required prior to each examination.

(b) The Alabama Department of Public Safety shall issue proper receipts for the examination fee and shall properly transmit all moneys received by it for deposit in the State General Fund. (Acts 1980, No. 80-530, p. 829; Acts 1995, No. 95-191, § 1.)

The 1995 amendment, effective June 15, 1995, in the first sentence of subsection (a), deleted "be required to" preceding "pay," substituted "an examination fee" for "a fee," and deleted "to conduct examinations in the county of the applicant's residence" following "designated by the Director of Public Safety," and made nonsubstantive changes.

ARTICLE 1A.

UNIFORM COMMERCIAL DRIVER LICENSE ACT.

§ 32-6-49.19. License fees; term of licenses.

For the purpose of defraying the cost of issuing commercial drivers' license, the probate judge or license commissioner shall collect for each Class A commercial driver license the sum of $45.00; the sum of $35.00 for each Class B commercial driver license; the sum of $15.00 for each Class C commercial driver license, provided, however the fee for any school bus driver license shall be $15.00 and such license shall be restricted to the operation of a school bus and noncommercial vehicle. These licenses shall be issued for a period of four years. (Acts 1989, No. 89-878, § 19; Acts 1990, No. 90-577, p. 982.)

ARTICLE 2.

LICENSE TAGS AND PLATES.

Division 5.

Disabled Veterans.

§ 32-6-131. Rules and regulations; wrongful acquisition or use.

Detention for minor traffic violation. — Defendant was driving a motor vehicle with an improper tag; this was a misdemeanor offense in violation of this section, and therefore, deputy had the right to arrest defendant and take him into custody. Callahan v. State, 557 So. 2d 1292 (Ala. Crim. App.), aff'd, 557 So. 2d 1311 (Ala. 1989), cert. denied, 498 U.S. 881, 111 S. Ct. 216, 112 L. Ed. 2d 176 (1990).

Division 6.

Personalized License Tags or Plates.

§ 32-6-150. Issuance and sale of tags or plates for motor vehicles, motorcycles, and motor-driven cycles.

(a) Owners of motor vehicles, motorcycles, and motor-driven cycles who are residents of Alabama, upon application to the judge of probate or commissioner of licenses complying with the state motor vehicle laws relating to registration and licensing of motor vehicles and payment of the regular license fee for tags or plates as provided by law for private passenger, pleasure motor vehicles, motorcycles, or motor-driven cycles and the payment of an additional annual fee of $50, shall be issued personalized license tags or plates upon which, in lieu of the numbers prescribed by law, shall be inscribed special letters, figures, numbers, or other marks, emblems, symbols, or badges of distinction or personal prestige or a combination of these as are approved for and assigned to the application by the Department of Revenue.

73

(b) Except for license tags or plates for motorcycles or motor-driven cycles, the special marks or badges of distinction shall include distinctive commemorative tags, assigned by the Department of Revenue for each of those public and private four-year colleges or universities and Athens College participating in the commemorative tag program and the Environmental Commemorative Tag Program. The commemorative tags shall be issued, printed, and processed in the same manner as other personalized tags are in this chapter. The fee for the commemorative tags shall be the amount provided in subsection (a). The commemorative tags shall be valid for five years and shall be replaced at the end of the period with conventional tags or other personalized tags. Payment of the required motor vehicle license fees and taxes for the years during which a new vehicle license plate is not issued shall be evidenced as provided for in Section 32-6-63. The board of trustees of the respective colleges and universities shall design, or have designed, the commemorative tag for a college or university subject to approval by the Commissioner of Revenue and in compliance with all laws and regulations. The Department of Environmental Management for environmental commemorative tags shall design, or have designed the personalized environmental commemorative tag or plate, subject to approval of the Commissioner of Revenue and in compliance with all laws and regulations except that Section 32-6-54 shall not apply to personalized environmental commemorative tags or plates.

(c) The Troy State University commemorative tags issued January 1, 1987, through October 31, 1987, shall continue to be valid without payment of the additional fee provided in this section until the expiration date in the year 1992, or until otherwise becoming invalid or expired provided the regular annual license fees continue to be paid each year.

(d) Each college or university desiring a commemorative tag shall pay to the Department of Revenue the sum as the commissioner may require to cover the cost of production of the tags requested by the college or university before production occurs.

(e) The Department of Environmental Management shall pay to the Department of Revenue the sum the commissioner may require to cover the costs of production of the personalized environmental commemorative tags before production occurs. (Acts 1975, 3rd Ex. Sess., No. 144, p. 387, § 1; Acts 1985, No. 85-411, p. 373; Acts 1988, No. 88-127, p. 181, § 2; Acts 1991, 1st Ex. Sess., No. 91-794, p. 189, § 1; Acts 1992, No. 92-622, p. 1464, § 2; Acts 1993, 1st Ex. Sess., No. 93-880, p. 144, § 4; Acts 1995, No. 95-529, § 1.)

The 1993, 1st Ex. Sess., amendment, effective October 1, 1993, in subsection (a), substituted "judge of probate" for "probate judge," deleted "except as provided in subsection (b)" preceding "the payment," deleted "such" preceding "special letters," inserted "a" preceding "combination," and substituted "of these" for "thereof"; rewrote subsection (b); and in subsection (d), substituted "the sum" for "such sum," substituted "the college" for "such

college," and deleted "any such" preceding "production occurs."

The 1995 amendment, effective September 29, 1995, in subsection (a), inserted "motorcycles, and motor-driven cycles," inserted "motorcycles, or motor-driven cycles," and deleted "state" preceding "Department of Revenue"; and in subsection (b), added "Except for license tags or plates for motorcycles or motor-driven cycles" in the first sentence, and substituted "subsection (b) of this section" for "subsection (a) of this section" in the third sentence.

Code Commissioner's note. — Acts 1992, No. 92-622, which amended this section, in § 1 provides: "It is the intent of the Legislature to establish an Alabama Environmental Education initiative; to supplement environmental programs; to improve and maintain Alabama's environment; to create and sustain an environmental education program; to provide a basis to support environmental education programs of the various state agencies; and to create, with the assistance of the Alabama Education De-partment, an environmental education curriculum. For this purpose, the Environmental Personalized and Commemorative Tag Program, and the Alabama Environmental Education Fund are established. Further, the Alabama Legislature desires to provide a commemorative tag program to recognize certain veterans."

In 1995, the Code Commissioner inserted "subsection (a)" for "subsection (b) of this section" in the third sentence of subsection (b) to correctly reference the appropriate subsection.

§ 32-6-156.1. Distribution and appropriation of fees.

Any fees collected pursuant to Section 32-6-150 for environmental commemorative tags shall be distributed to the Alabama environmental education fund and are appropriated each year to the Department of Environmental Management. Funds appropriated to the Department of Environmental Management shall be used for environmental education. The expenditure of the funds appropriated shall be budgeted and allotted pursuant to the Budget Management Act and Article 4 of Chapter 4 of Title 41 (commencing with Section 41-4-80). The fees represent a charitable contribution from the purchaser to the Alabama environmental education fund. (Acts 1992, No. 92-622, p. 1464, § 3.)

Division 8A.

Members of Ancient Arabic Order of Nobles of Mystic Shrine.

Effective date. — The act which added this division becomes effective September 1, 1994.

§ 32-6-192. Issuance of distinctive license tags to members.

(a) A member of the Ancient Arabic Order of Nobles of the Mystic Shrine for North America who is the owner of a motor vehicle and a resident of the state may be issued a distinctive license tag or plate bearing the words "The Ancient Arabic Order of Nobles of the Mystic Shrine" across the top portion of the tag or plate and bearing its logo between the county identification number and the actual license number. The member shall make application to the judge of probate or license commissioner, comply with the motor vehicle registration and licensing laws, pay the regular fees required by law for license tags or plates for private passenger or pleasure motor vehicles, and pay an additional fee of twenty-five dollars ($25).

(b) The tags or plates shall be issued, printed, and processed like other distinctive and personalized tags and plates provided for in Chapter 6 of this title. The tags or plates shall be valid for five years and may be replaced with either a conventional, personalized, or new "Ancient Arabic Order of Nobles of the Mystic Shrine" tags or plates. Payment of required license fees and taxes for the years during which a new tag or plate is not issued shall be evidenced as provided in Section 32-6-63. (Acts 1994, No. 94-695, p. 1335, § 1.)

§ 32-6-193. Distribution of proceeds.

The net proceeds of the additional revenues derived from sales of tags pursuant to this division, less administrative costs, including the cost of production of the tags, shall be distributed by the judge of probate or license commissioner to the Juvenile Health Care Board of the City of Piedmont, Alabama. (Acts 1994, No. 94-695, p. 1335, § 2.)

§ 32-6-194. Transfer of tags or plates.

The distinctive license plates or tags issued pursuant to this division shall not be transferable between motor vehicle owners, and in the event the owner of a vehicle bearing the distinctive plates sells, trades, exchanges, or otherwise disposes of the motor vehicle, the plates shall be retained by the owner to whom issued and returned to the judge of probate or license commissioner of the county, who shall receive and account for the tags or plates as provided in this section. In the event the owner acquires by purchase, trade, exchange, or otherwise a vehicle for which no standard plates have been issued during the current license period, the judge of probate or license commissioner of the county shall, upon being furnished by the owner proper certification of the acquisition of the vehicle and the payment of the motor vehicle license tax due upon the vehicle, authorize the transfer of the distinctive license plates or tags previously purchased by the owner to the vehicle, which plates or tags shall authorize the operation of the vehicle for the remainder of the then current license period. In the event the owner of the distinctive license plates or tags acquires by purchase, trade, exchange, or otherwise a vehicle for which standard plates have been issued during the current license year, the judge of probate or license commissioner shall, upon proper certification of the owner and upon delivery to the official of the standard plates previously issued for the vehicle, authorize the owner of the newly-acquired vehicle to place the distinctive license plates or tags previously purchased on the vehicle and use the plates for the remainder of the then current license period. The notice of transfer of ownership shall be made of record by the judge of probate or the license commissioner.

Any person acquiring by purchase, trade, exchange, or otherwise any vehicle formerly bearing the distinctive plates may, upon certification of the fact to the judge of probate or license commissioner of the county and the payment of the fee now required by law, purchase standard replacement plates for the vehicle which shall authorize the operation of the vehicle by the new owner for the remainder of the license period. (Acts 1994, No. 94-695, p. 1335, § 3.)

Code Commissioner's note. — In 1995, the Code Commissioner inserted "on" in the next-to-last sentence of the first paragraph.

§ 32-6-195. Return of plates upon termination of membership.

Upon termination of membership with the Ancient Arabic Order of Nobles of the Mystic Shrine, an applicant to whom a distinctive license plate was issued under Section 32-6-192 shall, within 30 days, return the plate to the judge of probate or the license commissioner of the county of the applicant's residence. (Acts 1994, No. 94-695, p. 1335, § 4.)

§ 32-6-196. Replacement plates.

If a distinctive license plate deteriorates to the point where inscriptions thereon are not discernible, the owner or lessee may obtain a replacement plate free of charge. (Acts 1994, No. 94-695, p. 1335, § 5.)

Division 11.

Medal of Honor Recipients and Prisoners of War.

§ 32-6-250. Distinctive plate authorized; no fee required.

A distinctive permanent license plate shall be issued to any resident of the state who is a recipient of the Medal of Honor or the Purple Heart Medal or who is a duly recognized American prisoner of war, or who is an American who was a duly recognized prisoner of war while serving with a formal American ally force, for use on a private motor vehicle registered in the recipient's name. There shall be no fee or tax for such license plate, except Purple Heart Medal recipients shall pay ad valorem taxes on vehicles for which such distinctive plates are issued, and no recipient shall receive a plate for more than one vehicle. (Acts 1981, No. 81-699, p. 1176, § 1; Acts 1982, No. 82-571, p. 1063, § 1; Acts 1991, No. 91-657, p. 1244, § 1.)

Code Commissioner's note. — Acts 1992, No. 685 and Acts 1992, No. 698 provide that it was the intent of the legislature in passing Act 91-657, which amended this section, that winners of the Purple Heart Medal be issued a distinctive license plate emphasizing that the bearer of said license plate has indeed won the Purple Heart Medal. The State Finance Department and Department of Corrections are to use the design that has previously been transmitted to them by the Alabama Chapter, Military Order of the Purple Heart. Since most of the recipients of the Purple Heart Medal are now senior citizens, the State Finance Department and the Department of Corrections are to commence production and distribution of the distinctive tag as soon as is conceivably possible.

Acts 1993, 1st Ex. Sess., No. 93-880, § 5, provides: "Sections 32-6-250 to 32-6-255, inclusive, shall continue to apply to veterans awarded the Purple Heart Medal."

§ 32-6-251. Distinctive design of tags.

The special plates shall be of the same size as regular motor vehicle license plates, distinguished by the letters MOH or PHM to be of a different color scheme and design to any other vehicle tag in this state, or POW to be of the same color scheme as other distinguished military tags in this state, whichever distinctive design applies, the nature of which shall be prescribed by a committee to be appointed by the chief legislative sponsors of this division. (Acts 1981, No. 81-699, p. 1176, § 2; Acts 1991, No. 91-657, p. 1244, § 2.)

Code Commissioner's note. — Acts 1992, No. 685 and Acts 1992, No. 698 provide that it was the intent of the legislature in passing Act 91-657, which amended this section, that winners of the Purple Heart Medal be issued a distinctive license plate emphasizing that the bearer of said license plate has indeed won the Purple Heart Medal. The State Finance Department and Department of Corrections are to use the design that has previously been transmitted to them by the Alabama Chapter, Military Order of the Purple Heart. Since most of the recipients of the Purple Heart Medal are now senior citizens, the State Finance Department and the Department of Corrections are to commence production and distribution of the distinctive tag as soon as is conceivably possible.

Acts 1993, 1st Ex. Sess., No. 93-880, § 5, provides: "Sections 32-6-250 to 32-6-255, inclusive, shall continue to apply to veterans awarded the Purple Heart Medal."

§ 32-6-252. Transfer of plates.

Code Commissioner's note. — Acts 1993, 1st Ex. Sess., No. 93-880, § 5, provides: "Sections 32-6-250 to 32-6-255, inclusive, shall continue to apply to veterans awarded the Purple Heart Medal."

§ 32-6-253. Construction of provisions; penalty for violation.

Code Commissioner's note. — Acts 1993, 1st Ex. Sess., No. 93-880, § 5, provides: "Sections 32-6-250 to 32-6-255, inclusive, shall continue to apply to veterans awarded the Purple Heart Medal."

§ 32-6-254. Use and transferability; permanence; use by surviving spouse.

The use and transferability of such plates shall be the same as the method used for national guard and air national guard plates as provided in sections 32-6-111 through 32-6-114. Provided, however, said license plates shall be permanent in nature and shall not be reissued each year. A recipient shall be entitled to keep his license plate for life. Provided further, upon the death of any recipient, the surviving spouse shall be entitled to retain said distinctive permanent plate, at no fee or tax, except that surviving spouses of Purple Heart Medal recipients shall pay ad valorem taxes due, for one private motor vehicle owned by the surviving spouse for the remainder of said spouse's lifetime or until her remarriage. (Acts 1981, No. 81-699, p. 1176, § 5; Acts 1982, No. 82-571, p. 1063, § 1; Acts 1986, No. 86-621, p. 1209; Acts 1991, No. 91-657, p. 1244, § 3.)

Code Commissioner's note. — Acts 1992, No. 685 and Acts 1992, No. 698 provide that it was the intent of the legislature in passing Act 91-657, which amended this section, that winners of the Purple Heart Medal be issued a distinctive license plate emphasizing that the bearer of said license plate has indeed won the Purple Heart Medal. The State Finance Department and Department of Corrections are to use the design that has previously been transmitted to them by the Alabama Chapter, Military Order of the Purple Heart. Since most of the recipients of the Purple Heart Medal are now senior citizens, the State Finance Department and the Department of Corrections are to commence production and distribution of the distinctive tag as soon as is conceivably possible.

Acts 1993, 1st Ex. Sess., No. 93-880, § 5, provides: "Sections 32-6-250 to 32-6-255, inclusive, shall continue to apply to veterans awarded the Purple Heart Medal."

§ 32-6-255. Rules and regulations.

Code Commissioner's note. — Acts 1993, 1st Ex. Sess., No. 93-880, § 5, provides: "Sections 32-6-250 to 32-6-255, inclusive, shall continue to apply to veterans awarded the Purple Heart Medal."

Division 12.

Fire Fighters.

§ 32-6-270. "Fire fighter" and "retired volunteer fire fighter" defined.

(a) As used in this division, unless the context clearly requires a different meaning: "Fire fighter" means a current member or members of, or a retired member or members from, a paid, part-paid or volunteer fire department of a city, town, county or other subdivision of the state or civilian federal fire fighters or of a public corporation organized for the purpose of providing water, water systems, fire protection services or fire protection facilities in the state; and such words shall include the chief, assistant chief, wardens, engineers, captains, firemen and all other officers and employees of such departments who actually engage in fire fighting or in rendering first aid in case of drownings or asphyxiation at the scene of action.

(b) As used in this division, the term "retired volunteer fire fighter" means someone that has retired from performing the required duties of a fire fighter on a voluntary basis at a certified volunteer fire department, wherein, those duties were performed for at least 10 years and said person has attained the age of 55 years old. (Acts 1982, No. 82-550, p. 909, § 1; Acts 1989, No. 89-917; Acts 1991, No. 91-579, p. 1066, § 1.)

§ 32-6-272. Preparation and issuance of plates or tags; lists of eligible fire fighters; additional fee; use of plates or tags.

The distinctive license plates here provided for shall be prepared by the commissioner of revenue and shall be issued through the judge of probate or license commissioner of the several counties of the state in like manner as are other motor vehicle license plates or tags and such officers shall be entitled to their regular fees for such service. The chief of each certified volunteer fire department and each federal fire department shall submit to the Alabama forestry commission by October 1 of each year a list of fire fighters from his department who are eligible for the distinctive license plate or tag. The fire fighters' personnel standards and education committee shall submit to the Alabama forestry commission by October 1 of each year a list of certified fire fighters who are members of paid or part-paid fire departments and who are eligible for such distinctive license plates or tags. The forestry commission shall submit to the probate judge or license commissioner of each county by December 1 of each year a list of the certified fire fighters in the county who are eligible for the distinctive license plate or tag under this division. Applicants for such distinctive plates shall present to the issuing official proof of their identification. If such applicant's name is on the list furnished by the Alabama forestry commission to the probate judge or license commissioner, the fire fighter shall be issued the requested number of distinctive license plates or tags upon the payment of the regular license fee for tags, as provided by law, but shall not be required to pay the $3.00 fee. The distinctive license plates or tags so issued shall be used only upon and for personally-owned, private, passenger vehicles (to include station wagons and pick-up trucks) registered in the name of the fire fighter making application therefor, and when so issued to such applicant shall be used upon the vehicle for which issued in lieu of the standard license plates or license tags normally issued for such vehicle. (Acts 1982, No. 82-550, p. 909, § 3; Acts 1986, No. 86-456, p. 833; Acts 1989, No. 89-944; Acts 1991, No. 91-579, p. 1066, § 2.)

Division 14.

"Helping Schools" Tags.

§ 32-6-300. Issuance authorized; fee; term of validity; design.

(a) Owners of motor vehicles who are residents of Alabama, upon application to the probate judge or commissioner of licenses, complying with the state motor vehicle laws relating to registration and licensing of motor vehicles and payment of the regular license fee for tags or plates as provided by law for private passenger or pleasure motor vehicles, and the payment of an additional annual fee of $15.00, shall be issued license tags or plates which shall bear the words "Helping Schools."

(b) Such tags shall be issued, printed and processed in the same manner as other personalized tags are in this chapter. Such tags shall be valid for five years and shall be replaced at the end of the period with either conventional tags or other personalized tags, or with new "Helping Schools" tags. Payment of the required motor vehicle license fees and taxes for the years during which a new vehicle license plate is not issued shall be evidenced as provided for in section 32-6-63. The state department of revenue shall design, or have designed, the "Helping Schools" tag in compliance with all laws and regulations. (Acts 1990, No. 90-668, p. 1288, § 1.)

§ 32-6-301. Use of net proceeds.

The net proceeds of the $15.00 additional revenues derived from sales of "Helping Schools" tags as provided for in this division, less administrative costs including the department of revenue's cost of production of such tags, shall be distributed by the probate judge or license commissioner to, as nearly as practicable, the school district in which said funds were generated to be used for the purchase of classroom supplies and equipment in grades K through 12 of the public schools of such school district. (Acts 1990, No. 90-668, p. 1288, § 2.)

Division 14A.

"Retired Educator" License Tags or Plates.

Effective date. — The act which added this
division became effective May, 4, 1994.

§ 32-6-302. Commemorative motor vehicle tags for certain educators.

(a) Owners of motor vehicles who are residents of Alabama and who are receiving monthly retirement checks from the Teachers' Retirement System of Alabama, or who are receiving monthly retirement checks from an education retirement pension program from any other state, shall be eligible to apply for and receive "Retired Educator" commemorative or personalized license tags or plates as provided in this division. Owners of motor vehicles who are residents of Alabama and who are currently employed by a public education school system, college, university, institution, or who are active and contributing members of the Teachers' Retirement System, or who are employed by the State Department of Education, shall be eligible to apply for and receive "Educator" commemorative or personalized license tags or plates as provided in this division.

An applicant to receive a "Retired Educator" or "Educator" commemorative or personalized license tag or plate for private passenger or motor vehicles shall meet the following criteria:

(1) Apply to the appropriate judge of probate or commissioner of licenses as the case may be.

(2) Comply with the state motor vehicle laws, relating to registration and licensing of motor vehicles.

(3) Pay the regular license fee for license tags or plates as provided by law for private passenger or pleasure motor vehicles.

(4) Pay an additional annual fee of twenty-five dollars ($25) for the "Retired Educator" tag or license plate and fifty dollars ($50) for the "Educator" tag or license plate.

(5) Present documentation or certification to the appropriate judge of probate or commissioner of licenses, as the case may be, that the applicant is either receiving a monthly allotment as a retired education employee; or, in the case of "Educator" tags or license plates, is currently employed in public education as provided in this section.

(b) Upon meeting all of the criteria, the applicant shall be issued a personalized motor vehicle license tag or plate upon which, in lieu of the numbers prescribed by law, shall be inscribed special letters, figures, numbers, or other marks, emblems, symbols, or badges of distinction or personal prestige, or combination thereof, as are approved for and assigned to the application by the State Department of Revenue.

(c) The distinctive commemorative tags provided for in this division shall be issued, printed and processed in the same manner as other personalized tags in Section 32-6-150. The distinctive commemorative tags shall be valid for five years and shall be replaced at the end of the period with conventional tags or other personalized tags. Payment of the required motor vehicle license fees and taxes for the years during which a new vehicle license plate is not issued shall be evidenced as provided for in Section 32-6-63.

(d) The Commissioner of Revenue shall approve the distinctive design of the tags or plates provided in this division, and the approval shall be subject to submission of the design by the Education Tag Advisory Committee, which committee shall be strictly voluntary and the members shall serve without pay or remuneration. The Education Tag Advisory Committee shall consist of three members who shall be appointed by the Alabama Education Association. The design of the distinctive tag shall be subject to approval of the Revenue Commissioner and shall comply with all applicable laws and regulations pertaining to car tags and licenses, except that Section 32-6-54 shall not apply to this division.

(e) Fees collected pursuant to this division shall be transmitted timely to the State Treasurer. After payment to the Department of Corrections for its costs of manufacture and administration of the commemorative tags, the balance shall be transferred by the State Comptroller into the Penny Trust Fund established by Amendment 512 of the Constitution of Alabama of 1901, and as provided in Chapter 15A of Title 41.

(f) Fees paid pursuant to this division represent a charitable contribution from the purchaser to the Penny Trust Fund. (Acts 1994, No. 94-708, p. 1374, § 1.)

Division 15.

Pearl Harbor Survivors.

Code Commissioner's note. — Acts 1990, No. 90-769, which enacted this division, in § 6 provides: "The provisions of this act shall be construed to be cumulative to any laws or parts of laws relating to motor vehicle license plates or distinctive license plates."

§ 32-6-310. Distinctive plates authorized.

Any person who was a member of the United States armed forces on December 7, 1941, was on station or offshore at a distance not to exceed three miles, during the hours of 7:55 a.m. to 9:45 a.m., Hawaii time, during the attack on the island of Oahu, territory of Hawaii, and received an honorable discharge from the United States armed forces may, upon application and subject to the provisions of this division, be issued distinctive motor vehicle license plates or tags identifying said persons as Pearl Harbor survivors. (Acts 1990, No. 90-769, p. 1571, § 1.)

§ 32-6-311. Design of plates; issuance; fees; proof of qualification; use on private vehicle.

Said license plates shall be of a design to be prescribed by the commissioner of revenue, provided said plates shall bear the words "Pearl Harbor survivor" and prominently display the seal of the Pearl Harbor Survivors Association. The distinctive license plates shall be prepared by the commissioner of revenue and shall be issued through the probate judge or license commissioner of the several counties of the state in like manner as are other motor vehicle license plates or tags, and such officers shall be entitled to their regular fees for such service. Applicants for such distinctive plates shall present to the issuing official such proof as required by the commissioner of revenue that the qualification requirements of this division are met. When such applicant presents proof satisfactory to the commissioner, the applicant shall be issued the requested number of distinctive license plates or tags upon the payment of the regular license fee for tags, as provided by law, and the additional payment of a fee of $3.00 for each plate issued. Said applicant shall pay the additional $3.00 fee for each license plate issued in the future, however in those years in which a decal is issued said applicant shall pay the regular license fees for tags, as provided by law. The distinctive license plates or tags so issued shall be used only upon and for personally-owned, private passenger vehicles (to include station wagons and pick-up trucks) registered in the name of the person making application therefor, and when so issued to such applicant shall be used upon the vehicle for which issued in lieu of the standard license plates or license tags normally issued for such vehicle. (Acts 1990, No. 90-769, p. 1571, § 2.)

§ 32-6-312. Plates not transferable between owners; return of plates; transfer to other vehicle.

The distinctive license plates issued pursuant to this division shall not be transferable as between motor vehicle owners, and in the event the owner of a vehicle bearing such distinctive plates shall sell, trade, exchange or otherwise dispose of same, such plates shall be retained by the owner to whom issued and by him returned to the probate judge or license commissioner of the county, who shall receive and account for same in the manner stated below. In the event such owner shall acquire by purchase, trade, exchange or otherwise a vehicle for which no standard plates have been issued during the current license period, the probate judge or license commissioner of the county shall, upon being furnished by the owner thereof proper certification of the acquisition of such vehicle and the payment of the motor vehicle license tax due upon such vehicle, authorize the transfer to said vehicle of the distinctive license plates previously purchased by such owner, which plates shall authorize the operation of said vehicle for the remainder of the then current license period. In the further event the owner of such distinctive plates shall acquire by purchase, trade, exchange or otherwise a vehicle for which standard plates have been issued during the current license year, the probate judge or license commissioner shall, upon proper certification of such owner and upon delivery to such official of the standard plates previously issued for such vehicle, authorize the owner of such newly-acquired vehicle to place the distinctive plates previously purchased by him upon such vehicle and use same thereon for the remainder of the then current license period. Such notice of transfer of ownership shall be made of record by the probate judge or the license commissioner.

Any person acquiring by purchase, trade, exchange or otherwise any vehicle formerly bearing such distinctive plates shall be authorized, upon certification of such fact to the probate judge or license commissioner of the county and the payment of the fee now required by law, to purchase standard replacement plates for such vehicle which shall authorize the operation of such vehicle by the new owner for the remainder of the license period. (Acts 1990, No. 90-769, p. 1571, § 3.)

§ 32-6-313. Initial preparation and furnishing of plates.

Such distinctive plates or tags shall be prepared and furnished for the licensing year commencing October 1, 1989, and thereafter as is provided by law for the issuance of other license plates. (Acts 1990, No. 90-769, p. 1571, § 4.)

Division 16.

Square and Round Dance Tags.

Effective date. — The act which added this division became effective September 1, 1993.

§ 32-6-330. Acquisition; design.

Upon application to the judge of probate or license commissioner, compliance with motor vehicle registration and licensing laws, payment of regular fees required by law for license tags or plates for private passenger or pleasure motor vehicles, and payment of an additional fee of $5, owners of motor vehicles who are residents of Alabama shall be issued license tags and plates bearing the words "Square and Round Dance" across the top portion of the tags and plates, upon which, in lieu of the numbers as prescribed by law, shall be inscribed distinction words or marks designed by the Department of Revenue. These tags or plates shall be valid for five years, and may then be replaced with either conventional, personalized, or new "Square and Round Dance" tags or plates. Payment of required license fees and taxes for the years during which a new tag or plate is not issued shall be evidenced as provided for in Section 32-6-63. The Department of Revenue shall design, or have designed, the "Square and Round Dance" tags or plates. The tags or plates shall be issued, printed, and processed like other distinctive and personalized tags or plates provided for in Chapter 6 of Title 32. (Acts 1993, No. 93-635, p. 1089, § 1.)

§ 32-6-331. Disbursement of proceeds.

The net proceeds of the additional revenues generated by the $5 fee for the "Square and Round Dance" tags or plates, shall be disbursed according to Sections 40-12-269 and 40-12-270. (Acts 1993, No. 93-635, p. 1089, § 2.)

§ 32-6-332. Transferability.

The distinctive license plates or tags issued pursuant to this division shall not be transferable between motor vehicle owners, and in the event the owner of a vehicle bearing the distinctive plates sells, trades, exchanges, or otherwise disposes of the motor vehicle, the tags or plates shall be retained by the owner to whom issued and returned to the judge of probate or license commissioner of the county, who shall receive and account for the tags or plates as provided in this section. In the event the owner acquires by purchase, trade, exchange, or otherwise a vehicle for which no standard tags or plates have been issued during the current license period, the judge of probate or license commissioner of the county shall, upon being furnished by the owner proper certification of the acquisition of the vehicle and the payment of the motor vehicle license tax due upon the vehicle, authorize the transfer of the distinctive license tags or plates previously purchased by the owner to the vehicle, which tags or plates shall authorize the operation of the vehicle for the remainder of the then current license period. In the event the owner of the distinctive license tags or plates acquires by purchase, trade, exchange, or otherwise a vehicle for which standard plates have been issued during the current license year, the judge of probate or license commissioner shall, upon proper certification of the owner and upon delivery to the official of the standard plates previously issued for the vehicle, authorize the owner of the newly-acquired vehicle to place the distinctive license tags or plates previously purchased for the vehicle and use the tags or plates for the remainder of the then current license period. The notice of transfer of ownership shall be recorded by the judge of probate or the license commissioner.

Any person acquiring by purchase, trade, exchange, or otherwise any vehicle formerly bearing the distinctive tags or plates may, upon certification of the fact to the judge of probate or license commissioner of the county and the payment of the fee now required by law, purchase standard replacement plates for the vehicle which shall authorize the operation of the vehicle by the new owner for the remainder of the license period. (Acts 1993, No. 93-635, p. 1089, § 3.)

Division 17.

Distinctive License Tags.

Effective date. — The act which added this division became effective October 1, 1993.

§ 32-6-350. Legislative intent.

(a) It is the intent of the Legislature to establish an Alabama Veteran Tag Program to recognize certain veterans.

(b) The owner of a motor vehicle who is a resident of this state and who is an eligible veteran pursuant to subsection (c) of this section may be issued a distinctive license tag pursuant to this division. The veteran shall make application to the judge of probate or commissioner of licenses, comply with state motor vehicle laws relating to registration and licensing of motor vehicles, pay the regular license fee for a tag as provided by law for a private passenger or pleasure motor vehicle, and pay an additional fee of $3 for the initial issuance of the tag.

(c) The distinctive license tags in the Alabama Veteran Tag Program shall include veterans of the United States Armed Forces exposed to dangerous levels of radiation due to the atomic bomb and weapon testing from 1944 to 1962, Vietnam veterans, Korean War veterans, World War II veterans, veterans of the Battle of the Bulge, and veterans of Desert Shield/Desert Storm. The distinctive tags shall be issued, printed, and processed in the same manner as other distinctive tags as provided in this chapter. The payment of the required motor vehicle license fees and taxes when required by this section for a year during which a new vehicle license plate is not issued shall be evidenced as provided in Section 32-6-63.

(d) The Vietnam Veterans of America (VVA), Alabama State Council for the Vietnam veterans distinctive tag and the Department of Veteran Affairs for the other distinctive veteran tags shall each respectively design or have designed the distinctive veteran tags, subject to approval by the Commissioner of Revenue and compliance with all laws and regulations. An applicant for a Vietnam veteran tag shall be a Vietnam era veteran and the local veteran's affairs officer in the county in which application is made for the distinctive tag shall certify all Vietnam veterans eligible for a Vietnam veteran distinctive tag. An applicant for other veteran distinctive tags shall be a veteran of the appropriate conflict or otherwise qualify for a veteran tag as authorized by this section, and shall be certified as eligible by the Department of Veteran Affairs.

(e) The distinctive license tags shall not be transferable between motor vehicle owners and shall be subject to the same provisions of law related to the transferring of distinctive motor vehicle tags provided in Section 32-6-154 or as otherwise provided by law or regulation of the Department of Revenue. (Acts 1993, 1st Ex. Sess., No. 93-880, p. 144, § 1; Acts 1995, No. 95-528, § 1.)

The 1995 amendment, effective July 31, 1995, substituted "local veteran's affairs officer in the county in which application is made for the distinctive tag" for "Vietnam Veterans of America (VVA), Alabama State Council" in the second sentence of subsection (d).

§ 32-6-351. Active reserve identification tag.

Effective January 1, 1994, a resident of this state who is an active member of the United States Armed Forces Reserve may obtain a distinctive motor vehicle license tag or tags signifying service in the Armed Forces Reserve upon presenting to the judge of probate or commissioner of licenses an active reserve identification card. The distinctive motor vehicle license tags authorized by this division shall be issued in the same manner, under the same conditions, and for the same fees due, if any, as distinctive motor vehicle tags are issued to active members of the National Guard. (Acts 1993, 1st Ex. Sess., No. 93-880, p. 144, § 2.)

§ 32-6-352. Promulgation of rules.

The Department of Revenue may promulgate any rules necessary to carry out this division. (Acts 1993, 1st Ex. Sess., No. 93-880, p. 144, § 3.)

Division 18.

Members of Fraternal Order of Police.

Effective date. — The act which added this division became effective January 1, 1995.

§ 32-6-360. Issuance of license tag or plate to members of Fraternal Order of Police.

(a) A member of the Fraternal Order of Police who is the owner of a motor vehicle and a resident of the state may be issued a license tag or plate bearing the words "Fraternal Order of Police" across the top portion of the tag or plate upon which, in lieu of the numbers prescribed by law, shall be inscribed distinctive words or marks provided by the Department of Revenue. The member of the Fraternal Order of Police shall make application to the judge of probate or license commissioner, comply with the motor vehicle registration and licensing laws, pay the regular fees required by law for license tags or plates for private passenger or pleasure motor vehicles, and pay an additional fee of ten dollars ($10).

(b) The tags or plates shall be issued, printed, and processed like other distinctive and personalized tags and plates provided for in Chapter 6 of this title. The tags or plates shall be valid for five years and may be replaced with either a conventional, personalized, or new "Fraternal Order of Police" tags or plates. Payment of required license fees and taxes for the years during which a new tag or plate is not issued shall be evidenced as provided in Section 32-6-63. (Acts 1994, No. 94-614, p. 1132, § 1.)

§ 32-6-361. Proceeds.

The proceeds of the additional revenues generated by the ten dollar ($10) fee for the "Fraternal Order of Police" tags and plates shall be deposited in the General Fund. (Acts 1994, No. 94-614, p. 1132, § 2.)

§ 32-6-362. Appropriation to offset initial costs.

As a first charge against revenues collected under this division, to offset its initial costs in administering these collections, there is appropriated to the Department of Revenue for the fiscal year ending September 30, 1994, the sum of three thousand dollars ($3,000). The Legislature shall appropriate to the department for each fiscal year the amount of money necessary to offset any expenses the department incurs in administering and enforcing this division. (Acts 1994, No. 94-614, p. 1132, § 3.)

§ 32-6-363. Distinctive license plates or tags not transferable.

The distinctive license plates or tags issued pursuant to this division shall not be transferable between motor vehicle owners, and in the event the owner of a vehicle bearing the distinctive plates sells, trades, exchanges, or otherwise disposes of the motor vehicle, the plates shall be retained by the owner to whom issued and returned to the judge of probate or license commissioner of the county, who shall receive and account for the tags or plates as provided in this section. In the event the owner acquires by purchase, trade, exchange, or otherwise a vehicle for which no standard plates have been issued during the current license period, the judge of probate or license commissioner of the county shall, upon being furnished by the owner proper certification of the acquisition of the vehicle and the payment of the motor vehicle license tax due upon the vehicle, authorize the transfer of the distinctive license plates or tags previously purchased by the owner to the vehicle, which plates or tags shall authorize the operation of the vehicle for the remainder of the then current license period. In the event the owner of the distinctive license plates or tags acquires by purchase, trade, exchange, or otherwise a vehicle for which standard plates have been issued during the current license year, the judge of probate or license commissioner shall, upon proper certification of the owner and upon delivery to the official of the standard plates previously issued for the vehicle, authorize the owner of the newly-acquired vehicle to place the distinctive license plates or tags previously purchased upon the vehicle and use the plates for the remainder of the then current license period. The notice of transfer of ownership shall be made of record by the judge of probate or the license commissioner.

Any person acquiring by purchase, trade, exchange, or otherwise any vehicle formerly bearing the distinctive plates may, upon certification of the fact to the judge of probate or license commissioner of the county and the payment of the fee now required by law, purchase standard replacement plates for the vehicle which shall authorize the operation of the vehicle by the new owner for the remainder of the license period. (Acts 1994, No. 94-614, p. 1132, § 4.)

§ 32-6-364. Return of license plates upon termination of membership.

Upon termination of membership with the Fraternal Order of Police, an applicant to whom a Fraternal Order of Police license plate was issued under this section shall, within 30 days, return the plate to the judge of probate or the license commissioner of the county of the applicant's residence. (Acts 1994, No. 94-614, p. 1132, § 5.)

§ 32-6-365. Replacement plates.

If the Fraternal Order of Police license plate deteriorates to the point where inscriptions thereon are not discernible, the owner or lessee may obtain a replacement plate according to Section 40-12-265. (Acts 1994, No. 94-614, p. 1132, § 6.)

Division 19.

Letter Carriers.

Effective date. — The act which added this division became effective July 25, 1995.

§ 32-6-380. Definition of "letter carrier."

The words "letter carrier" as used in this division, unless the context clearly requires a different meaning, means only those persons who are employed by the United States Postal Service and who are employed as letter carriers or who are retired from the United States Postal Service as letter carriers. (Acts 1995, No. 95-400, § 1.)

§ 32-6-381. Issuance of license tags and plates to letter carriers.

Letter carriers, who are residents of Alabama, upon application to the judge of probate or license commissioner, compliance with motor vehicle registration and licensing laws, payment of regular fees required by law for license tags or plates for private passenger or pleasure motor vehicles, and the payment of an additional fee of $3.00 to be used for production and administration costs, shall be issued license tags and plates bearing the logo of the National Association of Letter Carriers between the county identification number and the actual license number. These tags or plates shall be valid for five years, and may then be replaced with either conventional, personalized, or new "Letter Carrier" tags or plates. Payment of required license fees and taxes for the years during which a new tag or plate is not issued shall be evidenced as provided for in Section 32-6-63. The Department of Revenue shall design, or have designed, the "Letter Carrier" tags or plates. The tags or plates shall be issued, printed, and processed like other distinctive and personalized tags or plates provided for in this chapter. (Acts 1995, No. 95-400, § 2.)

§ 32-6-382. Transfer of tags or plates.

The distinctive license plates or tags issued pursuant to this division shall not be transferable between motor vehicle owners, and in the event the owner of a vehicle bearing the distinctive plates sells, trades, exchanges, or otherwise disposes of the motor vehicle, the tags or plates shall be retained by the owner to whom issued and returned to the judge of probate or license commissioner of the county, who shall receive and account for the tags or plates as provided in this section. In the event the owner acquires by purchase, trade, exchange, or otherwise a vehicle for which no standard tags or plates have been issued during the current license period, the judge of probate or license commissioner of the county shall, upon being furnished by the owner proper certification of the acquisition of the vehicle and the payment of the motor vehicle license tax due upon the vehicle, authorize the transfer of the distinctive license tags or plates previously purchased by the owner to the vehicle, which tags or plates shall authorize the operation of the vehicle for the remainder of the then current license period. In the event the owner of the distinctive license tags or plates acquires by purchase, trade, exchange, or otherwise a vehicle for which standard plates have been issued during the current license year, the judge of probate or license commissioner shall, upon proper certification of the owner and upon delivery to the official of the standard plates previously issued for the vehicle, authorize the owner of the newly-acquired vehicle to place the distinctive license tags or plates previously purchased on the vehicle and use the tags or plates for the remainder of the then current license period. The notice of transfer of ownership shall be recorded by the judge of probate or the license commissioner.

Any person acquiring by purchase, trade, exchange, or otherwise any vehicle formerly bearing the distinctive tags or plates may, upon certification of the fact to the judge of probate or license commissioner of the county and the payment of the fee now required by law, purchase standard replacement plates for the vehicle which shall authorize the operation of the vehicle by the new owner for the remainder of the license period. (Acts 1995, No. 95-400, § 3.)

Code Commissioner's note. — In 1995, the Code Commissioner inserted "on" in place of "for" after "or plates previously purchased" in the third sentence of the first paragraph to effectuate apparent legislative intent.

§ 32-6-383. When tags to be prepared and furnished.

The distinctive plates or tags shall be prepared and furnished for the licensing year commencing October 1, in the year following the passage of this division, and thereafter as is provided by law for the issuance of other license plates. (Acts 1995, No. 95-400, § 4.)

Division 20.

Lions Club International.

Effective date. — The act which added this division became effective November 1, 1995.

§ 32-6-390. Issuance of distinctive license tags or plates to members.

(a) A member of the Lions Club International who is the owner of a motor vehicle and a resident of the state may be issued a distinctive license tag or plate which shall be produced and designed by the Alabama Department of Revenue. The member shall make application to the judge of probate or license commissioner, comply with the motor vehicle registration and licensing laws, pay the regular fees required by law for license tags or plates for private passenger or pleasure motor vehicles, and pay an additional fee of twenty-five dollars ($25).

(b) The tags or plates shall be issued, printed, and processed like other distinctive and personalized tags and plates provided for in this chapter. The tags or plates shall be valid for five years and may be replaced with either a conventional, personalized, or new "Lions Club" tag or plate at the additional fee of twenty-five dollars ($25). Payment of required license fees and taxes for the years during which a new tag or plate is not issued shall be evidenced as provided in Section 32-6-63. (Acts 1995, No. 95-532, § 1.)

Code Commissioner's note. — In 1995, the Code Commissioner deleted "and the actual license number" at the end of the first sentence in subsection (a) because the language fails to fit within the context of the sentence and appears to have been incorrectly retained while textually consistent language was deleted by amendment.

§ 32-6-391. Distribution of net proceeds.

The net proceeds of the additional revenues derived from sales of tags pursuant to this division, less administrative costs, including the cost of production of the tags, shall be distributed by the judge of probate or license commissioner to the Alabama Lions Sight Conservation Association, Incorporated, to be administered by its board. (Acts 1995, No. 95-532, § 2.)

§ 32-6-392. Transfer of tags or plates.

The distinctive license plates or tags issued pursuant to this division shall not be transferable between motor vehicle owners, and in the event the owner of a vehicle bearing the distinctive plate sells, trades, exchanges, or otherwise disposes of the motor vehicle, the plate shall be retained by the owner to whom issued and returned to the judge of probate or license commissioner of the county, who shall receive and account for the tags or plates as provided in this section. In the event the owner acquires by purchase, trade, exchange, or otherwise a vehicle for which no standard plates have been issued during the current license period, the judge of probate or license commissioner of the county shall, upon being furnished by the owner proper certification of the acquisition of the vehicle and the payment of the motor vehicle license tax due upon the vehicle, authorize the transfer of the distinctive license plates or tags previously purchased by the owner to the vehicle, which plates or tags shall authorize the operation of the vehicle for the remainder of the then current license period. In the event the owner of the distinctive license plates or tags acquires by purchase, trade, exchange, or otherwise a vehicle for which standard plates have been issued during the current license year, the judge of probate or license commissioner shall, upon proper certification of the owner and upon delivery to the official of the standard plates previously issued for the vehicle, authorize the owner of the newly-acquired vehicle to place the distinctive license plates or tags previously purchased on the vehicle and use the plates for the remainder of the then current license period. The notice of transfer of ownership shall be made of record by the judge of probate or the license commissioner.

Any person acquiring by purchase, trade, exchange, or otherwise any vehicle formerly bearing the distinctive plates may, upon certification of the fact to the judge of probate or license commissioner of the county and the payment of the fee now required by law, purchase a standard replacement plate for the vehicle which shall authorize the operation of the vehicle by the new owner for the remainder of the license period. (Acts 1995, No. 95-532, § 3.)

§ 32-6-393. Return of plates upon termination of membership.

Upon termination of membership with the Lions Club International, an applicant to whom a distinctive license plate was issued under this division shall, within 30 days, return the plate to the judge of probate or the license commissioner of the county of the applicant's residence. (Acts 1995, No. 95-532, § 4.)

§ 32-6-394. Replacement plates.

If a distinctive license plate deteriorates to the point where inscriptions thereon are not discernible, the owner or lessee may obtain a replacement plate upon payment of the $3 fee for the cost of manufacturing the plate. (Acts 1995, No. 95-532, § 5.)

Division 21.

"Olympic Spirit" License Tags or Plates.

Effective date. — The act which added this division became effective July 31, 1995.

§ 32-6-400. Issuance of distinctive tags and plates.

Upon application to the judge of probate or license commissioner, compliance with motor vehicle registration and licensing laws, payment of regular fees required by law for license tags or plates for private passenger or pleasure motor vehicles, and payment of an additional fee of twenty-five dollars ($25), owners of motor vehicles who are residents of Alabama shall be issued distinctive "Olympic Spirit" license tags and plates. These tags or plates shall be valid for five years, and then shall be replaced with either conventional or personalized tags or plates. Payment of required license fees and taxes for the years during which a new tag or plate is not issued shall be evidenced as provided for in Section 32-6-63. The distinctive "Olympic Spirit" license tags or plates shall bear the official United States Olympic Committee logo and the words "Olympic Spirit" on the plates and shall be produced and designed by the United States Olympic Committee and the Alabama Sports Foundation. The tags or plates shall be issued, printed, and processed like other distinctive and personalized tags or plates provided for in this chapter. (Acts 1995, No. 95-552, § 1.)

§ 32-6-401. Production costs; distribution of proceeds.

The production costs shall be paid monthly to the Department of Corrections by the Alabama Sports Foundation, and the foundation shall be provided with a monthly report detailing revenue by county from the Alabama State Comptroller. Proceeds from the additional revenues generated by the twenty-five dollars ($25) for the "Olympic Spirit" tags or plates, less administrative costs, shall be submitted monthly by the Alabama State Comptroller, to the Alabama Sports Foundation which shall remit one-half of the net proceeds to the United States Olympic Committee for the general operation of its amateur sports program. (Acts 1995, No. 95-552, § 2.)

§ 32-6-402. Transfer of plates or tags.

The distinctive license plates or tags issued pursuant to this division shall not be transferable between motor vehicle owners, and in the event the owner of a vehicle bearing the distinctive plates sells, trades, exchanges, or otherwise disposes of the motor vehicle, the tags or plates shall be retained by the owner to whom issued and returned to the judge of probate or license commissioner of the county, who shall receive and account for the tags or plates as provided in this section. In the event the owner acquires by purchase, trade, exchange, or otherwise a vehicle for which no standard tags or plates have been issued during the current license period, the judge of probate or license commissioner of the county shall, upon being furnished by the owner proper certification of the acquisition of the vehicle and the payment of the motor vehicle license tax due upon the vehicle, authorize the transfer of the distinctive license tags or plates previously purchased by the owner to the vehicle, which tags or plates shall authorize the operation of the vehicle for the remainder of the then current license period. In the event the owner of the distinctive license tags or plate acquires by purchase, trade, exchange, or otherwise a vehicle for which standard plates have been issued during the current license year, the judge of probate or license commissioner shall, upon proper certification of the owner and upon delivery to the official of the standard plates previously issued for the vehicle, authorize the owner of the newly-acquired vehicle to place the distinctive license tags or plates previously purchased on the vehicle and use the tags or plates for the remainder of the then current license period. The notice of transfer of ownership shall be recorded by the judge of probate or the license commissioner.

Any person acquiring by purchase, trade, exchange, or otherwise any vehicle formerly bearing the distinctive tags or plates may, upon certification of the fact to the judge of probate or license commissioner of the county and the payment of the fee now required by law, purchase standard replacement plates for the vehicle which shall authorize the operation of the vehicle by the new owner for the remainder of the license period. (Acts 1995, No. 95-552, § 3.)

Code Commissioner's note. — In 1995, the Code Commissioner inserted "on" in place of "for" after "or plates previously purchased" in the third sentence of the first paragraph to effectuate apparent legislative intent.

Division 22.

Supporters of Alabama Forests.

Effective date. — The act which added this division became effective November 1, 1995.

§ 32-6-410. Issuance of distinctive tags and plates.

Upon application to the judge of probate or license commissioner, compliance with motor vehicle registration and licensing laws, payment of regular fees required by law for license tags or plates for private passenger or pleasure motor vehicles, and payment of an additional fee of fifty dollars ($50), owners of motor vehicles who are residents of Alabama shall be issued distinctive "Alabama Forests" license tags and plates. These tags or plates shall be valid for five years, and shall then be replaced with either conventional or personalized tags or plates. Payment of required license fees and taxes for the years during which a new tag or plate is not issued shall be evidenced as provided for in Section 32-6-63. The distinctive "Alabama Forests" license tags or plates shall be produced and designed by the Alabama Department of Revenue with the advice and consent of the Alabama Forestry Commission. The tags or plates shall be issued, printed, and processed like other distinctive and personalized tags or plates provided for in this chapter. (Acts 1995, No. 95-553, § 1.)

§ 32-6-411. Establishment of Forest Stewardship Education Fund; distribution of proceeds.

(a) There is hereby established a separate special revenue trust fund in the State Treasury to be known as the "Forest Stewardship Education Fund," whose purpose is to promote the professional management of trees and related resources and to educate the general public regarding the contribution that trees and related resources make to the economy and environmental quality of this state.

(b) Proceeds from the additional revenues generated by the fifty dollars ($50) for the "Alabama Forests" tags or plates, less administrative costs, shall be submitted monthly by the Alabama State Comptroller to the Forest Stewardship Education Fund. Receipts collected under the provisions of this division are to be deposited in this fund and used only to carry out the provisions of this division. Such receipts shall be disbursed only by warrant of the State Comptroller upon the State Treasurer, upon itemized vouchers approved by the State Forester; provided that no funds shall be withdrawn or expended except as budgeted and allotted according to the provisions of Sections 41-4-80 through 41-4-96 and 41-19-1 through 41-19-12, and only in amounts as stipulated in the general appropriations bill or other appropriation bills. The additional fees represent a charitable contribution from the purchaser to the Alabama Forestry Commission. The funds may be used by the Alabama Forestry Commission or may be used through grants from the Alabama Forestry Commission to other organizations. (Acts 1995, No. 95-553, § 2.)

§ 32-6-412. Transfer of plates or tags.

The distinctive license plates or tags issued pursuant to this division shall not be transferable between motor vehicle owners, and in the event the owner of a vehicle bearing the distinctive plates sells, trades, exchanges, or otherwise disposes of the motor vehicle, the tags or plates shall be retained by the owner to whom issued and returned to the judge of probate or license commissioner of the county, who shall receive and account for the tags or plates as provided in this section. In the event the owner acquires by purchase, trade, exchange, or otherwise a vehicle for which no standard tags or plates have been issued during the current license period, the judge of probate or license commissioner of the county shall, upon being furnished by the owner proper certification of the acquisition of the vehicle and the payment of the motor vehicle license tax due upon the vehicle, authorize the transfer of the distinctive license tags or plates previously purchased by the owner to the vehicle, which tags or plates shall authorize the operation of the vehicle for the remainder of the then current license period. In the event the owner of the distinctive license tags or plates acquires by purchase, trade, exchange, or otherwise a vehicle for which standard plates have been issued during the current license year, the judge of probate or license commissioner shall, upon proper certification of the owner and upon delivery to the official of the standard plates previously issued for the vehicle, authorize the owner of the newly acquired vehicle to place the distinctive license tags or plates previously purchased on the vehicle and use the tags or plates for the remainder of the then current license period. The notice of transfer of ownership shall be recorded by the judge of probate or the license commissioner.

Any person acquiring by purchase, trade, exchange, or otherwise any vehicle formerly bearing the distinctive tags or plates may, upon certification of the fact to the judge of probate or license commissioner of the county and the payment of the fee now required by law, purchase standard replacement plates for the vehicle which shall authorize the operation of the vehicle by the new owner for the remainder of the license period. (Acts 1995, No. 95-553, § 3.)

§ 32-6-413. Alabama Forest Stewardship Education Committee to administer fund.

(a) The Alabama Forest Stewardship Education Fund shall be administered by the Alabama Forest Stewardship Education Committee. The committee shall be appointed by the Alabama Forestry Commission and composed of the following members:

(1) One member of the Alabama Association of Consulting Foresters.

(2) One member of the Alabama Treasure Forest Landowners Association.

(3) One member of the Urban Forestry Association.

(4) One member of the Society of American Foresters.

(5) One member of the Alabama Farmer's Federation.

(6) One member of the Alabama Forest Owners Association.

(7) The chair of the Board of Registration for Foresters, or his or her designee.

(8) The Dean of the Auburn University School of Forestry, or his or her designee.

(9) The Executive Director of the Alabama Forestry Association, or his or her designee.

(10) The State Forester, or his or her designee, who shall serve as chair of the committee.

(b) The first six members who are appointed to the committee shall initially serve two-year terms. At the expiration of the two-year terms, the members will serve staggered three-year terms as designated by the chair of the committee. Each of the members appointed from the association, society, or federation listed in subdivisions (1) through (6) of subsection (a) shall be appointed by the Alabama Forestry Commission from a list of three names submitted by the State Forester. (Acts 1995, No. 95-553, § 4.)

Code Commissioner's note. — In 1995, the Code Commissioner inserted "of subsection (a)" after "through (6)" in subsection (b) to complete the reference to the specified subdivisions.

Division 23.

Supporters of Alabama Jaycees.

Effective date. — The act which added this division became effective December 1, 1995.

§ 32-6-420. Issuance of distinctive license tags and plates.

Upon application to the judge of probate or license commissioner, compliance with motor vehicle registration and licensing laws, payment of regular fees required by law for license tags or plates for private passenger or pleasure motor vehicles, and payment of an additional fee of fifty dollars ($50), owners of motor vehicles who are residents of Alabama shall be issued distinctive "Alabama Jaycee" license tags and plates. An officer of the Alabama Jaycees who is verified as an officer by the Alabama Jaycees headquarters may request that a distinctive license tag or plate be issued to him or her, which identifies the applicant as a Jaycee officer. These tags or plates shall be valid for five years, and may then be replaced with either conventional, personalized, or new "Alabama Jaycee" tags or plates. Payment of required license fees and taxes for the years during which a new tag or plate is not issued shall be evidenced as provided for in Section 32-6-63. The distinctive "Alabama Jaycee" license tags or plates shall be designed by the Department of Revenue with the advice of the Alabama Jaycees. The tags or plates shall be issued, printed, and processed like other distinctive and personalized tags or plates provided for in this chapter. (Acts 1995, No. 95-726, § 1.)

Code Commissioner's note. — In 1995, the Code Commissioner inserted "advice" for "ad- vise" in the last sentence for grammatical pur- poses.

§ 32-6-421. Distribution of proceeds.

Proceeds from the additional revenues generated by the fifty dollars ($50) minus the production and administrative costs for the "Alabama Jaycee" tags or plates shall be submitted monthly by the Department of Revenue or other appropriate official to the Alabama Jaycees Foundation which shall distribute the proceeds to various charities as directed by the Birmingham Jaycees with the approval of the Alabama Jaycees Executive Board. (Acts 1995, No. 95-726, § 2.)

§ 32-6-422. Transfer of plates or tags.

The distinctive license plates or tags issued pursuant to this division shall not be transferable between motor vehicle owners, and in the event the owner of a vehicle bearing the distinctive plates sells, trades, exchanges, or otherwise disposes of the motor vehicle, the tags or plates shall be retained by the owner to whom issued and returned to the judge of probate or license commissioner of the county, who shall receive and account for the tags or plates as provided in this section. In the event the owner acquires by purchase, trade, exchange, or otherwise, a vehicle for which no standard tags or plates have been issued during the current license period, the judge of probate or license commissioner of the county shall, upon being furnished by the owner proper certification of the acquisition of the vehicle and the payment of the motor vehicle license tax due upon the vehicle, authorize the transfer of the distinctive license tags or plates previously purchased by the owner to the vehicle, which tags or plates shall authorize the operation of the vehicle for the remainder of the current license period. In the event the owner of the distinctive license tag or plate acquires by purchase, trade, exchange, or otherwise a vehicle for which a standard plate has been issued during the current license year, the judge of probate or license commissioner shall, upon proper certification of the owner and upon delivery to the official of the standard plate previously issued for the vehicle, authorize the owner of the newly-acquired vehicle to place the distinctive license tags or plates previously purchased on the vehicle and use the tags or plates for the remainder of the current license period. The notice of transfer of ownership shall be recorded by the judge of probate or the license commissioner.

Any person acquiring by purchase, trade, exchange, or otherwise any vehicle formerly bearing the distinctive tags or plates may, upon certification of the fact to the judge of probate or license commissioner of the county and the payment of the fee now required by law, purchase standard replacement plates for the vehicle which shall authorize the operation of the vehicle by the new owner for the remainder of the license period. (Acts 1995, No. 95-726, § 3.)

CHAPTER 7.

MOTOR VEHICLE SAFETY-RESPONSIBILITY ACT.

Purpose of the Alabama Automobile Insurance Plan. — A primary purpose of the plan is to establish a procedure for the equitable distribution of risks assigned to insurance companies and to preserve for the public the benefits of price competition by encouraging maximum use of the normal private insurance system, and the plan's intended purpose of protecting the general public from uninsured or underinsured motorists is a legitimate government end. Weaver v. Champion Ins. Co., 567 So. 2d 380 (Ala. Civ. App. 1990).

The assignment of policies to subscribers on a semi-random basis is a reasonable means of effecting the purposes for which the plan was designed. Weaver v. Champion Ins. Co., 567 So. 2d 380 (Ala. Civ. App. 1990).

Assignment of policies with limits in excess of minimum limits. — The Alabama Automobile Insurance Plan's practice of assigning policies with limits in excess of the minimum limits of coverage mandated by the Alabama Motor Vehicle Safety-Responsibility Act, §§ 32-7-1 through 32-7-42, did not exceed the plan's authority. Weaver v. Champion Ins. Co., 567 So. 2d 380 (Ala. Civ. App. 1990).

The state may rationally require insurance companies to service the needs of its citizens as a condition to doing business in the state. Weaver v. Champion Ins. Co., 567 So. 2d 380 (Ala. Civ. App. 1990).

§ 32-7-1. Citation of chapter.

Collateral references.
"Excess" or "umbrella" insurance policy as providing coverage for accidents with uninsured or underinsured motorists. 2 ALR5th 922.

§ 32-7-2. Definitions.

For the purposes of this chapter, the following terms shall have the meanings respectively ascribed to them in this section, except in those instances where the context clearly indicates a different meaning:

(1) DIRECTOR. The Director of Public Safety of the State of Alabama.

(2) JUDGMENT. Any judgment which shall have become final by expiration without appeal of the time within which an appeal might have been perfected, or by final affirmation on appeal rendered by a court of competent jurisdiction of any state or of the United States, upon a cause of action arising out of the ownership, maintenance or use of any motor vehicle, for damages, including damages for care and loss of services, because of bodily injury to or death of any person, or for damages because of injury to or destruction of property, including the loss of use thereof, or upon a cause of action on an agreement of settlement for those damages.

(3) LICENSE. Any license, temporary instruction permit, or temporary license issued under the laws of this state pertaining to the licensing of persons to operate motor vehicles.

(4) MOTOR VEHICLE. Every self-propelled vehicle which is designed for use upon a highway, including trailers and semitrailers designed for use with the vehicles (except traction engines, road rollers, farm tractors, tractor cranes, power shovels and well drillers) and every vehicle which is propelled by electric power obtained from overhead wires but not operated upon rails.

(5) NONRESIDENT. Every person who is not a resident of this state.

(6) NONRESIDENT'S OPERATION PRIVILEGE. The privilege conferred upon a nonresident by the laws of this state pertaining to the operation by him or her of a motor vehicle or the use of a motor vehicle owned by him or her in this state.

(7) OPERATOR. Every person who is in actual physical control of a motor vehicle.

(8) OWNER. A person who holds the legal title of a motor vehicle, or in the event a motor vehicle is the subject of an agreement for the conditional sale or lease of the motor vehicle with the right of purchase upon performance of the conditions stated in the agreement and with an immediate right of possession vested in the conditional vendee, or lessee, or in the event a mortgagor of a vehicle is entitled to possession, then the conditional vendee, or lessee, or mortgagor shall be deemed the owner for the purposes of this subdivision.

(9) PERSON. Every natural person, firm, copartnership, association or corporation.

(10) PROOF OF FINANCIAL RESPONSIBILITY. Proof of ability to respond in damages for liability, on account of accidents occurring subsequent to the effective date of the proof, arising out of the ownership, maintenance, or use of a motor vehicle in the amount of $20,000, because of bodily injury to or death of one person in any one accident, and, subject to the limit for one person, in the amount of $40,000 because of bodily injury to or death of two or more persons in any one accident, and in the amount of $10,000 because of injury to or destruction of property of others in any one accident.

(11) REGISTRATION. Registration certificate or certificates and registration plates issued under the laws of this state pertaining to the registration of motor vehicles.

(12) STATE. Any state, territory or possession of the United States, the District of Columbia or any province of the Dominion of Canada. (Acts 1951, No. 704, p. 1224, § 1; Acts 1993, 1st Ex. Sess., No. 93-903, p. 192, § 1.)

The 1993, 1st Ex. Sess., amendment, effective August 31, 1993, substituted "those damages" for "such damages" at the end of subdivision (2), substituted "the vehicles" for "such vehicles" in the middle of subdivision (4), inserted "or her" in two places in subdivision (6), in subdivision (8), substituted "of the motor vehicle" for "thereof" and substituted "the con-ditional vendee" for "such conditional vendee," and in subdivision (10), substituted "the proof" for "said proof," substituted "$20,000" for "$5,000.00," substituted "the limit" for "said limit," substituted "$40,000" for "$10,000.00," and substituted "$10,000" for "$1,000.00."

Cited in Davis v. Cotton States Mut. Ins. Co., 604 So. 2d 354 (Ala. 1992).

§ 32-7-5. Report required following accident.

The operator of every motor vehicle which is in any manner involved in an accident within this state, in which any person is killed or injured or in which damage to the property of any one person, including himself or herself, in excess of two hundred fifty dollars ($250) is sustained, shall within 30 days after the accident report the matter in writing to the director. The report, the form of which shall be prescribed by the director, shall contain only the information necessary to enable the director to determine whether the requirements for the deposit of security under Section 32-7-6 are inapplicable by reason of the existence of insurance or other exceptions specified in this chapter. The director may rely upon the accuracy of the information unless and until there is reason to believe that the information is erroneous. If the operator is physically incapable of making the report, the owner of the motor vehicle involved in the accident shall, within 10 days after learning of the accident, make the report. The operator or the owner shall furnish additional relevant information as the director shall require. (Acts 1951, No. 704, p. 1224, § 4; Acts 1984, No. 84-301, p. 672, § 1; Acts 1995, No. 95-260, § 2.)

The 1995 amendment, effective June 26, 1995, substituted "within 30 days" for "within 10 days" in the first sentence; deleted "as may be" preceding "necessary to enable" in the second sentence; substituted "there is reason" for "he has reason" in the third sentence; and made nonsubstantive changes.

Code Commissioner's note. — Acts 1995, No. 95-260, § 1 provides: "The intent of this act is to increase the length of time for a person who has a motor vehicle accident to file an accident report required by the Motor Vehicle Safety Responsibility Act. It is the further intent of this act to allow a person who has proper documentation, security, or insurance to cover the accident, but who fails to timely file the report and has his or her driving privilege suspended, to have the driving privilege reinstated without charge."

Requiring debtor to submit accident form subsequent to bankruptcy. — Alabama department of public safety's (ADPS) requiring debtor to submit an Accident Report

Form SR-13 subsequent to the filing of the petition in bankruptcy was not a police power protected by 11 U.S.C. § 362(b)(4); therefore, in effectuating the respective suspensions, the ADPS acted in contravention of the automatic stay imposed by 11 U.S.C. § 362(a). In re Kuck, 116 Bankr. 821 (Bankr. S.D. Ala. 1990).

Section 32-10-1 was not applicable. — Where driver argued that a "non-contact" accident did not fall within the language of § 32-10-1, that section was not applicable where driver faced the suspension of her driver's license as mandated by § 32-7-6, and this section provided that every operator of a motor vehicle "which is in any manner involved in an accident" is subject to § 32-7-6; driver's appeal to circuit court was entitled "Petition Under Alabama Motor Vehicles Safety Responsibility Act 704," and in that petition driver acknowledged being involved in an automobile accident. Worthy v. State Dep't of Pub. Safety, 599 So. 2d 629 (Ala. Civ. App. 1992).

§ 32-7-6. Security required; exceptions; suspension of licenses and registrations.

(a) If 20 days after the receipt of a report of a motor vehicle accident within this state which has resulted in bodily injury or death, or damage to the property of any one person in excess of two hundred fifty dollars ($250), the director does not have on file evidence satisfactory that the person who would otherwise be required to file security under subsection (b) of this section has been released from liability, or has been finally adjudicated not to be liable, or has executed a duly acknowledged written agreement providing for the payment of an agreed amount in installments with respect to all claims for injuries or damages resulting from the accident, the director shall determine the amount of security which shall be sufficient in his or her judgment to satisfy any judgment or judgments for damages resulting from the accident as may be recovered against each operator or owner.

(b) The director shall, within 60 days after the receipt of the report of a motor vehicle accident, suspend the license of each operator and all registrations of each owner of a motor vehicle in any manner involved in the accident, and if the operator is a nonresident the privilege of operating a motor vehicle within this state, and if the owner is a nonresident the privilege of the use within this state of any motor vehicle personally owned, unless the operator or owner or both shall deposit security in the sum so determined by the director. Notice of the suspension shall be sent by the director to the operator and owner, not less than 10 days prior to the effective date of the suspension, and shall state the amount required as security. Where erroneous information is given the director with respect to the matters set forth in subdivisions (1), (2), or (3) of subsection (c) of this section, he or she shall take appropriate action as provided within 60 days after receipt by the director of correct information with respect to these matters. Upon applying for reinstatement for suspension imposed under this section, no reinstatement fees shall be assessed if proper documentation is provided to the director that acceptable insurance was in effect at the time of the motor vehicle accident.

(c) This section shall not apply under the conditions stated in Section 32-7-7 nor in any one of the following if:

(1) The operator or owner if the owner had in effect at the time of the accident an automobile liability policy with respect to the motor vehicle involved in the accident.

(2) The operator, if not the owner of the motor vehicle, if there was in effect at the time of the accident an automobile liability policy or bond with respect to the operation of motor vehicles not owned by him or her.

(3) The operator or owner if the liability of the operator or owner for damages resulting from the accident is, in the judgment of the director, covered by any other form of liability insurance policy or bond.

(4) Any person qualifying as a self-insurer under Section 32-7-34, or to any person operating a motor vehicle for the self-insurer.

No policy or bond shall be effective under this section unless issued by an insurance company or surety company authorized to do business in this state unless the motor vehicle was not registered in this state, or was a motor vehicle which was registered elsewhere than in this state at the effective date of the policy or bond, or the most recent renewal thereof. The policy or bond shall not be effective under this section unless the insurance company or surety company, if not authorized to do business in this state, shall execute a power of attorney authorizing the director to accept service on its behalf of notice or process in any action upon the policy or bond arising out of the accident provided, that every policy or bond is subject, if the accident has resulted in bodily injury or death, to a limit, exclusive of interest and costs, of not less than twenty thousand dollars ($20,000) because of bodily injury to or death to one person in any one accident and subject to the limit for one person, to a limit of not less than forty thousand dollars ($40,000) because of bodily injury to or death of two or more persons in any one accident, and, if the accident has resulted in injury to or destruction of property, to a limit of not less than ten thousand dollars ($10,000) because of injury to or destruction of property of others in any one accident. (Acts 1951, No. 704, p. 1224, § 5; Acts 1965, No. 578, p. 1074; Acts 1984, No. 84-301, p. 672, § 2; Acts 1995, No. 95-260, § 3.)

The 1995 amendment, effective June 26, 1995, in subsection (a), deleted the former heading for the subsection which read: "Security required unless evidence of insurance; when security determined," and deleted "to him" following "satisfactory"; in subsection (b), deleted the former subsection heading which read: "Suspension," substituted "personally owned" for "owned by him" in the present first sentence, divided the former first sentence into the present first and second sentences by deleting "provided that" at the end of the present first sentence, in the present third sentence, deleted "hereinbefore" preceding "provided," and substituted "by the director" for "by him," and added the present last sentence; in subsection (c), deleted the former subsection heading which read: "Exception," and added "in any one of the following if" in the introductory language, substituted "The operator" for "To such operator" in subdivisions (1) through (3), deleted "nor" at the end of subdivision (3), substituted "Any person" for "To any person" in subdivision (4); in the last paragraph, in the first sentence, substituted "unless the motor vehicle" for "except, that if such motor vehicle," and substituted "than" for "that," and divided the former first sentence into the present first and second sentences; and made nonsubstantive changes.

Code Commissioner's note. — Acts 1995, No. 95-260, § 1 provides: "The intent of this act is to increase the length of time for a person who has a motor vehicle accident to file an accident report required by the Motor Vehicle Safety Responsibility Act. It is the further intent of this act to allow a person who has proper documentation, security, or insurance to cover the accident, but who fails to timely file the report and has his or her driving privilege suspended, to have the driving privilege reinstated without charge."

Absent express legislative intent, the 1984 amendment to this section could not be applied retroactively to an uninsured motorist policy which was renewed prior to the effective date of that amendment. Granite State Ins. Co. v. Styles, 541 So. 2d 1062 (Ala. 1989).

Due process argument relating to license revocation not applicable to suspension. — Where in support of her due process argument, driver cited Mechur v. Director, Dep't of Public Safety, 446 So. 2d 48 (Ala. Civ. App. 1984), for the proposition that the suspension of driving privileges without determination of guilt, thus interfering with the pursuit of a livelihood, is a violation of due process of law; Mechur, however is a driver's license revocation case which involves a person who had been convicted of DUI (driving under influence) twice in a five-year period; the court of appeals did not find that case to be applicable to the suspension case. Worthy v. State Dep't of Pub. Safety, 599 So. 2d 629 (Ala. Civ. App. 1992).

Section 32-10-1 was not applicable. — Where driver argued that a "non-contact" accident did not fall within the language of § 32-10-1, that section was not applicable where driver faced the suspension of her driver's license as mandated by this section, and § 32-7-5 provided that every operator of a motor vehicle "which is in any manner involved in an accident" is subject to this section; driver's appeal to circuit court was entitled "Petition Under Alabama Motor Vehicles Safety Responsibility Act 704," and in that petition driver acknowledged being involved in an automobile accident. Worthy v. State Dep't of Pub. Safety, 599 So. 2d 629 (Ala. Civ. App. 1992).

The trial judge properly substituted the limits of liability set out in city ordinance for the limits set forth in this section. St. Paul Fire & Marine Ins. Co. v. Elliott, 545 So. 2d 760 (Ala. 1989).

§ 32-7-8. Duration of suspension.

The license and registration and nonresident's operating privilege suspended as provided in Section 32-7-6 shall remain suspended and shall not be renewed, nor shall any license or registration be issued to that person for a period of three years or until:

(1) The person shall deposit or there shall be deposited on his or her behalf the security required under Section 32-7-6; or

(2) Two years shall have elapsed following the date of the suspension and evidence satisfactory to the director has been filed with him that during that period no action for damages arising out of the accident has been instituted; or

(3) Evidence satisfactory to the director has been filed with him or her of a release from liability, a final adjudication of nonliability or a duly acknowledged written agreement, in accordance with subdivision (4) of Section 32-7-7. In the event there shall be any default in the payment of any installment under any duly acknowledged written agreement, then, upon notice of default, the director shall forthwith suspend the license and

registration or nonresident's operating privilege of the person defaulting which shall not be restored unless and until:

    a. The person deposits and thereafter maintains security as required under Section 32-7-6 in the amount the director may then determine; or

    b. Two years shall have elapsed following the date when the security was required, and during that period no action upon the agreement has been instituted in a court in this state. (Acts 1951, No. 704, p. 1224, § 7; Acts 1959, No. 72, p. 478; Acts 1993, 1st Ex. Sess., No. 93-903, p. 192, § 2.)

The 1993, 1st Ex. Sess., amendment, effective August 31, 1993, in the introductory paragraph, deleted "so" preceding "suspended," deleted "such" preceding "license," and substituted "that person" for "such person"; in subdivision (1), substituted "The person" for "Such person" and inserted "or her," in subdivision (2), substituted "Two years" for "One year," substituted "the suspension" for "such suspension," and substituted "that period" for "such period," in subdivision (3), in the introductory paragraph, divided the former first sentence into the present first and second sentences, and in the present first sentence, inserted "or her" and deleted "provided, that in" following "Section 32-7-7," and in the present second sentence, added "In," deleted "such" preceding "default," and substituted "the person" for "such person," in paragraph a., substituted "The person" for "Such person," substituted "the amount" for "such amount," and deleted "as" preceding "the director," and in paragraph b., substituted "Two years" for "One year," substituted "the security" for "such security," substituted "that period" for "such period," and substituted "the agreement" for "such agreement."

§ 32-7-11. Custody, disposition and return of security.

Security deposited in compliance with the requirements of this chapter shall be placed by the director in the custody of the state treasurer and shall be applicable only to the payment of a judgment or judgments rendered against the person or persons on whose behalf the deposit was made, for damages arising out of the accident in question in an action at law, begun not later than the period of time provided in section 6-2-38(l), with regard to actions for injury to the person or rights of another not arising from contract, or any successor statute of limitations, for general negligence, following the date of such accident or within the said period of time following the date of deposit of any security under subdivision (3) of section 32-7-8, or to the payment in settlement agreed to by the depositor of a claim or claims arising out of such accident. Such deposit or any balance thereof shall be returned to the depositor or his personal representative when evidence satisfactory to the director has been filed with him that there has been a release from liability, or a final adjudication of nonliability, or a duly acknowledged agreement, in accordance with subdivision (4) of section 32-7-7, or whenever, after the expiration of the said period of time following the date of the accident or from the date of any security under subdivision (3) of section 32-7-8, the director shall be given reasonable evidence that there is no such action pending and no judgment rendered in such action left unpaid. (Acts 1951, No. 704, p. 1224, § 10; Acts 1990, No. 90-665, p. 1281.)

§ 32-7-12. Matters not to be evidence in civil actions.

Cross references. — For this section being commented on by new Rule 501, Alabama Rules of Evidence, effective January 1, 1996, see the Advisory Committee's Notes to new Rule 501 in the 1995 Cumulative Supplement to Volume 23.

§ 32-7-15. Suspension to continue until judgments paid and proof given.

Collateral references.

Validity, construction, application, and effect of statute requiring conditions, in addition to expiration of time, for reinstatement of suspended or revoked driver's license. 2 ALR5th 725.

§ 32-7-22. "Motor vehicle liability policy" defined; policy provisions.

(a) A "motor vehicle liability policy," as the term is used in this chapter, means an owner's or an operator's policy of liability insurance, certified as provided in Section 32-7-20 or Section 32-7-21 as proof of financial responsibility, and issued, except as otherwise provided in Section 32-7-21, by an insurance carrier duly authorized to transact business in this state, to or for the benefit of the person named in the policy as insured.

(b) The owner's policy of liability insurance:

(1) Shall designate by explicit description or by appropriate reference all motor vehicles to be insured; and

(2) Shall insure the person named in the policy and any other person, as insured, using any motor vehicle or motor vehicles designated in the policy with the express or implied permission of the named insured, against loss from the liability imposed by law for damages arising out of the ownership, maintenance, or use of such motor vehicle or motor vehicles within the United States of America or the Dominion of Canada, subject to limits exclusive of interest and costs, with respect to each such motor vehicle, as follows: $20,000 because of bodily injury to or death of one person in any one accident and, subject to the limit for one person, $40,000 because of bodily injury to or death of two or more persons in any one accident; and $10,000 because of injury to or destruction of property of others in any one accident.

(c) The operator's policy of liability insurance shall insure the person named as insured in the policy against loss from the liability imposed upon him or her by law for damages arising out of the use by him or her of any motor vehicle not owned by him or her, within the same territorial limits and subject to the same limits of liability as are set forth above with respect to an owner's policy of liability insurance.

(d) The motor vehicle liability policy shall state the name and address of the named insured, the coverage afforded by the policy, the premium charged for the policy, the policy period, and the limits of liability and shall contain an agreement or be endorsed that insurance is provided under the policy in accordance with the coverage defined in this chapter for bodily injury and death or property damage, or both, and is subject to all the provisions of this chapter.

(e) The motor vehicle liability policy need not insure any liability under any workmen's compensation law nor any liability on account of bodily injury to or death of an employee of the insured while engaged in the employment, other than domestic, of the insured, or while engaged in the operation, maintenance, or repair of any motor vehicle nor any liability for damage to property owned by, rented to, in charge of or transported by the insured.

(f) Every motor vehicle liability policy shall be subject to the following provisions which need not be contained in the policy:

(1) The liability of the insurance carrier with respect to the insurance required by this chapter shall become absolute whenever injury or damage covered by the motor vehicle liability policy occurs. The policy may not be cancelled or annulled as to that liability by any agreement between the insurance carrier and the insured after the occurrence of the injury or damage. Any statement made by the insured or on his or her behalf and any violation of the policy shall not defeat or void the policy.

(2) The satisfaction by the insured of a judgment for injury or damage shall not be a condition precedent to the right or duty of the insurance carrier to make payment on account of injury or damage.

(3) The insurance carrier shall have the right to settle any claim covered by the policy, and if the settlement is made in good faith, the amount of the settlement shall be deductible from the limits of liability specified in subdivision (2) of subsection (b) of this section.

(4) The policy, the written application for the policy, if any, and any rider or endorsement which does not conflict with this chapter shall constitute the entire contract between the parties.

(g) Any policy which grants the coverage required for a motor vehicle liability policy may also grant any lawful coverage in excess of or in addition to the coverage specified for a motor vehicle liability policy, and the excess or additional coverage shall not be subject to this chapter. With respect to a policy which grants any excess or additional coverage, the term "motor vehicle liability policy" shall apply only to that part of the coverage which is required by this section.

(h) Any motor vehicle liability policy may provide that the insured shall reimburse the insurance carrier for any payment the insurance carrier would not have been obligated to make under the terms of the policy except for this chapter.

(i) Any motor vehicle liability policy may provide for the prorating of the insurance by its terms with other valid and collectible insurance.

(j) The requirements for a motor vehicle liability policy may be fulfilled by the policies of one or more insurance carriers which policies together meet the requirements for a policy.

(k) Any binder issued pending the issuance of a motor vehicle liability policy shall be deemed to fulfill the requirements for a policy. (Acts 1951, No. 704, p. 1224, § 21; Acts 1993, 1st Ex. Sess., No. 93-903, p. 192, § 3.)

The 1993, 1st Ex. Sess., amendment, effective August 31, 1993, inserted "or her" throughout this section; in subsection (a), substituted "the term" for "said term," substituted "means" for "shall mean," and substituted "in the policy" for "therein"; in subsection (b), substituted "The owner's" for "Such owner's" in the introductory paragraph, in subdivision (1), deleted "with respect to which coverage is thereby" following "motor vehicles" and substituted "insured" for "granted," and in subdivision (2), substituted "in the policy" for "therein," deleted "such" preceding "motor vehicle," inserted "designated in the policy," substituted "the named insured," for "such named insured," substituted "$20,000" for "$5,000.00," substituted "the limit" for "said limit," substituted "$40,000" for "$10,000.00," and substituted "$10,000" for "$1,000.00"; in subsection (c), substituted "The operator's" for "Such operator's" and substituted "in the policy" for "therein"; in subsection (d), substituted "The motor vehicle" for "Such motor vehicle," substituted "for the policy" for "therefor," substituted "under the policy" for "thereunder," and substituted "for bodily injury" for "as respects bodily injury"; in subsection (e), substituted "The motor vehicle" for "Such motor vehicle" and deleted "such" following "or repair of any"; in subsection (f), substituted "in the policy" for "therein" in the introductory paragraph, in subdivision (1), divided the former first sentence into the present first, second and third sentences, and in the present first sentence, substituted "the motor vehicle" for "said motor vehicle" and deleted "said" following "occurs," in the present second sentence, added "The" and deleted "no" following "damage," and in the present third sentence, added "Any," substituted "any violation" for "no violation," inserted "not," and substituted "the policy" for "said policy," deleted "such injury" in two places in subdivision (2), in subdivision (3), substituted "the settlement" for "such settlement" and substituted "of the settlement" for "thereof," and in subdivision (4), substituted "for the policy" for "thereof" and deleted "the provisions of" preceding "this chapter"; in subsection (g), in the first sentence, substituted "the excess" for "such excess" and deleted "the provisions of" preceding "this chapter," and substituted "any excess" for "such excess" in the second sentence; deleted "the provisions of" preceding "this chapter" in subsection (h); substituted "by its terms" for "thereunder" in subsection (i); substituted "the requirements for a policy" for "such requirements" in subsection (j); and deleted "such" preceding "a policy" in subsection (k).

Collateral references.

Liability of insurer to insured for settling third-party claim within policy limits resulting in detriment to insured. 18 ALR5th 474.

§ 32-7-23. Uninsured motorist coverage; "uninsured motorist" defined; limitation on recovery.

I. GENERAL CONSIDERATION.

Purpose of section, etc.

The purpose of the statute is to provide coverage for the protection of persons insured thereunder who are legally entitled to recover damages from the owners or operators of uninsured motor vehicles. Auto-Owners Ins. Co. v. Hudson, 547 So. 2d 467 (Ala. 1989).

It is the purpose of the Uninsured Motorist Act, and thus, the public policy of the state, that Alabama citizens purchasing automobile liability insurance are to be able to obtain, for an additional premium, the same protection against injury or death at the hands of an uninsured motorist as they would have had if the uninsured motorist had obtained the minimum liability coverage required by the Motor Vehicle Safety Responsibility Act. Champion Ins. Co. v. Denney, 555 So. 2d 137 (Ala. 1989).

The purpose of this section is to protect insured persons who are legally entitled to recover damages from owners or operators of uninsured motor vehicles. An uninsured motorist insurance carrier can not limit or restrict that coverage. Star Freight, Inc. v. Sheffield, 587 So. 2d 946 (Ala. 1991).

Provisions of subsection (a) are mandatory if motor vehicle liability policy is issued. — Alabama makes no distinction between uninsured and underinsured motorist coverage; the two are looked upon as one and the same. Furthermore, Alabama is not a compulsory insurance state where neither residents nor nonresidents are required to have insurance either to obtain a driver's license or to secure vehicle registration or to travel through the state; however if a motor vehicle liability policy is issued in this state, the provisions of subsection (a) are mandatory. Best v.

Auto-Owners Ins. Co., 540 So. 2d 1381 (Ala. 1989).

The plain meaning of subsection (c) of this section is that an injured person covered under a multi-vehicle policy may stack the uninsured/underinsured motorist coverage for additional vehicles covered within the policy, limited to "the primary coverage plus such additional coverage as may be provided for additional vehicles, but not to exceed two additional coverages." State Farm Mut. Auto. Ins. Co. v. Fox, 541 So. 2d 1070 (Ala. 1989).

Absent express legislative intent, the 1984 amendment to this section could not be applied retroactively to an uninsured motorist policy which was renewed prior to the effective date of that amendment. Granite State Ins. Co. v. Styles, 541 So. 2d 1062 (Ala. 1989).

The purpose of consent-to-settle clauses in the uninsured/underinsured motorist insurance context is to protect the underinsured motorist insurance carrier's subrogation rights against the tortfeasor, as well as to protect the carrier against the possibility of collusion between its insured and the tortfeasor's liability insurer at the carrier's expense. Lambert v. State Farm Mut. Auto. Ins. Co., 576 So. 2d 160 (Ala. 1991).

Subrogation not allowed. — This section makes no provision for subrogation in uninsured motorist cases. Star Freight, Inc. v. Sheffield, 587 So. 2d 946 (Ala. 1991).

"Umbrella policy" not motor vehicle liability policy.

In accord with the bound volume. See Sweatt v. Great Am. Ins. Co., 574 So. 2d 732 (Ala. 1990).

Underinsured motorist coverage defined. — Underinsured motorists coverage, by definition, does not duplicate liability coverage but is coverage in excess of liability coverage, and is available to a claimant only after the claimant has exhausted available liability coverages; it differs from typical uninsured motorist coverage because uninsured motorist coverage takes the place of nonexistent liability coverage. Dillard v. Alabama Ins. Guar. Ass'n, 601 So. 2d 894 (Ala. 1992).

Underinsured motorist coverage applies where the negligent or wanton tortfeasor has some liability insurance.

Underinsured motorist coverage is a type of uninsured motorist coverage that does not apply unless the sum of the limits of liability under all bodily injury liability bonds and insurance policies available to an injured person after an accident is less than the damages which the injured person is legally entitled to recover. Dillard v. Alabama Ins. Guar. Ass'n, 601 So. 2d 894 (Ala. 1992).

Underinsured motorist coverage pays in excess of existing liability coverage, where the liability coverage is inadequate to fully compensate the claimant. Alabama Ins. Guar. Ass'n v. Hamm, 601 So. 2d 419 (Ala. 1992).

When benefits are paid under the claimant's uninsured/underinsured motorist policy and the tort-feasor's liability insurer is insolvent, the benefits are paid as uninsured motorist benefits; such payments will offset the obligation of the Alabama Insurance Guaranty Association dollar for dollar up to the policy limits. Dillard v. Alabama Ins. Guar. Ass'n, 601 So. 2d 894 (Ala. 1992).

If the insolvent company issued liability coverage for the tort-feasor, a claimant can recover uninsured motorist coverages available to the claimant, but cannot then recover the full amount of the insolvent insurer's liability coverage from the Alabama Insurance Guaranty Association, irrespective of whether the claimant has been made whole. Alabama Ins. Guar. Ass'n v. Hamm, 601 So. 2d 419 (Ala. 1992).

Uninsured motorist (UIM) coverage, paid by the Alabama Insurance Guaranty Association on an insolvent insurer's UIM policy, is not offset by a recovery against other liability insurance coverages, because UIM coverage does not duplicate the liability coverage. Alabama Ins. Guar. Ass'n v. Hamm, 601 So. 2d 419 (Ala. 1992).

Subrogation right waived. — Insurer by its refusal to consent to settlement or to timely advance the amount of the settlement offer, effectively waived its right to be subrogated, and the insured's acceptance of the settlement from the tortfeasor's liability insurer does not affect their rights under their own underinsured motorist insurance policy. Lambert v. State Farm Mut. Auto. Ins. Co., 576 So. 2d 160 (Ala. 1991).

Where an insurer attempted to extend or expand its right of subrogation, so as to recover its payment of uninsured motorist insurance proceeds in the event plaintiff recovered from any party, regardless of whether that party was an uninsured motorist, the agreement contravened this section. Star Freight, Inc. v. Sheffield, 587 So. 2d 946 (Ala. 1991).

Since recognizing the tort of bad faith in Alabama, this court has held that mere negligence or mistake is not sufficient to support a claim of bad faith; there must be a refusal to pay, coupled with a conscious intent to injure. Georgia Cas. & Sur. Co. v. White, 582 So. 2d 487 (Ala. 1991).

Delay of uninsured motorist benefits. — The ultimate issues of whether an insurer's payment of stacked uninsured motorist benefits was delayed with the intent to injure or whether, under the circumstances, the delay was reasonable, are issues of fact for the jury. Georgia Cas. & Sur. Co. v. White, 582 So. 2d 487 (Ala. 1991).

An action for bad faith refusal to pay cannot be maintained by an estate when the actions of the insurance company giving rise to the claim of bad faith refusal to pay occurred during the life of the insured. Georgia Cas. & Sur. Co. v. White, 582 So. 2d 487 (Ala. 1991).

Where the extent of liability and the extent of injury had been determined before the death of the insured so as to convert the contract for insurance into a contract for payment, and facts sufficient to state a cause of action for bad faith refusal to pay were alleged, the estate, the party entitled to be paid, can maintain an action for bad faith refusal to pay. Georgia Cas. & Sur. Co. v. White, 582 So. 2d 487 (Ala. 1991).

For a case finding that the circumstances under which an insurance company refused to pay stacked uninsured motorist benefits (i.e., liability had been established and the amount had been established) did not, as a matter of law, constitute mere negligence or mistake, see Georgia Cas. & Sur. Co. v. White, 582 So. 2d 487 (Ala. 1991).

Cited in Jones v. Allstate Ins. Co., 601 So. 2d 989 (Ala. 1992); Wilson v. Madison County, 601 So. 2d 479 (Ala. 1992); Gibson v. Alabama Ins. Guar. Ass'n, 601 So. 2d 416 (Ala. 1992); Davis v. Cotton States Mut. Ins. Co., 604 So. 2d 354 (Ala. 1992).

Collateral references.

Automobile uninsured motorist coverage: "legally entitled to recover" clause as barring claim compensable under workers' compensation statute. 82 ALR4th 1096.

Insured's recovery of uninsured motorist claim against insurer as affecting subsequent recovery against tortfeasors causing injury. 3 ALR5th 746.

Liability of insurer to insured for settling third-party claim within policy limits resulting in detriment to insured. 18 ALR5th 474.

Uninsured or underinsured motorist insurance: validity and construction of policy provision purporting to reduce recovery by amount of social security disability benefits or payments under similar disability benefits law. 24 ALR5th 766.

II. WHO IS COVERED.

Proceeds payout governed by Wrongful Death Statute when insured party deceased. Sprouse v. Hawk, 574 So. 2d 754 (Ala. 1990).

IV. LIMITS OF LIABILITY.

The phrases "any one contract" and "within such contract" in paragraph (c) refer to a single insurance contract. There may be no significant difference between five single-vehicle insurance policies and one insurance policy covering five vehicles, as insurance company contended. However, the legislature clearly directed its limitation of stacking of uninsured/underinsured motorist coverage to a single policy covering multiple vehicles. American Economy Ins. Co. v. Thompson, 643 So. 2d 1350 (Ala. 1994).

Subsection (c) must be construed to give effect to its plain language, which only allows injured persons who are insureds under a particular policy to stack. Where claimant was not an insured under the uninsured motorist provisions of either of two policies, she had no right, legal or equitable, to claim any benefit under either of those policies. Putman v. Womack, 607 So. 2d 166 (Ala. 1992).

When subsection (c) does not apply. — Subsection (c), which allows stacking of up to three coverages under one multi-vehicle insurance contract, does not apply to an attempt by a passenger in another person's insured vehicle to stack uninsured motorist coverages under separate single-vehicle insurance policies on vehicles not owned by him or occupied by him at the time of his injury. State Farm Mut. Auto. Ins. Co. v. Faught, 558 So. 2d 921 (Ala. 1990).

Provision in subsection (c) does not apply where insurer issues five separate single vehicle policies. — The provision in subsection (c) of this section, that limits an insurer's liability under the uninsured/underinsured coverage to the primary coverage plus two additional coverages, does not apply where the insurer issues five separate single-vehicle policies rather than one multi-vehicle policy. State Farm Mut. Auto. Ins. Co. v. Fox, 541 So. 2d 1070 (Ala. 1989).

Stacking is limited to one policy or contract of insurance. Powell v. State Farm Mut. Auto. Ins. Co., 601 So. 2d 60 (Ala. 1992).

Limitation of stacking directed to single policy covering multiple vehicles. — The phrases "any one contract" and "within such contract" refer to a single insurance contract. There may be no significant difference between five single-vehicle insurance policies and one insurance policy covering five vehicles. However, the legislature clearly directed its limitation of stacking of uninsured/underinsured motorist coverage to a single policy covering multiple vehicles. State Farm Mut. Auto. Ins. Co. v. Fox, 541 So. 2d 1070 (Ala. 1989).

It is not unconstitutional to deny stacking of uninsured motorist coverages to an injured passenger who does not happen to be a resident of the named insured's household when the insurer has issued separate policies to the named insured, when stacking of those coverages would be allowed for such a passenger if the insurer had covered all of the named insured's vehicles under the same policy. Allstate Ins. Co. v. Alfa Mut. Ins. Co., 565 So. 2d 179 (Ala. 1990).

Injured passenger was not entitled to stack uninsured motorist coverage. — Injured passenger, who was not a named insured under the policy covering the vehicle in which she was injured, and who was not a resident of the named insured's household, was not entitled to stack the uninsured motorist coverage of a separate policy that covered a separate and distinct vehicle belonging to the insured and was insured by the same insurer but was not involved in the accident. Allstate Ins. Co. v. Alfa Mut. Ins. Co., 565 So. 2d 179 (Ala. 1990).

When tortfeasor's insurer offers to pay maximum liability and damages exceed underinsured coverage. — When the tortfeasor's liability insurer has offered to pay the maximum of its liability limits, and it is undisputed that the damages exceed that amount and, further, exceed the amount of underinsured coverage available, the insured should give its underinsured motorist insurance carrier notice of this offered settlement and the underinsured motorist carrier should consent to the settlement and forgo any right of subrogation for any underinsured motorist coverage it may subsequently pay, or else pay to its insured the amount offered by the tort-feasor's insurer and preserve its right of subrogation. Auto-Owners Ins. Co. v. Hudson, 547 So. 2d 467 (Ala. 1989).

V. PROCEDURE.

"Legally entitled to recover damages," etc.

In accord with the bound volume. LeFevre v. Westberry, 590 So. 2d 154 (Ala. 1991).

For procedural guidelines to be followed in all instances where rights of insured and underinsured motorist insurance carrier may conflict, i.e., subrogation rights, absence of carrier consent to release, see Lambert v. State Farm Mut. Auto. Ins. Co., 576 So. 2d 160 (Ala. 1991).

Burden of proving uninsured status may fall on insurer. — Although claimant has initial burden of showing that tortfeasor was uninsured, this burden shifts to the insurer if claimant can show that he used reasonable diligence to ascertain the uninsured status of the tortfeasor and that such information was unobtainable. MIC v. Williams, 576 So. 2d 218 (Ala. 1991).

Time for maintaining bad faith action dependent upon facts of each case. — When is a carrier of uninsured motorist coverage under a duty to pay its insured's damages?

There is no universally definitive answer to this question or to the question when an action alleging bad faith may be maintained for the improper handling of an uninsured or underinsured motorist claim; the answer is, of course, dependent upon the facts of each case. LeFevre v. Westberry, 590 So. 2d 154 (Ala. 1991).

The legislature did not intend that the insured would have to sue and receive a judgment in his or her favor before bringing an action alleging bad faith. LeFevre v. Westberry, 590 So. 2d 154 (Ala. 1991).

For a discussion of the procedures an insurer must follow when its insured has notified it of a claim under the uninsured/underinsured motorist coverage provision of an automobile liability policy, see LeFevre v. Westberry, 590 So. 2d 154 (Ala. 1991).

"Outrageous" conduct not shown. — Insurer's conduct in delaying payment to insureds as a result of an automobile accident with underinsured, who was also insured by the insurer, was not "so outrageous in character and so extreme in degree as to go beyond all possible bounds of decency, and to be regarded as atrocious and utterly intolerable in a civilized society"; thus, insured could not recover damages for the tort of outrage. State Farm Auto. Ins. Co. v. Morris, 612 So. 2d 440 (Ala. 1993).

Reasonable diligence determination must be made upon the facts in each case. An admission by the insurer or its agent would clearly have probative value on the question of whether the tortfeasor was insured or an affidavit, deposition, or even letter [from the owner or driver of the automobile] to the effect that they were uninsured at the time of the occurrence should control, although it must pertain to the time of the occurrence. MIC v. Williams, 576 So. 2d 218 (Ala. 1991).

Reasonable diligence evidenced by claimant sufficient to shift burden on establishing uninsured status where claimant hired a process server to try to locate car driver, who made several trips to possible residences of the driver, also checked the city directories for two cities, checked at the tag registration offices and made several phone calls but did not locate the driver. MIC v. Williams, 576 So. 2d 218 (Ala. 1991).

Waiver of underinsured benefits. — Although insured notified underinsured motorist insurance carrier of the possibility of a claim and of the fact that the tortfeasor had some insurance coverage, but he did not notify carrier of his settlement with the alleged tortfeasor and the tort-feasor's carrier until after he had settled and executed a release, he waived his right to underinsured motorist insurance benefits. Allstate Ins. Co. v. Beavers, 611 So. 2d 348 (Ala. 1992).

§ 32-7-24. Notice of cancellation or termination of certified policy.

Cited in Aplin v. American Sec. Ins. Co., 568 So. 2d 757 (Ala. 1990).

§ 32-7-27. Money or securities as proof.

(a) Proof of financial responsibility may be evidenced by the certificate of the State Treasurer that the person named in the certificate has deposited with him or her $50,000 in cash, or securities that may legally be purchased by savings banks or for trust funds of a market value of $50,000. The State Treasurer shall not accept the deposit and issue a certificate pursuant to this section and the director shall not accept the certificate unless accompanied by evidence that there are no unsatisfied judgments of any character against the depositor in the county where the depositor resides.

(b) The deposit shall be held by the State Treasurer to satisfy, in accordance with the provisions of this chapter, any execution on a judgment issued against the person making the deposit, for damages, including damages for care and loss of services, because of bodily injury to or death of any person, or for damages because of injury to or destruction of property, including the loss of use of property resulting from the ownership, maintenance, use or operation of a motor vehicle after the deposit was made. Money or securities so deposited shall not be subject to attachment or execution unless the attachment or execution shall arise out of an action for damages as provided in this subsection. (Acts 1951, No. 704, p. 1224, § 25; Acts 1993, 1st Ex. Sess., No. 93-903, p. 192, § 4.)

The 1993, 1st Ex. Sess., amendment, effective August 31, 1993, in subsection (a), in the first sentence, substituted "in the certificate" for "therein," inserted "or her," substituted "$50,000" for "$11,000" in two places, and substituted "that" for "such as," and in the second sentence, substituted "the deposit" for "any such deposit," substituted "pursuant to this section" for "therefor," and substituted "the cer-tificate" for "such certificate"; and in subsection (b), in the first sentence, substituted "The deposit" for "Such deposit" at the beginning and towards the end, substituted "the person" for "such person," and substituted "of property" for "thereof," and in the second sentence, substituted "the attachment" for "such attachment" and substituted "provided in this subsection" for "aforesaid."

§ 32-7-28. Owner may give proof for others.

Collateral references.
Application of automobile insurance "entitle-ment" exclusion to family member. 25 ALR5th 60.

§ 32-7-31. Duration of proof; when proof may be cancelled or re-turned.

Cited in Aplin v. American Sec. Ins. Co., 568 So. 2d 757 (Ala. 1990).

§ 32-7-35. Assigned risk plans.

Purpose of the Alabama Automobile Insurance Plan. — A primary purpose of the plan is to establish a procedure for the equitable distribution of risks assigned to insurance companies and to preserve for the public the benefits of price competition by encouraging maximum use of the normal private insurance system, and the plan's intended purpose of protecting the general public from uninsured or underinsured motorists is a legitimate government end. Weaver v. Champion Ins. Co., 567 So. 2d 380 (Ala. Civ. App. 1990).

The assignment of policies to subscribers on a semi-random basis is a reasonable means of effecting the purposes for which the Plan was designed. Weaver v. Champion Ins. Co., 567 So.

2d 380 (Ala. Civ. App. 1990).

Assignment of policies with limits in excess of minimum limits. — The Alabama Automobile Insurance Plan's practice of assigning policies with limits in excess of the minimum limits of coverage mandated by the Alabama Motor Vehicle Safety-Responsibility Act, §§ 32-7-1 through 32-7-42, did not exceed the plan's authority. Weaver v. Champion Ins. Co., 567 So. 2d 380 (Ala. Civ. App. 1990).

The state may rationally require insurance companies to service the needs of its citizens as a condition to doing business in the state. Weaver v. Champion Ins. Co., 567 So. 2d 380 (Ala. Civ. App. 1990).

§ 32-7-39. Expenses of administering chapter. Repealed by Acts 1993, 1st Ex. Sess., No. 93-903, p. 192, § 5, effective August 31, 1993.

CHAPTER 8.

UNIFORM CERTIFICATE OF TITLE AND ANTITHEFT ACT.

ARTICLE 1.

GENERAL PROVISIONS.

§ 32-8-1. Short title.

The overall plan of the act shows exclusive attention to maintaining records of the identity and ownership of vehicles; persons who buy cars are entitled to rely on the accuracy of such elements of that tracing system as certif-

icates of title and Vehicle Identification Number plates, and a subsequent purchaser of a car is within the class of persons who are the beneficiaries of the duty not to falsify identification numbers or certificates of title. Johnny

Spradlin Auto Parts, Inc. v. Cochran, 568 So. 2d 738 (Ala. 1990).

Chapter establishes standard of conduct. — Although this chapter does not create an independent cause of action in tort, that does not mean that the chapter does not establish a standard of conduct for persons or corporations who come within its terms. Trailmobile, Inc. v. Cook, 540 So. 2d 683 (Ala. 1988).

Obligation to furnish buyer with certificate was written into contract by operation of chapter. — Even if the contract did not specify that seller of trailers was obligated to furnish buyer with the certificates of title upon satisfaction of the lien, that obligation was written into the contract by operation of this chapter. Trailmobile, Inc. v. Cook, 540 So. 2d 683 (Ala. 1988).

§ 32-8-2. Definitions.

For the purpose of this chapter, the following terms shall have the meanings respectively ascribed to them in this section, except where the context clearly indicates a different meaning:

(1) CURRENT ADDRESS. A new address different from the address shown on the application or on the certificate of title. The owner shall within 30 days after his address is changed from that shown on the application or on the certificate of title notify the department of the change of address in the manner prescribed by the department.

(2) DEALER. A person licensed as an automobile or motor vehicle dealer, manufactured home dealer, or travel trailer dealer and engaged regularly in the business of buying, selling or exchanging motor vehicles, trailers, semitrailers, trucks, tractors or other character of commercial or industrial motor vehicles, manufactured homes or travel trailers in this state, and having in this state an established place of business.

(3) DEPARTMENT. The department of revenue of this state.

(4) DESIGNATED AGENT. Each judge of probate, commissioner of licenses, director of revenue or other county official in this state authorized and required by law to issue motor vehicle license tags, who may perform his duties under this chapter personally or through his deputies, or such other persons, as the department may designate; the term shall also mean those "dealers" as herein defined who are appointed by the department as herein provided in section 32-8-34 to perform the duties of "designated agent" for the purposes of this chapter; such "dealers" may perform their duties under this chapter either personally or through any of their officers or employees.

(5) IMPLEMENT OF HUSBANDRY. Every vehicle designed and adapted exclusively for agricultural, horticultural or livestock raising operations or for lifting or carrying an implement of husbandry and in either case not subject to licensing or registration if used upon the highways.

(6) LIEN. Every kind of written lease which is substantially equivalent to an installment sale or which provides for a right of purchase, conditional sale, reservation of title, deed of trust, chattel mortgage, trust receipt, and every written agreement or instrument of whatever kind or character whereby an interest other than absolute title is sought to be held or given on a motor vehicle or manufactured home.

(7) LIENHOLDER. Any person, firm, copartnership, association or corporation holding a lien as herein defined on a motor vehicle or manufactured home.

(8) MANUFACTURER. Any person regularly engaged in the business of manufacturing, constructing, assembling, importing or distributing new motor vehicles or manufactured homes, either within or without this state.

(9) MANUFACTURED HOME. A structure, transportable in one or more sections, and which is built on a permanent chassis, and not designed normally to be drawn or pulled on the highway except to change permanent locations, but is designed to be used as a dwelling, with or without a permanent foundation, when connected to the required utilities, including the plumbing, heating, air conditioning and electrical systems, if any contained therein. It may be used as a place of residence, business, profession, trade or for any other purpose, by the owner, lessee, or assigns and may consist of one or more units that can be attached or jointed together. Except for article 1 (definitions), wherever in chapter 8, Title 32, as amended, the terms vehicle or motor vehicle shall appear, they shall be deemed to refer also to manufactured homes.

(10) MOTOR VEHICLE. Such term shall include:

a. Every automobile, motorcycle, mobile trailer, semitrailer, truck, truck tractor, trailer and other device which is self-propelled or drawn, in, upon or by which any person or property is or may be transported or drawn upon a public highway except such as is moved by animal power or used exclusively upon stationary rails or tracks;

b. Every trailer coach, and travel trailer manufactured upon a chassis or undercarriage as an integral part thereof drawn by a self-propelled vehicle.

(11) NEW VEHICLE or MANUFACTURED HOME. A motor vehicle or manufactured home that has never been the subject of a first sale for use.

(12) NONRESIDENT. Every person who is not a resident of this state.

(13) OWNER. A person, other than a lienholder, having the property in or title to a vehicle or manufactured home. The term includes a person entitled to the use and possession of a vehicle or manufactured home subject to a security interest in another person, but excludes a lessee under a lease not intended as security. Under any lease-purchase or installment sales agreement where a governmental agency, either city, county or state, is the lessee or purchaser with a security interest or right to purchase, such lessee or purchaser shall be the owner for purposes of this chapter.

(14) PERSON. Such term shall include every natural person, firm, copartnership, association or corporation.

(15) POLE TRAILER. Every vehicle without motive power designed to be drawn by another vehicle and attached to the towing vehicle by means of a reach or pole, or by being boomed or otherwise secured to the towing vehicle, and ordinarily used for transporting long or irregularly shaped loads such as logs, poles, pipes, boats or structural members capable generally of sustaining themselves as beams between the supporting connections.

(16) SCRAP METAL PROCESSOR. Any person, firm, or corporation engaged in the business of buying scrap vehicles or manufactured homes, automotive parts, or other metallic waste by weight to process such material into scrap

113

metal for remelting purposes, who utilizes machinery and equipment for processing and manufacturing ferrous and nonferrous metallic scrap into prepared grades, and whose principal product is metallic scrap.

(17) SCRAP VEHICLE or MANUFACTURED HOME. Any vehicle or manufactured home which has been crushed or flattened by mechanical means or which has been otherwise damaged to the extent that it cannot economically be repaired or made roadworthy.

(18) SECURITY AGREEMENT. A written agreement which reserves or creates a security interest.

(19) SECURITY INTEREST. An interest in a vehicle or manufactured home reserved or created by agreement and which secures payment or performance of an obligation. The term includes the interest of a lessor under a lease intended as security. A security interest is "perfected" when it is valid against third parties generally, subject only to specific statutory exceptions.

(20) SPECIAL MOBILE EQUIPMENT. Every vehicle not designed or used primarily for the transportation of persons or property and only incidentally operated or moved over the highway, including but not limited to: ditch-digging apparatus; well-boring apparatus; road construction and maintenance machinery such as asphalt spreaders, bituminous mixers, bucket loaders, tractors other than truck tractors, ditchers, leveling graders, finishing machines, motor graders, road rollers, scarifiers, earth-moving carryalls and scrapers, power shovels and draglines, and self-propelled cranes; and earth-moving equipment. The term does not include manufactured homes, dump trucks, truck-mounted transit mixers, cranes or shovels or other vehicles designed for the transportation of persons or property to which machinery has been attached.

(21) STATE. A state, territory or possession of the United States, the District of Columbia, the Commonwealth of Puerto Rico or a province of the Dominion of Canada.

(22) TRAVEL TRAILER. A vehicle without motive power, designed and constructed as a camping vehicle or a temporary dwelling, living or sleeping place and designed to be drawn or pulled on the highway, but not including folding or collapsible camping trailers and manufactured homes as defined herein.

(23) USED VEHICLE or MANUFACTURED HOME. A motor vehicle or manufactured home that has been the subject of a first sale for use, whether within this state or elsewhere.

(24) VEHICLE OR MANUFACTURED HOME IDENTIFICATION NUMBER. The numbers and letters on a motor vehicle or manufactured home designated by the manufacturer or assigned by the department for the purpose of identifying the motor vehicle or manufactured home. (Acts 1973, No. 765, p. 1147, § 1; Acts 1985, 2nd Ex. Sess., No. 85-939, p. 249; Acts 1987, No. 87-806, p. 1581, § 1; Acts 1989, No. 89-918, § 1; Acts 1991, No. 91-694, p. 1340, § 6.)

§§ 32-8-4, 32-8-5. Repealed by Acts 1992, No. 92-186, § 80, effective October 1, 1992.

§ 32-8-13. Offenses constituting misdemeanors.

Obligation to furnish buyer with certificate was written into contract by operation of statute. — Even if the contract did not specify that seller of trailers was obligated to furnish buyer with the certificates of title upon satisfaction of the lien, that obligation was written into the contract by operation of statute. Trailmobile, Inc. v. Cook, 540 So. 2d 683 (Ala. 1988).

ARTICLE 2.

CERTIFICATE OF TITLE.

§ 32-8-39. Contents and effect of certificate.

Certificate of title is only prima facie evidence of ownership, etc.

A certificate of title is not conclusive evidence of ownership, because ownership can be established by other evidence. Crowley v. State Farm Mut. Auto. Ins. Co., 591 So. 2d 53 (Ala. 1991).

Absence of ownership. — The absence of ownership indicated by the absence of a certificate of title can be rebutted by other evidence of ownership. For example, ownership or a transfer of ownership can be established by evidence of a party's taking possession of the vehicle; by evidence of a bill of sale that manifests an intent to sell and transfer the vehicle and to grant dominion and control over it; and by evidence of a transfer of money for the vehicle. Crowley v. State Farm Mut. Auto. Ins. Co., 591 So. 2d 53 (Ala. 1991).

Although title was in father, debtor had equitable interest in car. — Car was property of the debtor's estate; although bare legal title was in the father, the debtor had an equitable interest in the car; debtor made all payments on the car, made the down-payment and trade-in, was listed as insured on a policy of insurance, negotiated a refinancing, and was in possession of the car. In re Rutledge, 115 Bankr. 344 (Bankr. N.D. Ala.), aff'd, 121 Bankr. 609 (Bankr. W.D. Ala. 1990).

Cited in Buchannon v. State, 554 So. 2d 477 (Ala. Crim. App. 1989).

§ 32-8-46. Transfer of ownership — By operation of law.

Cited in Crum v. Southtrust Bank, 598 So. 2d 867 (Ala. 1992).

§ 32-8-49. Suspension or revocation of certificates.

(a) The department shall suspend or revoke a certificate of title, subject to the appeal provisions of Chapter 2A of Title 40, when authorized by any other provision of law or if it finds:

(1) The certificate of title was fraudulently procured or erroneously issued; or

(2) The vehicle has been scrapped, dismantled or destroyed.

(b) Suspension or revocation of a certificate of title does not, in itself, affect the validity of a security interest noted on it.

(c) When the department suspends or revokes a certificate of title, the owner or person in possession of it shall, immediately upon receiving notice of the suspension or revocation, mail or deliver the certificate to the department.

(d) Should any person fail to comply with the provisions of subsection (c) of this section the department shall seize and impound the certificate of title which has been revoked. It shall also be the duty of any peace officer, on notification to him by the department of the failure of a person to mail or deliver a revoked certificate of title to the department, to seize and mail or deliver to the department the revoked certificate of title. (Acts 1973, No. 765, p. 1147, § 25; Acts 1992, No. 92-186, p. 349, § 14.)

ARTICLE 3.

SECURITY INTERESTS.

§ 32-8-60. Excepted liens and security interests.

The Uniform Certificate of Title and Antitheft Act, § 32-8-1 et seq., does not provide for the creation of a security interest between used automobile dealers who hold automobiles for sale. Crum v. Southtrust Bank, 598 So. 2d 867 (Ala. 1992).

§ 32-8-60.1. Security interest not created where rental price may be adjusted by reference to amount realized upon sale.

In the case of motor vehicles as defined in section 32-8-2(10), notwithstanding any other provision of law, a transaction does not create a sale or security interest merely because the transaction provides that the rental price is permitted or required to be adjusted under the agreement either upward or downward by reference to the amount realized upon sale or other disposition of the motor vehicle. (Acts 1991, No. 91-549, p. 1012, § 1.)

§ 32-8-61. Perfection of security interests.

No provision for period of time to file security interest. — While the Uniform Certificate of Title and Antitheft Act provides the exclusive method of perfecting a security interest in a motor vehicle covered by the Act, it does not explicitly provided a time period within which the security interest must be perfected. Landmark Chevrolet, Inc. v. Central Bank, 611 So. 2d 1043 (Ala. 1992).

Twenty-day measure of "substantially contemporaneous" for certificate of title perfection. — The court adopted the strict requirement of the 10 to 20-day measure of "substantially contemporaneous" under Section 547(c)(1)(B) of the Bankruptcy Code. The court would apply the 10-day period of Section 547(e)(2)(B) of the Bankruptcy Code to non-purchase money security interests not perfected via certificate of title and the 20-day period of subsection (b) for certificate of title perfection. W.T. Vick Lumber Co. v. Chadwick, 179 Bankr. 283 (Bankr. N.D. Ala. 1995).

Cited in Hill v. McGee, 562 So. 2d 238 (Ala. 1990).

§ 32-8-64. Release of security interest.

Obligation to furnish buyer with certificate was written into contract by operation of statute. — Even if the contract did not specify that seller of trailers was obligated to furnish buyer with the certificates of title upon satisfaction of the lien, that obligation was written into the contract by operation of § 32-8-1 et seq. Trailmobile, Inc. v. Cook, 540 So. 2d 683 (Ala. 1988).

§ 32-8-66. Exclusiveness of procedure.

Cited in Hill v. McGee, 562 So. 2d 238 (Ala. 1990).

ARTICLE 4.

ANTITHEFT LAWS.

§ 32-8-86. Removed, falsified or unauthorized identification number, registration or license plate; seizure of vehicle, part, etc., when number altered, etc.; disposition of forfeited property.

Act is applicable to subsequent purchaser of car. — The overall plan of the Uniform Certificate of Title and Anti-Theft Act shows exclusive attention to maintaining records of the identity and ownership of vehicles; persons who buy cars are entitled to rely on the accuracy of such elements of that tracing system as certificates of title and Vehicle Identification Number plates, and a subsequent purchaser of a car is within the class of persons who are the beneficiaries of the duty not to falsify identification numbers or certificates of title. Johnny Spradlin Auto Parts, Inc. v. Cochran, 568 So. 2d 738 (Ala. 1990).

Once state shows that vehicle has, etc.

In accord with the bound volume. See State v. 1980 Chevrolet Corvette, 568 So. 2d 1233 (Ala. Civ. App. 1990).

Section 20-2-93 inapplicable to subsec- tion (h). — The language of § 20-2-93 has no effect on the forfeiture of the automobile in proceedings instituted pursuant to subsection (h). Glover v. State, 553 So. 2d 131 (Ala. Civ. App. 1989).

Substitution of 1986 V.I.N. plate in place of 1983 plate constituted fraud. — Replacement of 1986 Vehicle Identification Number (V.I.N.) plate by employee of auto parts company constituted a suppression of the fact that car was not what the V.I.N. plate represented it to be, that is, a 1986 Camaro with a factory-installed V.I.N. plate; by riveting the 1986 plate into the place where the 1983 plate had been, auto parts company suppressed material fact it had a duty to disclose to subsequent purchaser of car. Johnny Spradlin Auto Parts, Inc. v. Cochran, 568 So. 2d 738 (Ala. 1990).

§ 32-8-87. (Effective October 1, 1996) Dismantling, destroying or changing identity of vehicle; certificates of title to be cancelled; salvage certificates; dealer transport license; responsibilities of insurance company upon settlement of claims; "total loss" defined; penalties regarding removal, sale, etc., of vehicle identification numbers, certificates, etc.; restrictions on transfer of salvage vehicles; application for inspection of salvage vehicle; inspection fee; "component parts" defined; "rebuilt" certificate of title.

(a) Each owner of a motor vehicle and each person mentioned as owner in the last certificate of title who scraps, dismantles, destroys, or changes the motor vehicle in such a manner that it is not the same motor vehicle described in the certificate of origin or certificate of title shall as soon as practicable cause the certificate of origin or certificate of title, if any, and any other documents or information required by the department to be mailed or delivered to the department for processing. The department shall, with the consent of any holder of liens noted on the surrendered certificate, enter a cancellation upon its records. Upon cancellation of a certificate of origin or certificate of title in the manner prescribed by this section, the department shall cancel all certificates of origin or certificates of title and all memorandum certificates in that chain of title. A certificate of title for the vehicle shall not again be issued except upon application containing the information the department requires, accompanied by a certificate of inspection in the form and content as specified in this section.

No motor vehicle for which a salvage or junk certificate has been issued by this state or any other state shall be driven or operated on the highways or other public places of this state. A vehicle which is in this state and for which a salvage certificate has been issued, and the vehicle is being restored to its operating condition which existed prior to the event which caused the salvage certificate of title to issue, may be moved to and from repair points as necessary by the rebuilder to complete the restoration or may be moved as permitted by the Department of Revenue for inspection or for any other purpose. A valid Alabama dealer license plate shall be displayed on the vehicle during its movement. A person who violates this subsection shall, upon conviction, be guilty of a Class C misdemeanor and shall be punishable as required by law.

(b) When the frame or engine is removed from a motor vehicle and not immediately replaced by another frame or engine, or when an insurance company has paid money or made other monetary settlement as compensation for a total loss of any motor vehicle, the motor vehicle shall be considered to be salvage. The owner of every motor vehicle in which total loss or salvage has occurred shall, within 72 hours after the total loss or salvage occurs, make application for a salvage certificate of title and forward to the department the certificate of origin or certificate of title to the motor vehicle, whereupon the department shall process the certificate of origin or certificate of title in a manner prescribed by law or regulation. An insurance company which pays money or makes other monetary settlement as compensation for total loss of a motor vehicle shall at the time of payment or monetary settlement obtain the vehicle's certificate of origin or certificate of title and, as soon as practicable after receiving them, shall forward them along with their application for a salvage certificate, to the department for processing. In the event the payment or monetary settlement was made because of the theft of the vehicle, which shall be considered a total loss as defined in this section, the insurance company shall forward the vehicle's properly assigned certificate of origin or certificate of title as provided herein, to the department as soon as practicable after the vehicle is recovered. When a stolen motor vehicle has been reported to the department in compliance with this section and is later recovered, and for which a salvage certificate has been issued, the owner recorded on the salvage certificate shall assign that certificate to the purchaser. A person who violates this subsection shall, upon conviction, be guilty of a Class C misdemeanor and shall be punishable as required by law.

(c) If an insurance company acquires a motor vehicle in settlement of an insurance claim and holds the vehicle for resale and procures the certificate of origin or certificate of title from the owner or lienholder within 15 days after delivery of the vehicle to the insurance company, and if the vehicle was not a total loss as defined by this section, the insurance company need not send the certificate of origin or certificate of title to the department but, upon transferring the vehicle to another person, other than by the creation of a security interest, the insurance company shall complete an affidavit of acquisition and disposition of the motor vehicle on a form prescribed by the department and deliver the certificate of origin or certificate of title, affidavit, and any other documents required by the department to the transferee at the time of delivery of the motor vehicle.

(d) For the purposes of this section, a total loss shall occur when an insurance company or any other person pays or makes other monetary settlement to a person when a vehicle is damaged and the damage to the vehicle is greater than or equal to 75 percent of the fair retail value of the vehicle prior to damage as set forth in a current edition of a nationally recognized compilation of retail values, including automated data bases, as approved by the department. The compensation for total loss as defined in this subsection shall not include payments by an insurer or other person for medical care, bodily injury, vehicle rental, or for anything other than the amount paid for the actual damage to the motor vehicle. A vehicle that has sustained minor damage as a result of theft or vandalism shall not be considered a total loss. Any person acquiring ownership of a damaged motor vehicle that meets the definition of total loss for which a salvage title has not been issued shall apply for a salvage title, other than a scrap metal processor acquiring such vehicle for purposes of recycling into metallic scrap for remelting purposes only. This application shall be made before the vehicle is further transferred, but in any event, within 30 days after ownership is acquired.

(e) It shall be unlawful for the owner of any junkyard, salvage yard, or motor vehicle dismantler and parts recycler or his or her agents or employees to have in their possession any motor vehicle which is junk or salvage or a total loss when the manufacturer's vehicle identification number plate or plates, authorized replacement vehicle identification number plate or plates, or serial plate or plates have been removed, unless previously required to be removed by a statute or law of this state or another jurisdiction. A person who violates this subsection shall, upon conviction, be guilty of a Class C misdemeanor and shall be punishable as required by law.

(f) It shall be unlawful for a person, firm, or corporation to possess, sell or exchange, offer to sell or exchange, or to give away any certificate of origin, certificate of title, salvage certificate of title, manufacturer's identification number plate or plates, authorized replacement vehicle identification number plate or plates, serial plate or plates, or motor vehicle license plate or plates of any motor vehicle which has been scrapped, dismantled, or sold as junk or salvage or as a total loss contrary to this section, and every officer, agent, or employee of a person, firm, or corporation, and every person who shall authorize, direct, aid in or consent to the possession, sale or exchange, or offer to sell, exchange, or give away such certificate of origin, certificate of title, salvage certificate of title, manufacturer's vehicle identification number plate or plates, authorized replacement vehicle identification number plate or plates, serial plate or plates, or motor vehicle license plate or plates contrary to this section, shall, upon conviction, be guilty of a Class C misdemeanor and shall be punishable as required by law.

(g) The department is authorized to issue a salvage certificate of title for a fee of $15.00, on a form prescribed by the department which shall provide for assignments of this title. The salvage certificate of title is to replace a certificate of origin or certificate of title required to be surrendered by this section. The department shall prescribe necessary forms and procedures to comply with this subsection.

(h) It shall be unlawful for a person to sign as assignor or for a person to have in his or her possession a salvage certificate of title which has been signed by the owner as assignor without the name of the assignee and other information called for on the form prescribed by the department. A person who violates this subsection, upon conviction, shall be guilty of a Class C misdemeanor and shall be punishable as required by law.

(i) Every owner of a salvage or junk motor vehicle who sells or transfers the vehicle to any person other than to a scrap metal processor for purposes of recycling into metallic scrap for remelting purposes only, shall provide at the time of the sale or transfer a properly executed assignment and warranty of title to the transferee in the space provided therefor on the salvage certificate of title or junk certificate of title or as the department prescribes. A person who willfully violates this subsection shall, upon conviction, be guilty of a Class C misdemeanor and shall be punishable as required by law.

(j) The department may issue a certificate of title to any motor vehicle for which a salvage certificate has been issued by this or any other state, and the vehicle has, in this state, been completely restored to its operating condition which existed prior to the event which caused the salvage certificate of title to issue, provided that all requirements of this section have been met. No certificate of title shall be issued for any motor vehicle for which a "junk" certificate has been issued or for a vehicle which is sold "for parts only."

(k) Every owner of a salvage motor vehicle designated a 1975 year model and all models subsequent thereto which is in this state and which has been restored in this state to its operating condition which existed prior to the event which caused the salvage certificate of title to issue shall make application to the department for an inspection of the vehicle in the form and content as determined by the department. Each application for inspection of a salvage vehicle which has been so restored shall be accompanied by all of the following:

(1) The outstanding salvage certificate or out-of-state title previously issued for the salvage vehicle.

(2) Notarized bills of sale evidencing acquisition of all major component parts (listing the manufacturer's vehicle identification number of the vehicle from which the parts were removed, if parts contain or should contain the manufacturer's vehicle identification number) used to restore the vehicle and bills of sale evidencing acquisition of all minor component parts.

Notarization shall not be required on bills of sale for minor component parts; provided that a notarized bill of sale which lists the manufacturer's vehicle identification number of the vehicle from which the parts were removed, if parts contain or should contain the manufacturer's vehicle identification number, shall be required for a transmission.

(3) Evidence that the owner is a licensed motor vehicle rebuilder as defined in Section 40-12-390.

(4) The owner shall also provide a written affirmation which states the following:

a. That the owner has rebuilt the vehicle or supervised its rebuilders, and what has been done to restore the vehicle to its operating condition which existed prior to the event which caused the salvage certificate to issue.

b. That the owner personally inspected the completed vehicle and it complies with all safety requirements set forth by the State of Alabama and any regulations promulgated thereunder.

c. That the identification numbers of the restored vehicle and its parts have not, to the knowledge of the owner, been removed, destroyed, falsified, altered, or defaced.

d. That the salvage certificate document or out-of-state title certificate attached to the application has not to the knowledge of the owner been forged, falsified, altered, or counterfeited.

e. That all information contained on the application and its attachments is true and correct to the knowledge of the owner.

(*l*) The application fee for each inspection of a restored vehicle shall be $75.00, payable by certified funds to the department, which shall accompany the application.

(1) All application fees received by the department shall be applied toward the personnel and maintenance costs of the vehicle inspection program and the vehicle inspection program shall be conducted by the office of investigations and inspections of the department. Upon receipt of the application for inspection, application fee of $75.00, its supporting documents, and title fee of $15.00, payable by certified funds to the department, the department shall require an inspection to be made of the title and the vehicle by qualified agents or law enforcement officers of the department.

(2) The inspection and certification shall include an examination of the vehicle and its parts to determine that the identification numbers of the vehicle or its parts have not been removed, falsified, altered, defaced, destroyed, or tampered with; that the vehicle information contained in the application for certificate of title and supporting documents is true and correct; and that there are no indications that the vehicle or any of its parts are stolen. The certification shall not attest to the roadworthiness or safety condition of the vehicle.

(m) Component parts are defined as:

(1) PASSENGER VEHICLES.

a. Major components:

1. Motor or engine.

2. Trunk floor pan or rear section and roof.

3. Frame or any portion thereof (except frame horn), or, in the case of a unitized body, the supporting structure which serves as the frame, except when it is a part of the trunk floor pan, or rear section and roof.

4. Cowl, firewall, or any portion thereof.

5. Roof assembly.

b. Minor components:

1. Each door allowing entrance to or egress from the passenger compartment.

2. Hood.

3. Each front fender or each rear fender when used with a rear section and roof.

4. Deck lid, tailgate, or hatchback (whichever is present).

5. Each quarter panel.

6. Each bumper.

7. T-tops, moon roof, or whichever is present.

8. Transmission or trans-axle.

(2) TRUCK, TRUCK TYPE, or BUS TYPE VEHICLES.

a. Major components:

1. Motor or engine.

2. Transmission or trans-axle.

3. Frame or any portion thereof (except frame horn), or, in the case of a unitized body, the supporting structure which serves as the frame.

4. Cab.

5. Cowl or firewall or any portion thereof.

6. Roof assembly.

7. Cargo compartment floor panel or passenger compartment floor pan.

b. Minor components:

1. Each door.

2. Hood.

3. Grill, except on one ton or smaller trucks.

4. Each bumper.

5. Each front fender.

6. Roof panel and rear cab panel.

7. Each rear fender or side panel.

8. Pickup box.

9. Body or bed.

(3) MOTORCYCLE: COMPONENT PARTS.

a. Engine or motor.

b. Transmission or trans-axle.

c. Frame.

d. Front fork.

e. Crankcase.

(n) A salvage vehicle which has been restored in this state to its operating condition which existed prior to the event which caused the salvage certificate of title to issue shall be issued a certificate of title which shall contain the word "rebuilt."

(o)(1) Each salvage vehicle restored or rebuilt in this state which is required to be inspected by the department pursuant to subsection (*l*) and for which a certificate of title may be issued pursuant to subsection (n) shall be issued a decal, plate, or other emblem as prescribed by the department to reflect that the vehicle is rebuilt. The decal, plate, or other emblem shall be attached to the vehicle in a place and in a manner prescribed by the department.

(2) A person who willfully removes, mutilates, tampers with, obliterates, or destroys a decal, plate, or other emblem issued and attached to a salvage vehicle pursuant to this subsection is guilty of a Class A misdemeanor punishable as provided by law.

(p) Each person who sells, exchanges, delivers, or otherwise transfers any interest in any vehicle for which a title bearing the designation "salvage" or "rebuilt" has been issued shall disclose in writing the existence of this title to the prospective purchaser, recipient in exchange, recipient by donation, or recipient by other act of transfer. The disclosure, which shall be made at the time of or prior to the completion of the sale, exchange, donation, or other act of transfer, shall contain the following information in no smaller than 10 point type: "This vehicle's title contains the designation 'salvage' or 'rebuilt'." (Acts 1973, No. 765, p. 1147, § 41; Acts 1985, No. 85-650, p. 1010, § 2; Acts 1987, No. 87-806, p. 1581, § 1; Acts 1988, 1st Sp. Sess., No. 88-730, p. 127, § 3; Acts 1989, No. 89-863; Acts 1995, No. 95-406, § 1.)

For this section effective until October 1, 1996, see the bound volume.

The 1995 amendment, effective October 1, 1996, substituted "A" for "Any" throughout the section; in the second paragraph of subsection (a), deleted "However" preceding "A vehicle" in the second sentence, and deleted "transport (DT)" preceding "license plate" in the next-to-last sentence; in subsection (d), substituted the language beginning "a vehicle is damaged" for "it is deemed to be uneconomical to repair the damaged vehicle" in the first sentence, and added the last two sentences; in subsection (f) substituted "or plated" for "plate(s)" throughout the subsection, deleted "the provisions of" following "total loss contrary to" and also preceding "this section, shall, upon conviction"; deleted "the provisions of" following "comply with" in the last sentence of subsection (g); added the language beginning "to any person" and ending "for remelting purposes only" in the first sentence of subsection (i); deleted "Howev-er" from the beginning of the last sentence in subsection (j); in subsection (k) deleted "however" preceding "that a notarized bill" from the second sentence in subdivision (2), substituted "That the owner has" for "He" in paragraph (4)a, and substituted "That the owner" for "He" in paragraph (4)b, added "That" in paragraphs (4)c, (4)d, and (4)e; in subsection (*l*), in subdivision (1), in the first sentence deleted "Alabama department of revenue" following "conducted by the" and added "of the department" to the end, and in the last sentence deleted "Alabama" following "officers of the" and deleted "of revenue" from the end; in subsection (n) deleted the former second and third sentences relating to component parts; added subsections (o) and (p); and made nonsubstantive changes.

Code Commissioner's note. — In 1995, the Code Commissioner deleted "of this section" following "subsection (*l*)" and "subsection (n)" in subdivision (1) of subsection (o) because the language was surplusage.

CHAPTER 9.

TRUCKS, TRAILERS AND SEMITRAILERS.

Article 2.

Size and Weight.

Sec.
32-9-20. Schedule of restrictions.
32-9-25. Exemptions — Length.

ARTICLE 2.

SIZE AND WEIGHT.

§ 32-9-20. Schedule of restrictions.

It shall be unlawful for any person to drive or move on any highway in this state any vehicle or vehicles of a size or weight except in accordance with the following:

(1) WIDTH. — Vehicles and combinations of vehicles, operating on highways with traffic lanes 12 feet or more in width, shall not exceed a total outside width, including any load thereon, of 102 inches, exclusive of mirrors or other safety devices approved by the State Transportation Department. The Director of the State Transportation Department may, in his or her discretion, designate other public highways for use by vehicles and loads with total outside widths not exceeding 102 inches, otherwise; vehicles and combinations of vehicles, operating on highways with traffic lanes less than 12 feet in width, shall not exceed a total outside width, including any load thereon, of 96 inches, exclusive of mirrors or other safety devices approved by the State Transportation Department. No passenger vehicle shall carry any load extending beyond the line of the fenders. No vehicle hauling forest products or culvert pipe on any highway in this state shall have a load exceeding 102 inches in width.

(2) HEIGHT. — No vehicle or semitrailer or trailer shall exceed in height 13½ feet, including load.

(3) LENGTH. — No vehicle shall exceed in length 40 feet; except, that the length of a truck-semitrailer combination, semitrailers, including load, used in a truck tractor-semitrailer combination, shall not exceed 57 feet and semitrailers and trailers, including load, used in a truck tractor-semitrailer-trailer combination, shall not exceed 28½ feet each. Semitrailers exceeding 53½ feet shall only be operated on highways designated pursuant to Section 32-9-1 and shall only be operated when the distance between the kingpin of the semitrailer and the rearmost axle or a point midway between the two rear axles, if the two rear axles are tandem axles, does not exceed 41 feet and if the semitrailer is equipped with a rear underride guard of a substantial construction consisting of a continuous lateral beam extending to within four inches of the lateral extremities of the semitrailer and located not more than 22 inches from the surface as measured with the semitrailers empty and on

a level surface. For purposes of enforcement of this subdivision, lengths of semitrailers and trailers refer to the cargo carrying portion of the unit. Truck tractor units used exclusively in combinations transporting motor vehicles may directly carry a portion of the cargo, provided that the combinations are restricted to truck tractor-semitrailer combinations only and provided further that the overall length of these particular combinations shall not exceed 65 feet; except that the overall length of stinger-steered type units shall not exceed 75 feet. No truck tractor-semitrailer combination used exclusively for transporting motor vehicles shall carry any load extending more than three feet beyond the front or four feet beyond the rear of the combination. No other vehicle operated on a highway shall carry any load extending more than a total of five feet beyond both the front and rear, inclusive, of the vehicle.

(4) WEIGHT.

a. The gross weight imposed on the highway by the wheels of any one axle of a vehicle shall not exceed 20,000 pounds, or such other weight, if any, as may be permitted by federal law to keep the state from losing federal funds; provided, that inadequate bridges shall be posted to define load limits.

b. For the purpose of this section, an axle load shall be defined as the total load transmitted to the road by all wheels whose centers are included between two parallel transverse vertical planes 40 inches apart, extending across the full width of the vehicle.

c. Subject to the limit upon the weight imposed upon the highway through any one axle as set forth herein, the total weight with load imposed upon the highway by all the axles of a vehicle or combination of vehicles shall not exceed the gross weight given for the respective distances between the first and last axle of the vehicle or combination of vehicles, measured longitudinally to the nearest foot as set forth in the following table:

COMPUTED GROSS WEIGHT TABLE:

For various spacings of axle groupings

Distance in feet between first and last axles of vehicle or combination of vehicles	Maximum load in pounds on all the axles				
	2 axles	3 axles	4 axles	5 axles	6 axles
8 or less	36,000	42,000	42,000		
9	38,000	42,500	42,500		
10	40,000	43,500	43,500		
11		44,000	44,000		
12		45,000	50,000	50,000	
13		45,500	50,500	50,500	

Distance in feet between first and last axles of vehicle or combination of vehicles	Maximum load in pounds on all the axles				
	2 axles	3 axles	4 axles	5 axles	6 axles
14		46,500	51,500	51,500	
15		47,000	52,000	52,000	
16		48,000	52,500	58,000	58,000
17		48,500	53,500	58,500	58,500
18		49,500	54,000	59,000	59,000
19		50,000	54,500	60,000	60,000
20		51,000	55,500	60,500	66,000
21		51,500	56,000	61,000	66,500
22		52,500	56,500	61,500	67,000
23		53,000	57,500	62,500	68,000
24		54,000	58,000	63,000	68,500
25		54,500	58,500	63,500	69,000
26		56,000	59,500	64,000	69,500
27		57,000	60,000	65,000	70,000
28		59,000	60,500	65,500	71,000
29		60,000	61,500	66,000	71,500
30			62,000	66,500	72,000
31			63,500	67,000	72,500
32			64,500	68,000	73,500
33			65,000	69,000	74,000
34			65,500	70,000	74,500
35			66,500	71,000	75,000
36			67,000	72,000	76,000
37			68,000	73,000	77,000
38			69,000	74,000	78,000
39			70,000	75,000	79,000
40			71,000	76,000	80,000
41			72,000	77,000	81,000
42			73,000	78,000	82,000
43			74,000	79,000	83,000
44 and over			75,000	80,000	84,000

Except as provided by special permits, no vehicle or combination of vehicles exceeding the gross weights specified above shall be permitted to travel on the public highways within the State of Alabama.

No vehicle or combination of vehicles shall be permitted to operate on any portion of the Interstate Highway System of Alabama that shall have a greater weight than 20,000 pounds carried on any one axle, including all enforcement tolerances, or with a tandem axle weight in excess of 34,000 pounds, including all enforcement tolerances, or with an overall gross weight on a group of two or more consecutive axles produced by application of the following formula:

$$W = 500 \left(\frac{LN}{N-1} + 12N + 36 \right)$$

where W = overall gross weight on any group of two or more consecutive axles to the nearest 500 pounds, L = distance in feet between the extreme of any group of two or more consecutive axles, and N = number of axles in group under consideration; except, that two consecutive sets of tandem axles may carry a gross load of 34,000 pounds each, provided the overall distance between the first and last axles of the consecutive sets of tandem axles is 36 feet or more; provided, that the overall gross weight may not exceed 80,000 pounds, including all enforcement tolerances. Nothing in this section shall be construed as permitting size or weight limits on the National System of Interstate and Defense Highways in this state in excess of those permitted under 23 U.S.C. Section 127. If the federal government prescribes or adopts vehicle size or weight limits greater than or less than those now prescribed by 23 U.S.C. Section 127 for the National System of Interstate and Defense Highways, the increased or decreased limits shall become effective on the National System of Interstate and Defense Highways in this state. Nothing in this section shall be construed to deny the operation of any vehicle or combination of vehicles that could be lawfully operated upon the highways and roads of this state on January 4, 1975.

  d. For purposes of enforcement of this subdivision, all weights less than or equal to the sum of the weight otherwise prescribed by this subdivision, plus an additional weight to be calculated by multiplying the weight prescribed by this subdivision by one-tenth (.10) that shall represent a scale or enforcement tolerance, shall be deemed to be in compliance with the requirements of this section, and shall not constitute violations thereof. No evidence shall be admitted into evidence or considered by the trier of fact in any civil action unless the evidence proffered would tend to prove that the weight of the vehicle exceeded the amount provided in this subsection. Nothing in this paragraph d. shall restrict or affect the right of any defendant to place in evidence such evidence tending to prove the defendant was in compliance with this section.

  e. Dump trucks, dump trailers, concrete mixing trucks, fuel oil, gasoline trucks, and trucks designated and constructed for special type work or use shall not be made to conform to the axle spacing requirements of paragraph (4)c of this section; provided, that the vehicle shall be limited to a weight of 20,000 pounds per axle plus scale tolerances; and, provided further, that the maximum gross weight of the vehicles shall not exceed the maximum weight allowed by this section for the appropriate number of axles, irrespective of the distance between axles, plus allowable scale tolerances. All axles shall be brake equipped. Concrete mixing trucks which operate within 50 miles of their home base shall not be required to conform to the requirements of paragraph (4)a of this section; provided, that the vehicles shall be limited to a maximum load of the rated capacity of the concrete mixer, the true gross load not to exceed 66,000 pounds, and all the vehicles shall have at least three axles, each with brake equipped wheels. It shall be a violation if the vehicles named under this subdivision travel upon bridges designated and posted by the Transportation Director as incapable of carrying the load.

f. If the driver of any vehicle can comply with the weight requirements of this section by shifting or equalizing the load on all wheels or axles and does so when requested by the proper authority, the driver shall not be held to be operating in violation of this section.

g. When portable scales are used in the enforcement of this section, the axles of any vehicle described or commonly referred to as tandem or triaxle rigs or units (that is, vehicles having two or more axles in addition to a steering axle), the group of tandem or triaxles shall be weighed simultaneously, and the total weight so derived shall be divided by the number of axles weighed in the group to arrive at the per axle weight, except that if any one axle in the group exceeds 20,000 pounds in weight, it shall not exceed the weight of any other axle in the group by more than 50 percent. When portable scales are used to determine the weight of a vehicle pursuant to this section, the operator of the vehicle will be permitted to move the vehicle to the nearest platform scales certified by the Department of Agriculture and Industries and operated by a bonded operator within a distance of 10 highway miles, accompanied by an enforcement officer to verify the accuracy of the portable scales used in determining the vehicle weight. If the weight of the vehicle is shown by the platform scales to be within the legal limits of this section, the operator of the vehicle shall not be held to be in violation of this section.

h. The governing body of a county, by appropriate resolution, may authorize limitations less than those prescribed herein for vehicles operated upon the county highways of the county.

i. The State Transportation Department may post or limit any road or bridge to weights less than those prescribed by this section. It is the legislative intent and purpose that this section be rigidly enforced by the State Transportation Department, the Department of Public Safety and any other authorized law enforcement officers of the state, any county, or city and incorporated towns.

j. Two and three axle vehicles being used exclusively for the purpose of transporting agricultural commodities or products to and from a farm and for agricultural purposes relating to the operation and maintenance of a farm by any farmer, custom harvester or husbandman may not be made to conform to the axle requirements of paragraph (4)a of this section or the gross weight requirements of paragraph (4)c of this section. (Acts 1927, No. 347, p. 348; Acts 1932, Ex. Sess., No. 58, p. 68; Acts 1939, No. 484, p. 687; Code 1940, T. 36, § 89; Acts 1943, No. 179, p. 159; Acts 1947, No. 210, p. 72; Acts 1955, No. 245, p. 560, § 1; Acts 1959, No. 413, p. 1052, § 1; Acts 1961, No. 686, p. 980; Acts 1963, No. 295, p. 762, § 1; Acts 1965, No. 879, p. 1645; Acts 1966, Ex. Sess., No. 334, p. 476; Acts 1975, No. 922, p. 1829, § 1; Acts 1979, No. 79-792, p. 1445, § 1; Acts 1979, No. 79-795, p. 1453;

Acts 1985, 2nd Ex. Sess., No. 85-912, p. 188, § 2; Acts 1989, No. 89-631; Acts 1993, No. 93-308, p. 459, § 1; Acts 1994, No. 94-305, p. 539, § 1; Acts 1995, No. 95-758, § 1.)

The 1993 amendment, effective May 3, 1993, inserted "or her" in the second sentence of subdivision (1); in subdivision (3), substituted "57 feet" for "53 feet" in the first sentence, added the present second sentence, in the present fourth sentence, substituted "the combinations" for "such combinations," and added the language beginning "except that," and substituted "the combination" for "such combination" in the next-to-last sentence; in subdivision (4), in the last paragraph of paragraph c, in the first sentence, substituted "the consecutive sets" for "such consecutive sets," and substituted "the overall gross weight" for "such overall gross weight," in paragraph e, substituted "the vehicles" for "such vehicles" throughout this paragraph, substituted "the true gross load" for "such true gross load," and substituted "all vehicles" for "all such vehicles," and substituted "the load" for "such load" in the last sentence, substituted "the driver" for "said driver" near the end of paragraph f, substituted "the county" for "such county" at the end of paragraph h, and in paragraph i, substituted

"may post" for "for cause, shall have the right to post" in the first sentence, and deleted "the provisions of" preceding "this section" in the second sentence.

The 1995 amendment, effective August 8, 1995, substituted "State Transportation Department" for "State Highway Department" throughout this section; deleted "provisions" following "with the following" in the introductory language; and in subdivision (4), rewrote paragraph d, substituted "transportation director" for "highway director" in the last sentence of paragraph e, and deleted "the provisions of" following "enforcement of" in the first sentence of paragraph g.

Code Commissioner's note. — In 1995, the Code Commissioner restored the figure "44,000" to the "4 axles" column and deleted the figure from the "2 axles" column on the "11" line in the "Computed Gross Weight Table" in paragraph c. of subdivision (4) to correct a typographical error and to set out the table, which was not amended, as it appeared in 1994.

§ 32-9-25. Exemptions — Length.

There shall be exempt from this article as to length, detachable wind deflection devices which have been approved by the state highway department, loads of poles, logs, lumber, laminated wood building materials, structural steel, piping and timber, and vehicles transporting same. Trucks, trailers and semi-trailers which are constructed and used exclusively for the hauling of livestock, shall also be exempt from the restrictions of this article as to length, but shall not exceed 65 feet in length. (Acts 1939, No. 484, p. 687; Code 1940, T. 36, § 94; Acts 1949, No. 607, p. 939; Acts 1979, No. 79-430, p. 677; Acts 1979, No. 79-792, p. 1445, § 1; Acts 1993, No. 93-630, p. 1076, § 1.)

The 1993 amendment, effective May 13, 1993, in the first sentence, deleted "the provisions of" preceding "this article," and inserted

"laminated wood building materials" following "lumber," and in the second sentence, deleted "however" following "but."

CHAPTER 10.

MOTOR VEHICLE ACCIDENTS.

§ 32-10-1. Accidents involving death or personal injuries.

Legislature intended § 32-10-2 to be fulfilled under section instead of § 32-10-3. — Evidence was sufficient to charge defendant with the crime of leaving the scene of the accident under this section although defendant did not violate the mandates of § 32-10-3 which this section requires upon the stop of the driver; since § 32-10-3, which addresses a driver's duty upon striking unattended vehicles, cannot be reconciled, with the requirements and nature of the offense described in this section, the legislature intended to provide that the requirements of § 32-10-2 be fulfilled upon the "immediate stop" of the driver of the vehicle causing the damage or injury. Mayfield v. State, 545 So. 2d 89 (Ala. Crim. App.), rev'd on other grounds, 545 So. 2d 92 (Ala. 1988).

"Non-contact" accident. — Where driver argued that a "non-contact" accident did not fall within the language of this section, this section was not applicable where driver faced the suspension of her driver's license as mandated by § 32-7-6, and § 32-7-5 provided that every operator of a motor vehicle "which is in any manner involved in an accident" is subject to § 32-7-6; driver's appeal to circuit court was entitled "Petition Under Alabama Motor Vehicles Safety Responsibility Act 704," and in that petition driver acknowledged being involved in an automobile accident. Worthy v. State Dep't of Pub. Safety, 599 So. 2d 629 (Ala. Civ. App. 1992).

Culpability issue should have been in jury charge. — Trial court erred when it refused to give defendant's requested jury charges concerning the requisite intent and mental state for the offense of leaving the scene of the accident; this section contains no language indicating that it is a strict liability crime, and thus, the issue of the appellant's culpability should have been presented to the jury in the court's jury charge. Turner v. State, 584 So. 2d 864 (Ala. Crim. App. 1990).

Enhancement of sentence. — Where appellant was convicted of robbery in the first degree, the trial court properly used a conviction for leaving the scene of an accident, a violation of this section, to enhance his sentence even though that conviction did not occur under Title 13A of the Code of Alabama. Powell v. State, 624 So. 2d 220 (Ala. Crim. App. 1993).

Habitual Felony Offender Act. — Sentencing provisions that specifically include the provisions of the Habitual Felony Offender Act do apply to sentencing for a violation of this section when such violation involves death or personal injury. Martin v. State, 625 So. 2d 455 (Ala. Civ. App. 1993).

Trial court did not err in refusing to give this oral requested charge, which stated as follows: "If an injury is inflicted under such circumstances as would ordinarily superinduce the belief in a reasonable person that injury would flow or had flowed from the accident or collision, then, its [sic] the duty of the operator to stop this vehicle"; there was no question that the appellant knew that his vehicle had struck the victim's, the appellant stopped and he gave the victim an incorrect name, address, and telephone number. Where a charge does not properly apply to the facts of the case, the charge may be refused. McCorvey v. State, 642 So. 2d 1351 (Ala. Crim. App. 1992).

Collateral references.

Sufficiency of showing of driver's involvement in motor vehicle accident to support prosecution for failure to stop, furnish identification, or render aid. 82 ALR4th 232.

Sufficiency of evidence to raise last clear chance doctrine in cases of automobile collision with pedestrian or bicyclist—Modern cases. 9 ALR5th 826.

Necessity and sufficiency of showing, in criminal prosecution under "hit-and-run" statute, accused's knowledge of accident, injury, or damage. 26 ALR5th 1.

§ 32-10-2. Duty to give information and render aid.

Legislature intended this section to be fulfilled under § 32-10-1 instead of § 32-10-3. — Evidence was sufficient to charge defendant with the crime of leaving the scene of the accident under § 32-10-1 although defendant did not violate the mandates of § 32-10-3 which § 32-10-1 requires upon the stop of the driver; since § 32-10-3, which addresses a driver's duty upon striking unattended vehicles, cannot be reconciled, with the requirements and nature of the offense described in § 32-10-1, the legislature intended to provide that the requirements of this section be fulfilled upon the "immediate stop" of the driver of the vehicle causing the damage or injury. Mayfield v. State, 545 So. 2d 89 (Ala. Crim. App.), rev'd on other grounds, 545 So. 2d 92 (Ala. 1988).

Failure to perform any one of multiple duties violates statute. — Where defendant initially stopped his vehicle after colliding with another occupied vehicle, which was the first among several statutorily imposed duties under such circumstances, the defendant's failure to remain at the scene and exchange certain information with the driver of the other vehicle did not entitle the defendant to a "lesser included offense" jury instruction since the "leaving the scene" statute imposes multiple duties and the failure of one so involved to perform any one of the statutorily imposed duties constitutes a violation of the statute. Mayfield v. State, 545 So. 2d 92 (Ala. 1988).

Collateral references.

Sufficiency of showing of driver's involvement in motor vehicle accident to support prosecution for failure to stop, furnish identification, or render aid. 82 ALR4th 232.

§ 32-10-3. Duty upon striking unattended vehicle.

Legislature intended § 32-10-2 to be fulfilled under § 32-10-1 instead of this section. — Evidence was sufficient to charge defendant with the crime of leaving the scene of the accident under § 32-10-1 although defendant did not violate the mandates of this section which § 32-10-1 requires upon the stop of the driver; since this section, which addresses a driver's duty upon striking unattended vehicles, cannot be reconciled, with the requirements and nature of the offense described in § 32-10-1, the legislature intended to provide that the requirements of § 32-10-2 be fulfilled upon the "immediate stop" of the driver of the vehicle causing the damage or injury. Mayfield v. State, 545 So. 2d 89 (Ala. Crim. App. 1986), rev'd on other grounds, 545 So. 2d 92 (Ala. 1988).

§ 32-10-6. Penalty for violation of sections 32-10-1 through 32-10-5.

Statute is not unconstitutionally vague. — This statute does not fail to apprise a defendant of the nature and cause of an accusation against him because the statute establishes an offense as a felony and as a misdemeanor; the statute is not unconstitutionally vague since, from a reading of the statute, a defendant can be reasonably apprised of the accusation against him or her and of the possible penal consequences. Mayfield v. State, 545 So. 2d 89 (Ala. Crim. App.), rev'd on other grounds, 545 So. 2d 92 (Ala. 1988).

§ 32-10-11. Accident reports confidential.

Cross references. — For this section being commented on by new Rule 508, Alabama Rules of Evidence, effective January 1, 1996, see the Advisory Committee's Notes to new Rule 508 in the 1995 Cumulative Supplement to Volume 23.

Collateral references.

Discoverability of traffic accident reports and derivative information. 84 ALR4th 15.

CHAPTER 13.

ABANDONED MOTOR VEHICLES.

§ 32-13-4. Notice of sale; hearing; appeal.

Trial court did not commit reversible error when it determined that subsection (a) of this section was controlling in this case and that repair shop owner failed to meet the notice requirement under that code section. In this case, the name of the owner of the vehicle was known. The repair shop owner should have exercised due diligence in attempting to locate an address for truck owner prior to publishing the notice in the newspaper, pursuant to subsection (b) of this section. There was no evidence as to the efforts made to locate truck owner, only a statement in an affidavit that another owner of repair shop made an attempt to locate truck owner prior to publishing the notice of the sale in the newspaper. DeRamus Exxon, Inc. v. Wyatt, 636 So. 2d 450 (Ala. Civ. App. 1994).